On Competence

⋃⋃⋃⋃⋃⋃⋃⋃⋃⋃⋃⋃⋃⋃⋃⋃⋃⋃⋃⋃⋃

*A Critical Analysis
of Competence-Based Reforms
in Higher Education*

Gerald Grant

Peter Elbow

Thomas Ewens

Zelda Gamson

Wendy Kohli

William Neumann

Virginia Olesen

David Riesman

On Competence

A Critical Analysis of Competence-Based Reforms in Higher Education

Jossey-Bass Publishers
San Francisco • Washington • London • 1979

ON COMPETENCE
A Critical Analysis of Competence-Based Reforms in Higher Education
by Gerald Grant, Peter Elbow, Thomas Ewens, Zelda Gamson,
Wendy Kohli, William Neumann, Virginia Olesen, and David Riesman

Copyright © 1979 by: Jossey-Bass, Inc., Publishers
433 California Street
San Francisco, California 94104
&
Jossey-Bass Limited
28 Banner Street
London EC1Y 8QE

Library of Congress Catalogue Card Number LC 79–83572

International Standard Book Number ISBN 0–87589–405–4

Manufactured in the United States of America

JACKET DESIGN BY WILLI BAUM

FIRST EDITION

Code 7909

The Jossey-Bass Series
in Higher Education

Preface

On Competence examines the foundations, understandings, meanings, and import of the movement toward competence-based education in American colleges and universities. It derives from a grant from the Fund for the Improvement of Postsecondary Education (FIPSE) of the United States Department of Health, Education, and Welfare. During the 1970s, FIPSE encouraged a number of colleges and universities to develop competence-based curriculums, and in 1974 it sponsored the authors of this volume for three years of fieldwork and analysis of these reforms. We interpreted this research opportunity as a chance both to understand the conceptualization and evolution of a striking experiment within American education and to probe the meanings of competence itself within American life. The following chapters report our findings.

A word should be said as well concerning what this book is not about. The most rapidly spreading use of the term *competence* occurs today in the phrase "minimum competency testing," referring to laws that have been enacted or proposed in thirty-three states requiring students in elementary and secondary schools to pass standardized tests at a specified level. New York, for example, administers a statewide minimum competency examination in reading and mathematics at the high school level. Although this minimum competency testing movement in the schools stems from some of the same roots as the competence-based education movement in colleges, our book does not focus on that movement or even on the "competency-based" teacher education and certification movements. Instead, it views the problems of competence in America through the prism of efforts at the undergraduate college level to develop competence-based curriculums in the liberal arts and in a variety of occupations besides schoolteaching.

Altogether, we completed nine case studies of such competence-based programs as part of the project, five of which are published in Part Three of this volume. Each of the members of the project team developed a case study separately, but we did not work in isolation. By sharing our field notes, we looked over each other's shoulders; and, during the course of the study, we all visited each of the case study institutions together to do fieldwork in common. At the same time, each of us examined a critical problem of competence-based education common to all or most of the sites, and these analyses form the basis of the chapters in Part Two.

A preliminary version of our work was published as a two-volume report by the Syracuse Research Corporation at the conclusion of the grant from FIPSE (Grant, 1977). This book, however, is by no means simply an edited version of that report. During a fourth year of analyses in 1978, we circulated drafts of our chapters to colleagues and practitioners and on several occasions made additional trips to the field. Most of the chapters were revised more than once; some were virtually reconceptualized. Material from only one chapter—Chapter Nine on the College of Human Services —has been published elsewhere (Grant and Riesman, 1978), since work on it was supported by a grant from the Carnegie Corporation as well as from FIPSE. Two chapters herein did not appear in any form in the preliminary report: the opening chapter on the foundations of competence-based education and the concluding chapter on methodology. On the other hand, this book could not include everything produced by the project or published in the preliminary report. It would take at least fifteen volumes to publish all the field notes, research papers, and other interim contributions by such members of the project as Harry Brill, Ronald Carino, Jonathan Daube, Nancy Jones, Samuel McCracken, and John Watt, and by various associated consultants, including Robert Daly and Elena Paolillo. Their important contributions should not go unrecognized here, even though their work is not reproduced in the following pages.

The prologue and first two chapters of the book seek to put today's competence-based experiments in context. So much writing about education—particularly under the headings of "innovation" and "policy proposals"—portrays a landscape where no shadows are cast. Unidimensional figures are boldly invested with momentary enthusiasms and gallop forward blissfully ignorant of history. Yet the historical imagination is usually what one most needs in thinking about education, and one must go back at least a hundred years to see ahead for ten. Thus, in the prologue I attempt to define the competence movement and to illuminate its variations in the context of earlier reforms at the secondary school level.

Next, in Chapter One David Riesman offers an examination of the societal concerns that have prompted the development of the competence-based movement in recent years. Among them, he notes that we Americans have lost our earlier feelings of omnipotence. We have learned that more efficient automobiles can be made abroad and that other countries can cope with crises such as oil embargos more effectively than we can. We have even come to fear that our problems—environmental degradation, Malthusian perils, and nuclear terror among them—may have outrun our capacities for solution.

In Chapter Two, William Neumann moves from social concerns to the educational initiatives that have prepared the ground for today's reform efforts. Some critics have sought to identify present competence-based experiments solely with behaviorism or with the "efficiency" movement within education. Although Neumann's account of the antecedents of the movement shows that the behaviorists were a major influence, it also points out the highly complex roots of today's efforts.

If these opening chapters indicate that competence-based education is in some ways an old-fashioned response to new problems, the five chapters in Part Two examine in greater detail its actual response to these problems. In Chapter Three, for example, Peter Elbow analyzes the transformation in the role of the teacher that typically occurs in competence-based programs. Although other observers might have focused on different issues than we did, it would be difficult for any of them to avoid some discussion of this change for the instructor. Elbow brings us inside the classroom and even inside the consciousness of a teacher who is struggling to rethink his or her task in the very fundamental ways demanded by the competence-based format. He anticipates the objections to this format that might be raised, say, by an Oxford don—in particular the serious question of whether and in what sense the teacher must compromise his or her sense of vocation by submitting to an emphasis on more clearly specified and assessable outcomes.

In Chapter Four, Wendy Kohli and I explore the new modes of assessment that have been developed in competence-based programs. The requirement that students demonstrate competence in aspects of some role forces new assessment procedures, and competence-based programs place greater emphasis on diagnosis and self-assessment than is characteristic of many traditional programs. However, these modes are not without their own conceptual and practical difficulties, and faculty who might consider employing competence-based assessment techniques will want to turn as well to the back of the book and the compendium of these procedures compiled by Susan E. King.

The relation of the competence-based movement to the traditional liberal arts on the one hand and to professional preparation on the other is explored in the two subsequent chapters. In Chapter Five, Thomas Ewens examines the actual practices of teachers in the competence-based mode at several liberal arts colleges against the background of traditional understandings of the liberal arts in European and American education. Ewens confronts the possibility that the crisis in liberal education today may be that many faculty members, although sincere and expert within their disciplines, are themselves no longer liberally educated. He senses that competence-based reforms may be a way of renewing faculty conversation about the nature of liberal education and about the practical outcomes one can reasonably expect it to achieve; this process in itself, Ewens thinks, may help faculty to become more liberally educated.

In Chapter Six, Virginia Olesen then considers the impact that the competence-based movement may have on reform of the professions. Her chapter bears particularly on the question of whether competence-based programs can serve as models for continuing education and recertification of practicing professionals in medicine, pharmacy, law, and other fields; but questions of assessment and of who has the power to set professional standards are also critical dimensions of her analysis.

In Chapter Seven, Zelda Gamson prefaces our presentation of case studies of five competence-based programs with her analysis of the problems of innovation that leaders of these programs have had to face and in some way resolve. As she shows, such programs have a high mortality rate; beyond the problems of new faculty roles, new assessment techniques, and new expectations, they must concern themselves with the elemental problems of acceptance and survival.

In Part Three, our five case studies—of Alverno College, the College for Human Services, Mt. Hood Community College, Florida State University, and College IV of the Grand Valley State Colleges—occupy Chapters Eight through Twelve and, we hope, make vivid all the complex and sometimes surprising interconnections that can affect the fate of any reform.

Following these institutional case studies and preceding Wendy Kohli's annotated bibliography of other sources about competence-based education, I give in an epilogue a summary of our own research methods, treating our project itself as a case study and showing some of the messy surprises we encountered. This methodological case study may be of most interest to those readers who want to know what we learned about interdisciplinary team efforts in the social sciences from our three years of work on this project as such a team. But the general reader will also find there an account of how we moved from the immersion in the data of case studies, such as those reported in Part Three of the book, to the kinds of inferences and analyses that comprise the chapters in Parts One and Two.

We owe perhaps our greatest debt to our hosts and fellow teachers at the institutions where we did our fieldwork. We learned more from them than appears in these pages, and most of us on the project team now think differently about what we do as teachers as a result of the interviews so generously given and the observations so ungrudgingly permitted. The nature of our work required us to keep imposing on our sources as we drew upon them to respond to drafts of these chapters, and sometimes to revisions of revisions. Our respondents allowed themselves to be co-opted as coresearchers without complaint.

Acknowledgments

Besides their help, my colleagues and I wish to acknowledge the contributions of other individuals and groups to particular chapters. For Chapter One on society's demands for competence, David Riesman would like to note the assistance he received from the Lilly Endowment and the Exxon Education Foundation that made continued work on the chapter possible well past the end of support for the project from FIPSE.

For Chapter Six on competence-based education and professional reform, Virginia Olesen wishes to acknowledge helpful comments on the first draft from her colleague and friend, Arlene Kaplan Daniels. In addition, she adds: "As always, Jane Tabata Usami of the Department of Social and Behavioral Sciences, University of California, provided essential and excellent technical support. Conversations with Cynthia Nelson of the American University in Cairo, Anne David and Sheryl Ruzek of the University of California, San Francisco, and Elvi Whittaker of the University of British Columbia also enriched my thinking. Finally, acknowledgments are due faculty, administrators, staff, and students at the sites studied, particularly Mt. Hood Community College, as well as two additional schools not in the main study—the University of Minnesota School of Pharmacy and the Southern Illinois University School of Medicine."

For Chapter Ten on Mt. Hood, Olesen wishes to note: "Mary Taylor Hassouna helped clarify my thinking with useful ideas on diffusion models; members of my family, through generous gifts of their time and support, made possible my participation on the project team during a long illness in the family; and, most importantly, the administrators, the former and current faculty, and the students of Mt. Hood, along with members of the Oregon State Board of Nursing, generously shared ideas and time in their harried circumstances and sensitive situations, and members of the college administration and nursing commented insightfully on drafts of the case history."

And for Chapter Eleven on Florida State University, David Riesman wishes to thank everyone who responded to earlier drafts: Alan Bayer, Anne Belcher, Louis W. Bender, Peter Bennett, Neal Berte, Gordon Blackwell, Pat Brantingham, Willis Caldwell, Frances C. Cannon, Albert W. Collier, Wesley Collins, Thomas Corcoran, Eugene J. Crook, Arthur Dorlag, Daisy Parker Flory, Dianne F. Foote, Phillip C. Fordyce, Harold Goldstein, Fred Groomes, Joseph Grosslight, Gifford Graham Hale, John Harris, Pauline Haynes, Emilie Henning, Joe Hiett, Wiley Lee Housewright, Roger Kaufman, Robert E. Knott, Harold Korn, William T. Lhamon, Roland Liebert, Sharon MacLaren, Edward E. McClure, Robert McTarnaghan, Stanley Marshall, Robert Mautz, John Merrill, Robert Edward Mitchell, Robert Morgan, Charles W. Nam, Homer Ooten, Richard Rubenstein, Richard Rubino, Ray Solomon, Robert A. Spivey, Harold Stahmer, Fred G. Standley, Jerome H. Stern, Charles Swain, Augustus B. Turnbull III, Gary W. Woditsch, E. T. York, Jr., and John Zeugner.

As director of the project, I would like to make special note of the gift of a sabbatical by the trustees of Syracuse University, which gave me an additional year to work on this report with the assistance of grants from the Hazen Foundation and the Spencer Fellow Fund of the National Academy of Education. I also owe thanks to Deans David Krathwohl and Burton Blatt, and to my department chairman, Thomas F. Green, for generous leave policies that sustained this work, and to my colleagues Vincent Tinto and Emily Haynes, who shouldered burdens in my absence. Another kind of burden caused by my absences in the bouts of fieldwork the project required cannot be easily acknowledged. That burden fell on Judith Dunn Grant, who somehow managed to be faithful both to her own career as a teacher and to do double duty as the parent of our three children. I hope that Susan, Sarah, and Robert Grant will not one day be the harshest critics of this book.

My co-authors and I especially want to thank Susan King, a consultant to the project and now senior tutor in education at the University of Western Australia, for preparing the section on technical problems and publications in assessing competence.

Finally, the coordination of the research project involved amazing feats of diplomacy and ingenuity on the part of two administrative assistants, Ruth Bayo Ford and Anne C. Woodlen, who planned conferences, helped arrange fieldwork schedules, and assisted the members of the project team in myriad research tasks. Their competence was never in question.

Syracuse, New York   GERALD GRANT
February 1979

Contents

ꙍꙍꙍꙍꙍꙍꙍꙍꙍꙍꙍꙍꙍꙍꙍ

Part Two: Critical Issues in the Development of
            Competence-Based Programs

Part Three: New Programs for Increased Competence

Contents

The Authors

GERALD GRANT is professor, Departments of Sociology and Cultural Foundations of Education, Syracuse University

PETER ELBOW is a faculty member, Evergreen State College

THOMAS EWENS is associate professor of philosophy, LeMoyne College, and clinical professor of psychiatry, State University of New York Upstate Medical Center, Syracuse

ZELDA GAMSON is professor of sociology, Residential College, and of higher education, Center for the Study of Higher Education, University of Michigan

WENDY KOHLI is a doctoral student, Department of Cultural Foundations of Education, Syracuse University

WILLIAM NEUMANN is a doctoral student, Department of Cultural Foundations of Education, Syracuse University

VIRGINIA OLESEN is professor of sociology, Department of Social
and Behavioral Sciences, University of California School of
Nursing, San Francisco

DAVID RIESMAN is Henry Ford II Professor of Social Sciences,
Harvard University

On Competence

A Critical Analysis
of Competence-Based Reforms
in Higher Education

Gerald Grant   Prologue

Implications
of Competence-Based
Education

A few years ago the Philadelphia Welfare Department denied a
mother custody of her baby on grounds of incompetence. It was an
unusual case: The father was absent and the mother was a lifelong
quadriplegic whose shrunken limbs were virtually useless. The Welfare Department asserted she was unable to care for her daughter,
then five months old, even with daytime household help. But the
mother went to court to prove her competence. As spectators stood
in awe, she changed the child's diaper before the judge, using her
lips and tongue. She also demonstrated that she could type fifty
words per minute and play the organ—both by using her tongue.
The judge awarded her full custody of her daughter, commended
her courage, and commented, "You have proven that the physical
endowments we have are only a part of the spectrum of resources
that human beings possess" (*New York Times,* 1976).

It is such an incredible case and yet so characteristically
American—one cannot quite imagine its happening anywhere else.
It evokes the powerful innocence of American will, the "can do"
spirit that has always animated our national life, the refusal to be

1

denied the right to happiness on the basis of any a priori definitions or ascribed statuses or presumptions of incapacity by age, sex, or even the most infirming physical traits.

The case also shows that the competent are often defined as a residual category of all those who cannot be shown on some obvious ground to be incompetent. It highlights thereby the difficulty of talking about what we mean by competence other than by using the negative definition "non-incompetent." Perhaps no word has been used more frequently in recent years with less precision than *competence*. In an egalitarian culture, it is less invidious than the word *merit*, but more ambiguous. Competence is something all Americans admire, even if, when pressed, they are not quite sure what it means or whether they or society possesses it in adequate amounts.

This is a book about that unease and about efforts to remedy it through reform of college curriculums. A number of colleges— primarily in the nonelite sector of American higher education—have recently attempted to reconceptualize what it is they do, with the aim of being able to state that their students are competent *at* something or competent to *do* something rather than that they have accumulated so many course credits. This is the heart of competence-based educational reforms. And each of these colleges has faced the same problem as the Philadelphia judge: How does one decide whether someone is competent, and what constitutes an adequate demonstration of competence?

Variance and Definition

At most competence-based institutions, this problem has involved making assumptions about the kind of life roles that students will enter and decisions about what should constitute an adequate demonstration of ability or performance in these roles. At Florida State University in Tallahassee, for example, faculty in urban planning, marine biology, music, and several other departments began to ask themselves, as well as professionals in these fields, about the needed attributes of urban planners, marine biologists, and musicians. They then sought to ensure the achievement of these attributes through what they called a Curriculum of Attainments.

In the very different setting of lower Manhattan, faculty at the College for Human Services, serving poorly schooled welfare mothers and out-of-work men, asked what constitutes competence in the role of "human service" worker—broadly defined to include teaching, counseling, and social work—and then organized a unique grid of experiences to develop these skills in their unlettered but highly motivated students.

In Gresham, Oregon, faculty responsible for training nurses at Mt. Hood Community College had begun to doubt that the course content in traditional nursing programs led to effective performance at bedside. They devised a competence-based nursing program—strongly influenced by the behaviorist paradigm of learning—in the hope of making their nursing graduates more responsive to the needs of patients.

In Milwaukee, a desire to promote women into managerial and professional careers was one impetus for reform at Alverno College, influencing its efforts to devise ways for assessing the accomplishment of educational goals that too often remain clichés in discussions of what constitutes a liberally educated person—goals such as clear and critical thought, effective communication, and artistic appreciation. In new and quite remarkable ways, the Alverno faculty have tried to answer the question, How do we know our students have in fact learned to be competent in these ways, and how can we demonstrate it to a skeptical outsider?

These four institutions, described in case studies later in this volume, as well as others that have adopted the competence-based label, such as Sterling College in Kansas, Mars Hill College in North Carolina, and the Antioch School of Law in Washington, D.C., share a common concern for their students' competence. But beyond this, they are so diverse that the first challenge faced by observers of the competence-based movement is to ask if any more specific quality can be said to characterize them. In at least four ways their diversity is as great as their commonality.

Theoretical Orientation. Some competence-based programs, as in nursing at Mt. Hood, are heavily behavioristic: Their faculty focus on specific behaviors that can be measured and replicated. Others, as at Alverno, term themselves humanistic: Their faculty emphasize holistic performance that incorporates the broad values associated with the humanities and liberal education. And still others, as at Seattle Central Community College, are functionalist:

They attempt to analyze the major functions, typical operations, and skills comprising a role. Some programs, of course, incorporate elements of all these theoretical orientations in varying combinations; but those that rely chiefly on one of these points of view differ radically from those based on another perspective. For example, the behavioristically oriented variety of program was characteristic of many early experiments in competence-based teacher education, but to many observers, this stream of development has come to be so discredited that it threatens to pollute the river. As a result, some of the most promising competence-based programs that we observed have been eager to wash away any trace of the competence label, lest they be marked by the stain of behaviorism. (For a sampling of these critiques, see Smith, 1975.)

Scope of Role. A few competence-based programs tend toward a narrow view of training. The Mt. Hood program, for example, sees a close relation between the curriculum and preparation for a specific job, and in this way comes close to the model of traditional vocational training. In contrast, other programs take a broad view of what is implied by any role, occupational or otherwise—holding that it incorporates elements of citizenship, attitudes toward learning, understanding of the culture in which it is situated, and what John Dewey in his essay on the vocational aspects of education called a sense of purpose and a "direction of life activities" ([1915] 1966, p. 307).

Reform Intention. Some competence-based programs accept traditional definitions of a role and restrict their innovations largely to processes of education and means of preparation within the context of the existing conception of the role. Typified within our sample by Florida State University, they seek to maintain the existing occupational structure. Others, however, attempt to transform this structure. Our sample of institutions, funded for the most part by an agency bent on major reforms of postsecondary education, included a higher than average number with a strong reformist bias of this kind. Thus the College for Human Services exemplifies in its role of the human service professional those values of service and client advocacy that it believes are neglected by traditional professionals. At Mt. Hood, the nursing educators, while incorporating a behaviorist theoretical orientation, sought to question and change the traditional, doctor-defined relationships between nurses and their patients. And at the Antioch School of Law, the faculty have sought to reorient the legal profession toward serving the poor and disenfranchised and to elevate the status of criminal defender and trial work, traditionally derogated both in law school and legal practice.

Disciplinary Focus. In most of the experiments that we observed, the traditional academic disciplines were cast in a subordinate role. But the range of attitudes toward them was great. In a number of programs, departments and disciplinary forms of organization were abolished altogether; the disciplines were hardly recognized as relevant to the enterprise; and practitioners and faculty were thrown together in odd combinations of expertise. In others, as at Alverno, a dual structure of disciplinary and competence units was maintained. And in a few places, as at Florida State, the competence programs attempted to infiltrate, as it were, the dominant departments and sought to legitimate "applied" studies as a respectable part of their work.

These wide variations may help to explain the ambivalence about competence-based programs that one finds among their observers, including the authors of this book—as illustrated, for example, in later chapters by Peter Elbow's worries about the anti-intellectual attitudes of some competence-based reformers and by Thomas Ewens's concern that in some ways competence-based education may be a complicated travesty of liberal education. But some ambivalence is necessary. One cannot be "for" or "against" competence-based education any more than one can be "for" or "against" testing. Armchair dismissal or unqualified acceptance of competence-based education, as with testing, is likely to be wrongheaded. One has to ask: What kind of competence program? For what purposes? Under what conditions?

But despite this diversity within the competence-based movement, we can nonetheless identify the boundaries that define a competence-based program or institution. Our attempts at definition never completely satisfied all the members of our own project team, some of whom found exceptions to nearly every general statement about the movement. But we largely agreed on this early working definition or criterion: *Competence-based education is a form of education that derives a curriculum from a specification of a set of outcomes; that so clearly states both the outcomes—general and*

*specific—and the means by which they will be assessed that faculty,
students, and interested third parties can make reasonably objective
judgments with respect to student achievement or nonachievement of
these outcomes; that tends to conceive learning experiences in terms
of these outcomes; and that certifies student progress on the basis
of demonstrated achievement of these outcomes.*

  This definition failed, however, to distinguish a competence-
based approach from that of most more conventional programs,
since every college catalogue contains a general statement of the
institution's anticipated or hoped-for "outcomes," followed by
specifications in terms of course requirements of how to fulfill them.
At such a general level, almost every institution could consider itself
competence-based because of its concern for outcomes. It thus
seemed important to ask whether the outcomes of the clearly
competence-oriented institutions tended to be conceived in any
characteristic way, and this question led to another definition:
*Competence-based education tends to be a form of education that
derives a curriculum from an analysis of a prospective or actual role
in modern society and that attempts to certify student progress on
the basis of demonstrated performance in some or all aspects of that
role. Theoretically, such demonstrations of competence are independent of time served in formal educational settings.*

  Some of us remained uneasy with this definition's emphasis
on roles, even if broadly construed, feeling that it made the definition less applicable to the programs at competence-based liberal arts
colleges than at others. But taking into account this reservation, we
believe this definition provides a way to identify the participants in
the competence-based movement. In virtually every institution we
examined, the faculty have at some point analyzed the subsets of
skills, knowledge, and personal requirements necessary for competence in a role, even though this may be a very generalized role,
such as a liberally educated person or a human service worker.
Often this analysis has involved observations of actual performance
in the role, interviews with exemplary performers of the role, or
surveys of clients about what expectations they hold for competent
performance in such roles. Equally important, these institutions have
sought to assess and approve student progress by means of performance directly related to this role, and they have tended to grant
credit, degrees, or other awards more on the basis of these assess-

ments than on the basis of time spent in the program. For them, as for the advocates of "mastery learning," student achievement becomes the hoped-for constant, with time and the academic calendar the variable.

Context

In terms of its current role within American education and society, the competence-based movement can best be understood as a response, at the level of higher education, to the debates beginning nearly a century ago over the future of the American high school—debates that shaped the progressive education movement and the reaction to it during this century. In recent decades, America's higher education system has been undergoing an expansion similar to that which began at the turn of the century for its secondary school system. In both cases, changes in scale have forced major changes in form and structure. In 1880, only 1 percent of the high-school-age population attended high school; but by 1930, 47 percent was enrolled. That expansion over fifty years almost exactly foreshadowed the enrollment curve at the college level in the nearly fifty years since 1930.

The arguments over competence-based education today are also similar to those of the protagonists in the secondary school debate of the 1890s and early 1900s. They involve the adequacy of the higher education system to absorb and effectively educate its new clientele, vastly expanded in numbers and highly varied in background. Whether one calls this clientele the "new students," the "bottom third," or "nontraditional students," one is referring to students who have not previously been educated at this level of the system. And the debate about them has become more intense as the proportion of the age grade continuing to this level has approached or surpassed half. When the rising tide of new students reaches this level, only three responses are possible: (1) Turn students away by restricting admissions or providing incentives for youth to enter the work force, (2) absorb the new students in existing programs and structures, or (3) change the structures and the system to meet the needs of the new students.

Near the turn of the century, the secondary system consisted of a sprinkling of public high schools and a network of private academies. These were oriented to the academic requirements of the colleges in the same way that until recently many colleges were oriented to the graduate and professional schools. When the influx of new students into the high schools began, the first response was to defend ever more strongly the traditional values of academic training. Presidents Nicholas Murray Butler of Columbia and Charles W. Eliot of Harvard led the famous Committee of Ten on Secondary School Studies to make the proposal in 1893 that four years of "strong and effective mental training" (Rippa, 1969, p. 470) would be the best preparation for all students, whether bound for college or work. The ideal curriculum they recommended deviated little from the traditional academic subjects and was more rigorous than most college students encounter today (Latin, Greek, mathematics, English, French, German, history, and the sciences). Butler and Eliot were emphatic that this curriculum was as fitted for the youngster headed for work as for college: "Every subject which is taught at all in a secondary school should be taught in the same way and to the same extent to every pupil so long as he pursues it, no matter what the probable destination of the pupil may be, or at what point his education is to cease" (Rippa, 1969, p. 466).

But within a few decades, the high school population had increased from 360,000 students to five million and the progressive movement developed two major counterthrusts to Butler and Eliot's prescription of a purely academic and disciplinary emphasis. One major line of development grew out of the progressive concern for clean, rational government and efficient schools. If schools were going to serve the masses, they needed to be more practical and efficiently run. R. Freeman Butts has noted that the advocates of social efficiency have not had a good press from revisionist historians "because of their overly enthusiastic acceptance of business ideals of management efficiency and their belief that education ought to perform the function of social control on behalf of the predominantly business society in a modernizing nation. . . . The primary purpose of education for social control, then, was not to acquire knowledge as such or simply to develop academic power; it was to prepare the individual for his role in an urban, industrializing, and capitalist society" (1978, p. 191). The most widely publicized examples of the efficiency wing of the progressive movement were the reports issued between 1915 and 1919 by the Committee on Economy of Time in Education of the National Education Association. This concern for a more rational, cost-effective, and practically useful curriculum has been a major theme of the competence-based movement.

But the other, more Deweyan wing of the progressive movement, which David Tyack (1974, pp. 196–197) called the "pedagogical progressives" in contrast with the efficiency concerns of the "administrative progressives," also reappears in current debates. The pedagogical progressives were concerned about democratic social development and spoke about the "project method," the "activity curriculum," and other ways to "meet the individual needs" of children. That concern for social development reached an early crest with the publication of the Cardinal Principles of Education by the National Education Association's Commission on the Reorganization of Secondary Education. Again, Butts summarizes the era: "What the seven Cardinal Principles did was to shift the emphasis in school away from preoccupation with the academic and intellectual disciplines and to broaden the social role of education almost beyond recognition. The 'constants' were now to be thought of in terms of the common social needs and activities required of all individuals, rather than subject matters to be mastered. Variation and differentiation appropriate to differing individuals could be served in connection with vocation and leisure, but the goals of cohesion should be achieved by common studies having to do with health, family, knowledge-acquiring skills, and democratic citizenship" (1978, p. 194).

By the late 1940s, this aspect of the progressive movement had eventuated in the life adjustment curriculum, which produced a sharp conservative reaction to what was regarded as a watered-down curriculum without intellectual rigor or discriminating standards of achievement.

At the same time, debate continued over the fate of strictly manual or vocational training. Should it take place alongside academic subjects, should it be given in separate schools to youth who were sorted out by examination or other means as suited for "manual" careers, or should vocational training become the responsibility of industry and unions in apprenticeship systems. The high value that American society has always placed on equal educational opportunity militated against early "streaming" into separate paths or any premature closure of educational options. The compromise that was shaped from all these impulses generally brought all youth together under one roof. In the American comprehensive high school, all students to some degree participated in a common "civics" curriculum but were tracked for most of their studies in so-called general (or business), academic or vocational curriculums.

And at the postsecondary level today, Americans are reluctant to impose rigid controls or to seal the fate of some students upon high school graduation. It has become fashionable of late to emphasize the stratified nature of the American higher educational system, underscoring the separation of students into community, four-year and university levels, and differentiation within levels by student selectivity and aptitude. Yet even the two-year or community colleges in America have followed the comprehensive pattern, and nearly half of their students now transfer to four-year colleges or universities. In addition, students who would have been considered woefully underprepared for college a decade or two ago now enter four-year colleges and universities in large numbers directly from high school.

Hence, competence-based education has been a means of raising again the questions of how and in what ways these "new" students should be served. Analogously, we are now past the point at which Butler and Eliot argued that the traditional values of academic training would be the best medicine for all. Instead, there is widespread skepticism that formal course work should remain the only pathway to a credential, and there is doubt that traditional course content bears much relation to the future performance of many students. In effect, competence-based education represents an attempted synthesis of the same congeries of forces that entered the debate over the development of the secondary system. In their various manifestations, competence-based reformers have attempted to subordinate the traditional disciplines to some conception of competence, to be responsive to the concern for greater efficiency and cost effectiveness, to seek a closer fit between an ever more costly system of higher education and the needs of a technological society for highly skilled workers, and to place more emphasis on developing social and cooperative skills. All these were elements of the progressive debate sketched above. But the synthesis attempted by the competence movement also takes the reaction to the progressive movement into account, particularly the attacks in the 1950s and early 1960s on the excesses of the life adjustment curriculum and its presumed loss of standards. Hence, the competence-based movement joins egalitarian hopes to an insistence on clear standards of assessment and—at least thus far—reasonable standards of achievement for all students.

At the societal level, then, these are the forces, infused with concern over the erosion of competence in many areas of American life, that shape the context in which specific institutional initiatives toward competence-based approaches have been taken. As yet we have had no clear statement of the principles that govern these institutional efforts, similar to the statement provided by the Progressive Education Association in 1919. Nor has the competence movement yet produced any major thinker to provide the conceptual and theoretical underpinnings for competence-based programs in the way that Dewey served the progressive education movement. Indeed, we may never have a fully worked out theory of competence-based education comparable to his for the progressive movement. Nonetheless, competence-based education is now sufficiently mature that conclusions about its educational impact, if not its theory, can be advanced, even if they are based on a small sample of institutions and must be offered tentatively.

Impacts

From the institutional point of view, the major impact of adopting a competence-based approach is to shift more of an institution's resources from the best to the average and below-average students. These "invisible" students, formerly given C's or D's for endurance and passed along, become highly visible in a competence-based format and no longer merely slip through the institution unnoticed. The competence approach forces a redistribution of faculty labor to them: A higher proportion of the faculty will spend more time teaching these students basic skills and helping them achieve specified outcomes than in traditional schools.

Whether these additional efforts actually lead to a net increase of societal competence remains an open question. The dropout rate for competence-based programs seems high, perhaps because of the very demands they make on students,[1] and we have yet seen no clear evidence that students who complete the programs are in fact more competent or employable than similar students from traditional programs. The data are just not available to make such comparisons, and they may never be. For all the reasons discussed later in Chapter Four, demonstration of adequate performance in aspects of a role at one point in time cannot be considered predictive of performance in a role at a later time under changed circumstances. But there is no question among leaders of the movement that competence-based education does lead to a net increase in societal competence, and this is one of the strongest dynamics driving competence reforms. If the movement can eventually show that it serves average or new students more effectively than do traditional curriculums without greatly increasing costs, it will be bound to gain more widespread public and legislative support. At the same time, this heavy workload with middling students is one of the strongest sources of faculty resistance to competence programs.

Turning to the movement's impact on students, the new modes of assessment developed in competence-based programs appear promising. Assessments are very often put to diagnostic use, and students exercise considerable initiative in choosing when and how often to be assessed. The use of student peers as assessors and the practice of demanding self-assessments seem to produce nondefensive and modestly self-confident students—although this impact,

[1] It is difficult to assess dropout data, since dropout rates are higher among poorer and underprepared students, who are overrepresented at the institutions in our sample. But among these institutions, dropout rates were particularly high at the College of Public and Community Service at the University of Massachusetts at Boston, and in the urban planning program at Florida State University. At Boston, only 61 of 300 students completed the program; at Florida State, only 3 of 16 students elected to continue in urban planning at the end of the first year. Elsewhere the completion rates were higher: At the College for Human Services, close to half of the students completed the two-year program; at Mt. Hood, 67 percent of the nurses remained in the program; and at Alverno, 85 percent completed the first year. And although we do not have dropout figures for Seattle Central Community College, overall enrollment in its competence-based management program declined over two years from 164 to 146 students.

too, must remain subject to reconsideration until we have had more experience with and more careful analysis of these programs.

But while the impact on students is considerable, competence-based education is essentially a faculty reform. It goes to the root of the relationship between faculty and students and requires faculty members to rethink their role. Even tenured faculty—already uneasy with the new emphasis on student evaluation of teaching—must learn to be competent at new skills. They must move away from the lectern and learn to teach in other settings and in other forms of interaction with students; they must spend less time performing themselves and more time observing the performances of students. Those faculty who have relied primarily on paper and pencil tests of knowledge or on demonstration of intellectual abilities must devise a wider range of assessments, often involving simulations or live performances of various kinds that attempt to assess human capacities and personal attributes beyond the purely intellectual. Faculty must also be willing to spend enormously greater amounts of time in assessment than has typically been the case in more traditional programs.

For faculty, competence-based education also initiates a process of interdisciplinary dialogue about the desired outcomes of a college education and the means to assess them. An individual faculty member's autonomy in designing his or her course syllabus thus gives way to an interrogation about what he or she can teach that will contribute to developing these outcomes. The result of this process for faculty is that they often change their primary reference group from that of the "invisible college" of their disciplinary peers throughout the nation to that of their immediate colleagues in the local institution, including new "colleagues" who are often practitioners in the fields that students will enter. In the process of forming these new collegial relationships, faculty must open their teaching to peer inspection and open themselves to peer criticism outside disciplinary channels in a radically different way. In fact, one of the most threatening aspects of a competence-based curriculum for many faculty, particularly in its early stages, is that it exposes their competence or incompetence to discuss, in a clear and nontechnical way, the application of their subject to the roles for which students are being prepared or to the outcomes under consideration.

In addition, competence-based approaches lead to a strong emphasis on "accountability"—on holding faculty and institutions responsible for teaching students to achieve certain outcomes. All students generally submit to external assessments of their competence, and these assessments can be a means of determining the relative success of various teachers measured against the same standard and of obtaining information about the performance of the institution and the curriculum as a whole. Faculty members are also accountable to curriculum committees, which have the power to gauge the appropriateness of courses to outcome goals; thus course planning is no longer the province of the individual teacher or the teacher's disciplinary guild. The process of curriculum revision and course design in competence-based programs often leads to a coordinated syllabus, sometimes expressed in condensed form as a "grid" of outcomes and prescribed experiences. In this respect, syllabi in competence programs come to resemble those characteristic of the elementary and secondary schools: imposed rather than individualistic, standardized rather than idiosyncratic. Because of this, competence-based education may be said to be the first tertiary education reform.

Prospects

One cannot at this point predict widespread adoption of competence-based education throughout American higher education. As Zelda Gamson's analysis in Chapter Seven shows, competence-based programs have had a high mortality rate. Perhaps because of their very demands, they have not proved particularly attractive to students; and in institutions where the faculty have the power to resist imposed change (such as well-established institutions with tenure), it has been difficult to win the loyalty of faculty to a competence-based approach. Thus the programs at Florida State University have come to a virtual standstill, and a substantial segment of the Alverno College faculty has resigned, while those remaining have protested to the college's board about the competence approach and its manner of implementation.

Looking to the future, we must acknowledge some major concerns about the competence-based movement as a movement. As a response to the needs of today's new college students competence-

based education may be as subject to excesses as was the life adjustment curriculum at the secondary level. If competence-based programs eventually show that they serve new students more efficiently
than conventional programs do and the movement thus turns into a
bandwagon, it could produce a renewed attack on the institution of
tenure, particularly in those institutions serving the new students.
And because the competence format makes it difficult to defend
"research faculty" work schedules for any faculty members, even at
graduate levels, its impact would be greatest in nonelite universities
where large undergraduate programs provide the tuition dollars to
finance what are regarded as cushy working conditions for the
graduate faculty. If these assaults were successful, they could ultimately lead to a further stratification of American higher education
and the creation of an even more career-oriented sector of institutions similar to the polytechnics in Great Britain.

Even in the absence of this bifurcation by institutional type,
competence-based education could become a means of further
bureaucratizing some sectors of higher education. It is a reform that
could easily lend itself to the thickening of a middle layer of managers, curriculum specialists, assessment experts, and record keepers
who would hold faculty accountable to the outcomes that these
factotums have specified. In such a bleak scenario, a competence-
based curriculum would be a vital adventure only in its formative
stage when faculty were launched on a new dialogue about purposes. In the second or third generation, however, the curriculum
could become a routinized, lifeless grid, all the more difficult to
change because of the paraprofessional and managerial jobs dependent on its continuance.

In our most pessimistic mood, my colleagues and I fear the
movement could degenerate into a grand hoax, a perpetuation of an
illusion that students are more competent when all that has been
done is to reshuffle the old deck while mumbling some new jargon.
The semblance of reform and its substance are very different things,
yet the American philanthropic and governmental sponsors of innovation have often paid very dearly for the former without realizing
the latter. In the next decade, many postsecondary institutions will
find themselves underenrolled, and they might seek support under
the competence label without accepting its rigors. The reimposition
of requirements on their students that high competence would de-

mand might be too much for them to risk because of their understandable fear of losing student customers in a buyers' market.

We thus remain ambivalent about the competence-based
movement. Indeed, we worry more about it as a possible bandwagon
than as an institutionally generated reform, for we do not believe that
any program can or should be imposed across the board or upon any
designated subset of students or faculty. But within a pluralistic framework of reform and institutional self-determination, we believe that
much has been learned in competence-based approaches that merits
wider attention. Most important, the process of faculty discussion
about outcomes and assessment practices can have significant benefit
for institutions, as Thomas Ewens illustrates in Chapter Five. In
addition, after a decade of remissions in the curriculum, during
which students have been allowed to pick and choose their courses
at will, the competence approach renews the corporate authority of
the faculty and reduces the anxieties of individualistic bargaining
characteristic of the recent era of student-faculty relations.

Moreover, unlike the minimum competency-testing movement at the secondary school level, which has been justifiably
criticized as ridiculously easy[2]—in New York, the high school exam
asks students to write the time shown on a clockface—competence-
based reforms at the college level have not set a bare minimum of
performance as the standard for all. On the contrary, at least in
the first generation, they have tended to be maximalist, not minimalist. Their emphasis on outcomes has led faculty to entertain
demanding, if not awesome, expectations of competence. Thus we
think experiments in competence-based education should be encouraged on a selective basis at more institutions—in particular, at those
institutions where a significant portion of the faculty displays a
readiness to undertake a fundamental reconsideration of what it is
they are trying to achieve, and where faculty seek to prepare

[2] As this book went to press, the New York Board of Regents adopted
a much stiffer test requiring high school level performance in basic academic
subjects, which generated a controversy among school officials who assert
that thousands of students will thereby be denied high school diplomas. In
response, Education Commissioner Gordon Ambach proposed that students
who flunked the test be given "certificates of achievement," a compromise
adamantly opposed by Regent Kenneth Clark, a black psychologist, who
favors a single rigorous standard for all pupils.

students both to fulfill a useful role in society and to be intelligently critical of that role and of the society's ordering of roles. In such institutions, a competence-based approach is likely not only to serve students well but to renew the faculty's sense of vocation, even at the cost of transforming—while not abandoning—their relationship to their disciplines.

We would make four recommendations toward that end to educators, institutions, and funding agencies:

First, they should foster greater dissemination of what has been learned in the experiments undertaken thus far under the competence-based label.

Second, they should provide more opportunities for exchange of faculty and for visits by faculty to such institutions as Alverno or the College for Human Services, where major programs have been developed whose accomplishments and difficulties have been made visible by continuous scrutiny and self-criticism.

Third, they should encourage the development of new modes of assessment and the further refinement of methods already developed in competence-based experiments.

And fourth, they should sponsor more precise comparative studies of the long-range effects of competence-based programs as compared with more traditional forms of higher education, particularly to assess benefits for the so-called new students.

Despite the three years our project team spent in the field— longer than most "evaluations" of other educational experiments —our time was too short and our charter too limited, particularly in terms of the kinds of data we could reasonably ask institutions to produce, for us to answer that question of comparative effects of traditional and competence-based education. Nonetheless, we had enough of a look to convince us of the promise and possible benefits of the competence-based approach, in spite of its potential dangers as a movement. As the following chapters on critical issues, along with the case studies later in this volume attest, there is much to commend in competence programs. If these chapters have value, they will serve not as a prescription for reform or as the final word on competence-based education, but as a means for understanding a major reform movement and as an aid for more educators to rethink their own goals, desired outcomes, and competence.

David Riesman   1

Society's Demands
for Competence

ῼῼῼῼῼῼῼῼῼῼῼῼῼῼῼῼῼῼ

Competence-based education has many of the qualities of a social movement or rather of a set of overlapping social movements. As with any such movement, one has to ask: Why has competence-based education manifested itself just now, in the last half-dozen years or so; and why has it taken so many, indeed protean, forms?

If something is felt to be amiss with America's level of competence, or with the means by which individual competence can be recognized or credentialed, it is no surprise that educational institutions should be asked to supply a remedy. Our schools and colleges have for some time been expected to solve an endless list of social problems, whether these be racial injustice, inequalities of income, inadequate nutrition and health care, an apathetic and alienated citizenry, or lack of intercultural understanding. Remedying incompetence is but one more burden—and a natural one at that—to be placed on our educational institutions.

But what is there in the current American climate of opinion that leads to a general societal concern for competence, or, stated inversely, to the belief that many Americans, in various age cohorts and not merely the young, are insufficiently competent for the widely evident tasks of society? There seem to be at least four major sources for this concern and for the competence-based education movement to which it has given rise.

Demand of the Times for Increased Competence

Perhaps the most immediately plausible explanation for this concern over competence is that levels of competence once thought at least tolerable for a society moving at a slower pace are quite inadequate for a society whose internal management is growing steadily more complicated. Consider, too, the amount of knowledge that individuals must master to conduct themselves competently and to have the self-confidence that comes from believing themselves competent.

Today, in fact, belief in one's own competence is no longer enough, and a demand for demonstrated competence now motivates much of education. This demand underlies much of the insistence on continuing education and even relicensure in the major professions, and it aims both to uncover cases of self-delusion about one's competence and to prevent apathetic resignation about maintaining one's competence. To this end, large corporations not only provide intensive training through specialized in-house schools, such as the General Motors Technical Institute, but also send their employees to midcareer management programs, such as that for Sloan Fellows at M.I.T., or to short-term courses for managers and labor leaders, which the Harvard Graduate School of Business Administration offers. Many institutes bring lawyers up-to-date on the everchanging intricacies of the Internal Revenue Code, of antitrust law, and of other specialized fields of law; and pressure is increasing to improve advocacy among the trial bar, long known within the profession for playing it by ear. Continuing medical education programs see to it that doctors keep up with advances in medical knowledge, especially doctors who are not part of a large university medical complex. Similar efforts encourage teachers to return for additional certificates and degrees with the incentive of raises in salary, if not that of released time. Less well-established efforts at "faculty development" in higher education have resulted from the present stasis in the academic profession and from the hope of making tenure less of a lifetime resting place. Postdoctoral fellowships offer updating and training in new fields within the academic disciplines. To reach the top in the major professions today would thus seem to require a far greater degree of cognitive complexity and conceptual clarity than in an earlier era, and certainly to remain on top requires far more. There is more to know in general; there is more to know about the specialty on which one focuses; and there is a more continuous production of new knowledge that requires sifting, even if much of it must be discarded as unproven or redundant.

This intense concern for competence—this sense that time may be running out for us unless we increase our competence—is a relatively recent development in American life, having arisen since Hiroshima and Nagasaki and having been precipitated most directly by Sputnik. From the beginnings of American self-consciousness, there have been repeated doubts about American competence, but not until recently have they become widespread. For example, among Puritan divines and those who listened to them, the questions that mattered were whether one was saved, was godly or God-fearing, or, in the various evangelical revivals, could be born again in Christ. Building a competence, in the old-fashioned sense of a craft or qualification, might be taken, as Max Weber observed in *The Protestant Ethic and The Spirit of Capitalism,* as a possible sign of belonging to the elect, of being saved, but it was no certain sign: piety counted more than craftsmanship or learning. And in addition to such religious currents that encouraged resignation and fatalism, a strong minority intellectual tradition in America rejected worldly definitions of competence, as illustrated by the writings of that competent surveyor, Thoreau. Thought and contemplation, not practical success, were world enough for some. But more commonly, Americans thought of themselves as sufficiently competent—indeed, as more competent than any other people. Educated. Americans might look to Europe for models of science, culture, and art, but others reacted defensively against foreign models with a vulgar and still not uncommon boosterism.

Even as recently as the Second World War, the United States appeared to retain its image both abroad and at home, as a "can do" country. It emerged from the war with both its enemies and allies prostrate and dependent upon it for economic recovery and even for survival and with a general glow of good feeling about its level of competence. At that time, the atom bomb could be seen as symbolizing American achievement (although of course it was an international achievement "made in America"). Only thereafter did the threat of destruction of the planet by nuclear weapons begin to grow, a threat that was later heightened by Sputnik. While the uses to which this Russian achievement was put by American educators and politicians seemed fundamentally to alter prevailing American attitudes about our superior competence, one might in fact have drawn a more ambivalent lesson about American ability from a closer look at the actual record of Americans during the Second World War. Many who took part in the war effort were brought face-to-face, often for the first time, with gross incompetence. Many war industries were frightfully mismanaged, and only our over-whelming bounty of natural resources, manpower, and—for the first time in heavy industry in any quantity—womanpower, allowed us to supply our allies and later our own military services with the matériel needed to overwhelm the enemy. It was not wise general-ship but partially self-defeating bombings and vast expenditures of ammunition that accomplished this victory. (How many Americans recognize that both radar and the jet engine were invented not by Americans but by the British?) When training for military service, GIs soon learned the common expression "SNAFU" (in polite trans-lation, "Situation Normal: All Fouled Up") as the result of their experience with our neglected peacetime military command, itself supplemented by half-trained ROTC cadres, who were often, in the absence of complete air and artillery superiority, no match for the *Wehrmacht*. Underneath the appearance of superiority, ineptitude was rampant, just as underneath the veneer of patriotism, cynicism was rife concerning the legitimacy of governing institutions, although it did not approach the levels of cynicism found among the far less representative GIs who were drafted or recruited to fight in Vietnam.

Critical observers drew similar lessons from what seemed to them the needless expansionism of the Mexican and Spanish-Ameri-can wars and the brave but often needless slaughter of the War Between the States, as well as from a closer, more differentiated look at American history in general. Thus Alexis de Tocqueville reports in *Democracy in America* that he asked an American sailor why

American sailing ships (much like American stagecoaches and steamboats of the same epoch) were often hastily constructed and not notable for seaworthiness. The sailor responded that any ship would soon be obsolete, so rapid was the progress in mechanic arts. It is important to recall Tocqueville's sailor because of the common supposition that commercial advertising is responsible for built-in obsolescence, but both conspicuous consumption and conspicuously wasteful production long preceded the development of advertising and were accompanied by a disregard of careful craftsmanship. Even in our own time, when New England mills have sought to remain viable by importing tool-and-die men from the United Kingdom, careful craftsmanship has been in limited supply in the United States, its evidences preserved in museums, and its living exemplars treasured like museum pieces. Another example may be taken from Calhoun's study (1960), which demonstrated that American bridge and railway builders (mostly self-taught until West Point and later Rensselaer Polytechnic Institute began to professionalize engineering) possessed less mathematical competence and hence made less conservative allowances for possible error than British engineers, with not infrequent and spectacularly disastrous results, as bridges fell down and boilers blew up.

Tocqueville also noticed the cavalier treatment of the land by American farmers, who regarded their farms as real estate speculations to be sold to newcomers as the older settlers moved on to better land. A New York newspaper editor, Horace Greeley, visiting Kansas in the 1840s, observed that farmers, sitting on their isolated plots of land, were often indolent and that their separate houses (not clustered, village-style, in the European manner) were surrounded by castaway junk, much as today one can find debris scattered from northern New England to western Washington. Our mistreatment of the land in which the soil eroded and blew away was dramatically illustrated by the desperate flight of the Okies during the Great Depression—and the beginnings of soil conservation.

American tolerance of ineptitude has not been limited to agrarian life where, despite urban stereotypes, it is today perhaps the most important area in which American technology holds world leadership. The Great Depression (out of which the country emerged only as a result of the Second World War) demonstrated that industrial management did not know what work on the shop floor was really like. Eventually, it is true, managers were forced, through the blessing bestowed on unionization by the New Deal, to attend to the actualities of daily work. Management then began to learn. But this incompetence was followed, as in the railroad industry and, more recently, in the steel industry, by managerial abuse and union monopolistic opportunities to raise prices and wages and then by the eventual loss of monopoly positions to competitors—either to homegrown substitutes (competing forms of transport in the case of the railroads) or to substitutes from abroad (for example, foreign imports of steel). Indeed, in comparison with earlier American feelings of exalted or almost omnipotent competence vis-à-vis the rest of the world, we have discovered that many countries can make both technological and social inventions superior to ours; they can make more efficient automobiles, reduce infant mortality and general morbidity, and, as in the notable case of Japan, manage such crises as the oil embargo with greater social cohesion and compliance of citizens.

What appears to be incompetence and sloppy workmanship shows up at all social levels in the United States, often to the astonishment of foreign visitors who have taken at face value America's image of itself as an efficient country. According to Maccoby, the high production costs of many large and apparently efficient corporations are elevated by distrust between labor and management: Resentment appears not only in decreased effort and increased absenteeism, but in active sabotage; managerial inspections then intensify worker distrust, leading in a vicious circle to still more inspections. In the automobile industry, on which we Americans have prided ourselves, poor workmanship has led to an almost chronic recall of cars for defects, which have managed to pass series of inspections. And even our prisons and insane asylums, once models for the rest of the world (our prisons were what attracted Tocqueville and his companion Beaumont to the United States), are no longer regarded as sources of national pride.

It may be that the problems humanity has faced have always outrun the immediate capacity to resolve them, but today we are far more aware of the discrepancy than when H. G. Wells penned his famous phrase describing education as a race between ignorance and catastrophe. Since Sputnik we have become aware of dangers of environmental degradation in the land, the air, and the oceans. Not only have we witnessed the potential exhaustion of easily attainable natural resources but we have also been reminded of the grave danger of famine, having crossed the Malthusian line in Bangladesh and in the Sahel in 1973. We now realize that much of our farming is highly dependent on petroleum for fertilizer, insecticides, machinery, and transport, and perilously dependent on diminishing water tables for irrigation. Finally, we know that no Malthusian peril equals the continuing threat of nuclear devices or other perhaps about-to-be-invented weapons of mass annihilation, whether such weapons might be used out of national intent, political fanaticism, or mere inadvertence. Even high competence, we fear, may not be sufficient to avoid the looming problems of the future.

As noted earlier, once Americans decide to call something a problem, we tend to turn to education with the assumption that every problem has a solution. Just as West Point and Rensselaer Polytechnic taught mathematics to supposedly no-nonsense engineers, so America's land-grant colleges came to epitomize education for competence in all fields of learning and endeavor—created as they were, according to the Morrill Act of 1862, "for the benefit of agriculture and the mechanic arts" by promoting "the liberal and practical education of the industrial classes in the several pursuits and professions of life." Setting out to raise the competence of farmers in cooperation with state and federal agencies in the agricultural extension services, these colleges controlled erosion and increased crop production through research and teaching. They turned out civil engineers who facilitated the development of extractive industries, undertook flood control, entered urban planning to try to solve the problems of massive metropolitan congestion, and added to the traditional federal involvement in geological and oceanic surveys a greatly improved system of weather forecasting, useful in everything from agricultural planning to airplane navigation. By the time of the Second World War, America's leading universities, both private and public, were among the institutions preparing psychoanalytically oriented anthropologists, who could examine the cultures of adversaries and allies alike, and their schools of civil affairs trained occupation forces for rehabilitating conquered Germany and Japan.

Following the Second World War, higher education became one of the most significant claimants for discretionary resources, whether public or private, as the United States embarked on a nearly continuous boom both in production and in consumer goods, in contrast to the postwar depression that had followed the First World War. GIs returned from the war to take advantage in unprecedented numbers of the GI Bill of Rights, and they brought a new seriousness to higher education in their search for the various kinds of competence that would assure them of employment. They were young "adult learners," rarely collegiate in the older style, and hence gratifying to serious faculty members, who did their best to respond to the needs of these students. At the same time, institutions were expanding to meet the enlarged numbers of those attending college. But even then, higher education was still overwhelmingly a local or at most a regional matter. There were no national competence-based movements since there was not yet a national concern for education except among a handful of leaders, and since state and local governments, as well as private philanthropy and private enterprise, were still geared to local markets for students and only peripherally to a national market for ideas. Since the GI Bill was a federal measure, however, many GIs, uprooted by the war, did not return to the colleges nearest their former homes but sought out institutions that in turn were becoming increasingly national; that is, these colleges saw the opportunity to improve their quality and selectivity, and with the recruitment of competing institutions extending into their own local catch basins, they had to go national to maintain, if not to enlarge, their enrollments.

Just as universities had used the leverage of the military services, such as the Office of Naval Research, to seek federal largesse during and at the end of the Second World War, so the Cold War, greatly intensified first by the Korean War and then by Sputnik, proved useful to universities, colleges, and schools alike in securing support for upgrading teaching, especially in mathematics, the sciences, and foreign languages. Under the patronage of the National Defense Education Act, it became respectable for university mathematicians and physicists to concern themselves with "the new math," "the new physics," and "the new biology"—cognitively quite abstract and complex forms of learning. Simultaneously with research into styles of learning and teaching undertaken by such diverse scholars as Jerome Bruner, Benjamin Bloom, and Jerome Kagan, these new approaches to math and science were introduced into the high schools through the Educational Development Corporation, the National Science Foundation (NSF) and similar agencies. (Many, possibly most, educators—and also many legislators, had they not been worried about attacks from potential political rivals—would have preferred to see the "Defense" label removed from this legislation, but they were not above accepting funds under any label to raise the level of scholastic achievement and to undertake a good deal of nonapplied, more or less "pure" scholarship.)

At the same time, as part of a number of concurrent developments, the Council on Basic Education was demanding a return to a more rigorous, if not traditional, curriculum. A strong reaction was also setting in against what was defined as "progressive" education by many upper-middle-class parents. Raised under either religious auspices or a secularized version of the Protestant ethic, and often under the hardship of the Great Depression, they were anxious lest their own children become hedonistic and slack, and they were inclined to see the public schools as soft. Ridiculing an emphasis on "life adjustment" and courses in subjects such as driver training, they pressured school officials to emulate the charmed circle formed by the few well-established private preparatory schools, the suburban public luminaries of New Trier and Newton, and such rare specialized citywide schools as the Bronx High School of Science; and they sought to create in the United States the equivalents of the German *Gymnasium,* the French *lycée,* or the Japanese secondary school, undistractedly geared to top-level cognitive performance.

In this post-Sputnik movement of educational reform, the responses ranged from "enrichment" and advanced placement programs for the gifted in high school to selective admissions and accelerated programs for the "superior" student in college. As part of this reform, a number of such technical devices as programmed learning that were later to flow into the competence-based education movements gained their initial impetus. But the first competence-based movement centered less on students or instructional methods than on school teachers and the adequacy of their teaching credentials and certificates. The M.I.T. physicist Jerrold Zacharias, who helped run many NSF-sponsored institutes with the aim of upgrading teachers so that they could handle the reorganization of subject-matter, liked to talk about developing "teacher-proof" curriculums that would allow bright students to proceed in school at their own pace, not held back by slower students or by instructors regarded as poorly trained in the teachers colleges of an earlier era. And many articulate parents thought that schools could be made accountable for the shortcomings of their students. They wanted to mandate through state law or local executive action that teachers be judged on the basis of how well their students performed and not by their possession of a teaching credential, which, in spite of all efforts to give schoolteaching professional status, was not considered truly meaningful.

The famous Coleman report, *Equality of Educational Opportunity* (1966), would later suggest how relatively unimportant the contribution of teacher training was to the level of academic achievement and cognitive learning in schools, compared to the influence of the home and the general atmosphere of the community. In contrast to these other factors, however, teacher training was particularly vulnerable to attack and accessible to government control. And although some of the main impresarios of the diverse impulses within the competence-based movements are to be found in schools of education, the competence-based movement against granting certificates to teachers on the basis of course credits alone did not arise primarily from within such schools. It arose instead among parents as represented on school boards and among taxpayers as represented in legislatures. These groups were concerned over the failure of school children to learn the basic skills required for minimal functioning in American society, including the ability to read, write, and do quantitative work at grade level or to do college-level work when admitted to college through what amounted to social promotion (whether by grade inflation or educational philosophy or the political clout of students and their parents.

Schoolteachers of course had always been vulnerable. In an earlier era, they were mostly women and were subjected in their overt moral behavior to the severest of community norms. After the epidemic of McCarthyism broke out, they had to watch their step not to be thought "pinkos," just as in the South they ran risks if they became identified as "nigger lovers." But what changed in the 1950s was that they became vulnerable from a new quarter—previously a source of protection for them on civil libertarian grounds—namely, the upper-middle-class parents of superior educational background, organized in the PTA or directly through the school board, who were asking not only why their Johnny couldn't read, but why he was reading science fiction rather than Shakespeare. To teachers, struggling not only against low status and low salaries but high vulnerability, lifetime credentials based largely on accumulated credits and earned degrees were professional protection, just as unionization and collective bargaining were later to become. But a vicious circle ensued. Credentialism intensified the feeling on the part of many legislators, school board members, and taxpayer groups that teachers could not be made accountable and that, once certified, they were as difficult to remove, whatever the level of their classroom performance, as tenured professors. One basic element of the competence-based movement involves, then, an effort to dispense with academic gatekeeping. It asks teachers and other professionals not what courses they have taken with what graded results and with what resultant certificates or degrees but rather what they can actually do or what they have in fact done, for which a still necessary, if vestigially meaningful, credential should be bestowed. (See Spady, 1977, for additional discussion of this point.)

Similar doubts about the competence of college and university faculty members have reinforced competence-based education in postsecondary institutions. Especially in public higher education, professors have increasingly followed the lead of schoolteachers down the road of collective bargaining, at times as a response to felt financial imperatives but no less often as a response to pressures for accountability. The mandates at even leading universities like Michigan and Texas as to the number of "contact" hours that faculty members should have with students reflect the common American

judgment once pungently summed up in a comment by former
Teamsters Union boss Dave Beck to Clark Kerr, then president of
the University of California: "How do you fellows get away with a
six-hour workweek, which even we powerful teamsters can't attain!"
Part of this pressure for accountability came from purely budgetary
motives. As higher education absorbed a larger share of state resources, both absolutely and relatively to other social services, there
was an understandable desire on the part of public officials to know
what was being purchased with these funds in the way of actual
performance by faculty. But in addition, it reflected a not negligible
backlash against faculty members who were believed to have
sympathized with, if they had not actively incited, the student protests and demonstrations of the 1960s. Here was a belief analogous
to that held in circles far beyond the reach of the work of the Council for Basic Education that schoolteachers infatuated with open
classrooms and other "permissive" innovations were responsible for
both the lack of discipline and the failures in the teaching of academic subjects in the public schools.

In the immediate post-Sputnik years, many of the wealthier
states competed with each other to develop not only their flagship
campuses but also many formerly regional comprehensive colleges
into "centers of excellence", in the terminology of the National
Science Foundation. State prestige and educational prestige then
. appeared to go hand in hand. Financial resources and entrepreneurial energies both seemed inexhaustible—one unobtrusive measure being the spread of distinguished university presses far beyond
the charmed circle of the previously eminent world-class universities.
But if the student beneficiaries took the opulence of their art centers,
athletic facilities, and handsome new residences for granted, they
resented the competitive pressures, which that very drive for excellence, along with the demographic boom, was producing. Faculty
members themselves brought up with heightened expectations did
not want to teach the basic skills of writing to the barely motivated
and ill-prepared students who were encouraged to attend college by
subsidy and exhortation, any more than departments of mathematics were prepared to teach "bonehead" math to high school
graduates who could hardly handle arithmetic, let alone algebra or
the calculus. The upshot was the beginning of the same cycle of

backlash and protective response already present in the schools, and
that in turn led to the emergence of competence-based programs in
colleges and universities.

Many public institutions, under pressure from state boards
of higher education, regents, and influential legislators, began to increase academic rigor and monitor faculty performance. At Florida
State University, the "Curriculum of Attainments" program, an
early competence-based curriculum that is described in Chapter
Eleven of this volume, got some of its original impetus from a
legislative mandate that all state universities in Florida should experiment with three-year degrees. This was certainly no new development in American higher education, but it was given new
visibility and impetus by one of the most widely circulated of the
Carnegie Commission reports, *Less Time, More Options: Education
Beyond the High School* (1971).[1] The very title, "Curriculum of
Attainments," judging from the writings of its initial proponent,
John Harris, was intended to signify a major concern with tightening
academic standards and with strengthening the academic spine of the
university through an emphasis on performance. Close to the "back to
basics" trend in some school systems, the report could be seen in one
aspect as an effort to regain ground lost during the 1960s. It wanted
to do this, however, not by reinstating core requirements and less
inflated grading but rather by insisting on a standard of what might
be called on-the-job performance by its graduates, a standard that
could not be surmounted by the fear or favor of faculty members,
the guile or charm of students, or the purchasing of term papers.
Rather than relying merely on grades assigned by professors for the
assessment of student achievement, the program set out to recruit
nonacademics from the community, the professions, and the world
of business as evaluators of student performance. In some measure,
its tests became external to the institution, hence partially and unevenly immune to its collective and individual vulnerabilities.

---

[1] For an account of the repeated efforts to establish a three-year degree
in American academia, see Rudolph (1977). Rudolph's account should be
illuminating to educational reformers as well as to historians because of its
discussion of the fluidity of the curriculum even in the supposedly sedate
colonial and postcolonial colleges in America, and of the successive waves of
innovation introduced by particularly significant institutional leaders such as
Andrew D. White of Cornell and William Rainey Harper of the University
of Chicago.

In sum, by the 1970s the need for increased competence among Americans was evident and a concern for improved education was widespread. Most important, there was underway a national competence-based education movement, which focused on the classroom capabilities rather than the credentials of teachers and on what students actually learned rather than on what teachers taught or what appeared in the syllabus or their lesson plans.

Demands for Different Kinds of Competence

Additional interest in competence-based education stemmed from a reaction to the preoccupation of the 1950s with a single dimension of competence that came to be symbolized by the phrase "scholastic aptitude" and by the seemingly all-important Scholastic Aptitude Tests (SATs) of the College Entrance Examination Board. As high schools graduated a larger and larger proportion of the adolescent age cohort, more and more of their graduates tipped, as real estate agents might say of neighborhoods, in the direction of college, and a meritocratic race was on. Gaining high SAT scores was the goal; emphasis was placed on quick learning, fast recall, and high grades in "academic" subjects; and the concept of competence as defined in terms of verbal and mathematical proficiency and as measured by SATs held increasing sway. Major private liberal arts colleges and universities concentrated on increasing their selectivity rather than on greatly expanding their enrollments, and some major state universities followed suit, becoming de facto selective even where state law required the admission of all high school graduates. (Students whose aptitudes seemed insufficient were either counseled to attend one or another of the growing network of community colleges or regional colleges and universities or sent home at Thanksgiving or Christmas, having had their chance, perhaps to try again elsewhere or even at the same institution later.)

Within higher education, the neighborhoods that had first tipped in this scholastic direction were not the undergraduate colleges of the increasingly research-oriented universities but their graduate and professional schools, which as early as the 1920s had begun to be as completely meritocratic as any French "*bachot*" or Japanese "examination hell." By the 1960s, however, this competition permeated almost all the undergraduate colleges that sent the majority of their graduates on to graduate and professional schools, as well as a number of others that nourished similar ambitions. If students had suffered in the pre-Sputnik era from the extravagantly collegiate and the antiacademic, in the post-Sputnik era they were subjected to a curriculum framed in terms of the subdividing specialties of increasingly autonomous academic departments. These departments all imposed a standard of performance that was merito-cratic along a narrow cognitive dimension: technical mastery of subject matter. If students had earlier been attuned to the peer pressures that Coleman described in *The Adolescent Society* (1961), they were now subjected to an increasingly powerful, almost an-archic, faculty, able to traumatize even the most scholarly students, who often came to feel inadequate as total human beings in a milieu tipped in the direction of highly competitive academic performance alone.

Among a minority of educators who took issue with this pre-occupation with verbal and quantitative skills were future leaders in the competence-based movements of the 1970s. They created courses in which students were assessed not through time-limited written tests of cognitive competence alone but instead through examination of their performance against a wide range of affective and cognitive criteria. They also created curriculums that would allow graduates to compete with other professionals on the basis of how well they performed on the job rather than of how well they scored on tradi-tional tests. A subtle shift occurred among these innovators in the kind of competence that they valued. It came to be a competence that was not "strictly academic," and it was to include the ability to make one's way in the nonacademic world, in the civic and occupational world, and in the world of one's own personal horizons. It was still traditionally American in its individualism, but the quali-ties defined as competence and thus sought for, nurtured, and re-warded were not traditionally competitive: They were rather the qualities of caring, of cooperation, of inventiveness, and—in the case of professional programs—of being able to provide superior profes-sional services that were more concerned with individual clients than with the institutional frameworks in which the services were delivered.

To take several examples, President Audrey Cohen and Dean Stephen Sunderland at the College for Human Services in New

York City, Sister Joel Read and her colleagues at Alverno College in Milwaukee, and Edgar and Jean Cahn at the Antioch School of Law in Washington, D.C., were all deeply interested in expanding definitions of competence and in increasing opportunities for students to develop competence. They were dissatisfied with prevailing levels of competence when measured in terms of who was served by society's professions and how professional service was rendered, and they desired to give people—both students and clients—the sense that they had a say in their own lives, that options were not closed to them, and that they could make choices, including refusals.

This concern for wider views of competence coincided with the growth of a general social belief—perhaps some would call it a new cynicism—that experts were generally incompetent and not to be trusted. Paradoxically, the graduates of the leading professional schools in medicine, law, nursing, and administration had been both more highly trained as specialists and subjected to increased dosages of social, psychological, and ethical materials to help them provide more humane as well as more technically competent service. But the new lessons did not always take; many graduates absorbed only the lucrative specialties of professional training and ducked the rest as "cultural garbage." And even when they did take, the rising level of expectation about the quality (including the humaneness) of service that the general population should receive and about the infallibility of judgment the professional should render increased the time and other pressures on professionals and made what was in fact often better service seem worse.

The College for Human Services combines this ideology of conflict between demanding clients and harried professionals—part of the increasingly corrosive hostility toward and cynicism concerning authority endemic in society and enormously heightened in the era of Vietnam and Watergate—with optimistic idealism. Its leaders sense that all too often those who possess technical competence do not exercise it humanely or conscientiously or in the interest of clients; they are self-serving, self-protective, and often slovenly in dealing with their clients, especially those among the less privileged. In a way, the college is saying that *professional* competence, no matter how expert, is not enough, and that by rendering those who are not expert dependent, it can even be counterproductive. What

is requisite instead is *humane* competence, which can be taught, or
at least modeled in such a way that it can be learned. According to
the college, doing so requires a combination of training in a few
basic skills—most specialized skills can be learned on the job—
and the cultivation of a kind of generic and resourceful compassion
in the whole gamut of human services, which are to be considered as
a unity rather than as a diverse set of specialized skills. (For an
eloquent discussion of this distinction between skills and capacities,
and the ambiguities and paradoxes in seeking to teach the latter—
qualities such as wisdom, loving, and grieving—see Holmer, 1977.)

Alverno College perhaps represents most clearly the view of
competence as consisting in large part of self-confidence and, therefore, sees the task of building competence as requiring the building
of self-confidence. The videotape that belongs to every Alverno
student illustrates this view both actually and symbolically: Its first
exposure is that of the student as a freshman giving a short prepared
speech on an assigned topic before the camera. The student views
this videotape with a faculty mentor who supportively helps her
criticize her own performance and improve her self-presentation.
The videotape reel becomes the student's own record, not of un-
interrupted successes necessarily, but rather, like tree rings, of
relatively continuous, if uneven, growth toward competence in wider
areas. The expectation of the Alverno faculty is that its students,
most of whom commute from home and are often the first in their
families to attend college, having accumulated a series of such
examples of increasingly competent performances in situations of
realistic stress—sometimes simulating the stresses experienced in
occupations and other times documenting actual stresses of occupational internships—will be empowered to move away from the
relative docility of lower-middle-class homes and will have available
to them a wider choice of modes of work and life than was apparent
to them when they entered Alverno.

Elsewhere, those in charge of several competence-based
nursing education programs believe that the traditional medical
hierarchy needs to be revised, just as the Antioch School of Law
believes that legal practice has to place greater emphasis on public
interest law and on serving the deprived instead of the clientele traditionally preferred by lawyers. Legal education, the faculty believe,

has to change so as to turn out lawyers who are broadly competent to practice law in the public interest rather than simply graduates who have satisfactorily mastered the cognitive content of the profession as it is represented in written tests. Such institutions, in seeking to change professional frameworks to make them more client-centered, are themselves trying to become more student-centered. Similarly, their interest in inculcating more diverse competencies is leading them to seek new ways of measuring and assessing qualities that go beyond scholastic achievement.

Half a dozen years ago, with such issues in mind, I visited the able and dedicated psychologists at the Educational Testing Service (ETS) in Princeton to discuss with them the feasibility of tests for what might be regarded as the affective side of competence—for example, projective tests that would give some indication as to the ability of individuals to endure frustration, to subdue narcissism, and to accept as well as exercise authority. The ETS officials asked how I thought one could go about creating such tests, which I insisted were more and more necessary as schools and college dispensed with requirements, creating a generation of students who could often do extremely well on aptitude tests but who had never come anywhere near the level of their potential competence. If such students were to be prepared to do what is called "independent study," and which frequently is neither, then one needed more than their SAT scores as a basis for evaluating their prospects to succeed in such self-paced work. To the idea that one could use Rorschach or Thematic Apperception Test materials for such analysis, the ETS officials threw up their hands: Such measures are typically unreliable indicators of how an individual is likely to behave in a real-life situation, and they are also subject to a host of problems that jeopardize fair interpretation and use.

Still, these capabilities warrant attention, and unobtrusive measures of them do exist. To illustrate, if I am sitting on an admissions committee, I am prepared to welcome applicants who, beyond a certain minimal level of scholastic aptitude, have been long-distance runners or cross-country skiers or swimmers, or have learned a difficult foreign language, such as Japanese or Hungarian, or who know how to play the oboe or bassoon or other instrument that requires long practice. Even in the more esoteric branches of scholarship (outside of such fields as mathematics, where to make an original contribution requires an early demonstration of enormously high cognitive competence), I believe that these moral and affective qualities of persistence and perseverance count for much more than is generally recognized. (To these I would add a quality for which there are few unobtrusive measures, namely, moral courage—a quality particularly hard to detect, since moral courage is sometimes indistinguishable from exhibitionism and ruthless or disingenuous ambition.) The competence-based education movements are not likely to provide the credibility for which their critics ask until the time comes—and quite conceivably, it may not come—when this work on assessment becomes sufficiently subtle and sophisticated to be able to measure with reasonably convincing accuracy the often impalpable qualities that some proponents claim they are already able to determine.

Pressure for More Opportunities to Gain Competence

Additional momentum for competence-based education has been provided by two social movements that are at once overlapping and at times in competition: civil rights and women's liberation. Although focused primarily on equality, the several elements of the civil rights movements of the 1960s did not deprecate competence and achievement; rather, they sought to widen, as Coleman's title *Equality of Educational Opportunity* (1966) indicated, the opportunity for previously excluded groups to become competent. Similarly, the aim of the women's liberation movements at the outset—and still today for many of those movements—has been to increase the pool of competence throughout society by bringing into the educated labor force at all levels and in all fields an actual majority of the population which had in many places previously been overlooked and discriminated against.[2] This concern of women

[2] For women in college and university positions, it would constitute a triumph to return to the situation of 1930, when one third of the total teaching profession was female. As Bernard (1964) observes, many of these earlier women scholars and teachers were unmarried or childless. Women of similar social position and education were less likely to go to graduate school in pursuit of the Ph.D. degree during the post–Second World War era of emphasis on the family and childrearing.

for access to education has corresponded, as the pool of high school graduates has begun to shrink, with the interest of educators in offering nonresidential and individualized programs for older people, who because of family circumstances or obligations of work cannot become full-time students in what was once regarded as the regular curriculum.

Both the civil rights movements and the later women's movements sought more than to open gates of opportunity in the formal sense for their previously excluded or only marginally included contingents. They did not assume that black males or women would simply make use of the decline of ascriptive criteria for social status and selection in order to win places in society through demonstrated cognitive competence on a strictly individualistic basis. Instead, they sought to use their ascriptive group and its special qualities as a positive element in a more broadly defined competence which would not only play down individual winning but would also emphasize assisting others through collective enterprises. One wing of the women's movements, for example, started to question the value of competitive individualistic achievement, just as many men who were winners at that game had begun to do.[3] And a number of competence-based programs, imbued with the social orientation of the women's and civil rights movements, have not only redefined competence and actively recruited the "new students" of whom Cross has written (1973) but they have also provided supportive and, if need be, compensatory services for these students. The open door through which the disadvantaged were recruited was not to become a revolving door: Virtually all of these students were somehow to be given appropriate credentials, which would permit them to compete on a professional level with graduates of other more selective institutions. The College of Public and Community Service of the University of Massachusetts at Boston, Seattle Central

[3] Hochschild (1975) gives a sensitive critique of the whole system of individualistic careers, rewards, and achievement. For a less happy account of the behavior of a small minority of liberationist women toward any one of their group who stands out or excels, and is therefore perceived to be engaged in a masculine ego trip, see "Joreen," now self-revealed to be Jo Freeman (1976). Riesman (1976) comments on the relation of this aspect of the women's movements to the problem of productivity—hence of competence—in an interdependent world.

Community College in Washington state, and such aforementioned institutions as Alverno College (which besides admitting younger women sought older women who wanted to begin a college education or were trying to complete a previously interrupted one) were all motivated in part by this desire to achieve not only equality of opportunity for previously disprivileged or excluded groups but equality of outcome for them.

Involved here are shifts in the foci of both the civil rights movements and the women's movements. As the emphasis changed from equality of opportunity to equality of outcome for particular groups, it was not enough to give high-scoring blacks, sometimes from privileged backgrounds, wider opportunities in selective educational institutions and occupations; it was necessary to assure that all who were admitted developed the stated competence, regardless of the time or effort involved. Similarly, it was not enough to open previously sex-segregated institutions to women; it was necessary to shift the moral tone, or emphasis, of the institutions away from competitive achievement and toward group achievement.

Competence-based programs naturally vary in the degree to which they emphasize the competing goals of individual achievement and equality of achievement. On the one hand, individual achievement was perhaps most unequivocally the basis of the Curriculum of Attainments program at Florida State University. This program was a reaction not to claims of social injustice or inadequacies in the treatment of students but instead to the tilt of the seesaw in favor of equality of results. Of course, Florida State University has, like other institutions, been involved in bringing previously excluded students, particularly nonwhites, into the university. But, as at other institutions, these students rarely enrolled in voluntary experimental programs, such as the Curriculum of Attainments. They did not want to be "guinea pigs," and they would rarely have been well advised to take a chance on as yet insufficiently tested programs, even if the very aim of the programs was mastery learning and, hence, in intention if not in practice, geared to students who needed more individualized guidance and instruction and more time to achieve mastery than better prepared students.

On the other hand, a number of other programs can be interpreted as deliberate efforts to prevent the race from being won

only by the swift, who presumably are those already advantaged;
rather, they hold that speed is not of the essence. In these programs,
as in mastery learning where there is no limit on the number of
trials or in pass/no credit grading where only successes are recorded,
students theoretically have an unlimited amount of time to establish
a competence. These programs are thus linked to such other mastery-
oriented and time-free contemporary movements as programmed
instruction, the Keller plan, computer-assisted instruction (a notable
example is the PLATO program at the University of Illinois in
Urbana). Closely linked in terms of time-free and often location-
free procedures, are the development of negotiated contracts as
devices for individualized learning. The pioneers are mainly private
institutions such as New College in Sarasota (now New College of
the University of South Florida), Johnston College of the University of Redlands, and Hampshire College. At the level of the
adult nonresident learner, and for some in the immediate post-high
school cohort also, public institutions have been among the pioneers,
notably Empire State College in New York with its many local
learning centers; Metropolitan State University in Minnesota; Justin
Morrill College of Michigan State University; and the cooperative
television-linked network whose headquarters are at the University
of Nebraska in Lincoln. In addition, the network of adult degree
programs now grows everywhere in the country at all levels of public
and private institutions, some with minimal quality control. Like
other efforts to create individualized settings for learning, these
competence-based programs involve a belief that many students of
all ages not only prefer but are better served by individualized learning. Since competence is, moreover, both a personal benefit to students and an ancillary benefit to society, such programs encourage
students to move at their own speeds rather than through traditional
calendrical and age-graded academic timetables.

Competence-based education thus illustrates the dialectic
common throughout American life and American education of
oscillation between an emphasis on liberty for individual achievement seen in highly competitive and individualistic terms and an
insistence on equality of outcome (as distinguished from equality of
initial opportunity) in which outstanding performance by some
individuals may seem less important than the advance of entire,

previously disadvantaged groups.[4] But by their emphasis on mastery, even those competence-based programs that aim to benefit all "new students" seek to avoid the possibility of sentimental "social promotion" and loss of standards simply by virtue of minority status or previous handicap. Rather, they are requiring that even these students develop adequately those kinds of competencies of which America and its social institutions stand in need.

But two difficulties confront these programs. First, although certain jobs and situations are well filled by people who have demonstrated endurance and pertinacity through repeated trials in overcoming a hurdle—as in the Keller plan, in many modular forms of teaching, and in time-free, competence-based programs—still, in some cases the cost to society of nurturing "slow but sure" performance may be too high. In fact, the ability to learn quickly may be in and of itself a competence in certain lines of work. Suppression of evidence about the length of time involved in learning a competence (as with a "sanitized" transcript in which only successes are recorded) will in the long run not prove beneficial to students, to competence-based programs, or to society as a whole.

Second, one of the seeming paradoxes of those competence-based programs which have focused on developing cooperative skills and assuring equality of results is that competence-based instruction itself is highly individualized. In fact, if there is any common thread that links various competence-based institutions together, it is scorn for the traditional classroom with its arranged rows of seats and its fifty-minute lecture to a group of students inevitably at different stages of cognitive development and at different levels of motivation. (Despite this scorn, only two of the institutions that our project team examined had actually abolished the classroom: College IV of the Grand Valley State Colleges, at least in its initial phases, and Justin Morrill College in its program for older persons.) What struck those of us who observed classroom settings in competence-based institutions (except for Alverno and Florida State) was the

[4] Lipset (1963) contends that this kind of seesaw has operated throughout postcolonial American history. If, for example, the emphasis on equality and the corresponding reduction of hierarchy and privilege go "too far" in terms of the specific economic and ideological problems of an era, there will be a reversal in favor of the demand to give individuals their heads in the name of liberty or achievement.

way in which students, if they came to class at all, showed up late and left early. At the College of Public and Community Service of the University of Massachusetts at Boston, attendance was never required. At the Antioch School of Law, attendance was spotty—uniquely so in my experience, compared to other law schools where, even today, what might be called countercultural insouciance has made little obvious headway—and some students would saunter in and leave again even though black instructors were discussing issues supposedly relevant to blacks, such as how to bring cases before the Equal Employment Opportunities Commission. These students failed to understand one meaning of competence: what it meant to be competent *as students* as well as refusing socialization to professional norms.

Yet regulated behavior is a necessary part of professional competence, and in my judgment educators unconcerned, for example, with students' lack of interest in routine or with their inability to master the minimum and concededly pedantic knowledge necessary to pass professional examinations fail to appreciate the degree to which these are unobtrusive measures of the absence of qualities essential in professional practice. A lawyer without the diligence to show up for class or to cram for the bar examination is likely to be a type (in a profession notorious for procrastination) who will let the statute of limitations run out on a client or will fail to check title to real estate properly or to make the appropriate motions in the course of litigation.[5] From my perspective, competence-based institutions, especially those aiming to help poorly prepared students cope with the problems of competence in the contemporary world, must run a very tight ship indeed. They must insist both on class attendance and on promptness, for these are precisely among those

[5] As a former practicing lawyer and law professor, I have been deeply interested in increasing clinical training within law schools and in making use of internships along the medical model. But I do not agree with those who claim that there is no relation between performance on the bar examination and usefulness as a lawyer, as has been claimed at Antioch and other law schools, and even more forcefully by the National Association for the Advancement of Colored People, which has brought suit against bar examinations on the ground of alleged discrimination against graduates of predominantly black law schools. I believe that these people are overly optimistic in assuming that clients will be well served by those incapable of passing what is generally the relatively low hurdle of the local bar examination.

affective or motivational attitudes necessary if one is to become competent. (For further analysis, see the discussion of the Legal Assistants Program at the College for Human Services in Chapter Nine of this volume.)

Fear of Decay

The fear of decay is a recurrent theme in the history of civilization. Indeed, as many observers have noted, the great revolutions of Western history have had strong restorationist, even nostalgic, elements hidden beneath the rhetoric of the progress that would ensue from destroying everything old and supposedly rotten and corrupt. Repeatedly, purist and puritanical movements have arisen on the premise of individual decadence and social decomposition and decay. Such attitudes were strong in the *fin de siècle* trends of thought in Europe at the end of the nineteenth century and were echoed in the United States primarily by older, middle-class elements of northern and western European origin dismayed at the arrival of the "unwashed masses" from central and southern Europe. Even earlier, in a novel ironically entitled *Democracy,* Henry Adams had portrayed Washington life as at once sterile, vulgar and corrupt. His later and influential *The Education of Henry Adams,* combined with the gloomy prophecies of his brother Brooks Adams, in *The Degradation of the Democratic Dogma* and other writings, probably had less impact on transatlantic thought than Oswald Spengler's cyclical imagery of foreboding in *The Decline of the West.*

As Americans became better educated and less provincial, more and more members of influential elites grew familiar with the pessimistic views of human nature expressed by writers from Thomas Hobbes to Friedrich Nietzsche. They were also exposed to similar doubts concerning social progress, doubts to be found not only in Thomas Malthus, but also in such more contemporary writers as Jacob Burckhardt and, more recently still, in such very different writers as Karl Popper and the professionally derided but still influential Arnold Toynbee. These wider, in some sense worldwide, moods of bleak pessimism for the future and this rejection of Enlightenment ideas concerning both man's nature and man's hopes provide a kind of semi-conscious backdrop for those Americans who have moved from the euphoria of the years immediately following the Second World War to the prevailing widespread sense of the ungovernability of democracy and the unmanageability of the contemporary industrial state. Some, with a nostalgia for their own American predecessors, contrast the reaction to Franklin D. Roosevelt's credibly expressed confidence that all we had to fear was fear itself, to the sinking of the dollar in the stock market when President Carter announced an anti-inflation program. Indeed, the battle against inflation is one source of the pressure for competence-based education for, just as the military complain that college ROTC programs are turning out semi-literate graduates who cannot handle sophisticated weaponry, so industrialists contend that the current levels of competence in American society are not just inadequate to meet the needs of an increasingly complicated present, but, like the dollar, have actually declined in absolute terms.

To illustrate this decline of standards, these critics point to the disintegration of the "work ethic," cynicism about accomplishment at all levels, the setting in of a kind of social passivity, the well-known decline of SAT and ACT scores, the increasingly evident inability of students to write coherent, well-organized prose, and an apparent decline in spans of attention that makes learning any difficult subject nearly impossible. Following the post-Sputnik calls for *increased* competence, these later critics seek to hold the line against *eroding* competence by instituting minimal standards for progress from one grade to another and minimal competence requirements for graduation from high school, admission to college, and even graduation from college and professional school.

There has always been a minority of Americans, chiefly among the elite, who have held that the majority were not only inept but growing increasingly incompetent. When Catholics began to arrive in large numbers in America, displaying compassion and good works among kinfolk and showing obedience to clergy, nativist reactions included the temperance movement, in part an anti-Catholic crusade and in part a protest against what were regarded as the self-indulgent habits of the newly arrived—habits that of course could easily be acquired by imitation of many of the successful among the already arrived (Gusfield, 1963). When the Irish responded to the hostility of the more settled, primarily Protestant

Americans by moving into municipal politics, where their general
ability to command the English language made them natural builders of coalitions among the non-English-speaking (and often
Catholic) immigrant groups, their taking over of municipal services
led earlier arrivals to think that government had fallen into corrupt
and incompetent hands—a phenomenon that we have seen repeated
with each successive wave of migration, including the most recent
internal migration, that of rural southern blacks to cities both North
and South. Such feelings had arisen much earlier on the national
scene at the time of what used to be called the Jacksonian Revolution, when the Virginia dynasty (along with several of the Adamses),
which had given the nation dignified if not always competent government, concluded that Andrew Jackson—a self-made frontiers-
man, slave-trader, and soldier—would lead the country to ruin.

In contemporary society, not only elite groups but also
the general population seem convinced that America has not
only grown slack but is getting worse. The fears expressed a quarter
century ago by upper-middle-class parents that their children were
becoming merely passive consumers, hedonistic and hostile to any
difficulty in learning, have in many families been realized; the peer
culture did prove stronger than the diminishing authority of parents
and other adults. Children have not only won independence from
reluctant adults but, in an era of emphasis on "children's rights,"
have been given independence by willing adults, including lawyers, educators and social scientists who speak very glowingly
about the natural spontaneity of youth and the dangers of repres-
sion. (For a penetrating critique of the focus on the individualistic
rights of children in the new vogue for "moral education," see
Bennett and Delattre, 1978.)

Today such fears are not confined to upper-middle-class
parents or to faculty members in the humanities who care about the
ability of their students to read and write, preferably in more than
one language. Concern is evident at many other social levels. It is
evident among parents, both white and black, and among taxpayers,
whether or not they are also parents of school-age children, who are
dismayed by the lack of discipline, the disorder, and the vandalism
in the public schools. Educated in an era of less instant gratification
and of more obligatory reading, writing, and class attendance, they

view social promotion, grade inflation, and the inability to sit still and learn that characterize contemporary students at all educational levels as a decline in quality. Blaming both the progressive movement and the innovative gurus of the 1960s counterculture, they demand that schools return to "basics." It remains a matter of debate, as it was among the members of our project team, whether there has in fact been any absolute regression in American levels of competence. But evidence for such a decline has been set forth by observers who make social and educational policy in American society, and their evidence deserves consideration.

Recently, for example, I had a chance to talk about the issue with I. F. Stone, a remarkable autodidact who never finished college and who has just now turned seventy. After giving up his *Weekly* and his regular column in the *New York Review of Books,* he began in his sixties to study Greek. He has since immersed himself with enormous enthusiasm in studies of classical Athens and its place in the Mediterranean world and has also undertaken scholarly researches into the work of the church fathers. My first discussion of incompetence with him was some years ago when he was editing the *Weekly.* He asked me if I could perhaps find a recent Harvard College graduate to serve as his assistant. I sent him several bright graduates—honors graduates at that—who admired him greatly, but he found them all wanting. Indeed, he was shocked to discover that graduates of a college he would have liked to attend were so ignorant of history and the classics, that they did not know foreign languages, and that they lacked serious bibliographical training. Last fall he gave a lecture at Kansas State University in Manhattan, Kansas, and found to his great surprise all the major classical commentaries and texts in its library. But he also discovered that no one had taken them off the library shelves for a number of years. Now he finds that there are few scholars with whom he can discuss the complexities he has uncovered concerning Plato, St. Jerome, and other early thinkers. He feels that the lack of imitation of, and even enrollment in, the two St. John's Colleges (at Annapolis and Santa Fe) is a symptom of the decay of what he sees as a great tradition of learning. By contrast, American University, where as a visiting professor he now has an office, gives credit in a course on the city of Washington for going to museums, art exhibits, and concerts—activities that he believes students should do on their own and for which credit is ridiculous. (Although American University seems quite severe in its demands in comparison with institutions that give "life experience" credit for nothing as illuminating as concert-going, Provost Richard Berendzen has been working to persuade the faculty to adapt a more coherent curriculum.) He does not deny that much of the earlier learning he admires was pedantic and pedantically taught, and he admits that there are still pockets of learning—possibly a much larger number than heretofore— which are lost in the larger landscape of the partially educated. But everywhere he sees pandering to students, with student evaluations of faculty as a way to intimidate faculty, and thus a great leveling process going on.

Stone's concerns are paralleled by symptoms of a seeming decline in what used to be called the "Protestant ethic" and today is often referred to as the "work ethic." Even as late as the Great Depression, this motivational element in the desire to perform competently had as yet scarcely been undermined by what later became a persistent question of *cui bono*? There was, it is true, a gnawing suspicion that economic and political institutions were faltering, and in metropolitan circles a small minority of individuals thought that the failure of these institutions would lead the country to adopt some brand of socialism. Yet hardly any union leaders questioned the fundamental status quo, and the shop steward protected the work force from the arbitrariness of the foreman without undermining, and often in fact supporting, the work ethic. Whatever the restrictions that existed on levels of output, workers continued to show up on Mondays and to believe, slightly revising the slogan of the times, in a "fair (but not excessive) day's work for a fair day's pay." A good illustration of the temper of the times was the Civilian Conservation Corps, in which young men from the cities were willing to work clearing firebreaks, building trails in the national parks, and doing similar chores under generally rugged conditions—willing both to learn the necessary new competence and to apply it.

By the 1950s, however, McClelland and his co-workers had developed projective tests for what they spoke of as "the need for achievement," in tandem with, or in contradiction to, the "need for affiliation," and Whyte's *The Organization Man* (1956) had given a picture of corporate complacency and conformity, a "social ethic," as contrasted with an individualistic ethic of achievement. *The Lonely Crowd* (Riesman, Denney, and Glazer, 1950) noted among other changes a shift from "inner-directed" motivation regarding work toward "other-directed" motivation for social approval.[6]

During the 1960s, in contrast to the spirit of the Civilian Conservation Corps during the Depression, young men in the Job Corps, especially Americanized nonwhite males, showed a far greater cynicism toward authority, a greater hedonism, and an unwillingness to continue working toward a distant goal or to acquire the necessary competence in the absence of immediate reward. Experience with the Peace Corps throughout the 1960s furnished additional evidence of a shift in values. The Peace Corps gave volunteers extraordinary opportunities to develop competences in unanticipated situations where they were often on their own. Where they were not on their own, however, they were likely to be extremely critical of authority, whether that of Peace Corps supervisors or host country nationals. (Indeed, an extraordinary demand for competence was placed on both trainers and overseas supervisors of volunteers, since they often could not command but had to coax and cajole.) Many volunteers, especially in the early years, made use of this opportunity to gain know-how, with the result of increasing their self-confidence and, in the plurality of cases, of altering their career plans on their return home. But many later volunteers took advantage of the Peace Corps simply for overseas junkets, and the rate of attrition overseas rose as high as 40 percent. Volunteers no longer so avidly sought know-how, when the question of "know-why" became enmeshed with doubts about America's mission in the world in general and in the host country in particular.

The recent coining of the pejorative term "workaholic"

[6] The concept of "need for achievement" contains a built-in paradox that haunts competence-based education. It is difficult to distinguish on the basis of a test or trial the need or motivation for accomplishment and competence in contrast to the need to be *thought* to have achieved or to be *perceived* as accomplished or competent. The achievement or accomplishment or competence of the craftsman is intrinsic, not based on recognition; the need for achievement in McClelland's sense, judging by the Thematic Apperception Test stories used to assess it, often rests on the desire to exhibit one's achievement.

signals a general societal disposition to deprecate those who work "too hard"—sometimes because they are trapped in situations where they conscientiously feel that they cannot stop because none of the scoffers will take their places. Peer groups, whether in a factory, a shop, or an educational institution, have always sought to set a level of effort which was less than optimal, though often more than minimal. But in a society increasingly unable to compete on the world market, whether with the Japanese, the Taiwanese, the Swiss, the West Germans, or the Scandinavians, there seem few counter-vailing pressures to these groups, in the form of appeals either to authority or to self-discipline and national pride. One result is the vicious cycle of efforts to increase mechanization in order to replace an incompetent work force, resistance in the form of unionization on the part of the work force that remains, increased unemployment, and a dangerous rise in calls for protectionism and in the xenophobia that would seek to justify it. Currently a whole gamut of ideologies, old and new, has been assembled to justify resistance to work. It takes no education to declare that one is bored or exploited and only a bit more to say, sometimes with faint echoes of Karl Marx, that one is alienated. Such verdicts on the employer or the work setting may, of course, be justified. But they are often verdicts on the person using the terms, and they do not automatically serve as justification for the level of incompetent performance one has managed to achieve and, either sporadically or more permanently, maintain.

Yet any careful analysis of the rise of antiwork ideologies would have to take into account the long tradition and importance of the antiwork ethic created by the small minority of white southern planters who, in the period of slavery and later, looked down on manual labor and despised what they regarded as Yankee com-mercialism and self-destructive drivenness. There is also the fact that surprisingly few southern blacks were infected with the cavalier out-look, as can be seen in such self-help settlements as the Sea Islands of Georgia or in such black enclaves as Muskogee, Oklahoma. The presently deprecated Booker T. Washington sought to get blacks to learn crafts and to adopt better farming practices, just as slaves in cities like New Orleans early developed into industrious craftsmen, caterers, and other small entrepreneurs. After the abolition of slavery, the inroads of white labor drove many blacks out of these occupations, just as much later the mechanized cotton-picker and, to some extent, the minimum wage forced blacks off the land and into the cities, where only recently, with the weakening of the black Protestant churches and of the extended family, many young blacks have become ultra-American in hedonist rejection of the work ethic.[7]

Such an analysis might also reinterpret the work of Coleman (1961) on the social climates of a selected group of Illinois public high schools during the 1950s. As noted earlier, Coleman's work seemed to indicate that there was considerable peer pressure against achievement and against competence, if competence was defined not as bare minimal performance but as stretching oneself to the limit of one's capacities. Coleman had given a questionnaire to high school students, asking the young men such things as whether they would rather be the academic leaders of their class or the athletic leaders, and asking the young women comparable questions dealing with the conflict between popularity and academic achievement. But Coleman's findings were perhaps more ambiguous than they at first seemed. In the topflight suburban schools in his sample, many students were already academically adept, and they were concerned with the missing (or potentially missing) elements of school life which were less individualistic than the attainment of good grades and which brought not only self-respect but peer comradeship.

Furthermore, while many Americans have indeed been stretched beyond the limits of their competence, other Americans have never had the opportunity to exhibit the competence they do possess. The poor workmanship for which employees are blamed leads employers to mechanize their jobs and put them out of work as a way of controlling incompetence. But what looks to employers like shoddiness or indeed sabotage on the part of the work force should not be taken at face value. To some extent, workers have

[7] Paradoxically and tragically, the citywide and distinguished black high schools created in cities with an already established black middle class after the Civil War, cities such as Baltimore, Washington, Atlanta, and New Orleans, were casualties of integration and/or the egalitarian destruction of supposedly elitist tracking systems. It was out of such schools that many of the black leaders of the present century came. See Hill (1970) and Sowell (1974, 1976).

been influenced by ideological judgments on the part of teachers
and the mass media, reflecting currents among academic and intellectual elites, that certain kinds of work are not "meaningful," and,
as indicated earlier, the women's movement has made a contribution to this assessment vis-à-vis many jobs traditionally occupied by
women. Furthermore, a more educated workforce has higher expectations as to what is "meaningful" work, including self-determination about the degree of supervision regarded as appropriate. In
consequence, Americans tend to have escalating expectations as to
what is essential to them. Wartime requirements and the imperatives
of national survival in the two world wars to some extent obviated
this second need: Bookkeepers knew why they had to become efficient craftsmen, and the only question then was know-how. But the
Vietnam War dramatized that even in the armed forces a lack of
know-why could have a debilitating effect.

What has been said suggests how ideological climates affect
our assessment of the competence of individuals; our desires to
simplify may hide contradictory tendencies. For example, we
have already referred to the jack-of-all-trades abilities of the capable
farmer today, managing not only a great variety of equipment, but
also making judgments about short-run and long-run trends in the
prices of farm commodities—an enterprise which involves taking
account of inflation, the monopolistic pricing of farm implements,
and possible scarcities of oil supplies and such other petrochemical
products as pesticides and fertilizer. And while it may be true that
we are running out of widely skilled tool-and-die makers in many
parts of the country, one has to lay against these losses in numbers
of unusually competent individuals the increased do-it-yourself
capacities of the average homeowner, impelled by both the high
prices (and often incompetence and dishonesty) of professional
repair personnel and the strong desire for self-reliance and individualism that remains an American norm. Currently many more
women than at any time since the Second World War are demonstrating competence in the world of jobs and careers, although a
perhaps smaller number either want or are able to perform the tasks
of parenting. And if we are talking about competence at cooperation and teamwork, many more women who once had been

privatized as housewives have now learned or are learning these skills through both athletics and employment.

What we lack are the social indicators which could definitively determine whether or not there has been an absolute decline in the level of competence with which work is done in America. In the private sector where there is a "bottom line," it appears that the rate of increase in productivity has fallen and at times has even been negative, but we do not know how to sort out the various factors that may be involved, such as a decline of available competence; the inability to dismiss clearly incompetent workers because of the elaborate grievance procedures followed by almost inevitable litigation making such efforts seem too costly in time, money, and morale; the effects in some areas of Affirmative Action, interpreted as requiring the employment of people not yet competent, but who must be and presumably are assumed to be capable of being trained to an appropriate level of competence; the ideologies already mentioned that are critical of "rate-busters" who supposedly overwork or who, by peer definition, are insufficiently "alienated"; and the growing hostility to and distrust of authority that has already been discussed as affecting especially the large organizations. And in the increasing proportion of the work force engaged in the "tertiary" or nonprofit sectors of the economy, it is the very difficulty of measuring productivity and the vast increase in social overhead costs that have led to the demands for competence, without clear evidence that competence has diminished in comparison with earlier eras in our history.

Another example illustrating how complex, if not impossible, is an overall judgment of historical changes in levels of competence involves the use of metrical indexes of cognitive competence. For even here the answers are by no means clear cut. So far as I have been able to determine, whatever measures one uses—Miller Analogies, IQ tests, SATs, Graduate Record Examinations, and medical and law school aptitude tests—the general intelligence of the population appears to have grown until at least the middle 1960s. "More" in terms of resources spent on education, including students' time, did not mean "worse," to use the famous phrase of Kingsley Amis about the expansion of British postsecondary education after the Second World War when he was convinced that more did mean worse.[8] The polemical question, "Why can't Johnny read?" was being raised at a time when, holding proportions constant, Johnny was reading more and better poetry and short stories than ever before in our history, along with art and music criticism and the new genre of film criticism. At the same time, Johnny was also doing advanced calculus in high school (Sally wasn't, but was instead reading and writing more poetry and short stories). If one assumes, as a number of scholars have, that some 10 percent of the population is motivationally and intellectually prepared for a liberal arts education that is cognitively oriented, then this 10 percent has remained reasonably stable as the absolute numbers of young people have grown and as more and more of them have poured into postsecondary education.

Admittedly there has been a decline since the middle 1960s in the level of cognitive competence measured by SATs and ACTs, a decline which takes account of the vast number of persons now taking these tests. Faculty members even in that small minority of colleges which today can still practice high selectivity because of their large number of applicants report that students, including those from professional families and leading public and private secondary schools, are arriving with much poorer preparation: Not only have they learned no foreign language, but they have learned a patois version of English that may show them to be fully egalitarian but leaves them unable to communicate and hence often unable to discover or to write about complex realities of thought and feeling. And sometimes, because of the loosening of requirements that was regarded as a necessary solvent for the student-faculty protests of the late 1960s, students can graduate from college, let alone from high school, without ever having written an essay of more than two or three pages.

However, faculty members who point to the inability of students to read and express themselves adequately are unlikely to take account of studies showing that textbooks in major fields of study,

---

[8] For a survey of and report on the proliferating literature about the ratio of costs to benefits of higher education, see Bowen (1977). He concludes that benefits do in fact outweigh costs.

such as Paul Samuelson's famous and repeatedly revised *Economics,* have increased not only the difficulty of their "readability" level but also the complexity of their ideas over the years, and that course examinations such as those at Harvard have become more and more demanding over a period of decades, going from simple, unidimensional frames of reference toward more metaphorical and complex ones.[9] Critics may also forget that in most fields where concepts have in fact become more intricate, more time may be needed by instructors to explain these concepts, and that in many fields, "readers" made up of research papers have often taken the place of traditional textbooks. At the same time, as many faculty have become more specialized and better trained themselves, their reading lists begin to seem like "advertisements for myself"—lists which, if taken seriously, would require the average diligent student to spend all of his or her time on a single course. Faculty members may cumulatively deceive themselves concerning how much of the reading they assign is actually going to be done and with what degree of intensity. The reality of student achievement is usually more complex than nostalgic recollection may indicate.

At any rate, it certainly seems much too early to say that hedonism has taken over the land when, at least in the selective colleges, students are competing as never before to enter the expanding medical schools, the larger number of national law schools, and increasingly sought-after graduate schools of business. In the 1920s, the "little magazines" which published "difficult" criticism, fiction, and poetry, had tiny circulations, whereas today the *New York Review of Books,* the much older *Partisan Review,* the British magazine *Encounter,* and many other literary and critical journals are being read by both an absolutely and a relatively larger number of individuals, even if it is not clear that these include the youngest cohort of students who have been brought up on the more instant gratifica-

---

[9] On textbooks see Santa and Burstyn (1977), whose controlled experiments on economics and psychology texts showed that students at Douglass College of Rutgers University with SAT scores around 520 learned difficult concepts more readily from earlier editions than from later editions of the same text; on Harvard tests see Perry (1970), who estimates that two thirds of the examinations involved multidimensional complexity rather than the simple "right" or "wrong" answers expected at the beginning of the century.

tions of movies and television and, often, on less nonobligatory reading.[10]

International assessments of what high school students know at various ages put the Japanese, the Scandinavians, and others in more meritocratic and homogeneous countries far ahead of the average American high school student, although it is still true that the ablest Americans are at least the equal of their counterparts in any other country. And declines in levels of cognitive ability undoubtedly occur, although undulations in SAT and ACT scores hardly qualify as indicators of a cataclysmic drop. Despite the work of the College Board's Advisory Panel on the Scholastic Aptitude Test score decline, headed by Willard Wirtz, we do not yet understand all the elements that have contributed to the recent decline—why, for example, the verbal scores for women have declined so markedly[11]—and we certainly cannot, as I have already argued, take one facet of cognitive competence as a judgment of the level of cognitive ability in the society as a whole. If we looked at young Americans not in terms of test scores but in terms of their ability to read musical scores, we might come to a somewhat altered con-

---

[10] An interesting finding reported by Bowen (1977) is that Reed College seniors in 1969 were doing less outside reading for pleasure and going to fewer museums and concerts than the same students had as freshmen four years earlier. It is not clear whether they were substituting a cocurriculum in political science, as many activists of the era did, concentrating on their specialties, engaging in the anti-intellectual hedonism which has been one aspect of the counterculture, or partaking in some combination of all these activities. See also Clark and others (1972) and, more generally, Bradshaw (1975).

[11] I have perhaps quixotic if not heretical views on at least one element affecting the verbal scores for women: the way most of our schools are organized. Putting junior high school young women in the same classroom with boys of near identical chronological age, under current practices of sexual intimacy and near-total peer control over norms of appropriate effort, results in the young women feeling that they must descend to the boys' level to avoid appearing superior to them, without acquiring the quantitative or spatial abilities that many of the boys possess. Females are more resonant than males to the attitude of those around them, both male and female. If we separated the sexes, perhaps especially in junior high school, and recruited more able men to teach literature in elementary school and more able women to teach natural sciences and mathematics at all levels of school, we might be able to produce less uneducated secondary school graduates and substantially raise test scores.

clusion. But these declines in test scores are a serious omen, even if no more than an omen: One's ability to read and write is not without salience as an indicator of the capacity to become broadly educated and capable of curiosity in a complex society where most experiences that can take us out of ourselves and our local enclaves will for most of us remain vicarious.

Nevertheless, even if we leave aside meaningful judgments based on test scores, it is possible to argue on the basis of quantity rather than quality that, among faculty members at least, "more means worse" in several respects. Price (1961), one of the first to note that over 90 percent of all scientists who ever lived are now alive, has also noted that mediocre science in a sense gets in the way of genuinely innovative science. Trow (1971) illustrates this theme in an essay entitled "Distractions," where he describes a professor watching a new faculty office building going up outside his window and realizing how many distractions the inhabitants of that building will create for him. Certainly the rural isolation, unattached or semiattached to a university, of an Edmund Wilson or a Lewis Mumford may be necessary for certain kinds of omnivorous learning and scholarship, particularly with the secularization and deliquescence of most monasteries and convents.

It may be that we suffer today from disillusionment because of an earlier belief that knowledge evolves in a unilinear way, a belief greatly heightened by those bombastic social scientists who, after the Second World War, contended that if the social sciences, or in their own preferred usage, the "behavioral sciences," were given the vast amounts of money put into the Manhattan Project, then we would learn enough to solve all the great social problems. No doubt, in certain technical fields, whether in the natural sciences or in philology or archaeology, one can move more rapidly toward the boundaries, because "we stand on the shoulders of giants." But in the human sciences, all we have to do is to read Aristotle's *Nicomachean Ethics* or *Politics* to realize that our understanding of society has advanced little if at all from the time of that small but extraordinary group of Attic Greeks and their fellow inhabitants of the Mediterranean world. The problems of political judgment which preoccupied Thucydides preoccupy us still; we understand more instances because we know more history, but this does not make us wiser, or more capable of comprehending the meaning of events, of other people's actions, or of our own lives.

Indeed, the grimmest prospect that already faces us is a decline in demands for competence among educators themselves. Teachers and faculty members are beginning to take for granted the levels of competence evident in their own preparation, and often do not realize that even their own teachers may never have known a cultivated person. By reading little, and by having few vicarious means of coming into contact, let us say, with the mind of the author of *Middlemarch*, they may reduce their expectations and challenges for their own students as a result. Having studied the cohort of faculty and schoolteachers now passing through the educational system at all levels, Dresch (1977) has arrived at the conclusion that competence, however defined, is likely to decline both absolutely and relatively in the years to come, insofar as it depends on educated faculty to provide both preparation in cognitive terms and in affective or motivational terms. In his view, while the strongest colleges and universities will be able to live off the "capital" of the able faculty they already have, they will be unable either to shift to new fields or to add new faculty, while the weaker institutions will, if private, in many cases disappear or, at best, become part of a public system where collective bargaining limits the level of effort faculty members are willing to put forth.

This fear finds its counterpart in the drive among state legislators and the many publics they represent to create the equivalent of a "bottom line" in nonprofit institutions and to hold those who manage them accountable for their "product" in terms of what graduates can accomplish rather than in terms of time served and credit gained on a course-by-course basis. This pressure to establish requirements for minimal competence at the post-secondary level will grow—just as the "Johnny can't read" issue has grown at the school level—since students are now in many cases graduating from college thanks to the same sort of grade inflation that has operated in the secondary schools—a kind of social promotion responsive less to the demand for equality of outcomes than to the desperate need of faculty for filling their classrooms in the face of a declining cohort of young people, and fearing to fail students on whom their own future and that of their department and institution depend because these students carry with them tuition and public subsidy. There may be no more than fifty institutions in the whole United States so heavily over-applied that the institution can take risks in making demands on students, but it does not follow even in these institutions that particular faculty or particular departments, fearing shifts in the fluid customer market, can afford to make demands. But even if faculty were more self-confident about their own personal futures and the future of their educational unit or institution, they would not necessarily possess the ability to cope with large masses of underprepared, poorly motivated, and often semivoluntary students. Many of these students are in attendance because of the very insistence on credentials which at least one branch of the competence-based movements is seeking at one and the same time to surmount for their own students and to delegitimate as societal barriers for all students.[12]

Faculty members are supposed to be professionals, subject to self-imposed demands, and are supposed to establish their own competence. It is here that competence-based education is likely to have its greatest impact. It seems clear that the core competence finally at stake in the competence-based movement is that of faculty members themselves, and only secondarily that of students or other professionals, whether nurses, social workers, or lawyers. Only a small minority of faculty members is willing, let alone eager, to monitor and to be monitored. But an influential number of faculty members, including some who have become administrators, have been responding less to legislative mandates and public pressures for accountability than to a concern intrinsic to education itself: the concern for what students can do rather than for what the faculty believe they have taught.

We come here to two paradoxes implicit in these efforts towards competence-based education. First, while on the one hand a powerful impetus comes from conservative elements among the groups responsible for financing and controlling higher education,

[12] Another increasing cadre of semivoluntary students are in college because in effect they are bribed to go; various grant programs serve as a kind of unemployment insurance, and as many students in unselective colleges will say of their attendance, or rather their quite intermittent attendance, "it beats working." For an early recognition of the negative consequences of bribing students to attend college, see Grant (1972).

on the other hand the motives of competence-based educators themselves are often liberal and even radical, both in terms of increasing access for previously excluded groups, of using mastery learning techniques to give students enough time and feedback to achieve even the most difficult of competences, and of monitoring their own performance. There was certainly no overt alliance between the relatively conservative individuals pressing for faculty and schoolteacher accountability on the one side, and the reformist administrators and faculty interested in self-accountability on the other. Indeed, in some of the public institutions concerned with competence-based education, there did not appear to be an awareness that reformist impulses and taxpayer backlash could coincide, as they have done in giving drive and visibility to the competence-based education movement itself and in challenging the whole credentialing apparatus—a system anathema to conservatives and reformers alike.

A second paradox lies in the fact that while educators who advocate competence-based approaches are often liberal, if not radical, they are perceived by many students and some other educators as reactionary because of their concern with the maintenance of standards. The hostility toward authority and toward constraint that have recently been endemic in young people, if not in the American population generally and traditionally, has been met on the side of school and college authorities by a variety of strategies, including an often sycophantic imitation of the young by the old. Competence-based education is one of the strategies that seeks to assure achievement and hence appears old-fashioned in spite of its radical procedures.[13] Its insistence that students demonstrate their competence and that faculty members increase their competence by learning to be mentors of student achievement rather than classroom performers for student approval is unlikely to be widely popular among students and faculty. But it will continue to grow more

[13] Margaret Mead has often declared that in the United States members of the older generation are always in the position of being immigrants (even if native-born) in the country of the young. See her *Culture and Commitment* (1970), a book which in some ways echoes Henry Ford's famous dictum that history is bunk. For an example of a "Tory" view, see Doenecke (1977). For a general discussion of the effect that the protesters and pressures of the 1960s had on curriculums, see Grant and Riesman (1978, Chap. 6).

urgent in an era in which the reimposition of requirements upon students, which were discarded as supposedly constraining spontaneity and freedom during the protest movements of the late 1960s, after having been progressively eroded by the development and spread of the elective system during the nineteenth century, is unlikely to occur, and this simply because most postsecondary institutions will find themselves underenrolled.

Prospects for the Future

While I have throughout this necessarily abbreviated essay emphasized the limitations of nostalgia, it would be a mistake not to take with the utmost seriousness the prospects of higher education in a period of at least relative decline in enrollments and of enormous consumer sovereignty. The current period of retrenchment follows directly on the heels of the great expansion of higher education that occurred in the 1960s. Underenrollment, both institution-wide and in departments overstaffed with tenured faculty, will increasingly become the norm, in spite of efforts to recruit older and part-time students who are also sought by the military and industry as well as by many profit-making institutions. More and more marginal students are now entering college, thus decreasing the general competence of the college population at least in academic subjects. Many of these students are in turn being taught by faculty members who themselves entered college in the great heyday of expansion when, as enrollments grew and new campuses sprang up, academic careers became attractive relative to other professional occupations. The top quality people who were first drawn into faculty positions began in the 1960s to give way to marginal people—people less commonly prepared at the most selective private and public research universities and sometimes less well prepared even by those schools.

Many of these only marginally qualified faculty quickly became tenured under rules set in the earlier era of an almost continuously expanding professoriate and before institutional leaders were prepared to recognize the coming decline, although it had been predicted by a number of writers. (See, for example, Cartter, 1966, and Riesman, 1969.) Tenure rules set by the American Association of University Professors do not distinguish between what

might be termed "beauty queen" fields, such as mathematics—
where a department can usually decide early as to a new instructor's
cognitive capacities (although with little chance for assessing long-
term growth or willingness to teach students who are not themselves
planning to major in the discipline)—and what one might term
"wisdom" fields, such as comparative literature or history, where
later decisions would be preferable. Sometimes young professors
were given tenure even in their late twenties to hold them.
More recently, with the growth of participatory democracy and
the student "vote," the scholarly and often deprecated mandate of "publish or perish" was succeeded by the often antischolarly
mandate of "teach or perish," and faculty gained tenure by prevent-
ing more scholarly people from even being considered for open
positions. This has also been true of some natural scientists who are
likely to become obsolescent in due course if they do not continue
their scholarship and research. Even they have not been eager in a
situation of general stasis or retrenchment to have as younger colleagues those whose research re-ignites the scholarly superegos that
many of them have sought to shed in making clear their dedication to teaching (meaning by this, keeping in touch with their
discipline and their academic colleagues) and some form of "community service."

　　Furthermore, it takes very little observation of the ablest
students in selective colleges today to see how extensive is the "brain
drain" in the natural sciences away from graduate school and a
possible academic career into the secure field of medicine, and how
even more severe is the drain of potential academicians—and even
of some actual academicians who have had difficulty finding positions of expected quality—into law schools. Even graduate schools
of management and of business administration are now attracting
capable undergraduates despite their earlier allergies toward large
organizations. Students might find positions in academia, but they
tend to overaggregate the big picture, made bleaker even for affluent
families by inflation.

　　If the most capable faculty taught lower-division courses for
the least qualified students, as I have repeatedly urged on both
faculty and administrators, there might be a chance for redeeming
deficiencies in the public schools (which in turn reflect deficiencies

in the family, church, and neighborhood) and for reversing the spiral of decline within education that Dresch and other critics foresee. But today it is often the least capable faculty who are teaching the worst prepared students. Note, for example, the unwillingness of most people trained in English literature, despite the present paucity of jobs, to undertake the handicraft task of teaching basic writing skills to semiliterate students. With the decline of the young adult population, colleges and universities could well assign better faculty to teaching not only the basic skills of reading, writing, and mathematics but also the no less essential knowledge of world history and of other cultures required for understanding and coping effectively with the contemporary world. There has been much discussion about how faculty might be prepared or retrained for this role of teaching those skills which were taken for granted in an era when only a small proportion of the population finished high school— *Change* magazine and other journals, for example, issue documents and associations run workshops on faculty development. My own observations, however, do not make me sanguine that many faculty are likely to be truly converted to this task: They will still be dependent for their own self-esteem and that of their departments on attracting student traffic into upper-level specialized courses, whether this serves student needs or only student wants. Only the most unusually dedicated mathematician, for example, along with the reject who has concluded that he will never be a Gauss or an André Weil, is willing to teach what used to be termed "bonehead" math where there will be limited opportunity to exhibit the elegance of the craft.

Finally, except for a tiny minority of institutions—among them, those that are competence-based and the small and underenrolled campuses of St. John's Colleges in Annapolis and Santa Fe—faculty have not been able to agree on a core curriculum or on what kind of core achievement or competence graduates should be expected to demonstrate in cognitive, let alone affective, terms. Even in those few institutions where student applications are not a problem this is true; thus neither the presidentially sponsored Bressler Commission at Princeton in 1971–1973 nor the excellent faculty committee chaired by as respected a faculty leader as Professor Robert Dahl at Yale were able to persuade their respective faculties

to agree on a set of requirements: no department was willing to
concur that the subject it taught was less essential than any other.
At Amherst, President John William Ward has sought but failed
to restore what had been in an earlier era one of the most demanding core curriculums for entering students to be found anywhere in
the United States. A similar fate is likely to overtake the much-
publicized efforts currently under way to establish a core curriculum
at Harvard, despite the massive efforts exerted by Dean Henry
Rosovsky and by the Committee on the Core Curriculum chaired by
professor James Q. Wilson. Neither the vocal undergraduates nor
the individualistic faculty in Harvard's departments are much more
likely to agree than they were at Yale, Princeton, and Amherst. If
that is true, it will overly sanguine to expect agreement among
faculties at many less comfortably oversubscribed institutions.[14]

Competence-based education cannot solve all these student,
faculty, and curricular problems, but it does address all of them and
makes its own demands about them. For students—even the
marginally prepared—it demands that they become self-motivated
learners who take an active part in their own education, as against
the traditional caricature of students as receptacles either bored or
eagerly being filled with knowledge, and that they demonstrate
adequate performance in order to graduate, as against being promoted for endurance alone. For faculty—even the tenured in—it
requires that they do more than pass on the often outdated knowledge they learned at the esoteric fringes of their discipline in graduate school and become instead mentors, models, and in some
measure quasi-parental figures—a new kind of teacher with a different timetable of work, since the personal relationship involved in the
mentor role is no easier to interrupt despite the pressures of the
regular academic calendar than are other close ties. And for the
curriculum—even the elective and the individualized—it insists
that outcomes be agreed on in advance by faculty and that students

[14] For a discussion of developments in learning theory and of concerns
about the weakening of requirements in the undergraduate liberal arts curriculum which helped give rise to competence-based developments in some
liberal arts colleges prior to the offer of government support or the pressure,
as in competence-based teacher education, of legislative mandate, see
Woditsch (1977) and Spady (1977).

be assessed on these outcomes not simply by individual faculty members and often by evaluators who are not themselves faculty members.

Given the strain of these expectations on both students and faculty, it is hardly surprising that, as Zelda Gamson's companion chapter on the diffusion and implementation process makes plain, the competence-based education movements have not spread rapidly over the academic landscape. Few students have embraced their new responsibilities without qualms; few faculty members are yet comfortable in their new roles and even fewer have been trained for them. Even if one makes the heroic effort to become, for example, a mentor in such a program, Zelda Gamson's Chapter Seven suggests the still fugitive nature of such commitment, the rapidity with which one can "burn out" when engaged in an effort for which there are few models and for which, despite all that is said these days about more flexible incentive systems, little support exists beyond local faculty colleagues. Certainly faculty in most institutions of any size or faculty possessing any capacity even now for upward mobility have been suspicious of the movement, for the student freedoms granted in the 1960s and earlier have been faculty freedoms as well—the freedom to teach their own thing, and the freedom outside of teaching to do their own thing. Under the regimen of competence-based education, they realize, there may be very little "outside" of teaching. The development of programs, the arguments about standards and valid assessments, the discovery and adjustment of mismatchings between student and program, the effort at careful evaluation—all are inevitable, and all mean that the work of competence-based education is never done. Indeed, in most of the self-proclaimed competence-based institutions that we have examined, such education can hardly be said even to have begun; and at Florida State it has come to an almost complete halt. Those few institutions, such as Alverno and Mars Hill, which have managed in spite of considerable resistance from faculty, some students, and influential constituencies to convert some skeptics, have had the benefit of persistent and tough-minded presidents. These leaders were prepared to lose faculty members who were unwilling to live up to the new expectations, as well as students who were not prepared for the new demands put on them. Other originators have often turned out, as Zelda Gamson also makes clear, not necessarily to be capable, scrupulous, and long-term implementers.

One encouraging exception is an institution that does not fly the competence-based banner, one that I have independently studied, namely, Worcester Polytechnic Institute (WPI) in Massachusetts. There, as at Alverno and the College for Human Services, an effort at rejuvenation began internally (however, under a former president). There was concern for the Institute's survival, as well as for the quality of engineers and scientists it was turning out in an era when technology was no longer regarded as an unequivocal blessing and could not be divorced from wider social and ethical concerns. Over a period of some years, a home guard faculty (again as at Alverno, many of them alumni) produced a document entitled *The Two Towers,* as the basis of a plan under which a new president then gained governmental and private philanthropic support. It is a plan which could well be called competence-based. Not only do students, after counselling, admit themselves, and then proceed with their program at their own pace (class attendance no longer being required) but they qualify for graduation through a week-long written and oral "competency examination." A humanities minor culminates in a research paper and successful completion of a major technical project—an "interactive" project which links technological work with the social sciences and which can be carried out at one or another of the links that WPI has established with such governmental agencies as the Council on Environmental Quality in Washington. It is a drastic shift for one of the most traditional of institutions preparing students for one of the most traditional sets of professions. But contrary to what had been my own initial fears, the faculty does not appear to be exhausted, even though a number of them have become dangerously remote from their original disciplines as a result of involvement, perhaps overinvolvement, in the new plan. Their momentum may reflect the general conservatism of the institution and its milieu: WPI has not attracted faculty or many students who want to make everything new, to have a hand in every decision. Nevertheless, WPI does face some of the chronic problems endemic to all serious changes in faculty role, from emphasis on lectures to emphasis on mentorship; thus, the rather limited PhD programs feel jeopardized by what they see as an undue preoccupation with the major task of baccalaureate education, and faculty who are stretching themselves to accommodate "interactive" projects outside their areas of expertise often fear that they will lose touch with the latter. Yet to date, WPI may be counted a success story, an augury that competence-based efforts elsewhere are both feasible and desirable.

In sum, as we have had in the past a boom-and-bust economy in the United States, so we have had in effect boom-and-bust cycles of overgeneralization about social and educational developments in American society, passing in less than a decade from egregious optimism about national progress to scarcely less shallow assumptions of total national depravity and despair. Today, as we confront the human as well as the technological structures we have erected, those who struggle against ineptitude in education and shoddiness in society may despair, just as some political scientists and governmental reformers, struggling with entrenched civil service echelons, sometimes wish that the old spoils system and the old political machines could be restored. Critics of education may be unjustifiably nostalgic for the past, even as the critics of civil service forget the horrors of the spoils system, and they may have forgotten what might be thought of as the first law of reform: that every reform will breed unexpected deleterious consequences, leading to the need for new reforms. This law of the unanticipated consequences of purposive social action is one of the few established findings of social science, and it is one of the sources of the current mood of despair and powerlessness which haunts so many Americans today. But neither nostalgia nor despair is justified. As Worcester Polytechnic and the other institutions studied for this volume illustrate, competence-based education can help alleviate some current educational problems, even though, like any other reform, it will eventually breed consequences that lead to further reforms. Thus I do not take lightly the swings of fashion in thought; indeed, I disparage and regret them because they tend to have a self-confirming quality. We need both social demands for competence and insistence on it by educators at all levels. Despair, fashionable though it may be, is no more helpful in mobilizing energy to this end than was the belief in automatic progress.

William Neumann 2

Educational Responses
to the Concern
for Proficiency

Researchers looking for the antecedents of today's experiments in competence-based education find themselves going in a variety of directions all at the same time. Thus both Ralph Tyler (1975) and David Riesman (see Chapter One) draw upon very broad and diverse historical sources in attempting to explain the rise of these experiments. No doubt the competence-based education movement has a variety of antecedents in earlier movements—including those for efficiency in education, vocational education, progressive education, and instructional technology. Striking parallels can be found between the efficiency movement of the 1920s, for example, and several features of current competence-based programs. Advocates of competence-based education generally contend that it is both cost and time efficient, and the competence-based programs at Florida State University were precipitated directly in response to a mandate from the state legislature for a time-shortened degree.

Similarly, certain basic features of progressive education and the philosophical work of John Dewey are unmistakably present in competence-based education. An obvious emphasis on learning by doing, a recognition that education takes place outside as well as within the classroom, efforts to make educational experiences as realistic as possible, attempts to involve members of the community, and a concept of designing education to prepare for life roles can all be found both in today's competence-based programs and in Dewey's *Democracy and Education* ([1915] 1966).

The effects of enduring American ideals and major crises in American life are also apparent in competence-based programs. In an excellent historical account, Veysey (1965) has shown how the principles of utility and democracy had triumphed in American higher education by the beginning of the twentieth century over elitist and "nonpractical" concepts of liberal culture and research, such as research for research's sake. The same principles appear today in competence programs. They place high importance on the usefulness of education. Their emphasis is not on what you know but on what you can do. They put into practice Alfred North Whitehead's definition of education as "the acquisition of the art of the utilization of knowledge" (1949, p. 16). And their democratic orientation is evident in their commitment to equal educational opportunity for diverse groups of "new students," in their elimination of traditional grade level distinctions between students, and in their equalization of the stature of all fields of instruction—as evidenced at Alverno College in Milwaukee, where traditional subject-matter distinctions have tended to disappear.

The experiences of two world wars have also left indelible marks on competence-based programs as well as on American education in general. The tendency of these programs to stress mastery learning and to incorporate performance tests as assessment and learning instruments may be seen as the result of wartime education and training experiences. The contingencies of wartime learning did not allow for partial learning. It was important that students learn quickly, but it was absolutely essential that they learn *completely*. And the only truly reliable means for determining whether students had mastered their assignments was the performance test. The final part of every training course had its solo flight, whether it was flying a B-29, repairing a radar unit, or cooking breakfast for five-hundred men.

In addition, ideas from developmental psychology have had a powerful impact. Compared to those, on the one hand, of orthodox Freudian psychoanalytic theory, which saw the child as struggling to cope with internal libidinal demands intensified by family interaction, and, on the other hand, of traditional learning theory, concerned with the details of stimulus and response, the work of Jean Piaget and of Ernest Schachtel emphasized from separate perspectives the desire of young people to learn, to explore, to master their world, to become competent. The semi-Freudian ideas about stages of growth by Erik Erikson, the writings of Jacob W. Getzels, and the research of Robert W. White all contributed to this sense of the development of youngsters as a search for competence—a search for puzzles to be enjoyed and solved and of problems to be confronted and overcome. Perhaps most important, White's concept of competence in his widely quoted essay, "Motivation Reconsidered: The Concept of Competence" (1959), made many educational psychologists and teachers aware of the concept and its relation to education.

Each of these sources of competence-based education invites further and more detailed investigation than is possible within the scope of this book. But focusing on the key feature of competence-based education as defined in the Prologue—namely, its tendency to develop a curriculum from an analysis of roles to be filled on completion of the educational program—two broadly divergent approaches to curriculum design seem particularly worth examination here as both historical and theoretical bases for current experiments. One is heavily behavioristic or functional, defining roles and building curriculums in terms of highly refined, specifically stated skills or functions. The second approach is much more humanistic, viewing life roles from a holistic perspective and building curriculums that incorporate elements of culture, personality, and citizenship. As Gerald Grant notes in the Prologue, early efforts at competence-based teacher education built on the behavioristic or functional approach; but some of the other programs studied for our project adopt the humanistic orientation, which challenges and moderates the strictly behavioristic approach.

Behavioristic and Functional Antecedents

The search for antecedents of contemporary educational and training programs that are based on an analysis of specific behavior or functions to be performed within certain roles leads back to the first decades of this century, to the principles of scientific management and job analysis, and to their exposition by one man.

Frederick W. Taylor: Scientific Management and Job Analysis. The general impact of the ideas and work of Frederick W. Taylor on American education has been well documented by Callahan (1962), but he does not discuss in detail the area of Taylor's work which bears directly upon the antecedents of competence-based education. That area involves, specifically, the relationship between two of Taylor's "four great underlying principles of management": the first principle, the development of a true science for each element of a person's work, that is, job analysis; and the second, the scientific education and development of the worker (Taylor, [1911] 1947, p. 36).

The concept of job analysis, or the systematic analysis and dissection of occupations into a number of component steps and processes, did not begin with Taylor (Uhrbrock, 1922). Personnel and employment officers in industry had for some time used an elementary form of job analysis in their work in hiring and placing employees, but Taylor's development and use of job analysis for time and motion studies in *The Principles of Scientific Management* crystallized interest in job analysis and brought it up to the level of a science. The new science, according to Taylor, was basically a very simple process: "Each job should be carefully subdivided into its elementary operations, and each of these units should receive the most careful time study" ([1911], 1947, p. 7).

Taylor's development of the concept of job analysis would prove infinitely useful for the selection and placement of workers, but more important were its implications for the training of employees. Still, although Taylor saw the potential value of using job analysis to structure the training program of employees, he did not develop this relationship to any great degree. The extent of his use of job analysis for training consisted of drawing up carefully detailed instruction sheets which specified the steps to be followed in doing a job; these would be given to both workers and management, and management (usually the foreman) would demonstrate the new "scientific" manner in which the job should be performed. It remained for someone other than Taylor to articulate the relationship between job analysis and education, to show that job analysis would reveal not only the most efficient manner in which to carry out a task but also the most efficient manner in which to train someone to fill a job or role.

The entry of America into the First World War and the resulting demands imposed upon educators to train competent tradesmen and technicians provided the impetus for the further development of Taylor's work in the direction of coordinating job analysis and education. The efforts of the Committee on Classification of Personnel, the Committee on Education and Special Training, and the United States Shipping Board reflect the influence of Taylor's ideas and their extension into educational programs that derive their curriculum from an analysis of roles to be performed and that certify student achievement on the basis of demonstrated performance in a relatively time-free context.

The First World War was the first major mechanized war, and the first to require the inclusion of large numbers of skilled tradesmen and technicians in the military. American entry into the war confronted the War Department with the immediate task of increasing the regular army from 45,000 men to several million. To build an army this size, thousands of skilled tradesmen and specialists were needed; the first army requisition, in March 1918, called for 85,960 skilled tradesmen. It became apparent that the draft alone would not supply the required numbers, and that the army would have to train soldiers in various skills and trades. In addition, it was necessary to balance the needs of the military for skilled tradesmen with the needs of vital war industries. It was in the interest of filling the needs of the latter of these two groups that Charles R. Allen joined the training staff of the United States Shipping Board in 1917.

Charles R. Allen: The Instructor, the Man and the Job.
Prior to joining the staff of the shipping board, Allen had spent
three years as a special agent for vocational education for the
Massachusetts State Board of Education under Commissioner David
Snedden, himself a prominent figure in vocational education. Allen
was thus well qualified for a task that consisted of turning skilled
riveters, boilermakers and other mechanics into instructors for the
thousands of inexperienced workers coming into the shipyards. His
assignment on the training staff provided Allen with the opportunity
to refine and polish his educational ideas, and shortly after the end
of the war he published a book, *The Instructor, the Man, and The
Job* (1919), which embodied his thought on the education and
training of instructors for vocational education. Allen's book, which
was to become a classic text, provides unmistakable evidence of
Taylor's influence.

"The first operation" in the instructional process, Allen tells
the future teachers, is the determination of what is to be taught, and
that is based upon the results of a trade analysis:

> Analyzing the trade simply means listing out all
> the things that the learner must be taught if he is to be
> taught the complete trade. If the trade is that of a car-
> penter, the instructor notes down all the different jobs
> that a carpenter has to do. If it is plumbing, or book-
> binding, or machine shop work, the same listing of jobs
> must be carried out. If, in addition to the jobs themselves,
> there are certain special words (technical terms) whose
> use he must know, or special tools whose names he must
> be able to remember, or constructions or computations
> which he must be able to make, or special safety pre-
> cautions that he must take, these must also be listed
> completely. The point in each case is to make a complete
> list of all that the man must know when the instructor
> has trained him for the complete trade [Allen, 1919, p. 43].

Allen placed great emphasis upon the importance of the
trade or job analysis as the foundation upon which the training program was to be structured: "Getting out a correct and complete
analysis and then classifying correctly is the key to the whole prob-

lem of getting an effective order of instruction. If the analysis is not complete, the instructor will omit things the man should be taught if he is to be completely trained" (p. 211). Using the trade analysis as a guide for identifying component skills to be learned, Allen proposed that a number of learning units or "blocks" could be identified which would each represent the specified skills to be developed and which could be arranged according to difficulty, beginning with the simplest and progressing to the most complex.

The learning blocks were to be so defined and organized as to permit a student to enter at whatever level he was prepared for, and the time factor was to be deemphasized, thus providing for a high degree of individualization: "Not only should the training work be so organized that a man can be admitted to an instructional group at any time but the organization should be such that each man can progress through the course of training required for his particular case as rapidly as his individual capabilities will admit. A 'bright' man should not be held back by men who are less 'bright' nor should a 'slow' man be speeded up in an attempt to make him keep up with the fast man. Each man should be allowed to travel at his own best gait" (p. 228).

The measure for determining progress from block to block was to be complete mastery of the subject or skill in each block. Allen rejected the more traditional method—that of evaluating the amount a person has learned in a fixed period of time and then advancing him—as inappropriate for vocational education: "The difficulty with this organization so far as trade training is concerned is that, if a man is to be taught to do a job, he must be entirely taught, so that he can do that job, not half taught, or two-thirds taught, but entirely taught. If the fixed time interval is used, a slow man can be thoroughly taught fewer jobs than a fast man, but he must be thoroughly taught when he is taught" (p. 228). As to the means for determining complete mastery, Allen's first choice was the performance test, that is, to put the instructed man up against the actual job which he has been taught to perform successfully. In those instances where a performance test was not available, a student could be evaluated by means of recitation, discussion with the instructor, or a written exam.

The book was an immediate success. In its introduction,

Charles A. Prosser, the executive director of the Federal Board for Vocational Education, praised it as "the most important contribution yet made to industrial and trade training. It deals with the most vital of our problems—the proper selection and training of competent instructors" (Allen, 1919, p. v). So impressed was Prosser that after the war ended he invited Allen to join his staff. Allen's ideas now had national exposure, and he embarked upon a long and active career in vocational and industrial education.

While Allen was busy training instructors in the shipyards, however, two committees of the War Department were also actively involved in developing innovative training techniques. The Committee on Classification of Personnel and the Committee on Education and Special Training had different but related tasks, and it was the success of their joint efforts which was largely responsible for the remarkable effectiveness of the War Department's training program.

The Committee on Classification of Personnel. This committee was established by the War Department initially to provide for the placement of skilled personnel within the army. In addition, the Committee on Education and Special Training needed accurate definitions of various army jobs and detailed information about the qualifications required of each soldier-tradesman to send to all of its 57 training sites. The Committee on Classification responded by using job analysis to assemble the *Trade Specifications and Occupational Index,* which provided precise definitions of the duties and specifications for each of the 714 civilian trades and occupations the army used, and also specified the trade needs for each branch of the army. This information was shared with the Committee on Education and distributed to all of the training sites.

Although the *Trade Specifications and Occupational Index* aided in the classification of personnel, the army soon found that its methods of selection—which generally consisted of a questionnaire and an interview—were not sufficiently accurate. For a variety of reasons, including dishonesty among recruits and variance among interviewers, large numbers of men were being inappropriately and inefficiently selected for trade and occupational training.

In an attempt to solve this problem, the Committee on Classification formed the Army Trade Test Division. The work of this division and its final product, the trade test, is reported in detail in a book written by a member of the division, James Crosby Chapman, and titled *Trade Tests: The Scientific Measurement of Trade Proficiency* (1921). Taking a cue from practices in American industry and the British army, the Army Trade Test Division turned to the performance test as the instrument for evaluating both applicants and students or trainees. Chapman and his associates developed performance tests for each of the many trades required by the military. Many of these tests are contained in the book along with a chapter on occupational analysis and a chapter explaining how the trade tests can be adapted for training purposes.

Chapman's training plan is similar to Allen's, and again Taylor's influence is apparent. Using the *Trade Specifications and Occupational Index,* Chapman would break each trade into a number of component jobs. These jobs would be carefully analyzed, a precise instruction sheet would be drawn up for each component task, and these instruction sheets would then be given to the student. The jobs would be arranged according to difficulty, and the performance test would be used to evaluate student progress. One interesting difference between Chapman's and Allen's work is that Chapman would accept a percentage of mastery of performance at each job as a criterion of assessment and progress: "If the learner can answer a predetermined proportion of the questions, if the product that he has turned out, when rated by standard methods, scores a reasonable percentage of the maximum, then, and not until then, will this particular stage in the process of learning be passed. The accomplishment of the job, with a reasonable degree of success, success being defined in purely objective terms, is the signal for advancement to the operation next in sequence" (1921, p. 407).

While it is known that the *Trade Specifications and Occupational Index* was widely distributed and used among the various training institutions under the supervision of the Committee of Education and Special Training, there is no information available which indicates the extent to which the division's or Chapman's thoughts on the design of training programs influenced these institutions.

The Committee on Education and Special Training. Created by the secretary of the War Department in February of 1918, this committee had the primary responsibility for meeting the army's needs for skilled tradesmen; and, not surprisingly, the military turned to industry to find its educational direction. Channing R. Dooley, the manager of the educational department of the Westinghouse Electric and Manufacturing Company of Philadelphia, was appointed educational director for the committee.

Dooley's task was formidable. In addition to almost staggering demands in terms of numbers and time constraints, Dooley had to coordinate training programs at 157 different institutions that were engaged in training soldiers for 67 different trades. Out of practical necessity, he organized a rather loose, decentralized administrative structure, which resulted in a good deal of autonomy and diversity among the training programs of the participating institutions. The results of the committee's work were indeed remarkable; within the first six months of its existence, the committee trained and delivered to the army over 100,000 men, and an additional 40,000 men were ready by the time the armistice was signed (Dooley, 1919).

Although the committee did issue some general guidelines for the design of the training program, its mandate to the participating institutions was to adopt those methods of instruction which would best train the men in the shortest time (Dooley, 1919). Consequently, there was considerable diversity in organizational and instructional techniques among the different training programs. Significantly, however, in the final report to C. R. Mann, the chairman of the advisory board for the committee, Dooley describes one system as being superior to all the others:

> Best results were obtained in schools that had the courses organized into a series of jobs. In these schools the job was the unit as opposed to a period of time. A man was given a job to do and not merely assigned to a job for a scheduled period of time. In such courses as that of auto mechanics the entire work was divided into the major units of engine work, chassis work, carburetor work and electrical work which included ignition, lighting and self-starter. Further subdividing arranged the whole course into a series of what might be termed minor units. The men progressed as they developed ability in

performing each successive job or unit. This method of instruction permitted a careful grouping of the men at the beginning of the course on the basis of their previous experience and capacity to progress in the course. The capable men were thus enabled to advance as rapidly as they grasped the instruction and were not retarded by the weaker men. Men with previous experience and native ability could complete the entire course in the two-month period while others found it all they could do to develop a working knowledge of the carburetor, the engine, or the chassis, or at most a combination of a few of these units. Individual instruction not only is advisable but becomes a necessary part of the method. Instructions in the form of job sheets were given to the men. These assigned a specific job and contained questions which invited definite study of important features. Performance tests as opposed to written tests were advocated, as the basis upon which to rate the men [Dooley, 1919, p. 11].

The success of these training programs astonished everyone, including their designers: "Farmers totally ignorant of the tinsmith trade produced work of commercial quality including the making of their own patterns and involving principles of descriptive geometry; bank clerks did excellent work in pattern making; real estate agents acquired great skill and enthusiasm in electrical wiring; garment workers who had never seen a piece of hot iron became good general blacksmiths. Complete failures were so rare as to be recorded negligible" (Dooley, 1919, p. 12). Clearly these noteworthy results can be attributed in part to the high degree of motivation exhibited by the students, who were, after all, preparing to go to war; and also, in part, to the effects of the strict military discipline they were living under. But the design of the educational and training programs—specifically, the key elements of individualization, evaluation by performance, promotion based on mastery, the modularization and systematic program structure, the use of self-instruction manuals or "job sheets," the emphasis on exit requirements or outcomes, and the derivation of a curriculum closely coordinated to the results of a role analysis—all these contributed to the success of the programs.

The Lessons of Wartime Training. The accomplishments of

the wartime training programs and their special features did not go unnoticed, particularly by the members of the committees responsible for their design. As was true of Allen and Chapman, two members of the Committee on Classification, Herbert Toops and Arthur Kornhauser, published work drawn from their wartime experiences.

An associate of Chapman's in the Army Trade Test Division, Toops shared Chapman's interest in the adaptation of trade tests for use in education, and his book *Trade Tests in Education* (1921) came out the same year as Chapman's. Toops presents the case for the adoption of trade or performance tests in vocational education in words which could just as easily have come from some proposals for competence-based education:

> Only until very recently has trade skill and knowledge been measured in more refined terms than subjective personal judgements of "skilled man" and "helper," "successful" and "unsuccessful," "competent" and "incompetent." Army trade tests solved this problem for the army; adaptations of the method may solve the problem for our vocational schools. Graduates of our vocational schools are at present of equal merit, so far as measure of their merit goes, for they all receive diplomas. Industry wants a more accurate measure of their hiring worth; and the school desires to recognize the varying merit of its product. Unless the prospective employer can successfully rate the human product of the vocational school, he is at a loss to know in placing a graduate of a vocational school in industry whether he should adopt a course different from that followed in the case of any other applicant for the job. The average employer is skeptical of the value of the "book learned" tradesman. His skepticism, we must believe, is not directed toward vocational school graduates as against particular exceptional individuals in the past who have happened to fail when given the test of industry, the test of doing the job itself [Toops, 1921, p. 1].

Having underscored the value of performance tests, Toops goes on to explain just how a trade test can be constructed and administered by educators. But he then reverses himself somewhat and claims that, while the performance test is good, it is not as efficient as a "multiple-choice trade test," which is much more "objective" and timesaving. Written as a practical, and not theoretical, guide to the adaptation of army trade tests to education, the book contains many examples of how trade skills can be standardized and evaluated through written multiple-choice exams.

Kornhauser had also served on the Committee on Classification of Personnel and, like Chapman and Toops, was convinced of the value of trade tests—he called them "performance job tests"—and other unique features of the training program developed during the war. Kornhauser's "Plan of Apprentice Training" (1922), which appeared in the *Journal of Personnel Research* and had been given a trial run by the Scott Company, was an effort at making apprentice training more effective and efficient through the army's training methods.

Kornhauser systematically arranged the whole of apprentice training into a series of "natural divisions" or jobs. Bearing in mind the two principles of individualization and of stating specific objectives, he operationalized his plan with the following features:

1. The progress of an apprentice is determined by the ability he shows in his work. There is no set time for any part of the course.
2. Proficiency as a basis for advancement is measured by job tests and oral examinations; also by ratings given foremen and supervisors.
3. Student manuals consisting of specified job tests and trade questions serve not simply as a measure of progress. They are at the same time goal, stimulus, and means of instruction.
4. The presence of known specifications of accomplishment places a definite goal before instructor and students. This serves both to stimulate the apprentices and to give point and direction to the training, thus markedly shortening the time required in acquiring skill [Kornhauser, 1922, p. 217].

The plan of apprentice training developed by Kornhauser does contain the essential features of the military program, and its subsequent widespread adoption by industry demonstrates its transition from wartime training to peacetime industrial education.

In another attempt to spread the concepts of the military training program to the greater educational community, Charles R. Mann, who had been chairman of the advisory board for the Committee on Education and Special Training and who was later to become president of the American Council on Education, wrote an article called "The Technique of Army Training" (1922) for *School and Society* in which he summarized the "best" practices of the military. In his article Mann emphasized the use of job analysis for establishing the "special objectives" of the educational program, the modularization of the subjects, the establishment of specifications or acceptable standards of accomplishment, and the use of objective tests of proficiency. The ideas that came from the First World War training programs were eventually to have a great influence on practices in vocational and industrial education, but it was their impact on the field of curriculum studies that was to bring them into the limelight of educational practice.

The Science of Curriculum-Making. While military, industrial, and business training programs were rapidly becoming "scientific," the study and practice of education was also experiencing the effect of the scientific revolution. This was especially apparent in the emergence and growth of the field of curriculum studies in the 1920s.

Franklin Bobbitt, identified by Callahan as one of the most influential subscribers to Taylor's ideas, wrote the first full-length book devoted entirely to the curriculum. Among the wide range of issues covered by Bobbitt's book, *The Curriculum* (1918), there appeared a section on "Scientific Method in Curriculum-Making" in which he presented the case for the study of the curriculum: "The technique of curriculum-making along scientific lines has been but little developed. The controlling purposes of education have not been sufficiently particularized. We have aimed at a vague culture, an ill-defined discipline, a nebulous harmonious development of the individual, an indefinite moral character-building, an unparticularized social efficiency, or, often enough nothing more than escape from a life of work. Often there are no controlling purposes; the momentum of the educational machine keeps it running. So long as objectives are but vague guesses, or not even that, there can be no demand for anything but vague guesses as to means and procedure. But the era of contentment with large, undefined purposes is rapidly passing. An age of science is demanding exactness and particularity" (1918, p. 41).

The scientific technique Bobbitt proposed begins with an *activity analysis,* which is simply another term for job analysis, only in this case the "job" to be analyzed is life: "The central theory is simple. Human life, however varied, consists in the performance of specific activities. Education that prepares for life is one that prepares definitely and adequately for these specific activities. However numerous and diverse they may be for any social class, they can be discovered. This requires only that one go out into the world of affairs and discover the particulars of which these affairs consist. These will show the abilities, attitudes, habits, appreciations, and forms of knowledge that men need, these will be the objectives of the curriculum. They will be numerous, definite, and particularized. The curriculum will then be that series of experiences which children and youth must have by way of attaining those objectives" (p. 42).

Bobbitt's use of activity analysis to derive curricular objectives required the articulation of those objectives in terms of real-life activities. These objectives stated as particular activities were the forerunners of what are today referred to as behavioral objectives (Eisner, 1967). Indeed, Ralph Tyler, who has been called "the father of behavioral objectives," was a student of Bobbitt's at the University of Chicago.

It was one of Bobbitt's contemporaries, W. W. Charters, who elaborated upon Bobbitt's work on curriculum-making and widely disseminated it through numerous publications. Although, in essence, they all involved the same procedure as a job analysis, Charters advanced the use of the activity analysis (1922), the functional analysis (1924a), the difficulty analysis (1926), the duty analysis (1926), the trait analysis (1924b), and the information analysis (1926), all for the same purpose: curriculum construction. But the development of the concept of the trait analysis is probably Charters' unique contribution to the process of analysis and curriculum construction: "A trait analysis should always accompany an activity analysis. In building a curriculum it is not sufficient to find out what people have to do and give them instructions in the performance of the duties. Much depends upon traits of personality, such as accuracy, neatness, courtesy, and firmness. As a matter of fact college-trained teachers who fail in a vocation seldom make a failure because of lack of information or technical skill. The causes of failure are weakness of personality. Consequently, a teacher training institution must pay direct, explicit, and persistent attention to the development of the proper traits of personality. What has to be done is not so important as how it is done; and the standards of performance are set by the traits of personality and the character of the worker" (1924a, p. 218).

The trait analysis was conducted simply by interviewing experts and qualified judges in the field, and finding their consensus. It became a permanent feature of Charters' method of curriculum construction, this construction consisting of four steps: Steps one and two, which were carried out concurrently, were the functional analysis and the trait analysis; step three was the use of the results of these analyses to determine the basic subject matter; and step four was the arrangement of the material in teaching order with special regard to the lessons of psychology.

The 1920s were the heyday of job analysis and curriculum construction, and W. W. Charters was undeniably its leading figure and most prolific proponent. Although a major part of the work continued to be in industrial-trade and vocational areas, important efforts were made to adapt the procedure for professional education and more traditional academic subjects. As a professor of education at the Carnegie Institute of Technology, Charters helped guide the work of two Carnegie researchers, Strong and Uhrbrock, who conducted a study of the use of job analysis in designing a curriculum for the training of executives for the printing industry. Their study, which appeared as *Job Analysis and the Curriculum* (1923), was important because it made an early attempt to adapt job analysis to a profession, served as an early model for later studies, and included an excellent bibliography on job analysis.

An article on the use of job analysis in vocational curriculum-making appeared in the yearbook of the National Society for the Study of Education in 1924 (Kitson, 1924), and in that same year, a special issue of *The Journal of Educational Research* was devoted solely to articles on "Educational Objectives for Colleges and Schools of Education" and "Job Analysis and the Training of Teachers." Both Bobbitt and Charters were among the contributors, and the following year Charters began the famous Commonwealth Teacher Training Study. This study, published in 1928, was probably the most thorough job analysis in history. Charters' entire analytic scheme was employed, and more than two million activities and points of information regarding teaching were amassed. After being reviewed and evaluated by juries of teachers, administrators, and professors, these activities were then reduced to about a thousand. This list became known as "The 1001 Activities of American Teachers" and was used by many teacher training institutions in curriculum development (Tyler, 1975).

The extent to which job or activity analysis had been accepted by educators as a means for curriculum-making may be judged by the regard paid it in the composite statement of the committee on curriculum-making which appeared in 1926 in the yearbook of the National Society for the Study of Education. In Section III, "Curriculum-Making and Scientific Study of Society," the committee wrote: "Curriculum-making will increasingly make use of scientific procedure. The materials of instruction (individual and group activities of children, reading, open forum discussions, excursions, what not) will be chosen in the light of the analysis and appraisal of the activities in which people, old and young, most universally and permanently engage. This is just as necessary in the case of the finer types of appreciation as in the case of the most highly specialized skills. Not only will the materials of instruction emerge from a scientific study of society, but, in addition, the discovery of the sound purposes of education will be furthered by such study" (in Rugg, 1926, p. 15).

Later that year the Teachers College Contributions to Education Series published a monograph by Walter Jones, *Job Analysis and Curriculum Construction in the Metal Trade Industry* (1926). In this book Jones proposed the use of the "project method" to build a curriculum of projects based upon a job analysis of metal tradesmen's work. While there was nothing very new in its design, it did represent an attempt to wed two of the "hottest" educational techniques of the day, job analysis and the project method.

Interest in job analysis and curriculum construction began to decline in the 1930s as the influence of progressive education became more widespread and reached college curriculum-makers. The major features of the First World War training programs had by the 1930s become firmly established principles of vocational and industrial training, but times were difficult and industries were laying off employees, not training them. There was, however, at least one redoubt in which these training concepts flourished.

The Civilian Conservation Corps and Unit Instruction. Along with the goal of providing immediate employment for thousands of the unemployed, the Civilian Conservation Corps (CCC) also had as a primary objective the development of skills in their enrollees which would make them employable on the open market. To this end a program of "unit instruction" was instituted in several camps. Unit instruction was considered an improvement on military methods (Rice, 1940), but descriptions of such instruction reveal few, if any, differences between it and the military training programs it was drawn from. (It is interesting to note that C. R. Mann once again appears in an advisory role, this time as a member of a national advisory committee supervising the educational programs of the CCC. His influence may be detected in the operation of unit instruction.)

Toward the end of the 1930s, when it became clear that the United States would be drawn into a war for which it wasn't prepared, there was a resurgence of interest in the First World War programs. The National Industrial Conference Board published a booklet in 1940 called *Quick-Training Procedures* which summarized the report of Dooley's committee, and Dooley—who had been appointed director of the Training Within Industry branch of the War Manpower Commission—wrote the introduction for an industrial training manual, *How to Train Workers for War Industries: A Manual of Tested Training Procedures* (1942). Sponsored by the American Management Association, this manual was a compilation of articles written for business executives by business executives describing various quick-training programs and practices.

The new wartime training programs operationalized by industry and the military bore remarkable similarity to the training programs of the First World War. Charles Prosser tells the story of how a representative of the War Department, General Frank McSherry, in 1939 found the plans for the 1918 training programs, became very enthusiastic about them, and urged the War Department to adopt them again (Todd, 1945).

Lessons from Wartime Training: Another War. The considerable demands by the military for trained specialists in 1918 seem almost paltry when compared to the requisitions of the Second World War. Education and training programs were carried out on a magnitude unsurpassed in history. More than ten million men and women became "experts" in a vast range of activities, many of which were highly technical. That education and especially higher education would be affected by these training programs was to be expected. More than six hundred colleges and universities, along with thousands of professors and other educators, participated to some degree in military training.

To ensure that what was of value in these programs would not be lost to American educators after the war ended, the American Council on Education, with funding from the Carnegie Corporation and the General Education Board, appointed a commission under the leadership of Alonzo P. Grace to conduct a two-year study of the implications of military experiences for civilian education. Their general report, *Educational Lessons from Wartime Training* proclaimed no "educational atom bombs," but it did provide solid evidence for the validity and effectiveness of several educational practices: "Out of the experience of the armed services in the training of twelve million men it is clear that new concepts have emerged to take their places besides our presently held concepts in general education about the importance of the objective, the need for curricular revision in the light of social change and scientific advancement, the desirability of adjusting the curriculum to the individual, the relatively greater effectiveness of learning experiences that involve doing rather than only listening or reading, the importance of instructors' guides and of suitable materials and aids in the implementation of a particular course or program, and the power of motivation and learner purpose in attaining objectives" (Grace, 1948, p. 99).

Increasingly one could find certain distinctive features of the trade training program appearing in educational programs for more professional military roles, such as those for engineers, medics, and pilots. The literacy program that the military designed was individualized and modularized, had very clear objectives, and was time-free. Advancement depended upon mastery of material as demonstrated in performance tests. The one feature which the commission stressed as having the most important implications for civilian education was that of designating specific goals or objectives for courses and instruction. The objectives were the foundation upon which to design the course of training and later became the basis for evaluating student progress.

The test for evaluating the degree to which objectives were reached was most often a practical or performance test, and the commission recommended its more general utilization by educators: "It is important to note that the armed services used actual tests of performance of the required skills whenever practicable. The best practical test of a radio mechanic is to place before him several devices that he will be expected to keep in repair, each of which has a defect which he is required to locate and correct. Such tests were used in the final examinations of radio operators and mechanics. Similar tests were used in many other technical courses, wherever they could be devised, to supplement pencil-and-paper achievement tests. Possibly a similar type of practical testing could be used far more widely in liberal and professional education than is now the case" (Grace, 1948, p. 29).

Significantly, the members of the commission—themselves all civilian educators—drew special attention to the basic differences between military training and civilian general education. Although granting that civilian educators are faced with more complicated problems of teaching emphasis and that their goals are necessarily much broader than those of the armed services, the commission members felt that the efficiency and effectiveness of military training, often in highly complex technical activities, constituted "an open challenge to civilian educators to think about the objectives of American schools and colleges" (Grace, 1948, p. 100).

Training Research and Education. There was little governmental or military interest, and certainly no money, for the study of training programs after the First World War, but the situation was just the opposite following the Second World War. Military interest in training research not only continued unabated but, in fact, increased. During the 1950s and 1960s the Department of Defense sponsored hundreds of psychologists to conduct training research. In 1957, for example, it was reported that the military employed a minimum of 729 psychologists. Members of the American Psychological Association (APA) established a division of military psychology, and an enormous body of psychological literature on learning and training was generated.

Glaser (1962), who conducted some of this research and has written widely on the implications of training research for education, reports that one of the primary concerns of these psychologists has been with the development of techniques of task analysis as a means of behaviorally specifying performance objectives. Robert Gagne (1965b), also active in training research and a former president of the division of military psychology of the APA, feels that this emphasis on behavioral objectives is critically important in the design of effective instruction. He himself looks on task analysis as the most useful technique for arriving at statements of training objectives in behavioral terms. Both Gagne and Glaser readily admit that their use of task analysis as a principle in training programs was based upon the earlier work of another training psychologist, Robert Miller. Glaser, for example, writes: "A primary example of the analysis of instructional goals is the notion of task analysis developed in the military context by Miller. Such procedures should provide information to assist the designer of a course of instruction in making design decisions. Furthermore, factual data of this kind can combat prejudices and ritualistic practices about what is relevant or nonrelevant—to criterion performance" (1965a, p. 155).

Miller (1962), in his own work, uses the term "task" interchangeably with the term "job" and talks about "parts" of tasks, "functions" of tasks, and task "activities." Task analysis is, quite simply, an attempt to identify the variety of tasks in a job. Each task in turn can be divided into several subtasks. The subtasks are then arranged in a task sequence, which is specially arranged to facilitate transfer of learning from task to task. The outcomes of task analyses are referred to as "task descriptions" and these serve as instructional goals.

Gagne (1962a) considers the use of task analysis for the design of training programs as the most effective means of instructing individuals to develop motor skills, sequence skills (that is, learning to do things in their proper order), and such higher order skills as troubleshooting or problem solving. In his presidential address delivered at the annual meeting of the division of military psychology, Gagne attests to the superiority of the technique of task analysis over other learning principles: "If I were faced with the problem of improving training, I should not look for much help from the well-known learning principles like reinforcement, distribution of practice, response familiarity, and so on. I should look instead at the technique of task analysis, and at the transfer, and the sequencing of subtask learning to find those ideas of greatest usefulness in the design of effective training" (1962a, p. 90).

It is no surprise that both the military training programs and recent developments in experimental psychology have exerted a strong influence on the design of many current educational programs, and especially competence-based education. But, significantly, not all educators adhere to the behavioristic-functionalistic approach. There are educators, including some involved in the design of competence-based education programs, who reject this atomized, highly particularized view of education. They would call these programs "training" and not education. The distinction being made here between training and education rests upon the degree of specificity with which program objectives are described. Glaser puts it well: "If the end products of the learning process can be rather precisely specified, as, for example, learning to use a slide rule, then it can be said that the student is being trained to use a slide rule. On the other hand, if the behavioral end-products are complex and present knowledge of the behavior makes them difficult to specify, then the individual is educated by providing a foundation of behavior which represents approximations to the behavior it is wished that the student will eventually perform, for example, being a creative scientist" (1962, p. 4).

Within Glaser's statement lies the crux of the contrast between behavioristic and humanistic perspectives on competence-based education. Although they construct their curriculums with the intention of preparing students for certain roles, and fairly specific ones at that, some competence-based education programs profiled in our study, such as those at the College for Human Services and the teacher preparatory program at Syracuse University, take a much broader, less particular, approach in the design of their curricular experiences.

The Humanistic Challenge

The often dramatic successes of the behavioristic and functional approach to education in part explains its present ascendancy in American educational practice, yet some competence-based programs, through their broader conception of roles, demonstrate the persistent humanistic influence that challenges and moderates some of the excesses of the more prominent orientation.

John Dewey. Perhaps the most articulate challenge to the strictly behavioristic and functional approach to education can be found in the work of John Dewey. In *Democracy and Education* (1915) Dewey forcefully rejects the atomistic, task-specific curriculum of some educational programs:

> We must avoid not only limitation of conception of vocation to the occupations where immediately tangible commodities are produced, but also the notion that vocations are distributed in an exclusive way, one and only one to each person. Such restricted specialism is impossible; nothing could be more absurd than to try to educate individuals with an eye to only one line of activity. In the first place, each individual has of necessity a variety of callings, in each of which he should be intelligently effective; and in the second place any one occupation loses its meaning and becomes a routine keeping busy at something in the degree in which it is isolated from other interests. No one is just an artist and nothing else, and insofar as one approximates that condition, he is so much the less developed human being; he is a kind of monstrosity [Dewey (1915), 1966, p. 307].

Like Bobbitt, Dewey claims that the dominant role for which education must prepare one is life. Life involves not one role, but a multitude of roles. An occupation is just one role; other roles include being a family member, a friend, a member of some political group, or a colleague. There is a natural tendency to think of a person in terms of his occupational role because it is this role which distinguishes a person, but this should not cause one to ignore or deny the other roles a person must fill. Clearly where Bobbitt's perspective on life is static (life as a number of identifiable activities), Dewey's is vibrant, growing. According to Dewey, the dominant vocation of all human beings at all times is living, that is, intellectual and moral growth.

Dewey dismisses the narrow task-specific curriculum as injurious to both the individual and society. A lack of breadth in educational experiences inhibits individual development and restricts possibilities for growth, thus making it very difficult for the individual to find "his own right job." Equally damning of the job-specific curriculum is Dewey's sense that it is essentially undemocratic. It deprives students of the social meaning of the careers for which they are preparing and doesn't equip them to be critical or independent of the occupational roles thrust upon them: "To predetermine some future occupation for which education is to be a strict preparation is to injure the possibilities of present development and thereby to reduce the adequacy of preparation for a future right employment. To repeat—the principle we have had occasion to appeal to so often, such training may develop a machine-like skill in routine lines (it is far from being sure to do so, since it may develop distaste, aversion, and carelessness), but it will be at the expense of those qualities of alert observation and coherent and ingenious planning which makes an occupation intellectually rewarding. In an autocratically managed society, it is often a conscious object to prevent the development of freedom and responsibility; a few do the planning and ordering, the others follow directions and are deliberately confined to narrow and prescribed channels of endeavor" (Dewey [1915], 1966, p. 310).

The inclination towards specialization in educational programs that were vocationally oriented was, Dewey thought, natural and to be expected, but it was up to educators to restrain it, "so that the scientific inquirer shall not be merely the scientist, the teacher merely the pedagogue, the clergyman merely one who wears the cloth, and so on" (p. 308). The ideal curriculum designed by Dewey to prepare students for a specific occupation, which of course is part of one's vocation, would be broad indeed: "An education which acknowledges the full intellectual and social meaning of a vocation would include instruction in the historic background of present conditions; training in science to give intelligence and initiative in dealing with material and agencies of production; and study of economics, civics, and politics, to bring the future worker into touch with the problems of the day and the various methods proposed for its improvement. Above all, it would train power of readaptation to changing conditions so that future workers would not become blindly subject to a fate imposed upon them" (p. 319).

The powerful logic of Dewey's pronouncements demands a broader conceptualization of programs that claim to educate, not simply to train students.

Stephens College. This broader perspective can be found in the later work of the founding fathers of task analysis and curriculum construction, Franklin Bobbitt and W. W. Charters. In the late 1930s Stephens College in Missouri asked W. W. Charters to develop a curriculum specially designed to meet the needs of women. Charters responded with his typically ambituous use of the task analysis and the difficulty analysis, but from a slightly broader perspective than he had taken in the past. He asked more than three hundred women, some married and some unmarried, some employed outside the home and some not, but all college graduates, to keep diaries for several weeks in which they were to record their activities, their problems, and their thoughts. He then analyzed the diaries, and from a list of over seventy-five hundred items he abstracted seven broad areas common to all women's activities and needs. The seven areas, which served as the foundation for the curriculum at Stephens, included: communications, appreciation of the beautiful, social adjustment, physical health, mental health, consumers' problems, and philosophy of living. To this list the faculty at Stephens added an eighth area, "a knowledge of science in terms of life needs." Despite the detailed list of activities and intensive analysis, the curriculum developed at Stephens was intentionally broad. B. Lamar Johnson, dean of instruction at Stephens, noted that "the curriculum is conceived broadly, for it includes the sum total of the student's college experience, in the classroom and in the library, in the dormitory and on the athletic field, in the laboratory and in the sorority room" (1939, p. 128).

The curriculum developed at Stephens College demonstrates a blend of the behavioristic and functional and the humanistic schools of thought. A similar blending is also apparent in the curriculum developed at Rollins College in Florida during the 1930s.

Rollins College. In January 1931, Hamilton Holt, the ambitious and sometimes erratic president of Rollins College, invited John Dewey and Goodwin Watson of Columbia University's Teachers College, along with several other prominent progressive educators, to a highly publicized conference on curriculum for the College of Liberal Arts. Participants in the conference were strongly influenced by a two-part article by Watson on "What Should College Students Learn?" that had appeared in the November and December 1930 issues of *Progressive Education* (Butts, 1939). Watson charged that increasing public demands for equality of educational opportunity called for a new and more effective college curriculum. He proposed an "ideal but practicable" curriculum that would eliminate traditional academic subject divisions and replace them with several broadly conceived departments which would represent more appropriately actual life experiences. The seven departments, which were remarkably similar to the seven areas that Charters identified for Stephens College, included: health, homemaking, purchasing and consumer activities, leisure-time experiences, vocation, citizenship, and philosophy of life.

Students would not take courses within these departments, but instead would engage in various "project enterprises" of which Watson said: "Considered as life situations in all their varied ramifications, they will help the student to become more competent in the affairs of modern social life" (1930, p. 400). While projects would occupy the activities of students in all seven departments, special attention was drawn to the projects in the department of citizenship, which called for an activism on the part of students not unlike that required by the College for Human Services: "Projects in this department will be highly realistic; they will take the student out of the classroom into the life of his community, county, state, and nation. If he discovers that the methods of providing playgrounds, caring for the insane, or censoring moving-pictures is highly inadequate, according to the best standards of judgment his study reveals, it should be his business, not merely to write a term paper about it, but to participate in the actual work of improving the social structure where it is at fault. This realistic approach to the problems of the world as it is will break down prejudices and open many new fields for study" (p. 401).

Although Watson claimed that one of the virtues of his new curriculum was that it would individualize education and provide interested students with the opportunity to specialize, he was opposed to an emphasis on specific vocational training. In addition, he would ensure against overspecialization by requiring that students gain a certain minimum of experience in each of the seven departments.

Reports of the conference were written by John Palmer Gavitt (1931a, 1931b) and Goodwin Watson (1931), but it was not until some months after the conference that President Holt announced that Rollins would have a new curriculum: "Under the new plan, which is a departure from standardized college practices, the student body will be divided into an Upper and a Lower Division. New methods of evaluating a student's work have been evolved, with the consequent abandonment of the present system of credits and grades, thus permitting the elimination of the time element in completing a college course and placing the work of the student on an 'accomplishment basis' " (McHale, 1932, p. 83).

At Rollins College, the responsibility for taking the initiative in education was placed upon the shoulders of the student: subject matter was still organized into courses, but courses were not required. One gained certification of attainment not through attendance, but through demonstration of certain definite levels of accomplishment: "Furthermore the student is no longer held back by the lockstep system of mass education. He can go ahead as far and as fast as his ability will allow" (Holt, 1930a, p. 372). A document submitted by Rollins College for inclusion in the yearbook of the National Society for the Study of Education describes the essential features of the new Rollins curriculum:

>But in place of the system of evaluating a degree in terms of credit hours, grades, and terms of residence, there has been substituted one in which the student who desires admission to the upper division of the college will be required to demonstrate to the satisfaction of a board of admissions that he has met the requirements for such admission; and, further, the upper division student who is a candidate for a degree will in like manner have to demonstrate to a special committee that the work which he has accomplished is of such character and of sufficient amount to warrant his recommendation for the degree. The committees are given great discretion as to the methods they may follow in evaluating the work of any given student and it is quite probable that the methods employed will vary with the student. The plan provides for no required courses. Instead of this it prescribes certain definite accomplishments and leaves the student a choice of methods by which he may fulfill the requirements. The college will offer, and probably the majority of the students will take, courses in which they will acquire the materials necessary for the satisfaction of the requirements; but there is nothing to prevent a student satisfying the requirements by purely independent work or by work carried on under the informal guidance of a member of the faculty. The conference plan of instruction will be retained [McHale, 1932, p. 84].

The objective of the new curriculum was simply stated as the "hope" that the student would be "better prepared to meet conditions prevailing outside the college."

The new curriculum at Rollins included the following features, many of which are characteristic of more behavioristic attempts at competence-based education: individualization, modularization as reflected by the projects, establishment of objectives referred to as "definite accomplishments," mastery learning, evaluation based upon student demonstration of accomplishment, the elimination of required courses, efforts to make educational experiences realistic and practical, and the elimination or deemphasis of time as an evaluative factor in education. While the Rollins Plan shared several features of behavioristic competence-based education programs, it differed in one crucial aspect; it was based upon a very broad curricular objective, namely, to prepare students to meet conditions outside the college.

Final Observations

Competence-based programs tend to be eclectic, incorporating various characteristics of different types of educational programs and practices. In many of them, such relatively new concepts as programmed instruction, behavioral objectives, and mastery learning coexist comfortably with age-old educational concepts like individualization, self-paced learning, and learning through practical experience. But despite this eclecticism of practice, these programs tend toward one or the other of two major theoretical orientations or philosophical approaches: the behavioristic and functional view on the one hand or the humanistic and holistic on the other. Their choice of perspective affects all facets of their operation, including instructional practices and assessment techniques. As the case studies later in this volume illustrate, some programs can blend facets of both orientations, rather than espousing only one or the other. The aim of this chapter, however, has not been to baptize one orientation or the other, but to make the nature of these choices more explicit by uncovering their histories.

Peter Elbow   3

Trying to Teach
While Thinking
About the End

A student knocks on the office door. He enters and says, "I wanted to talk to you about the paper you handed back today in class. You gave me a B minus. I don't really see from your comments what's the matter with it. I really worked hard on it. It really answers the questions. It's carefully done. You don't really point out anything seriously wrong with it."

The teacher tries to remember what he was thinking when he graded the paper. He leans back and looks out the window. Sighing wearily and wishing he hadn't, he begins to talk about things being a bit vague here and there, about missed opportunities. He contemplates saying, "Yes, it's true you don't really say anything wrong, and I'm not just grading on style, but there's something missing. The paper doesn't measure up. And it's not just a matter of my own prejudice or pleasure. I have a definite sense of an external standard for an A paper, and this doesn't make it. But I can't tell you exactly what you should have done. There are many things you might have done." But he knows from experience that this kind

95

of candor only makes things worse. He settles for pointing out some ambiguity of thought, some poor writing, and some specific points he can learnedly rebut.

Is there a teacher who has not experienced this kind of scene? The account can be shaped to suit one's prejudices: either into the story of a virtuous student victimized by a bumbling, incompetent teacher or into the story of a teacher with a sense of the best that humankind has thought and done, heroically trying to preserve civilization against the insidious erosion of callow youth. But either way, I see that student in my mind's eye, going on to major in engineering or education, then going on to graduate school, all the while muttering, "There's no excuse for asking students to do something if you can't specify exactly what constitutes a good job," and finally growing up to invent competence-based education.

In this essay I attempt to explore the effects on college level teaching of a competence-based approach. I start by describing the most direct and straightforward effects of a competence approach upon teaching, and I then explore some of its paradoxical effects— paradoxes I see in the spirit of the competence approach itself. Finally I address the question that has perplexed me most during this inquiry, that is, whether a competence approach rules out or inhibits certain styles or temperaments in teaching.

Since competence-based education tells you to start by determining the competencies you want students to attain—the outcomes—and only then to plan your teaching to fit them, its effects on teaching would seem to depend almost entirely on what those competencies are. But there is little agreement within the movement about the nature of competencies. That is, they can be oriented toward *performance* or *knowing how to* (for example, play the following musical pieces up to a certain standard, or solve this particular problem); or they can be oriented toward *knowledge* or *knowing that* (for example, explain the difference between the baroque and classical styles; or describe the theory of problem-solving). In addition, competencies can be oriented toward disciplines (for example, the department of music at Florida State University has competencies entirely within that discipline); or they can be what are called *generic competencies* that cut across disciplines (for example, "communicating" or "critical thinking" at Alverno College in

Milwaukee—where students work on attaining these generic competencies through course work in different disciplines). And finally,
competencies can simply be small or big: There are scores of
competencies a student must attain in only one nursing course at
Mt. Hood Community College, in Gresham, Oregon, while at
Alverno there are only eight competencies required for the bachelor's
degree. (Of course, each of the eight Alverno competencies is
broken down into six levels; and conversely the myriad Mt. Hood
nursing outcomes are clumped—even across courses—into large
categories, for example, "asepsis" or "patient comfort." Still, some
programs feel crowded and some feel expansive because of a
tendency to think in terms of small competencies or big competencies.) In the end, however, the most interesting and important
effects of the competence approach on teaching seem to me to
transcend these variations among competencies and to result from
the basic competence situation itself in which outcomes—and often
assessments—are devised and made public in advance and teaching
is planned to fit them.

Direct Effects

*Foremost among the effects of competence-based education
on teaching is that it breaks up the role of the college teacher into
many different parts.* I never thought the organization of higher education was simple until I had to think about competence-based
education. But it is. Just divide knowledge into areas, handing the big
areas to departments and the small ones to individual teachers. Let the
students sign up, give everyone your blessing, and ask for grades at
the end of the quarter (making sure, however, to collect payment at
the beginning of the quarter). I get great pleasure from seeing this
simplicity, but as with so many innocent pleasures, it is experienced
primarily in retrospect. Where I used to see just a college teacher
teaching, now I often see an array of distinct functions:

1. Devising the competencies: writing out in advance the knowledge
   and skills a student must have to get credit.
2. Validating the competencies: going to the outside world to determine whether these are the competencies people really need

for certain jobs or studies or tasks, or whether these are the competencies people really want for whatever goals they might have.
(Strict constructionists insist that the educational institution has
no right to decide by itself what should be taught.)

3. Designing the instruction: figuring out what subject matter,
   activities, and materials should be used to help students get these
   competencies.
4. Early diagnostic testing: finding out whether students are suited
   for this instruction or need special help or perhaps already have
   the competencies.
5. The teaching itself.
6. Late diagnostic testing: determining whether students are ready
   for certification, for example, giving a "practice final"; this also
   tells teachers which parts of their teaching worked and which
   parts did not work.
7. Certifying: making up and giving tests to see who gets credit.
8. Advising: not just helping students clarify their own goals and
   find their way through the complexities of the institution and its
   regulations, but also helping students figure out the best ways to
   do these things.

Of course we didn't see different people performing each one
of these functions, but the competence approach, with the opening
wedge of asking you to specify outcomes and assessments in advance, invites you to distinguish among all these tasks that used to
be simply the overall job of the college teacher. This tendency to
distinguish functions helps explain why these programs are so expensive in time and dollars. Theoretically, of course, the mere conceptualization of different functions shouldn't cost more time or
trouble, but once you begin to separate functions, you tend to increase the amount of work.

Imagine, for example, two teachers from similar or overlapping disciplines who have decided to collaborate in an outcome-
oriented fashion. Each figures out the competencies that the students
must have by the end of the course and puts these in writing. Each
agrees to assess the other's students at the end. Even though there is
no time spent on validating the competencies, on extra advising, on
alternate learning paths or on committee meetings, nevertheless this
proto-competence program would cost both teachers additional

time: to figure out and write down their competencies clearly enough so that the other could test for their presence or absence in students; to work out assessments; and to *do* assessments carefully enough to trust them with students they hadn't worked with for perhaps fifteen weeks.

Second, competence-based education attacks the role of "professor." The higher the status of the college or the university, the more likely that its teachers are called professors and that they have complete jurisdiction over all teaching functions. In particular, they would feel affronted if someone started telling them what they should cover in their courses or how they should grade their students. ("Are *you* trying to tell *me* who gets credit in *my* course?") In effect, society hands students to the professor and says, "Teach them what you will; then decide whether they learned it and deserve credit. You don't have to tell what the component parts of your course are or what your criteria are for giving credit." That, really, is the entire educational transaction, apart from counseling, registration, and administration. Of course, departments supposedly ensure to society that professors are responsible and competent. But being nothing but groups of professors, departments are in a ticklish position for this regulatory function. Although they can be decisive in refusing tenure to a member for lack of good research and publication, they seldom ensure that teachers teach competently.

But competence-based programs are apt to take some of these functions out of professors' hands: They seldom have unilateral power over what the outcomes should be—and sometimes no power at all—and often they will be partially or wholly unconnected with the assessment function. It is no accident, then, that competence programs are not usually found at high-status colleges. Many of them are at places where the faculty members are not called professor and where—before the program was instituted—the faculty had little autonomy or sovereignty compared to what is taken for granted at high-status colleges and universities.

Though a competence program can be a vehicle for a faculty to renew and reorganize its collegial control over the curriculum (see Chapter Five), the competence-based approach invites lessened faculty control. There is often a distinct animus against "professors" among people in the movement—an animus I also sensed in some of the staff at FIPSE—and in many of these programs, faculty do not feel their usual control over the curriculum. As one dissatisfied faculty member said, "We don't own the curriculum anymore. The administration does." Sometimes it is indeed the administration, but more often, in fact, it is a matter of new groupings of faculty working out the curriculum together; when these groups are not organized along departmental lines, some faculty members experience a loss of control.

In addition, if there is to be a real process of validating the competencies—going outside the academy to see what others think ought to be taught—then clearly the faculty's sole responsibility for deciding what should be taught is diminished. As most readers will know, many legislatures are getting into the competence-based act and specifying the things that ought to be taught. Many college teachers are content to let legislatures specify what should be taught in primary or secondary schools, but are very offended if they specify what colleges or universities should teach. (The Supreme Court, too, has ruled that primary and secondary school teachers are not entitled to the academic freedom enjoyed by college professors.)

Specificity of outcomes, separation of functions, and alternate learning packages make manifest something that has always been true but which conventional curriculums make it easy to overlook, namely, that students can learn without teachers but teachers cannot teach without students. In some programs there is significant investment in auto-instructional packages, and some use of them by students. But what I see as a more decided trend than the elimination of teachers is the use of such adjunct persons as undergraduate tutors and nonprofessional counselors, helpers, and mentors.

There is also a special kind of teaching in competence-based education programs that perhaps is not so much teaching as it is high-level advising, that is, helping a person learn things which you don't happen to know much about yourself. It is not surprising that these programs make heavy use of words like "mentor" and "facilitator" for people in quasi-teacher roles who do things that are hard to describe clearly. The skills required of these people are not the traditional ones asked of college professors, namely a profound knowledge of what is to be learned, but rather a sensitivity to and sympathy with the student, as well as a special feeling for styles and modes of learning.

In competence-based programs of professional training, there is a widespread tendency to hire yet another kind of nonprofessional teacher, that is, "practitioners" or people who actually work at the jobs or do the things for which the students are preparing. Practitioners help in validating competencies—in making sure that the learning is indeed preparation for the real thing. What these teachers lack in teaching experience they are supposed to compensate for by bringing into the classroom an emphasis on actual performance and the standards of the "real world." They are to help students see a connection between the classroom and the work they may do later in life.

In most cases it is cheaper and less troublesome to hire these non-regular teachers for part-time positions with no fringe benefits. They need not be involved in meetings or in policy decisions and they often must accept conditions of employment that regular teachers would find unacceptable.

There is an obvious reason why competence-based programs can use these teachers: It is easier for nonexperts to teach a subject when they are provided with an explicit statement of teaching outcomes, with a lesson plan or full outline for the course, and when they don't have to design or administer any exams. (It is especially helpful if the program has built alternate learning paths: opportunities for dissatisfied or disgruntled students to learn in some other way instead of staying around and disrupting the class.)

Another potential loss of professionalism and perhaps status for professors involves the important word *accountability*. If you separate the instructional function from the assessment function, you have a way to measure—or at least to seem to measure—the output or productivity of the teacher that seems more accurate than the present method of just counting how many students take a teacher's course or pass the examination.

> I think of College IV where adjunct part-time teachers are paid per mastered credit; that is, they do not get paid unless the student passes. (The student gets three tries.)
>
> But a story from Mars Hill College in North Carolina shows why you cannot measure teacher output unless you also measure input. Three sections of intro-

ductory calculus were taught by three teachers. One of
the sections, taught by a new teacher, did poorly; the
next quarter this section was taught by someone who
was acknowledged to be an excellent teacher, and it still
did just as poorly. The original teacher was vindicated.
(How many of us can be so fortunate in having our deepest
feelings corroborated: "I know they're not learning
much, but my students are a bad lot.")

Different schools have handled this potential dethroning of
the professor in different ways. Florida State University had professors at the start and has tried to keep them in the competence
setting. Seattle Central Community College opted for part-time
practitioners, yet the regular faculty are not seen by many as "professor types" (that is, few have PhD degrees and they are not expected to do research; there is, however, tenure). The College for
Human Services was able to establish its own breed, since it started
from scratch. Teachers are crucial—probably the central characters
in the life of the institution—but they are not given "professorial"
perquisites and dignities, and definitely not tenure. Justin Morrill
College at Michigan State University offers the ultimate insult and
forgoes teachers altogether, but given their university context, they
probably had to choose either full-fledged professors or none at all.

Alverno has the most viable solution to the problem of
teacher-dignity and teacher-role. The English teacher, for example,
still chooses what plays or stories to teach in her course, and she
doesn't have to change from English teacher to teacher of, say,
"values" or "critical thinking"; yet she has an added responsibility
to be on a competence committee and to teach those plays or
stories in such a way as to help students pass assessments in critical
thinking or valuing or whatever the competence happens to be.

*Third, competence-based education usually forces teachers
to rethink what they teach.* In some of the competence-based programs, teachers end up teaching subject matter that is new to them.
But usually it is a matter of reorganizing what they teach—and in
doing so, reconceptualizing it. For example, someone might say to
me, "To teach with a competence approach, you have to know
precisely what you teach," and I might reply, "I do know precisely
what I teach. Chaucer." But he would then go on to say, "But that

isn't what I mean. What does this 'Chaucer' look like when it occurs in a student—that is, what changes do you hope will occur in your student from studying Chaucer with you?" Now I might answer, "I expect the student to change to the extent that he will be able to write the following correct answers to the following questions about Chaucer." (And I would pass muster with the behavioral objectives people if I had specified those questions and answers with the right kinds of precision.) But most of the people at the schools our team visited wouldn't be satisfied with that answer. They are looking for something bigger. They are indeed idealists, and I might protest that they want me to delude myself into having grander objectives than a teacher of Chaucer has any right to have. But these idealists would not be deterred. They would reply, "Yes, but by studying Chaucer, what new or better ways of looking at the world, looking at the self, dealing with books, do you hope to produce in those students?"

I think of Terry Anderson at Antioch Law School in Washington, D.C., who used a consultant to help him in an interesting empirical approach to competence teaching. He was teaching constitutional law, but what was he really teaching and testing for? Knowledge of cases? If so, what kinds of cases? Analytical thinking of a certain sort? A certain conception of "the law"? Lucidity of prose? Creativity? Finally, how well did his testing match his teaching? He had the consultant observe his teaching, assignment giving, test making, and test grading to help him answer these questions. He did not set out with the grandiose plan of restructuring his whole curriculum or teaching something brand-new. He simply wanted to determine what he was actually doing. But learning more clearly what he was actually doing led him to make some changes—none really earthshaking—which nevertheless made a big difference to him and his students. In short, he still teaches for the most part what he was teaching, but he now has greater control and intentionality in his teaching. His empirical approach strikes me as wise. Like most teachers, I would probably give a stupider answer to the question, "What should a student get from studying, say, Chaucer?" than the

answer you could get if you watched my teaching behavior and extrapolated from the *best* parts of it. My
answer to the big fat abstract question would likely be
naive and dominated by my favorite theories and hobby-
horses, and it would lack the sophistication and shrewd-
ness that have probably developed in my behavior over
the years. Yet, on the other hand, much of my teaching
behavior may well be blind or misguided or ineffective—
or simply aimed at goals that I don't approve of when I
see them in the plain light of day. When I am thus confronted with all the answers that can be extrapolated
from my behavior, I can get the benefit of conscious
conceptual thought without having to put up with its
shortsighted naiveté.

*Fourth, competence-based education helps teachers get more
taught.* A competence-based program gives you better grounds for
refusing credit in a course, but most programs simply cannot survive—either with the administration or with their constituency—if
they flunk too many students. And since you can't just give C's or D's
to those students who have the general picture but don't really have
mastery, you are in a sense "stuck." You really do know they lack
genuine mastery, and you now have the means to help them attain
it; that is, you can allow them to take more time and use different
routes to learning. In short, the competence structure increases the
likelihood of having to bring more students to the point of mastery.
And it is precisely those students who have difficulty learning the
material in the normal length of time and by the normal methods
of teaching-and-learning—those students who usually get a C or a
D—who are the most difficult to teach.

I think of two students in music at Florida State
University. One joined the program because she was in a
hurry to finish college, and it would give her the chance
to move ahead more quickly. She soon saw that she
wouldn't go faster, but that she would learn more and
better. The other student said that she joined because,
having asked an older, regular student about a problem
with which she needed help, she was told, "Oh, I don't

know, I took that last year." This made her decide to
join a program where she would really know what she
learned.

The teachers that thrive in these programs often seem to
have been bothered in the past by the large number of students who
passed courses without really attaining the given knowledge or
competence. They are exhilarated at finally having an approach
which ensures that their students really will learn. I talked to a
whole range of teachers who were initially very skeptical about a
competence approach, but when they finally saw the results on the
learning of their own students, they became enthusiastic supporters.
This feeling is especially strong among teachers with poorly
prepared students. One teacher described the competence approach
primarily as a way for the teacher to maintain high standards when
she has a classroom full of such students. It is easy for teachers with
poorly prepared students in non-competence-based curricula to become completely demoralized. The low level of success among the
students causes teachers to become cynical and tired. Sometimes
they try to teach the few students in each class that they think can
grasp the material and sometimes they just go through the motions.
This leads to what I think is a common mood in teachers: a feeling
that students are clods, that culture and civilization are crumbling,
that there's nothing to do but make cynical, sarcastic jokes. It is a
mood of failed hope—of the very hope combined with idealism
that made them go into teaching in the first place. Since it is not
politically possible to flunk all the students, teachers end up giving
passing grades for performances that they really think are worthless.
Thus that smell of sour idealism. The competence approach seems
to help teachers get out of this swamp by allowing them to *demand*
more.
But if the competence approach usually helps teachers raise
C, D, and F performances up to what we might call a B or B minus
level, does it invite B plus and A performances to sink to mere
mastery—or at least those B plus and A performances which were
the product of grade-hunger alone? I didn't hear any teachers make
this complaint. Besides, many of these programs retained conventional grades along with the competence approach.

Fifth, the competence approach is liable to make the teacher feel more exposed. Teachers must submit their teaching to external review of various sorts. Before the course begins, the outcomes and the assessment procedures—often the tests themselves—must be published to students and to colleagues. This is very different from merely publishing a course description. Often outcomes and assessments must be judged by colleagues to see whether the course will fit with generic college-wide competencies. For example, at Alverno the English teacher must write a module to show how her teaching of the short story will really help students pass a certain assessment level in, say, critical thinking.

> I think of my visit to Cynthia Stevens' class at Alverno when she showed me her course outline for the whole semester: a huge and impressive lesson plan spread over two sides of legal-size paper, containing not just headings but well-thought-through, concrete topics and activities. Then when I sat down with some students and they happened to open their notebooks, I was surprised to see the same two sheets of paper. I realized that I had simply assumed, without thinking, that the teacher would not hand out this plan to her students.

Of course, the competence teacher's teaching is more nakedly exposed when, at the end of the semester, it is revealed how many students passed an assessment administered by someone else. If a large number of students don't pass, it is threatening to the teacher.

> I think of a teacher at the College for Human Services in New York City during a meeting of an assessment committee that was on the brink of failing a student. He gave many reasons why this decision didn't seem fair: It was partly the college's fault, partly the fault of the internship setting which was a poor learning situation. But he finally blurted out, "It's not fair to punish her for *my* shortcomings as a teacher."

Sixth, competence-based education invites the separation of the teacher from what is taught and invites a collaborative relation-

ship between teacher and student. Traditional college professors are invited by their central role in the educational transaction to be an embodiment of what is taught. They are by definition experts in the subject. They contain the thing to be learned inside them and hence are invited to become people who profess, people who stand up in front of students and say, in effect, "Get what is inside me inside you. Look at me; listen to me; be like me. I am important." It follows, of course, that professors are gatekeepers who contain within themselves criteria for judging whether the student knows the subject. They are not obliged to publish those criteria or have them validated by someone else. They may indeed conclude that those criteria in their purity cannot be explicitly or publicly articulated— or at least not in such a way that they can be understood by any but the few other experts who also possess this knowledge.

A competence-based program, on the other hand, since it requires the specification and publication in advance of outcomes and assessment procedures, invites the separation of the teaching and the assessment functions. Someone other than the teacher may be the gatekeeper or wielder of standards for the subject. Our team saw different persons teaching and assessing in roughly half the cases that we observed. I believe that this separation has important consequences because of the different psychological stance toward the student implied in the teaching role and the assessing role. If you want to increase your chances of success in the teaching role, you will take a stance that communicates to students in one way or another that you believe they can learn the material and that you are not deterred by words or behavior on their part that try to claim they are incapable. But if you want to increase your success as an assessor in smoking out facile work that doesn't really represent mastery, you must adopt the opposite stance and assume that students don't know the material; you must be as critical as possible and refuse to be influenced by confident or impressive appearances.

When teachers and assessors are different persons, teachers have a kind of "coach" or "ally" role: They are helping the student pass a test given by someone else. They are rewarded by adopting the hypothesis that the student can learn. The student needn't be afraid to reveal weakness or ignorance to the teacher since the teacher isn't the certifier. The student can get better help from the teacher and thereby increase chances of passing the test by being open and honest with the teacher.[1]

I was impressed by the numbers of competency teachers who were allies with their students and avoided the difficulties that arise in the conventional arrangement, where the student is apt to look upon the teacher as the enemy who must be conned, psyched out, or evaded. Because these teachers haven't so much authority vested in them as gatekeepers of their subject matter, they are more approachable. A more collaborative relationship can spring up. These teachers aren't forced into the role of keeping the purity and integrity of their subject matter from being defiled by the unwashed. They are not so likely to be hurt or insulted if students hate "their" area or are dismal at it.

> I think of Wes Collins, who teaches music at Florida State University. He was actually pleased that the assessment committee for his wind students was likely to have people of different persuasions about embouchure or lip position. Although he had always tried to cover the subject matter well, he knew he had tended to teach his view and think in terms of it. Now he had to make sure his students could defend any point of view to a hostile assessor.

Even when the instruction and assessment are done by the same person—as we saw in many cases—the competence approach helps teachers deal better with these conflicting roles and hence have a better relationship with students. When the assessment instruments are spelled out publicly in advance, teachers can be more explicit

---

[1] I am not asserting a simpleminded resemblance between a teacher's actual style in the flesh and the role of teacher or assessor. That is, someone may be particularly good as an assessor and therefore shrewdly critical in detecting hidden shortcomings in student answers and yet nevertheless be warm and cordial in manner. On the other hand, someone particularly skilled in the teacher role may use a negative tone of voice for positive expectations, saying, in effect, "OK you bastards, I'm going to *make* you learn this stuff and I don't care how much it hurts!" This may seem a nasty snarl from a mean teacher, but it is nevertheless a declaration that all can learn. Such a teacher is not the certifier who refuses credit but rather, as it were, the marine sergeant marshaling his rigors to help his platoon win the prize.

about judgments, using clearly specified criteria that neither they nor the students are so apt to confuse with the teacher's own person.

In a noncompetence-based situation, on the other hand, where assessments are seldom spelled out clearly in advance, and where the teacher must therefore try to embody both the teaching and the assessing roles, the path of least resistance is simply to lean more toward one or the other, and hence be better as teacher or assessor. Thus teachers tend to drift into being—as students like to say—"hard" or "easy." Until my visits to competence programs, I had never seen so many teachers who manage to be both hard and easy—both very demanding in their standards and yet very supportive and positive as teachers. I think the separation of teaching and assessment functions helps make this possible.

> I asked John Millay, sociology teacher at College IV of Grand Valley, whether he ever had difficulties switching from the teaching to the assessing role with the same students. He said that since he had started teaching in an outcome-oriented fashion, he had never had a difference of opinion with a student—or even bad feelings—about an assessment decision. This is a result, he said, of the fact that the competence approach forces him to publish to students at the beginning not only the outcomes for the course, but specifically what the assessment will be. In effect, he must say, "Here's the final exam. The course will try to teach you to give good answers to the following questions. Here are the criteria I'm going to use to decide what's a good answer and what isn't."

Seventh, competence-based education invites collaboration among teachers. A college ought by definition to be collegial, but college teachers seldom have to agree with each other. College teaching is the vocation for individualists. In most competence-based programs we observed, however, faculty members had to work out collectively the competencies and the criteria for successful performance. This process almost always involved struggle at first but in the end usually produced more cooperation and understanding. It was seldom a matter of a simple tug of war between pre-existing positions. Usually brand new conceptualizations had to be forged. Most faculty members appreciated improved collegiality and the resulting new insights into subject matter.

Eighth, competence-based education invites collaboration among students. I think of the biology students at Florida State University spending a lot of time together in a lounge, talking and helping each other out. The competence approach means that such students are not competing against each other for grades on a curve in a zero-sum game (if he scores higher, I necessarily score lower). All are simply working for mastery. There is usually less time spent in class, and students are more on their own. Many of them find peer collaboration to be an enjoyable and effective method of learning. Where programs provide space and suitable conditions for this kind of collaboration, it seems to occur (except when the students are working adults).

There is another link between the competence approach and student collaboration. When I first noticed that many teachers broke their classes down into small groups, I just assumed this was a matter of temperament—which no doubt it was. But then I looked more closely at the tasks that they were setting for their students. I realized that a competence approach pushes a teacher to articulate what is to be learned in such a way that there are clearer criteria for determining whether a given answer is satisfactory or not. A competence setting, that is, would tend to discourage such tasks as "Discuss the poem," and would instead encourage such ones as "How is the mood of the poem or the response of the reader affected by specific images? Be sure to discuss three of them." Given this second task, a group of students on its own can certainly be expected to collaborate in distinguishing strong and weak responses and coming up collectively with its best answer. With the global task, "Discuss the poem," on the other hand, a teacherless group is more apt to flounder unproductively and slide into the thoughtless morass of, "Well, that's your opinion, and this is my opinion." When all questions are like "Discuss the poem" or "Discuss the influence of Russia on global politics," the only thing students can do with their answers is hand them in to the authority and wait for the verdict. And because it is so often a verdict based on unstated criteria, the student is likely to quarrel with it or fail to understand it.

I hadn't realized before that it was possible to take complex issues, work out criteria, and get students to engage in collaborative learning.

I think of the College for Human Services. It first decided that to be a good human services worker involves, among other things, the ability to establish a professional relationship on the job. Only then did it try to decide what a professional relationship is characterized by. (Their students are apt to be rejected as nonprofessionals at agencies.) Having defined the characteristics of a professional relationship, students can more competently discuss a fuzzy issue, such as whether a person is behaving professionally with colleagues, and can come to agreement with assessors as to their verdict.

I think also of the following observations by Zelda Gamson, of our project team, about Allan Wurtzdorf's class at Alverno:

The class I observed was just beginning to work on competency two, level three, which attempts to get students to analyze the relationship between environmental settings and behavior. The twenty-one students were divided into five groups. They were quietly talking about the settings, usually single rooms, which they had been asked to observe. Each student was first to describe her setting to the other members of the group in great detail and then go on to identify the potential psychological impacts of that setting. An interesting discussion started in the group I observed about one of the younger student's dormitory room. Two older women in the group began drawing out information about how the young student and her roommate used the room, and it became very clear that the room was primarily a social space and not a study space. The older women asked whether the young student or her roommate used the desk (the answer was no), where they studied (the answer was on their beds), what they kept on their desks (the answer was knicknacks and various things they dumped when they came into the room). The older women were beginning to develop hypotheses about why the younger women did not use the desks as study spaces and about the impact of the design of the dormitory room and the larger dormitory setting on students living there. An altogether intelligent discussion. I only had a

few fleeting minutes with Allan Wurtzdorf, who circulated from group to group. He did say to me that he
loved teaching this way and had enjoyed developing the
module for the environmental psychology course. He
noted that since "everything is laid out, you don't have
to justify what you are doing and students know what is
expected of them." I found it an interesting exercise and
an enviably focused way of dealing with what could be
either very fuzzy or, at the other extreme, very technical
material.

*Ninth, competence-based education encourages students to
be less passive and to take more responsibility for their own learning.* At first I wondered whether spelling out everything so clearly
might not reduce students to obedient followers of orders. When I
didn't see that happening, I began to realize that it can be liberating
for students to have everything spelled out and that the most common cause of student passivity is leaving things unspecified. When a
teacher publishes only a brief course description and doesn't spell
out on opening day how things will work, he is in effect saying to the
student, "Just follow me, just trust me, don't ask questions. I will
take charge of all decisions."

I think that learning depends on personal investment more
than on anything else. I thought that to spell everything out might
diminish investment, but I saw students investing themselves more
in competence programs than I usually see them do in traditional
curriculums. I finally realized the source of my confusion: Leaving
things open and unspecified adds to my investment as a teacher. It
gives me room for choice and adventure and excitement. I can do
things on the spur of the moment, change directions three weeks
into the course because of a new thought. But it is seldom that I or
many other college teachers are willing to share fully this choice
over options with students. Therefore, leaving things open gives me
more options, but it tends to give students less sense of choice and
control.

There are a number of what might be called *negative* measures of the initiative and responsibility required of students by
competence-based programs. In virtually every program that allows
flexible timing, students procrastinate in coming to take their tests

and get credit. The pipelines get clogged. Credit (full time equivalent) is not generated as quickly as in a normal program. I saw many programs resort to this or that device to get students moving along; for example, compulsory appointments with advisors at certain intervals. Teachers were often having to hunt down students and say, "Look, you know it well enough; come on in for the assessment on this unit so you can start working on the next."

What is the problem? Are the students in flexibly paced programs just wasting time? This didn't seem to be the case. Many students, it is true, didn't know how to organize and budget their time. This problem was most serious with adolescents and disadvantaged students; middle-class adults did better. But the main factor here is a major psychological change when students have any choice over scheduling their assessments. In normal curriculums, students sign up, work as hard as they want, probably harder just before the exam, and then take the exam because they have to; it is the appointed day. In the time-flexible format students must do something: They must go to the test, not just wait for the test to come to them. When a student makes this act and says, "I want to be tested now," his or her whole relationship to learning becomes very different. That student has taken much more responsibility and is thrust into being much more adult. At times I even found myself wondering whether this responsibility might not be too much of a burden, especially for young or disadvantaged students. That feeling grew when a teacher told me, in a very relieved tone: "They don't blame the teacher anymore; they blame themselves."

This need for student initiative and responsibility seems widespread in the programs, though none, as I recall, specify these qualities as competencies. Not all students, of course, demonstrate responsibility. To handle this problem, some programs simply set up procedures so that less initiative is needed, at least at first, while others simply allow those who don't develop initiative to drop out. Dropout rates are high in many programs, and I think this is the main reason.

Finally, competence-based education invites the individualization of learning. The competence movement, of course, does not have a monopoly on individualized learning. Methods like the Keller Plan have gone far in adapting it even to completely traditional curriculums. Nevertheless, the impulse to individualize learning seems unusually strong in many competence programs. Many of the teachers feel that one of the main purposes of putting learning into a competence format is so that people can learn at their own speed and in their own style. In most of the programs that our team observed, the teacher sat down individually with each student at least once, even if the format was primarily a group one.

But we also saw many hindrances to individualization. For one thing, most registrars cannot deal with students starting or stopping courses at any time, and most business offices don't know how to make out bills unless people are enrolled for a quarter or a semester. Secondly, all the individual interactions take a great deal of teacher time—usually more time than there is in a week. And on top of everything else, students often *want* to sit in the same room with others as part of the learning process. This may be just the persistence of the old Adam—"it doesn't feel like school without *class*"—but I believe that people often need the support, encouragement, and solidarity they get from groups. Some programs that started out with the emphasis entirely on individual, one-to-one interactions found it necessary to institute some kind of group meetings.

Paradoxical Effects

Among the paradoxes in the spirit of competence-based education is its orientation to intellect. We see here the grand old American pragmatic anti-intellectual tradition that says talking isn't real, only doing is real. Performance is stressed. Outcomes are usually roles, jobs, tasks—not just knowledge, and certainly not just knowledge for its own sake. There is an animus against what is merely "academic"; against teachers who just teach theories, ideas, and words; against students who can pass tests with good writing and fancy language but may not be "really competent." The spirit of the competence movement is anti-baloney—and baloney is usually seen as something verbal and conceptual.

Yet I am struck by how central and pervasive in the competence-based movement is a certain kind of intellectuality: an emphasis upon—almost a preoccupation with—analytic self-consciousness. You are always supposed to know what you are doing and why you are doing it. You must have chosen your outcomes or goals, you must have some awareness of how and why you arrived at them, you must figure out how to break them down into parts so that you can measure progress toward them, and you must figure out criteria for demonstrating when you have attained them. In short, the movement is anti-intuitive. It attracts people who enjoy analysis and classification.

> I think of Sister Joel Read, president of Alverno, saying that there are two kinds of people in the world: those who understand the historical process and group process and insist on clarity and organization of ideas; and the "intuitives." It took me a minute to realize that "intuitive" could be a bad word. Especially—*mea culpa*—from a woman.
>
> I also think of Diana Dean, architect of the nursing program at Mt. Hood, saying that teachers must have heightened self-consciousness, must analyze; it's not good enough for them just to know the larger outcomes—they have to know all the specific behaviors that make up the larger outcome.

College teachers traditionally lack such self-consciousness about the process of teaching. It is traditionally felt that attention is better given to the subject matter than to pedagogy. Teaching is seen as something inherently mysterious. Metaphors for teaching are apt to come from realms judged inimical to analysis or self-conscious scrutiny: Teaching is like a delicate human encounter, like love, like sex. You destroy it if you try to shine a bright light upon it. People in the competence-based movement have little patience with this kind of thinking. To them, if something is important, it's worth figuring out.

And it is true enough that college teachers are characteristically unclear about their goals. Many haven't even decided what *kind* of things their goals are; that is, they haven't made it clear to themselves whether their goals consist of effects upon student behavior, effects upon student character or personality, effects upon their own behavior or knowledge, or effects upon published knowledge. If you don't know what your goals are, you can hardly know whether you are attaining them. You are liable to be blown about by the conflicting cues of popularity, scholarly eminence, success in "winning discussions," or simply feeling good as you walk out to the parking lot at the end of the day. Teachers traditionally deal in what is fuzzy, unseen, mysterious, inner—in what can easily seem indistinguishable from baloney.

Some of the mystery is no doubt inherent in teaching. Certainly, if you think of teaching in any lofty sense—trying to influence character, trying to influence or improve society (and who, really, ever became a teacher without harboring deep down some goals such as these?)—you are usually in the dark about the effectiveness of your teaching. How can you possibly have a clear sense at the end of the day, of the year, even of the decade, whether you are making progress toward these goals? (Thus, there is the same fantasy in the collective unconscious of all teachers: the great hero drops in and says, "I owe it all to you and your teaching ten years ago. I hated it then, but now I want to *thank* you for making me do all those things.")

But the intellectual tendency in competence teachers won't let you off the hook just because your ideals are whoppers and in a sense unrealizable. These people will insist on analytic self-consciousness and say, "I see. Yes. So you want to create 'better people'? Fine. Now tell me what these better people might look like or things they might do that would distinguish them from ordinary people." And before you know it, they will have you specifying some outcomes that you could actually try to attain— and not only that, but begin to measure your success—and not only that, but all this while engaged in teaching Chaucer or physics or accounting.

Competence teachers often have a special anger against those who actually take pride in being intuitive, who say they can't state their goals and criteria or that it would destroy their human integrity or academic freedom to do so; who say no one else could assess the students in their course or assess them as teachers because no one else is competent in exactly these standards or criteria.

Our own project team, as visitors and observers of competence-based programs, received some of this resentment and anger. If you believe in making goals and criteria explicit, you could scarcely help but be suspicious of our team since we hadn't formulated—much less published—any explicit goals or criteria for our investigations beyond agreeing to write case studies of the evolution of these programs. You would experience us as unprofessionals simply fooling around.

But this emphasis on analytic self-consciousness in the movement is not just in reaction to the characteristic vagueness of the educational enterprise. The very involvement in a competence approach heightens your conscious analysis of your own teaching behavior: "What am I really trying to teach? What would that competence look like in a person who successfully learned it? How could I distinguish a person who has learned it from one who hasn't? How should I teach it? How can I express my outcome so that someone who wasn't engaged in the teaching could distinguish a student who had learned it from one who hadn't?" In some places teachers forced themselves to answer yet another layer of difficult questions: "Why should someone study with us? What good for the college or society is there in our teaching what we teach?" And even: "What in society needs changing that we can try to change with our teaching?" To insist not only on asking these questions but also on giving answers concrete enough to lead to specific teaching activities is a massive enterprise in forcing-yourself-to-decide-what-you-are-doing-and-why.

> I think of Frances Prindle at Seattle Central saying that her happiest period as a teacher came during the early days of trying to plan a competence-based daycare program when all the teachers constantly got together informally in meetings and parties to try to figure out what qualities a daycare teacher really ought to have.

Certain things follow from this heightened self-consciousness. One is an increased analytical self-consciousness about subject matter. And when teachers achieve this kind of self-consciousness, they tend to become excited about their discovery and want to pass it on to their students. Thus, many programs don't merely ask that a student do something or know something. They want meta-knowledge or second-stage learning too: knowing *what* you are doing; knowing *about* your knowing. Merely getting the task done is not good enough, and hence all the self-evaluations in these pro-grams. I couldn't figure out the connection at first. I associate stu-dent self-evaluation with the kind of "old fashioned" personalistic non-outcome-oriented experimentalism of places like Antioch or Goddard. But I soon realized that this analytic self-consciousness in teachers makes them try to foster it in students too. It is also true, however, that teachers are not always successful in passing on this enthusiasm for analytic self-consciousness; in fact, some students are intimidated or drop out.

Many programs emphasize—especially in their admissions publicity—that they will give students credit for what they learn in life or on the job. But often students do not in fact get this credit if they just grew into a job and got good at it by learning prag-matically. They have to know the theory too. In the Seattle Central problem-solving competence, for example, no one could satisfy it just by learning how to solve problems in a management setting. The assessment instrument insists that the person know the "theory of problem solving." (The competence almost implies that the stu-dent has to solve problems the way the theory says they are solved.)

A final consequence of the analytic self-consciousness in com-petence programs is a high emphasis on planning. I had never before seen so many teachers who planned so much. One would often see teachers who worked out lesson plans for the whole term, and these seldom seemed to be the kind of fake lesson plans that some public school teachers make because their supervisors require them to.

In all these ways, then, I sense a highly analytic self-con-sciousness alongside the mood of anti-intellectuality.

Is the spirit of competence-based education egalitarian and anti-elitist? It is certainly anti-elitist in the common sense of the word. There is a spirit in the competence-based movement that says anyone can learn and that, except for diagnosis, it is immoral to have assessment at the entrance to educational institutions. Hard-nosed, door-closing assessment only belongs at the exits or conclu-sions of the educational experience. People in the movement are very aware that no elite colleges are involved in competence-based education and tend to view elite colleges as the enemy. They see elite colleges as rooted in norm-referenced assessment and rank-ordering—that is, as using education to distinguish superior people from the rest. There is a spirit in elite higher education that says, "Education is not really teaching people to know or do things. Yes, of course, we do that, but that's not the point. The point is to find out who has a first-class mind. That takes time—as long as three or four years. People can look good after only a year or two but turn out to lack real quality. What they know doesn't matter; indeed it's better if their minds are not too cluttered up with facts and ideas, otherwise they can't really think straight." The Oxford Greats program is, as it were, the *locus classicus* of this spirit. Studying Greek and Latin didn't make a better governor of India, but it was a good chance to see who had quality.

A high proportion of the programs that we looked at have a definite mission to move society in a more democratic, egalitarian direction. (Sometimes this is stronger in the wording of the grant proposal than in subsequent behavior, and may be an example of verbal operant conditioning by FIPSE.) There is a feeling that elite institutions and elite teachers have unfairly dominated the very conception of what educational institutions and teachers are supposed to be like, that this situation has operated to the disadvantage of the majority of citizens, and that competence-based programs are going to start changing things around.

Yet the competence-based approach, with its insistence on complete learning or mastery, reflects a kind of puritanism that is itself elitist. It's quality they are after. The "real thing." The teachers set extremely high standards and demand from the student large amounts of self-management, initiative, and—perhaps at the root of all such qualities—confidence that one *can* make it. But it is precisely these qualities that are often in short supply in the disadvantaged students whom these anti-elite programs sometimes specifically seek.

I think here of the nursing program at Seattle Central (for students who couldn't get into other nursing programs), which a few years ago became self-paced.

Almost none of the students finished. I think too of my conversation with a black teacher at Florida State University who was weighing the pros and cons of a merger between the university and a nearby black college. She noted that an outcome-oriented curriculum seemed to be just what disadvantaged black students need: They wouldn't then have to be the "dumb" ones in the back of the class, get lower grades, or hold the class back since all students can learn at their own speed. Yet her own experience teaching in such curriculums made her realize that it is precisely the disadvantaged students who are the first to drop out of these programs. And they drop out quietly; a competence-based program never has to fail anybody. These students just don't have the self-confidence to persist, especially when they must work very independently. This becomes a comfortable situation for an institution or a teacher who doesn't really want to deal with disadvantaged students. It reminds me again of the teacher who said, "They don't blame the teacher anymore; they just blame themselves."

My conclusion, then, is that competence-based institutions and teachers can make their egalitarianism really functional—since they are raising standards at the same time as they are opening doors wider—only if they are terribly shrewd, tireless, and well-planned in giving extra help and support to underprivileged students. For, really, the competence approach fits elite students best, that is, it fits confident, well-prepared students who can say, "Just tell me what I need to know and don't bother me with your classes and lectures. I'll tell you when I'm ready. Now get out of my way, I'm in a hurry." And, it is the highly elite institution, really, that is naturally closest to the competence approach. It is of the essence at Harvard and Oxford, for example, not to care whether students go to classes or lectures, not to care anything about process but only about outcomes: papers and exams. The difference is that elite schools, with their goal of trying to identify the most talented—and their implicit equation of talent with the ability to deal with the unexpected—tend to leave outcomes unstated; in an elite school, it would seem against nature to hand out the final exam on the opening day as so many competence teachers do in one form or another.

Somewhere between elite, confident students for whom the competence approach is natural, and underprivileged, poorly prepared students who must struggle to find the confidence and self-management skills necessary, there is a third population: adults who are already functioning in society. The competence approach seems just right for these autonomous and functioning, but not necessarily middle-class, students. They can set their own schedules; they know how to take charge of themselves because as functioning adults they've learned that no one will do it for them; and also—because they are adults—they are in a hurry and don't want to waste time.

Is competence-based education hostile to professing? While it is unambiguously hostile to professors, it is ambivalent about professing: standing up there and putting yourself at the center of the stage, asking students to look at you and listen to you, in a sense even to ingest you or fall in love with you. Many good teachers do this kind of professing, and many people learn best and fastest from such teachers. As Socrates pointed out, we fall in love with beautiful or wise persons more easily than with beauty and wisdom. But this kind of teaching can just as easily be described in hostile terms: ego tripping, limelighting, narcissism. Whatever way you describe it, however, it appears at first as though competence people are against it. Here is a typical comment: "I could no longer give myself up to the process of doing what I enjoyed doing in my teaching. I had gotten too self-conscious about outcomes." She discovered that doing what she enjoyed doing, was used to doing, and felt good doing, didn't in fact bring the outcomes she desired.

Competence teachers insist on taking themselves out of the center and focusing instead on the student and the things the student has to master. They are likely to characterize traditional and elite colleges as places where teachers just go into classrooms and talk about whatever interests them in an ego-centered way. I found competence teachers as good as their prejudice. That is, they didn't let themselves be in the limelight. They were often mentors, helpers, facilitators—people who helped students manage their own learning. And I began to reflect—being myself something of a teacher-centered teacher—that this is asking a great deal. Yes, it may be good for students, but can one really sustain a whole teaching career on such a selfless stance? After all, students don't have to be in our classrooms very long but we do. Even if we don't deserve the satisfaction that comes from being in center stage, can we teach with passion and intensity for very long with no direct ego gratification? The dynamic competence teachers that I saw teaching with passion and intensity—the many good ones—can they really keep it up for five years? Ten? Twenty? Aren't the involvement and intensity consequences of the newness? Aren't most teachers who sustain themselves as passionate teachers really engaged in a kind of narcissism? I suspect they are.

Nevertheless, I found it necessary to think further about this issue, and about what these teachers had told me. Suddenly I realized that, although they aren't professing in that limelighting way, they are engaged in something equally arrogant and, in a sense, self-centered. And they admit it openly. That is, all these impressive teachers said to me in one way or another that they were committed to the new approach because it permitted them to have more of an impact on the student than conventional teaching did. It permitted them to shape or change the student more.

> I think of Milton Ford in College IV at Grand Valley sending a student home with a module on literary criticism. After only three or four hours of work but in accordance with certain strict guidelines, the student comes in to discuss the reading and the written responses. Milton remembers saying to himself with amazement, "I've *done* something to that student's mind" (and not just changed that student's behavior with run-on sentences). He never had a sense of making this much impact in conventional teaching.
>
> I think of Cynthia Stevens at Alverno saying, "Competence-based education is a radical infringement on the right of teachers to manipulate students." But later in the same conversation she admitted that she does indeed have a strong personality, that she wants students to feel even her personal impact, and most of all that she feels she can have a bigger impact on students through her competence-based teaching. Admittedly the kind of impact she wants to have is for them to become more independent, autonomous, critical people—people who

figure things out for themselves. Yet this laudable goal
cannot be called anything less than an attempt to mold
personality to her own specifications.

These teachers are thus willing to give up professing from
center stage but, for many of them, only in the interest of greater
effectiveness in shaping students—if not to their own image, at least
to their own consciously chosen specifications. If you lob them a
kind of classic liberal question, "Do you really think it's right or
valid or honest for teachers to play with people's minds like that and
try to change people's character and behavior?" you will find them
ready at the net to smash it home: "All teachers are engaged in playing with people's minds. It's dishonest to pretend otherwise. Your
only choices are whether to know what you are doing, and whether
to be effective at it." I now realize that this kind of mission, given
the success that many of these teachers seem to have, could sustain
teachers for a whole career.

Is competence-based teaching student-centered? When I
think of student-centered teaching I think of something in the tradition of Antioch and Goddard—personalistic, often loose, sometimes
anarchistic. All these qualities are pretty squarely the opposite of
what one finds in competence-based programs. Student-centered
teachers are often anti-puritan, anti-work ethic, while I find a strong
puritan work ethic in these new programs. Student-centered enterprises tend to let students determine their own goals and outcomes,
and student-centered teachers are usually oriented away from assessment. By contrast, the spirit in competence programs is for firm
criteria set long before the student arrives and never bent for the
benefit of some particular student; and all teaching is directed toward tough, bottom-line assessment. The spirit, in short, is very
hard-nosed.

Yet competence-based teachers do tend, in the last analysis,
to be student-centered in a crucial sense; whatever you teach, you
must always state it in terms of *what it would look like embodied in
a student.* Thus, no matter how puritan, tough-minded, or assess-
ment-centered the teaching is, an important part of the teacher's
attention must always be focused on the student, the student's needs,
and how the student will internalize the subject. This is one of the

reasons why one-to-one conferences tend to play a bigger role in competence programs than in conventional teaching.

Is competence-based education inimical to learning by immersion? The classic case is learning by literal immersion: Throw 'em in the water so they'll swim. Immersion teaching in higher education is represented by the teacher who deliberately talks over the heads of students and engages in a conversation with a couple of the brightest ones—or with herself—while the other students must flounder, and feel lost, and only gradually begin to get a feel for what is going on. Learning by immersion, when it works, tends to produce fast and extensive learning: entire gestalts. Language teachers, for example, have made explicit the principle that if an instructor has to explain everything and get students to understand everything, the class can move only at a snail's pace compared to what is possible if the instructor just forges ahead, doing it "too fast." However, learning by immersion—as with language learning by this method—always entails disorientation and frustration for the learner. And learning by immersion doesn't always work because the learner is liable to give up. Also, it is tinged with a kind of elitist flavor since, in a sense, that's just what it is: just throw them in the water and see who has quality. It tends to be elitist college teachers who prefer the talk-over-their-heads method.

The mood of analytic self-consciousness in the competence movement produces an understandable prejudice against the chaos and elitism of the immersion style. The competence procedure asks teachers to figure out exactly what they want to teach, and this process tends to inspire them to work out the component parts of a course and the best incremental and rational order for presenting them. I sensed a prejudice against just plunging into the thick of things. But if it is demonstrated that such a method does work in achieving certain outcomes, competence-based teachers will certainly go along. Indeed they won't settle for "just plunging in"; they will try to analyze what kinds of plunging in work best for what kinds of teaching. In addition, competence-based education stresses learning through life experience, job experience and simulation, and these tend to be experiences of learning by immersion, with all of its advantages and disadvantages: speed; having to wait in disorientation for the new gestalt; and failure for the timid and nonpersistent.

Sometimes an early practicum component of a curriculum, which is supposedly just a way of learning, functions in fact as a kind of mechanism to weed out students who would be difficult to teach— students who are not temperamentally suited to the competency.

Impact on Teaching Styles and Temperaments

Does competence-based education rule out or inhibit certain styles or temperaments in teaching? This question, I realize finally, is what drew me deeper and deeper into a fruitful perplexity during the three years of our study. The tongue returns to the aching tooth. I can answer yes quickly enough: I do see a slight narrowing in the range of styles of teaching in the programs I visited. But from almost the beginning I had an intuitive sense that this question can also be answered no. Now I think that my intuition was also right.

Let me start by posing the question in its most extreme or biased form—a form, however, that reflects the real fears of many thoughtful teachers: Does competence-based education reduce the teacher to a coach merely drilling people to pass exams? Does the competence approach kill all true education or deeper thinking? If outcomes are trivial and teachers lazy or unimaginative, and if assessment procedures are stupidly mechanistic and inappropriately precise, these fears would be realized. But we did not see outcomes or teachers or assessments of that sort, nor did we see those dismal results.

But what if we move to a more moderate form of the question: Does competence-based education lead students and teachers to be predominantly pragmatic? Not simpleminded or trivial or blindly mechanical, mind you, but does it lead to a slight narrowing in the range of human styles, away from creativity, intuition, play, humor, and purely disinterested curiosity? Is the spirit of competence teaching, in short, the spirit of instrumentalism?

I do think, in fact, that the spirit of instrumentalism predominates in the programs we saw. The movement attracts pragmatic, no-nonsense people: "If you can't justify everything in advance, you are falling down on the job and you are unprofessional. You must always know what you are doing. If you haven't figured out your goals and outcomes and planned your activities on the basis of them, you are irresponsible." There is a puritan prejudice against intuition, play, irony, and humor. And certainly the path of least resistance in a competence-based program is simply to teach to the examination.

But I don't think that competence-based teaching has to be dominated by a spirit of instrumentalism or pragmatism or that its full range of possibilities has been exploited in what I saw. For one thing, historical factors have played a large role in creating the present instrumental spirit. The approach appeals most obviously to schools of professional training where the instrumental spirit, understandably, is already strong. Teachers of nursing, even of law, have always tended to have outcomes in mind since they can so easily imagine how the student will have to perform in the hospital or in the courtroom. And even when teachers in professional schools try to put these pictures to one side and teach more toward disinterested inquiry, students tend to wrench pragmatic goals back to center stage. We saw very few liberal arts colleges with competence-based programs, and it will probably take much longer for such colleges and for teachers opposed to instrumentalism to see that a competence approach might be helpful.

In addition, the competence-based movement is clearly reacting against elite higher education with its tendency to proclaim, after Aristotle, that learning for some purpose is always inferior to learning for its own sake alone. If more liberal arts colleges and more colleges of higher status were to try out a competence-based approach—a huge "if," I admit—I believe that the spirit of competence-based teaching would be considerably expanded. I believe, in fact, that every kind of teaching would be fostered.

I base this prediction partly upon some of the teaching I actually saw, and partly upon analysis of what seems to me possible.

The only liberal arts college I saw using a competence approach was Alverno. Although the teachers there tended somewhat toward the instrumental in their neglect of the intuitive and creative dimension when working out the competencies that characterize a liberally educated person, nevertheless they articulated deeply intelligent outcomes which seemed to permit and invite all kinds of teaching. For example, the assignment mentioned earlier in which students were asked to describe a room in terms of its effect on users was an instrumental teaching procedure, perhaps, but also one that invites the intuitive and the unexpected.

I also saw how the very instrumentalism of a competence program can paradoxically permit a teacher to be shoddily noninstrumental. I am thinking of a lecture I heard at one of our sites. It was a boring, rambling, poorly organized, and badly presented performance. There was no sense of outcomes, direction, or planning. Such lectures are not uncommon in higher education, but what seemed new was seeing how students were able to get considerable value out of this poor performance because of the competence-based curriculum it was part of. From talking to some of them afterwards, I discovered that though they didn't like the lecture, they knew what they needed, what to look for in the chaos. I could see that they weren't just tuning it out with those obvious manifestations of boredom or anger—slumped bodies and glazed eyes—which are so familiar in traditional college lecture halls, where students don't really know what they need to know. The students I saw were able to take a more active, shaping role in getting what they needed out of an unshaped performance.

Also, because the competence approach helps teachers specify goals, it thereby helps teachers figure out their own private agendas better, and, as a result, some teachers seem to expand and enlarge the kinds of goals they work for.

I saw many small examples of this, but I think particularly of Arlene Fingeret teaching adults basic competencies in math and reading. As a result of her analysis of the students, she adopted the following competencies in addition to basic math and reading: (1) knowing more specifically when you are stuck by recognizing the signs—from a feeling in your stomach to the way you clench your fist to a special kind of drowsiness; (2) having a whole repertoire of conscious options you can choose among when you are stuck—from various plans or algorithms for attacking the problem, to more intuitive plans for sneaking up on the problem, to being able to ask for help, all the way to having the choice of saying, "The heck with it, I quit"; (3) having the confidence in a school setting to take risks and follow hunches and not feel that you must always know how to do a task correctly the first time; (4) gaining a political and cultural understanding of schools in our society so that you don't blame yourself as incompetent and helpless if you have not yet learned to read or do math. Fingeret worked very hard on these supplementary competencies in addition to the math and reading—harder in fact than the students were comfortable with. Yet the students all passed the assessments on math and reading and achieved higher scores than were usually achieved by concentrating on those subjects alone.

I see this as the story of a teacher who refused to be restricted by the official or assigned competencies (not that she by any means scorned teaching basic math and reading) and as the story of how an emphasis on outcomes helped her become more conscious and explicit than she would otherwise have been about a very different set of outcomes. Obviously she had already developed an interest in these goals in her previous teaching, but she had not worked them out so clearly or taught with them in mind so explicitly before. The official goals forced her into a dialectic process that in turn allowed her to be clearer about her own special agenda as a teacher and how to realize it. At one point in our conversation, I termed "subsidiary" the competencies she had added in that they helped lead the students to do a better job at the stated ones. She bristled. "They're *more* important," she said.

As I think about this woman who, on the one hand, teaches competencies much more practical and pedestrian than most college teachers feel they should have to stoop to, but who, on the other hand, teaches more than most college teachers try for, namely, a basic change of consciousness, I recall a sentence from the writing of James Chapman: "The old distinction between what is practical and what is theoretical tends to disappear. Precisely the same element of information may be theoretical if given at one time and essentially practical if given at another" (1921, p. 408).

Perhaps, for the sake of argument and at the risk of selling her short, we can see Fingeret as representing the spirit of enlightened and flexible instrumentalism. But the additional question that interests me is, How *far* can one go in a competence-based format away from instrumentalism? I have, to be frank, a certain personal stake in behavior that is not goal oriented—even in nonsense. I structure my exploration around three pointed questions:

First, in a competence-based program, can I teach a course in a new area or on a question I cannot answer or around a book I wish to explore for the first time? That is, can I teach toward goals but not know how to get there? Can I make my teaching a journey of exploration for me as well as for the students? I recently taught a course in Shakespeare, and that is not my main field; I am about to teach a course in peace studies, an area not even in my discipline; Gerald Grant, who headed our research project, taught a seminar in assessment as a way to learn about it. Would these enterprises be possible in a competence-based format?

The answer seems to depend on the nature of the outcomes. If they were *in* the new subject matter, I wouldn't know enough about that subject matter to specify the outcomes in advance. The last thing I would figure out at the end of the semester—if I were lucky—would be what is really important. But if, on the other hand, the competencies were not *in* the subject matter but were more generic, then I think I could set out on my exploration and have my adventure in a competence-based setting. That is, I could teach Shakespeare in such a way as to help students attain competence in, say, critical thinking or literary exploration or how to get literature and their own experience to interact. These would be fruitful interactions between generic competencies specified clearly in advance and new and different subject matter looked at in terms of them. Some of the most powerful teaching we saw was a result of this kind of interaction.

Second, in a competence setting, can I teach toward no goal? Can I teach for purely disinterested inquiry? Can I have learning entirely for its own sake? Surely this refusal to consider ends goes

squarely against the competence approach. But here again, the
competence approach itself forces me to think more clearly about
what I mean by my question. First of all, is it the student or the
teacher I am asking about? If I want students to engage in disinterested inquiry and become better at it, I don't see any reason
why this cannot be taken as an educational goal, an outcome, a
competence. Frankly, I am not impressed with the ability of most
colleges to foster the love of disinterested inquiry in students. I think
faculty members might do better if they actually specified this kind
of inquiry as a competence and planned teaching and learning
situations specifically for the sake of fostering it. There is nothing
logically inconsistent or empirically impossible about getting students
to take as a goal the ability to engage in behavior that is not
oriented toward a goal. I suspect that most higher education does
not suffer from too much concern for disinterested inquiry but
rather from too little—pieties to the contrary notwithstanding.

But what if my goal is for *me,* as a teacher, to engage in
purely disinterested inquiry. Can I be purely noninstrumental as a
teacher in a competence-based format? Can I, that is, teach without
having a clue where I'm going? Without even knowing what the
real question or problem is? This, after all, describes where one
often finds oneself in any serious inquiry. Here again we stumble
upon another sense of the word "professor" that seems diametrically
opposed to the spirit of competence-based education. That is, the
professor, in traditional lore, is a comically impractical chap, hope-
less at getting where he wants to go, always forgetting where he set
out for in the first place, always digressing, always forgetting the
point: "Let's see now. What was I talking about?"

If I do this purely exploratory teaching in such a way that
students actually learn competencies stated somewhere in advance,
it would be appropriate although it may require a certain benevolent
stage managing by someone else, for example, discreet notices posted
somewhere that say, "Elbow thinks he's teaching Chaucer, but really
he's teaching writing or epistemology." Or perhaps I am teaching
Chaucer but in a very peculiar way. A competence system can be
especially useful here because it enables students to study and get
credit in Chaucer (or in some particular competence) without having to endure the teaching of the "Chaucer person." In conventional

curriculums, there are many students who don't take subjects because, though they wish to pursue the subject, they don't want to work with the teacher involved. Often a class is ruined by being half-filled with students who cannot or will not benefit from the teacher's approach or style, yet to get credit they have to undergo this person's instruction. Without that disgruntled half, the teacher and the remaining students often flourish.

But what if I really don't help students toward stated outcomes with my teaching, or if I cannot get a producer or stage manager to make my performance available to the right students at the right time? Then I'm in trouble in a competence-based program. I may be thrashing around in the dark in a wonderful way—producing all kinds of growth for me and even producing outcomes in students that are grand but not called for in the curriculum. Presumably that is not enough. The astringent spirit of the competence approach would give an uncompromising answer: "Yes, creative drifting is important, but you'll have to do it after class or at home or as part of your research. While you are teaching, you'll have to find some way to help students toward the stated outcomes—unless you can persuade us to adopt your new outcomes."

But I venture to suggest that many of us who say that our teaching is a journey of disinterested inquiry into the unknown are not really behaving as unpredictably as we like to believe. For just as the absentminded professor is likely in fact to be quite predictable—he is engaging in instrumental behavior designed to produce specific outcomes in a process which his wife or students can describe clearly even if he cannot—so too we may very sincerely say at the beginning of the semester, "I don't know where this course is going to end up; we'll just have to follow the process of reasoned inquiry where it leads us," yet the student who took a course from us last semester is likely to know just where we will end up. In short, many of us who say we engage in disinterested inquiry have intentions and goals that for some reason we prefer to know incompletely or not at all. The competence-based people would say that we have a duty to become more aware of our goals and take more responsibility for our intentions.

Third, are certain goals or outcomes unsuitable for a competence approach? Are the "deep" goals of "true" education, as opposed to those of training and professional education, unattainable by the very act of choosing or stating them as outcomes? Does instrumental consciousness prevent us from arriving at certain destinations? Are there butterflies we cannot grasp with goal-oriented fists? Aristotle says that we cannot teach metaphorical ability. Socrates suspects that we cannot teach virtue. Others say we cannot teach growth or tolerance for ambiguity or lovemaking or how to empty your mind.

In short, I wish to explore as directly as possible the suspicion that a goal-oriented approach is inherently limiting—at least in certain realms. This suspicion is quite widespread; otherwise the word *methodical* wouldn't so often connote *dumb*. I admit to the suspicion myself. For one thing, it seems to me that people who care too desperately about knowing exactly what they are doing and why, what the goal is, and how terms are defined, often have a tendency to run away from ambiguity, uncertainty, and contrary voices from within and without—a tendency which leads to behavior that is dogmatic, inflexible, and sometimes just plain stupid. If people listen only to voices they understand or proceed only according to plan, they cut themselves off from half their intelligence. In many situations, nothing is more likely to preclude good thinking than defining terms at the start. For another thing, certain kinds of learning seem to take place only if people remove their shoulders from the harness of a goal for a while and engage in noninstrumental behavior. Most wise teachers have a sense of the paradoxes involved in learning: how the hardest things are often learned only when students stop trying or stop practicing. I can think of a whole range of non-goal-oriented activities that lead to deep learning: play, exercises for learning how to meditate, free association in psychoanalysis, free writing. Many of these are exercises in learning to not-try, to unclench, to remove the shoulder from the harness.

But my reflections on competence-based teaching have helped me finally to realize that, even though these may be instances of not trying and even of removing the goal entirely from mind, it is incorrect to call them instances of *not having a goal*. Most of them are activities worked out, in fact, to help people achieve particular goals, but to help by taking away an excessive consciousness of the goal. The techniques often involve learning to take loops, detours, or roundabout paths. I end up suspecting, then, that there is nothing one cannot adopt as an educational goal or outcome, but that certain goals must be worked toward with great tact and intelligence, and others with a wise indirection. I suspect that the slippery, tricky goals all involve organic development or personal growth.

If, for example, one were to adopt as outcomes for teaching the stages of moral development enumerated by Kohlberg (1977) or the cognitive stages set forth by Perry (1970), one would have to be wise and subtle. I can well imagine ineffective, perverse, or even harmful teaching toward these outcomes. But that doesn't mean the attempt is wrong or doomed to failure; witness the many successful examples of people who do indeed intentionally help others attain growth or other subtle developmental goals. Admittedly these people are often called "parents" or "counselors" or even "employers" rather than "educators." But the mere fact that they are not formal educators doesn't mean they don't sometimes adopt these goals quite consciously.

I think, at this point, of Outward Bound, one of the many institutions arising in our culture which can variously be described as providing education or therapy or simply intimacy—institutions lying somewhere between school and family. Outward Bound programs adopt and announce such goals as courage, confidence, the ability to give and receive support from a group, and even maturity. They do amazingly well at attaining such goals. But they do a characteristic dance with respect to outcomes, that is, they shuffle around what is focal and what is subsidiary—what you have your eye on and what you don't. (See Polanyi, 1958.) They arrange things so that the student's attention gets fully occupied with what could in a sense be called "subsidiary goals"—getting to the top of the mountain, getting something to eat, or not getting killed. At the time, it might seem odd to call these goals "subsidiary," but that is the whole point: they are pressing enough to take your mind off the tricky developmental goals—which is just what is needed with tricky goals. But taking your mind off a goal is not the same as not having it for a goal. And teachers in Outward Bound do not take their eyes off the developmental goals.

If anything can be taught, can anything be assessed? That is a more difficult question to answer. It may well be that part of the wisdom and subtlety required for the teaching of developmental goals involves refraining from direct or blatant assessment of them or at least of assessment at certain points in the learning process. An Outward Bound experience could be called all teaching and no assessment; that is, if students make it through the "semester," they automatically pass the "final." Or perhaps we should call it all assessment and no teaching; that is, if students make it through the final, they can skip the course. A somewhat similar ambiguity about teaching and assessment emerges in some competence programs. Ostensibly they are interested in separating teaching and assessment, but their very exploration of new forms of assessment and instruction often serves to muddy the distinction. Many of the assessment procedures at Alverno and the College for Human Services—the places that set outcomes most involved with human growth and development—are clearly functioning as learning procedures.

We can finally be clearer, then, about the paradoxical answer to the question for this section; namely, does competence-based education exclude certain *styles* or *temperaments* in teaching? But we must first distinguish between two dichotomies that are similar and easily confused. To start with, there is the dichotomy between two *temperamental styles*: a pragmatic, no-nonsense style of always keeping your shoulder to the wheel, always knowing exactly what you are doing and why, never fooling around, and never leaving anything ambiguous; versus the contrasting style of inviting intuition, ambiguity, play, and some thrashing around in the dark. But that dichotomy between temperamental styles is different from a dichotomy between two *general strategies*: a strategy of formulating your goals and priorities as clearly as you can, and trying to think clearly and awarely about how to attain them, versus a strategy of simply going along by instinct or intuition or tradition or habit, without examining assumptions, and of seeing where you come out.

Now obviously, people who have a goal-oriented temperament are more likely to choose a goal-oriented strategy. And that is what we see at this moment in the competence-based movement. But the strategy and the style don't have to match. In my own case, for example, I realize that I can adopt a more goal-oriented strategy without changing my more non-goal-oriented temperament or giving up some of my favorite non-goal-oriented learning activities, such as games or free writing or interludes of unstructuredness. Indeed, because I have begun to adopt a more goal-oriented strategy for attaining some of my subtler educational goals, such as growth, creativity, and metaphorical thinking, I am beginning to use non-goal-oriented teaching activities more consciously and to better effect. I conclude, then, that competence-based education, though it is a goal-oriented strategy, need not foster only goal-oriented styles and pragmatic temperaments in teachers.

Conclusions

First, for teaching in a competence program, much depends on the outcomes and assessments. Indeed a competence-based program *is* the outcomes and assessments. You can teach however you want as long as you succeed in preparing the students for the assessments. If the outcomes are trivial or the assessments blindly mechanistic, you can still teach how you want, but you will have to swim against the tide of trivialization or bad faith.

But second, although you can teach any *way* you want in a competence-based program, you probably cannot teach *what* you want as freely as most faculty members can at high-status colleges. The competence approach is a vehicle for allowing new constituencies—adminstrators, colleagues, and legislators, for example—. to have a share in deciding what will be taught. (Perhaps having to put up with these new constituencies led the programs we saw to exclude almost entirely the most obvious new constituency for helping decide what should be taught, namely, students.)

Third, we did not often see the competence-based approach used stupidly or in bad faith, but it is probably true to say that the system lends itself to such uses. For the competence approach represents, among other things, a more unified, integrated, and tightly organized way of putting together an entire curriculum. If stupidity or malevolence were in the saddle, they could be more pervasive and damaging in their effects than in traditional colleges and universities, which are organized around departments and thus have the not inconsiderable benefits of anarchy: Parts of the organism are blessedly immune from influence by other parts.

But fourth, although we did not see competence-based education narrowed to a vehicle for triviality or bad faith, I at least did not see it broadened out as much as it could be into a vehicle for the fullest spectrum of styles and temperaments in teaching. This will not happen until the approach is used by a wider range of people and institutions. For the competence approach is understandably most attractive to people with a goal-oriented temperament and to institutions of professional training where there is already an obvious outcome: a job or profession. The competence approach is indeed helpful for such persons and institutions, but I judge it particularly helpful for those people and institutions who are most likely to be suspicious of it: people with a non-goal-oriented temperament, and colleges of liberal arts where there is woeful disagreement as to the purposes of the education given.

Fifth, even though competence-based education has more to do with outcomes and assessments than with what kind of teaching is used, the teachers played a central role in the programs we saw. When teachers get involved in competence programs, they tend to become enthusiastic. But why do they become this way over programs that take so much out of their hides? I think it is because the approach helps them to teach better and thereby to feel more sense of accomplishment. It both forces and helps teachers to figure out more clearly what they have been trying to do, to become more aware of their latent assumptions and premises, and often to go through this process collaboratively with colleagues. The result tends to be teaching that is more intentional, effective, and energized.

But sixth, I don't see how it could be anything but scary to contemplate teaching in a competence-based program for any teacher in higher education who, like myself, has never taught in one. In any program, I would look for assurance: (1) that faculty members will have a major role in determining the outcomes and assessment procedures; (2) that the outcomes will be broad and deeply intelligent and not neglect the larger dimensions of human growth nor the special dimensions of intuition and creativity; and (3) that a feedback loop will operate in *both* directions. It will not just use assessment to provide feedback on the effectiveness of teaching, but it will use the experience of teaching to provide feedback on the validity of the outcomes and assessments. To put it bluntly, if my students fail the assessments, we will not just ask what's wrong with my teaching. We will also ask whether the students are perhaps not ready or able to attain these outcomes; whether perhaps the outcomes are desirable but very lofty (for example, if the outcome sought is a change of consciousness, only 10 percent success might be cause for celebration); and whether perhaps I had instinctively veered in my teaching toward new and better outcomes which we should adopt instead of the present ones.

Such assurances are no doubt hard to secure, but without them, I doubt whether many faculty members in colleges and universities can be induced voluntarily to try a competence approach, despite what I hope I have shown to be its obvious benefits.

Gerald Grant
Wendy Kohli

4

Contributing to Learning by Assessing Student Performance

Why does assessment—the evaluation or appraisal of the skills, traits, and abilities of persons—assume such importance in competence-based educational programs? Perhaps no other form of education typically invests so much student time or faculty resources in formal and informal modes of assessment. The reason for this emphasis is not just a matter of new techniques, although a number of competence-based programs have adopted videotape exercises, elaborate simulations, and third-party judging to assess students. Nor have practitioners in this realm achieved any major breakthroughs or "solved" any of the complicated problems of predicting successful performance that have plagued testers for generations. What seems clear is that competence-based education engenders a radical reorientation of attitudes about and responsibilities for assessment. This chapter describes that new orientation, analyzes some of its practical and conceptual problems, and summarizes what we regard as its most hopeful outcome.

A Reorientation of Attitudes Towards Assessment

Three major characteristics underlie this reorientation to assessment: (1) an egalitarian concern that emphasizes "failure-free" opportunities to demonstrate competence according to criteria made explicit in advance of the test; (2) a utilitarian emphasis that fosters skepticism about the usefulness of what has been learned until it has been publicly assessed as relevant to achieving a defined competence; and (3) a managerial attitude that seeks ways to hold faculty more accountable for teaching all students and to compare the performance of teachers by assessing the relative success of their students when measured against common benchmarks.

Egalitarianism. Americans have pursued the ideal of equality of opportunity with greater devotion than any other society in history, but that very pursuit has increased anxieties about inequality. A nation that encourages virtually everyone to make use of his or her opportunities insists on a competition in which some become "more equal" than others. A major portion of the responsibility for ensuring fairness in such a competition—or at least for giving the appearance of fairness—has traditionally fallen on the schools and colleges. The Jeffersonian ideal of an intellectual aristocracy based upon meritocratic selection is deeply imbued in our educational history. American society has demanded that the schools devise a rational means of selecting those students who should be given special opportunities or advanced levels of training. As the first nation that attempted to provide universal primary and then secondary education, it was not accidental that America invented the giant corporate test makers and scorers, such as the Educational Testing Service (ETS), which have performed the function of helping educational institutions grade, select, and sort millions of students each year. (See Hawes, 1964.) And though such a process has created some resentment, it has generally been accepted in preference to nonmeritocratic bases of selection.

Thus, although teachers have resisted nationally standardized tests if it meant they must "teach to the test" or if they perceived these tests as a check on their own performance, they have never raised serious objections to the corporate test makers who shared the burden of designing rational systems of selection and prediction. This is not surprising. Teachers have agreed with the ideal of meritocratic selection and have tolerated assessment as a necessary adjunct of a meritocratic system. But they have viewed their usual assessment tasks—grading themes, checking lab exercises, reading dissertations, sitting for oral examinations—as an onerous duty, often a bore. Whenever they have had the power to do so, they have put the burden of these tasks on assistants. But, whether teachers could escape these assessment chores or not, they have regarded them as impediments to what they look upon as the central activity of teaching, namely, a transaction between themselves and pupils characterized by growth and learning.

In other words, the process of assessment has not traditionally been assumed to be a learning experience itself. The test comes "after" the learning in order to see "how much" learning has occurred in one student relative to others or to some norm. Thus an assessment is frequently a grade or a number that conveys little information other than a relative ranking. That an eighth grade girl received an A in mathematics may mean that she can do algebra (if she enrolled in an honors class in Winnetka) or that she can do long division (if she attends a one-room school in Appalachia). Although most traditional tests can be used diagnostically, they are seldom experienced that way. They are experienced as a competition leading to a summative judgment expressed in a rank or a number. As Dreeben (1968) has pointed out, one of the most significant things children learn as part of the "hidden curriculum" in modern schools is to cope with competition and to accept treatment of themselves in "objective" categories.

Yet every assessment can also be a learning experience in a more conscious sense. Most persons have sometimes experienced assessments that convey considerable information: a thoughtful boss who tells you why you are not being promoted, a therapist or friend who assesses features of your personality, or a coach who points out aspects of your performance on a videotape of last

Saturday's game. These are judgments about relative performances, but they are not experienced simply as rankings. They are experienced as learning. This is one of the major themes of competence-based education, namely, that assessment itself can contribute greatly to learning.

Most of those in competence-based programs would take the position that American society has been too concerned with excellence for a few. The outcome, they would argue, has been to stamp many students as failures. Society concentrates resources on the most able students while the herd slips through with C's and B's and very little competence. The thrust of the first wave of competence-based programs is to set fairly high but explicit and reasonable standards by which all will be assessed. This assures that most students will meet those standards and that teachers will be more accountable if students do not.

To achieve an egalitarian goal without sacrificing standards, competence-based education employs "criterion-referenced" rather than "norm-referenced" assessment. Criterion-referenced assessment measures the *degree of attainment* according to some defined standard, while norm-referenced assessment measures the *relative behavior* of two or more individuals from some defined population. In using criterion-referenced assessment, teachers in competence-based programs do not posit a so-called "normal curve" in which the teacher expects so many students to get A's, so many to get B's, and so many to fail. The teacher does not give an algebra test and then hand out A's to the top ten scorers. Instead, the criterion may be, "Can solve six of eight quadratic equations within fifty minutes." The expectation is that most students will be able to satisfy the criterion, given enough teaching, practice, and the desire to do so.

With this orientation, there is less penalty for failure: It is believed that the student suffers less from harsh comparison with others and is less subject to what often seem like ex post facto and arbitrary faculty grading practices. On the contrary, the assessment can be largely a learning and diagnostic experience under the guidance of a sensitive and supportive teacher. Indeed, most competence-based institutions operate on the "pass-forget" principle and do not count or record failures. At Mt. Hood Community College in Gresham, Oregon, unsuccessful trials are not called "failures" but "learning opportunities." And finally, as part of this orientation, such institutions emphasize self-pacing, whereby students often decide individually when they will be assessed.

Utilitarianism. Perhaps we can understand why the utilitarian theme—that is, skepticism about what has been learned until it has been publicly assessed—becomes a focus of competence-based reforms by considering the process faculty in these programs typically follow. It is difficult to think about competence in the abstract. We tend to associate competence with a complex of skills and qualities comprising a role; we tend to think of people as being competent "at something." This is so even with quite generic skills such as problem solving. We want to know: competent at problem solving in what context? A competent architect, or a competent mathematician?

Even competence-based programs within the liberal arts usually have some specific set of applied roles in mind. Thus Alverno College in Milwaukee originally described its program as "liberal learning in a management context" and pointed its students toward attaining competence as managers. The competence-based program in music at Florida State University aims toward the role of music educator, and the College for Human Services in New York City emphasizes the roles of counselor, social worker, and teacher. In contrast, more traditional colleges and faculty have generally placed emphasis upon achieving competence in a particular discipline. Their implicit question has always been: Is this student making progress toward becoming a competent historian, chemist, mathematician, or philosopher? Traditional professional schools have had a more practical orientation than this, but even here many faculty members have simply assumed that what they teach is relevant to what professionals do.

Faculty in competence-based programs make no such easy assumptions. Ordinarily, they begin with an analysis of the role to derive a curriculum that will supposedly be more relevant to it. The burden is upon teachers to show that what they teach relates to performance in the role. Hence Alverno initiated its reforms by asking faculty why their subjects should be taught. Antioch Law School in Washington, D.C., questioned the relevance of typical casebook methods for preparing lawyers to perform such tasks as interviewing and negotiating, which typify the daily grind for many lawyers. This questioning forces a major shift in perspective upon many faculty. It means that they can no longer rely on the usual paper and pencil tests to indicate normative performance in a discipline. Assessments grounded in the logical structures of the disciplines have to be supplanted by judgments—heretofore made in the work place—about performance in a role. Academics are asked to make judgments that are no longer purely "academic." In the music program at Florida State University, faculty have to make sure not only that a student is a good flutist, but that she knows several ways to teach the flute and other instruments. At Alverno College, teachers do not assume that a student who writes an A theme can communicate on her feet much less that she can effectively organize informational inputs from several sources into a rational plan of action, as she might have to do in a job. Specific exercises have been devised to assess the student's performance in the ways just mentioned, and the English program has been subsumed under a curriculum of communication skills pointed toward competence in the managerial role.

For assessment in competence-based programs, then, a wide range of evidence is considered relevant. Faculty in more traditional institutions measure a student against the abstract standards of a discipline and rule out, by design, considerations of nonintellectual attributes. That is, the conventional norm observed in the academy is that one should not confuse ideas and persons. One should judge only the intellectual merit of the argument, not the interpersonal skills of the student who advances it. It is "mind" that matters, not personality. But competence-based programs try to assess other attributes as well: persistence, interpersonal skills, aggressiveness, and initiative. As noted in the *Chronicle of Higher Education* (1978), efforts to develop these kinds of assessments are spreading to major medical and law schools. Thirteen medical schools have asked ETS to develop dependable measures of the interpersonal skills used in clinical practice. Another ETS study sponsored by the American Bar Association and the Law School Admissions Council seeks ways to measure student qualities that correlate with competence in such aspects of the lawyer's trade as negotiating and settling cases or performing effectively in the courtroom. For faculty embarked on competence-based reforms, however, assessments of this kind are not means of excluding students via the admissions process but are evaluations that all students, once admitted, undergo. Hence, the question arises of what responsibility faculty have for developing students' interpersonal skills or for inculcating particular values.

Explicitness about value orientations is, however, only one of the issues that faculty in competence-based programs encounter. A second is explicitness about the measures and criteria by which students demonstrate competence in a role. Hence at Antioch the work place has been literally recreated within the school by means of a teaching law firm in which students interview clients, prepare briefs, and argue in court. Antioch law students interview "clients" played by actors, and these interviews are videotaped for criticism and evaluation. The lawyering skills of students must be demonstrated in the law clinic. Students assigned, for example, to the Child Advocacy Clinic have their performances evaluated on a scale derived from the clinical faculty's perception of what a beginning lawyer should be able to do.

At Mt. Hood Community College, the "classroom" is a virtual duplication of a modern hospital wing, complete with two fully equipped operating rooms. Students must demonstrate their ability to do such things as give intravenous injections and bathe patients. The College for Human Services places students on the job three days a week in a variety of agencies that provide human services. They are asked to demonstrate their competence in a series of "constructive actions" of progressive difficulty reflecting the change-oriented goals of the college.

In the Seattle Central Community College day care program, evaluators assess students who are working with children, and they try to agree whether the students achieve the desired outcomes. An effort is made to find indicators of competence, including such qualities as "showing warmth" or "relating well with children." Seattle Central personnel have agreed upon three indicators of how well students relate to small children: (1) the appropriateness of the questions they ask the children; (2) how the student gives or does not give help; and (3) the brute fact of how much energy and attention is devoted to care—does the student, for example, even hear the child off to one side who needs attention?

The teaching centers connected with the Syracuse University

Teacher Education program also provide an integrated practical learning experience for students by requiring them to demonstrate their skills in real classrooms. Assessments are made periodically by regular teachers, faculty supervisors, and the students themselves. At Florida State University, competence-based practicums are part of the evaluation for music education and nursing majors, although in these fields, competence-based assessment differs little from that in more standard programs, where assessments have long been performance-based. Among the exercises performed by Alverno students is the in-basket test that simulates office decision-making situations.

Competence-based educators have not invented new forms of assessment so much as they have employed already existing techniques in new areas of the curriculum and with new participants in the assessment process—as in jury assessments involving practitioners in the field students hope to enter. At Florida State, for example, marine biologists from state agencies have served as jurors; at Antioch, practicing attorneys have evaluated students interviewing a client; Milwaukee business executives have served on panels at Alverno College; and at Seattle Central, students have submitted portfolios containing memos, grant proposals, and other written documents produced on the job to juries for review. And competence-based institutions are employing technological aids in the process. The videotape is particularly helpful as a means of recapturing a performance so as to better diagnose and assess it. Antioch Law School has developed an exercise in which the student critiques a simulated videotaped interview between a lawyer and a client and then analyzes his own performance as an interviewer compared with that of the lawyer. Seattle Central, Florida State, Syracuse, and Alverno also make use of videotaping in their assessments.

Managerial Attitude. Competence-based education tends to evaluate faculty by assessing the relative success of different teachers' students against explicit and common benchmarks. Explicit criteria of the nature commonly employed in competence-based programs are often rejected by faculty in more traditional programs as too constraining. Yet, as Thomas Ewens shows in Chapters Five and Eight of this book, faculty discussion leading to the adoption of these criteria can be of fundamental educational importance: One of the things a competence-based program does is reveal the ability or inability of members of the faculty to talk about these matters. And in applying assessment criteria, faculty as well as students are required to reveal the quality of their judgments and the depth of their knowledge. Judgments that were previously quite private are now open to wider scrutiny. Written work in a number of competencies at Alverno, for instance, is judged by both the faculty member conducting the course and an assessor who does not have direct responsibility for instruction. Each has a voice in deciding whether the student has fulfilled the competence requirement, and they meet to discuss their application of the criteria to particular papers. In developing their courses, faculty are not restricted to satisfying competency levels, but whatever competency levels they do claim to satisfy in the course are submitted to other faculty committees, which not infrequently contest such claims. Hence the faculty member must develop a rationale for what she or he is teaching in terms of some defensible outcome.

Outcome-oriented education makes faculty answerable for the content they teach as well as for what is learned by their students. Once faculty provide a rationale for what they are teaching, they are held responsible for the acquisition of this material by their students. With explicit criteria stated in advance, and with assessments made in relation to these criteria, faculty are held accountable for the number of students who meet these criteria. Explicit criteria also make possible the assessment of previous learning, whereas much of traditional higher education provides no means of assessing prior learning other than evaluation of credit earned in courses.

Our fieldwork at ten colleges indicates that most competence-based programs are not "minimalist" in terms of assessing competence. If anything, once forced to be explicit about outcomes, faculty generally set high standards of competence. Thus competence-based education tends to establish a fairly rigorous standard for the "C" student in institutions with a large number of "C" students. On the average, more is required of these students than would be in programs that are not competence-based. In fact, this is one of the appeals competence-based education has for faculty at these institutions—it provides a corporate bulwark for raising the *average* performance of all students. In management terms, then, competence-based education develops *corporate* responsibility for assessment and for student performance, in contrast to the individual responsibility found in traditional programs.

Conceptual and Practical Problems

As we have seen, the developers and practitioners of most competence-based programs have established new orientations toward assessment. Yet these orientations themselves raise some difficulties.

Criterion and Norm-Referenced Assessment. The distinction commonly made in competence education between criterion-referenced and norm-referenced assessment may be overdrawn. This distinction between the *degree of attainment* according to some defined standards and the measurement of *relative behavior* of two or more individuals is meaningful to competence-based programs because it reduces emphasis on the ranking of students and promotes egalitarianism. But it can be argued that the "defined standards" of criterion-referenced evaluation are derived from a normative consensus of what is required, for example, of a well-trained nurse or teacher; and in this sense, a student's performance is measured in terms of his or her level of attainment "relative to" the normative standards of a defined population. This confusion is captured in an observation by a member of our research group: "The goal of competence-based education is to move away from norm-referenced assessment—to move away from marking on a curve to specifying what the student is able to do. This is easier said than done, for the attempt to specify what has to be done tends to result in competency statements that are simply too hard—competency statements that require a person to do everything that a whole group of planners ever admired. If you require all the competencies and all the components, no one will get a certificate. Or else you will covertly start grading on a curve. But since you're not supposed to grade on a curve, you will tend to pass those people who *seem* to satisfy *all* the indicators."

One can ask whether a test based upon some norm of what a competent performance is can be purely "criterion-referenced," even if a student's performance is not graded along a curve. Although competence-based institutions strive for "objective" assessments based on criteria met, they can't easily resist the demand to make judgments about the *quality* of a performance. Quadratic equations can be solved laboriously or elegantly. One is seldom interested only in whether a student can make a pot; instead one usually wants to know if the pot will hold water, or if it is pleasing in appearance, or how it compares with pots others have made or with pots that the same student made a month ago.

Second, one can ask whether "time-to-completion" does not become the hidden assessment in most criterion-referenced tests. Probably more than 98 percent of the nation's twenty-year-olds could satisfy the criterion of changing a flat tire, but those who can't do it in less than an hour are unlikely to be hired by a garage owner, much less by a driver in the Indianapolis 500 who is looking for a helper on his pit crew. Proponents of criterion-referenced assessment would argue that one can admit the existence of a "pit-crew" bias in the wider society without letting it contaminate educational assessment. Thus Mt. Hood Community College allowed students to "slow pace" if they wished and placed no limits on the number of trials its students could attempt. But since most of the assessments involved various kinds of laboratory exercises, equipment already put away had to be unpacked for the "slow-pacers," and this was often irritating to faculty. As a result, pressures developed over time for students to move along as a group.

Whose Standards? In terms of the second orientation of assessment in competence-based programs—that towards utilitarianism—reaching agreement among the faculty on standards of competence presents a major problem. What standards are going to be applied? Whose standards are they? And what happens when assessors disagree about the application of a particular standard?

The expectations and norms governing performance in a role are to a large extent shaped by a particular social or organizational context and a particular value orientation. In deriving and assessing the components of successful role performance, it matters greatly what values one accepts. If one's definition of a successful lawyer is based on the standards of Ralph Nader's organization, then one's method of assessment ought not to reflect the requirements of a

Wall Street firm serving multinational corporations. Presumably, lawyers for both the Wall Street firm and Ralph Nader's group have some skills in common; but if one is assessing competence in a role, then one is no longer talking about law in the abstract. Antioch Law School, for example, is explicit on this point, selecting students who have rejected a Wall Street career in favor of serving the poor and disenfranchised. Antioch requires its students to live with poor black families in Washington during their first weeks in law school and it builds its curriculum around a teaching law firm in which students handle cases for indigent clients.

Similarly, the competence-based program in nursing at Mt. Hood Community College began by asking patients their view of competent nursing. Patients emphasized different aspects of the nursing role than those that doctors have traditionally valued. Patients valued nurses who personalized care, made the patient feel important, respected privacy, sympathized with the grieving and terminally ill, explained why certain procedures were performed, and gave information about the purposes and likely effects of various medications. Some doctors have always encouraged nurses to do these things, but the norm has been that nurses tell the patient as little as possible. In some states, until quite recently, nurses were not even allowed to tell a patient the name of a medication, unless it was insulin for a diabetic patient. Much of the nurse's role has been to keep the patient quiet and obedient, not give him or her ammunition with which to "pester" the doctor. The contrasting implications for assessment of the latter nursing role as compared with the former are obvious.

The difficulty in agreeing on standards indicates the fundamentally subjective quality of assessment, even when standards are supposedly explicit. A juror in the marine biology program at Florida State noted that it was no easier to make judgments about competence or excellence from students' jury presentations than from a paper that a student might write. Furthermore, as David Riesman's study of the Florida State program in Chapter Eleven reveals, a jury assessment does not eliminate the problem of norm-referencing. In fact, the sequence in which students appear may affect their rating. Jurors tend to set a norm based on what they regard as "best performance," and if the first students to go before the jury that day are the "best," then it becomes difficult for those who follow.

The subjective element may be reduced by structuring the assessment in precise and "objective" terms. But human judges can never eliminate all personal bias, regardless of the degree of explicitness of the criteria, as this excerpt from the field notes vividly illustrates:

> There was also a discussion among the assessors as to what degree they should require students to convey information in written form and to what degree they could rely on their observations of students in field clinics and so forth. One faculty member also said bluntly that she liked the student's written reflections, "but I don't know whether she's competent or not." She also said she was not sure how members of the committee were variously "reading these documents," a problem that we encounter again and again in this matter of assessment. One can have so-called new means of assessment . . . but one still has the problem of different standards being applied by different persons who are doing the actual assessment.

This debate over standards gets down to the question, not only of value orientations, but also of who decides what constitutes the critical variables of performance for any profession. Whatever "indicators" one uses to define competence are derived as a subset of considerations from one's general ideology or value orientation. But this does not mean that the attempt to become more explicit and objective in assessment is worthless. Another way to look at this is to say that competence-based education is a means of making precisely these kinds of value orientations more explicit.

Some kinds of human assessments are consensual judgments by those participating in an activity: Who among us should be first violinist? Others may have opinions about it, but their judgments will not necessarily carry any weight. Although one can indicate some general standards, it is impossible to specify in advance precisely what the criterion will be that will determine who will be first violinist. It will be that person among us who is "best." The attempt to be precise about it beforehand is felt as a violent distortion of the activity itself. There are some "outcomes"—creativity, for example—that are known in a precise way only after they have happened. Psychologists who have studied creativity have concluded that one cannot devise tests that certify creative competence or predict it. One can only point to creative products or works after they have appeared. (See, for example, MacKinnon, 1962. Nor does intelligence, measured on standardized tests, correlate significantly with creativity, as MacKinnon discovered in his studies of creative architects, mathematicians, writers, researchers, physical scientists and engineers.)

Teachers in traditional disciplines, particularly in the more elite sectors of academe, have this same attitude toward their subject. The kind of assessment used in competence-based programs is seen as a vulgar distortion of the activity, the cold hand of measurement crushing the butterfly of creativity. Judgments about what philosophy is, what mathematics is, or what sociology is can only be made by colleague participants. They are judgments measured against what is best in the field, ultimately against a universe of discourse stretching through time. Faculty members perceive themselves as initiating students into this discourse, and the outcomes are not stated in the form of criterion-referenced tests. The outcomes that are desired have to do with styles of inquiry, appreciation of complexity, knowledge of fact and theory, and development of critical intelligence. Such teachers are teaching for themselves as much as for students, especially in the research-oriented universities that dominate the academic landscape in America. The graduate seminar is the ideal, a mutual inquiry with student colleagues, a voyage of discovery, with the outcomes partially unknown. (See Chapter Three.)

It may be possible to limit the negative aspects of the explicit and particularistic emphasis of competence assessment by differentiating among the purposes of an assessment. It is certainly possible to argue for the need to assess for specific skills and particular bits of knowledge, for their own sake as well as for the sake of a larger goal. In this sense, assessment of discrete acts and skills does not become trivial and reductionist. In our fieldwork, we were impressed with those teachers who struggled to protect the intellectual and educational integrity of their programs at the same time as they tried to be precise and explicit about the outcomes they wanted their students to attain. Many were familiar with the criticisms of the competence-based teacher education movement with its heavy reliance on behavioral objectives and its general absence of a synthetic understanding of what and who a teacher is. This excerpt from the project team's field notes portrays such a tension:

> The assessors must be able to support their opinions; they cannot just say, "She did a lousy job"; they have to give specific examples, and here of course the running notes they kept are important, although it occurred to me that the overall judgment of competence was in fact the likely one made, and then justified by appropriate illustrations. But in the case of each competence level, both students and assessors are given a whole series of cues by which competence is defined, although, here again, the cutting up of competence into little bits seems to me to present problems. For example, to judge whether a student has "sufficient understanding" of contemporary events, she must accurately answer "a majority of the questions addressed to her"; but such a quantitative reckoning may leave out of account a subtlety shown in response to particular questions. Still, the point is to get students to be specific and concrete, and to tie the concrete to the more general, logically rather than inchoately.

In dealing with the problem of "the whole versus the sum of its parts," the following questions might be posed to avoid some of the reductionist tendencies in outcome-specific education: Do the assessors have a vision of what constitutes a competent person or competent performance in a role—a vision of the whole? Do the specific assessments along the way bear a logical relationship to making judgments about the performance as a whole—or toward learning the components necessary for holistic performance? Is it possible to make judgments about the parts without considering the whole? (Do faculty really make an overall judgment and then seek "illustrations" to justify it, rather than "adding up" discrete performances to see if the whole passes?) These are dilemmas that bear upon any assessment, of course, and not problems that can be solved in any final sense by competence-based or more traditional educators; but progress on them among competence-based educators will reduce the suspicion of the traditionalists as well as set a standard for their own assessments.

Practical Difficulties. In attempting to achieve greater accountability—what we have called the management orientation of competence-based programs—a number of practical difficulties have arisen.

First, in nearly every program under study, developers underestimated the amount of time and resources needed to conceptualize and implement satisfactory assessments. In most cases, assessors did attempt to keep up with program development. But some programs have never practiced the elaborate assessment exercises they planned, and many have reverted to standardized paper and pencil tests that are easier to administer and less expensive. This reversion may be accelerated now that many institutions no longer receive external support for the costly development of performance-based assessment. This erosion may undermine the very existence of many competence-based programs, let alone their new approaches to assessment.

Second, while students often find approval by external examiners or jurors to be confidence-building, they often delay appearances before juries because the possibility of failure in such a setting seems especially traumatic. Thus in many of the "self-paced" assessment exercises typically found in competence-based programs, rates of "slow-pacing" and even "non-pacing" are high. For example, at Grand Valley State Colleges, College IV began as a completely modularized, self-paced program; but by the end of the first term the average completion rate was less than two credits per student. Moreover, jurors cannot always be relied upon. Although practitioners may volunteer eagerly at the outset of such experiments, some programs have found that enthusiasm wanes quickly. Florida State eventually canceled external jury assessments in several programs because of the frequent "no-shows" by volunteer jurors.

Third, competence-based programs are not exempt from the traditional measurement problems of constructive and predictive validity. (See Jackson and Messick, 1967; and King's chapter in this volume.) The assumption that adequate performance on

criterion-referenced tests predicts that students will be able to perform adequately on the job is problematic. There is no absolute
distinction between performance tests and other kinds of tests.
Performance tests are considered to be "relatively realistic," and
they try to "simulate" real world and occupational experiences.[1] But
if a performance measure is to be interpreted as relevant to "real
life" performance, it must be taken under conditions representative
of real life situations. The "representativeness" of the simulated
performance is judged according to the degree that the simulation
approximates the real situation and yields indicators that clearly
and accurately represent the actual performance. Thus, the most
valid performance test places the student in an actual job situation—
for example, the Antioch law student who works in the school's
teaching law firm or the student at the College for Human Services
who serves an internship. But most performance tests in competence-
based programs select only one aspect of the real job. The in-basket
test at Alverno College, for example, puts a student in the situation
of an executive who must figure out what actions to take based on
the information in her in-basket. Although such a test does measure
analytic ability, which may be important for the job in question, it
does not necessarily predict whether the student will actually become
an effective manager. That may depend upon a combination of
such other qualities as persistence, and the ability to get along with
co-workers, and upon other unique or unpredictable aspects of the
particular contexts. Thus such assessments may have important outcomes for learning or may help diagnose student weaknesses, but
their predictions are not so reliable as some seem to believe.

Fourth and finally, even if competence-based programs can
develop adequately representative performance testing, they will still
face other challenges. Some models for performance testing are
partially derived from industrial or military settings and may be less
suited to academic experiences. Certainly to transplant a technique
from one environment to another will have some unanticipated

[1]Several of the essays in Keeton (1976) bear upon this discussion,
particularly those by Coleman and by Tumin. The classic study by the
Office of Strategic Services in the Second World War, *Assessment of Men*
(1948), remains perhaps the best discussion of attempts to predict performance on the basis of rather ingenious simulations.

consequences if one is not aware of the assumptions underlying the technique. Qualities of conformity and deference that are highly valued in military and industrial settings, for example, may not serve educational ends. Job-related performance testing may have to be supplemented by more traditional academic evaluations to ensure these ends. In summary, then, the reorientation towards assessment in competence-based programs displays the following features:

- It is usually criterion-referenced, characterized by criteria that are explicit and known in advance; determining these criteria, as well as deciding whether they have been achieved, typically involves agreement among faculty members and often the participation of outsiders.
- It minimizes the invidious distinctions of norm-referenced grading and emphasizes "failure-free" self-pacing in which the student decides when he or she will be assessed—an option that can lead to procrastination and low completion rates but that also encourages learning and growth from the assessment process itself.
- It emphasizes assessment of student performance in actual or simulated roles, and thus directs the attention of faculty and other professionals to the components of these roles and to adequate assessment of their representative components.
- It enables assessment of competence or learning whenever or wherever it has occurred and thus does not require that students "serve time" in taking courses—although, in practice, most do so.

Importance of Self-Assessment

Beyond these outcomes, however, competence-based education employs students themselves in formal assessment roles whenever possible. So far, we have not said much about this outcome, but of all that stem from the reorientation of assessment in competence-based programs, the employment of students in assessment roles is one of the most significant. Competence at self-assessment is, of course, an overarching kind of competence required in the modern world. While it would require several volumes to give an adequate historical and sociological account of the development over several centuries of the modern self-consciousness about assessment, certainly no one would deny that the demand for increased competence in the assessment both of self and of others has been a critical feature of the transition from traditional societies to complex modern societies. When men were bound by ties of land and kin, when they were born into their roles instead of being forced to make choices about them, assessment was not such a pervasive aspect of everyday life. But modern man is continually evaluating his "contracts" in a network of shifting obligations and commitments.

Self-assessment and student assessments of their peers are features of most competence-based programs. At Justin Morrill, for example, incoming students are asked to assess their levels of proficiency on thirty-seven separate competencies as part of the admissions process. The students must provide a rationale justifying each of their ratings on the self-assessment form, and describe the experiences that have significantly contributed to the levels of competence claimed. Students also describe what action they will take to remedy deficiencies. If faculty members disagree with the student's assessment, then the differences are worked out in an interview.

Alverno College has developed, through videotape, perhaps the most sophisticated kinds of self-assessments, some of them adapted from exercises used for management selection at the American Telephone and Telegraph Company. A cumulative record of each student's performance is compiled on a videotape reel so that she has a visual transcript of her progress over four years. The following excerpt from the field notes of our project team describes a student undergoing an assessment for the first-level competence in communication skills. The student must analyze a three-minute talk she had taped a week earlier. To pass this first-level competence, the student need not give a good talk but must show that she can recognize her strengths and weaknesses:

> Not much was scheduled for the Assessment Center that morning other than a feedback session for a freshman who was coming in for the first look at the videotape she had made on the assigned topic, "Should There be Entrance Requirements for College?" After obtaining the student's permission, the faculty member

took me into a room behind a one-way mirror where I could see a slightly plump, nervous, young woman named Joan looking up at a television screen.

The speech that appeared on the screen was a terrible, almost incoherent performance. It was obviously painful for the student to look at it. In fact, she kept averting her eyes and occasionally slapping her forehead softly in disbelief at the image before her. I scribbled these notes as I watched: "garbled speech, stumbled, voice too low, poor transition from point to point, exceedingly nervous, lost train of thought, little eye contact, little development of argument, false stops and starts, and ends with a slogan that makes no point."

I also graded the sheet before me, giving her "no" on all six criteria. Joan began to fill in the rating form as the faculty assessor, a pleasant woman of about forty, sat patiently beside her. She did not hurry the student or express disapproval in any way. After Joan had completed the form, the assessor went over each point. The student had given herself negative ratings on five of the six categories. The assessor had given her six "no's" as I had. Thus, they had agreement on five, so she informed the girl that she had passed. "You don't have to do a smashing job," said the assessor. "You must be able to look at [the tape] and make an objective critique, and you did."

The assessor began her critique by saying it was obvious that the girl was frightened, and Joan nodded vigorously in assent. She assured her that that was perfectly natural, that many students are frightened by the television equipment, and that she knew Joan could overcome her fears and learn to give a clear and stimulating speech. She pointed out the ways in which Joan had been hesitant, mumbled and didn't speak clearly or crisply. She spoke about her lack of voice projection and poor eye contact, although she complimented her on occasional lively facial expressions. She reminded Joan of the need for voice variety, asking her to think of changes of tone and gesture in family dinner table conversation. Then she turned to questions of organization of her talk, pointing out that Joan had never really addressed the question of entrance requirements nor taken a position on it. The conversation went on in this way for nearly twenty minutes with the student gradually taking a more active part in the analysis. At the close the assessor suggested she work on some of her skills in the speech lab before attempting the next level assessment.

The Alverno exercise illustrates several aspects of the new orientation towards assessment. It is a criterion-referenced rather than a norm-based assessment. Criteria are stated explicitly in advance. Although the idea that most questions are not susceptible to a simple yes or no answer is bred deeply into most academics, the criteria for this talk do capture the subjective and arguable points most of us would agree are important elements of an effective speech. Most important, the student herself is asked to judge the speech act as a complex whole—no small matter, of course, since it demands a critical self-consciousness that lies dormant among many students. (The experience is so novel for some that they cannot do the rating until the tape has been run two or three times.) And she receives approval for recognizing her weaknesses, which is a precondition to working on them.

Such student self-assessment at Alverno College is a recurring feature of its program, and in later stages students who have completed certain competence levels often join faculty or outside assessors in judging students who are attempting to pass those competencies. Students thereby develop the meta-competence of self-assessment. Such exercises also help them develop a sense of detachment and to view themselves objectively. The process of assessing one's performance on a videotape is a way of standing outside the self, of holding a mirror up to one's own performance. In exercises where students are employed as assessors of others, the students undergoing the trial are encouraged to be nondefensive, knowing they will be judging peers the next time around. In judging others, and in comparing the reasons that they give for their judgment with those of faculty and outside judges, students are learning to exercise their critical faculties in a profound way. In exercises such as the student's analysis of her own three-minute talk, where the student compares her self-rating with that made by a faculty member, a student learns to invite criticism and to recognize the limits of her own competence.

Of course, it would be naive to argue that competence-based programs are unique in these ways. One can sometimes learn to be more detached and less defensive in a good seminar. Students also compare their performance to that of others in many traditional settings. There is nothing intrinsic to competence-based education that restricts the growth of these qualities to that domain. But many of the assessment practices commonly employed in these programs do facilitate such growth in a uniquely powerful way, and that seems to us the most promising thing about the new orientation we have described. Assessment in competence-based programs does not necessarily improve prediction, but it can make a large contribution to learning.

Thomas Ewens 5

Analyzing the Impact
of Competence-Based
Approaches
on Liberal Education

ᘁᘁᘁᘁᘁᘁᘁᘁᘁᘁᘁᘁᘁᘁᘁᘁᘁᘁ

To ask oneself whether and in what sense competence-based education is or might be liberal education is a challenging and frustrating
exercise. One is forced to explicate one's own understanding of
liberal education and at the same time assume the position of judge
regarding those competence-based programs that aim at liberal
education—no two of which are exactly alike. The problem is
severe, even if approached with modest hopes. As Strauss (1968)
points out, we lack authoritative traditions for judging liberal education, since the greatest minds contradict one another regarding it.
Let me thus say at the outset that in part I think competence-based
liberal education is an original and useful approach to some of the
problems and processes of liberal education and that in part I
think it is a complicated travesty of liberal education. In answer to

the question, "Is competence-based liberal education really liberal education?" I must respond ambiguously: "Yes, it is, but it might be!"

Traditional Liberal Education

Given the extraordinary array of conflicting theories and practices that pass for liberal education in our pluralist culture, it seems impossible to give a definition of liberal education that would adequately characterize even a significant minority of liberal arts colleges. I have therefore adopted the following strategy here: In order to discuss liberal education with at least a modicum of intelligence, I employ the device of using *heuristically* one interpretation of traditional liberal education—an interpretation that is very classic, and doubtless, in the eyes of some, very conservative. It is a distillation of the interpretations to be found in Aristotle, Thomas Aquinas, John Henry Newman, and, in our day, Jacques Maritain, Robert Hutchins, Mortimer Adler, and such other writers as J. Glenn Gray and Vincent Smith. (One need not agree with this interpretation to recognize, I hope, its heuristic usefulness.)

There is no doubt that the central concern of traditional liberal education as exemplified by these writers is the pursuit of knowledge for its own sake. It is informed through and through by a desire (*phila*) for theoretic knowledge (*sophia*): its goal, its central purpose, its overriding aim is, in Newman's exact phrase, "philosophical knowledge." This is the highest, the most noble, the most fundamental and at the same time the most pleasurable knowledge available to mortals. This is the truth that frees one not only *from* the enslavements of ignorance, bias, passion, the multifarious idols of human adulation, and the merely pragmatic concerns of the workaday world but also *for* an examined life, a life whose transcendent values and possibilities of realization have been recognized, examined, and thought through to the very fundaments, a life therefore which can be intelligently and lovingly lived within the horizons of a properly human world: the true, the good, the beautiful.

In the traditional theory of liberal education, the unity of knowledge intended was metaphysical. Historically, this unity has been based on confidence in the ability of men and women to know the structure of reality, a structure seen as an ordered hierarchy of intelligibilities. Thinkers in this tradition have sought knowledge of the principles that are the source of intelligibility of a given domain, but what they have sought above all else has been knowledge of the ultimate principles of all things. Aristotle called such knowledge first philosophy or natural theology: what later came to be known as metaphysics. To it, in the Middle Ages and thereafter, was added speculative theology based on what believers considered to be the revealed word of God. In both cases, it was metaphysics/theology that provided the theoretic unification of all the rest. Although all theoretic knowledge was worthy of pursuit for its own sake, this was preeminently true of metaphysics. All the other "sciences" were ultimately for it: metaphysics/theology was the only truly liberal knowledge.

In the traditional view, the proper concern of "higher" education was the "highest" things that could be known by men and women and those things were not men and women and their works (and so not the humanities or the human sciences) or, still less, the things lower than men and women (and so not the physical and the natural sciences) but things higher than men and women, that is, the gods. Knowledge of the gods, it was felt, ennobled human beings and inspired them to become, in their various ways, like unto the gods.

The traditional curriculum reflected this structure but was organized pedagogically according to the order of learning, that is, the movement from things "more knowable by us" (for example, history and literature) to things "more knowable in themselves" (for example, the sciences and philosophy). Thus the trivium (grammar, rhetoric, dialectics) was concerned with the order of discourse and was instrumental in nature. The quadrivium (arithmetic, geometry, astronomy, music) was concerned with quantitative orders of reality. These orders were considered more superficial than the orders of reality revealed by philosophy and theology but were thought to be uniquely accessible to the understanding of young students. This program was preparatory to the study of the higher, more universal, and synthesizing orders that were the provinces of philosophy, theology, and law. A conscious, sixteenth-century effort to institutionalize this conception can be seen in the *Ratio Studiorum* devised by the Jesuits; their program involved six years of grammar and rhetoric, three years of philosophy, and four years of theology. Its influence on successive centuries was considerable. Such a hierarchical, metaphysical vision of the unity proper to liberal education is common to Aristotle, to Aquinas, and to Newman.

That vision has long since been shattered. Although glimpses of it can still be caught in the St. John's colleges (Annapolis and Santa Fe), in Thomas Aquinas College (Thousand Oaks, California), and in some other, often religiously oriented, liberal arts colleges, this metaphysically grounded vision of liberal education seems to many to be of merely historical interest. Not only has modern science thrown off the yoke of metaphysical/theological hegemony, but theologies and philosophies have taken to revealing themselves as queens, nay ever so humble maidens, without clothes, and have in fact been nonchalantly ravished by the sciences of man. Fideism in theology, the generally nonspeculative nature of contemporary religious studies, empiricism and positivism in philosophy, and the generally antimetaphysical tenor of contemporary philosophical writing have all undermined the intelligibility of classical liberal education. Indeed, the very principles that structured it are currently declared unknowable or worse: "myth," "transcendental illusion," "metaphysical gibberish."

Even those who consider metaphysics something more than foolish talk are no longer sanguine about the possibility of achieving a theoretic unification of our knowledge. Doubtless the task of articulating our knowledges into a coherent unity remains on the horizon of the philosophic effort, but the horizon continually recedes from our view. Not only is there no commonly accepted unification of our various discourses from the standpoint of theory but the unification of even a single discipline or field seems beyond the possibilities of any one person. Disciplines, specialties, and sub-specialties multiply at a staggering rate. What remains is a nostalgia, a parlous and inchoate desire for unity which expresses itself in the relatively recent vogue of inter-, multi-, and trans-disciplinary studies.

This lack of a theoretically unified focus for our academic pursuits is reflected in the condition of the faculty members who are responsible for liberal education. They are grouped in a disarray of disciplines to which they owe their primary allegiance. There are chairpersons for physics, for biology, for sociology, psychology, and history, but the vision which ought to inform the whole of liberal education in all its parts is the responsibility of no one: It is relegated to distribution or breadth requirements, to the limbo of general education, or to the uninformed choice of eighteen-year-olds. The abdication of their responsibility by faculties has been widespread, and although the pendulum seems to be swinging back from some of the more harrowing inanities of the later 1960s (with competence-based liberal education contributing, perhaps, in some small measure to this swing), a reasonably coherent faculty vision of the goals of liberal education is still almost everywhere lacking.

Why should it be otherwise? Professors are socialized into the disciplines. Not only do many of them have no clear idea of what liberal education has been, is, or might be, but they are not liberally educated themselves. They are sincere, intelligent, and competent in their particular disciplines; but they are not liberally educated—and they are not for the obvious reason that the majority of our colleges and universities have long since ceased being seriously concerned with liberal education. They have been concerned rather with specialization. This increasing specialization in all fields of knowledge dictates the work in the graduate schools whence the nonliberally educated professors come. The same emphasis on specialization in turn perverts the traditional liberal arts colleges not only in the form of professors whose interests are likely to be narrow even within the limited confines of their own disciplines but also in the form of programs that for years have been oriented to preparing students for graduate schools, where the dreary cycle repeats itself. This of course is news to no one. As Daniel Bell's (1966) account of past efforts to revitalize the liberal arts curriculums at Chicago, Harvard, and Columbia makes clear, this complaint has been constant for a hundred years.

In Chapter One of this report David Riesman has brilliantly limned the social, economic, political, and cultural contexts that have given rise to a widespread national demand for competence. Those contexts are of course also relevant to competence-based liberal education (CBLE). Although in quite different ways and with varying degrees of commitment, CBLE institutions have also adopted competence-based modes of education in the hope that they might: (1) survive; (2) respond to the needs of several new clienteles, for example, college-age students who are failure prone and generally ill prepared or older students with a wealth of life and work experiences who now need or want academic credentials; (3) break the faculty monopoly on knowledge and on the times and places of its acquisition; (4) take account of and manage the knowledge explosion; (5) promote interdisciplinary work and, generally, break down the disciplinary divisions and satrapies of knowledge; (6) render more flexible the temporal and spatial constraints of traditional education; (7) foster independent, self-paced learning; (8) provide a structure which promotes faculty development and renewal on a continuing basis; (9) respond to internal and external administrative demands for accountability and cost efficiency, and, doubtless, irrigate their parched gardens with a sprinkle of federal dollars.

    CBLE is a response to many problems, some of them more or less clearly recognized from the beginning, others not. Certainly one of these problems concerned the needs of new students who were living under a set of social, economic, and political circumstances markedly different from those which characterized an earlier world of liberal education. As we will see, CBLE is in large measure an effort to shape liberal education so as to meet what are thought to be the needs of these new students. But there is another, less obvious, problem to which CBLE may be seen as a response: the problem of faculty in liberal arts colleges. What needs to be said at this point is simply that, if it makes sense to see CBLE as a response to certain problems within liberal education and, in particular, to certain problems within liberal arts faculties, then CBLE challenges and interrogates all of us interested in liberal education. However we ultimately judge these new initiatives, many of the problems they are meant to address are of general import. In examining CBLE's approaches to these problems we must, at least implicitly, examine our own.

Competence-Based Liberal Education

    If one is aware of the heteroclite band of drummers in today's liberal arts colleges; if one has glimpsed something of the

mysterious odysseys students and faculty undergo as they pursue the
uncertain venture of trying to become educated; if one recognizes
the staggering diversity inherent in the institutions and agents of
liberal education—then one is likely to regard the task of specifying
the outcomes of liberal education as a rather large one. Might it not
be far more prudent to chant the mystagogical pieties with which
we habitually envelop our doings than to seek clarity about something as nebulous as the outcomes of liberal education?

Yet theorists ancient and recent have always sought to do so
and, in their own ways, the advocates of competence-based education seek to do so now. Aristotle was expressing what he thought to
be the outcomes of liberal education when he said: "An educated
man should be able to form a fair, off-hand judgment as to the
goodness or badness of the method used by a professor in his exposition. To be educated is in fact to be able to do this; and even the
man of universal education we deem to be such in virtue of his
having this ability. It will, however, of course, be understood that
we only ascribe universal education to one who in his own individual person is thus critical in all or nearly all branches of knowledge,
and not to one who has a like ability merely in some special subject.
For it is possible for a man to have this competence in some one
branch of knowledge without having it in all" [1937, p. 643]. Newman was likewise trying to describe the result of liberal education
when he wrote: "That perfection of the intellect, which is the result
of education, and its *beau ideal,* to be imparted to individuals in
their respective measures, is the clear, calm, accurate vision and
comprehension of all things, as far as the finite mind can embrace
them, each in its place, and with its own characteristics upon it"
([1852] 1959, p. 160).

Aristotle himself is, arguably, the only person who ever
realized his portrait of the liberally educated person, and George
Schuster suggests apropos of Newman's *beau ideal* that such a synthetic vision as Newman extols "is possible only with God" (1959,
p. 42). Both Aristotle and Newman thought it important to determine the end of liberal education in terms of its fullest achievement,
but in practice they were willing to settle for something less than the
ideal. Newman, for example, cheerfully admits that "there are few
minds susceptible enough to derive from liberal education any sort

of virtue adequate to those high expectations. We must be contented therefore to lower our panegyric to this, that a person cannot avoid receiving some infusion and tincture, at least, of those several qualities" (1959, p. 190).

These classic examples of Aristotle and Newman may serve to give some perspective to the difficult task of specifying the outcomes of liberal education in terms of a given set of competencies. Between Aristotle's fair, off-hand judgments or Newman's tinctures and infusions on the one hand, and various sets of competencies on the other, there is one obvious similarity: they are all outcomes whose presence or absence reasonably knowledgeable people can determine without too much trouble. Aristotle and Newman were naming the effects by which one could tell if a certain form of education "had taken"; if it makes sense to do that, then it surely makes sense to take the next step and to ask questions like this: *Can* this student make fair, off-hand judgments regarding the suitability of given methods in given contexts? *Can* the student show that he or she is properly tinctured and infused? *Can* the student demonstrate the possession of this or that set of competencies? We may smile at the notion of a properly tinctured and infused student, but granted the need for further specification, it does not seem foolish to ask these sorts of questions or to expect that they can be answered in fairly forthright ways.

It is just such a no-nonsense approach that proponents of competence-based liberal education take to their subject. In seeking to identify the basal competencies that would characterize the liberally educated person, they are doing much the same thing as Aristotle and Newman did when they sought to tell us how we could tell one if we saw one, and they are doing so in considerably greater detail than either Aristotle or Newman did.

The evidence for this outcomes-based approach to liberal education is derived from the experiences of several institutions. One is Alverno College in Milwaukee—the only institution in our sample that is primarily a liberal arts college and that has put its entire curriculum on a competence basis—and another is Justin Morrill College of Michigan State University—whose competence-based program is primarily an assessment program that involves neither courses, departments, nor teaching as these are ordinarily understood. In addition, there are competence-based courses in the liberal arts at Florida State University; there are clusters of courses in the traditional areas of liberal education at College IV of the Grand Valley State Colleges in Michigan and in the College of Public and Community Service at the University of Massachusetts at Boston; and there is a liberal arts tincture diffused throughout a professionally oriented curriculum at the College for Human Services in New York. Finally, a number of other liberal arts colleges beyond our project sample have conceived and begun to implement competence-based liberal education programs, including Mars Hill College in North Carolina, Our Lady of the Lake University of San Antonio, Bowling Green State University in Ohio, and Sterling College in Kansas.[1]

Among these pioneers of competence-based liberal education are several small, explicitly Christian colleges able to call upon motivations and mobilize commitments unlikely to be as intense in more secular or in larger institutions. In the late 1960s, they were faced not only with student and faculty restiveness of the sort then common throughout most of higher education but also with declining or potentially declining enrollments, with fears of not surviving, and, perhaps most significantly, with the reality of students less well prepared—often much less well prepared—than an earlier decade of students: students whom Cross (1973) has named the "new students." Each of these institutions had undertaken extensive curricular reviews and engaged in some curricular experimentation before hitting on the notion of structuring their curriculums in terms of clearly stated outcomes or competencies. At Alverno, for example, during one of the seemingly endless series of faculty meetings that had punctuated efforts at curricular revision over a three-year

[1] This evidence on competence-based liberal education is much less extensive than that on competence-based education in general for the other chapters in this book, but this paucity is compensated by several factors: A considerable body of literature on competence-based liberal education has been produced by these colleges; we were able to draw on a year's fieldwork as well as a site visit by the entire project team—some twenty-five person-days in all—at Alverno College, whose competence-based program was in a number of ways the most advanced and the most fully implemented of all the programs studied; and members of the project team interviewed faculty at a number of other liberal arts colleges, including those named above.

period, somebody wondered aloud whether the college might not consider structuring its entire program in terms of the outcomes that it sought to achieve—and this idea, apparently unanticipated, led to the radical revision of its program. Other institutions had similar experiences at about the same time.

At all these institutions the movement toward what came to be known as competence-based liberal education seems initially to have been self-generated; unlike a number of other institutions in our sample, these liberal educational institutions had been effectively engaged in rethinking the goals, processes, and contents of liberal education in terms of outcomes before FIPSE announced its "special focus" program in competence-based education and some federal money thus became available. They began on their own, trying to do better what they had already been doing or to reform their enterprise so that it would better fit the needs of new students and the requirements of new circumstances. In the process, it became apparent to some of these institutions that they were also doing something original and distinctive in structuring the whole educational program around a set of competencies, although it was generally after the fact that this was discovered. Most of these institutions did not know exactly where they were going or how they were going to get there. They did know that some changes were necessary and they were willing to risk themselves and their resources on a daring and laborious new venture.

A simple listing of the sets of competencies that such schools as Alverno evolved lacks any sense of the dramatic human contexts from which they emerged. In each case, the set finally agreed upon, even when that set was, so to speak, taken off the shelf—the shelf on which Bloom's *Taxonomies of Educational Objectives* (1956), Phenix's *Realms of Meaning* (1964), and Dressel's *College and University Curriculum* (1968) are found—was preceded by an enormous amount of faculty involvement, discussion, reflection, and argument over many months and, in some cases, years.

Because of limitations of space, only the generic outcomes or competencies which different faculties have judged to be commensurate with a liberal education can be listed here. Examples of the detailed specification of these general principles or statements into the levels and component parts that constitute the programs must be left to the case studies in this volume and to the descriptive literature produced by these colleges. But here are some general examples:

Alverno College

1. Develop effective communications skill (communication).
2. Sharpen analytical capabilities (Analysis).
3. Develop workable problem-solving skill (Problem-Solving).
4. Develop a facility for making value judgments and independent decisions (Valuing).
5. Develop facility for social interaction (Social Interaction).
6. Achieve understanding of the relationship of the individual and the environment (Environment).
7. Develop awareness and understanding of the world in which the individual lives (Contemporary World).
8. Develop knowledge, understanding, and responsiveness to the arts and knowledge and understanding of the humanities (Humanities).

Mars Hill College

1. A graduate of Mars Hill College is competent in communication skills (Communication).
2. A graduate of Mars Hill College can use knowledge gained in self-assessment to further his own personal development (Personal Knowledge).
3. A graduate of Mars Hill College comprehends the major values of his own and one foreign culture, can analyze relationships of values between the cultures, and can appraise the influence of those values on contemporary societal developments in the cultures (Cultural Values).
4. A graduate of Mars Hill College understands the nature of aesthetic perception and is aware of the significance of creative and aesthetic dimensions of his own experience which he can compare to other cultures (Esthetics).
5. A graduate of Mars Hill College understands the basic elements of the scientific method of inquiry, applies this understanding by acquiring and analyzing information which leads to scientific conclusions and appraises those conclusions (Sciences).

6. A graduate of Mars Hill College has examined several attempts to achieve a unified world view and knows how such attempts are made. The graduate is aware of the broad questions that have been posed in the history, philosophy, and religion of western civilization and can assess the validity of answers given to these broad questions in terms of internal consistency, comparative analyses, and his own position (Humanities).

One last list. As this is being written, the dean of an institution that has not been noted for its interest in CBLE and which is not among those in our sample has brought forth his own list of basal competencies after more than two years of faculty debate:

Harvard College

1. An educated person must be able to think and write clearly and effectively.
2. An educated person should have a critical appreciation of the ways in which we gain knowledge and understanding of the universe, of society and of ourselves.
3. An educated American, in the last third of this century, cannot be provincial in the sense of being ignorant of other cultures and other times.
4. An educated person is expected to have some understanding of, and experience in thinking about, moral and ethical problems.
5. We should expect an educated individual to have good manners and high aesthetic and moral standards.
6. An educated individual should have achieved depth in some field of knowledge.

In many ways these lists are unexceptional. Others like them have been generated by curricular committees for as long as there have been curricular committees.[2] As in other such exercises, the

[2] Well before there was anything known as a competence-based movement in liberal education, Stanley Idzerda, then dean of the college at Wesleyan University, summed up a conference on "the challenge of curricular change" sponsored by the College Entrance Examination Board, in the following way: "If nothing else, I may conclude that the particularistic Tower of Babel we have created in our time makes us look back to a simpler

language of these competence statements is not always constrained
by a sense of modesty. Indeed, there must be some scholars who
would be quite content if, after a lifetime of effort, they were able
to claim some measure of competence to understand the major
values of their own culture, to appraise the influence of those values
on contemporary societal developments, and to have attained re-
flective and critical perspectives on their personal and social growth
and on the quality of their interpersonal relationships. The competencies themselves are of very different sorts; for example, a
facility for effective social interaction is surely a different kind of
thing and is differently acquired than is an understanding of the
basic elements of scientific method, and the ability to make discriminating moral or esthetic judgments differs again from these.
There is, too, a good deal of overlap between some of the competencies, for example, analysis and problem solving. Though they
are intended to be reasonably inclusive, none of the lists set up by
CBLE institutions pretend to be exhaustive, and it is not difficult
to think of competencies that might have been included but rarely
are, for example, creativity, intuition, physical skills. Problem solving is often mentioned but never problem raising. Although each
of these lists is in principle a description of the liberally educated
person, there is sometimes a curious hesitancy internal to one or
another list regarding the adequacy of the list itself. Thus Alverno,
after enumerating seven competencies, adds the catchall competence of "knowledge, understanding, and responsiveness to the arts
and knowledge and understanding of the humanities"; another
institution includes a competency that requires the student "to
demonstrate experience in a concentrated examination of a problem
or topic through the techniques of the entire range of the liberal

---

and more self-confident set of ends. As I perceive these ends, they seem to run
in a continuum. The first end we appear to want is *competence*. We want a
student to be able to learn, to grow, and to have those skills that will enable
him to learn more. We want him to acquire competence in every tool and
every language that will help him to receive, to feel, to hear—to restructure
his experience so that he can both control it and be open to new experience"
(1966, p. 149). Idzerda then describes the additional ends in the continuum—
confidence, creativity, contemplation, courage, commitment, and compassion—but fails to say how we are to know if these ends are actually achieved.

arts." Any list of the outcomes of liberal education is likely to run into similar problems, and these lists are no exception.

What is exceptional is the decision to put the demonstrated achievement of a set of competencies, rather than a given set of required or elective courses, at the center of an educational program and to do so in such a way that all the parts of the program are defined by the set of competencies. Two basic requirements of a competence-based liberal education program are (1) a statement of outcomes and (2) a statement of the standards or criteria by which these outcomes will be assessed. The latter must be clear enough to allow faculty, students, and interested third parties to make reasonably objective and nuanced judgments with respect to the achievement or nonachievement of the stated outcomes. Is this principle being applied by the traditional liberal arts college that makes some statement of its general goals or intended outcomes and then declares that these are to be achieved by means of courses assessed according to the grading system listed in the catalogue? I think most will agree that the answer is no. Outcomes in CBLE programs must be specified in much greater detail than is ordinarily required in traditional programs. Further, it is the achievement of these outcomes that is credentialed, not the mere amassing of a given number of course credits. The definition of competence-based education given by O'Connell and Moomaw is explicit on this point: "A competency-based curriculum (CBC) consists, basically, of three components: (1) explicit statements of competencies learners are to acquire; (2) procedures for assessing achievement of competencies; and (3) learning experiences specifically designed for the attainment of the competencies" (1975, p. 1). This definition implies further that the components of the competencies are in each case explicitly assessed according to specific standards that are derived not from a general normative ranking of comparative performances but from the concrete behaviors appropriate to the components of the competence in question.

Note particularly here the words *concrete behaviors*. Competence-based liberal education not only controverts traditional practice by its emphasis on the assessment of specified competencies but it also controverts the traditional view of liberal education by its concern for behavior rather than for theoretic knowledge. Traditional liberal education, these proponents say, is not competence based, but knowledge based, and the knowledge it is based on is theoretic knowledge or more exactly, *merely* theoretic knowledge, characterized as "a detour from life into some ivy-covered sanctuary, just theory and cognitive level of knowledge" (Brownlee, 1974) or mere "information" (Alverno College, 1975). Russell Edgerton, formerly deputy director of FIPSE and now executive director of the American Association for Higher Education, points out that competence-based liberal education goes "beyond the notion that simply knowledge or understanding is to be the outcome of learning" (O'Connell and Moomaw, 1975, p. 6). It is concerned instead with competence that "involves not only knowledge but skills and attitudes" (pp. 5–6), and that involves "not just knowing but freedom of observation and of judgment exercised in behalf of purposes that are intrinsically worthwhile" (p. 46). What is required is "the competence to employ . . . knowledge effectively" (Alverno College, n.d.) and "not just theory and cognitive levels of knowledge but student involvement through the affective and psychomotor levels of learning" (Brownlee, 1974). In short, whatever the role of theoretic knowledge in relation to competence, competence is understood to involve something more than such knowledge.

As it is commonly understood, traditional liberal education is *for* the education of the intellect. Its principal value is that of knowledge for its own sake. What competence-based liberal education is for is expressed in different ways. The competencies actualize "the power to frame purposes and to execute or carry into effect purposes so framed" (Knott, 1975, p. 46); they "relate knowledge directly to what society needs and expects" and make students "more effective in practical ways in whatever roles [they] choose" (Alverno College, 1975, p. 4); they enable students "to use information, do something worthwhile with it, to make it work for them and others" (Alverno College, 1975, p. 20); they allow students "to perform a number of tasks and roles," "to do what they know" and thus to be "qualified to participate effectively in life" (Brownlee, 1974); they are the abilities requisite to becoming "a whole person—in short, a person who is competent" (Brownlee, 1974)'.

As portrayed in the literature of the CBLE movement, traditional liberal education is organized in terms of the disciplines. Its fundamental experiences are content-based courses in which teachers are the preeminent "dispensers" of knowledge, students the largely passive "receptacles" of knowledge. It is also time-based ("doing time") : so many courses over so many years to be traversed in "lockstep." It assumes that its processes will produce students possessed of a dazzling array of competencies, skills, and abilities, but in fact its processes are not designed to do this and generally do not do it in spite of what catalogues and commencement orators are prone to claim. Its criteria of assessment are normative and their principal function is to "sort people out" (this is bad; it is non-egalitarian, and tags some people as "losers"). It is elitist (this is even worse, for a variety of confused reasons). Insofar as proponents of CBLE are to some extent reacting against traditional liberal education, there will inevitably be an element of caricature in their portrait. They almost but not quite say that the principal products of these reified forms, materials and roles are the "elegant imbeciles" whom Newman ([1852] 1959) mentions.

Since in principle CBLE requires only that the student demonstrate the achievement of the competencies, teacher-dominated and time-bound courses are no longer the only or even the most important learning experiences available. The curriculum in some cases includes "all learning situations on and even off campus" (Brownlee, 1974). Teachers function less as "dispensers" of knowledge, more as "facilitators" of learning. The major responsibility for learning is the student's. The emphasis is "not on what the teacher teaches but on what the student learns" (Knott, 1975, p. 4), "not on a set of subjects but on the process of learning and on student responsibility for learning" (Brownlee, 1974). Since learning can go on in a variety of settings and times, CBLE promotes considerable flexibility in student itineraries and diversity of learning styles. The uniformities are neither contentual nor pedagogical nor temporal—there is great variety here—the uniformity lies rather in the set of competencies. These are meant to give coherence to all the activities of the college. Whatever the materials, times and places of instruction, whatever the roles of faculty and students, these are the outcomes for which the institution holds itself accountable at each step in the process. As the more important of these processes, namely, teaching and assessment, are the subjects of separate essays in this volume, I will concentrate here on the nature of the goals.

Competence and Liberal Education

Competence for what?

Let us recall that the arts which the ancients considered liberal were so considered because their purpose was the attainment of the mind's own good: truth. The truth they were concerned with was not practical or artistic truth—truth useful for doing something or making something—but theoretic truth: truth recognized as a value in itself; truth for its own sake. Practical and artistic knowledge, by contrast, were not considered valuable in themselves but only in terms of what they allowed one to do or to make. Newman ([1852] 1959) expresses the traditional view with elegant economy: theoretical knowledge, which he calls philosophical knowledge, "is liberal education."

Strictly speaking, the liberal arts and liberal education are not the same thing, although there is a certain amount of overlap between them. The liberal arts, whether classic or contemporary, are only prelude to and instrument for liberal education. Liberal education either presupposes (as in Europe) or includes (as in this country) a degree of mastery of these arts, but it is generally understood to consist in some mix of the physical, biological, and behavioral sciences, along with mathematics, history, literature, philosophy, and theology. Its traditional hallmark is scientific or philosophical knowledge. Liberal education, in Newman's phrase, is university education.[3]

---

[3] What "university education" might mean in the peculiar historical context of the American "liberal arts" college poses a familiar conundrum. A bachelor's degree in the arts or sciences does not signify merely preparatory, preuniversity education, but neither does it quite signify university education, even when it includes a major in one of the disciplines.

In fact, CBLE programs are cast in the mold of the four-year American college and typically include some version of a major concentration in

The liberal arts are arts, that is, they involve making or producing or constructing, but they are not practical arts; rather, they are speculative arts. Their concern is speculation, not in the pejorative sense common today but in the sense of speculative or theoretic knowledge as contrasted with practical knowledge. They are called liberal because of the kind of knowledge for which they are the instruments: theoretic or scientific or philosophical knowledge, knowledge freer than all other forms of knowledge because independent of desires other than the desire to know. In other words, the liberal arts, traditionally understood, derive their liberal character from the free and independent nature of the knowledge they serve.

As we will see in more detail further on, the liberal arts *also* have their practical functions and uses. Here it is enough to recall that the liberal arts are liberal because of the nature of the end that they serve.

I want now to say two things about the lists of competencies from Alverno and Mars Hill colleges insofar as they relate to liberal education: (1) it seems to me beyond doubt that most, perhaps all, of the generic competencies listed earlier are analogous to the logical, linguistic and mathematical arts of the ancient trivium and quadrivium; (2) but they are, properly speaking, analogous to the classic liberal arts only to the extent that theoretic knowledge retains a central place in competence-based liberal education. Whether theoretic knowledge does in fact retain such a place is in doubt. I will discuss these two points briefly before taking up the question of the role of practical knowledge in competence-based liberal education.

---

one of the disciplines or some form of preprofessional training. Were CBLE solely concerned with a contemporary version of the liberal arts designed for students who have not yet achieved any significant mastery of these arts, then the situation would be much clearer than it is. Were this the case, we could hail CBLE as a pioneer of a future two- or three-year American college of the liberal arts which would be just that: a college of the liberal arts. There would be, I suspect, great advantages to such a limited, clearly circumscribed version of CBLE, but for fairly obvious historical and institutional reasons this is not the model that extant programs incarnate. The latter are concerned not only with the liberal arts; they are concerned also with liberal education. And so the competencies they seek to develop are not only arts but also involve theoretical and practical knowledge.

What does a student "do" when he or she "does" communication, analysis, or problem solving, if not involve himself or
herself in very specific ways with the "makings" of the spirit, that
is, with the constructs by which the mind orders its materials? These
and other generic competencies are arts because they involve, not
doing or acting, but making or producing or constructing. As Vincent Smith says:

> The liberal arts are arts because they involve con-
> struction. The logician makes definitions and arguments,
> the grammarian makes sentences and paragraphs, the
> rhetorician orders his expressions . . . mathematics as
> an art constructs numbers and figures. Music, as a
> mathematical art, makes harmonies, and, as mathemat-
> ical, astronomy and other branches of mathematical
> physics make special constructions like the eccentrics
> and epicycles of Ptolemy, the ellipses of Kepler and
> Newton, the operators of Schroedinger. Sciences that are
> not arts—such as metaphysics, strictly natural science,
> and sacred theology—do not construct their objects but
> find them ready-made outside the mind. If there is any
> construction in these sciences of objective things, the
> constructive character arises from the logical mathe-
> matical instruments used by the sciences in question and
> not from the matter actually being studied through the
> instruments applied. The construction comes from the
> fact that these other sciences employ logic [1960, pp.
> 97–98].

Although it is not possible here to analyze the parts, sub-
components, and levels, of the various generic competencies, I
believe such an analysis would show that the processes and operations grouped under headings such as "communication," "analysis,"
"synthesis," "problem-solving," "humanities," or even "valuing" encompass and illustrate most of the constructions that in times past
were the province of the logical, linguistic and mathematical arts.
Interestingly, at Alverno and Mars Hill, communication, which
tends to be the most clearly worked out of the competencies at
these schools and elsewhere, specifically includes the materials of

grammar, logic and rhetoric, as well as several of the mathematical arts. But in different ways and combinations, analysis, synthesis, problem solving and much of what is included under sciences and humanities are likewise arts. Of them and their role in CBLE it is appropriate to say, as does the catalogue of St. John's College (Annapolis): "The primary function of the liberal arts has always been to mediate men's understanding, to give conscious form to knowledge through systems of signs accommodated to men's intellects—that is, words and numbers. Traditionally, the liberal arts were seven in number: grammar, rhetoric, logic—the arts of language; and arithmetic, geometry, music and astronomy—the arts of mathematics. In contemporary terms, man practices such liberal arts as analyzing, thinking, writing, speaking, and deciding as he used verbal symbols; man practices such liberal arts as counting, measuring, deducing, and demonstrating as he used mathematical symbols."

Indeed, one may be tempted to push the parallel between the old wine and the new bottles even further. The ancients recognized two sources of new knowledge: learning by discovery and learning by instruction; two fundamental mental operations: induction and reasoning (or syllogism); and four basic forms of argument: demonstrative, dialectical, rhetorical and literary. No doubt what is known has grown immeasurably since the Middle Ages, but is it not likely that the specifications of the generic competencies reflect these sources of knowledge, these mental operations, these forms of argument as basic to what is called "communication," "problem solving," and "analysis"? Whatever the advantages of the new taxonomies and their translation into competencies it seems appropriate to regard many of these competencies as arts in the classic sense.

One may of course wonder whether these competencies are only new bottles and whether the spiritual stuff being decanted is really the old wine. Does the rearrangement of the classic *artes liberales,* or their contemporary equivalents, in terms of one or another list of competencies provide any new insights into what these arts are about? By and large I do not think so. But there is one possible exception. Gary Woditsch of Bowling Green State University has derived a set of what he calls "genotypic" competencies from a variety of sources in the behavioral science literature of this century. He claims that the intensive research in the field of cognition lends credence to the proposition "that there are generic cognitive capabilities, that these are not genetically fixed but in significant ways educable, and that their state of development is highly predictive of, among other things, what gains an individual can realize from subsequent formal education" (Woditsch, 1977, p. 7). Without claiming that his list is exhaustive, he (1977, p. 36) names five such competencies:

1. Selective attention: ability to control the class of stimuli which receive conscious focus.
2. Sustained analysis: a capacity to probe a complex situation until all its components are identified.
3. Analogizing: a capacity to test known relationships for similarity with those potential to a new situation.
4. Suspension of closure: prioritizing (synthesizing) factors before shaping solution.
5. Autocensorship: testing a solution covertly, before affirmation.

If the assumption underlying Woditsch's extrapolation is correct, namely, that there are identifiable and relatively invariant genotypic competencies that are at play in all cognition, then it seems to me that the competence-based movement, in liberal education and elsewhere, would be possessed of a new epistemological basis for its endeavors. These genotypic cognitive competencies would be the deep structures, the invariant a priori forms at play in all learning much in the way that Chomsky claims that there are certain highly abstract principles of organization at play in the acquisition of language.

In Woditsch's schema the development of these genotypic competencies would be the business of liberal or general education— in effect, the first two college years. Their phenotypic articulation and elaboration in specific contexts, for example, the disciplines, would be the business of the third and fourth college years and, indeed, of all future learning. The genotypic competencies, however, remain context-free: they are universal modes of organization. The various arts by which we order the materials of our knowing would themselves be illustrative of these deeper structures, and the liberal arts might well remain the preferred (but not the only) means for raising these deeper structures or capacities to a given level of performance.

We need not attempt to judge here the validity of Woditsch's neo-Kantian conception of what competence-based education is trying to get at—namely, basal cognitive competencies—but his conception does have an exemplary clarificatory power in that it delimits the domain of competence to *cognitive* competence and in that it offers nonarbitrary grounds for a list of competencies.

Woditsch's conception, moreover, makes explicit something of value that is implicit in all the different lists of competencies: all of them name or refer to analogous types of mental operations. For example, analysis in physics is not the same thing as analysis in biology and neither of them is the same as analysis in literature or in metaphysics. But analysis in any one of these areas is analogous to that engaged in in the others. In making explicit the analogicity of these different operations, the competence named "analysis" dramatically emphasizes a central feature of liberal education: the transferability (the ana-logicity) of its characteristic procedures from one domain to another. No less a traditionalist than Scott Buchanan observes:

> The great advances in the last three hundred years are usually celebrated as the successive triumphs of empiricism in science. It may seem absurd to say that this is the latest battle cry of the grammarians, but it is connected with the next previous battle cry which argues for the retention of Greek and Latin grammar in the school curriculum on the ground that students trained in these grammars were quicker and keener in scientific observation. The psychological controversy about transfer of ability from one subject matter to another always hangs on the discovery of common properties in the subject matters. It is not hard to find them in this case. As great an observer as Galileo spoke of his work in mechanics as decoding the book of nature, and he even gives us the middle language by which he made his translations, namely, mathematics. The trick in finding the

common ground for the bookworm grammarian and the observer of nature is not a difficult one. There is no more trickery in it than finding that Greek translates into English. It is only necessary to take stock of the languages one knows. There is the language in which we speak and write as members of the English culture group. There is also the language of an imagery in which we speak to ourselves and perhaps our families or best friends. There is the language of our gestures both conscious and unconscious. There is the language of our daily rituals such as washing, eating with knife and fork, wearing neckties and trousers or skirts; by all these we say that we belong to European culture and believe its rules of prudence. But back of all these lies the nonartificial world of nature or as much of it as we are sensitive to, and all our languages, in so far as we are judged to be sane, bear an analogical correspondence to this basic language [Buchanan, 1938, pp. 27–28].

If we ask the faculties that devised the different lists of competencies: Do these lists name the competencies of the contemporary "liberal artist"? they might well respond: Yes, the rosters are perhaps incomplete but that is not important; there is nothing sacred about the seven liberal arts of tradition.

Granted that, however, the question concerning ends with which we began immediately arises: competence for what? Are these competencies really intended to be the competencies of the liberal artist? Are they instruments intended to be used in the further pursuit of liberal education? Or are they to be understood in a quite different sense, for example, as useful in helping one to earn a living in Milwaukee? In other words, what is the role of theoretic knowledge in competence-based education? Are the competencies, above all, the instruments of liberal studies or not? And if not, what happens to the delicately poised edifice of liberal education? There are two things to be said here: (1) that theoretic knowledge has a role in competence-based liberal education; (2) that there is a question whether that role is not only compromised but subverted by the emphasis of competence-based liberal education on the practical.

A number of observers, skeptical of the behaviorist tendencies of the competence-based movement and disdainful of the effort to "quantify the unquantifiable," are inclined to scorn its incursions into liberal education as just one more aberrant pursuit of technicist phantasms on the part of "educationists" who know not what they do. For them CBLE can only be a low-grade form of training in which anything resembling theoretic knowledge and the tradition of humane learning is largely irrelevant. Others, struck by the egalitarian, strongly antiintellectualist tone of some of the CBLE rhetoric, annoyed by its boosterism and its tendency to caricature traditional academic values, distrustful of its repetitive insistence on doing, on know-how, on effectiveness, on action, are inclined to dismiss CBLE as a utilitarian travesty of liberal education, an archetypically American espousal of managerial pragmatism, a thinly veiled capitulation to the forces of vocationalism and professionalism.

If only on the basis of the sampling cited above, it would be difficult to deny that there is an antiintellectualist tone, a utilitarian cast to the CBLE rhetoric, as well as elements of exaggeration and of caricature. This is distasteful; but, more importantly, it is misleading. Even the more dubious aspects of this rhetoric are capable of—and, I believe, merit—a more benevolent interpretation than they are often accorded.

It should not be forgotten that proponents of CBLE are reacting against an entrenched and powerful tradition as well as, in many cases, a good chunk of their own pasts. They also represent small, hitherto unheard and unheard of institutions, some of which have been catapulted into the vanguard of a nationally modish movement. A certain amount of exaggeration, caricature of traditional ways, and outright bombast are probably inevitable. Nor are some of the more obstreperous leaders of the movement incapable of using the outrageous statement, claim, or charge for their own political purposes. But one need not take the rhetoric of CBLE any more seriously than one is inclined to take the rhetoric of traditional liberal education. In both cases one is better advised to consider actual practice.

In practice, CBLE's emphasis on the practical ends of liberal education does not mean that theoretic knowledge ceases to have a central role in CBLE. Although we have argued that some of the competencies are arts—indeed, liberal arts—and others involve practical knowledge, it remains true that "understanding" and its cognates are the terms most often used in the descriptions of generic competencies. That the understanding in question is often theoretical understanding seems certain. Although CBLE does emphasize the competencies and the processes of education more than it does a sacrosanct set of disciplinary contents, it should not be imagined that the importance of theoretical knowledge as it is articulated by and in the disciplines is ignored. In those institutions (for example, Mars Hill and Our Lady of the Lake) that have derived their sets of competencies from the work of Phenix, the competencies are themselves expressions of the methods of inquiry and the modes of understanding characteristic of a cluster of related disciplines. Thus the competence variously labeled "understanding the environment," "problem solving," "acquisition and use of knowledge," or simply "sciences" in fact refers to the modes of inquiry and understanding in the natural sciences; the competence called "synthesis" or "synoptics" or "humanities" in fact refers to the modes of inquiry and understanding in history, philosophy, and theology. Phenix (1964, p. 10) himself insists that "the content of instruction should be drawn entirely from the fields of disciplined inquiry." Similarly, at Alverno, where the competencies are not so directly tied to specific disciplines, it remains true that their competencies are taught *through* disciplinary contents. Moreover, even at Alverno, which has devised some remarkable procedures for the assessment of its competencies, most of the assessments are still quite traditional and content based.

The competencies may indeed—unquestionably do—involve more than theoretic understanding but the important point here is that many of them *do* involve such understanding as of course the disciplines themselves do. At Justin Morrill, at Alverno, at Mars Hill, professors who have taught in CBLE programs claim that they are able to teach *more* of their disciplinary content than ever before. In other words, they find that they are able to pursue farther and in more detail the theoretic understandings, which are the fruits of disciplined inquiry, while at the same time emphasizing the liberal arts, which are the instruments of such inquiry.

On this crucial issue CBLE literature often belies CBLE practice; there is, as we noted, a tendency in the literature to dismiss theoretical knowledge as "mere theory" or, even worse, "mere information," but in practice theoretic knowledge and its pursuit seems to retain a central place. Newman's realistic and modest requirement that a student not be able to "avoid receiving some infusion and tincture" of "philosophical knowledge" appears to be easily met in CBLE programs.

Nonetheless, the question arises whether the role traditionally accorded to theoretical knowledge pursued for its own sake can be meaningfully maintained in programs oriented in large measure to practical outcomes. Though skeptical that it can be, I do not know the answer to this question. There is some evidence that there are many mansions in the house of competence-based liberal education, and these programs may develop in quite unanticipated ways. Meanwhile, theoretic knowledge does remain central to competence-based liberal education, but it is not the only or even the predominant end of the educational process. Practical knowledge is equally valued; indeed, it is somewhat more equally valued than is theoretic knowledge.

Competence-based liberal education manifests a significant shift of emphasis with respect to the ends of liberal education: a shift from the primacy of the theoretic to the primacy of the practical. Before exploring this shift in more detail, let us recall that traditional liberal education, although primarily concerned with theoretic knowledge—with its transmission where it is possessed, with the search for it where it is not—is also concerned with practical knowledge, if in a carefully circumscribed way. As already noted, its interest in how things are made is limited to the arts by which the mind constructively orders its products: the liberal arts. Its interest in how things are done is limited to the kind of doing that is of preeminent importance in human life: moral and political action. Its concern here is with the practical, normative knowledge of how human actions are to be ordered—with, therefore, the principles of moral and political action insofar as these principles can be a subject of teaching.

Practical knowledge of how things are made (things which, unlike the liberal arts, exist outside the mind, for example, painting, sculpture, music, or dance) has no legitimate place within the traditional understanding of the curriculum of liberal education, and that for two reasons: these arts are by definition not liberal, and they cannot be learned by instruction from a teacher. They are learned rather by practice or by following the example and counsel of a master, a mentor, or a coach. They are not the business of a college but of an atelier or a conservatory. Similarly, practical knowledge of how human actions other than those of the moral and political life are to be performed also has no legitimate place in the curriculum of liberal education as classically understood but is rather the concern of vocational or professional schools.

Now it is clear that competence-based liberal education controverts these traditional views in a number of ways. To begin with, theoretic knowledge—Newman's philosophical knowledge—is no longer the keystone that holds the edifice together. On the contrary, proponents of competence-based liberal education proclaim as clearly as can be that what is wanted is not just knowledge, and certainly not "mere" theoretic knowledge, but the skills, abilities and attitudes that enable one to use knowledge effectively. Such practical knowledge, as the Alverno catalogue (1975–76, p. 5) unabashedly puts it, is "the most important part of a truly 'liberal' education." Indeed, it is even claimed that this practical knowledge of which the competencies are the component parts is the kind of wisdom which should characterize "the whole and effective individual" or "the whole person, that is, the competent person."

Competence for what? In a number of instances this personalist rhetoric seems to suggest that the competencies in question include certain moral competencies, for example, the ability to do something "effective" or "worthwhile" or the ability to become "a whole person." Presumably these are morally good things to do or to be (Query: Is it a morally good thing to be a whole person? Response: I should say so!), and in that sense, along with its other benefits, competence-based liberal education would enable us to teach moral virtue. That would be a fine thing indeed, but some may think that there is a potential confusion that occasionally afflicts the rhetoric of the competence-based movement with regard to practical education of "the whole person."

There are many different practical knowledges, skills and

abilities that men and women possess, and most of these, in themselves, are value-neutral: they can be used to serve any ends. The ability to analyze, to communicate, or to solve problems is equally useful to businesswomen, thieves, saints, swindlers, and college presidents. But there is one form of practical knowledge that is not value-neutral, namely, the ability to judge correctly in the moral and political affairs of men. Such knowledge, though it is knowledge, is rooted in and cannot exist without moral rectitude, which is more than knowledge. It exists only in the morally good person. It is the habitual ability to give reasoned expression to what is, truly, worthwhile in human life: the ancients called this ability practical wisdom. And if there is a practical knowledge which ought to characterize the whole person, it is surely practical wisdom in this sense. But such wisdom is the end of all the educational agencies within a culture, not of formal education.

Competence for what? What kinds of artistic or practical knowledge does competence-based liberal education foster? Does it foster the speculative, the fine, the useful arts? Is it engaged in promoting the knowledge and skill requisite for a competent nurse, business administrator, community action leader, lawyer, doctor, plumber? One of the problems in the literature of competence-based liberal education is that all these different artistic and practical activities tend to be lumped together as an indiscriminate know-how, ability, skill, or competence. Some distinctions would be helpful, particularly with regard to the practical functions of the liberal arts. Unfortunately, there is a tendency to confuse the practical functions of liberal education and the proper ends of liberal education. This is of course not at all unique to competence-based liberal education, but it is competence-based liberal education that we are concerned with here.

Different programs emphasize different kinds of practical knowledge, but in fact the CBLE institutions we have some knowledge of are career-oriented in specific ways. Alverno, for instance, promotes what is called "liberal learning in a management context," and the practical goal intended is to provide the student with the means—the know-how—to assume various sorts of "managerial" roles, especially in nursing and in education. To a greater or lesser extent, depending on the program, liberal education is identified with the knowledge and skills requisite to be a nurse or teacher or manager or something called a "change agent." Current CBLE practice emphasizes the job-related nature of the skill it promotes. The reasons for this are complex. They reflect the reformist tendencies of CBLE (see, for example, Chapter One) and they also involve a "hard sell" directed to what are thought to be the needs of particular student clienteles.

From the standpoint of traditional liberal education, this kind of career-oriented education is not liberal education at all. The underlying problem here is of course not unique to competence-based liberal education; few indeed are the American "liberal arts colleges" that have not made a variety of concessions to, and compromises with, the careerism, vocationalism, and professionalism rampant in our culture. Proponents of competence-based liberal education, as well as others, like to justify their own compromise in this regard by pointing out that liberal education has always been professionally oriented: to theology, law, and teaching in the Middle Ages, to teaching and the learned professions today. That many people educated in liberal arts colleges have in fact gone on in these fields is no doubt true but it does not seem valid to infer from this that liberal education is therefore professionally oriented. The fact that many people educated in liberal arts colleges go into the professions "proves" only that many people educated in liberal arts colleges go into the professions. It tells us nothing about the nature of liberal education.

This issue cannot be further debated here but one can ask questions about this career-orientation of competence-based liberal education. For example: if one is going to include the practical knowledge and skill appropriate to nursing or accounting in the curriculum of liberal education, is there any reason *in principle* to exclude car repair and basket weaving? In other words, what criterion can one use to decide which types of practical knowledge should be included within the curriculum of liberal education? Proponents of competence-based liberal education seem to have no clear opinion on this matter.

In fact, CBLE would seem to confuse this issue in new ways. In grouping different kinds of arts and practical knowledges under common competence etiquettes, CBLE tends to undermine any meaningful distinctions among disciplines or kinds of practical knowledge. To the extent that the kinds of practical knowledge (or of theoretical knowledge, for that matter) appropriate to philosophy, history, literature, accounting, nursing, classroom management and medical technicianship all count as "analysis" or "problem solving," CBLE would seem to obviate even the possibility of distinguishing between liberal education and professional or vocational or career education. There may indeed be some analogies among analyses in philosophy, in chemistry, in history, in medicine, and in automotive repair, but there are also important differences; unless all education is to be dubbed "liberal education," some account needs to be taken of these differences.

The crucial issue here is what one takes to be the proper end of liberal education; if that end is, as the ancients thought, knowledge pursued for its own sake, then these various kinds of practical and artistic knowledges and skills, however valuable they are in themselves, are not the proper business of liberal education. On this view, the only "doings" worthy of attention in liberal education—and then from a theoretic point of view—are moral and political action. All these competence-based liberal education programs include a competency, generally called "valuing," that roughly corresponds to moral and political philosophy as normative disciplines. The ancients would have stopped there; they would have limited their curricular concern with practice to the philosophy of human action; they would not have thought it their business to turn out Jacks and Jills of all trades.

There is, however, another and somewhat more benevolent way of regarding competence-based liberal education's insistence on practical competencies. I suggested above that theoretical knowledge continues to play a role in competence-based liberal education even though the emphasis on the practical tends to subvert that role and, thereby, to undermine what traditionally would have been considered central to liberal education. Let us imagine now a college in which the role of theoretical knowledge retained its primacy of place but in which there was a lively interest in the competence-based liberal education movement. How might that movement be interpreted and adapted to such a "traditional" liberal arts college? Let me suggest two ways.

First, insofar as theoretic knowledge remained at the center of the formal education process, there would be no confusion about what the competencies as liberal arts were for: they would be *for* theoretic knowledge, useful *for* the physicist, the chemist, the biologist, the social scientist, and the philosopher *as theoreticians*. But that is not all that they would be for.

Second, our traditional college would avoid the even more serious confusion of mistaking a *practical function* of liberal education for the proper end of liberal education. Clear on the distinction between the *theoretic ends* of liberal education and the *practical functions* of liberal education, our traditional college could afford to ignore the misleading and confused rhetoric of some parts of the competence-based movement and to concentrate on what may be its real contributions to a more vital and responsible liberal education.

It has always been supposed that liberal education has a practical function. The judgment of the tradition that theoretical knowledge is the heart of liberal education is itself a practical, moral judgment. Such an education, it was thought, is eminently practical for a human being since it best fits the person for a truly humane life. It has also been supposed that the liberal arts, as well as liberal studies, though worth pursuing for their own sakes, are also useful in making rational decisions in the varied realms of human action. Something that is an end in itself, theoretic knowledge, for instance, or sex, can also be a means to other ends. "Although the useful is not always good," Newman reminds us, "the good is always useful," and on that principle he bases his classic statement of the usefulness of liberal education:

> And so, as regards intellectual culture, I am far from denying utility in this large sense as the end of education, when I lay it down that the culture of the intellect is a good in itself and its own end; I do not exclude from the idea of intellectual culture what it cannot but be, from the very nature of things; I only deny that we must be able to point out, before we have any right to call it useful, some art, or business, or profession, or trade, or work, as resulting from it, and as its real and complete end.

Again, as health ought to precede labour of the body, and as a man in health can do what an unhealthy man cannot do, and as of this health the properties are strength, energy, agility, graceful carriage and action, manual dexterity, and endurance of fatigue, so in like manner general culture of mind is the best aid to professional and scientific study, and educated men can do what illiterate cannot; and the man who has learned to think and to reason and to compare and to discriminate and to analyze, who has refined his taste, and formed his judgment, and sharpened his mental vision, will not indeed at once be a lawyer, or a pleader, or an orator, or a statesman, or a physician, or a good landlord, or a man of business, or a soldier, or an engineer, or a chemist, or a geologist, or an antiquarian, but he will be placed in that state of intellect in which he can take up any one of the sciences or callings I have referred to, or any other for which he has a taste or special talent, with an ease, a grace, a versatility, and a success, to which another is a stranger. In this sense then, and as yet I have said but a very few words on a large subject, mental culture is emphatically useful [Newman (1852), 1959, pp. 181–182].

Even more germane to our present subject is the magnificent exordium with which Newman ends his essay on "Knowledge and Professional Skill":

If then a practical end must be assigned to a university course, I say it is that of training good members of society. Its art is the art of social life, and its end is fitness for the world. It neither confines its views to particular professions on the one hand, nor creates heroes or inspires genius on the other. Works indeed of genius fall under no art; heroic minds come under no rule; a university is not a birthplace of poets or of immortal authors, of founders of schools, leaders of colonies, or conquerors of nations. It does not promise a generation of Aristotles or Newtons, of Napoleons or Washingtons, of Raphaels or Shakespeares, though such miracles of nature it has before now contained within its precincts. Nor is it content on the other hand with forming the critic or the

experimentalist, the economist or the engineer, though
such too it includes within its scope. But a university
training is the great ordinary means to a great but ordinary end; it aims at raising the intellectual tone of
society, at cultivating the public mind, at purifying the
national taste, at supplying true principles to popular
enthusiasm and fixed aims to popular aspiration, at
giving enlargement and sobriety to the ideas of the age,
at facilitating the exercise of political power, and refining
the intercourse of private life. It is the education which
gives a man a clear conscious view of his own opinions
and judgments, a truth in developing them, an eloquence
in expressing them, and a force in urging them. It
teaches him to see things as they are, to go right to the
point, to disentangle a skein of thought, to detect what is
sophistical, and to discard what is irrelevant. It prepares
him to fill any post with credit, and to master any subject
with facility. It shows him how to accommodate himself
to others, how to throw himself into their state of mind,
how to bring before them his own, how to influence
them, how to come to an understanding with them, how
to bear with them. He is at home in any society, he has
common ground with every class; he knows when to
speak and when to be silent; he is able to converse, he is
able to listen; he can ask a question pertinently, and gain
a lesson seasonably, when he has nothing to impart himself; he is ever ready, yet never in the way; he is a
pleasant companion, and a comrade you can depend
upon; he knows when to be serious and when to trifle,
and he has a sure tact which enables him to trifle with
gracefulness and to be serious with effect. He has the
repose of a mind which lives in itself, while it lives in the
world, and which has resources for its happiness at home
when it cannot go abroad. He has a gift which serves
him in public, and supports him in retirement, without
which good fortune is but vulgar, and with which failure
and disappointment have a charm. The art which tends
to make a man all this is in the object which it pursues as
useful as the art of wealth or the art of health, though
it is less susceptible of method, and less tangible, less
certain, less complete in its result [Newman ´(1852), 1959,
pp. 191–192].

Though language in our day seems no longer capable of such lofty diapasons, some of what Newman says here is not different in principle from what the proponents of CBLE also say. CBLE has taken as one of its ends the promotion of some of these practical functions of liberal education. To be sure, these practical functions are, in the traditional economy, functions of a theoretic end, but for the moment we need only note that CBLE takes these practical functions with great seriousness. Such skills and abilities, such casts of mind and delicacies of manner, such a wondrous display of *savoir faire* as Newman here praises have ever been claimed to be the inseparable adjuncts of liberal education and to be its uses and its practical ends. There may be some irony in Newman's portrait. In his day as in ours, the practical usefulness of liberal education for some Oxonians consisted largely in a knowledge of which tweeds to wear on which occasions; and surely this admirable concatenation of an ideal gentleman's exquisite competences no more characterized the scruffy Dublin teenagers who passed through Newman's noble hands than they do the ordinary graduates of our university colleges. But that is just the point in a way. Similar claims *have* always been made for liberal education but they have generally remained mere claims; self-serving, indolent, almost always unverified suppositions. Though their ideal of the liberally educated person is hardly the aristocratic English clubman Newman extols, proponents of CBLE take seriously the acquisition of some such set of competencies as a practical end worthy of liberal education. Along with "philosophical knowledge," the realization of these competencies is also considered central to liberal education. CBLE makes this explicit and structures much of its educational endeavor in such a way as to assure, insofar as it can, that these competencies will in fact be acquired. Rather than count on serendipity and wishful thinking in this domain, CBLE marshalls intelligence and requires performance.

Of course many of the qualities which Newman mentions in his extraordinary paean are not learned by instruction, but his example is invoked to make a general point about the kind of practical and artistic knowledge that, on this view, CBLE seeks to foster. It seems to me that it can be characterized as a certain cleverness, dexterity, flexibility, or adroitness that comes from having done a great variety of things, such as analyzing chemical compounds and

economic situations, solving problems in physics, literary interpretation, and pedagogy, communicating statistical information, aesthetic
appreciations, and moral values. Here is where the transferability of
the liberal arts from the domain of the speculative to that of the
practical is relevant: the skills of the liberally educated person are
also useful for formulating clear alternatives and making reasoned
choices in the realm of practical action. Those competencies which
are neither speculative arts nor proper to theoretic understanding
are the components of a general practical knowledge: a set of
trained, general capacities or skills or abilities that can be brought
to bear in a broad variety of circumstances. There are of course
more particular forms of practical knowledge. Vocational or professional programs designed to train carpenters or nurses or lawyers
would have to identify the specific components of the particular
forms of practical knowledge that are carpentering, nursing, lawyering. This need not be the task of liberal education.

   The assumption that liberal education is useful in these practical ways underlies the traditional claim that liberal education
prepares for no one of the professions or callings of life but that it
prepares for them all. Proponents of CBLE are well aware of this
but they think that they have broken new ground here. For good
or for ill, CBLE emphasizes these practical aspects of liberal education more than traditional liberal education does, and it does this
in two ways: along with but inseparable from the other components
of competence, these practical aspects are at the center of the educational endeavor; they are also verified, that is, assessed, somewhat
differently in traditional liberal arts programs. In the long run it is
perhaps in this latter area of careful and detailed assessment that
CBLE will be seen to have made its most important contribution.
Though student acquisition of many of the liberal and practical arts
is often assessed in ordinary paper and pencil ways, other assessments are also used. Since all students are required to demonstrate a
certain level of competence in these skills, and to do so in quite
specific ways, there would seem to be greater assurance in CBLE
that students do achieve these levels than there is in less specific,
curved grading systems. More importantly, as both Chapters Three
and Four in this book indicate, the imaginative teaching strategies
and assessment instruments in CBLE seem to promote a highly

critical awareness of the nature of these arts. Judgments are difficult to substantiate here, but since CBLE requires that teachers (or others) spend much more time on assessment and be much more clear about what it is they are assessing than traditional liberal education does, it seems likely that increased critical awareness is an outcome. Moreover, the assessment procedures themselves often involve diagnostic teaching of a tutorial sort. Learning in such a situation is, more often than not, not learning through instruction but through practice, through emulation, or through simply doing it the way you are told, through what R. L. Stevenson called "sedulous apery." The teacher here becomes a coach or mentor who communicates a certain style and taste and feel which cannot be learned through instruction. The principles of logic, perspective, or grammar can be learned through instruction but to construct a logical argument or paint a picture or write a paragraph requires something more. In insisting that students not only know the principles but know how to use them effectively in practice, and in carefully and critically assessing their ability to do so, CBLE does well what is often done badly or not at all in more traditional settings.

An Outcome

It is axiomatic, I believe, that an innovation in liberal education is worthwhile in the measure that it contributes to the liberal education of faculties. If it does that, it is also likely to be good for students.[4] In my view, the principal effect of competence-based

---

[4] There is no section on student outcomes in this essay because it is too early to be able to say much, if anything, about this subject. Some professors and administrators claim that students in competence-based liberal education programs are more able than equivalent students educated under the old programs at their institutions, presumably because of competence-based liberal education; some students see themselves as more able than their peers at other institutions, presumably for the same reason. Other students and faculty members are not so sure. In addition, in the early years of some of these programs, student dropout rates have been quite high—over 25 percent in the first two years at Alverno, for example. Faculty turnover has also been considerable. No doubt there are a number of reasons for this, but dissatisfaction with one or another aspect of competence-based liberal education is probably one of them.

Looking to the future, what might be relevant measures of student

liberal education programs to date—the most evident single outcome if one prefers that language—has been its contribution to the liberal education of faculties. Here at least the claim of the competence-based movement that process is more important than content would seem to apply. At least in some instances, the process of developing and implementing a competence-based program has itself constituted a kind of continuing faculty seminar in liberal education.

The decision of a faculty to rethink their activities and their goals in terms of outcomes initiates a process that, if it is seriously pursued, can lead a faculty to rethink the very bases of what they take to be liberal education. Ordinarily, the question of the nature of liberal education is not directly addressed—it is a discomfitting question whose discussion is easily dismissed as fruitless—but it inevitably comes up when one is attempting to name the effects by which one could recognize that significant liberal education had taken place. For an entire faculty to engage in such an interrogation and to do so over a period of many months, as happened at Alverno College and at Mars Hill, is striking. Even if nothing had come of it—and for a long time it seemed to many faculty members involved that nothing would come of it—this kind of "philosophical" discussion, even indirect, of the nature of liberal education is a worthwhile outcome. It is just the kind of conversation that ought to be going on in colleges of arts and sciences but almost never seems to be.

One does not undertake an innovation like competence-based education in order to have a conversation, but once the specific questions raised by an outcomes-oriented approach are encountered it is difficult for faculty members to avoid a public discussion of their philosophies of education and a recognition of their corporate responsibility to articulate a vision of liberal education. Such a dialogue concerning the ends of liberal education has always been an essential part of liberal education, but it is not unusual to find faculty members who have never seriously engaged in that dialogue. In those places where it has been tried, competence-based liberal

outcomes in competence-based liberal education programs? Over what time span? With all the other measuring going on in these programs, a long-range comparative study of student outcomes here would seem both appropriate and useful. Newman thought his gentleman would be one in real life, not in the artificial and constructed circumstances of a battery of discrete assessment procedures.

education seems to have helped to bring these faculty members out of their caves. Individuals find themselves required to think about both their disciplines and their teaching in new terms and eventually to question whether what they are doing and how they are doing it is in fact related to the achievement of given competencies. Once a competence-based liberal education program is underway, such discussions tend to become commonplace. Faculty members now share at least some common aims and some common problems, for example, how is the textual analysis I do in my Chaucer course related to the analysis she does in organic chemistry? Are there comparable presuppositions or levels of complexity? Is there any discernible progression in the sophistication of the analysis between my sophomore poetry course and my senior seminar on the erotic elements in the poetry of Elizabeth Bishop? If so, what are the components of this progression? Are they comparable with what is being done in the advanced chemistry courses? Once begun, such a process, like psychoanalysis, is likely to be interminable. It is a process that can lead to new and greatly expanded colleague networks and can propel faculty beyond the confines of their own disciplines. It can promote, as Peter Elbow shows in provocative detail in Chapter Three of this volume, much more critically conscious teaching than conventional programs do. It can even happen that faculty members engaged in such ongoing discussions with colleagues in other disciplines find themselves unable to "avoid receiving some infusion and tincture," in Newman's splendid phrase, of liberal education. Certainly the professors who have involved themselves in this process claim at least this.

There is a further advantage to the process. The competencies in terms of which one is asked to rethink one's discipline and one's teaching are, broadly considered, a contemporary version of the ancient liberal arts. Discussions of analysis in literature and chemistry can lead one beyond traditional disciplinary concerns, and a prolonged concern with analysis, its different types and levels and nuances, can lead one to predisciplinary concerns. It can lead to a critical, professorial mastery of the liberal art of analysis; likewise with the other arts of competence. A mastery of these arts is in principle a presupposition of all of the disciplines, for professors and students alike. But not all professors are confident of their mastery here and students are sometimes even less confident of theirs. Competence-based liberal education can involve a kind of rediscovery of the liberal arts on the part of professors, in behalf of the students. To the extent that it does so, it tends to emphasize the predisciplinary at least as much as the disciplinary. Here it is the processes of analysis, communication, and problem solving that are more important than any particular content. The choice of the great books is left to the professor, but the great books are in some ways secondary to the great processes, that is, the arts of analysis, of communication, of problem solving, and others. The unexamined process is not worth living! The central business here is not placating the disciplinary superegos or even transmitting the shards of a common culture but helping the young to acquire the instruments of scientific and practical understanding: some of the arts of competence.

The arts of competence. Always the question remains, "Competence for what?" But however one answers that question, it is worth noting that a given set of competencies offers *a* form of unification to the varied activities we name liberal education and in that sense CBLE provides at least a partial response to some of the problems within liberal education sketched earlier in this essay. Whether one understands the competencies as liberal arts or as different practical functions of liberal education, they are in any case no longer the private affair of one or another department but the common objectives of the whole college. Competence-based liberal education tends to loosen the grip of the disciplines on the structure of liberal education, to lead professors to expand their interests outside of their disciplines, in short to promote among the faculty an interest in a crucial sort of liberal education: their own. For that at least faculties should be held accountable.

In using heuristically one interpretation of traditional liberal education, we have, in a way, put CBLE to a severe test, one which, in all probability, very few contemporary programs of "liberal education" could meet successfully. Whether CBLE is liberal education according to this standard remains an open question. And perhaps one would want to reject this standard, but that is just the point: CBLE forces us to reinterrogate our standard of liberal education. Is CBLE liberal education? Who is to judge? And on what grounds?

Virginia Olesen   6

Employing
Competence-Based
Education for
the Reform
of Professional
Practice

୲୨୲୨୲୨୲୨୲୨୲୨୲୨୲୨୲୨୲୨୲୨୲୨୲୨୲୨

The professions in America, long regarded as the sacred repositories of idealism and service, in the last decade have become one of the most contentious areas of national life:

- Patients, transformed to the new role of "consumer" and unhappy with health care costs, demand that medicine come under regulatory scrutiny.
- Physicians and nurses, ever edgy about the overlap of their pro-

fessional domains, become more so with proliferation of new work for nurses and new group forms of practice for physicians.

- Lawyers, initially swept up in the era's rising adversary proceedings and malpractice suits against physicians, increasingly find themselves the targets of such suits.
- Social workers are beleaguered by pressures from clients and strained with regulatory considerations governing eligibility for, nature of, and dispersal of all types of assistance.
- Those who are dispossessed, whether by virtue of sex, ethnicity, religion, or physical handicap, view professional roles and practice as elitist bastions to be breached by their numbers in the interests of redressing old inequities and assuring new services.

At the root of these complex problems lie two essential questions: What place have the professions in American society? And how are practitioners performing the work mandated to them by professional privilege and public assent?

These questions are not new, of course, to the American mind. They have informed much of the history of the professions in America, and, given the place of the professions in American life, it is likely they will continue to do so. Recently, however, some professional training programs and schools have attempted to respond to these concerns with an educational philosophy known as competence-based education. The encounters with this educational view raise the following questions—questions that form the focus of this essay: How are demands for reform in the professions accommodated by reform impulses in the competence-based movement? What are, to use the very language of competence-based education, the possible "outcomes" of this approach? Is there anything innovative or distinctive about uses of competence-based education in professional curriculums that has not characterized those curriculums previously? Where, if at all, will reform be realized with this educational philosophy? What do the practitioners, implementors, and others associated with this movement say with respect to the major issues in American society that the professions face, those that they may create and those that they attempt to solve? What does the competence-based movement contribute to the improvement of professional work, to performing the professional mandate in a more useful way?[1]

These two sets of key questions, one from the side of the professions and the other from the perspective of the competence-based movement, are presented as a way of understanding the points at which the concerns of the professions and the themes within the competence-based movement converge. That movement is complex, diffuse, and highly variegated. To assume that a first-hand infusion of competence-based ideas or a straightforward adoption of its elements has taken place in professional schools would be far too simple, but the links between competence-based ideas and education in some medical or nursing programs are relatively clear, for instance at Mt. Hood Community College, near Portland, Oregon, where an innovative nurse-educator brought precise behavioral management to the college, or at Southern Illinois University's medical school, where physicians in charge of the new curriculum sought out educators expert in mastery learning and competence-based education. The question of the links, however, while important to understanding the dissemination of competence-based ideas and subsequent changes in education for the professions, is of less concern in this essay than the potential for reform that competence-based education seems to afford those professions whose schools or training programs adopt variants of it. What precisely transforms reform impulses in the competence-based movement into catalysts for change in professional practice and place of the professions must await other analyses. For now our task is to comprehend what we know about competence-based education and its contribution to professional reform. To do that, it would be useful to review briefly

---

[1] This essay holds that the term *profession* refers to a certain type of occupation that is not necessarily one of the classical trio of law, medicine, or theology (Becker, 1962). Although it is true that the characteristics of (a) esoteric knowledge, (b) admission of neophytes by highly qualified individuals, (c) and dispersal of sanctions for inadequate performance are not shared to the same degree by social workers, doctors, engineers, pharmacists, nurse practitioners, ministers, and schoolteachers, to name but a few, professions are occupations wherein performance—that is, both tasks and human service—is regulated by those already admitted to the guild on the basis of the particularized knowledge they possess.

the history of reform in American professions and then to discuss in detail the meanings of competence-based education and where trends and themes in this movement offer the potential for reform.

Trajectories of Reform

The distribution of competence within recognized professions and the regulation of those who could be admitted to the ranks are by no means new issues. Joubert, a sixteenth-century French physician, collected and published folk remedies of the time so that "empirics" and "midwives" who utilized these remedies and were thought to be incompetent and dangerous could be better controlled (Davis, 1975). Indeed, prompted by lack of competent or even adequate care for the wounded at Scutari during the Crimean War, Florence Nightingale undertook, among her many other reforms, the upgrading of nursing care through the recruitment of gentlewomen who would receive thorough training in a hospital, something which did not exist for the "nurses" of the day.[2]

In the United States, the issue of competence in the professions must also be understood as an arena in which long-standing tensions among egalitarianism, individualism, and social ascent have been in play. The relationships among the contemporary professions of law, nursing, and human services are no exceptions to this; indeed, some of these relationships and their origins can best be interpreted in light of this triumvirate of American cultural themes. Whereas in the United States during the eighteenth century, efforts were made to differentiate the professions and elevate standards, this gave way in the nineteenth century to the leveling impact of Jacksonian democracy and the attempt, for instance, to permit all those of moral worth to practice law in New York State (Calhoun,

---

[2] Attempts to reform the professions frequently focus on recruitment of trainees, as the Flexner report indicated. Both Florence Nightingale's effort and those of the College of Human Services focus on moral attributes of social class membership as the key: Nightingale sought gentlewomen of good station for training to improve standards in nursing, the College stresses recruitment of poor persons, particularly from depressed ethnic minorities to educate in order to utilize their backgrounds for the enrichment of human services. In both instances training would channel the desired attributes to improved professional performance.

1965). This was the era wherein legislatures withdrew compulsory medical licensure, took away recognition from medical associations, discarded hierarchic distinctions among lawyers, and loosened restrictions on who could practice law, and when congregations asserted preferences for a more exciting and less authoritative ministry.

These leveling influences in turn gave way in the late years of the nineteenth century and the first decades of the twentieth to increased concern in the professions with standards of practice and education. This concern reached a climax with the Flexner report on medical education in 1919, a veritable scalpel that cut to the bone of the medical establishment, occasioning threats against Flexner's life and the institution of lawsuits against him (Stevens, 1971). The surge of reform in practice and standards also touched law and theology through the investigations of the U.S. Bureau of Education. Such private foundations as Carnegie, that had supported the Flexner inquiries,[3] were thus joined in the reform movement by the federal government. These reforms, it should be noted, focused primarily on the institutional contexts of medical education (diploma mills where teaching conditions were filthy and equipment was nonexistent), the background of students (who henceforth would have to hold the bachelor's degree before starting medical school), and the content of the curriculum (scientifically based medicine would come to be the rule) rather than the upgrading of adequate performance, though it was hoped this would follow.

The report's consequences were far reaching. For all its inadequacies, pre-Flexner medicine did allow those without privileged position to enter medical studies and practice. This was not subsequently possible, and medicine was fixed as an elite profession to which only those who had access to the university could aspire (Junitz, 1974). The impact of the report intertwined medical

[3] The interesting historical point which should not be lost here is that the major earlier reforms in the professions of medicine, law, and theology were instituted through the work of the Carnegie Foundation and in nursing by another private foundation, Russell Sage. The role of FIPSE in the study on which this essay is based is both similar and contrasting: Although a federally funded agency and subject to congressional scrutiny, the Fund in its organization functions essentially as a foundation within government.

education with the hospital, as well as with the university, adding further to the complexities that we know today.

The surge of late nineteenth-century professionalism also influenced legal education, prompting a movement away from apprentice training in law offices. A Carnegie commission, headed by Alfred Z. Reed, studied legal education, but the commission report did not have the sweeping effect of the Flexner document. Instead, it was the concern of practitioners themselves for public protection against unscrupulous lawyers that led to increased emphasis on standards of performance, bar examinations, and the movement of law schools into universities, where the case method emphasizing principles rather than the practice of law become ensconced (Thorne, 1973). The importance of the law school was further enhanced when most states began to require graduation from law school as a prerequisite for taking the bar examination. Only California, Pennsylvania, Rhode Island, and Vermont now offer the option of sitting for the bar with four years of experience reading and preparing cases in a licensed attorney's office in lieu of law school. Correspondence courses, unaccredited law schools, and fly-by-night entrepreneurs, in addition to the better night schools, still survive to train people for law—thus providing access for nonelite students that the upgrading of medicine shut off—but the contrasts between these types of legal education and the university schools constitute major parameters in framing subsequent careers in law.

More recent pressures for adequate clinical training in legal education antedated, but were also spurred by, demands rising out of the civil rights movement of the 1960s and 1970s for equitable access to legal services. David Riesman has pointed out to me that David Kavers, founder of the Duke University Law School's *Journal of Law and the Social Sciences,* had been talking about clinical legal education and a two-year law course several decades before the civil rights movement. These clinical courses, as one observer has noted, in most schools do not transform the curriculum; they are additions, and in some have led to little more than clerical experience for the students involved (Thorne, 1973). Partisans argue that these courses prepare new lawyers who will be familiar with clients and practice, while opponents score the intrusion of practice into the acquisition of legal theory.

The concern of educators for reform in nursing—in contrast to medicine and law—has long been tied to behavioral outcomes emphasized in the curriculum. Those reforms in the late nineteenth century drew from the practice-based Nightingale system. Indeed, Nightingale herself participated in the reforms by correspondence to ensure that stress would be placed on early hospital experience for students. (In contrast to medicine, where many students do not see a patient until the second or third year of training, most nursing schools assign students to patients within the first weeks of training.) Historically, nursing in America has searched ceaselessly for evaluation methods that would enhance education and result in a better "product" (the profession's term, not this author's), this search originating in part because of the early association of nursing education with educational psychology at Columbia's Teachers College.

These tendencies have been heightened by the shift of nursing education away from hospital schools, where it had been located from 1873 onward, to universities and then to community colleges. This move was further prompted by the American Nurses Association's controversial position paper of 1965 in which it was resolved that the basic educational level for professional nurses was to be the bachelor's degree and the minimum for technical nurses the associate of arts degree. This resolution, the focus of considerable debate within the profession between educators and practitioners, merely carried forward what early leaders had promoted and what two major reports on the reform of nursing education, the Goldmark Report of 1923 and the Brown Report of 1948, had strongly recommended. This emphasis, however, necessitated that both types of programs, university and community college, place even greater stress on behavioral outcomes. University schools found that they had to assure that their graduates, trained in theoretical materials as well as in practice, could in fact practice well, while community college faculties wanted to secure their newly achieved place in the health care field with graduates who could perform competently. This would make the community college curriculum in whatever field a fertile place to root competence-based education, for as Thomas Ewens has commented, the competence-based emphasis would license these and other colleges to claim that their graduates were as well educated as those of university or traditional programs.

In these several professions, reformers hoped for improved performance by stressing the recruitment of better students (for example, by restricting admission to medical schools to university graduates.) They thought that altering the site of preparation would lead to beneficial change: medical schools were linked to the hospitals, law schools emerged to supplant the law office as the site of apprentice training, and nursing programs left the hospital for universities. Reformers also attempted to upgrade curriculums; thus, a number of the leading schools of medicine (Western Reserve, for example), law (Yale), and nursing (University of California at San Francisco) introduced the social sciences in an effort to humanize professional practice.

But what was not emphasized in these gropings for improved professional practice was the development of concern for what the professional did, once he or she had graduated. Where professional reform took education as its locus, graduates were assumed to be adequate, competent, efficient, and ethical: it was assumed that exposure to the educational program resulted in absorption of the necessary skills and virtues. Those responsible for professional training in the post-Flexner era and beyond were concerned with educating a competent practitioner, of course, and were competence oriented in that sense. But they did not demand that students demonstrate competence in the performance of most professional *tasks,* even if students were required to show they had mastered the *content* of the curriculum presumed to be relevant to competent practice, and their programs were thus not competence based in the modern sense. Examinations for state licensure in dentistry in California are perhaps an exception to this, those examinations being conducted by observation and evaluation of actual practice on a patient.

Perhaps this failure to consider demonstrated competence as a basis for graduation from professional schools (if not for the certification or licensure of practitioners) lay in the idealism of the professions. Faculty in most schools were themselves practitioners who were considered representative of the ideals of the profession, and it was thought that as role models for students their skills and knowledge would engender competence in students. Moreover, students, motivated by the ideals of the physician, lawyer, nurse, social worker, or pharmacist, would surely perform adequately in light of those ideals of service to others. Cloaked with the moral responsibilities of service, they were placed above questions of competence, since to practice medicine, law, nursing, social work, or pharmacy was a near-sacred form of activity pursued in the interests of one's fellows, the good of society, the enhancement of mankind.

Then, too, this failure to require demonstrated competence in graduates may have been the result of a cognitive lag. Residues of the earlier reforms may well have led educators in the profession to believe that their programs were in fact competence-based. After all, would not the graduate who is admitted to practice be competent, having been trained by those already in possession of the particular knowledge and skills that constitute the heart of the profession? (This assumption overlooks that students can learn negative, even incompetent, performances from instructors who use sarcasm, humiliation, or excessive stress in their teaching. See Mendel and Green, 1965.) And besides, there were few follow-up studies in those years to determine how well graduates performed; competence could thus be assumed for every physician or lawyer who avoided malpractice suits, every nurse who kept a job, all social workers who were not reprimanded, and all pharmacists who ran profitable drugstores.[4]

The events of the 1960s and 1970s shook these views. Spurred by the militance of the civil rights movement, minority groups demanded better and less costly medical care, equal access to legal services, and better teaching to enable their children to climb out of the barrios and ghettos into a richer life. Setting their sights on the all-Caucasian, all-male preserves of the major professional training schools, minorities and women argued that they had been shut out long enough. Their opportunity to share in the sacrosanct responsibilities of professional care had been stunted too long; their chance to move upward in American society through

[4] One exception to this was an earlier study that suggested that some practitioners ought to be decertified as incompetent (Peterson and others, 1956). Subsequently, other studies (Mechanic, 1974; Turner, Helper and Kriska, 1974; Cooper, 1976; Doyle and Ware, 1977) have in fact begun to redress this deficiency in medical education, as has certain work in nursing (Lewin, 1977; Kramer, 1974; Olesen, 1973).

the powerfully elevating professional training programs had been denied too often. Simultaneously, both the belief that the professions operated humanely and justly and the assumption that competent practice was an automatic consequence of exposure to professional schooling came to be questioned (Millman, 1977).

At the same time the growing complexities—both technical and bureaucratic—of the settings where professional services were received (hospitals, schools, and public service agencies) increasingly frustrated and depressed the average, as well as the deprived, citizen. Dehumanization became the watchword and citizen complaints escalated. Costs of educating children, receiving the attentions of a physician, buying drugs from a pharmacist, or taking a case to court also spiraled upward. Public disenchantment with dehumanized and costly professional services in every sector from teaching through medicine came ever more frequently to public attention. The very frequency and prevalence of the complaints, criticisms, and lawsuits catalyzed consciousness raising about inadequate and incompetent services and about the place of the professionals who render those services. This dynamic gives no sign of abating.

These events energized impulses for reform in American professions which had become stultified by the professions' own and others' images of their practice and place in American life. What are these reform impulses? They include demands for (1) increased access to professional training, (2) greater excellence in that training, including development of greater sensitivity to human needs in the trainee, and (3) alteration of the profession and thus of society at large. Before examining how these impulses for reform achieved some salience in competence-based education programs, it will be useful to review the meaning of competence-based professional education in general.

Competence-Based Professional Education

This discussion uses the definition of competence-based education offered by Gerald Grant in the Prologue: "Competence-based education tends to be a form of education that derives a curriculum from an analysis of a prospective or actual role in modern society and that attempts to certify student progress on the basis of demonstrated performance in some or all aspects of that role. Theoretically, such demonstrations of competence are independent of time served in formal educational settings." Professional programs, of course, also prepare students for definite occupational roles that they enter either by passing state licensure examinations (medicine, law, nursing, pharmacy, teaching), or through affiliation with a specific professional field where licenses are not necessarily at issue (urban and regional planning), or through role definitions made by students themselves in the areas of advocacy and social change (human services, public and community service).

Grant's definition also highlights a number of crucial features of competence-based professional education—not only the reform aspects of certain programs but the innovative features as well. First, to derive a curriculum from an analysis of the professional role may not seem, on the surface, particularly striking, since some professionals, particularly in nursing, medicine, and law, would argue that this in fact is what has historically been the case. Thus medical or nursing students spend blocks of time in medical, surgical, and pediatric settings, learning the way practice is organized. However, the analysis of the professional role that has occurred in such competence-based programs as Mt. Hood's nursing program, the Antioch School of Law, and the University of Minnesota's pharmacy program literally atomized this role, breaking it, particularly at Mt. Hood, into highly discrete tasks and behaviors. These endeavors involved the assistance of professionals in the field, and, in the case of nursing at Mt. Hood, the cooperation of patients who were asked what they thought nurses do, based on their experience with nurses. While the University of Minnesota's pharmacy program did not derive its curriculum from panels of professionals and consumers, it uses such panels for its assessment program. This consultation with practicing professionals and consumers links its academic pharmacy program to the actual world of practice.

Second, this effort to tie the learning of professional skills closely to their practice attempts to bridge the ever-present gap between educators in professional schools and practitioners in the real world into which students will graduate. The importance of this effort, carrying an impetus for reform, cannot be underestimated, for the tensions between educators in professional schools, who believe themselves to be in the vanguard of professional innovation, and practitioners in the fields, who see themselves as in touch with practice "as it really is," are endemic in every professional field, creating problems both for educators who prepare students, practitioners who receive them, and—not least of all—the students who find themselves unwitting carriers of educational innovations, in the form of new practice learned, into settings where the innovations are neither known, nor understood, nor appreciated. (See Olesen, 1973, for a description of the problem that a baccalaureate-degree nurse has in being accepted as a college-educated nurse bearing many of the newer ideas in nursing care.) Thus, the core feature of competence-based professional education in some institutions involves bridging this long-standing tension between educators and practitioners. To this end, the urban planning and nursing programs at Florida State University use juries of professional practitioners from the community to evaluate students' competence, and the College for Human Services in New York City uses agencies to certify student progress. Many community college or baccalaureate nursing programs attempt to seek the opinions of staff nurses about student progress, but the Florida State program goes further in giving the nonacademic nurse on the evaluating jury the same power as the academic faculty to certify or refuse to certify students.

Third, these programs graduate students only after certifying them as competent in their professional role. This certification takes various forms in different programs; the College for Human Services demands completion of a "constructive action" by which the student demonstrates human services skills and competence—a project that the student must define, outline, and, if possible, undertake independently. The College of Public and Community Service of the University of Massachusetts at Boston developed certificates in key areas (housing and community development, human growth and development, legal education, cultural studies, individual and society, management and transformation of institutions, essential skills), and awards these certificates for performance of the competencies specified in each area. Mt. Hood Community College demands that nursing students perform timed nursing tasks in the practice laboratory before going on to the wards. Southern Illinois University's medical school elaborated very precise learning modules that are to be passed in each problem unit, at the end of which a cumulative module must be completed as well. Throughout these and all the other competence-based professional education programs analyzed, the outcomes have been made explicit in advance, the ways to reach the outcomes have been set out in great detail, and these ends and means have been in full view of both students and faculty.

Fourth, this emphasis on student mastery of competencies, whether by time trials in a nursing laboratory at Mt. Hood or by an argument in court for a client at Antioch Law, has not necessarily meant that instructors are relegated to the past. Where nursing or medical students, for example, have contact with patients in situations involving serious consequences for patient and student alike if errors occur, faculty guidance remains necessary. But some pressure is taken off the instructor, particularly with the use of modularized learning packages (one such package describes fully what Southern Illinois students are expected to learn about renal problems, and another tells what the Mt. Hood student should know about and be able to do for cardiac arrest) and when students receive ample opportunity for rehearsal and retrial, often at their own individual pace.

Fifth, these programs all involve the final element noted in Grant's definition: flexible time. They make use of flexible time in different ways, however. At Florida State, for example, movement through the curriculum of attainments is not time-bound in any way. At Southern Illinois, the medical students cannot accelerate their programs and the curriculum is not "open-ended." But because the demands on their time are not yet well analyzed and understood, students have an opportunity to repeat modules, blocks, and even years, if necessary. Some element of contracting or stretching time is apparent in all competence programs. This may be a matter of times to learn very precisely defined tasks, such as learning to measure blood pressure correctly in the Mt. Hood nursing laboratory, or a question of a total program, such as taking several extra years to complete the program or accelerating through it in much less time than usual. The idea that students can handle time differentially, whether in a finite way or broadly across the curriculum, is itself innovative in professional education, where the usual way students progress through professional programs is in lockstep. Opportunities to extend or shorten the length of study add, however, to faculty burdens, for students who are out of sequence, whether moving more slowly or more quickly than their fellows, need special attention, attention that becomes added to the usual round of faculty work. At Mt. Hood, for instance, instructors had to administer tests for slow or fast pacers at the same time they were working with students who were progressing normally.

To summarize, the points where elements of competence-based education appear in the professional programs reviewed here include the precise specification and articulation of components of the professional role (sometimes stated as behavioral outcomes), the assistance of practitioners and clients in this articulation, the certification of students only on demonstration of these components of professional role behavior (sometimes with the help of practitioners), and the use of individualized strategies that permit alteration of usual time frames. Some of these elements are particularly reformist and innovative in bridging the gap between professionals and practitioners.

Reform in Professional Education

The three demands for reform in professional education that competence-based programs attempt to meet are: (1) *increased access to professional education for denied groups,* (2) *excellence in professional practice,* and (3) *alterations of the structure of the profession and of society.*

Access for Denied Groups. Educators in professional schools seeking to reform their programs would recast this question of access as an issue involving retrieval, recruitment, and retention of denied and dispossessed students. Admissions policies designed to bring minorities and women into law and medicine, males into nursing, and the underprivileged into the fields of human or community services can be undertaken without reference to competence-based reforms. Such policies, however, benefit from certain features commonly associated with competence-based education. In every program studied (including one of the two programs not in the immediate sample for the FIPSE study) the competence-based curriculum allowed disadvantaged or unusual students to make use of individualized pacing. Some of these programs have already been discussed in the previous section and need not be reviewed here. But we can note that at the College of Public and Community Service, students develop individual learning plans that they follow in completing their certificates and that take into account their age, life goals, and future interests. Seattle Central uses a similar system in its managerial program. At Florida State University, the pacing elements in the nursing program allow students to move as quickly or as slowly as they need to.

Self-paced systems, however useful, cannot assure retention of some students whose background is so seriously disadvantaged that even pacing cannot help. At the Antioch Law School, for instance, only a disappointingly low 10 percent of the disadvantaged minority students who initially completed the program were able to pass the bar exams, resulting in the recognition that basic skills had to be in hand and that acceleration and tutoring could not overcome the lack of these skills. Antioch subsequently set higher test score requirements for admission. Similarly, at Mt. Hood, not even the fast- and slow-pacing system could accommodate the problems inherent for males in learning a "woman's" profession—the initial dropout rate of the male students exceeded their percentage in the program—and some administrators were concerned that students who should not be retained were able to continue because they could slow their pace greatly.

In spite of these shortcomings, the competence-based ideal of freeing students from the rigid constraints of time provides professional schools with the possibility of retaining unusual or "different" students and doing so in ways that are not seen as invidious. This strategy of flexible time is an answer to traditionalists' complaints about lowered standards; thanks to the variable time frame, it is possible to train new students to acceptable standards, which in some instances had been derived from practitioners and consumers. The import of this reform can scarcely yet be estimated. In nursing at Mt. Hood and medicine at Southern Illinois University, for example, students can be retained, yet faculty members can assure

Table 1. Elements of Competence-Based Education and Reform Impulses in Ten Professional Programs

School	Reform Issues Which CBE Elements in Program Address			
	Access to Training for Denied Groups	Excellence in Professional Practice	Alteration of the Profession or of the Social Order	Special Characteristics of Program Vis-à-Vis Other Training Programs in the Profession
Alverno College (Nursing)	Pacing provided	Alverno learning process plus some nursing competencies	No	Mix of Alverno learning process in pre-nursing year plus some in nursing program organized on non-block system. "No obsolete products."
Antioch School of Law	Pacing provided	Lawyering skills defined	Yes: graduates to bend legal profession more towards service to the poor	Interpersonal skills stressed as well as case learning. Skills derived from consultation with lawyers. School is also law firm where students "intern."
College for Human Services	Variation in time allowed for completing "constructive actions"	Areas of excellence, constructive actions	Yes: graduates to become change agents, socializers of others, for example, clients	Utilization of students' backgrounds as resource; jobs negotiated for students as part of program; agencies also charged with student assessment.
University of Massachusetts, Boston College of Public and Community Service	Individual learning plan	Certificates in key areas of competencies	Yes: students to become advocates of social institutional change	Certification of competence gained elsewhere.
Florida State University (Nursing, Urban Planning)	Pacing possible	Curriculum of Attainments	No	External assessors acting as final juries in fields in which students are graduating.

	Pacing	Assessment scheme		
University of Minnesota (Pharmacy)			No	Competencies and assessments identified through panels of faculty, students, practitioners and consumers of pharmacist's services.
Mt. Hood Community College (Nursing)	Pacing possible	Nursing competencies articulated	No	Nursing competencies built on patient panel idea of nursing behaviors; timed lab rehearsal of tasks prior to ward assignment.
Seattle Central Community College	Pacing	Certificates for passing competencies (not courses), assessment seminar	Partial	Recognition of students' backgrounds as preparation of new image of self as manager.
Southern Illinois University (Medicine)	No fast pacing; recycling	Integrated competencies	No	Cumulative competency objectives to assure maintenance of competencies once achieved.
Syracuse University (Teacher Training)	Pacing possible	Mini-courses	No	Close integration of teacher training with teachers in field.

Note: Detailed information on these competence-based programs and the orientations to reform are available in case studies that may be obtained from Syracuse Research Corporation, with the exception of the University of Minnesota School of Pharmacy and Southern Illinois University Medical School, which were not in the sample studied by the Project Team. Information on those programs may be obtained by writing Thomas Cyrs, Jr., director, Competency-Based Pharmacy Curriculum, University of Minnesota, Minneapolis, Minn. 55455; and Reed Holland, director, Competence-Maintenance Program, Southern Illinois University School of Medicine, Springfield, Ill. 62708.

themselves that their own professional standards will be met. Yet, as at Antioch and Mt. Hood, reformers not infrequently found that even with variable timing, admissions standards had to be raised to adjust their idealism to the realities of low completion rates or excessive student difficulties.

Excellence in Practice. This reform impulse characterizes the goals of the whole range of programs. Practice here is defined as exercise of professional skills and as achieving more humane relationships with clients. To accomplish this, Mt. Hood stresses the personalizing of nursing care along with the performance of technical skills, and the Antioch Law School emphasizes interviewing and effective ways of relating to clients as essential skills for lawyers. To assure excellence, assessment procedures are finely honed. Indeed, at Mt. Hood, a precise behavioral management system that faculty thought crucial for assessment in their competence-based program proved too precisely honed for students' taste and led to a major crisis. Other programs, mindful of the gap between education and practice, have charged agencies where students have jobs to help with assessment. Still other programs name juries of practicing professionals to evaluate students as they finish their professional training. Alverno's faculty, which did not want to produce "an obsolete product," has interleaved the "Alverno learning process" in the nursing students' first-year preparatory courses and throughout the curriculum. (The "Alverno learning process" refers to competence-based programs that utilize both individualized learning in key areas and community juries.)

Another and bolder strategy to achieve excellence is found in those programs where students' own backgrounds and experiences are deemed worthy resources for the improvement of professional practice. At the College of Public and Community Service, as well as at Seattle Central, students can be certified for competence gained earlier elsewhere in life, and at the College for Human Services, life experiences of former addicts, "street people," and the urban and minority poor are regarded as a resource for the enrichment, improvement, and alteration of human services. This represents a new type of "professional knowledge" of a very special sort not acquired in the classrooms or schools of social work, and thus not available to even the most well-intentioned professional educated in the usual school of social work (Rieff, 1974).[5] As one student at College for Human Services put it, "We [the former outsiders] are now getting the credentials, but there's a lot more than there is in the books, a lot more which *we* know." This utilization of disadvantaged people's knowledge as a key to excellence is seen by the college to exert a multiplier effect, for their persons, their histories, and their influence on and for equally disadvantaged clients are all harnessed to better services for those clients.

A different approach to the question of excellence, through the "nested competency" concept, is used at Southern Illinois University's medical school. Educators and physicians, working together, agreed that it could not be assumed that once a competency—in understanding cardiac problems, for example—was gained, it would necessarily be retained. They therefore developed a series of cumulative competency objectives to ensure that competencies, once learned, will be rehearsed and reintegrated at a later point in the curriculum. This ideal is implicit at a number of other institutions, particularly in those where juries evaluate students at the conclusion of their programs, but Southern Illinois is unique in making it explicit in its competence-based program.

In sum, the impulse to reform professional services through educating a more competent practitioner takes several forms in these programs: highly specific assessment modes, participation of practitioners in the evaluations of students, use of students' background and prior knowledge as resources for the types of service they will give, and reinforcement and reintegration at a later point of competencies learned earlier in the program.

Alteration of the Profession and of Society. Of the three reform impulses discussed here, this one is not widely characteristic of competence-based programs. It is found most clearly in only three programs—Antioch School of Law, the College for Human Services, and the College of Public and Community Service. (It was present only to a degree at Seattle Central, where students were asked to

[5] Interestingly enough, many of the assumptions in the Women's Health Movement, also prominent at the time that the College for Human Services started, parallel those of the college; for example, shared knowledge between client and practitioner, an alteration in the reward system, and transformation of the services system through the interaction of change agents with others (Marieskind, 1975; Ruzek, 1978).

"retool" themselves to become managers.) The reform expected here is more than the honing of an excellent, humane practitioner in the modes described above; it is nothing short of the reconstruction of the profession and society. Thus Antioch Law School tries to add to lawyers' counseling and interviewing skills a keen awareness of social injustice so that they will subsequently utilize legal resorts to redress social inequities; the College for Human Services seeks to socialize human services workers who, as one faculty member put it, in our field notes "will shake up the system and its institutions," and the College of Public and Community Service has similar hopes for its change agents.

Illustrative of this emphasis and its attendant ideals is the following statements by Deans Jean Camper Cahn and Edgar S. Cahn, founders of the Antioch Law School, from the 1975 catalogue: "Law schools must begin to discharge their duty to the larger society on an institutional basis by changing the type of training provided lawyers, by institutional involvement in the operation of the legal system and by serving as a primary 'brain bank' for ideas, expertise, and manpower to design, test, and implement models for institutional change within the legal system" (inside back cover). Field notes from this project disclose that administrators at the College of Human Services held that citizens had been drawn into new responsibilities in the education, training, and improvement of all human services because of the inadequate provision of basic and necessary services. They also criticized professional credentials, which, in their eyes, failed to ascertain through testing whether professionals were still qualified.

What is demanded in the reform agendas of these two schools is at once similar and divergent: Antioch Law School envisions law as the instrument of social change for betterment of society through more adequately trained lawyers—adequacy being defined here as a concern with social justice. But the alteration of law itself is not envisioned, nor is there any attempt to envision a different type of lawyer-client relationship. Service will still be dispensed by the lawyer and received by the client, hence perpetuating what has been called elsewhere, in an insightful critique of the health care system, "the post office model of receipt and delivery" (Nelson, 1976). This vision may lead to a better society, but it does not seek a different, postbureaucratic society. Its strategy is to seek improvement through changed socialization patterns and alteration of legal institutions rather than through a deprofessionalized state.

The College for Human Services, in contrast, seeks to explode the idea of "profession" and to go beyond the current concepts of professional practice and society by dissolving the boundaries between esoteric professional and lay knowledge in the human services, by reconceptualizing the locus of personal responsibility, and by placing on both professional provider and nonprofessional receiver the responsibility of service. This program, advocating as it does mutual participation, comes close to what has been described as a truly "participatory system" in which traditional lines of receipt and delivery are blurred and the client, as well as the professional, becomes a "provider" and "evaluator" of service and competence. Its vision is quite distinct from that of the achievement of a better society through skilled manipulation of legal institutions by socially conscious, competent lawyers.

It is important to note that the goal of the College for Human Services goes beyond the laudable reform goals of those other programs analyzed here that strive for greater excellence of performance in their graduates but whose graduates' admission to practice is dependent not only on holding a degree but also on passing examinations articulated by the state.[6] If the College for Human Services is allowed by New York State to grant the master's degree (its application, initially rejected, is being reconsidered), its graduates will not be confronted with the necessity of passing a credentialing examination—most of them will enter careers in teaching, social work, or related fields where state licensing exams are not required. Other competence-based programs that seek to alter the structures of professions or of society are limited by the

---

[6] In reaching for advocacy through a competence-based program, Antioch Law School seemed to lose part of the legal substance in the offerings given its students, yet the necessity to adhere to American Bar Association standards for curriculum disillusioned the activist students it recruited. They could not come to terms with the professional parameters that the school would have to incorporate if it were to remain accredited. As it was, some Antioch students transferred because they came to prefer traditional law school training and to look upon the Antioch certificate as worthless. At Seattle Central, where attempts are made to upgrade persons for managerial posts with a certificate, students commented that, whereas the program directors downgraded degrees, the same directors expected students to work for a certificate no one had heard of.

extent to which their graduates face state licensure or credentialing and by the degree to which any new certificate would be recognized and valued. In such fields as pharmacy, medicine, and teaching, attempts at licensure reform, raise the question of traditional professional prerogatives, and these attempts are further complicated in such professional fields as nursing, where education occurs in several levels of schools. Thus competence-based community college nursing programs that would include innovative curriculum materials have not been allowed to venture onto the academic turf of baccalaureate schools—as, indeed, Mt. Hood learned when its patient assessment and public health course came too close to offerings deemed proper only for collegiate schools. And Florida State's competence-based program for first-time nursing students was abandoned in favor of a similar program for returning diploma nurses who wished to earn a bachelor's degree, since the Florida State faculty did not wish to replicate the entry-level training available at Florida's community colleges.

In sum, an attempt to alter the professions and society is not as widely found in competence-based programs as are attempts to ensure access to professional practice and to increase excellence in that practice, and those face obstacles in licensing and certification practices as well as in the limits of what professional programs can teach. But what seems clear in these programs with respect to all three reform impulses is that competence-based curricula tend to make *both* faculty and students highly self-aware and self-conscious about the program, the profession, and the prospects for the profession. The author's field notes contain the response of a Mt. Hood nursing instructor to the question of whether a competence-based approach is really any different from other nursing approaches. The reply exemplifies this self-consciousness:

> When she was a student nurse, she said, there was indeed a great emphasis on skills and performance. But she saw a specific and important difference between that approach and the current competence-based approach. In her years as a student, the nurses and her teachers insisted that she be able to perform tasks, but they looked at her whole performance and said yes or no, or perhaps graded her A, B, C, D, or E. Criteria used to be much more global and much more *subjective,* but now compe-

tence programs have clearer and more specific criteria of a fine-grained sort. This has two effects. Assessments are fairer because they are less subjective; there are publicly stated criteria. The second effect is that the student becomes more self-aware, more self-conscious, because the student knows the criteria upon which she's being judged. The instructor notes she's often in a position now where she is taking a student through an assessment and before she can say anything to the student, the student tells her, "Well, I think I'm going to have to go back and study such and such, I don't know it well enough." Because criteria are so clear, she simply helps students to see what they did and did not do well. The instructor added that she loves the way this puts the responsibility on the student—where it belongs. She concluded, "It's more work, but it's better."

The student becomes conscious of what must be done, and the instructor conscious of what has been left undone and remains to be done. Though this comment comes from one teacher, it could well have been made by a number of instructors and students in other competence-based programs. If it reflects what indeed goes on in those programs, it signifies that competency-based education is making crucial contributions to the professions.[7]

Further Prospects for Reform

In professions such as nursing, medicine, pharmacy, and law—to name some of those studied in this report—evaluation of

[7] It would be important to be able to say how well graduates of these programs performed in relation to graduates of traditional programs, but those data, except in anecdotal form, were unavailable at the writing of this chapter. Certainly graduates of Mt. Hood's nursing program had no difficulty finding jobs at hospitals or institutions, some of which—according to the student grapevine—thought that the Mt. Hood graduates were better prepared than other graduates in the Portland area. Another indicator of success would be the extent to which graduates successfully completed the state boards. On this score, thirty out of forty-seven graduates at Southern Illinois University's medical school passed the national medical boards, a showing that is comparable to student performance nationally. Whether students who graduate from competence-based programs perform as well as other graduates is also a question that involves consideration of costs. In general, competence-based programs are costly in terms of faculty time.

competent performance once the graduate is in the field rests primarily with other professionals and only in extreme cases with clients; for example, a patient who institutes a malpractice suit. But as is clear from a number of writings on the professions in general and on medicine in particular, model, professional evaluations of incompetent performance are not always forthcoming. Indeed, the very organization of professional practice may be at the heart of why mistakes, shoddy performance, outright chicanery, or dehumanization are not more severely chastized once they are recognized (Daniels, 1971; Freidson, 1970). (A five-part series in the *New York Times* during January 1976 estimated that about 5 percent of the medical profession is unfit or incompetent to practice and that 30,000 Americans are killed each year by faulty prescriptions.) Larger problems of professional structure and organization are involved, beyond the preparation of competent graduates. The alteration of standards of professional practice and evaluation, now hinted at in states where professionals must update themselves with continuing education in order to be relicensed, reaches beyond the professional training programs. Moreover, the locus of evaluation of competence in professional life itself also lies beyond the ken of professional schools.

Competence-based education would appear to be a potent model for such continuing education programs. In this regard the College for Human Services' model illustrates what might be done in order to achieve wider reform in professional practice by restructuring institutional settings as well as the client-professional relationship. So long as the professions are organized as they now are—divided into specialties, each with powerful control over knowledge and entry, and in some instances, such as medicine, with control over entry into related professions—broad and far-reaching reform of professional practice through altered self-regulation appears distant. Perhaps it is unrealizable short of reconstructuring the social order of which the professions are a part. But for the short run, competence-based education and its various elements appear to offer the professions avenues of reform that may ameliorate this problem of self-regulation. By providing access for the disadvantaged, assuring excellence in technical and human practice, and reducing tensions between educators and practitioners, competence-based programs give evidence that at least some self-reform can arise in the professions. Moreover, given the history and course of reform innovations, it may well be that competence-based education will not only help give rise to new types of professional education but will also provide further impulses for reform.

The greatly heightened self-consciousness of both faculty and students that characterizes these programs bears mention here, for it seems to reach to the very heart of the moral aspects of the professional mandate: the concern for self and others. It would be unrealistic to overlook the realities of professional structure and the locus of professional responsibility. The professional who has gained greater self-awareness cannot alone be the genesis of reforms that will lead to greater realization of competent practice throughout the professions. Yet in the face of those realities, it appears that professional training that does heighten consciousness of self as competent, that does increase self-evaluation, and that perhaps even leads to self-correction, as competence-based education seems to do, is especially valuable. Certainly it is preferable to an unthinking acceptance of one's self as a permanently certified and largely infallible professional, an attitude that in part has generated the very demands for reform that have been at issue in these pages.

Zelda Gamson   7

Understanding
the Difficulties
of Implementing
a Competence-Based
Curriculum

ᘓᘓᘓᘓᘓᘓᘓᘓᘓᘓᘓᘓᘓᘓᘓᘓᘓᘓ

Competence-based education is pedagogically a more radical alternative to traditional practices than many of the "soft" innovations of
the 1960s—experimental colleges, interdisciplinary curriculums, free
universities, student-initiated courses—and is, to some extent, a reaction to them. But people working on competence-base education
share with other innovators in education certain elemental concerns.
They cannot avoid at some point questions about what they are
doing and what their motives are. They have to secure support to
begin and to continue their programs. They need to attract sufficiently committed faculty and staff to weather the stress and
inevitable conflicts that come from doing something new. They

224

must find ways of binding faculty members to the task and of replacing those who do not work out. They have to find a balance between openness and structure at various stages in their development, while gaining the strength to withstand premature pressures from powerful outsiders to "produce." They must come to terms with the fact that they will never have enough resources, energy, or time to do everything set down in their original plans. At the same time, they are caught in the formless corona surrounding their plans—a mixture of individual hopes, ambitions, commitments, and personal and institutional histories.

How to keep these forces in balance with the realities of implementing something new is a major dilemma for any innovation.[1] But competence-based programs add several new and complicating elements to this general picture, as can be seen by examination of the colleges and universities included in the research project that led to this book; by a broader, more comparative view of the growth of competence-based education from its early development to the first stages of implementation between 1970 and 1977; and by observations of other reforms in American higher education over the past fifteen years.

Although there is no single conception of competence-based education—the programs in our study vary widely in many respects—nevertheless there are three important similarities among such programs that, in combination, make competence-based education unique: (1) the specification of educational outcomes reflecting successful functioning in life roles, (2) the view that instructional time is independent of the achievement of these outcomes, and (3) the certification of the achievement of the outcomes in a reasonably objective and verifiable way.

Competence-based education almost inevitably leads to a radical examination of educational first principles: What do we want our students to be able to know and do? How can we best

[1]These issues emerge concretely from studies of a variety of experiments in higher education in the United States over the last fifty years; see, for example: Duberman (1972), Gamson and Levey (1976), Grant and Riesman (1978), Lindquist (1977), and Riesman, Gusfield, and Gamson (1975). For useful theoretical discussions covering a variety of innovations, see Havelock (1971), Rogers and Shoemaker (1971), and Zaltman, Duncan, and Holbek (1973).

ensure that they will be able to achieve those outcomes? How do we know when they are achieved? Do credits really represent the achievement of outcomes that we think are important? Why should the amount of time it takes to achieve outcomes be defined in equivalent chunks called credits? Are the kinds of people who can achieve credits or outcomes a special, limited group? Aren't there a variety of ways people could learn beyond the regular class and course structure? How can we get faculty to go behind these questions to new solutions that will overcome the privacy of the individual classroom and that will bring faculty to collaborate more with one another? The responses that proponents of competence-based education have given to these questions have resulted in educational forms that tend to be highly *complex, interdependent* and *indivisible.*

Much has been said about the mechanical and jargon-ridden quality of the competence-based education movement. One obvious reason for the opacity of much competence-based language may be simply the unfamiliarity of educators with the complex task of specifying outcomes in ways that are amenable to assessment. Of course, it is easy to let measurement requirements take over and in the process to compile long lists of highly specific behaviors to be measured, as happened in many competence-based teacher education programs and in some in our own study (for example, at Mt. Hood Community College near Portland, Oregon, and Seattle Central Community College). But even in programs that attempt to keep to a streamlined and coherent list of outcomes, the amount of new understanding and technical mastery of the system itself is high compared to other kinds of innovations. A historian teaching in an interdisciplinary American culture course might be expected to familiarize himself with the related work of literary critics and sociologists, but in a competence-based program he would need to be conversant with the work of educational researchers and assessment specialists as well. Competence-based education, therefore, requires more time for the conceptual work involved in defining competencies. Once this is accomplished, the educational program, materials, and assessment instruments must be laid out in much greater specificity and detail than is typically done in higher education—this, of course, is one of the raisons d'être of competence-based education.

Any competence-based experiment that goes beyond restructuring a single course requires high degrees of interdependence. There needs to be a great deal of coordination among faculty, between faculty and assessors (teachers and assessors are often different persons in competence programs), and between the administrators of the program and the practitioners in it. The amount of emotional and intellectual interdependence among faculty that is fostered by competence-based education sharply exceeds that of other interdisciplinary programs, themselves unusually demanding in these respects. Competence-based education also has intended and unintended consequences for the nonacademic sectors of the institution in which it is housed. At the most obvious level, it is a great paper generator and places a strain on secretarial and printing services. Record keeping must be changed, sometimes in major ways. Admissions staff members need to be briefed and sometimes won over. Student counseling and orientation become critical backups to the program. Calculating program costs and student fees is difficult when the unit of achievement is a "competence" that can be demonstrated in a variety of ways at any point across a wide time span. Some of these implications follow from features that the competence-based approach shares with other innovations—for example, self-paced instruction or experiential assessment—but competence-based education is unique in the way it puts all of these features together.

As an innovation, a competence program is a package of interrelated items that are not easily unwrapped or purchased piecemeal. Its elements are tightly linked. For example, if there is a serious attempt to specify program-wide or college-wide competences, then some group must be responsible for reviewing the competence statements of individual faculty members or departments. Once this is done, there must be a specification of the grounds on which the competence will be demonstrated and assessed, whether in a course or in some other way. If any part of the assessment is to be done independently of a teacher, then assessors and assessment instruments must be developed and legitimated. Instruction, moreover, must be derived from competence statements as well as from assessments. Indeed, once the process of stating competences or outcomes has begun, it is difficult to resist the logic of its claim on most facets of teaching.

This complexity, interdependence, and indivisibility of competence-based education makes it difficult (but not impossible) for potential adopters to take only portions of developed competence-based programs. And its diffusion throughout an entire curriculum requires an effort nearly Herculean in its demands for leadership and coordination of whole faculties. Moreover, competence-based education was introduced into many schools at a particularly inauspicious moment. It appeared when colleges and universities were beginning to face economic stringencies, and this situation is likely to continue and even worsen in the near future. Like all innovations, competence-based programs must find the time, energy, and resources for development while simultaneously dealing with the constant need to attract and generate resources. Cost-cutters initially hoped that competence-based education might become a model for economical "processing" of large batches of students. As we shall see, however, this has turned out to be a vain hope.

Origins

There would have been no competence-based education "movement" outside of teacher education without active promotion from FIPSE. Some of the programs in our study would probably not have come into being at all without the availability of money from this fund, and a large number of existing competence-based programs were given a boost by grants from FIPSE and other sources.[2]

But why was FIPSE so interested in competence-based education in the first place? A young, activist agency with a reform mandate, it was influenced by the Newman Task Force, which in 1971 issued a report highly critical of the state of higher education. The report led to the formation, under the Educational Amend-

[2] College IV at Grand Valley State Colleges is a partial exception. After three years of support from FIPSE and the National Science Foundation for the development of its self-paced, modularized curriculum, College IV decided to introduce a competence-based curriculum. With ten full-time faculty, this has been an extremely slow process despite the fact that College IV has learning "packages" and a time-free design, which should facilitate a competence-based program. But the press of daily activities and internal problems prevented faculty from moving faster.

ments Act of 1972, of a government "foundation" that would enable colleges and universities to adapt to the changing conditions they faced in the 1970s. Russell Edgerton, an assistant to Secretary Robert Finch at the Department of Health, Education, and Welfare and a member of the Newman Task Force, directed FIPSE during its formation. He became its deputy director when Virginia Smith of the Carnegie Commission on Higher Education was appointed director in 1973.

In fulfillment of its mission to improve postsecondary education, FIPSE in 1974 defined a "special focus" program in competence-based education. In part, this was a response to several proposals it had received that focused on the outcomes of education. The decision to focus on competence-based education was seen by FIPSE as a way to achieve a number of aims. Staff at the fund gave high priority to the issue of accountability, to the need for more cost-effective education, and to the establishment of a more rational basis for certification. Staff members liked the language of competence, its specificity and exactness in articulating purposes and expected outcomes. Since the staff thought that institutions of higher education lacked clarity in defining outcome criteria, it liked the prospect of intervening in an institution at the point of outcome analysis (Jones and Kohli, 1975). Competence-based education seemed to be ready-made for FIPSE and, with the announcement of its special focus program, a new label came into general currency. FIPSE received hundreds of competence-based education proposals and, while it has since discontinued its special focus program, it still receives many proposals for grants to conduct programs using practices of competence-based education.

The appearance of a label is critical to the diffusion of any new idea or program, even if its meaning can be interpreted in a variety of ways—as happened at FIPSE and in the postsecondary community at large.[3] In this respect, competence-based education was almost an instant success. With unconsciously brilliant timing, FIPSE and the early competence-based programs brought together, under the competence-based education label, ideas and practices from the diverse (and often discredited) worlds of business, teacher

[3] Rogers, Eveland, and Klepper (1977) discuss the role of labeling in the diffusion of innovations.

education and the military—on this see William Neumann in Chapter Two—and applied them in new ways to the liberal arts and some of the professions. It drew on practices that often existed in isolation from one another—field studies, the Keller plan, assessment of prior learning—and endowed them with a new rationale and integrative principle. References to "competence-based education" popped up almost instantly in such publications as *The Chronicle of Higher Education* and at higher education conferences.

The staff at FIPSE was important not only in diffusing the competence-based education label and in simulating interest in it but also in providing the margin of support to struggling institutions and thus speeding up the implementation process. Various representatives of FIPSE have actively shaped development and implementation in countless ways on the sites included in this study, urging everything from broad institutional adoption to community participation.

FIPSE has had particularly powerful effects on the smaller, less well-known institutions in our study by offering visibility at a time when they badly needed it. Innovative administrators—again, particularly in the smaller colleges—have been strengthened, and innovative faculty have found protection under the fund's umbrella. On its side, FIPSE stood to gain credit in Washington and elsewhere for helping nonelite institutions, while not losing a great deal of credit should the institutions fail.

FIPSE has deliberately pioneered new "trade routes" across the country for innovators (see "Senators' Views . . . ," 1976). Leading practitioners of competence-based education are called on to consult with colleges contemplating a competence-based program; faculty from Alverno College, for instance, were invited to speak at a faculty workshop at College IV at Grand Valley State in 1975 when it was discussing a competence-based program. Workshops and conferences attended or sponsored by the leading proponents of competence-based education are supported directly or indirectly by FIPSE, which has set aside a portion of its budget for the dissemination of competence-based education.

By offering protection and the validation of a grant to non-elite institutions (and even to a few embattled innovators within the elite schools), FIPSE may have made a lasting contribution to higher education. The fund is unique, as far as I know, in underwriting regular meetings for directors of the projects it supports. These meetings enable representatives from FIPSE to convey their interests and values, and they allow people from the various projects to get together informally with one another—a most unusual idea in the history of innovation in American higher education, where reformers have tended to be fiercely independent, if not downright solipsistic.

In their extensive travels to the projects, FIPSE monitors carry word of what is happening at other places. Indeed, we have found that the staff's knowledge of what is going on in the institutions it supports—and in higher education generally—is detailed and sophisticated. Project directors turn to the staff of the fund for advice on a variety of questions.[4]

While FIPSE staff members disagree among themselves about the proper balance between information giving and intervention, I would say that the weight has fallen toward intervention. FIPSE's guidelines for proposals—requests for evidence of institutional commitment and broad impact—shaped the claims made in the proposals it received. This is, of course, not new in the funding world, and good grantsmen know how to package their proposals to meet all sorts of guidelines. In the case of FIPSE and of the people working in competence-based education, this was probably rather uncalculated. But with a reform as untried as competence-based education, it was difficult to know in advance how much money and effort would be required to implement it. In this respect, the grantors as well as the practitioners were hoping that it would all work out in the end—a doctrine characteristic of American innovators that David Riesman, paraphrasing Hirschman (1967), has called the "hidden hand."

Readiness. In general, the infusion of money from FIPSE was most effective when a reasonably large number of people at a

---

[4] At the time of this writing in 1978, most of the staff, as well as its two original directors, have left FIPSE. Thus the key people who backed the investment in competence-based education are no longer available for advocacy, informal support, and technical advice.

given institution recognized the need for something like competence-based education to accomplish some central goals. Motivation at such places was high and shared to some extent beyond those who submitted the grant application. But motivation was never enough. Human resources—people who were able and willing to carry on the complex activities that competence-based education requires—were even more critical. To some extent, the fund was able to buy up time, but it was never able to guarantee commitment (or talent). As we shall see, this was a significant issue in several of the programs, and one that was usually present from the beginning.

Some of the colleges in our study had attempted to implement something like competence-based education before a proposal to FIPSE was ever contemplated, sometimes even before the fund existed: The outside money fueled sparks that were already glowing. In other cases, the announcement of FIPSE's interest in competence-based education was the first spark. Somewhere between these extremes were programs that were struggling with problems for which competence-based education appeared to be a possible solution. Consider the institutions in our study in terms of their readiness for competence-based education:

Alverno College: Alverno already had quite a fire going before FIPSE opened for business; all it needed was a little stoking. As the events are described in Thomas Ewens' case study of Alverno in Chapter Eight of this report, faculty at the college began a fairly systematic and time-consuming process of self-analysis in 1969. Since then, Alverno has been struggling to define its liberal arts curriculum in terms of outcomes and performance rather than contents. Planning for such an outcome-oriented curriculum had already gone quite far before the proposal was made to FIPSE. "Competence" was at first regarded as an appropriate label to apply to a painstakingly homegrown curriculum, although later rejected as an inadequate and misleading description of what is now called the "Alverno Learning Process."

Antioch School of Law: A similar need for something like competence-based education existed at the Antioch School of Law, where the connection with competence-based education appeared to be a natural one. In asking what lawyering skills were required for an effective legal advocate, in the context of an innovative law school set up on a clinical model, Antioch was faced with the problem of specifying outcomes and assessing them. But while some of the faculty were wrestling with these questions, they knew little about what was going on elsewhere under the "competence" label. Antioch's grant proposal to FIPSE was submitted without much faculty involvement or commitment. When the money came, Antioch was not prepared to make full use of it. A new experimental college with a late 1960s flavor, peopled with its share of political activists, rebels, and iconoclasts, Antioch had not yet settled the fundamental question of governance—who had authority over what—when it applied to the fund.

College for Human Services: This college had also been struggling with the problem of outcomes before FIPSE came on the scene. Indeed, the fund's interest in competence-based education may have been influenced by the presence of Audrey Cohen, the president of the college, on the Newman Task Force. In a variety of ways and through its different incarnations, the College for Human Services had been attempting to define what a competent professional was and had even begun to devise an assessment scheme for student performance that included clients, professionals, and faculty, as well as students. When FIPSE opened in 1973, the college's staff was ready with a strategy for building a curriculum around student performance in human services agencies.

College IV, Grand Valley State Colleges: When College IV opened in 1973, it of course had to deal with all the problems of getting started. While designing a curriculum, the faculty and administration were also working on student recruitment, record keeping, advising, and tutoring. The crucial difference between College IV and the other new colleges was that its curriculum was designed from the beginning to be self-paced, modularized, and organized around objectives. Its proposal to FIPSE was entirely the work of its first dean, Robert Toft; he selected the faculty for their commitment to and experience with self-paced instruction. So at College IV, need and motivation were not in question; the money from the fund was going to help the college do what it was designed to do, with full support from the administration of Grand Valley and from its own faculty. As we shall see, this consensus did not guarantee smooth sailing even at the beginning and certainly not as time passed, nor did it fully prepare the faculty for the work involved in designing a competence-based curriculum a few years later. But at the beginning, at least, College IV's grant from FIPSE was beautifully suited to its needs and activities.

The College of Public and Community Service, University of Massachusetts at Boston: This college received its grant from FIPSE at the time of its opening. Like Antioch and the College for Human Services, the College of Public and Community Service struggled to define its programs in terms of the performance of students as professionals committed to social change and humane service. This goal was entirely consistent with the university's highly publicized "mandate" to serve the city of Boston. The proposal to FIPSE was produced by the dean and a small planning group in March 1973. Meanwhile, faculty were being recruited with a variety of pictures of the college—in these, competence-based education was at most an afterimage. Students had to be recruited, the curriculum had to be designed, and the materials for it prepared. All this was going on while the fledgling college was caught in the Byzantine politics of the university and beginning to mirror these politics internally.

Florida State University: The Curriculum of Attainments at Florida State University is a product of administrative enterprise. In a paper describing this curriculum John Harris, then director of the university's division of instructional research, outlined a way of dealing with student performance in terms of outcomes that would not be bound either in time or in mode of instruction by the traditional course structure. Harris submitted a proposal for the Curriculum of Attainments to the regents under a Florida State University mandate to develop time-shortened degrees. He was given permission to seek outside funding for his idea and eventually obtained that funding from FIPSE. In the meantime, the initiative for lining up departments to pilot the Curriculum of Attainments program came from Harris and his associate, Gary Peterson. There was certainly no clamor from the departments to participate in the program: if anything, Harris and Peterson—with the crucial backing of several administrators and a department chairman—needed to prime the pump. Once interest was stimulated, Harris and

Peterson could offer support to three pilot departments for the development of the program.

Mt. Hood Community College: The nursing program based on behavioral objectives at Mt. Hood, under the leadership of Diana Dean, who had become interested in competence-based education several years before, was in place in 1971. The FIPSE grant to Mt. Hood in 1973 was for refining the curriculum and for establishing cost-effective procedures; it helped revive faculty who were worn down after two years of planning the competence program without being given adequate released time from regular teaching and supervisory duties.

Seattle Central Community College: Fortuitous circumstances led to the establishment of competence-based programs at Seattle Central. In an atmosphere of activity and energy created by the president of Seattle Central, an associate dean for curriculum development and instruction wrote a proposal to FIPSE to assess the college's curricular needs, especially in interdisciplinary planning. This elicited a request from the nursing and day care programs for help in developing a management curriculum which later became the basis for the competence-based management program at Seattle Central.

Thus, the competence-based programs in this study varied considerably both in the need that existed for them and in the human resources available to make optimal use of the grants they received. While it is impossible to give a precise ordering, Alverno and the College for Human Services appear to have been ready for competence-based education in a way that Seattle Central and Florida State were not. The involvement of Seattle Central and Florida State in competence-based education seems somewhat fortuitous, the result of the availability of funds or the ideas of a particular individual. Somewhere in the middle were Antioch and the College of Public and Community Service; there appeared to be a need for competence-based programs at these schools, but not optimal institutional conditions.

Institutional Context. Other forces besides need and readiness shaped the programs in our study. The particular contexts and mix of people and politics determined the ways competence-based programs took root and grew. For example, in our study, there were at least four patterns of relationship between the programs and their institutions:

1. Competence-based education as the basis for a complete curricular reorganization (Alverno College and the College for Human Services).
2. New institutions that began with a competence-based program (College of Public and Community Service and College IV in its initial self-paced curriculum).
3. New institutions that had a competence-based program as one component (Antioch School of Law and College IV's later competence-based program).
4. Competence-based programs within a larger, older unit (The CBE programs at Seattle Central and Mt. Hood, and the Curriculum of Attainments program at Florida State).

Programs within larger, older institutions do not have to face the problem of organizing a full range of services (admissions, record keeping, library and printing facilities) in the same way that programs in new institutions must. This advantage may be double-edged, however, since those working on the competence-based program may be lulled into thinking that the existing staff and practices will meet their needs. This is rarely the case since competence-based education requires changes in many different parts of the institution. Moreover, programs that are part of an older institution face the problem of conflicting pulls on faculty and administrators (and, in some cases, on students) from the larger unit. They must compete with other units for money and students, and there will be conflicts over educational goals.

In contrast, new institutions have the advantage, if they are aware of it, of shaping all their activities to the requirements of the competence-based program. This advantage also applies to the recruitment of faculty, staff, and students. It is much easier to recruit staff and students for a new program than to change people accustomed to the old ways. However, the necessity of attending to all these matters *and* of designing a competence-based curriculum at the same time places a heavy burden on new institutions, which typically have inadequate lead time. As a faculty member at the

College of Public and Community Service put it, "We were asked to design and to fly an airplane at the same time." An outside grant can help overcome some of these problems, but not completely.

Initiation

Certain general conditions seem to be necessary for the successful initiation of any new program that involves a fairly substantial change.[5]

It is clear, first, that strong, unswerving *support from the top* is crucial, especially when faculty support is not great. Because competence-based education is so new and so difficult to envision in practice, advocacy and resources from the highest levels are necessary. It may even be that a fait accompli is preferable to long deliberation by the faculty, since the only way to see the benefits of a competence-based program is to jump in and start one. The next condition is *the formation of a core group connected to and supported by the top leader but with sufficient responsibility and resources to move quickly.* The core group must be drawn from the faculty and must command their respect. Widespread faculty endorsement is not essential at this stage but it is important that faculty not be mobilized in opposition. The critical group at this point is a core group willing to act as vanguard and organizer. To win faculty support, or at least to defuse critics, it is crucial that the competence-based program be seen as *answering central institutional problems* or as being *linked to core values.* Here, intellectual vision—and an articulate representative of competence-based education—can be powerful in winning the skeptical and sustaining the convinced.

When these three conditions are met, *prior supportive practices or values* speed up the early stages and, even more, the implementation of a program. For competence-based education, such practices have usually included at least one of the following: the definition of faculty roles consistent with those required by the program; previous collaborative work among faculty members; a nondepartmental structure; new forms of assessment; nontraditional

[5] The following sources have been helpful to the author in formulating these conditions: Clark (1970), Hefferlin (1969), Rogers and Shoemaker (1971), Sarason (1972), and Zaltman, Duncan, and Holbek (1973).

pedagogical techniques, such as modules, programmed instruction, self-pacing, and field studies or internships. But along with these sources of flexibility, a certain amount of *institutional stability* seems necessary; since competence-based education requires so much energy and coordination, other more compelling institutional needs can interfere with its development. Financial difficulties and ambiguity or conflict about governance are particularly destructive of the initiation of a new program.[6] Finally, *ancillary needs,* such as recruitment, record keeping, counseling, and materials production, must be anticipated.

At the point of their initiation, each of the programs in our sample had rather strong support from the top, and most had some supportive practices that eased the entry of competence-based education. Half had a core group ready to begin working on the program, but less than half were operating in a situation of institutional stability. When it came to anticipating ancillary needs, even the exemplary programs ran out of steam. None paid enough attention ahead of time to questions of student recruitment, orientation, counseling, and retention. Few anticipated the voracious appetite of competence-based education for paper, computer time, and record keeping.

Alverno College: At Alverno, the transition to activities supported by FIPSE was barely perceptible. President Joel Read provided strong, forceful leadership from the top for competence-based education. A core group of people was prepared to continue the work that it had begun some years earlier. Two faculty members in particular, Austin Doherty and Georgine Loacker, had played a role in academic planning since the earliest days of Alverno's self-examination, and they stood ready to carry the competence-based program forward.

I do not want to overstate the extent of general support at

---

[6] Illness and turnover plagued the leadership of five of the competence-based programs during the period we studied them. Diana Dean's illness in the fourth year of the Mt. Hood program, Robert Toft's resignation in College IV's second year, changes at the upper administrative levels and Marci Catanzaro's illness at Seattle Central, the departure of John Harris as the Curriculum of Attainments program began at Florida State, and Dean Jean Cahn's illness at Antioch were serious disturbances during implementation. Other departures—of key faculty members and administrative supporters at FSU, a dean at Antioch, a whole faculty at Mt. Hood—upset the progress of competence-based education at those institutions.

Alverno for competence-based education, for we know that Sister Joel Read, a woman of considerable toughness and grit, weathered serious challenges from faculty and staff who differed with her less on values than on tactics and style. But by the time of our study, most of the dissidents had either departed, converted, or given up. And although Alverno had its share of turnover, this did not occur in the crucial leadership positions. Furthermore, Sister Joel held the power to fire, since Alverno did not have a system of faculty tenure. The question of *whether* the college should adopt competence-based education never came to a vote of the faculty as a whole.

Alverno was driven by a value system vividly articulated by Sister Joel, and the competence-based program was a way of linking this value system to the kinds of students that it educated. To harness competence-based education to its core values, it designed a liberal arts program from a conception of the intellectual and emotional qualities its students needed to pursue business and professional careers. Clarity about its goals, tasks, and students meant that it had a theme, a "saga" in Clark's terms (1970), to guide the development of its program. The "saga" emerged during a breakthrough event that occurred in 1971, later recalled in quasi-religious tones. The breakthrough came during a meeting that itself followed many fruitless meetings; it seemed to be genuinely collective; and it set the college in a direction that is still being pursued. (Thomas Ewens describes this breakthrough in Chapter Eight.)

What emerged from the breakthrough at Alverno was less important than the direction it set: It served as a guide for the development of learning experiences and assessments and helped the college design the curriculum in a relatively orderly, structured way.

Some supportive structures and practices were already in place when Alverno received its grant from FIPSE. An off-campus program already had set a precedent for students to work outside regular courses. An academic task force set up after the breakthrough meeting laid the foundation for faculty from different departments to work together, and the same task force was also important in setting up an assessment center. Finally, conversations early in 1972 with managers at the Wisconsin Bell Telephone Company led to the development of Alverno's assessment program, which adapted several techniques from Bell Telephone.

Of course, there were mistakes in planning, and the effects of these gradually emerged. Alverno, with a curious myopia that it shares with the other competence-based projects in this study, paid little attention to the implications of its new program for student recruitment and retention. While faculty and administrators were busy planning the competence program for the freshman class entering in 1973, little was done to secure support from the admissions staff or even to explain the new program to it. Consequently, these staff members were unable to articulate the program in comprehensible terms to prospective students and their parents; they may even have unintentionally conveyed their own sense that it was a strange, newfangled contraption. Enrollments at Alverno the following year were down, and admissions and recruitment continued to be sore points.

Antioch School of Law: At Antioch, it is possible to discern a number of forces that smoothed the way from the beginning for the competence-based program. It was clear that competence-based education would be focused on the clinical side of the curriculum—its main concern would be with defining and assessing lawyering skills, and motivation was high to make progress in that area. Despite constant struggles over governance and over what balance to strike between educational aims and social objectives the students and faculty did not challenge the fundamental character of Antioch as a clinical law school. Antioch had succeeded as well in creating a new faculty role—the "scholar-practitioner." Thus, there were faculty at Antioch who were likely to be able to implement the competence-based program once it was designed.

The crucial question at Antioch was that of responsibility for designing the program. The faculty members who were supposedly responsible claim that they had not been informed until the money for implementing the program came in. Planning shifted among a small group of faculty members, with Edgar and Jean Cahn—founders and deans of Antioch—carrying ultimate responsibility. A task force was assembled that included three educational consultants who had helped write the grant proposal. These consultants were to continue working at the law school, but for a long time their role was poorly understood—and, indeed, resisted—by many of the faculty.

As only one small part of the total life of the Antioch School of Law, competence-based education has been constrained by power struggles between the administration and the faculty that culminated in the unionization of the latter, and by the departure of a number of faculty members. Faculty, including those on the task force, have been run ragged from trying to discharge their teaching and clinical duties and at the same time going to court and keeping records. The competence-based program at Antioch, from the beginning, has been unable to attract a leader who was both committed and credible. Nor has there been a solid core group. Although the deans initiated the program and were committed to it, they have lacked the time or the credibility in the eyes of the faculty to play a forceful role in promoting it.

College for Human Services: Parallels between the College for Human Services and Alverno are striking. The college's transition to FIPSE support was barely perceptible. President Cohen provided strong leadership comparable to that of President Read at Alverno; key members of the faculty working on competence-based education had been through the various shifts in the college, some since 1965 when Cohen had founded the Women's Talent Corps. Like Sister Joel Read, Cohen weathered student and faculty resistance, and she too held the power to fire, since the college also did not have a system of faculty tenure.

Like Alverno, the College for Human Services was driven by values clearly articulated by its leader. These values grew from a vision of the humane professional who is committed in a realistic way to changing the human services profession. They provided the ideological basis for the development of competence-based education—a development sparked by a catalytic event comparable to the breakthrough meeting at Alverno. (Gerald Grant describes these meetings in Chapter Nine.) The resulting grid of competences and levels in the College for Human Services curriculum is less vivid on paper than it is in action, in the same way that a numbered diagram cannot convey the movement of a play in a football game. But the significance of this grid for the college's competence-based curriculum cannot be overemphasized. Analogous at the college level to teachers' manuals in the schools, it enormously clarified the task of working through a college-wide competence-based curriculum.

As at Alverno, supportive structures and practices were already in place. Before its breakthrough, the college had already listed some competences of the human services profession. From its beginning, it had a combined classroom and on-the-job curriculum. It had already created a new faculty role—the coordinating teacher—who was responsible both for supervising and observing students on their jobs and for classroom teaching. Most important of all, its service ideals attracted a predominantly female faculty sufficiently flexible and devoted to work in a highly demanding, nontraditional setting for relatively low salaries.

Finally, like Alverno, the College for Human Services was forced to pay close attention to the implications of its program for its students. Once a master's degree program became a possibility, the college began to recruit more selectively. While it still drew from low-income minority groups, entrance requirements were raised and the admissions procedure was formalized to screen out "losers" and select "winners"—by personality characteristics as well as by academic criteria.

College IV, Grand Valley State Colleges: College IV's competence-based program began three years after the opening of the college and soon after the departure of its visionary founder and central figure, Robert Toft. His departure followed a series of confrontations with the faculty and a variety of practical difficulties, the most disturbing of which were low enrollments. The competence-based program at College IV is the only one in our study that was formally adopted by the faculty and for which there was no external financial support. The College IV faculty saw a competence-based program as a way of achieving curricular coherence and of introducing applied, vocational subjects into the liberal arts curriculum. As a result, it was hoped that CBE would attract and hold students to a greater extent than the college had yet been able to do. From the beginning, the College IV faculty planned the introduction of competence-based education in a slow, phased way that would make use of the instructional modules that they had been assiduously designing since the founding of the college.

College of Public and Community Service: The initiation of this college's competence-based program was beset with difficulties. While the college had the outline of a competence-based program when it opened in 1973, this outline had neither competence statements nor assessments that could be used in designing the curriculum. Furthermore, some of the faculty were reluctant to accept the planners' definition of the college's curriculum, particularly the competence-based aspects of it. Since there was already considerable disagreement among the faculty about the goals of the college, a good deal of discussion focused on why the college needed a competence-based program, as well as on how it should be formulated. In the orientation of new faculty prior to the opening of the college, the competence-based program was understandably given less attention than governance, organization, curriculum, and student recruitment. The faculty—and some were not hired much more than a month before registration—did not understand what competence-based education was nor how it could be used to help in curriculum development. The planning group itself had neither the technical nor the practical expertise to be very convincing about the virtues of a competence-based education. Most significantly, as John Watt points out in his notes on the college: "The primary factor that attracted faculty to the college was its commitment to urban reform. This commitment predated its commitment to competence-based education and had remained central to the college's mission. . . . No clear-cut case existed prior to fall 1973 as to how exactly competence-based education would contribute to the urban reform mission of the college."

Thus, as at Antioch, the College of Public and Community Service had other questions to settle before it could turn competence-based education to its own uses. Faculty were suspicious of the whole competence-based effort, and divisions among the faculty and between the faculty and administration began to appear. While the faculty managed to put together a full-fledged competence-based certification system covering all requirements for graduation by mid-November 1973, John Watt's research gives no indication that the faculty's skepticism about competence-based education had dissolved by that time. It was not clear that there would be a group on the faculty who would carry it out.

There were elements supportive of the competence-based program at the college that were to emerge later as the curriculum began to take form. In combining professional training with the liberal arts the College of Public and Community Service, like

Antioch and the College for Human Services, could not depend on the traditional disciplines for curricular content or criteria for performance. Internships and practical application were built into the very mission of the college. While they differed in their personal agendas and goals for the college, the faculty themselves generally shared an interest in reform—of urban institutions, of the professions, of career education, and of higher education in general. They may not have understood exactly what competence-based education entailed, but most were willing to work in a college that was not organized according to familiar disciplines, courses, credits, and grades. The newness of the college hindered the development of a competence-based program in the short run but probably facilitated it in the long run.

Florida State University: The Curriculum of Attainments program at Florida State University began with the recognition that it would be a pilot program with only a small number of students; departments and faculty would participate on a voluntary basis. Just as the program began, the founder of the Curriculum of Attainments program, John Harris, left Florida State and his associate, Gary Peterson, took over. It is difficult to speak of the initiation of the program as a whole beyond these conditions, since each participating department followed a different pattern. Most depended on a single faculty member to take the initiative in developing the program, although nursing had several faculty members who worked actively in promoting its curriculum of attainment program.

Mt. Hood Community College: Mt. Hood's competence-based program in nursing began auspiciously with solid support from the college's central administration for its magnetic leader, Diana Dean. While some faculty left during the developmental period, she was able to attract and hold a committed core group. Following her death in 1975, this group continued to work together until a crisis led to the resignation of most of the core faculty.

Seattle Central Community College: Somewhat ironically, the initiation of the competence-based management program at Seattle Central coincided with the departure of the president who had encouraged the group that wrote the original proposal. As a first step, two young people were hired to administer the program: Marci Catanzaro, a tenured member of the nursing faculty, and

Rick Venneri, who had worked with the president. Although Catanzaro had been instrumental in designing outcome-oriented curriculums in nursing and Venneri was a specialist in traditional, non-competence-based forms of assessment, neither had been involved in writing the original proposal. They were never able to provide strong intellectual leadership for the program, nor was there a core group ready to carry it forward. Most of the teaching was done by people on part-time appointments to the program.

Implementation

Having actually to *do* something inevitably gives rise to new problems even under the best-laid plans. Initiators almost always underestimate the amount of time and energy required for development, so that, for example, when a program is supposed to become operational, materials are not ready and procedures have not been worked out. Problems can become particularly acute when those who must teach a new curriculum are not the same ones who planned it. Implementors, unless they have been drawn into planning in the early stages, will rarely have the same interests and skills as initiators. The forces that supported and encouraged initiators may not be shared by the implementors. And the sense of starting something new and shaping it in a way that reflects one's own history and situation—what practitioners of "planned change" call "ownership"—is then difficult to achieve.[7]

Role of the Faculty. Most competence-based programs are attractive to administrators because they offer a way of attaining certain institutional goals: visibility, a more effective curriculum, better teaching, more students. For some administrators, the goals of reform are deeper and less provincial—improving client services, changing a profession, increasing access to higher education, redefining the liberal arts.

Competence-based education, even on a modest scale, requires major changes in faculty performance, as Peter Elbow notes in Chapter Three. It objectifies not only what students have learned

[7] For the varieties of theories and practices included under "planned change," see Bennis and others (1976), Havelock (1971), Lindquist (1977), and Sikes, Schlesinger, and Seashore (1974).

but what faculty have taught. The control of faculty implicit in competence-based programs is one reason that these programs have been initiated most frequently at nonelite schools, where the balance of power is weighted more heavily on the side of the administration. In the elite sector, curricular change, even when stimulated by an administrator, must bump through a gauntlet of senatorial courtesies and interdepartmental treaties. But regardless of the prestige of the school or the power of the administration, implementation of an innovation eventually rests with the individual faculty member. There is simply no way around this fact, however much some administrators might want to avoid or postpone it, and it is a fact no less true of competence-based education than of most other teaching innovations.

In all of the programs in our study, competence-based education has led to intensive, often constant interaction between students and faculty—in classes, in one-to-one instruction and tutoring, in intern or job settings. This has placed a great strain on faculty who were also devoting their energies to designing new courses and assessment materials and going to what seemed like an endless round of meetings. Since competence-based education involves additional efforts and burdens for everyone concerned, at least at the beginning, initiators have the crucial task of convincing faculty that the extra work will benefit them and their students. The earlier that faculty become involved in designing the program, the more likely they are to support it later as implementors. And the earlier the leaders of the competence-based education effort appeal for faculty support and anticipate possible sources of resistance, the smoother the implementation. The programs in our sample varied considerably in the degree to which their faculty understood—let alone supported—their institution's commitment to competence-based education. Consider several examples:

Alverno College: Wide faculty participation preceding implementation of competence-based education at Alverno broadened the initial core group that had been pressing for the changeover to a competence-based program. Dissidents had resigned or been forced out. And while some resistance remained among faculty, there was enough support for and understanding of the program to carry it out when it began in the fall of 1973. Moreover, a structural change that combined competence divisions with disciplinary divisions helped the implementation of competence-based education considerably. Eight competence divisions, one for each competence in the curriculum, were made responsible for curriculum development and for assessment and teaching modules, while the disciplines were made responsible for content. Each member of the faculty became a member of both a disciplinary and a competence division. Although there were various organizational and political problems involved in the reorganization, this was the critical organizational machinery for achieving wider faculty involvement, legitimation, and accountability in the program.

Antioch School of Law: The storm-filled implementation of competence-based education at Antioch tempers my earlier dictum about the necessity for faculty support, for I think it is fair to say that the competence efforts proceeded at the college without much faculty support. Early on, the faculty managed to agree about the skills involved in lawyering. The first area, interviewing, was identified and competencies were worked out for it. Like the professional faculty at the College of Public and Community Service, Antioch faculty began to recognize the value of competence-based education for assessing students in the clinical part of the curriculum (but not in the classroom law courses). The various conflicts at Antioch between the faculty and the administration—and the resultant suspicion of competence-based education on the part of the faculty—slowed down its implementation.

College of Public and Community Service: It was not until its third year that the College of Public and Community Service implemented its competence-based program. John Watt notes in his study of the college that there was a continuing difficulty in relating the competence-based liberal arts centers to the professional centers. While faculty members spent great amounts of time refining definitions and standards for the competence program, other faculty saw competence-based education as competing for their time—and perhaps more importantly, for the college's identity as a school for public and community service. Competence-based education was resisted particularly by the liberal arts faculty of the college, while the professional faculty began to see it as a way of organizing their curriculums and better evaluating student performance. Efforts by the administration to resolve the conflict, including the employment of outside consultants, were rebuffed by the faculty.

Florida State University: If Antioch and the College of Public and Community Service faced active faculty resistance to competence-based education, some of the other colleges encountered a pervasive and frustrating faculty indifference. Such an attitude can be said to characterize the majority of faculty at Florida State University, many of whom had not heard of their university's Curriculum of Attainments even when it was operating at its height.

Seattle Central Community College: Seattle Central's program was hampered from the beginning by a part-time faculty that were initially hired to develop materials they would not necessarily teach. Seattle Central faculty never developed a sense of identification with the program, and not many people at the college cared about the program's attempt to define management learning outcomes.

Finally, if faculty commitment is necessary, it is not sufficient by itself, as both College IV and Mt. Hood teach us. Both colleges attracted faculty who were strongly committed to their programs, had helped to develop them, and were on the ground to implement them. And yet the competence programs at both colleges ran into such serious difficulties with students that they were eventually undone.

Role of Students. Any curricular blueprint will require reworking when the students arrive. Because students had not been involved in the conceptualization or initiation of any of these programs, all of them had to come to terms with their students. This meant more time and more tooling-up than planners had expected. Indeed, it is astonishing to realize that so soon after a decade of student activism, an innovation as thoroughgoing as competence-based education could take hold in some institutions with so little student involvement. I suspect, in fact, that most students would vote against competence-based education if they were asked. Not wrongly, they would see it as too demanding and too exposing, a covert way of reintroducing requirements and raising standards.

As a new approach, competence-based education must justify itself to students as well as to faculty. Competence programs, however, have the intended effect of bringing out deficiencies as well as strengths in students. Some students will accept such exposure if they think it will help them learn better, become better people, get better jobs. But such benefits are not always apparent to students, and competence-based programs must show them that following program grids and taking frequent assessments is in fact worthwhile, compared to more traditional education. Students at our sample institutions were clearly not convinced of this, as witness two examples.

Alverno College: Many Alverno students rebelled or dropped out in the first year of the competence-based program, and the college has had a difficult time building up its enrollment to achieve the stability it needs. (But this is true of many small, denominational liberal arts colleges.) The first group of students entering a competence-based program are like any first cohort in an experimental program: They complain about feeling like "guinea pigs" while basking in the glory of being "special." At Alverno, when students in the first group dropped out, word began drifting back to Alverno's traditional clientele that all was not right for them at the college. It is a tribute to Alverno that students, two years after the program began, were able to organize a forum to voice their criticisms.

Mt. Hood Community College: Although the first group of students to go through Mt. Hood's "write-say-do" behavior modification program staunchly defended it, the second group to enter the program rebelled. Appealing over the heads of the faculty to the top administration, this group complained about the failure to include students in curriculum planning, about the high dropout rate and about the "dehumanizing" effects of the program's precise behavioral counting system. By the time the crisis had played itself out, only a curriculum design and one original faculty member remained.[8] The dependence of the program on its founder, Diana Dean, combined with wavering administrative backing, meant that the nursing program was vulnerable to attack in Dean's absence. As Virginia Olesen notes in her case study of Mt. Hood in Chapter

[8] At Mt. Hood, what began as an exciting new program with adequate internal funding, grants, full administrative support, lead time, a charismatic leader, and a core of committed faculty ended in disaster. In contrast, some other programs that began less auspiciously—the College of Public and Community Service, for example—have managed to grow stronger. Thus go our general theories of change. Chance and serendipity play their part.

Ten of this volume, students became the unforeseen implementors of competence-based education. In passively resisting and eventually rebelling against a powerful assessment system that displayed their weaknesses and forced them to attend to discrete elements of behavior, they actively shaped and altered the program.

While Mt. Hood is an extreme example of student impact, it is an instructive case because it illustrates many of the difficulties that arose in the implementation of other programs. Active student resistance tended to be centered on issues of evaluation and adequate preparation for the demands of the program. As dramatically as students at Mt. Hood, Antioch students brought suit in the first year against the college for its use of letter grades. A confrontation between Audrey Cohen and students at the College for Human Services in 1972 brought to the surface dissatisfaction with basic skills instruction. And students at the College for Public and Community Service pressed the college to recognize prior learning and to transfer credits, as well as to clarify the relationship between certificates and classes.

Beyond active student resistance, attrition and low enrollment were serious problems at Alverno, College IV, the College of Public and Community Service, and in some of the programs at Florida State University, Mt. Hood, and Seattle Central. To some extent this was a function of unrealistic assessments of the student "market" for an unusual program; this was clearly the case at College IV and at Seattle Central. But the problem of student enrollment was exacerbated by the belief on the part of competence-based education advocates that it is a system that can work with anyone. In practice, it requires students high in personal initiative, maturity, and tenacity. Although it represents itself in antielite language, it is one of the most demanding systems in higher education. It says: "Don't just stand there, *do* something. Don't just *be* in college, demonstrate what you can *do* with your courses, your work experience, your thoughts. If you can show us what you can do, we guarantee that you will be able to achieve certain goals in your future life." According to proponents of competence-based education, anyone can become competent, given enough time and attention. But rarely is there enough time and attention, so competence-based education works in the same way as other social and educational reforms—those who need it least benefit most.

The programs that depended on self-pacing—as competence-based programs in their pure form should—found that students were unable or unwilling to pace themselves. College IV, for instance, which operated completely on self-pacing, discovered that students would simply disappear after enrolling for one or two modules. Students at the College of Public and Community Service did not take assessments or attend classes in sufficient numbers over a period of several years. Mt. Hood students varied a good deal in their progress, and some strain between "fast-pacers" and "slow-pacers" began to appear. But more important, slow student progress at these different schools meant low credit generation, a problem that no college, particularly a public one, can ignore.

As a result of these problems and despite their claims about wanting to work with nontraditional students, all of the programs had to come to terms with the quality and commitment of their students. As Etzioni (1975) notes, commitment can be ensured by carefully selecting members and by controlling their experiences within the organization. At the beginning, the competence-based programs did neither. By ideology or by circumstance, they found themselves with an unselected student body and a demanding new curriculum. Little effort went into finding out whether entering students had the requisite skills or backgrounds to handle the demands being placed on them. For a system that depends so heavily on assessment, it is curious that so few of the programs at the beginning assessed their entering students.

As time passed, the programs began to attend more to these matters. Although Antioch and the College for Human Services continued to draw from a nontraditional pool, they became much more careful about selecting the "right" students at the point of entry. Both colleges designed complicated application processes that included interviews and a variety of criteria matched to their goals. At the same time, they raised the minimum levels on traditional academic criteria. The College of Public and Community Service became more attractive to well-prepared middle-class people, particularly older women. Several of the Curriculum of Attainments programs at Florida State (urban and regional studies, music, religion) also worked with high-ability students.

Even more important, each of the programs eventually introduced orientation programs for their students. Under pressure from students, College IV realized, soon after it opened, that it would have to explain its self-paced, modularized system in a more systematic manner. Along with Alverno College, the College for Human Services, the College of Public and Community Service, and College IV at Grand Valley devised an orientation course as a method of encouraging students to begin planning their educational programs.

Administrative Snags and Human Resources. The implementation of competence-based education depends heavily on certain mechanics: printing and making available a variety of learning materials; designing, scheduling, and recording assessments; keeping track of faculty and student participation at various stages.[9] To some degree, all of the programs in the study ran into a variety of administrative and mechanical snafus, and students were most likely to complain about these problems in the new program. Again and again, we heard about various sorts of disorganization at the beginning. Consider examples drawn from two schools.

College IV, Grand Valley. College IV's reliance on printed modules required special arrangements with the printer. The central library and bookstore were more important to the College IV program than to the other colleges at Grand Valley since College IV relied entirely on instructional materials packaged in small units. Since registration and assessment could occur at any point, a flexible way of recording enrollment and student progress was needed. Eventually, systems were worked out to accomplish these ends but they were chaotic at the beginning. Registration and records of student progress were handled manually for a long time. And given the cavalier attitudes faculty typically have about completing forms on time, not all of the problems could be blamed on red tape.

Relationships with support offices are political as well as administrative. Zealous, ambitious innovators tend to ignore these offices, yet they can make life miserable for a new college or pro-

---

[9] For a discussion of these matters and of implementation of competence-based education in general, see the excellent paper by Huff (1975).

gram. Robert Toft, the founder of College IV, worked out a computer program for processing students, but neglected to persuade the people in the computing center to learn how to use it. Although he was himself convinced that there were many students clamoring for his college, he failed to convince the director of admissions, who (rightly) thought otherwise.

Mt. Hood Community College: Mt. Hood ran into difficulties with its narrative transcript system of recording student progress. In 1975, these records were kept in the program files rather than in the registrar's office because of the great expense involved in storing the data on the computer in earlier years. At Mt. Hood, students could present themselves for testing at any point, and so equipment had to be in place and faculty had to be available at all times to monitor the tests. Self-pacing also created problems, as at College IV, with registration and accounting. Some students, the slow-pacers or nonpacers, would show up in initial registration figures but not complete their work during the term for which they had registered. Meanwhile, they might have taken up a considerable amount of faculty time. Fast-pacers, similarly, would start on new materials and take up faculty time in the middle of a term but not appear as a "load" until later.

These problems of College IV and Mt. Hood have implications for costs and workload planning for all competence-based programs. "Formula" funding in public institutions clearly squeezes those competence-based programs that are self-paced and allow students to enroll at any time. As we have seen, there are many services integral to the operation of CBE—assessment, advising, tutoring—that are not reflected in tuition paid for a particular course or module. All colleges have these "hidden" costs but they are usually manageable. In competence-based education, however, these "extras" are the essence of the innovation itself. Moreover, since students who enter these demanding programs are often underprepared, competence-based programs are better described as "time-lengthened" than as "time-shortened."

How to charge for these services—and what the unit should be if it is not credits or courses—is a problem many advocates of competence-based education have begun to address (see Meeth, (1975).

It is fairly clear at present that competence-based education has not solved the question of the costs of a college education. By my calculations, it takes a minimum of three years from initiation to achieve a fairly "debugged" running version of a competence-based program, assuming some of the development costs are underwritten by outside agencies. There are, in addition, "donated" services that are incalculable. Unpaid consultants and assessors helped Alverno and the other programs in a variety of ways. Supervisors in job settings, unpaid faculty, and community assessors have provided extra margins. Without such volunteers, it would take extraordinary leadership and faculty commitment to implement a large-scale program in three years. And even with outside funding, it is clear that the competence-based programs we have studied have depended on the willingness of administrators and faculty to "give more." As one of the leaders said, "We took a lot of hide from the faculty." Everywhere we went, we saw exhausted, ragged faculty. There is a limit to how far human resources can be stretched (even if they appear in the form of supremely energetic nuns). Again, three years seems to be as long as most faculty can last on enthusiasm and shared values. Beyond that, they must be able to feel that there will be an end to constant experimentation and marathon workshops.

Administrators seemed jauntier and more resilient than faculty: They were the people who had begun the competence programs, and they believed in the virtue of what they had wrought. Even so, attrition among administrators has been very high, and this is quite demoralizing for those who remain behind. Alverno and the College for Human Services have held onto their top leadership, but they represent the exception rather than the rule. It would do well to recognize that administrative turnover in competence-based programs is likely. If administrators are failing, they will leave as soon as they can, perhaps to start another innovative program or, more typically, to settle down in a duller but more restful traditional job. If they are succeeding, they will be lured by another institution looking for an innovator who survived. In either case, planners should build in a succession principle from the beginning or at least single out a likely individual or group of people who can carry on when the leader departs. This is why I have emphasized the importance of a core group during the initiation phase. It is a way of preparing a second generation of leaders.

Institutionalization and Impact

What are the short- and long-term implications of competence-based education? The programs in this study cannot unequivocally answer this question for us since they are at different stages of development and even the oldest of them, Alverno, is still barely institutionalized. Yet I can at least summarize what the status of these programs was in 1977, as a possible indicator of competence-based education's impact.

Alverno College: Tough-minded realism in the service of a vision characterizes Alverno. Its competence program—the most mature one in our study—is well on its way to being institutionalized, if its resource base remains relatively secure.

Antioch School of Law: Antioch is more problematic. Much depends on the outcome of the power struggle between the administration and the faculty and on the impact of unionization on Antioch's innovative aspects. At the time of this writing, the competence-based component maintains a precarious hold on the clinical side of the law school.

College for Human Services: Like Alverno, this college's competence program is well on its way to being institutionalized and may even be adapted as a model for other human services programs around the country. But it too requires a relatively secure resource base.

College IV, Grand Valley: The competence-based component at College IV, barely begun in 1977, depends on the extent to which it is able to move under its new dean to redirect its liberal arts curriculum.

College of Public and Community Service: This college's struggles with competence-based education may have reached some resolution with the hiring of an experienced evaluation expert, and a curriculum plan that begins to integrate its liberal arts and professional objectives.

Florida State University: An administrative shake-up and the reassignment of Gary Peterson, the Curriculum of Attainments administrator, meant that institutionalization depended on the willingness of the participating departments to pick up the cost of their Curriculum of Attainments programs when the money from FIPSE ran out. In 1977, it appeared that this was not going to happen.

Mt. Hood Community College: At Mt. Hood, little remains of the "write-say-do" behavioral modifications; the new faculty members who took over the program in 1975 implemented the nursing program all over again and, in doing so, learned to appreciate the conception underlying the competence-based program they had inherited. Nevertheless, new people have brought new, often critical ideas to the original design.

Seattle Central Community College: The Seattle Central program does not appear to have a long-term future, given the fact of frequent administrative turnover and reorganization. Only a few courses from the original curriculum remained in 1977.

An attempt to assess the long-term impact of competence-based education on higher education would be foolhardy at this date, but it is clear already that it has had some effects on colleges and universities beyond the circle of early innovators who received grants from FIPSE. Competence-based education pioneers are asked to speak at conferences and to consult with other colleges interested in aspects of competence-based education. Alverno received a dissemination grant from the Kellogg Foundation, and the College for Human Services is attempting to transport its model to other human services programs. Materials from competence-based programs are circulating at countless colleges, and new assessments and instructional modules are being produced regularly. "Competence" has become an important catchword in political and social commentary.

Yet the glamour has worn off competence-based education in educational circles. Alverno itself has rejected the competence-based education label in favor of its own brand. At this writing, competence-based education has not penetrated the upper reaches of academia—the elite liberal arts colleges, the major research universities, and the disciplinary associations. Interest in competence-based approaches remains strongest in community colleges and in less elite liberal arts colleges.

While most writers have emphasized that the greatest contribution of competence-based education has been to the assessment of performance, I suspect that this aspect will be diffused least well. Performance assessment is expensive, unfamiliar, complex, and least consistent with current educational practices, particularly in liberal arts curriculums. Rather, I would say that the influence of competence-based education will come from stimulating the examination of outcomes. For all of its difficulties, it is clear that competence-based education has profound effects. Once past the travail of reaching agreement about conceptualization and design, many faculty have said that competence-based education forces them to examine themselves in new ways as teachers. They think that their students learn more, and they feel more authentic as teachers. They say that working with other faculty in new ways is difficult but also exhilarating. Indeed, the process of defining the outcomes of education—regardless of the result—can itself be a deeply moving experience for faculty. What at first is often resisted as administrative pressure and interference comes later to be seen as a way of defining central institutional goals or of arriving at a new conception of the liberal arts or the professions. Competence-based education, then, can offer a powerful tool to reconceive and reorganize a curriculum.

Competence-based education is also beginning to delineate a new conception of the faculty role, of the faculty as a collectivity, and of disciplinary boundaries. While competence-based education may have appealed to some funding agencies and to administrators because of its implications for faculty accountability, it is more often a tool for faculty development and self-examination. In his project notes, Thomas Ewens describes these effects at Alverno: "One of the effects of competence-based education is to level all hierarchial differences among different content areas. Once the philosopher, the physicist, the historian . . . begin to see themselves as all doing, in a sense, the same thing—for example, analysis, level 2—their perception of themselves, their colleagues, and the relative importance of their respective content areas tends to change. They begin to open themselves to the concerns of other disciplines in a way that they had not done before. So too, faculty colleague networks have changed [as a result of] newly developed interdisciplinary interests. The implementation of the new program has, in effect, been an important element in the liberal education of the faculty."

While I think it is premature to speak of a "second-generation" of competence-based programs, it is possible to see the adaptation of aspects of competence-based education—although they may not be identified as such—to local needs and terrains. In one place, it may be in assessing experiential learning and field studies. In another, it may be in attempting to conceptualize a total curriculum in outcome terms. Somewhere else, it may simply be in teaching a new course on problem solving.

These are signs of the influence of the competence movement as it has diffused beyond the first generation of innovators. Although the early competence-based programs began from an alliance between energetic administrators at a few struggling colleges and the staff of an ambitious, young federal agency, the wider appeal of competence approaches depends on more diverse and more local conditions. Purists will undoubtedly object that later generations are not "really" doing competence-based education, and they will probably be right. But, as with any innovation, people will choose what they need, adapting the work of others to their own uses. Such pragmatism seems healthy—even inevitable.

Thomas Ewens   8

Transforming
a Liberal Arts
Curriculum:
Alverno College

Alverno College is a small liberal arts college for women located on
a fifty-acre campus in a middle- and lower-middle-class neighborhood on the strongly ethnic south side of Milwaukee, Wisconsin. As
of 1976, its full-time equivalent enrollment was about 650. The college is owned and operated by the School Sisters of Saint Francis
under a predominantly lay board. Roughly 60 percent of the faculty
is lay, predominantly female; the remainder are members of the
School Sisters of Saint Francis (SSSF). Essentially a liberal arts college, Alverno offers strong programs in nursing, music, and education. In September 1973, Alverno began to implement a competence-based curriculum of liberal education with that year's
freshman class. By the fall of 1976, all four years of the college
curriculum had become competence-based. This case study describes
the development and the implementation of that program.

The Alverno of today resulted from the merger of three predecessor institutions that the School Sisters of Saint Francis had operated in Milwaukee for many years: a normal school (founded in 1887); a music conservatory (founded in 1922) that later became St. Joseph's College of Music; and a three-year nursing program (begun in 1890) run in conjunction with the Sacred Heart Sanitarium. The merger of the three schools was completed in 1948, Alverno received its accreditation in 1951, and it moved to its present campus in 1953.

The creation of Alverno was the work of a small group of sisters under the leadership of Sister Augustin, the first president of the college. Although the college began to accept a few lay students in the early 1950's—a number that increased to 50 percent of the student body by the end of that decade—it quickly settled into the tranquil and unexceptional life of other institutions of its kind, part college and part seminary. But if the merger into a liberal arts college had been accomplished in theory, the professional orientation of the component elements nonetheless remained strong in practice: a professional-vocational strain had influenced Alverno's history from its inception. Nonetheless, while training nuns and more and more lay women for careers in nursing, high school teaching, and other professions, Alverno operated as a liberal arts college, and, from all accounts, it was possible to get from it a solid liberal education in addition to preprofessional education.

The great majority of the sisters presently on the faculty at Alverno received their undergraduate education in the college, and except for high school teaching or stints as teaching assistants while in graduate school, most of them have not taught elsewhere. Because most of the faculty and administrators are over forty and very few are under thirty five (the average age in the order itself is well over fifty), they were formed and began their professional careers while Sister Augustin and her age-group peers were in control at the college.

Like other orders of religious men and women, the School Sisters of Saint Francis were profoundly affected by the tensions and opportunities stemming from the spirit of renewal that the Second Vatican Council produced in the Catholic church. Though the order has its share of women who were something less than enthusiastic about the reforms of religious life that came in the wake of the council, other members were in the forefront of those militating for a new conception of the roles and appropriate training of religious women in the church. Indeed, many of those responsible for the educational changes still underway in the college had earlier brought about significant changes in the order at large. In many cases they had had to forge a new understanding of themselves as religious women or, simply, as women, and found themselves required by both circumstances and personal choice to change both the order and the college to which they were committed. Yesterday's renegades became today's reformers, and their zeal and personal style are in part a reaction to the institutional viewpoints that they have discarded. Their advent to positions of authority in the college coincided with a period of considerable turmoil within the order and upheaval within the college in the late 1960s—a period that marked the beginning of the transition leading to the innovative program that characterizes Alverno today.

Before picking up the thread of that story, another skein of historical and cultural background is worth noting. Alverno today emphasizes not only "knowing what" but "knowing how to." It insists on setting precise objectives, demands performance, encourages initiative, independence, self-pacing, and self-mastery, and in general canonizes competence. But these were not always the qualities associated with religious life fifteen or twenty years ago, much less in the latter part of the nineteenth century, when the School Sisters of Saint Francis first established themselves in this country from Germany. Historically the order's efforts were directed toward girls and young women from families of relatively modest social, economic, and cultural backgrounds similar to those from which many of the sisters themselves come. But a number of today's leaders complain that, although the order gave them an excellent education of a traditional sort, it did little to fit them for effective, competent living outside the convent and the parameters of traditional female roles. Thus it is not surprising that these women should be so concerned with "worldly" competence, skills, and abilities and so dedicated to doing for their students what was not done for them. As the Alverno College catalogue (1975, p. 5) proclaims, their students "will be prepared for the world [they] live in . . .

will have the background and motivation to continue learning . . . will be more effective in practical ways in whatever world [they] choose." When the winds of change hit Alverno in the late 1960's, these women did not try to attract a new clientele, racial or other, as so many similar institutions did. They continued to work with the same type of young women they had always worked with— in a recent year 75 percent of Alverno's students received some form of financial aid—but they had a new sense of what these students needed and a willingness, born of their own recent experiences in the order, to experiment with new structures and procedures to meet this need.

Toward a More Exciting Place

In 1968 a number of events occurred that are relevant to these structures and procedures. Most important among them, the governing board of the order instituted a new policy that henceforth no young woman would be accepted into the order without a college degree. Prior to that time, the great majority of entrants had come to the order straight from high school and eventually matriculated at Alverno, which had been averaging 125 young sisters in its freshman class. Now sister-students were given the option of returning to their home bases in fourteen states for their education, and over 300 of them exercised this option in March and left Alverno. At about this same time, 19 sister-faculty members also left Alverno to pursue their professional work elsewhere. Not long before, long-simmering dissensions in the nursing department had boiled over, and many faculty there were restive and dissatisfied, as were the students. In February, a new board of directors, composed of ten sisters and five lay people, had been appointed. At its first meeting, in March, Sister Augustin resigned as president, effective in July.

Among the candidates for the presidency was Sister Joel Read, who was named acting president in July and president later that fall. She had graduated from Alverno in 1948 and, after completing a master's degree in history at Fordham, had taught full time at the college since 1955. From 1961 to 1967 she had been the chairperson of the history department. In 1967 she had taken the lead in trying to organize the faculty and, the following year, she had been elected as the faculty representative to the new board of trustees. In 1967 she had also been named to head a steering committee within the order whose mission was to plan the reorganization of the order in the dramatically changed circumstances in which it then found itself.

Another candidate for president, Sister Bernarda Handrup, a physicist by training, was named academic dean of the college; and from 1968 to 1970 Read and Handrup tried to make things more effective while holding the college together, but student and faculty dissatisfaction did not disappear. Alverno reflected the turmoil in colleges and universities across the country in the 1968–69 academic year. Thus at the faculty institute in May 1969, dissatisfaction among students and faculty was the principal subject of discussion. Who should decide the content of courses? Is the marking system relevant or should it be junked? Are typical lecture courses and the enforced passivity of students the best or the only way to teach and learn? Such questions were the order of the day, and from them a dialogue began to grow among faculty and between faculty and students.

In the fall of 1969 this incipient dialogue was adroitly put to work as a vehicle for change by means of a series of events innocuously entitled "September 1969." This was a three-day series of presentations and discussions intended to give faculty and students the opportunity to raise questions concerning their respective roles and the locus of responsibility for learning. In follow-up meetings, the faculty discussed every aspect of faculty and student life. At first, meetings were held in the departments. Later, an Educational Policy Committee was set up, as well as other committees on the January Interim term, evaluation of students, interdisciplinary course and experience, departmental organization into broad majors, flexibility in degree requirements, and evaluation of faculty members. Like many faculty discussions, these never really got anywhere. Alternative futures, possible approaches, and grandiose schemes were not lacking; tons of memos were generated; and yet discussion often seemed an end in itself, and the overall process remained inconclusive. Nonetheless, there was some sense of movement, principally in a raising of consciousness in the college, especially among the faculty. It was a time of exploration and recurrent glimmers of hope, of a gradually dawning recognition that, if only they would, they could chart a new direction for the college.

Then, in March 1971, an event occurred that everyone regards as a crucial moment in Alverno's search for a more exciting way to learn. A faculty meeting had been convened to discuss general problems of liberal education. The nursing faculty had not been invited but had showed up anyway. Things were not much different than they had always been at such meetings until, out of the blue, one faculty member wondered whether they might not conceive their curriculum in terms of outcomes rather than in terms of contents and fixed exposure times. Strangely, there is no consensus about whose voice it was, but the idea quickly galvanized the entire group. Indeed, many people speak of this intervention in quasi-sacral terms. In listening to them, one imagines that the faculty had been wandering about in the desert for many months when, as though from on high, a voice cried out; a great hush fell upon the group; insight flooded the assembled spirits. The manna of outcomes was at hand!

The voice may have cried out in the wilderness, but the way of the outcomes had been anticipated in a number of ways. President Read had been regularly urging faculty to ask themselves: Why should anybody study with them? What did they have to offer a student? What was different about what they were doing? Since 1969 there had also been a group of freshman teachers who met at lunch on Fridays to discuss the problem of teaching freshmen. They had dubbed themselves the CIA—the "Committee to Investigate Academia"; they were generally interested in sharing and inventing ways to deal with problems common to all of them. By 1971 a more formal group of freshman teachers had been organized. The dean had set up freshman seminars of fifteen students in each field, and the teachers of these seminars had begun to meet and to concentrate on some common abilities they were attempting to foster, for example, communication and analysis.

Moreover, Sister Elizabeth Glysh, whom Read had brought to Alverno in 1969 to help write grant proposals, had prepared a model for a supportive services program for disadvantaged students in late 1970 and early 1971. This model, which included a segment with flow charts and used such language as "conduct performance—

objective oriented instruction," could be described as a competence-based program in germ. Glysh herself makes no such claim but she does think that some of the things she and others had done in establishing this program had prepared for an emphasis on outcomes. Her own reaction to the voice episode was: "Well, they are finally beginning to catch on."

Perhaps most importantly, Sister Georgine Loacker and some of her colleagues in the English department, had begun to examine with great seriousness not only the problem of freshman English but the problem of English as a requirement in a liberal arts college. Why was it necessary? What good did it do? What exactly was necessary for such a course? They had been willing to throw out the course in freshman composition altogether and to re-think from the beginning what it meant to be an English major. They finally identified nine objectives whose accomplishment, in their view, would constitute a valid English major, and they had begun to experiment with these objectives while still retaining the old structure of the English major program. A sample objective required that a student understand the validity of both a critical response and an emotional or subjective response to literature, yet be able to distinguish between them: that she understand how to test a subjective response critically, with questions "Why?" and "How?" Their efforts did not work out as well as they would have liked, for the students quickly realized that it was enough to fill the old requirements and that they did not really have to bother themselves unduly about the new objectives. But an effort was underway to redefine radically the curriculum in one key disciplinary area not in terms of such traditional content as the nineteenth-century novel or Elizabethan drama, but in terms of a set of objectives that cut across all the standard courses.

At least one other preparation for the way of the outcomes deserves to be mentioned. In 1965–66 the SSSF, as an order, undertook a thorough rethinking of their common life, of their administrative structures, of their style of government, and so on. In the past, their individual communities had been organized in the traditional hierarchical fashion under a local mother superior. In the Alverno College SSSF community, which includes not only the professors and administrators at Alverno but a number of other sisters engaged in other work, this style of internal governance was done away with in 1966. Within the overall community, they decided to organize themselves in small, self-constituted affinity groups ranging from a single person to a group of ten. To avoid potential conflicts as best they could, each such group was asked to state, as explicitly and as precisely as possible, the criteria for membership in their group. These criteria, of course, reflected the different types of religious and personal commitments of the various members of the community. No one was excluded from any group, but, if she wanted to join an already constituted group, she would have to be governed by the criteria for membership. If that was the style of life she wanted, fine; if not, it would be better for her to find another group more suited to her personal interests. Each group would be responsible for organizing its own life as it saw fit. For the past ten years, one group of five has included among its members Sisters Joel Read, Austin Doherty and Georgine Loacker.

In short, regardless of who spoke the fateful words at the March 1971 faculty meeting, it is plausible to think that any one of seven or eight different persons could have spoken them. The immediate upshot of this meeting was that the steering committee proposed a series of questions to the various departments and committees with a view to preparing an agenda for the faculty institute to be held in May. As expressed in "Historical Development of Competence-Based Learning at Alverno," (1973b) these questions were:

1. What kinds of questions are being asked by professionals in your field that relate to the validity of your disciplines in a total college program? In other words, what are the burning issues? What is your department's position on these? How are you dealing with these current problems in a general education course and in the work for a major in your field?
2. What are you teaching that is so important that students cannot afford to bypass courses in your department(s)?
3. If we expect general education requirements in terms of expected outcomes rather than in terms of courses, what contribution does your department make to them?
4. How do you see your department in relation to other disciplines?

5. For the professional departments (nursing, education, music, physical education, medical technology): in what way are courses in your department integrated into the liberal arts college so that they differ from those in a purely professional school?

The same document continues by saying that "what began as a question of outcomes of general and professional education became a question of outcomes of liberal education." Although divided on any number of points, the faculty came to unanimous agreement at the May 1971 faculty institute that at least four outcomes were essential to any liberal education: problem solving, communications, involvement, and valuing. Thus did the efforts of the previous two years finally coalesce and come into focus: a potentially revolutionary framework for rethinking the curriculum of Alverno College had been agreed upon.

In the fall of 1971, the faculty began to grapple with the still vague notion of a curriculum that would be defined in terms of outcomes. The decision was made that the committee structure for that year would involve the entire faculty as a curriculum committee divided into subcommittees for each of the four outcomes that had been identified. In November Dean Handrup sent a memo to all the departments requesting them to assess the four outcomes from their points of view. Did they agree with those statements? Are there more specific goals that they would urge? Do these four outcomes encompass all the major outcomes that could reasonably be said to characterize liberal education? Are there other outcomes that they would suggest? A great variety of responses were received, including "broad integrating perspectives," "awareness of historical evolution of ideas," "mastery of content," "development of a person," and "international awareness."

The four subcommittees were asked to analyze and refine further their particular outcome in the light of the responses that had been received. These subcommittees—each averaging about twenty faculty members plus some students—were not particularly efficacious. But cumbersome as they were, these committees *were* fairly effective in allowing faculty to probe, to explore, and to accustom themselves to what was an unfamiliar and sometimes threatening way of looking at a curriculum, at the place of their own disciplines within it, and—not least—at their own roles as professors in a liberal arts college. These subcommittees were to continue their work throughout the 1971–72 academic year. Nominally coordinating this activity was Dean Handrup; but here, as later, her role does not seem to have been the decisive one. Throughout this voyage into the unknown, President Read's hand was firmly at the helm. She was beginning to have some sense of where things might be going, and along with some of her close faculty allies, she was initiating, pushing, and facilitating the process and forcing the action. The faculty members, of course, were doing the major share of the work during this still exploratory, transitional phase. Meanwhile, some other inputs were sought and/or arrived on the scene and served to punctuate the change underway. An outside consultant ran a workshop on the processes of change and, it seems, seriously complicated matters by succeeding in a day and a half in organizing the latent opposition to what was being attempted. The college invited other experts to organize a workshop on testing. A group from Antioch ran an institute on innovative forms of education. These useful exercises gave some minor legitimation and encouragement to a faculty now spending a considerable amount of time in meetings, but they do not appear to have had any decisive impact. Alverno finally developed an almost entirely self-generated program. In July 1973, they received a major grant from FIPSE but by that time Alverno had already laid out, at least in outline, a plan for the future.

An important input at this time came from the vice-president for administration, Dan Riedy, a former professor of management at the Milwaukee School of Engineering. He had never been much involved in the academic affairs of the college, but he was concerned with packaging and marketing Alverno's projects, and he was aware that the faculty was doing a lot of talking about their four outcomes without making much apparent headway with them. As a management specialist, he had one absolute principle: "Either you react to change or you manage it." He prided himself on his management point of view and took keen pleasure in working with charts, matrices. Earlier, he had been struck by the fact that his engineering students were good at analyzing the pieces of a process but rarely arrived at an overall view of it. To help them think deductively about the affairs of a business operation, he had constructed a very elaborate matrix that supposedly situated all the pieces of a complex operation in a coherent whole—the kind of thing Steinberg might have devised had he gone to a business school.

Riedy was interested in integrating the liberal arts with management, and the college's new concern with outcomes and objectives fitted nicely into his management point of view. Even better, these outcomes could be fitted into his matrix. To create a significantly different Alverno product, Riedy worked up a series of twelve goals on the one hand and nine strategies to develop these goals on the other, all of which had been transposed, with slight changes, from his original matrix.

Riedy presented this matrix to the faculty group. Although the faculty did not understand it very well, Riedy had in fact provided the faculty with a new context and a new instrument: Liberal education in a management context suggested a way not only of marketing Alverno to a potential student clientele but at the same time a way of packaging and marketing Alverno's students for the Milwaukee business and professional communities in which most of them would eventually seek jobs. Alverno would provide a liberal education, but their students would also be habituated to the rationality characteristic of postindustrial capitalism. As the college catalogue (1975, p. 7) was later to express it, their graduates would not only have knowledge "but would know what to do with it in practical ways"; they would not only have "information" but also "the training and ability to use it, do something worthwhile with it, make it work for them and for others."

Such a context was not uncongenial to President Read and those in the college who share her views. Read is herself committed to analytical procedures and management techniques. Her earlier experience in both the order and the college had convinced her that one problem common to both was the simplistic level of analysis with which people too often contented themselves. In her first address to the faculty after becoming president, she had made a point of criticizing the informal way of dealing with issues that had been customary in the college. She had insisted on the necessity of more formal management structures and a less "familial" organization of the community. Read tends to divide the world into those who understand historical process and insist on conceptual clarity and organization and those who are more intuitive by nature, do not understand change, and love muddling their way through. She sees herself as a process-oriented, modern, clear-minded, and decisive executive—which indeed she is. An attractive woman who can be charming, she is not the intuitive, empathetic, all-caring "mother-type" superior. In fact, she and a number of her associates and allies seem often to be in rather vehement reaction against traditional stereotypes of "eternally feminine" nuns in general and *mother* superiors in particular. Read and some of her colleagues, then, responded favorably to the notion of liberal education in a management context. (It may well be that they themselves inspired Riedy's approach.) The management point of view that Riedy had contributed was to become increasingly important in the process of curriculum development over the next one and one-half years although Riedy himself, except for an occasional and informal consultant role, played little further part in it.

More immediately important to the developments in 1972, however, was Riedy's matrix for plotting goals and strategies. At Alverno, as so often elsewhere, this simple instrument seems to have come as something of a discovery. For committees that had been actively but inconclusively treading water on the oceans of the unknown, Riedy's grid was a kind of life buoy. It gave a new handle to the four quite amorphous outcomes that the faculty had agreed upon, and seems to have given a new sense of direction to the efforts of the various committees.

Sister Austin Doherty of the psychology department took it upon herself to attempt to relate and refine the four outcomes in terms of Riedy's matrix, an effort that was then continued by the Curriculum Committee. Finally, in the spring of 1972, a matrix establishing a set of outcomes as student goals and indicating a strategy for achieving them was presented to the entire faculty. This new matrix was the subject of discussion at the faculty institute in May 1972.

Academic Task Force

In spite of the apparent clarity that a grid lends to a process, it was at this point still not clear where the process was leading. Nor was everybody necessarily going in the same direction. Even divided into four subcommittees, the faculty as a committee of the whole was in some ways counterproductive. Read recognized that if progress was to continue, some of the faculty would have to be given time off to do the shaping and the refining that could not be done effectively by a large committee. In the summer of 1972, Read therefore constituted an Academic Task Force (ATF), naming Austin Doherty, Georgine Loacker, Brian Nedwek, and Jack Cooper as its members. The academic task force, then, was composed of two behavioral scientists (Doherty and Nedwek), an English professor (Loacker), and, for a short time, a musician (Cooper). There was nobody from the nursing faculty, education, music (once Cooper withdrew) or the natural sciences. However, there was a large chance that a "politically" balanced committee would be unable to do the work. Read set up the ATF, gave them the ball and told them to run with it. She would take the flack. In principle, the task force was a group of faculty peers; in fact two of them were more equal than the others: Doherty and Loacker quickly assumed the dominant roles, and, notwithstanding contributions by Nedwek and the collaboration of the faculty as a whole, the program that eventually emerged from the task force was in large measure their creation.

By reason of its composition, the personal style of its principal members, its administrative status and the nature of its work, the task force could hardly avoid becoming a focus of controversy. President Read, of course, knew this and she was ready to take the heat while leaving the task force free to work with the faculty and to create the program. The task force had in hand a general matrix that had been agreed upon by the faculty the preceding May, as well as the large amount of material that had been generated over the previous three years. They also had a strong sense of the import of their mission for the college and for themselves, but above all, they combined prodigious energy with fierce belief in their ability to create their own future. Doherty, Loacker, and Nedwek agreed that they would spend about one third of their time each week on task force work. Indicative of the work ethic that tends to pervade the atmosphere at Alverno is the fact that for them one-third time meant a minimum of twenty to twenty-five hours. There were few weeks when they were to spend "so little" time on task force affairs.

Significantly, they did not set out to develop a "competence-based" program as such. They were to rethink, review, and improve what was already a reasonably good educational program with a strong professional orientation. To specify outcomes and to be explicit about the processes by which they could be realized was not necessarily to do something radically different from what Alverno had been doing: It was to do what the college had been doing more consciously, more critically and more effectively. Once the faculty had decided to reconceive what they had been doing in terms of general outcomes, the task force then followed the logic of that choice without betraying the past. Thus for a number of months its members used the word "competence" only sporadically and incidentally; likewise, much of the other vocabulary now associated with the competence-based education movement emerged only very gradually in their discussions, although by the time that FIPSE's special focus program on competence-based education was announced in the spring of 1973, Alverno faculty had discovered that they had been speaking the language of "competence" all along— as indeed they had been. Even later, when they found themselves thrust into the forefront of the competence-based movement, people at Alverno continued to insist that they were attempting to do in a new way something that was really quite traditional.

The task force had inherited from the faculty institute of May 1972 the matrix with twelve goals, and they tried to work around those for some time with no great success. They were finally to reduce the eleven goals to eight outcomes, which they came to call "competences." This helped but it wasn't a program. In late November, Doherty recalls, they had the feeling that they must simply lock themselves in a room and "break the nut." This is almost literally what they did, and they achieved a major breakthrough: They hit on the idea of leveling the different competences, that is, specifying a series of sequential levels of achievement for each competence. With that step taken, others followed. After considerable discussion, they decided on six levels for each competence, and they had the skeleton of a program. There would be eight competences, each with six levels, and hence a system with 48 possible competence levels, as illustrated in Table 1. All students in the program would be required to achieve level four in all eight

Table 1. Competence Levels

Competence 1: Develop Effective Communications Skill
  Level 1—Identify own strengths and weaknesses as initiator and responder in communication situations of the following types, including a variety of audiences: Written, oral, use of graphs
  Level 2—Analyze written and oral communication situations
  Level 3—Communicate with clarity of message—exchange in communication situations of the following types, including a variety of audiences: written, oral, use of graphs
  Level 4—Demonstrate sufficient understanding of basic concepts of at least 3 major areas of knowledge to communicate in terms of them
  Level 5—Demonstrate understanding of communication as historical process involving development of meaning and form in relation to technological and cultural forces
  Level 6—Communicate effectively through coordinated use of 3 different media that represent contemporary technological advancement in the communications field
Competence 2: Sharpen Analytical Capabilities
  Level 1—Identify explicit elements of a work (A work may be an article, artifact, or process)
  Level 2—Identify implicit elements of a work
  Level 3—Identify relationships in a work
  Level 4—Analyze the structure and organization of a work
  Level 5—In the interpretation and/or creation of one or more works, develop new hypotheses, new conclusions, or new relations of materials and means of production
  Level 6—Produce a single work that demonstrates facility in 3 types of analysis: elements, relationships, organizing principles
Competence 3: Develop Workable Problem-Solving Skill
  Level 1—Identify the process, assumptions, and limitations involved in the scientific method
  Level 2—Formulate questions which yield to the problem-solving approach
  Level 3—Apply the problem-solving process to a problem
  Level 4—Apply the problem-solving process to a new area of knowledge (area different from problem in Level 3)
  Level 5—Design and implement original research project of sufficient complexity to involve direction of or collaboration with others
  Level 6—Demonstrate that problem solving is an assumed approach in one's own search for knowledge and one's reflection upon experience
Competence 4: Develop a Facility for Making Value Judgments and Independent Decisions
  Level 1—Identify own values
  Level 2—Demonstrate understanding of philosophy, history, religion, arts, and/or literature as reflection of values
  Level 3—Demonstrate understanding of relationship of values to scientific and technological development
  Level 4—Make value judgments for which you (a) identify viable alternatives and (b) forecast and weigh consequences
  Level 5—Demonstrate understanding of the validity of value systems differing from culture to culture

Table 1. Competence Levels (continued)

Level 6—Communicate value judgments effectively, either to defend them or to persuade others to them, and demonstrate commitment to them

Competence 5: Develop Facility for Social Interaction

Level 1—Identify and analyze own strengths and weaknesses in group situations

Level 2—Analyze behavior of others within a theoretical framework

Level 3—Evaluate behavior of self and others within a theoretical framework

Level 4—Demonstrate effective social behavior in variety of situations and circumstances—both private and public, within one's own culture

Level 5—Demonstrate effective social behavior in variety of situations and circumstances, beyond as well as on college campus, involving different cultures or subcultures and large as well as small groups

Level 6—Demonstrate effective organizational activity

Competence 6: Achieve Understanding of the Relationship of the Individual and the Environment

Level 1—Identify environmental components

Level 2—Identify relationships between individual attitudes, beliefs, values, behaviors, and environmental components

Level 3—Demonstrate an understanding of the interaction effects of cultural and physical setting upon individual and group behavior

Level 4—Analyze alternative courses of action regarding a particular environmental problem on the basis of their feasibility, cultural acceptability, and technical accuracy

Level 5—Assess the consequences of various courses of action in regard to a selected environmental problem and the likelihood that goals will be achieved

Level 6—Defend a choice among solutions to a particular environmental problem

Competence 7: Develop Awareness and Understanding of the World in which the Individual Lives

Level 1—Demonstrate awareness, perception, and knowledge of observable events in the comtemporary world

Level 2—Analyze contemporary events in their historical context

Level 3—Analyze interrelationships of contemporary events and conditions

Level 4—Demonstrate understanding of the world as a global unit by analyzing the impact of events of one society upon another

Level 5—Demonstrate understanding and acceptance of personal responsibility in contemporary events

Level 6—Take personal position regarding implications of contemporary events

Competence 8: Develop Knowledge, Understanding, and Responsiveness to the Arts and Knowledge and Understanding of the Humanities (Levels 1 and 3 of this competence are to be achieved for a total of 3 arts and/or humanities including at least 1 of each)

Level 1—For each selected art, express response to and demonstrate understanding of elements, and for each selected humanity, demonstrate understanding of the elements characteristic of its method

Table 1. Competence Levels (continued)

Level 2—Express response to and demonstrate understanding of one of the arts in relationship to other arts, and demonstrate understanding of an artistic work as an expression of philosophy, religion, or history

Level 3—Express response to and demonstrate understanding of the arts, and demonstrate understanding of the humanities, in both cases as expressions of interrelationships between the individual and society

Level 4—Demonstrate understanding of works of other cultures and their impact upon modes of expression of one's own culture

Level 5—Formulate independent judgments regarding the relative intrinsic and extrinsic values of artistic or humanistic expressions and persuasively communicate the significance of their worth

Level 6—Demonstrate facility of self-expression in one or more artistic or humanistic modes and commitment to their importance

Source: "Competence-Based Learning Program," Alverno College (mimeograph, n.d.).

competences. This would be roughly equivalent to two years work in the old program, enough for an associate of arts diploma. A student would receive that diploma whenever she had demonstrated proficiency through level four in all eight of the competences. Levels five and six in each competence would be more complex and difficult to attain than levels one to four and would ordinarily take a proportionately longer period of time to achieve. For a bachelor's degree, eight fifth or sixth competence levels (including at least one sixth) would be necessary—a total, then, of forty competence level units (CLUs) of the possible forty-eight (thirty-two plus eight). It was anticipated that these eight level five or six CLUs would be the equivalent, again roughly, of the work of the junior and senior years in the old program. The notion of a ladder or levels of competence was the breakthrough they had been looking for and it continues to be a distinctive feature of the Alverno program.

The task force was principally concerned with devising and working out the details of a curriculum model. But each important decision that it made with regard to the curriculum model had manifold ramifications for the rest of the college. For example, who would be involved in the curriculum being developed? A pilot group or the whole college? There was a considerable divergence of opinion on this issue, and it was, of course, a crucial issue from an administrative standpoint. President Read finally decided to put the entire college, starting with the freshman class entering the following autumn, on the new curriculum.

In some instances, already existing programs fitted nicely into the developing curriculum model and added a new dimension to it, for example, off-campus experimental learning. But in others, the development of the new curriculum would require fundamental revisions. As the character of Alverno had changed from that of a college composed predominantly of student-sisters to a predominantly lay student body, student development had become a central concern—accentuated by the contemporaneous search for new role models for women. In 1971 President Read had proposed a bridge with the worlds of business and social services in Milwaukee that would allow Alverno students to engage in off-campus learning. Certainly this program reinforced the notion of liberal learning in a management context and fitted well into the context of competence-based learning. The college curriculum was centered on notions of competence, and the whole field of career development was concerned with bringing students to realize that what they learn is practical.

After the skeleton of the program had been decided upon, assessment became a central issue. Loacker began to ask her colleagues on the task force, "How are we going to know if a student has achieved the goals that we have set for her? How are we going to count or measure this achievement?" Neither she nor any of the others had previously given this question much thought. But relatively early in their discussions of assessment, the members of the task force talked about developing their procedure in such a way that they could use outside assessors. At the same time they realized that they could not take all assessment out of faculty hands. They began to talk about an assessment center without having any clear idea of what such a center would be like or how it would operate.

At the same time that they had begun to bat around questions concerning assessment, Doherty, Loacker, and Read had been reading a series of essays on the theme of servants by Robert K. Greenleaf in connection with their religious and liturgical activities. Greenleaf had been a vice-president with AT&T, but this fact does not seem to have been recognized by these sisters until sometime later. Greenleaf is also a kind of homespun, religiously oriented

(Quaker) philosopher who has been concerned for many years, both while he was at AT&T and since, with the problems of building communities. His writings had a significant influence on Doherty, Loacker and Read. (These essays have since been collected in a book. See Greenleaf, 1977.)

Greenleaf influenced his readers at Alverno in a number of ways. He encouraged them to be concerned about "really teaching," about what students "really learn," about the outcomes here and now for the students, about creating a community here and now of this faculty across the artificial divisions of the disciplines. The combination of management expertise, humane concerns, and underlying religious motivation that Greenleaf articulates could not have been more congenial to the Alverno people. One senses in Greenleaf, as in some of the Alverno people, a creative tension between, on the one hand, typical American phantasms regarding efficiency and clear, no-nonsense statements of outcome and, on the other hand, intensely personalist and religious concerns, which combat these technicist phantasms, attempt to humanize them, and make them serve community.

In fact, Greenleaf had played a major role in the development of some of the assessment instruments which AT&T has long since been famous for. Loacker and Doherty were aware that the Wisconsin Telephone Company had developed a series of assessment instruments that were considered quite effective, and so they made an appointment with the president of the Wisconsin Telephone Company to inquire about its assessment techniques. He and the telephone company personnel were very generous with their help, not only in sharing their assessment techniques with Alverno and giving them copyrighted materials at no cost but also in loaning Alverno the services of their public relations manager who was responsible for school and college relations. In addition to helping the Alverno people familiarize themselves with the Wisconsin Bell techniques, Donna Dollace also helped to coordinate the recruitment, selection, and training of assessors from the business and professional community. Alverno has adopted and adapted a good number of the Wisconsin Bell techniques.

(Sometime later, Doherty and others were at a luncheon with the president of Wisconsin Bell, who gave Doherty a book by

Douglas Bray on assessment techniques. The book was dedicated to Greenleaf. Later that day, Doherty discovered that her Greenleaf was AT&T's Greenleaf. It is worth mentioning that in 1974, Doherty and Loacker went to Greenleaf's rural retreat in New Hampshire and invited him to be one of the speakers at the ceremonies celebrating the hundredth anniversary of the SSSF.)

Problems and Difficulties

To make an omelette one must crack eggs, and it was inevitable in creating a new program that some egos would get cracked. Alverno has factions, cliques, and malcontents, as does any institution. Faculty salaries are relatively low. At least through 1975 there was no tenure policy, and individual faculty were relatively powerless. Faculty turnover has apparently been relatively high, and many of the people have left in anger and bitterness. For Doherty and Loacker, it sometimes seemed, the emerging program was their religion. They became less tolerant of those who criticized "their program," more prone to regard questions or doubts or hesitations as obstructionism or hostility. As the months wore on, these attitudes were picked up by different subgroups of faculty and played back in the form of a variety of easily imaginable complaints.

Doherty and Loacker, as they themselves recognize, came rather soon to be regarded, with Read, as the administration. All three of them have strong, if very different, personalities. Although everyone at Alverno recognizes their intelligence, ability, hard work, and commitment, there are also many who find their styles difficult to take. In addition a number of faculty came to regard the collaborative exchanges with the task force as a vast charade intended to convince the faculty that they owned a program that was in fact being imposed on them from above. There was, as one faculty member puts it, a constant "finagle factor" designed to convince the faculty that the program was their program. Many other faculty members hotly contest this charge and point to the years of searching in common, the numerous faculty institutes, and the critical role that each faculty member by necessity has had to play in the creation and especially the implementation of the program that was agreed upon.

Another problem had to do with cognitive style, reflecting to some extent the divergent tendencies of the natural scientists and the humanists. Although there were notable exceptions, especially in biology, the natural scientists have been at best lukewarm about the new program. Both Dean Handrup and Sister Elizabeth Glysh had backgrounds in physics. Handrup left the college in the summer of 1974 after the first year's experience with the new program, and Glysh, whose title had become director of institutional research, feeling that her position was constantly being undermined, quit in October 1973. The natural scientists represent the most structured of the disciplines, and it is plausible to think that their resistance to what seems to be a kind of homogenization of the disciplines within a competence matrix stems from the highly structured nature of their own disciplines. At the other end of the spectrum are the complaints of some musicians, historians, and professors of literature, who tend to see the competence-based mode as reductive of the values, variously described as "intuitive," "transcendental," and "intangible," that they see as central to the liberal arts tradition and to their own teaching. Some openly scoff at "the Galahad complex" of the would-be innovators.

Another central source of conflict in the college is Read's personal style. In her first address to the faculty she had warned that she was not promising them a rose garden; nor did she expect one for herself. She is a person of outstanding ability and intelligence and is generally recognized as such. An intense person who has assumed great risks, she can also be curt, needlessly abrasive, and arrogant. She is loved by her allies, respected by many and hated by some. There is no doubt that she has often been unfairly criticized and that much of her own impatience and occasional harshness has stemmed from her frustration with the lack of faculty leadership. Nonetheless her forceful style has often exacerbated situations that were already difficult enough. For her, offense is clearly the best defense against those who might upset her plans. But her method of attack sometimes tends to destroy the good will that might otherwise be accorded her.

Read carries a heavy burden and, like many others at Alverno, she is grievously overextended. Active in the local community and increasingly on the national scene, attending to the ordinary responsibilities of a president, Read has also kept most of the changes in the college under her control. The principal administrators, such as Handrup, Glysh and Riedy, as well as a number of other staff and faculty people, left because of Read or were forced out by her, and a significant number of these departures seem to have been accompanied by mutual bitterness. Severe as these and other difficulties and problems may have been, they were neither unique to Alverno nor particularly surprising given the changes the institution was undergoing. And it needs to be emphasized that in spite of the turmoil and trauma, the process of change continued, the work got done, and the faculty and staff were able to fashion a remarkable new program of liberal and professional education. The faults of the administrators, such as they were, need to be viewed in the light of this impressive achievement.

Implementing the Program

Implementing a program of this scope under the constant time pressures that afflicted Alverno's every move was a herculean task requiring extraordinary ingenuity and persistence in the face of seemingly endless problems of morale, dissensions, and ordinary human weaknesses and oversights. Most imperative, once the decision was made to structure the program in terms of competences, was a reorganization of the faculty. Read named a policy committee composed of the department heads to work on this problem, dividing them into two working groups: (1) a group that would work with the old structure and see how it would accommodate the new matrix and (2) a group that would work with the new structure and see what ideas they could come up with. The findings of these two groups were then presented to the faculty and provoked a mare's nest of problems. Who would be responsible for what? Who would hire? Who would promote? Who would adjudicate disagreement? President Read proposed a hybrid solution: The disciplinary divisions would be maintained and be responsible for hiring and promotion, but in addition eight competence divisions would be created whose responsibilities would include curriculum, assessment, and the teaching modules for each level within the competency. Each faculty member would be simultaneously a member of a disciplinary division and a competence division of his or her choice. Under the circumstances, splitting the work into two parallel divisions based on competence and discipline seems to have been the only feasible arrangement. The decision to place each member of the faculty in one competence division was, however, something of a mistake. It resulted in competence divisions—in effect, working committees—that were too cumbersome to be very effective. Later on these problems were to some extent resolved when the competence divisions were reduced in size. They now range from four to seven members.

When the program was first implemented with the incoming freshman class in September 1973, other difficulties arose. The situation in the admissions office had been chaotic the previous spring: the students had not been recruited for the new program and in fact knew nothing about it. An elaborate orientation program had been devised, but it seems to have been an almost total failure. The students were exposed to new assessment procedures by assessors who were also new at the work, although they had received some training during the summer. There was of course no class ahead of these freshmen to help them out. Internal public relations seem to have been either inept or nonexistent. Although total enrollment in the college the previous year had been 1,145, there were only 208 students in the freshman class that inaugurated the competence-based program. By Christmas of 1973 about 80 of them had left, and by April 1975, 124 were gone. One can readily imagine the effect that this exodus had on the college and its administration. The admissions staff was demoralized. Many of them were not keen on the new program and were unable to explain it convincingly to students, parents, or high school counselors. The admissions director left and was not replaced for months. In March of 1974 the board additionally complicated the tasks of the recruiters by raising tuition by $300. Record-keeping and follow-up were done badly when they were done at all. By late fall 1974 Read realized the extent of the problem and took steps to reorganize the admissions effort. The lack of attention paid to recruitment and the other problems in the area of admissions have been perhaps the gravest weaknesses in the overall Alverno picture. Now, Alverno's overall goal is to enroll 300 freshmen each year and maintain an overall full-time enrollment of 1200 students.

Even without these foul-ups in recruitment and admissions, Alverno would have faced problems in presenting itself to its traditional clientele group. The college is still mainly dependent on local students from the middle class and lower-middle classes who, along with their parents, find it hard to adjust to the change in the college from a strictly Catholic institution with a convent halo to an ambitious liberal arts college that seeks a vanguard position in the education of women. To confront this clientele with a radically new program that is difficult to explain briefly, and even more difficult to understand, is to risk frightening off both parents and students. Nor has the negative feedback of the students who dropped out simplified the college's task. In spite of an enrollment problem, Alverno has therefore soft-pedaled the new program and tended to avoid too much local publicity while developing a whole series of activities to acquaint the local community with the new program gradually and indirectly. Even with older women and other continuing education students, for whom the new curriculum would seem to be ideally suited since it promises to validate competence acquired elsewhere, Alverno has made no concerted recruiting effort and has in fact lost ground with this clientele as the competition with other colleges and institutions in Milwaukee has picked up. Alverno's program is in the anomalous position of being better known on the national educational scene than it is locally.

Especially during the early start-up period, the new program itself was subject to all sorts of snags. Students were unsure what was afoot and unsure whom they could ask for information. Faculty were experimenting with the new program and had all they could do to keep a day ahead of the students. As noted, not all faculty were enthusiastic about the program, and a number worked to subvert it. Since validation materials were often not prepared, students had difficulties in achieving competence level units when they wanted to. There was no central clearinghouse for student complaints, and those responsible for the program soon became testy and defensive when student or faculty criticism arose. Their disposition was not improved by the alarming dropout rate in the charter class. Except for President Read and the de facto directors of the new curriculum, Loacker and Doherty, overall administration in the college was at best uncertain and indecisive.

In spite of this turmoil, the program was nonetheless implemented. Loacker and Doherty continued their relentless pace, but the implementation of the program really depended on a group of convinced and extremely hard working faculty who were not only in the classroom trenches every day but also carried major loads in the disciplinary and competence divisions. The program inevitably had shortcomings. Only the first four levels of each of the competences had been worked out in any detail. Some of the competences, such as environment and social action, had been less clearly articulated than others. The degree of difficulty on a given level across the competences varied rather widely. So, too, the developmental sequences in some competences—communications for example— seemed to be more clearly thought out than in others. Initially there was a tendency to try to pack too much into the first and second levels (although later the underlying rationale for the first four levels was more clearly demarcated). The content proper to the hard sciences appeared to be somewhat slighted in the competence specifications; many of the items in this area center on methodology and/or the philosophy of science. History was not altogether absent from the different competences yet the latter seem to be ahistorical in character. And Competence Eight—"develop knowledge, understanding, and responsiveness to the arts and knowledge and understanding of the humanities"—was curious and puzzling. It was in fact a catchall competence that covers an enormous range of the liberal arts, and its inclusion leads one to wonder to what extent the constellation of the first seven competences *can* do justice to a number of elements that most people would consider central to liberal education.

The faculty recognized the need to improve and refine the competence specifications as they worked with the new program. But they made the decision to give the first four competence levels a thorough tryout without extensive revision. Under the circumstances the decision was a reasonable, even a necessary one. After several years' experience, the fact that no major revisions have been necessary indicates the basic soundness of the specifications of these four levels and is a tribute to the very careful and original work that went into producing them.

The music department seems to have had the greatest difficulty in accommodating itself to the new program, but whether this difficulty was due to the program or to the music faculty is not clear. The nursing program, on the other hand, has flourished. The new curriculum has provided its faculty with an opportunity to create a nursing program no longer based on the medical model. The old divisions in nursing education, such as medical-surgical, pediatric, and psychiatric, that paralleled the divisions in medicine have been transcended and integrated in the new matrix. Nursing education has become more solidly rooted in a liberal education while maintaining everything necessary for a superior nursing education. There is already some evidence from clinical supervisors and others that student nurses in the competence-based program have acquired various nursing skills much more quickly than did the upper class of student nurses who did not take the new program. Not only are they more competent but there are signs that they may be more assertive and more independent than their predecessors. The new curriculum seems to have fostered long-sought changes in the content of nursing education as well as new role-images for women as nurses.

In 1975–76, the assessment done in the assessment center comprised only between 25 and 30 percent of the actual assessment of the competences. Of the first four levels in the eight competences, ten were being assessed in the assessment center. Levels five and six and assessment procedures for them were of course just coming on stream, so the percentage has probably gone up somewhat. Nonetheless, 70 to 75 percent of the assessing is currently being done in the courses or in course equivalents. New ways of assessing are constantly being worked out so that not all of this assessment in the courses is necessarily traditional paper and pencil assessment. The assessment that is not accomplished in courses or course equivalents is done in the assessment center. The first director of the assessment center, named in January 1974, was Judith Hart, who had previously spent eight years with IBM, the last four of them as a manager of administrative operations.

Assessment—especially some of the more complex assessments that Alverno regularly makes of its students—has proved exceedingly time consuming when compared, say, to a machine-scored, multiple-choice test or even an ordinary essay test. Alverno decided to rely insofar as possible on a group of volunteer assessors. At least in the beginning, the college was able to establish a list of nearly 100 assessors who were willing to spend three or four hours a month at the college. Roughly a third of them were drawn from the Milwaukee business and professional community; the other assessors were alumni, faculty, and students. These assessors brought outside viewpoints and expertise into the college, and at the same time the assessment program has been an occasion for the college to advertise itself.

In some of the first-level assessments, a student receives her validation if her assessment of herself corresponds fairly well with that of the assessor. On these levels the assessment procedure also functions as a diagnostic instrument. For example, Wisconsin Bell has a three-minute "stand up and talk" exercise in which a management trainee is asked to give a presentation in favor of promoting somebody in the company. As part of level one of the communications competence, the Alverno student is also asked to give a three-minute speech on an assigned topic. At Wisconsin Bell the speech and its assessment serve the company as selection devices, whereas at Alverno the speech, its assessment, and especially the feedback that takes place during the assessment are themselves important teaching devices. Typically, many freshman students, quite possibly being videotaped for the first time, if not also giving a speech for the first time, mumble, become incoherent, and in general give a perfectly awful performance. When asked to assess themselves on such items as appropriate voice techniques, bodily response, development of theme, or appropriate examples, they quite clearly recognize that they have miserably failed in all these areas. The assessor will of course have agreed that on all these points the performance was simply incompetent. But what is truly extraordinary and moving at Alverno is what happens next. The assessor gives a careful and sensitive critique of the student's performance, indicating why it was that she had done this or that and why many students are frightened during this experience. But above all, the assessor will suggest ways for the student to improve her performance as she works up the competence ladders. This conversation between the assessor and the student often lasts twenty minutes or longer. If the student has been able to recognize her shortcomings, she has "passed that validation," but what is important is the teaching situation that the process has permitted. One needs to have observed one of these sessions to realize what powerful teaching tools and learning experiences they can be. The student, who often enough still talks ordinary teenage nonspeak, has little bodily awareness, and thinks that voice projection means screaming at her mother, now learns how to become more self-critical. At the same time she is reassured that with work she can do a creditable job and is given all kinds of pointers and information that will enable her to improve her performance. In general, Alverno is very attentive to the fundamental skills involved in writing, reading, speaking, and listening. These skills are surely essential components of anybody's competence and Alverno's efforts to assure that their students will attain such competence are extremely impressive. Given appropriate assessment instruments, the key here, as in other areas of the Alverno assessment program, is student self-criticism coupled with knowledgeable and carefully detailed feedback to the individual student.

Another example of how assessment is used for diagnosis: Level One of Competence Five (social interaction) asks that the student be able to identify and analyze her own strengths and weaknesses in group situations. Five or six students are asked to discuss the comparative merits of a variety of candidates for a government position dealing with environmental questions. Students are given vitae of three or four candidates, along with fictitious newspaper clippings and editorials that are not distributed equally to all the students so that some of them have more information about one or another candidates than do the others. The group is thus given an agenda, a certain amount of material to work with, and differential exposure to materials so that, presumably, they will take different positions and argue with one another. Prior to the discussion each student is given a questionnaire in which she is asked to clarify her own goals in relation to the group goal. The discussion lasts forty minutes or so. The student is then given a questionnaire that asks her to evaluate the achievement of the goals she had stated for herself as well as other aspects of her social interaction. A second questionnaire asks her to evaluate the social interaction of each of her peers. Each of the (usually) three assessors focuses on two of the students and keeps a written account as the discussion proceeds. The assessors, and later the students themselves, are asked to evaluate whether the student responds to verbal and/or nonverbal cues from others; whether her responses facilitate the interaction; and whether the student stands up for her ideas. How does the student react when her ideas are contested by others? Does the student challenge the opinions and the ideas of others? How differentiated are the approaches that the student makes to different members of the group? After the discussion is over, the assessors attempt to reach consensus on the students whom they have been responsible for tracking. Once that is done, they compare their opinions of the student's performance with the student's self-evaluation, and with the student's evaluation by and of her peers. As part of the training provided for each of the assessors, Doherty and Loacker have prepared a manual outlining all the items of behavior that are to be evaluated for the level one assessments in each of the competences. The last paragraph of the instructions for the assessment of Competence Five, Level One, is illustrative of the emphasis placed on sensitive and discriminating feedback-evaluation to the student: "If we want to make the entire process [of evaluation] a learning situation for the student, we need to realize that she cannot learn from our judgment unless we can provide her with clear evidence to clarify what she does effectively and what she does ineffectively. The verification of this will be in our evaluation-feedback session with the student. If this session is to be more than a confrontation of judgments, with 'expert good judgment' winning out for its own sake or retreating out of misplaced sympathy, it must be a clarification session from which the student emerges with a clear perception of her own strengths and weaknesses in a social interaction situation" (*Competence Assessment Program*, 1973a, p. 57).

In using selected students as assessors and in some teaching situations, Alverno is effectively socializing them into the teacher role. In this it is following the lead of more elite institutions where advanced students often have an opportunity to teach or to think of themselves as the colleagues of their professors. This is a large jump for many Alverno students to make, but some of them do make it and the fact that they do seems to enhance the confidence of many of the others.

After the competences had been decided upon and the competence specifications and assessment procedures had been worked out, the next step in rendering explicit and detailed the outcomes of the new program involved modularizing the individual courses. Each professor had to rethink her or his course in terms of the different competence levels and to state clearly when, where, and in what way the course was contributing to a given competence and how the student achievement of that competence would be assessed and validated. This was a difficult and immensely time-consuming task. Submitting their courses to interdisciplinary peer review was, moreover, a new experience for faculty, and faculty sensitivities were understandably acute. In effect, modularization required a dramatic shift from a disciplinary basis to a competence basis and demanded that course contents be viewed not from a traditional disciplinary standpoint but in terms of an overall process in which all contents and disciplines were—in principle at least—equal.

Late in 1974, President Read asked Robert Pitman to accept the job of acting dean. Pitman had been at Alverno for twelve years teaching theater and dramatic performance. He had been president of the rather weak faculty senate, but he was in some ways an unlikely choice for dean, having shown little interest in administration. He had not been particularly involved in planning the new program and in fact was largely uninterested in it until he had recast his own course in dramatic literature in the competence-based mode. This had been a revelation to him. Not only did he feel he could teach much more than he ever had before but he was convinced that his students had learned much more and had learned it much more quickly than they ever had before. An intelligent and articulate man of considerable personal distinction, Pitman appears to have been generally well liked by his colleagues. At the same time he was accustomed to the chaos that precedes the opening of any play and was able to handle with equanimity and decision the constant contingencies and conflicts that are a director's daily bread. Pitman moved easily into his new position and in the spring of 1975 accepted the position of permanent dean. His presence on the scene helped to dissipate the rankled atmosphere and some of the animosities that seem to have characterized many relationships in the previous period. (Robert Pitman died in 1978; Sister Austin Doherty is now academic dean.)

In addition, several characteristics of the Alverno faculty were directly related to the success of the enterprise. The first is the still relatively high percentage of nuns on the faculty—40 percent. Without this core of faculty members able and generally willing to spend incredible amounts of time and energy to do the work at hand, it is doubtful that Alverno would have been able to mount its complex programs. A good number of these women are in their late forties and early fifties. Their dedication, enthusiasm, and willingness to engage themselves in the exhausting process of reform at Alverno are remarkable. Many have a sense of mission that provides an example for lay faculty who have in turn stretched themselves beyond usual limits. For many religious and lay faculty, Catholic or not, the new program at Alverno seems to be more than an academic innovation and involves something like a total moral commitment that must be passionately affirmed. Another important motivation lies in Alverno's mission to educate—some there would say liberate—the women students that the college attracts. Finally, the faculty as a whole has not been unmindful of the fact that the survival of the college is at stake. In any case, lay and religious faculty have accepted work loads and overloads that few faculties would countenance.

Another unusual feature of the Alverno faculty is that it does not enjoy the advantages or suffer from the drawbacks of a tenure system. Had there been a tenure system at Alverno, it seems unlikely that the college could have accomplished what it has. The faculty senate has lacked both power and direction. Chairpersons are appointed and have little power. The faculty has almost none of the traditional powers of a faculty so that individuals who stand against the prevailing winds find themselves in an exposed and uncomfortable position. The president and her appointees, whether in the administration or the faculty itself, are decidedly in control. In such a situation, manifestations of dissidence and opposition are circumspect and rather muted. Faculty morale had improved considerably

even by the time our research team visited the college in the fall of
1975, and later reports indicate that most of the faculty have become reasonably committed to giving the program a fair trial.

That said, it must be added that some faculty are still smart-
ing over the way competence-based education was imposed on them.
As a rule, it is not the substance of the new program that has been
the cause of this hostility and hurt but rather the manner in which
it has been implemented. Like administrators elsewhere, Read,
Doherty, and Loacker are commonly accused of reacting harshly to
criticism and of being unwilling to listen to other views. Quite
a few faculty, as well as some administrators, feel that their own
efforts have been insufficiently recognized. The tensions and conflicts
mentioned here exploded publicly in the fall of 1977 and winter of
1978 and were reported both locally and nationally. But even those
who are most critical of "the trinity" recognize and respect their
intelligence, their organizational talent, their capacity for hard
work, and their willingness to make hard decisions. Moreover, they
are given generous credit for the remarkable feats they have accomplished and the uncommon contribution they have made to the
renewal of the college.

Effects on Faculty and Students

The effect of the competence-based program on the faculty
is in some ways one of the most interesting outcomes of the program
to date. Contrary to the situation in a number of other institutions
embarked on competence-based education, the Alverno faculty was
not recruited for the new program and had to train itself in the
new ways demanded by the program. One effect of the program
has been that individual faculty are now, of necessity, much more
aware than they ever had been before of who is doing what in the
rest of the college. Another has been to level all hierarchical differences among different content areas. Once the philosopher, the
physicist, or the historian, begin to see themselves as all doing, in
a sense, the same thing, for example, analysis, at level two, their
perception of themselves, their colleagues, and the relative importance of their respective content areas tends to change. They begin
to open themselves to the concerns of other disciplines in a way

that they have not done before. So too, faculty colleague networks have changed in relation to newly developed interdisciplinary interests. The implementation of the new program has, in effect, been an important element in the liberal education of the faculty.

If there is a split in the faculty today, it is less that of insiders and outsiders or lay and religious than it is that of discipline based or competence based. This is probably a predictable outcome in competence programs that have become really operational, just as it is probably predictable that those who represent the most highly structured disciplines—the hard sciences and mathematics, for example—are most likely to find themselves in opposition to competence-based education. To some extent this has been the case at Alverno although there are professors of history, literature, and music who are something less than enthusiastic about the new program.

One faculty member observed that he felt like an engineer with a Ph.D. working as a mechanic in a Sears garage. The analogy is interesting. The doctoral level engineer has a detailed understanding of the mechanics of an automobile as well as of the scientific principles on which the engineering marvel represented by the automobile rests. The mechanic need only know how to fit the right pieces and parts (competence levels and their component parts) into the right places. This view is perhaps typical of those who have been professionally socialized within a given academic discipline and are more likely to feel loyalty to the distant arbiters of the discipline than they are to the dictates of a local innovation. At Alverno those who are still principally committed to their discipline are usually not among competence education's true believers. With a few exceptions, however, they recognize much that is worthwhile in the new approach and are willing to work with it. Still, there is an understandable tension. One does not advance one's career in most disciplines by writing and rewriting modules or by spending untold hours in competence division meetings, but it is doubtful if one can long survive at Alverno without doing these things. On the other hand, many at Alverno feel that the discipline-based/competence-based question does not pose a real antinomy and is used by some of their colleagues to mask other oppositions to the program. But for some it does pose an anguishing dilemma.

The changeover to the competence-based program at Alverno has also raised questions about the traditional conception of a professor in a liberal arts college and his or her appropriate training. Should competence-based education ever become a statistically significant factor in liberal education, this traditional conception is likely to be radically reexamined and the question of role identification would then become acute for liberal arts professors as a group, as it is now for some at Alverno.

Turning to the impact of the program on teaching, which with the learning that presumably accompanies it is the outcome for which Alverno holds itself accountable to its students and its other constituencies, the caliber of much of the teaching at the college suggests that the program is an excellent vehicle for fostering, even demanding, competent teaching. Certainly one of its most important effects on faculty is the extent that it has forced them to become more self-critical and knowledgeable about their teaching. One who merely reads through the competence specifications, the assessment procedures, and the other Alverno literature may be led to wonder what happens in such a system to the notion of a collegial, investigative role in the teaching situation; or to what extent classes become a kind of drill: clear, effective, and efficient but not much fun and not leaving much room for questions for which one does not already have answers. In general such anticipations are not verified by experience in the Alverno classrooms. To be sure there are classroom situations that are mechanical, perfunctory, and boring: competence-based education is not a panacea. In incompetent hands modularized course contents can easily become dull, and Alverno does not pretend to have banished numbed and numbing professors from the face of the earth. The competence-based mode at Alverno, however, forces even the least talented of teachers to organize their material better than they would otherwise, and it makes it very much harder for them to hide their daily atrocities from the public view. A statement often repeated by professors at Alverno seems to sum up the situation well, if perhaps too modestly: As a result of the competence-based program, the good teachers are no worse than they were, and at least some of the poor teachers are much better.

What matters here is not the presence of a few bad teachers, who can be found anywhere, but rather the extraordinary amount of exciting and creative teaching that is being done at Alverno in the new program. After spending many hours in the Alverno classrooms, one seasoned observer exclaimed, "I felt I saw more teaching per classroom minute than I have ever seen before." As Alverno conceives it, competence-based education puts a premium on developing student initiative and student independence. It encourages teachers and students alike to break out of the comfortable roles of lecturer and consumer of lectures roles. Although there is still a good deal of straight lecturing at Alverno, the predominant teacher model is not that of master (or mistress) professing *ex cathedra* but that of coach and mentor.

If teaching styles have changed at Alverno, so have the *foci* in the classroom situation. In the practice of good teachers, of whom there are a large number at Alverno, there now seem to be three explicit *foci* of their teaching. Competences and competence levels are not taught in the abstract but through a disciplinary content: the work of literature or the historical interpretation remains a central focus of the teaching. At the same time, however, the professor also focuses on the competence that she or he hopes to help the students attain in the act of studying the work of literature or considering different historical interpretations. In addition, the course module that is possessed by both teacher and students focuses the teaching-learning situation in such a way as to encourage the students to be more self-reliant, to learn to collaborate with one another, and to become less dependent on a teacher.

The key to all of this is the extremely detailed and carefully thought-out organization of the course itself. Course contents are chosen with great care and strategically plotted, and teaching activities are organized with an incredible degree of specificity. Although such organization does not encourage the leisurely, inspired (or not so inspired) ramble, it does make possible a very efficient use of classroom time, and many practitioners claim that they are able to teach much more than they ever did before. Yet this detailed organization of material does not seem to hinder the freedom of the classroom—indeed, it seems to enhance it in many cases. The high degree of organization allows the Alverno teacher to do very creative work with small groups and to put the burden of learning on the students while freeing him or her to engage in informal, coach-like assistance.

Something analogous to the constraints imposed by the highly structured course module and the freedom permitted to the teachers in the classroom can be found in the relation of the teacher to the program itself. The program is highly structured, militant, and imposed from above. Yet it is structured in such a way that the teacher does not feel that she or he has been deprived of the right to decide what is going to be taught. The teaching vehicle remains a course or a course equivalent in the teacher's discipline, and it is the teacher who chooses the content and the books for the courses as well as the way in which those materials will be organized. Peer review of course content, teaching strategies, and assessment methods is resented by some, but it has the important benefit of fostering a critical and professional concern for teaching without interfering with the teacher's right to decide what will go on in the classroom. There is, of course, the danger that once a professor has worked out her module and had it approved, the module will become a substitute for the yellowed sheaf of notes and be repeated semester after semester. In fact it seems that the opposite outcome is far more common. This mode of teaching and of organizing one's teaching tends to generate a dissatisfaction with what one has done and an effort to do it better with different materials, different arrangements, and different teaching and assessing techniques. At least among the better professors, the implementation in the classroom of the Alverno program has created a kind of college-wide laboratory for research and experimentation in teaching.

For both pedagogical and feminist reasons, the effort to make students more self-reliant is high on the Alverno agenda, and ways are constantly being sought to get the students to teach and learn from one another. Insofar as possible, the physical space of the college has been organized into a series of learning and resource centers, where students can work either individually or in groups at assigned tasks. This emphasis on student collaboration is particularly evident in the classroom. Whether they are discussing a text or going over homework assignments, students are continually invited to learn to discuss things with one another. These are not unstructured discussion groups in which students flounder around in a sea of common ignorance. The materials to be discussed have been carefully chosen ahead of time. The tasks assigned are often very simple, very pragmatic, and very explicit so that the students invariably have something to talk about. But the burden of the discussion is left to the small group. The professor is present and is prepared to answer questions if those questions are relevant and beyond the capacity of the group to answer at a given time, but many of the professors are very good about refusing to answer student questions if they think that the students are able or should be able to answer them for themselves.

It is probable that the constant effort at Alverno to articulate competency in such a way that there are objective, yes-no standards for deciding whether or not the competency has been achieved rubs off on the small groups in classroom discussion. Students can learn to collaborate with one another and to trust that they can figure things out on their own when they believe that reasonably objective standards exist. What is or is not true is not merely a matter of authority, and the students' principal task is not to figure out what the professor may think to be true, but simply to determine what is true and why it is true. And it is just this spirit of inquiry that the teachers try to promote. The tight organization structures and controls the teaching situation, but precisely because of this the teacher can more easily refuse to give answers and to assume a didactic role, placing the burden of learning on the students. Paradoxically, the teacher is able to exert more control over the students and yet let them be more free to find answers for themselves. And as the students begin to do this, they tend to become increasingly confident of their ability to do it.

Finally, as mentioned already, the Alverno program makes much more feasible the use of student teachers in a variety of situations. This is, of course, the model they want to encourage and the fact that they are able to socialize at least some of the students into the teaching role helps to underscore the responsibility of all of the students to become teachers as well as learners.

Just as Alverno did not recruit a new faculty to develop and implement a new program, so the college did not seek a new student clientele. In general, Alverno students come from relatively modest socio-economic and cultural backgrounds. They do not suffer from the cult of spontaneity. If anything, they suffer from the conventional docility of many middle- and lower-middle-class students, particularly those in first-generation families.

Alverno's program seems to be well fitted to these students. It seeks to make them self-conscious, but not along any particular ideological lines. By learning more about themselves and how others react to them, Alverno students—that is the explicit hope—are to become more like what they might be and to acquire a realistic sense of what is required to actualize their hopes. Those students who stayed—and more in succeeding classes did—seemed generally pleased with the program. They liked the fact that if they did badly on one or another assessment they were not penalized but could go through it again when they felt better prepared. In spite of all the difficulties the "guinea pig" classes had to face, they seemed convinced that their educational experience was worthwhile even when they did not fully understand its rationale. Not infrequently students recounted comparative anecdotes tending to show that they were receiving a much better education than were their friends at Mount Mary, the University of Wisconsin, or Marquette. The national attention and the stream of visitors Alverno attracted had an effect on everybody in the college, but perhaps especially upon the students. They recognized that their teachers were seriously concerned with helping them and that many of their teachers were extremely capable, but they nonetheless had to make an act of faith in the program itself. The great interest in what they were doing manifested by knowledgeable outsiders tended to confirm them in their faith.

Students were not, however, uncritical of the program. In the spring of 1975 a small group of students organized a forum in order to voice their criticisms and complaints. This would have been unheard of in the Alverno of earlier years, and it is perhaps one mark of the success of the program that the students organized and successfully brought off this forum on their own. The complaints and criticisms that surfaced there were at once revelatory of some of the strains and difficulties the program had run into and signs of a critical vitality that the program itself had fostered.

The forum originated from a class in small group behavior, whose seven members were concerned about a variety of problems that had arisen in the program but had not been resolved. Their solution was to organize the forum. They carefully planned an agenda that was, in effect, a resume of problems they had perceived. They invited faculty to attend but did not allow them to speak. Among their complaints were the following: Many of the modules for the courses were difficult to read, even unintelligible, and the learning experiences promised in the module were not in fact realized. They complained that many of the professors themselves did not seem to understand their own modules and were unable to explain them, even when the topic of the course was the "use and abuse of language"! They wanted to know the relationship between competence-level units and credits: How did the units translate into credits? What happened if one wanted to transfer to another school? They complained that they were often required to do work on competence units in one course that they had already completed successfully in other courses. There was, they thought, entirely too much of this repetition of units, and it was defeating one of the stated purposes of the program. They mentioned that papers were occasionally lost in the assessment center, that feedback on the assessments came late or sometimes not at all. They were not convinced that the feedback was always objective, and they questioned the competence of some of the assessors. They spoke out against what they called the self-protective and convent-like atmosphere at Alverno, and they identified some of the principal administrators as people who immediately went on the defensive when complaints or problems were brought to them and who were inclined to put down the students for voicing their complaints. They said that when problems arose there was no place they could go to seek adjudication of them. They felt that there was a real and serious lack of internal communication at the college.

This forum had a considerable effect on the faculty and the administration. The students' complaints were well thought out and delivered in a professional manner. The tone of their criticism was open and straightforward, devoid of hostility. Several months afterwards, the students who had organized the forum expressed the opinion that their complaints, for the most part, had been listened to and they thought that their initiative had been constructive and helpful. They also thought that there continued to be a great need for constructive student criticism. As one talked to these young women, it became clear that they were committed to Alverno and to the new venture and that their voices would become increasingly important to both. Such an outcome is one in which the college can rejoice. Whether the other outcomes for which the college holds itself accountable will be achieved remains to be seen.

Gerald Grant   9

Creating
a Nontraditional
College for
New Careers:
The College
for Human Services

The quarters of the College for Human Services are properly un-prepossessing. As befits honest reformers, the place is frugal, a bit drab, and hand-me-down. Most of its 200 students are mothers who have been on welfare, although in recent years there has been a slight increase in the number of men who have come to the college. About 60 percent of the students are black, 25 percent are Spanish-American, 12 percent are Polish-American (most of them recent immigrants), and the rest are other white or Oriental. Two mornings a week they come out of a subway at Varick and

Houston streets in lower Manhattan and enter a sooty building. On the eleventh floor they turn down a hall lined with offices that have been converted to classrooms. Some rooms have bright rugs, but there are few luxuries. A library of several thousand volumes is at one end of the hall; nearby is a student lounge with a few chairs and tables, but the students do little lounging because the two days they spend at the college are filled with classes and conferences from 8:30 A.M. to 5:00 P.M. The other three days of the week they are employed as interns in schools, hospitals, social work agencies, museums, and a variety of other training positions that comprise what the college calls the human services.

The college was created by Audrey Cohen, a determined visionary and radical. She is shrewd, tough—although suave when necessary—and a fighter. She still bristles at the mention of a *New Republic* article by Joseph Featherstone that claimed the college "was started by a handful of reformist middle-class ladies with the idea of training poor women for jobs as assistants to professionals" (1969, p. 1). Featherstone is partly right, although Cohen, as an egalitarian, resented being identified with a privileged class. She is reminiscent of the settlement house reformers of the nineteenth century and their notion of *noblesse oblige;* in her emphasis on service and practical competence and her criticism of traditional universities, she has much in common with Jane Addams and Lillian Wald. Yet her aims, which involve the reform of the professions at large and of higher education in particular, are even more ambitious than theirs.

Cohen was born in Pittsburgh and graduated in 1953 from the University of Pittsburgh with a degree in political science. She taught high school for three years, was active in the civil rights movement in Washington, D.C., and pursued graduate studies at George Washington University. In 1958 she founded Part-Time Research Associates, utilizing the talents of more than 200 married women in the Washington area to do research tasks for a variety of clients, and the experience proved to be an early illustration that performance does not necessarily correlate with credentials. When her husband changed jobs, she moved to New York and in 1964 founded the Women's Talent Corps, turning her energies away from the employment of suburban housewives to the placement of low-income black women in burgeoning federal programs.

In 1966, the Women's Talent Corps received a grant from the federal Office of Economic Opportunity not only to train these women but to create permanent jobs for them in the human service sector, beginning as paraprofessionals. At that time, the college did not talk so much about transforming the professions as it did about reducing the antagonism between professionals and the poor neighborhoods they were supposed to serve, although the seeds of its later emphasis on social change can be found even in its early history. Of the 120 women accepted for the initial program, 113 completed a thirty-week training cycle and were subsequently employed. The college was especially proud that it established a foothold for "new careers" in several agencies, as well as in schools where the title "educational assistant" was created to denote the pedagogical responsibilities of the women from the talent corps in contrast to nonteaching community aides. At the time, the college was convinced it had achieved an important goal by helping to create such new positions as case aide, lay therapist, and community liaison assistant, and felt these would be first rungs on career ladders, not dead-end, nose-wiping jobs.

The core faculty were described in a 1968 report as "hardheaded do-gooders"—women who, as volunteers and mothers, had had enough experience with incompetence among professionals to be unawed by credentials and jargon.[1] Most of the twenty faculty were white, perhaps one third were Jewish. There were two blacks and one Puerto Rican among them, including the vice-president, Laura Pires Houston, a Cape Verdean who had graduated from Smith College and earned a master's degree in social work at Columbia. Most of the white women had backgrounds in education or social work (only three had degrees in the field), and there were two lawyers and a few former journalists among them. Several were married to ministers or had studied theology. There were no men in the major administrative posts, and when we visited the college in 1970 we observed that lines of authority seemed more

---

[1] Detailed information about events at the College for Human Services can be found in its annual reports, and this chapter makes use of the reports issued between 1968 and 1972. For statistical data on such matters as income and completion rates of the college's students, see Hack, 1973.

loose and relaxed than would be typical of most male-dominated organizations.

Toward a Breakthrough

In those first years, the college laid the foundation for a new faculty role, that of the "coordinating teacher" who divided her time between supervising students on the job and, more importantly, acting as an advocate for students in establishing career ladders. A student assigned to a legal services office, for example, might begin with responsibilities no weightier than filing papers or answering the telephone. As the student learned more in class and on the job, the faculty member would negotiate increased responsibilities, such as legal research or initial client interviews. Eventually, in successful cases, the student would receive increased pay and a redefinition of job. Coordinating teachers also sought to identify supervisors at the agencies as potential "teachers" for the students: the college expected the agency to help make the job a learning experience. Since the students were supported by federal training grants (now by funds from the Comprehensive Employment and Training Act through the City of New York), the college gained leverage with the agency by making students available as "free" labor for the first year of training, after which the agency assumed half the cost. And although the college was founded in the days of Lindsay optimism, it has been able to continue operating in an era of Beame and Koch budgets. It believes that the need for preparing "human service workers" continues to be acute, projecting a demand for millions of additional jobs to provide adequate education, health care, and recreational services. (For data cited by the college here, see Pearl, 1973.)

In 1967, the college added a second year to its training program, and in 1968, applied to New York State for a college charter with authority to grant the associate of arts degree. The Department of Higher Education rejected the application on the grounds that most of the college's students had not graduated from high school, its faculty did not possess advanced degrees nor sufficient college teaching experience, and it did not have an adequate library or endowment. The students' median age was thirty-seven, and most scored below ninth-grade level on tests of verbal and mathematical ability. The reviewing officers praised the "social effectiveness of this dedicated and imaginative group of women," but concluded that the Women's Talent Corps lacked the essential characteristics of a degree-granting institution.

Although such a decision is usually regarded as final, Cohen chose to ignore the door that had been shut in her face. Noting that technically the decision was not binding on the final authority, the New York Board of Regents, she began a campaign for approval at that level. She asked for a review of the college's program by Alvin Eurich's Academy for Educational Development, which subsequently recommended its approval as a degree-granting institution. She also hired a lawyer to contest the endowment requirement. Some concessions were made to demands for specialist faculty within the college's interdisciplinary structure. Not least, the college initiated a broad campaign to generate political and educational support.

On the matter of admissions standards, the college argued that job performance did not necessarily correlate with previous credentials and that students should be admitted without regard to previous formal education if they could pass basic reading and math tests. In response to criticism that the college did not adequately evaluate student performance, the Educational Testing Service (ETS) was asked to advise whether tests had been developed that could be adapted to the college's program. When the ETS experts could furnish none, the college cited this as evidence of the need for it to develop new measures of student performance.

Internally, some faculty and students opposed seeking degree status; they feared that bending to bureaucratic requirements would mean sacrificing freedom to experiment. But other students were equally strong in their desire to obtain the "piece of paper" that opened doors in a diploma-conscious society. When it was suggested that the charter campaign would be an ideal project for the final unit of the first-year curriculum on social change, faculty members took sides. Some argued that the best way to learn about social change was to participate in an effort to win college status for themselves; others opposed the campaign on the grounds that it upset curriculum plans and coerced students. In the end a compromise was reached in which students could choose among several action projects. Many participated in the charter effort, organizing letter-writing campaigns, seeking support for the college in agencies where they worked, and collecting petitions. In 1970, the board of regents provisionally approved a college charter and the right to grant the associate degree for a period of five years.

Although buoyed by the successful charter campaign, the college was coming to realize that its early enthusiasm about establishing new routes to professional careers was naive. Although it was successful in getting women off welfare and employed in paraprofessional positions, the college was forced to conclude that its hoped-for career ladders were largely illusory. Some of its "paraprofessional" graduates were hard to distinguish from the professionals with whom they worked—apart from the size of their paychecks. Yet they found that the career ladders had too many steps and bumped into very low ceilings. The associate degree would help some graduates overcome hurdles to advancement on the job, but the college realized that it must not just find new pathways to advancement for its graduates but change both the pathways and the professions. A change in consciousness about the nature of the training the college wanted to give was occurring. Less emphasis would now be put on the concept of training paraprofessionals as helpers who could move upward in traditional channels, and more would be given to the idea that the helping professions themselves needed major reform if they were to emphasize "humane service." The college would uphold its primary mission of promoting integration and "opening up the system" to minorities, but it would be "equally concerned with changing human service institutions so that they become more responsive to human needs. The more the college works in this area, the clearer it becomes that the shortcomings of the present system affect the public at large, and that basic changes are needed in the way service is delivered to everyone. . . . To this end, it will seek to create a new kind of credential, a two-year professional degree based on a definition that emphasizes humane performance rather than simply academic knowledge" (College for Human Services, 1972, p. 64).

The new emphasis that Cohen was putting on reforming

the professions by seeking authority to grant a full professional certificate (and eventually a master's degree) created major tensions. When the college added a second year to its original thirty-week program, it hired more black and Spanish-speaking male faculty, some of whom opposed the move to a new credential, believing the college should concentrate on the more limited goal of "opening the system" to minorities. Students petitioned for three days of classes a week, saying two days were insufficient to improve their deficiencies in English and math. Members of the student council accused Cohen of being a politician who had duped outside agencies into thinking she was an innovative educator. "We do not want the College for Human Services to grant us a master's degree in two years when many of us feel we need remedial work," the students wrote. "We feel Mrs. Cohen has hit upon a great idea . . . that new routes in education should be carved out and performance should be as important as academic achievement. But she has made a joke of her own ideas. Our training is shabby, our academic classes are poor, and once again we feel we have been taken advantage of."

When Cohen fired the black director of the second-year program in 1972, charges of racism were raised, a boycott ensued, and some faculty resigned, as did the black chairman of the board of trustees. Cohen's resignation was demanded, and the faculty strike committee urged her replacement by a black or Puerto Rican president. Unlike many white liberals who have caved in under such demands, Cohen replied by answering her opponents' specific charges and noting the acceptance of the college's program by many agencies; she pointedly informed dissident faculty that the demand for her resignation was based on considerations of color, not performance; she hired a lawyer to defend her in the grievance hearings that were being pursued by the dismissed director; and when she was upheld, she proceeded to fire more than a dozen members of the faculty.

During this period, the college began to pay more attention to training in basic skills and to pursue more seriously a master's degree program. While continuing to recruit poor minority students, it also set out to raise entrance requirements. Although a diploma was not required, students increasingly had the equivalent of a high school education, and some had spent a year or more in community colleges. Starting salaries for new faculty rose from $8,500 to $13,500.

The new emphasis on basic skills was also influenced by the college's experience with the Legal Service Assistant program. A joint venture with Columbia University Law School, this was one of the most carefully investigated programs undertaken by the college. Students in the legal aid program spent one third of their time at the college, in its interdisciplinary core curriculum, one third at Columbia in courses in legal skills and analysis with special emphasis on so-called poverty law (welfare family law, landlord-tenant actions), and one third on the job as practicing legal aides. Of the twenty-three students initially accepted in the program, eighteen completed the first year. Sixteen of these were offered jobs and eleven of those sixteen continued to hold their jobs for the second year. Nine received special merit increases in the offices where they worked. Six of those hired for the second year earned considerable independence, frequently handling routine cases up to the point of courtroom appearance, when an attorney took over. Five performed limited legal tasks under close supervision, and five others worked as clerical aides and messengers (one operated a switchboard). The program thus made clear that some minority students with only grade school skills at entrance could rise in two years of an intensive program to perform "professional" roles. On the other hand, poor work habits and repeated lateness and absences constituted a major problem for five of the sixteen aides and a minor problem for four others. Only about one fourth of the students reached a professional level. (See Statsky, 1969 and 1970; also "Legal Service Assistants," 1970.)

Despite the success of the legal service program, the college decided to terminate it and to put its effort into developing new performance standards for a generic profession of human service. In effect, it ruled out the more specialized professions, such as law or medicine, and concentrated on social work, guidance and counseling, education, and other areas where there is no clearly defined or highly structured knowledge base underlying practice.

In a typically prescient essay Nathan Glazer (1974a) has noted that the schools that train social workers, teachers, city planners, or ministers have been dubbed "professional schools" by courtesy, since they do not rest on the same base of special or technical knowledge as the classic professions of law and medicine. These schools have courted status by replacing practitioners with scholars and researchers. Thus schools of education are increasingly staffed by psychologists, sociologists, historians, and philosophers rather than by master teachers or practitioners. But sociologists and psychologists may be more interested in their specialties than in the quality of service that practitioners deliver, and the most useful training for the "minor professions" of education and social work takes place on the job, despite clear and important links to the academic disciplines.

The problem faced by the College for Human Services was how to shape a curriculum that would draw on the disciplines in a way that would permit performance- or competence-based evaluation on the job. The college believed from the beginning that all work with people involves basic similarities and depends on a common store of concepts and techniques. But if professional standing in the minor professions was not tied to specialized knowledge in the traditional sense, what, then, was the basis for judging the competence of the human service professional? For the next several years, the college attempted to answer the question stated most cogently by Laura Houston: "What does 'professional' really mean in terms of service, of results?" (1970).

Medicine and law had answered that (1) initial entry into a profession must be controlled by certification through professional schools, and (2) only other professionals who possess the specialized knowledge and the privileged access to information about clients can judge the competence of practitioners. The college and other critics of the professions have argued that certification procedures in professional schools are inadequate because they rely on grades and formal requirements although research studies have shown that grades (except, perhaps, in the field of engineering) rarely relate to occupational success. (See Jencks and others, 1972.) Initial entry, they claim, has sometimes been unfairly restricted to protect a profit monopoly as much as to protect standards. They argue that lax supervision of some self-interested professionals has resulted in inadequate protection for clients as well as increased isolation from standards of humane service. (Anderson, 1973, gives support to this view.)

Thus, the college has attempted to devise an assessment system that includes clients as well as professionals, faculty, and student peers.

In the fall of 1971, after the decision had been made to pursue a professional certificate, the faculty organized itself into five committees: education, daycare, drug therapy, social work, and health professions. Each of these committees included some persons from the agencies where students had been placed. Each group attempted to define a standard of professional competence in that field, drawn from their own experience in supervision and observation, on the basis of job descriptions, association statements, licensing requirements, and performance.

By the spring of 1972, however, the faculty expressed frustration that they were not getting at generic "competencies." So in an effort to define the professional competence of humane human service workers, the college turned to empirical research and retained David McClelland, the Harvard social psychologist, and his private research firm, the McBer Company, as consultants. McClelland had recently written an article, "Testing for Competence Rather than for Intelligence" (1973), that appealed to the college in part because it argued that generic subsets of personal attributes underlying competence could be defined. The study done for the college by the McBer Company was an important step toward building a new competence-based curriculum. The company's research did not involve direct observation but relied on an analysis of ten critical incidents or events described by sixty-two exemplary human service workers who were selected by the college on the basis of its own observations in various agencies. While not imputing any "superior knowledge of professional performance" to the college, the company argued that the "college alone can define its mission" and that it was appropriate for them to define it in terms of producing practitioners resembling the sixty-two regarded as exemplary by the college.

As a result of its analysis, the McBer Company derived the following seven competencies (Dailey and others, 1974):

1. Strong faith that human needs can and must be met
   a. that every client can change and grow
   b. that attitude change is possible and is itself worthwhile
   c. that you can get the system to adjust to the needs of the individual at least some of the time
2. Ability to identify correctly the human problem
   a. by being a good listener and observer
   b. by being able to get other people to talk openly and freely
3. Ability to arrive at realistic, achievable goals in collaboration with clients
4. Imaginativeness in thinking of solutions to problems
   a. through use of own human relations skills
   b. through knowledge of resources and regulations
5. Persistence in pursuing solutions, often against hostile authorities
6. Ability to remain task-oriented under stress, hostility
7. Skills in getting interested parties to work together to arrive at common goals

As an example, the fifth competence of "persistence in pursuing solutions" was the outcome of an aggregate of the following events cited in the critical incidents: "Insisting on payments to a family with five children whose benefits were cut off because their father had died; staying with a suicidal person; reacting to direct and public criticism from immediate superior; overcoming the board's unwillingness to invest in a program for the foreign born; recognizing the gradualism inherent in changing a system by very sustained and patient effort; working in an impossible multiagency system to help an intolerable and overwhelming family situation in housing; facing overwhelming defeat." Many questions may be raised about the validity of the McBer Company's methods and the value of its findings, and the college did not adopt the report as such. Still, it became the basis of continued discussion among the faculty and was an important step toward the college's goal of basing its program on new definitions of competence and on new professional models.

When the faculty met in the spring of 1974 to work on the concrete details of the new curriculum for the class that would enter in the summer, the fruits of the long months of searching for new definitions and new directions finally began to be felt. After weeks of work, a light dawned, and two years later, faculty were still speaking of the euphoria of the "breakthrough." In retrospect, as in most quite complex matters, it seems rather simple. The group members discovered that they had been talking about two different kinds of competencies. On the one hand, students were asked to do something: "design and implement a learning-helping environment" or "conduct human service research." On the other hand, they were asked to concern themselves with certain aspects of performance: consciousness of their own values, or understanding the larger system within which an action was embedded. Thus the competencies were a statement of actions or functions, as well as of values or dimensions. It was the combination of the accomplishment with an awareness of its values that constituted a professional performance. In a sense, the "breakthrough" brought to awareness an aim as old as the sixteenth-century Jesuit ideal, *actione contemplativus,* acting with purpose and contemplative awareness. Like the Jesuits, the college also emphasized the need to judge human action in its fullness: "It is clear that the dimensions can only serve their purpose as a guide to learning and assessment if they encompass every significant aspect of performance. Any breakdown of performance into its supposed elements is, of course, artificial. Knowledge, skills, attitudes, the components into which learning is most commonly analyzed, are totally inappropriate for performance-based education because they disregard the active interplay of insight, experience, judgment, purpose, etc., that comprises a living performance. Instead of dealing in such rigid categories, the college has tried to develop the dimensions as a filter that makes it possible to focus on the various aspects of performance without forgetting their relationship to the whole" (College for Human Service, 1974, p. I:74).

This "whole" to be assessed by the college was called a "constructive action." The curriculum, as the student would encounter it, was arranged as a series of "constructive actions," and each student, in order to "act as a change agent, planning, researching and promoting progress to improve human service delivery," would concentrate his or her learning and experience on a series of constructive actions demonstrating different facets of competence.

The performance grid summarizing this development, which has remained the basic bible of the new curriculum, is shown in Figure 1, along with sample facets of the curriculum related to each of the eight competencies and five dimensions.

A "grid," no matter how neat it is or how much euphoria it induces, is not sufficient to establish a new profession. Now several steps were taken. The first was to use the new curriculum to seek authority from New York State to grant a degree certifying its students as masters of human services. A profession also needs wider recognition from funding sources, policy-making groups, educational institutions, and other professions. In June 1974, the college brought together a broad potential support group and made a simple announcement of a new profession of the human services. The most prestigious supporters at the conference were asked to form a task force to establish the new profession and win wider recognition of it. Others were politely ignored.

In August, the college explained its new curriculum and the research on which it was based in a two-volume proposal seeking the authority to grant the master's degree. The proposal highlighted three fundamental propositions the program was designed to test: (1) that disadvantaged persons may be exceptionally qualified to serve others with intelligence, purpose and humanity; (2) that a performance-based program can prepare professionals in two rather than the usual five or six years; (3) that a new profession, human services, can serve clients better by responding to needs rather than within boundaries defined by traditional professions (1974, p. I:5). Let us examine the curriculum from the student's viewpoint.

Operation of the New Curriculum

In the summer of 1975, at an admission session conducted by Jan Powell, a college counselor, and Pearl Daniels, the admissions director, one of the early arrivals was José Morales, who had been born in Puerto Rico and had worked in a New York shoe factory for twenty-three years. In March, when the factory had closed, his children had urged him to return to school despite his age of forty-one, and a friend who worked with his wife as a teacher's aide had told him about the College for Human Services. Like the other

	A. *Purpose* Describe appropriate and realistic purposes and demonstrate reasonable success in achieving them.	B. *Values* Demonstrate a clear understanding of your values and persistence in working for them.	C. *Self and Others* Demonstrate an understanding of yourself and others in relation to your purposes.	D. *Systems* Demonstrate an understanding of systems in relation to your purposes.	E. *Skills* Demonstrate an ability to make good use of necessary and appropriate skills in the achievement of your purposes.
Competencies / Dimensions					
I. Become an effective learner and potential professional, accepting the responsibility for identifying your learning goals and finding appropriate resources for achieving them.					
II. Establish professional relationships at the work site with coworkers and citizens.					
III. Work with others in groups, helping to establish clear goals and achieve optimum results.	Facet 3: Demonstrate reasonable success in helping a group to achieve its common purpose while working toward your individual purpose.	Facet 3: Describe your views on the issue of decision-making in groups and explain how your views affect your performance (Locke, Mill, Dahl, Lindblom, Galbraith, Ibsen).	Facet 3: Demonstrate an understanding of alternative approaches to working in groups and their applicability to specific situations (Maslow, Lewin, Schwartz, Bion, Thelen).	Facet 4: Demonstrate an understanding of groups as cultural units (Kluckhohn, Barnouw, Greenwood, Goode, C. P. Snow).	Facet 3: Demonstrate in appropriate circumstances the ability to test and learn new interpersonal techniques (Miles).

IV. Function as a teacher, helping people to define and achieve appropriate learning goals.				
V. Function as a counselor, helping people to resolve problems in a manner that promotes their growth and independence.				
VI. Function as community liaison, working with the people and resources of the community to meet community needs.				
VII. Function as a supervisor, taking the responsibility for teaching, encouraging, and enabling other workers to make the best use of their abilities on behalf of citizens.				
VIII. Act as a change agent, planning, researching, and promoting programs to improve human service delivery.				

Figure 1. The Performance Grid with Sample Facets in One Competency

seven applicants—six Polish-speaking applicants and one black—
who arrived for a group interview that morning, he had survived an
earlier screening. Powell and Daniels, in explaining the history of the
college, noted that it did not have the power to grant the master's
degree and that the agencies in which students would be placed
were not legally bound to hire them—students thus could finish the
program without acquiring either a degree or a job. Daniels warned
them of the demands and rigor of the program, of the impact it
would make on their lives and those of their families. The women
would need two babysitters—one as backup for the other. The
divorce and separation rate of the students was high. They would
receive a weekly stipend of $99.75 and free dental care in the first
year. In the second year, since part of the cost would be paid by the
agencies in the form of taxable salaries they would in effect suffer a
pay cut, and Daniels urged them to try to save part of their stipend
in the first year.

During the two-hour conversation that followed, students
were invited to introduce themselves, to say why they wanted to
come to the college, and to ask about any aspect of the program.
Daniels and Powell responded candidly to questions, but most of
their attention was focused on the interaction of the participants.
Throughout the morning they evaluated candidates on the basis of
eight criteria: (1) general appearance (dress, grooming, manners);
(2) communication ability (listens to others, waits for them to
finish, effectively expresses own ideas and opinions); (3) relevancy of
comments to group discussion (comprehension, appropriateness, understanding of what is taking place in group); (4) attitudes toward
peers (interest in peer comments, openness to other points of view);
(5) attitude toward group leaders (interaction, attention, quality of
relationship, any hostility toward authority?); (6) expressed social
concerns (awareness of problems and solutions, knowledgeability,
values, recognition of need for change); (7) demonstrated potential
for helping others (listening, evidence of warmth and empathy);
(8) academic motivation (willingness to try, readiness to see learning as a positive way to change society, others, and self). Daniels
and Powell made clear that the college sought insight into the attitudes and motivation of potential students. Selection was made with
a view toward the main goal of the program, that is, the training of

a highly motivated "humane" worker who listens, has empathy, sees need for change, and has the determination to get results.

Following the session, students spent the afternoon taking the college's own examinations while the interviewers compared their ratings. José Morales was appealing to both interviewers. They felt that this man who helped Spanish-speaking people fill out forms in the welfare office, who listened and showed enthusiasm, was "our kind of student." They admitted him at once. The examination that the students took was homemade. No nationally standardized tests are given: the college does not find these useful for its own diagnostic purposes, and many of its applicants resent such tests. The college instead follows the principle that even successful applicants should learn something from taking a test. Hence the first reading comprehension question is a short article from the *New York Daily News* that explains a simple test for diagnosing sickle-cell anemia, a hereditary disease found almost exclusively among blacks. There are also excerpts from Ralph Ellison's *Invisible Man* and an editorial by W. E. B. DuBois hailing the black soldier of the First World War: "Out of this war will rise an American Negro, with the right to vote and the right to work and the right to live without insult."

The college's ideology seeps into the model answer sheet used to grade exams. For example, on a twenty-five-word vocabulary test, the model answer for *professional* is given as "someone who has competence and commitment to serve." The word *service* is defined as "really helping." One of the questions following the DuBois editorial asks whether students would make the same arguments about the black soldier in the Vietnam War, and the answer sheet reads: "No. He was fighting other people of color. If there is a right side, it is more the Communists. There are no immediate benefits for the returning G.I. except a small G.I. Bill." But questions cast in this way constituted less than 20 points on a 385-point scale. It would be misleading to interpret the test principally as a device for screening out those with "incorrect" political views. In fact, the college's bias is more like that of a religious group seeking postulants who, having heard its call for service and social change, will be good candidates for the college's "ideology of citizen empowerment."

The exam also includes questions about the college, based on the materials distributed to students in advance and the explanations given to them in the admissions session. It concludes with a short math quiz. Morales scored 315 (250 is passing), displaying excellent comprehension but weak math skills. Of the eight, five were accepted, two rejected, and one provisionally admitted. Two of those admitted had a year of college, three were high school graduates, and Morales had completed the eleventh grade.

The admissions process, like the college itself, is compassionate but tough. Final admissions decisions are not made until the student completes a three-week trial in class—a true "performance test"—since the college is not only admitting a student but in effect is hiring him, since it acts as a proxy for various agencies. This, of course, makes dismissal more difficult, since to fail a student is essentially to "fire" him. But the college tries not to shirk that responsibility. Although it grants wide access, it does not guarantee exit. The reputation of the college rests on the performance of its students, and while it takes chances, it cannot risk many disasters on the job.

"Become an effective learner and potential professional" is the simple declaration students hear as they begin classes at the college. For most of them, the idea that one can learn more or less effectively is a novel one, but this, of course, is the "purpose dimension" of the "learning" competence, as set forth in Figure 1: "Demonstrate your readiness to work toward realizing your personal and professional goals and helping the college fulfill its mission by joining the college as learner and potential professional." Working on this first competency involves a course on the college and its unique language of "performance grids" and "constructive actions." In it, students are actually being asked if, on the basis of more detailed knowledge of what the place is about, they are ready to make a contract to pursue the college's goals. Particularly for students in a high-risk category (that may mean recent parole on a felony charge for some), this is a moment of commitment when they must decide if they "really want to get off the corner."

By the end of the four-week period devoted to the first competency, during which they spend five days a week at the college, students must write a proposal describing their personal goals over the next two years and outlining the steps by which they will reach them. In the process, they must demonstrate an understanding of how others will help them reach these goals (the "self and others" dimension), that they understand how the college's aims contrast with those of traditional professional education (the "systems" dimension), and how they can "determine and rank long- and short-range goals and develop alternative strategies for reaching them" (the problem-solving "skills" dimension). Students keep a log or diary during this first competency unit, which includes an exercise in assessing the values of the teachers they are encountering in class. Students also read autobiographies showing contrasting values and learning styles.

The remainder of the two-year program focuses on field placement, and the aggressive negotiating strategy used by the college in finding placements was illustrated on the day two staff members, Ruth Messinger and Bonnie Hall, went to the Manhattan Development Center to secure placements for fourteen students. They met with the heads of several mental health facilities, including institutions for mentally retarded children, community halfway houses, and mental health therapy centers. Of the group, Dr. Alphonse Sorhaindo was perhaps the most favorably disposed toward the college and was eager to have its students as interns. But others around the table were more skeptical. After polite probing of the curriculum, they voiced fears that shrinking budgets would force them to dismiss the college's students at the end of the program. But at this point Messinger explained that Audrey Cohen had negotiated with the associate commissioner of the Department of Mental Hygiene in Albany. He had agreed to find funds and "job lines" for fifty-five of her students at the completion of the two-year program. Messinger showed them a copy of that letter and promised that the college would hold the commissioner—not them— responsible for the jobs. This was typical of the college's strategy of negotiating job quotas at the highest level so that whenever possible local agencies were relieved of the burden of justifying new budget positions.

Although such high-level endorsement is crucial, the college must still win its way into individual agencies and obtain the director's signature on a seven-page contract, the heart of which reads: "The college and the agency agree to this relationship in order to: a)' develop appropriate new educational routes into the human service profession; b) plan and implement training leading to professional employment; c) jointly employ a system of performance-based assessment criteria that will ensure professional competence; d) initiate and implement procedures for acquiring the academic degrees and certification that will assure program graduates appropriate professional status; and e) provide skilled workers who, both during the course of the program and thereafter, will improve, supplement and expand human service delivery and demonstrate new and effective professional roles."

The contract then spells out the agency's responsibilities and declares that the college will help to devise the educational component of training on the job and will make a determination of what portion of time over the two-year period will be spent in work and what in study. By morning's end, the director, who had been consistently doubtful, agreed to take four students personally under his wing.

The most difficult and challenging task students face comes on the heels of the four-week competency unit on becoming "an effective learner," during which students are at the college five days a week. But with the second competency, ("establish professional relationships at the work site with coworkers and citizens"), they begin to spend three days each week on the job. In more than a few of the agencies that employ the college's students, a multitude of problems have developed in the course of integrating students into the work setting. Some supervisors are openly skeptical that these students— many without high school diplomas and just off welfare—are in fact potential professionals. At Morrisania Hospital in the Bronx ten positions in social work had been negotiated. But when the students showed up, they were found unacceptable for those positions, although ultimately they were allowed to remain in a variety of other human service capacities. Again, teachers in a public school to which two of the college's students had been assigned would not allow them into the teachers' lounge. And even where there is no hostility, students must overcome the common view that the College for Human Services is a community college preparing paraprofessionals. When students who have been treated like professionals by the college are placed in paraprofessional or subprofessional positions in agencies, it is difficult, if not impossible, for them to make the jump to professional status. The self-doubts of the students themselves (sometimes grounded in realistic self-appraisals of deficiencies in knowledge in specialized fields), the natural tendency to seek good relationships with coworkers (difficult if you are seen by paraprofessionals as a rate-buster on the way up), and the gatekeepers who protect existing positions with the tariff of the five-year master's degree compound the problems. One hears about these battles in visits to field sites: the efforts of students to gain access to client records, to professional staff seminars, or to other equivalents of the executive washroom. The outcomes of these struggles vary, of course, but even where the host agency is hospitable, students may be relegated to paraprofessional positions at the end of their training because of budget restrictions or lack of formal degree requirements.

The quality of the student placement is the linchpin on which the whole program turns. One model site is New York's Museum of Natural History, where a Spanish-speaking student works as a teaching aide in the Mexican wing. Here the college had tapped the resources of a doctoral-level museum staff that worked closely with the intern, tutoring him, guiding his reading in Mayan culture, and teaching him museum procedures. Similarly, at the Keener Clinic, a residential facility for retarded children, students rotated through internships in physical therapy, behavior modification techniques, and classroom training. They also participated in a weekly seminar under the direction of a Columbia doctoral student in psychology. In other placements, the college has not been as successful. At the Polish-Slavic Center in Brooklyn, for example, efforts to turn students into switchboard operators and envelope stuffers had to be halted.

After completing the first two competencies, by November many students, like José Morales, are in the midst of the third: "Working with others in groups, helping to establish clear goals." If he had somewhat lowered his high original expectations, Morales was by no means discouraged with the program. The only reservation he expressed was that perhaps the screening should have been tougher—fewer students would then be admitted with deficiencies in basic skills or with family problems. Yet it seemed remarkable to him that there were no drunks and nobody high on drugs in the college, given what he knew of other colleges in the city. He winced when it was suggested that perhaps classes should be tracked in skill areas—"tracking" was virtually a forbidden word—but on reflection he agreed that this was needed. Of course, if the college had been tougher, he might not have been accepted. His math was poor and he didn't know how to write a paragraph. In fact it wasn't until the second day of his skill class that he knew what a paragraph was. Now he could write one.

Morales said he was no professional yet, "not by a long shot," but he was learning. When he was admitted, he thought a mistake had been made. He didn't think he was ready or prepared to be a professional: "It was like telling me I was going to be chief surgeon at Mt. Sinai. What the hell am I going to do with a scalpel in my hand? I might cut myself." But after the first competency (which he called "the orientation period"), he had realized that it was possible "to take your own experiences in life, your own true feeling, and if you want to make a contribution to the community you can." He had also discovered values he didn't know he had—for example, the way his religion affected his outlook. He added, "I was—how do you say it?—I was fatalistic. . . . I was willing to just let things be, but coming here I learned you can really change things." His wife tells him he has changed, that he doesn't explode at the children so much. He's more likely to listen instead of brushing them away. But things weren't going that well on the job. He was not sure he was cut out to be a teacher (his job placement was as a teacher's aide in an alternative high school). Maybe he would do better at counseling. But one could talk about the problems—that was also a virtue of the college.

What distinguishes classes at the college is their attention to student field experiences; the common, cumulative curriculum tied to a series of student "constructive actions"; the subordination of disciplinary divisions of knowledge to the functional categories of the competency goals, and the lack of emphasis on reading or analysis of texts. Nothing is labeled psychology or sociology or economics. Many of the college's students, to be sure, would not know how to answer if asked whether they were learning any sociology. They are doing just that, of course, although not in a formal, structured sense. Adele Brody, a lawyer by training, teaches what in many sociology departments would be called a course on formal organizations. But the students do not read Seymour Martin Lipset, Peter Blau, or any of the other standard sources in this field. Brody distributes copies of agency budgets and teaches students how to read them to find out who makes decisions, or how informal structures may block a decision that originates in formal channels. Comparing the classes with those in sociology at Staten Island Community College, one student explained that "we are dealing with more realistic problems of people, of the agencies of the city." What did she mean by that? She replied, "To be effective in the situation. To analyze the client's problems—to know what is realistic, what is not. How to deal with a particular client, know yourself, know your emotions. Once you're in the agency, how to feel it out. Know who to go to see to get something done."

The reading lists in the formal curriculum guides are impressive. Under Competency V (counseling), for example, seventy-one books are listed, from Samuel Butler to Thomas Szasz, and include Sigmund Freud, Erik Erikson, Haim Ginott, Albert Camus, Robert Coles, Arthur Janov, Carl Jung, Karl Marx, Abraham Maslow, Friedrich Nietzsche, Wilhelm Reich, Carl Rogers, William Shakespeare, B. F. Skinner, and Tennessee Williams. Even many doctoral students would not be at ease with the range of literature listed! This is no modest list of 100 great books; it is closer to 1,000 (if one adds all the competencies). But in actuality, traditional reading of this sort has a low priority. The students' acquaintance with books is painfully thin. Faculty members acknowledge this by assigning only short articles or chapters, seldom books. Frequently key passages are read in class, an open acknowledgment that not many have read the assignment. There are few written assignments or "bookish" demands. The college stresses action. Students have hectic schedules, and the faculty are overburdened themselves. (In one class a faculty member announced a standard written assignment to be completed over the weekend. A student outburst followed—fists banged, there were loud groans and shouts of "We can't do it. No way!" The instructor backed down, but after class admitted that the students had not exactly demonstrated "professional behavior." She resolved not to be intimidated a second time.) One class was lackluster and withdrawn when the instructor attempted to get students to discuss an article on teaching methods by Ronald Hyman, but when he left the text and asked students what they would do in a tutoring center for forty-two high school students on a day when ten volunteer college tutors did not show up, the discussion covered all the strategies that one would find among a group of student teachers at Hunter College or Berkeley.

An observer might recoil from the notion that students who have such cursory acquaintance with the books that ask some of the most profound and disturbing questions about the human condition can be certified as human service workers. But should one compare these students with some ideal, or with what the average nurse or primary school teacher knows of Rousseau or Shakespeare? Furthermore, will reading Rousseau or Shakespeare improve their performance? Are not most liberal arts courses taught to students in social work and education chosen in an arbitrary way; do not they at best have only weak correlations with performance? Does not the foregoing disjunction between discussing Hyman and discussing what to do in a tutoring center simply confirm the Aristotelian distinction between theoretical and practical wisdom? To know something is not necessarily to be able to do it well. One cannot justify Rousseau or Shakespeare in relation to short-term rewards, even if one believes that traditional sources must be included in any professional curriculum on the grounds that human life is impoverished without them.

What of more specialized or technical knowledge? A teacher of mathematics obviously needs to know mathematics. A pharmacologist must understand certain branches of chemistry and biology. The college's position is that most specialized knowledge can be learned on the job. With no laboratories, the scientific knowledge imparted crucially depends on the resources devoted to students on the job, and here opportunities vary enormously.

Gladys King, a forty-five-year-old black student who interns as a counselor in an alternative high school in the Williamsburg section of Brooklyn, faces the problem common to many of the more able students at the college. In the competition for jobs, will she be better off if she trains for a specific position? She wants to be a counselor-teacher and has decided to take the necessary courses in a community college in the evening. Did she choose that avenue of training because she needed specific credentials or because she lacked knowledge to do the work she wanted to do?

"I really do need more academic preparation to feel educated as a whole person. Maybe it's a feeling of inadequacy on my part. I will probably end up doing the same work I am doing now [by which she meant counseling], but I would like to be a counselor-teacher. I need science courses, not more counseling courses. Also math courses. These are the courses I need to feel like a well-rounded person. To me a well-rounded person means an adequate person. So I can function better in my job. If I am asked to assist the math teacher or assist the science teacher, I would like to know that I am prepared for that."

Another area of technical knowledge that the college does not teach well would be called "tests and measurements" in a traditional catalogue. The prejudice (which may be a fair prejudgment in some instances) that most of these tests are bad or ill-used is imparted to the students, but they are taught little that will allow them to be sophisticated critics or users of such tests. The college's ideology also infects discussions of modern social science. For example, in one class the findings of Coleman (1966) were lumped with other "social theories that blame the victim for not learning." A film on the community organizer Saul Alinsky presented him as a model to be emulated without question, and much of the discussion about him sounded like a testimonial. While the fault lies somewhat in ideological bias, it is also a reflection of the faculty's limited knowledge. There are no sociologists at the college who are likely to have read the full *Coleman Report* and secondary analyses of it, and the faculty's disciplinary training in social sciences is not strong. But it does shine in other areas: interviewing skills, group dynamics, a detailed knowledge of how human resources agencies in New York work, and explanations of new laws affecting client rights in many sectors. Thus a deputy director of a mental health agency was surprised that students from the college who had been on the job only a few months were familiar with court decisions affecting the mentally ill that professionals on his staff had not read. Moreover, the students saw in the decisions implications relevant to improving the treatment of patients in his facility. The college also employs an excellent staff to teach basic writing skills to students who enter with severe handicaps in this area. Whenever possible, writing is taught in the context of reports or memos likely to be required on the job. During the first year students spend two hours a week in writing clinics. Some make extraordinary progress, but others do not, and poor writing ability is one of the most frequent criticisms one hears from supervisors of the college's students.

The best teaching grows out of the "constructive action" projects students must develop on the job. This kind of teaching—the college's trademark—is focused on clarifying and generalizing what is learned in the field and what needs to be learned in order to complete individual projects. Faculty sometimes grow weary, however, of students who do little or no reading and who tend to dismiss a theoretical point or criticize a position without really understanding it. Such students must be convinced that although a theory may not have a specific, immediate application to a client with a problem, it may be useful for understanding the role of the supervisor or the organizational setting in which one is working. Of course, much can be taught that does relate to the immediate, practical problem. The case method that has been so effective in training teachers, social workers, counselors, is utilized at the college for the study of real, rather than hypothetical, material.

In its attempt to push the pendulum of reform in the direction of more humane service to clients, the college sometimes uses rhetoric reminiscent of quotations from Chairman Mao, and its appeals to the students to act as change agents may strike some ears like the slogans of *agents provocateurs:* "We cannot doubt that the Human Service Society will become a reality. A massive change in the use of human power is coming in this century, and we must prepare for it now. It will be a change as great as that which took individual workers out of their ground-floor shops and into the assembly lines. The industrial age swept a whole society away in its path. The Human Service Society will mean an equally sweeping change, but the motive force will be a concern for the quality of individual human life" (College for Human Services, 1974, p. I:xi). But the day-to-day realities of the college, in contrast to the clarion calls in proposals to funding agencies, reflect a sober awareness that change usually comes a step at a time. A random sampling of student constructive action projects reveals the following quite modest proposals: to organize a school library; to publicize the community programs in the Henry Street Settlement House neighborhood; to open a "general store" in a high school selling pens, papers, and books to raise money for school teams and give students a sense of identity; to plan a program for the training of child care workers; to teach coworkers a simple vocabulary to converse by hand signals with deaf children; to make patients at Morrisania Hospital more aware of their rights.

The proposal to organize a school library competently described twelve tasks the student would perform, such as ordering and cataloging books and establishing a circulation flow. The student who wanted to plan a child care program needed a good deal of help. His folder included a confused miscellany of pamphlets—one on child care from birth to age eighteen, another on alcoholism and drugs. The student showed little awareness that he would need to draw upon the skills of teachers, developmental psychologists, nutritionists, and others to plan such a program. The Morrisania Hospital proposal was more typical; it involved discovering and publicizing a variety of patient rights and benefits.

Just as the proposals are not as radical as the rhetoric, faculty do not insist in practice upon rigid application of the rule that the client is always right. José Morales, for instance, eventually became discouraged in his teaching at an alternative high school. With the support of his coordinating teacher, he resigned the job and transferred to another agency. Though he eventually did go back to the school at the request of other students and faculty, the experience left him seriously doubtful whether he should pursue the profession. On some occasions the students have learned their lessons so well that they have come close to losing their jobs. A Spanish-speaking student working in the emergency ward of the Morrisania Hospital pressed for treatment for a patient who had been turned away by the doctor in charge. Since the doctor remained adamant, she appealed to higher authority. Subsequently, he sought her dismissal.

Clearly, the kind of assessment one receives often depends on who does the assessing. The doctor we have just mentioned "failed" the student, but the patients and other lay professionals in the hospital took her side. The college has tried to reflect this reality by establishing an assessment procedure in which clients, peers, supervisors, and faculty all participate, but in which the teacher makes the final decision. Assessment of constructive action proposals, written work, and on-the-job performance occur throughout the year, but the major evaluation comes with the year-end review of students. One year, the college's counseling staff and the agency supervisors were asked to fill out assessment forms responding to the dimensions of competence listed on the performance grid. Were students, for example, able to identify goals and understand systems? Nearly 90 percent of the agency supervisors returned the forms—a remarkably high proportion. Faculty and counselors then discussed each student's case in an attempt to make an overall assessment. The process was stimulating but also frustrating, because different parties put different interpretations on the criteria, and judgments about the same student diverged widely. Sometimes it was difficult to secure and evaluate clients' assessments, and the sheer amount of paper generated was overwhelming. The feeling began to grow that the college would have to rent another floor just to store the assessment forms. The data included not only the rating sheets but the student's entire portfolio, which one faculty member compared to a 400-page novel. He thought he could read four or five portfolios in a morning, but found he could hardly get through one in that time. (Significantly, the forms not only pertain to students; the college faculty follows its own preaching on assessment, with one of the most thoroughgoing faculty assessment systems in use. Students complete elaborate faculty evaluation forms at the end of every competence period, and faculty observe one another in their classes and in their supervisory roles in the field.)

In the spring of 1976 attempts were made to "standardize" and simplify the student assessment process; but now another basic problem arose. Should students be assessed only on *performance* of a constructive action? What if the proposal fails utterly but the student learns a great deal from the experience? Does the faculty have absolute or relative notions of what constitutes a good performance? Is it fair to a student to "fail" him or her at the year-end review? Must such a student repeat the entire year? After listening to a faculty committee discuss these matters, an observer was impressed with the committee's willingness to discuss so candidly the difficulties of what they were attempting and to raise questions that challenged some of the core ideas of the program.

In contrast to the elusive measures found on the assessment forms, faculty members use unambiguous indicators of performance when they talk informally about students they are supervising: Do they get to work regularly and on time? Do they participate in class and complete assignments? Can they write? Do they dress, look, and act like professionals? Are they serious and motivated? Perhaps it is a mistake to cast the language of assessment in the same language as the teaching goals of the program; a simpler set of terms might work better.

Sometimes real differences of opinion arise between faculty and agency supervisors. A supervisor at a social work agency told me that she considered three of the four students assigned to her to be unlikely candidates for professional status. They had serious deficiencies in reading, writing, and analytical skills. When the faculty member suggested that their greater empathy and understanding of clients should compensate for their deficiencies, the supervisor replied quite firmly that "just having lived is not enough." She insisted that sophisticated diagnostic skills were required to analyze the difficulties of problem families and write the reports demanded by the city agencies. When pressed further, the supervisor replied that a student's failure to write the reports well would mean additional burdens on the agency. As to diagnostic skills, she felt that three of the college's students were below bachelor's degree expectations and certainly not up to the level of a social worker with a master's degree who would be expected to "know enough about therapy to try to evoke the neurotic patterns that parents were afflicted with that led them to child abuse or whatever."

At another agency, the Keener Clinic, supervisors felt that the college's students might be at the bachelor's level, but not the master's, on two grounds: Their basic writing and math skills were low, and they lacked specialized knowledge. For example, the college's students would not know enough about psychological testing to administer and interpret a battery of tests. Could such skills be taught on the job? Yes, but more time would be required on the agency's part, and students would need stronger basic skills.

Reinforcing this view of deficiencies at the college, the New

York Department of Education in 1975 rejected the college's application for authority to grant the master's degree, principally on the ground that this degree would not be built upon a bachelor's program. The college again responded in some of the same ways as it had in 1968, seeking other avenues of support and trying to demonstrate that its students would have the equivalent of a bachelor's degree. But it also tried another tactic. Since the model could not be sold in New York, why not export it? Audrey Cohen obtained a grant to disseminate the college's program and began consulting at several colleges in California, Massachusetts, and Pennsylvania. Lincoln University in Pennsylvania expressed considerable interest. In 1976, its faculty, with the approval of the associate commissioner of higher education in Pennsylvania, approved a program modeled after the College for Human Services, although its exit requirements included a core academic program as well as standardized tests (Lincoln University, 1976). At this writing it appears that the acceptance of the model in Pennsylvania may improve the likelihood of its approval in New York, where the college resubmitted its application in early 1977, making distinctions in its program between the bachelor's and master's degrees. A branch of the college established in Florida was granted authority to award the master's degree in June 1977.

Reflections and Recommendations

Although the College for Human Services stands in this volume as an illustration of a competence-based reform, it is clear that this is but one of the many strands of reform the college has planned and encouraged. The other strands include devising new roles for faculty, granting access to the most deprived groups of students, and seeking to reform some professions by making assessment depend on the judgment of the client as much as on that of fellow professionals.

There are a multitude of contexts in which one could analyze the significance of these reforms attempted by the College for Human Services. One could challenge its most basic premise of the need for a "human service" society on the grounds that it makes more sense to strengthen the family through direct grant programs than to enlarge the army of paid professionals who perform family-like functions. But complex modern societies cannot do without bureaucracies, and few persons would disagree with the aim of making them more responsive to human needs. Although the college has rejected the term "paraprofessional" to describe its graduates because the term has come to mean a restriction of opportunities, there is a sense in which it has indeed hastened the development of needed paraprofessional resources. "Para-" can mean "near" or "alongside," as well as "subsidiary to." The college fosters a leavening of the professions, some of which have severely and arbitrarily restricted entry, and it seeks to supply, in the human services, the analogue of the physician associate, or paradoctor, in medical practice. The difficulties of establishing these roles and new performance measures within the framework of the various professions that the college places under the mantle of "human services" are, of course, enormous. But the achievements of the college, begun by amateurs in rented quarters on short-cycle budgets, are remarkable.

The program took ten years to develop. Not a long time as historians would measure it, but much longer than most contemporary American educational innovators are willing to wait: they expect to have committee meetings this month and a revolution next semester, even though most of the significant innovations in American education have not been successfully developed and institutionalized in less than a decade. Some of the college's faculty members have come and gone, but a core has remained. Audrey Cohen, whose tenure really began in 1964, was still president as of 1979; by contrast, the average term for college presidents is now less than five years.

While questions remain as to the adequacy of the faculty's training in the disciplines, few departmentally organized faculties could have sustained such a complex developmental process. Conventional disciplinary ambitions had to be abandoned by a faculty willing to devote itself for a decade to the task of testing the emerging ideas about a performance-based curriculum. It might have been possible to maintain the esprit of the college's faculty members within a larger university, particularly if they were organized as a subcollege or semiautonomous unit to protect their very different reward systems and forms of organization, but it could only have been done with great difficulty.

What does account for the high morale? Salaries are low, fringe benefits minimal, the workweek long, the academic year a full calendar year. The College for Human Services began as a volunteer college built with the talents of gifted women who worked full time for part-time salaries. Faculty were attracted by the ideals of the college, its sense of social mission, and its visible human accomplishments as students moved off welfare and began to rise in responsible jobs. The college also exemplifies the wisdom of thinking big but starting small. Its fundamental aim—to establish a performance-based and job-related curriculum designed to deliver improved service to clients—involved complex networks of funding sources, dozens of city agencies, supplementary task forces, and research consultants. But because the scale was small—never more than 200 students and about 20 faculty—the program was manageable. The faculty could meet as a committee of the whole, with the maximum opportunity for communication. Each new wrinkle of the common curriculum was tested and appraised by all. Collegial learning was maximized. Visitors and consultants were plied with practical questions about the next step in the curriculum development process. The faculty had a keen sense of the college's history and seemed to enjoy talking over earlier stages in the developmental process.

Though idealistic reformers, faculty members were resilient in the face of not infrequent setbacks—"hardheaded do-gooders," if you will. When students slipped, faculty were not crushed. Nor did they allow themselves to be defeated by the always present gap between hopes and outcomes. The practical, job-related realities of the program helped to protect them from the rigidities of their own rhetoric.

Underlying all the talk about competent performance was a true religious sense of dedication. Most faculty members recoiled at sloppy, uncaring performance. Their desire to restore idealism to service was a blend of the puritanism and evangelism typically found in reformers. Written materials sound like epistles to shore up lonely missionaries. The college asks for a commitment to its "way," to the belief that in service and in giving one will be reborn. The college asks this commitment even of visiting researchers, whom it would like to use to spread the word about its good works. The college also sees such researchers as potential converts to the form of education and assessment that it considers necessary for the creation of a new professional, social, and intellectual world.

The college can point to major accomplishments in its first decade. It has established itself, surmounted internal crises and strikes, invented a new curriculum, survived harrowing cutbacks in funds for the human services in New York, extended political support networks locally and nationally, and drawn together a faculty dedicated to its vision of social change. Yet in the decade to come, the college will face critical problems. It must find a way to sustain the morale of students whose jobs do not match the college's hopes, to refine the knowledge base that underlies its performance-based program, and to rationalize its proposed new degree structure to skeptical external audiences.

Although at present nearly one third of the college's students have had some college and fewer have been on welfare, most still face a radical transition as they leave homebound roles to meet the demands of both college and a new job—a total workweek of fifty hours or more. It is doubtful that many could survive that transition without the structure that the college's core curriculum provides or the support on the job that faculty furnish as both advocates and supervisors. The practical, step-by-step nature of the CHS "performance grid" has holding power for many of these students. Yet the curriculum of constructive actions also creates role conflicts of major proportions. Students are asked to become change agents, not just to hold their own as they learn the ropes, but to transform the professions by creating one that as yet is undefined. To have been chosen by the college was a major boost in confidence for most students, and for many the curriculum is a transforming experience. But they encounter serious obstacles in trying to adjust the college's hopes to the realities of the marketplace. Few attain jobs at the professional level, and, without degrees, all enter the job market at a disadvantage. Theoretically, it should be possible for mature adults with some college experience to earn a master's degree in two years in an intensive apprentice-study program. In practice, however, there are some serious objections that the college will need to meet:

First, the college will have to offer different degrees for different levels of competence, and distinctions will be difficult to make. Student placements, of course, vary greatly according to the level of the student's work, and the opportunities for learning on the job are also uneven—a problem that has been exacerbated by cutbacks in agency supervisory personnel.

Second, the college must assure the validity of its assessment system. The program specifies that students must "function" as counselors or teachers, but there is disagreement about what constitutes an adequate level of functioning. The problem is compounded by the conflating of personality and characterological values in a number of competency statements. For example, as part of the counseling competency, students are told to "demonstrate in counseling practice that you are flexible, tough, willing to risk yourself, resilient in the face of difficulty, optimistic and able to remain focused in confused or emotional situations." To some degree, all programs preparing teachers or social workers share similar difficulties in setting standards. No program can avoid subjective measures, nor would it be desirable to do so. But at the College for Human Services the subjective nature of the assessments is not offset by any nationally standardized measures or achievement tests. In adapting the college's program, Lincoln University in Pennsylvania required that students pass national undergraduate record exams at the level achieved by its college seniors, take mathematics proficiency exams, and complete a series of standard courses in psychology, sociology, statistics, and other subjects, in addition to demonstrating the eight competencies listed on the performance grid.

Third, the college must show that a generic degree in the human services will allow its students to enter a declining market in the face of competition from students with traditional preparation in such specific fields as psychology, education, and social work. It remains to be seen how well College for Human Services students can make their way outside the specific placements the college has negotiated for them as part of the training process. However, if they were armed with an accredited master's degree, it seems likely that some would be able to create new positions, as the college and its graduates have done in the past. Much will depend on the climate of client assessment that the college, among others, is able to create.

Fourth, the college needs to distinguish variations in performance and then tie them to degree levels. No one who has interviewed the college's students over the course of their two-year program would doubt that most who stay for the full course make extraordinary progress. However, they begin from different baselines and progress at different rates. A few do reach levels that seem equivalent to those of students with master's degrees from elsewhere—the degree seldom indicates high proficiency in America. Some are prepared for more useful and interesting work than they would otherwise qualify for, but do not go much beyond the paraprofessional level. Others perhaps attain the equivalent of the bachelor's degree. The college has lengthened its program from thirty weeks a year to fifty and has raised its entrance levels so that more students now enter with at least some college. It has also attempted to distinguish between bachelor's and master's degrees—it has dropped the associate degree—and has not been sentimental in its judgments about the competence of its master's candidates. Of 113 students who enrolled in the first "master's program" class in 1974, 76 were certified as having completed the first year, and 63 of these were hired for a second year by the agency in which they had been placed. Of that number, 58 were admitted to a second college year, and 51 won permanent positions in agencies in 1976. But in its petition to Albany for degree-granting powers, the faculty recommended only 12 of the original 113 students for the master's degree and 5 for the bachelor's; 10 students were classified as needing more time to complete all the "constructive actions" before a judgment could be made. Whether any college could continue with such low degree-completion rates is doubtful.

Finally, the invention of the college's performance grid was a genuine breakthrough for the faculty, but the task of "filling in the boxes" or showing the connections between theory and practice is an ambitious one. The college has a small faculty, and although it now has a few Ph.D.s where formerly it had none, the disciplinary training of the faculty has little depth. Like teachers in the normal schools of an earlier day, or law schools before they began hiring

Ph.D.s, the college's faculty are practitioners, not scholars. Most do not regard the disciplines as irrelevant, but they are skeptical that any particular knowledge base underlies performance in the human services. Their refusal to equate a list of courses with competence is admirable, and the college's performance grid has become a filter through which the faculty can search the disciplines for useful knowledge. That search is infused with an evangelical commitment to social change, a commitment that sometimes leads, however, to a debunking of what is not fully understood. The result is the development of a curriculum that, though at points truncated and even anti-intellectual, is nonetheless dynamic. The unresolved issue for the college is the question of how deeply the faculty itself needs to be grounded in the disciplines in order to make an intelligent search and to distinguish values from ideology.[2] Not every faculty member at the college needs a standard Ph.D.—far from it. But the faculty could benefit from a better mix of scholars and practitioners than it now has. Because the College for Human Services has achieved some recognition for the genuine advances it has made, it may be more willing and financially able to seek better trained faculty; however, whether or not it expands its faculty, the tension between knowledge and action will remain. Audrey Cohen would probably sympathize with Arthur Morgan of Antioch, who said, toward the end of his distinguished career, that he wished he had been more ruthless in eliminating faculty who "came here to teach [their] subject" and did not share his vision of the college as a "revolution" and "a way of life" (Clark, 1970, p. 40). Yet, as at Antioch, some faculty are both grounded in the disciplines *and* committed to social change. They demonstrate in their own work the competence of constructive action that the college expects not only of its graduates but of all professionals.

[2] Ideology does not here mean a conscious deception or lie, but what Karl Mannheim called the "cant mentality" that fails to uncover the incongruities in thought in "response to certain vital-emotional interests." See Mannheim, 1955, p. 195. To be aware of the danger of ideology in this sense is to recall Max Weber's assertion that "the primary task of a useful teacher is to teach his students to recognize 'inconvenient' facts—I mean facts that are inconvenient for their party opinions." See Gerth and Mills, 1946, p. 146.

Virginia Olesen **10**

Overcoming Crises in a New Nursing Program: Mt. Hood Community College

ꙮ

Eight miles east of Portland, Oregon, in the lush agricultural region of Gresham lies Mt. Hood Community College, named for the commanding peak that dominates the majestic Columbia and Willamette river valleys. Like the mountain, the college campus dominates a pastoral landscape of rich fields and prosperous farms. The main structure, built of rugged stone, signifies the school's solid community roots, although the complex of trailers and temporary modules that huddle at the rear strike a contrasting note of transitoriness. These buildings were the initial locale for a competence-based nursing program whose history of transition and alteration touches key issues in professional education and educational innovations well beyond the rural quietude of the Pacific Northwest.

　　Mt. Hood began in 1965 as a newcomer in a region already rich with educational resources, including such private schools as nationally known Reed College and the University of Portland, politically active Portland State University, and a number of other community colleges. Issues of competition and territoriality were thus crucial. For instance, its planners considered acquiring a local hospital as a site for clinical nursing practice; this was abandoned because that hospital was part of another community college district and hence off limits for Mt. Hood. Equally important were funding concerns, for many citizens of the college district believed that Mt. Hood's chief problem was financing. Prudent fiscal management was therefore mandatory from the outset.

Given these tensions generated by the competitive nature of local higher education and citizens' sensitivities about fiscal operations, the Mt. Hood board and administration attempted to balance offerings that would serve the community without high costs against those that would create an image of the college as being different from, if not better than, other institutions in the area. One strategy, which emphasized comprehensiveness, generated offerings in music, art and dance that proved attractive to minority students from urban Portland. Another emphasized service to the community by providing costly training in fields where jobs would await the college's graduates. Astutely, the administration foresaw the coming demands for manpower in health care fields and established an Allied Health Division that attracted increasing numbers of students to such programs as practical nursing and dental hygiene. In 1970, the administration of this division decided to provide an associate of arts nursing program that would exceed in quality those currently available in the community. The strategy was to revise and upgrade the division's already available licensed practical nurse program in order to outdistance others in the area. A vision of excellence thus preceded the conceptualization of competence as a base for the new program.

Nursing and the Strategies for Change

To transform their practical nurse program into a curriculum for registered nurses, the planners selected the concept of the career ladder, an idea in health care education that had already gained substantial national attention and acceptance, including the blessing of the National League for Nursing, the powerful accrediting body in nursing education, as well as the approval of the National Commission for the Study of Nursing and Nursing Behaviors. The career ladder envisions that individuals who train for roles in the health care system for which not too many specialized skills are required, such as nurse's aide or practical nurse, can use this training to enter higher degree programs—for the associate of arts, the baccalaureate, or the master's degree—without having to start all over again at the beginning of these programs. This steplike sequence, it was hoped, would encourage persons from deprived or minority backgrounds held down in lesser jobs to ascend to better positions where their talents and knowledge from the job as well as their classroom skills could be used. (In other parts of the country where the idea had taken hold, the vision of the career ladder implied a veritable host of Jacobs ascending the heights. Those heights, of course, in most places were cut off at the doors of medical schools. An exception was California, where Governor Edmund Brown, Jr., startled the citizens and medical establishment in 1977 by espousing a career ladder plan that would carry individuals up the rungs noted here, and into medical schools, a rare instance of extending the ladder to the top of the professional hierarchy.) These reasons made the concept of the career ladder ideally suited to Mt. Hood, which envisioned a trajectory of education for the nurse assistant from licensed practical nurse, on to the new associate of arts degree for registered nurse, and then to schools such as the University of Oregon's School of Nursing in Portland or Southern Oregon College in Ashland for the baccalaureate.

If the career ladder was the strategy for meeting Mt. Hood's commitments to the community, competence-based education would provide the high quality that was to differentiate Mt. Hood's program from all others. Several educational views then current in American nursing education might well have provided this quality; for example, an emphasis on problem-solving training or on learning from computerized or individualized packages. However, it was the ideal of precisely specified and assessed nursing behaviors in tasks customarily assigned to the nurse that provided the basis on which the college's licensed vocational nurse curriculum would be transformed into the new program. Competence-based perspectives were neither widely known nor used in American nursing education in 1970, although nursing education had historically been concerned with behavioral outcomes, such as the student's capacity to demonstrate skillful concern for patient safety and comfort. The idea of competence-based education in nursing was brought to Mt. Hood by Diana Dean, a nurse-educator from Eugene, Oregon, whose orientation to competence-based education derived primarily from her contacts with Ogden Lindsley, a psychologist at the University of Kansas, whom she had met while working on her master's degree there, and who continued to be her chief consultant as Mt. Hood developed its program. (See Lindsley, 1972; and Pennypacker, Koenig, and Lindsley, 1972.) In addressing the problem of how to teach certain psychiatric nursing skills, she had turned to a sociological theory based on interaction but rejected this because in her view it was not focused enough to help the learner. She then turned to the behaviorists in psychology whose ideas—of identifying measurable behaviors as the end product of training, of measuring learners against their own performance, and of rejecting the idea of failure and using instead the concept of learning opportunity— appeared promising to her.

Her appointment in 1970 as the coordinator of Mt. Hood's nursing programs and as the founder of its competence-based associate of arts registered nurse program was not the consequence of a national search among well-known figures concerned with this educational paradigm. Rather, she was selected as a result of personal contact with administrators in Mt. Hood's Allied Health Division, her reputation within the Eugene community, where she had directed a health services unit for a school district while completing her doctorate in special education at the University of Oregon, and, in her own words, because the administrators wanted the program "to be different and they had heard that I was different." A brilliant and forthright woman, a black in an almost totally white college, an aggressive leader in a profession where female passivity is both rewarded and criticized, she dominated the introduction and implementation of competence-based nursing education at Mt. Hood in ways that were not dissipated even after her untimely death from cancer in 1975, five years after the new program started.

The Context of Curriculum Construction

To begin curriculum construction, she inherited a well-prepared faculty of five members, all of whom held master's degrees in nursing from prominent university schools of nursing in Colorado, Oregon, Washington, and California at San Francisco. All had been on the faculty for some time, and all had an intense investment in the new program that they were to build. Administrative support for developing the program was generous. The college provided released time to nonnurse faculty to help the nurse faculty in concept development as well as the assurance of flexibility. The administration did not provide released time for the nurse faculty; the FIPSE grant made released time possible.

The new program opened in 1971 with thirty students, a number that increased to sixty in 1972 without added faculty. This doubling of students represented a geometric rather than an additive increase in faculty work. The extra newcomers needed, as new nursing students always do, extensive and time-consuming clinical supervision. Additionally, faculty also had to guide and instruct second-year students. These added students were not the only demands. As faculty refined the curriculum, they began to realize that neither traditional nursing education nor the newer taxonomic approaches of such figures in the behavioral objectives school as Bloom (1956) or Mager (1962) suited their purposes. Traditional nursing education—whether in the hospital, community college, or university—tends to invoke a high degree of self-consciousness in graduates, particularly in programs where interpersonal skills and problem-solving orientations are stressed (Olesen and Whittaker, 1968). However, in the view of the Mt. Hood faculty, these approaches, as they had found from teaching their own courses in traditional ways, failed to make clear what a nursing competency was, how to measure such competencies, and the connection between concepts undergirding practice and skills used in practice. They saw that students could learn to perform skillfully and correctly, but at the same time be unaware of why they did so. The faculty found the contributions of the behavioral objectives school of Bloom and others suggestive, but this work related primarily to the classroom or observable classroom behaviors and not to clinical or field settings that were, of course, crucial for nursing. A conceptual learning model that argued that no theoretical descriptions operate in the abstract appeared more attractive to them. The curricular elements, then, of the Mt. Hood program represented an innovative leap in two directions: making more explicit the means to reach the goals of traditional nursing education and extending the ideas of the behavioral objectives school. That leap, however, necessitated an evaluation mode keyed to the more precise demands of their new curriculum and in that mode lay the seeds of future trouble.

Faculty first described nursing behaviors as competencies, for example, taking temperatures, making beds, interacting supportively with patients, and assessing patient status. They then divided these competencies into concepts and skills on the reasonable grounds that the literature in nursing education is divided into materials on concept formation, cognitive processes, and skills demonstration. They focused on what they wanted students to be able to write, to say, and to do, that is, on the kinds of psychomotor skills that had to be demonstrated in simulation or clinical settings. Thus, the "write-say-do" curriculum model emerged.

The contrast between the initial curriculum and courses in the write-say-do model is illustrated by Table 1, which shows two versions of a second-year course. Table 1 also indicates that a number of important features of the curriculum, such as the counting and charting of behaviors, were in place before the write-say-do model emerged. The difference lies in the precise articulation of competencies and the behaviors in the write-say-do version of the course. Whereas respiratory arrest, for instance, was a concept to be learned in the previous course, this concept is now broken into discrete units to be rehearsed in the practice laboratory at Mt. Hood or performed on the wards and evaluated accordingly. Table 2, which provides an example of the concept of respiratory arrest and what competencies would be expected of the student in the write-say-do model, shows the explicitness with which competencies were stated. In short, relevant nursing behaviors of all types were atomized, scru-

Table 1. Nursing 201 (Advanced Nursing Skills) Before and After Write-Say-Do Model

	Before Write-Say-Do Model	After Write-Say-Do Model
Course Description	Indication of goals, procedures, and settings.	Goals and settings stated, but behavior procedures explicit.
Objectives	Identical.	Identical.

Course Proficiency	To receive a grade of B:
	1. Prepare acceptable class and clinical assignments on time.
	2. Prepare one acceptable nursing care plan per week with identification of the six behaviors (a-f) below.
	
	3. Keep count and chart a minimum of two patient behaviors.
	4. Keep count and chart a minimum of two patient behaviors in which student has effected change.
	5. Accelerate[a] five of the following six behaviors 1.2 times greater than the previous quarter by the sixth week and maintain to the end of the term:
	  a. Concepts used correctly.
	  b. Skills used correctly.
	  c. Personalizes patient care.
	  d. Teaches patient correctly.
	  e. Makes positive interpersonal relations.
	  f. Takes appropriate action on data collected.
	To receive a grade of A, the student must accelerate[a] all six of the behaviors listed above by the sixth week, and must maintain or accelerate them to the end of the term.
		1. Identical.
		2. Complete competencies and skills as outlined. (See example of one competency in Table 2.)
		3. In addition to items 1 and 2 above, a student must accelerate[a] four of the following five behaviors 1.2 times by the end of the term:
		  a. Applies nursing concepts correctly.
		  b. Makes accurate nursing interventions.
		  c. Teaches patient correctly.
		  d. Personalizes nursing care.
		  e. Makes positive interpersonal relations.
		
		Identical in terms of the behaviors listed above.

Course Outline	Rather generally described; thus, for cardiac arrest concept, the advanced nursing skills are noted as mouth-to-mouth resuscitation, airway insertion, closed chest massage, participation in simulated resuscitation procedures with no specificity as to writing, saying or doing.	Requirement for writing, saying, doing, accepted frequency and setting precisely are detailed for all concepts as per example in Table 2.

Source: Adapted from Appendices 1 and 2, Nursing Curriculum in a Write-Say-Do Model, Project Report 4.0, January 1974, An Investigation of the Cost-Benefits and Consumer Outcomes Related to Competency-Based Education in a Community College, pp. 1–4 and 1–9 respectively.

[a] Acceleration is based on how many times student had done the particular behavior, as well as on how many times the student had done the behavior incorrectly or missed an opportunity to do it correctly.

Table 2. Competencies Identified for the Concept of Respiratory Arrest Under the New Curriculum

Competencies	Write-Say-Do And Setting
1. *Lists* symptoms by which respiratory arrest can be differentiated from cardiac arrest: (a) absences of respiration (b) presence of pulse	*Written* classroom concept test
2. *Recites* steps leading to a diagnosis of respiratory arrest in 1a & 1b	*Said* in Practice Lab at least 1 time
3. *Performs* steps leading to diagnosis of respiratory arrest: (a) *Looks* at chest and sees no respiration; (b) *Feels* and confirms presence of pulse	*Done* in Practice Lab at least 1 time
4. *Initiates* treatment of respiratory arrest: (a) *Examines* oral cavity for vomitus—if present, scoops out; (b) *Hyperextends* neck; (c) *Inserts* oral airway; (d) *Administers* slow, evenly spaced breath into lungs	*Done* in Practice Lab at least 1 time
5. *States* action if (a) secretions or vomitus require removal; (b) a foreign object lodged in trachea	*Said* in Practice Lab at least 1 time
6. *Performs* defibrillation: (a) *Identifies* ventricular fibrillation from oscilloscope; (b) *Turns on* defibrillator; (c) *Selects* dose in Watt seconds; (d) *Applies* electrode jell to paddles; (e) *Activates* charge; (f) *Warns* others away from bed; (g) *Positions* paddles correctly; (h) *Discharges* current promptly; (i) *Reads* ECK pattern	*Done* in Practice Lab at least 1 time *Done* in Hospital at least 1 time
7. *Recites* action to take if defibrillation unsuccessful: (a) *Gives* principles governing reapplication of jell to paddles; (b) *States* point at which cardio-pulmonary resuscitation is initiated; (c) *Recites* definitive therapy after successful defibrillation	*Said* in Hospital at least 1 time
8. *Cleans* and stores paddles	*Done* in Hospital at least 1 time

Source: Adapted from Table 2, Example of Learner Competencies for Two Concepts, Cardiac and Respiratory Arrest, Write-Say-Do from *Nursing Curriculum in a Write-Say-Do Model, Project Report 4.0,* January, 1974, An Investigation of the Cost-Benefits and Consumer Outcomes Related to Competency-Based Education in a Community College, pp. 6–9. These concepts were among those taught in an advanced nursing skills class.

Note: Unlike behaviors related to certain concepts these competencies were not timed, though as the table makes clear, the minimum frequency of performance was indicated. Taking a blood pressure, for instance, which was a competency related to learning the concept of blood pressure, had to be done error free within 4 minutes at least one time in a timed test in the practice laboratory.

tinized and worked into a curricular setting where rehearsal in the nursing laboratory not only assured performance in actual practice at specified levels of speed and accuracy but was predicated on knowledge of why certain actions were being taken. For instance, in a basic test on the elements of circulation, the student would have to define circulatory failure, state two major causes for it, list eight observational behaviors a nurse would make of a patient in circulatory failure, explain why each observation is relevant to such a patient, and then briefly state the medical and surgical treatment in such a way as to include the rationale underlying each—all of this in fifteen minutes on timed performance. The students were not permitted to go on wards or perform even certain types of simple nursing tasks until they demonstrated these to the appropriate level of speed and accuracy in the nursing laboratory.

The nursing laboratory took on a Skinnerian ambiance with timers clicking and bells ringing as students attempted to take blood pressures, read thermometers, interpret electrocardiograms, and discern medication levels under the watchful eye of a faculty member or a student assistant with a stopwatch. Some students complained that timing such a complicated task, as, for instance, simulated catheterization, was inappropriate and constituted poor nursing practice. The timing of the test, in their eyes, did not take into account what they believed to be the necessary and courteous explanations to the patient about the procedure. At the same time, most students commented that completion of the timed trials meant that when they went to the wards they knew that they could perform the tasks to be assigned. Hospital nursing staff in their clinical teaching echoed this same view, a rather crucial one, for in other nursing programs many students going on the wards for the first time feel great anxiety about their skills and their performance.

In 1973 the founding coordinator had sought and received a year-long grant from FIPSE to refine the new curriculum, analyze outcomes, and establish a cost-benefit procedure. This grant called for a twelve-person consumer advisory group to work with faculty, and this group, along with the competence-based curriculum, brought Mt. Hood to the attention of national nursing circles—the curriculum having been selected to be part of the open curriculum study sponsored by the National League of Nursing.

The twelve-person patient panel was selected in 1973 by the nursing faculty to represent different health care treatments (for example, medical, surgical, and maternity)', as well as different ethnic groups, ages, and social backgrounds. Using Lindsley's rules for writing competence statements, the panel described a nursing behavior as a complete active movement that can be repeated, and that a complete stranger could agree had been performed. The panel's 225 statements were analyzed as representing categories of nursing competence as viewed by patients; for example, makes patient feel important, personalizes patient care, gives physical care, respects privacy, gives information, explains, interprets, and reinforces institutional policies, is adaptable, has pleasant manner, supports the grieving and terminally ill. These categories were similar to the three basic conceptualizations of nursing care that the faculty saw running throughout their curriculum: personalization, that is, maintaining the dignity of each person as an individual and adjusting services to her or his special needs and concerns; assessment, or gathering and utilizing relevant information from multiple sources to make decisions; and intervention, for example, nursing actions taken for potential therapeutic and preventive effects. These eventually became condensed into "program product behaviors" which students would count in order to be evaluated as they performed them.

A second grant from FIPSE for 1974–1975 provided faculty released time to develop conceptual logic for materials, specify multiple entry and exit competencies, and follow up the progress of students. Additionally, when the founder fell ill, FIPSE made it possible for her to maintain her position as project director until her death. It enhanced the innovative impulse of the faculty as well as assured the continuance of the program by placing it in the stream of new trends in higher education and opening both the faculty and the college to external influence from other educational innovations such as the narrative transcript and the evaluation of minimum standards for admissions. It is less clear that the grants provided a seed-bed for the introduction of competence-based education into other sectors of the college. The nurse faculty held several workshops for instructors in other fields, but only two persons were sufficiently excited to write competencies in their own fields and none rallied to the support of the nurse faculty when the program was later threatened. Much later, in the winter of 1976, the administrators seemed to see ideas from the competence-based nursing program beginning to seep into other faculty and other programs, for example, inhalation therapy. Once underway, the new curriculum itself added further burdens. Faculty had to do extensive paperwork when monitoring evaluation devices, and substantial investments of time were necessary to guide students who wished to accelerate or slow down. In straining the faculty's professional energy, these demands constituted unanalyzed costs that for the most part went unacknowledged and unrewarded by the administration. As the coordinator herself admitted, "Such a program takes a lot of hide from faculty."

Some faculty, unwilling to pay the high personal costs, uneasy with such a dynamic leader, and reluctant to accept the competence-based model, left between 1971 and 1974. They were perhaps also uncomfortable with some new types of students recruited in the program's liberal outreach (males and "hippies," for example) and may have sensed the difficulties that would come from the evaluation mode. But with one exception, this winnowing process produced a faculty that was committed to the program and willing to pay its high costs. Their willingness, however, was seriously strained when the founding coordinator underwent surgery for cancer in the summer of 1974 and the subsequent treatment and course of the illness removed her from direct, active participation in the program. Although other faculty handled her teaching load (without recompense to them) and one faculty member acted as an assistant coordinator, communicating between the faculty and her, at her home in Portland, eight miles away, the program suffered greatly, further straining faculty morale. Not surprisingly, however, given the faculty's heavy investment in the newly constructed curriculum, their response to the impending loss of this young, vital leader was to increase their own emotional and professional commitment, even as the costs of implementing the new program remained high and increased.

Self-Pacing

One of the program's competence-based features that did appeal to students was self-pacing, which allowed students to proceed as rapidly or as slowly as they wished. Such latitude, however, created problems for the faculty. Necessary equipment for timed tests, for instance, had to be available to students who were out of sequence with their classmates, and faculty had to be available to monitor the tests. If, for example, a student wished to be tested on taking blood pressure and the pressure cup had been stored from the previous quarter, the instructor would have to retrieve the equipment, set up the test, and arrange for the test at a time when other students were testing an entirely different skill.

Differential pacing also meant problems for the registrar. Some students who chose to fast pace would complete one course at midterm, start the materials for another course in the same quarter and perhaps finish it, but would be shown as registered for only one course without indication of the extra time spent and resources used. Worries about student credit and registration for these out-of-sequence courses emerged. Further, students could take incompletes if they had not met all their competencies for a particular course within the quarter but planned to finish their work out of sequence in a future term when they would not be registered for the class being completed. Thus registration figures did not reflect the drain on faculty time and energy, and the large number of incompletes created problems with student records.

The variable pacing plan created yet another difficulty among students themselves. Slow-pacing students reported that because they could not participate in class work with their peers, they had lost some of the support necessary to move through a program that was generally regarded as stressful by even the most favorably disposed students. Fast pacers, on the other hand, said that they found it necessary to explain carefully to their fellow students why they were accelerating, or else good relationships with them would not be maintained. These were crucial points. Many students agreed that either fast or slow pacing could jeopardize the high degree of cooperativeness existing among the nursing classes. Fast pacers added yet another concern, namely that fast pacing required a great deal of extra energy and time. From the view of administrators in the Allied Health Division, variable pacing was a mixed blessing; they thought it helped retain weak students.

Parallel problems with admissions also plagued the overworked faculty and, in the instance of high drop-out rates (caused by male students), came to be seen as consequences of the competence-based program. The college's open-door policy brought in unusual students, including a large number of males, for whom the stresses of training in a traditionally female profession were heightened by the innovative curriculum. Curiously, no attention had been given in the early planning to admissions policies that would fit recruits to the new program; some of the admitted students could handle the classroom and laboratory work but needed excessive tutoring and guidance on the hospital wards. A faculty-administration task force finally resolved some of the issues.

How then were graduates of this innovative program regarded in the nursing community? How did the graduates regard themselves? Judging from a follow-up study conducted by the faculty, and by comments made to this author during the fieldwork, the program and its count system clearly produced a graduate highly conscious of her or his own strengths and shortcomings. Of the graduates, 48.2 percent believed that the most valuable competency the program gave them was interpersonal skills. At the same time, more than half regarded themselves short of the mark in supervisory skills. Hospital supervisors interviewed in the follow-up study also thought this a shortcoming, as did supervisors whom this writer interviewed in the field. This, however, suggests lack of understanding, for associate of arts programs do not prepare nurses for supervision, though Mt. Hood graduates told this author that they sometimes experienced pressure on their first job to step up immediately to supervisory ranks. When the graduates were asked to evaluate their own education against programs with which they were familiar by virtue of contact with students from diploma or university schools in clinical sites, they replied that they thought more highly of Mt. Hood's program. The majority believed that the Mt. Hood program was equal to or better than other associate degree programs, diploma programs, or baccalaureate programs in four areas—instruction, curriculum content, clinical experience, and amount of class work. They drew the sharpest distinction between Mt. Hood and other community colleges, viewing Mt. Hood in a much more favorable light.

Trajectory of Crisis and Change

The spring of 1975 brought a series of events that described a trajectory of crisis as steep as any of the gradients on the student's count sheets. The death in April 1975 of the founding coordinator who had brought ideas about competence-based education to the college was not unanticipated. While faculty were genuinely grieved by her passing, her release from the ravages of her illness also liberated faculty and the acting coordinator from the strained circumstances of distanced and ambiguous communications. By the spring of 1975, faculty had worked out competencies for six of the seventeen nursing courses. In retrospect, the placement of those six courses in the curriculum appears to have influenced the course of later events. Three courses in the first year, one in the first quarter, and two in the second quarter had been completely revised. The other three courses for which competencies had been completed were in the first, second, and third quarters of the second year. This meant that all students, whether they chose to take just a licensed practical nurse certificate at the end of the first year or to continue through the second year to receive the associate of arts degree, were early, intensely, and continuously exposed to the competence-based curriculum and its assessment mode, the precise behavioral management system. The class that entered in the fall of 1974 was therefore the first class for which the competencies and the accompanying assessments were complete. This was the class whose discontent with the precise behavioral management system peaked in the summer of 1975.

As noted earlier, the crucial words in the rehearsal and performance of competencies at Mt. Hood were *speed* and *accuracy,* but they implied a third, *frequency.* Frequency became the measure of determining how many competencies were actually acquired in the clinical setting. It was thus related to the program's assessment mode, that is, the precise behavioral management system that began to loom larger in importance to the students than the program as a whole and that by the summer of 1975 became the focus of mass student protest.

The precise behavioral management system was developed to grade and to evaluate student performance at the critical points of the first and fourth quarter of their studies and at the end of the second year of the two-year program. Looking back for a moment at Table 1, it can be seen that in both versions of Nursing 201, students were expected to accelerate their performance on five or six key behaviors termed "program product behaviors," for example, in the write-say-do version, "applies nursing concepts correctly," "makes accurate nursing interventions," "teaches patient correctly," "personalizes nursing care," "makes positive interpersonal relations." (A complete list of these "program product behaviors" for the first and second years may be found in Table 3.)

The precise behavioral management system required that students and faculty record their performance on the program product behaviors daily and quarterly, generating a formidable amount of paperwork for both. For instance, a student would have to note down how many times he or she had given correct care in the area of patient comfort, had personalized patient care, had

Table 3. First- and Second-Year Program Product Behaviors

First-Year Program Product Behaviors

Judges interpersonal contact as sensitive (insensitive)
Applies new nursing concept or old concept in new and different way correctly (learning opportunity)
Applies old nursing concept correctly (learning opportunity)
Makes faculty contacts
Makes student decisions
Makes positive class contribution (learning opportunity)
Teaches patient correctly (learning opportunity)
Gives personalized patient care (depersonalized patient care)
Feels positive about patients (negative about patients)
Feels positive about college nursing program (negative)
Feels positive about peers (negative)
Feels positive about care given (negative)
Reaches proficiency in application of concepts in lab (attempts to reach)

Second-Year Program Product Behaviors

Uses interpersonal relations skills in which other person has (not) been taken into account in sensitive manner
Applies new nursing concepts or old concepts in a new and different way correctly (learning opportunity)
Applies old nursing concepts correctly (learning opportunity)
Teaches patient correctly (learning opportunity)
Feels positive about patients (negative)
Feels positive about Mt. Hood (negative)
Feels positive about nursing (negative)
Gives information to physician (receives)
Makes decisions using daily behavior chart (without chart)
Makes effective nursing intervention (ineffective)

Source: Appendix 4, Program Product Behaviors, *Nursing Curriculum in a Write-Say-Do Model, Project Report 4.0,* January, 1974, An Investigation of the Cost-Benefits and Consumer Outcomes Related to Competency-Based Education in a Community College.
Note: The first behavior is the correct behavior; that in parenthesis would be termed a "learning opportunity," a term used for incorrect behavior to avoid connotations of failure and to emphasize the idea that learning could occur from "mistakes" or "missed opportunities."

taught the patient something about his or her illness, or had given the physician information. Students also noted how many times they encountered a learning opportunity, that is, the incorrect perform- ance of the behavior or the missed opportunity to do it correctly. Both counts were charted on a special type of logarithmic paper on which ideal student progress would describe an ever steeper gradient. These data were stored in a computer program for retrieval and analysis. This type of precise behavioral analysis permitted not only fine-grained monitoring of student performance but the assessment of clinical sites—for example, the rate of acceleration that a student showed in a certain hospital—and finite evaluation of certain assign- ments to see how quickly or slowly they could be finished. Many faculty also used the precise counting system on their own behaviors both in their teaching and in other parts of life. Their counts were not used as assessments of faculty performance, but data on them were available in the computer should such an assessment have been desired.

From the students' point of view, expressed with varying de- grees of emotional intensity, the counting system produced great stress and anxiety, but little in the way of genuine learning. While they found the competence-based conception of nursing education to their liking, they believed that the count system was too intense an evaluative mode for a two-year program. Others noted that one could manipulate the daily counts so that the record showed the proper gradient of acceleration, a type of faking of which faculty claimed to be aware. Unhappiness with evaluation systems is by no means unusual in nursing education, where assessment of student performance historically has been painful and anxiety provoking for students, and the subject of continual debate, discussion, and con- cern among nursing educators. For some Mt. Hood students, how- ever, the count system generated particularly intense feelings. They felt that the count system dehumanized them, forced them to fake the counts, and was used illegitimately in counseling when it became the basis for personal evaluation.

Aware of student distress about the count system, faculty members attempted certain changes, for instance, reducing the num- ber of counts. Another portent of troubles to come occurred when a student whom the nurse faculty had deemed clinically unsafe became the center of a tense situation between the faculty and the administration. In the hierarchy of nursing values, none stands higher than patient safety, and hence perceived failure to achieve this standard constituted a very grave matter for the instructors. The administration's resolution of this situation seemed, in the faculty's eyes, to place student rights ahead of professional prerogatives and to constitute an affront to their professional values. But this incident, however predictive, had slipped into memory by the end of June when the entire first-year class of twenty-three students obtained an interview with the assistant to the president of the college to present a dossier of complaints about the faculty and the program. Faculty members were not invited nor were they present at the meeting. The administration, however, made it clear to students that this was not the usual mode of presenting such materials, which in the future should be forwarded through prescribed channels.

The students charged that the faculty failed to include their ideas on curriculum change and that the high drop-out rate was due to the new curriculum. They also criticized the stressful final faculty-student conferences and, not unexpectedly, the "dehumanizing" count system. Some days later they requested, by letter, an alteration in the count system. On July 14, the faculty was called to a meeting with the administration at which students' complaints were summarized; they were given five days in which to prepare an answer.

During that week, concerned about the climate of crisis and the effect it was having on their own teaching as well as on students on the wards, faculty canceled their clinical work and asked the college president for a week's emergency leave, which was granted. They then sought counsel from the State Board of Nursing and from the Oregon attorney general's office and were advised that they would not jeopardize themselves professionally should they resign. They decided, however, to stay at least through the summer, thus, ironically, making it possible for the very students who had lodged the complaints to complete their summer course work. According to informed observers, had they chosen to resign at that point, the board would have had no choice but to withdraw accreditation, as such is predicated, among other things, on the presence of qualified faculty.

In the meantime, the second-year students had rallied and on July 17 presented a letter of support for the faculty to the administration, although they acknowledged that some features of their program needed changing. That same day the faculty presented a written response to the administration's July 14 request, reviewing the history of the program and stressing the integral, indeed crucial, role of the precise behavioral modification system in nursing as an applied and precise science. While assuring the administration that they would remain through the summer, the faculty also indicated that if the first-year students could not accept the curriculum, then they should terminate at the licensed practical nurse level and seek other, more traditional nursing education elsewhere. The faculty alleged that the administration had not followed correct procedures regarding grievances against them, and they listed four conditions that had to be met if they were to remain after the summer term: (1) administrative use of correct procedures for handling student complaints, (2) attention to faculty rights, (3) continuation of the current curriculum, and (4) the appointment of the acting coordinator as permanent coordinator.

At a conclave on July 22 between faculty and administration, the faculty were advised that their four conditions were unacceptable. The administration hoped that the faculty would be amenable to program modification and improvement and would remain at the college but stated that if the faculty felt they could not continue, they were to request a release from contract by July 31—a somewhat ironical note, according to the faculty, since they claimed that they had received no contracts. On July 31 the faculty responded to the administration, noting the extensive investments of time they had made in developing the program, reaffirming their belief that decisions about nursing curriculum content and teaching methods should be made by nursing educators in conjunction with patients, students, and curriculum experts, and indicating that so long as differences existed around the issue of who should plan, implement, and evaluate the nursing curriculum, they would not return to teach at the college. The faculty met again with the State Board of Nursing, whose help had also been requested by the administration. The board asked the faculty to return, but the instructors stuck by their earlier requirement that the administration meet stated conditions.

By mid August the crisis had come to involve twenty-one graduates of the program who personally delivered a letter of support for the faculty to the administration. While acknowledging the sensitive nature of the count system, they praised the program and its emphasis on care of the "whole patient." This letter was forwarded to the Mt. Hood board and the State Board of Nursing. The issue was closed, however, for the search for a new nursing faculty had begun. The administration claimed that the resignations were due to its and the board's refusal to give in to the teachers' demands to set and control their own curriculum and program, holding that, "No department or division on this campus is autonomous" (*Oregon Journal*, August 27, 1975).

Thus, by the fall of 1975, a scant five years after the initial planning for the program, the program was in limbo and only one faculty member remained—she had been on vacation during the crisis and was not party to the events. Those who had developed the program were seeking other work in the tight nursing market in the Portland area, and the administration was trying frantically to fill the vacated positions with persons acceptable to the State Board of Nursing. Nothing had ensued from the supporting letters written by second-year students and graduates, members of the counseling staff, or an administrator of a large clinical facility, nor from the faculty's contact with the college faculty association. The instructors apparently had no natural allies in other programs or disciplines on the campus who would rally to their aid. The State Board of Nursing was not empowered to act on behalf of faculty in personnel disputes, but only on accreditation issues related to the quality of the curriculum. None of the dissident faculty were members of Portland's militant women's groups, which might have championed their cause. Moreover, the rapid development of the crisis necessitated focus on emerging events, leaving faculty with little opportunity to search for allies. Some members of the dissident group were reluctant to register complaints or take later action that "might get nasty." How successful those efforts might have been is problematic, for, as an observer not on the faculty put it, "With the college, student rights and community interests come first." The administration, sitting in a conservative college district with a high tax rate and mindful of the high costs of the nursing program, was understandably eager to return to a normal state of affairs. In death, as in life, the figure of the founder provided a symbol against which these events were interpreted, for the dissident faculty were said to be "not as tough" as she was, an ironic and curious interpretation in light of the instructors' strong stands about what they believed to be right in their program.

Denouement and Reconstitution

With the nursing program emptied of faculty a scant month before the start of the new school year, the State Board of Nursing emphasized to the college that accreditation would indeed be jeopardized if competent faculty and, in particular, a competent coordinator were not hired. The board mandated that two courses containing materials inappropriate for the community college curriculum—community health and patient assessment—would have to be altered and that the entire program would be under review for the coming year.

The fall term started with a brand-new cadre of locally recruited instructors with the exception of the holdover instructor who, as noted previously, had been on vacation during the summer's crisis. (This instructor provided a link between the old era and the new.) Whatever their knowledge of the summer's problems, the new instructors plunged into work on what they described in admiring tones to this writer as "a beautifully developed curriculum." They received in turn substantial moral support from the administration.

The faculty had been told they could defer teaching one quarter while they acquainted themselves with the program, but they chose to go ahead immediately. At the outset, however, they decided to use a modified behavioral management evaluation rather than the highly precise counting system that had evoked the crisis. Although the new coordinator believed that there was some benefit in the behavioral management system, the faculty, after debate, cut back on use of the count system in both the first- and second-year courses, thereby continuing the downward trend that had actually been started by the departed dissident faculty. Counts were later reduced from six behaviors to two and finally to one competency in each quarter. Grades were separated from the counting system. As a substitute for the controversial count system, some faculty at first used a mode based on development of nursing care plans, a classical teaching and evaluating device in nursing education. Under this method, the student writes out what will be done for the patient, and this description, as well as her observed behavior is evaluated. The faculty then adopted a system based on seven nursing behaviors (assessment, safety, efficiency, personalization, teaching, intervention and comfort) that were to point the student to competencies to achieve in clinical work. These behaviors, under the acronym ASEPTIC, would form the basis of self-evaluation and instructors' evaluation on a six-point scale from poor to excellent but would not be timed. Competencies were still to be timed in laboratory tests, however.

As the fall of 1975 got underway, it seemed as if problems with the count system would survive to plague the new faculty. Very early, some second-year students who would have been part of the summer's crisis complained that they still had to manipulate the data in order to get a satisfactory grade. These new second-year students had also vividly described to entering first-year students the difficulties of the competence-based program and its count system, but these descriptions did not generate further uprisings, particularly since faculty downplayed counting and graphing. The second-year students, however, put some of the new faculty to the test, giving one instructor a particularly hard time and in general savoring the sweet taste of the impact they had earlier made on the program. One faculty member commented: "The sense of power has made quite a difference for them. They know they had an instrumental hand in [the events of] last summer." At the same time faculty saw these students as being somewhat worried by the amount of influence they had and still a bit shaken by how close the program had come to being closed down in the summer, a closing that would have jeopardized their degrees and professional careers. The crisis lived on for a time in interpersonal tensions at clinical sites between the new instructors and former faculty members working there as well as in the difficulties in placing some of the student leaders in settings where their reputations as "troublemakers" had preceded them.

The first year, in the new coordinator's words, "had been tough." As the faculty came to the end of the year, they realized that they had to make changes in the curriculum, but had little time to do so. More particularly, they realized that much of the material taught was not relevant for the state board examinations. First-year students, arriving at that stage where they question every-thing, had suggested changes, for instance, in the mathematics course that they had to pass before they could be allowed to give medications. The faculty had also changed the student-faculty as-signment system so that students were assigned to one instructor rather than to two or three, a change much for the better in the new coordinator's view. Students had also asked for more lectures, a rather familiar cry in many schools of nursing.

Pacing also continued to present problems for the faculty. How, for example, should twelve slow pacers in the first year and twelve in the second year be handled when they came back into nursing courses from taking supporting courses in the social and biological sciences? The potential strain on teaching time and space in the Mt. Hood laboratory and on available clinical placements could be quite serious. To avoid this problem in the future, the faculty decided that students would have to declare three months in advance if they wished to pace themselves slowly. Thus slow and fast pacing, a feature of the innovative program, was succumbing to the practical difficulties created by differential pacing.

The year ended with the controversial count system fading as a viable element in assessment, but the basic conceptualization of nursing competencies as a groundwork for the program in the write-say-do model was sustained and supported, for the most part enthusiastically, by the new faculty. The course outlines written by the faculty show that major elements of the competence-based program were still in place, but there had been significant modifica-tions of the initial program. For example in N–216, Nursing for Acute Physical and Environmental Situations, competencies remained highly specific and thoroughly detailed with indications of what the student was to write, say, and do in what settings and with what frequency, very much as in the material earlier noted in Table 2. Course requirements called for students to seek out new opportunities to perfect skills, take at least one test during each class period, complete a weekly nursing care plan, prepare a group presentation, and indicate if they were unable to provide care for patients. A grade of B would be given for documented evidence of completion of course requirements and competencies. Students had to demonstrate advanced nursing skills in accordance with ASEPTIC concepts, engage in meaningful patient teaching, maintain rapport with patients, hospital staff, and peers, and show evidence of effective nursing intervention through utilization of basic concepts of ASEPTIC. Grades of A were to be given for documented evidence of all of the performances for a B but with evidence that there had been an improvement in the quality of total patient care exceeding that of the average student. Also required were completion of a fifteen-minute conference for the hospital staff on the student's ward and completion of an in-depth nursing care study.

Clearly, many of the elements of what had previously been termed "program product behaviors" were still at play under different names in the revised courses, but the element of timed evaluation, as well as the acceleration of those behaviors now subsumed under the ASEPTIC format, was missing. As with every innovation that passes from the hands of the originators into those of adapters, some elements were picked up that could be easily and congenially fitted into the new era, for example, specification of competencies on an ideal of nursing behavior, and the write-say-do model. But troublesome aspects, for example, the count system and the precise behavioral management, were left aside. Whether the new version of the innovative program would produce the same highly self-conscious and self-evaluative student as the older version had would remain open to question.

Thus the first year of the new era ended with the program transformed. That ending also marked the move from temporary trailers to handsomely furnished new quarters in the Allied Health Division's part of the main structures. With a touch of irony that could only have been unplanned, the second-year rebels, who had overturned the initial faculty and its innovative program, presented the new faculty, upon the occasion of the move to the new building, with a large, solidly rooted plant to grace their quarters.

Continuities: Portents of Further Change

Implementation of the competence-based innovation, altered by the students and further modified by the new faculty, continued in yet different directions with recruitment of more new faculty in the fall of 1976, some of whom were uncomfortable with the competence-based model, preferring, for example, modular types of instruction. These divergences in view were also reflected by the appearance of teaching styles that were no longer unified around a common and intensely held allegiance to the innovative program. What thus had begun to happen at Mt. Hood was the further alteration of an innovation by individuals who were not initially or even secondarily a party to it.

Other issues emerged from the policy of allowing students to repeat and rerun the competency trials and clinical behaviors. One student who had failed the crucial math test and who had been receiving illegitimate assistance from other students in completing her competencies—something which prompted the other students to complain to the new coordinator—had taken a competency test eight times before finally receiving an A. This particular case, as well as that of the student who had been judged unsafe by the faculty in the spring of 1975 and who was to be allowed to return to Mt. Hood, raised two crucial issues for faculty and administration: With certain competencies, to quote one instructor, "it's not a question of being able to perform the nursing skill *eventually,* it is a question of being able to perform the task or behavior *well.*" Administering shots, catheterizing a patient, reading a cardiogram, and most crucially of all, figuring the mathematical base of medications are examples of these skills. The second issue was that of chance: Could a student pass a competency by chance, but then not perform well again? This question implied that passing a competency does not necessarily guarantee that the skill can be adequately performed indefinitely. These troublesome questions occupied some faculty and administrators as the second year under the new coordinator ended in spring 1977.

This new era, however, was to give way to yet another chapter in the Mt. Hood story, for in January 1977 the "new" coordinator indicated her intention to retire, noting that she had not intended to become a coordinator when she came to the faculty in the fall of 1975 after the crisis. Her two years, however, had eased the program from a period of crisis into the new era and had seen curricular resolution of the state board's criticisms of the community health and assessment courses.

In the spring the administration and faculty selection committee picked as the last coordinator one of the faculty who had come with the new group in the fall of 1975. She would take the competence-based innovation into yet another era. She hoped for the opportunity to do long-range planning rather than respond to one crisis after another, and thought that returning the faculty to clinical affiliations, for example, the classical areas of medical-surgical nursing, maternal and child nursing, and psychiatric nursing could be accomplished by faculty organization. That she would continue implementation of the competence-based program seemed likely, given her use of the write-say-do model as well as of the precise articulation of competencies, though she preferred a more complete explanation of competencies to students than the original program had provided.

Thus, the Mt. Hood drama closes in these pages with a new set of players who will further transform the dreams of the founder, her dispossessed faculty, and even the "new" faculty of 1975. The key element that runs through all these phases—a closer and more self-conscious integration of behavior and concept in nursing performance than is usual in community college curriculums—could constitute a major contribution to nursing education in community colleges. It could propel Mt. Hood to the forefront of community college nursing education, as well as competence-based education. Whether it does so or not is the next phase of the drama.

Comments: Factors in a Model of Change

The Mt. Hood story contains elements that usefully provoke thought both about educational innovations in general and about the particular locales where such programs start. Two crucial conflicts emerged from the history of the program there. The matter of curriculum content, that is, the inclusion of courses in community health and assessment placed the college and the program in a sensitive situation vis-à-vis the powerful State Board of Nursing because those sectors of the program exploded the boundaries set for curriculum (and job entry levels) for community college programs. Thus, some attendant features of competence-based programs may exceed the educational constraints of particular settings. The second conflict arose from the initial faculty's views of the rights of professionals to regulate a professional curriculum, views that could not be accommodated in a college administrative structure where student rights and community interests had priority. Consequently, a competence-based program such as Mt. Hood's poses the critical issue, much explored in current research and thinking on organizations, of strains in the bureaucratization of professionals and professional education.

As for the competence-based curriculum, certain features played a large part in the flow of enforced change and bid to alter the program in the future. Although the founder and her faculty preferred to think of the elements of the curriculum (the articulation of competencies, the precise behavioral management mode of assessment, and differential pacing plan) as unified, inseparable, and not necessarily alterable parts of the whole, it would be useful here to separate out the storm center of the crisis: the timing and counting aspects of the precise behavioral management system. Though these were modes for determining how students could reach high levels of nursing skills, they became intertwined with the definition of overall nursing competence, overshadowing the very precisely stated nursing competencies. Why did these modes become the fulcrum of change? Why did the students exhibit such militance against them? Some speculative comments may be offered.

Nursing education, wherever it occurs, is stressful for students. Evaluation modes have long created anxieties for students and worries for instructors. In this respect Mt. Hood shares its problems with all of nursing education. What might have been additionally at work in the Mt. Hood program was the "discrete" nature of the count system and its requirement that various parts of life, the self, and nursing be separated into behaviors and then counted. Such an exercise essentially separates that which, in human knowledge, is integrated, global, and whole, if we are to follow Polanyi's (1967) views on "tacit knowledge." Thus, while a student could and would become highly self-conscious about these discrete behaviors, the separation of ordinarily integrated behaviors would be discomforting, particularly for students interested in the humanistic and holistic features of nursing, rather than in the discrete behavioral or scientific elements on which nursing care rests. Equally discomforting for some was the necessity to fake counts to achieve satisfactory grades. That student dissatisfaction with this element of the program became linked to militant protest suggests that these nursing students, like their peers in baccalaureate schools around the country, were the delayed beneficiaries of university and college protests that had peaked earlier while these nursing students were still in high school.

But such links remain dim in this story. Of clearer significance for the as yet unknown future of Mt. Hood are the following two elements: First, competence-based programs are constituted of many features, any one of which can become the focus for other events that will deflect the innovation in unforeseen directions. In this instance a powerful assessment tool, uncongenial to students, was that focus. Such programs are not homogeneous, but multi-faceted, each facet representing potentials for change or resistance to change, depending on the given structural features. Second, whereas administration and faculty in this case brought in and implemented an innovative program, the clientele ultimately became the unforeseen implementors, for they did not passively receive the new program but moved actively to shape and alter it. This would suggest that more than student progress and performance are the "products" of such programs, and that some of the student "outcomes" may well be found in the developing content and contours of competency programs. These outcomes will bear watching as Mt. Hood moves to the next stage of its history.

It is also apparent that the unforeseen inheritors of an educational innovation can become its implementors, as in the case with the "new faculty of 1975" and the even newer faculty of 1976. Though perhaps some purists and members of the original faculty would argue that the program was no longer a competence-based program—an argument that could take on numerous dimensions given the disagreements and difficulties of reaching consensus on what constitutes "a competence-based program"—the analysis here indicates that the unforeseen implementors, though abandoning the troubled assessment system, retained and modified the ideal of precisely described nursing behaviors that would reflect ideal nursing practice, based on patients' judgment. Those behaviors, being precisely stated, could be taught to students, without counting, timing and accelerating behaviors in such a way that grades and fates were tied to the timing gradients.

As the Mt. Hood story indicates, social interactions in an institutional context produce educational innovation but also generate a career for the innovation. If forceful and striking, that career may well transform the situation of individuals who actively contributed to the innovation, those who were implicated, and the institution of which all are a part. Moreover, such careers not only transcend the innovator and institution but live into new eras as a source for further change. At Mt. Hood, the innovators' dream became a drama with unwitting players, unforeseen scripts, and occasionally unmanageable properties, all of which share with the innovators the credit or blame for the fate of the innovation.

David Riesman **11**

Encountering
Difficulties
in Trying to Raise
Academic Standards:
Florida State
University

When FIPSE began in 1973 to provide "seed" money for ventures in competence-based education, its alert leaders recognized that in small, private, and often denominational colleges like Alverno, Sterling, or Mars Hill, dynamic leadership and cohesive interpersonal relationships might make possible a change in their whole

Note: There are some institutions my wife, Evelyn T. Riesman, and I have visited where we have felt constantly monitored, if not shown Potemkin villages, and where we have had to use the most tactful ingenuity we could muster to escape from what appeared to be benign nonneglect. The directors

approach to learning if financial aid from FIPSE could underwrite the high start-up costs of a new program. Such aid could in addition provide technical support for the program and a sense of colleagueship with other enterprises also financed by FIPSE. But what happened in these colleges would be unlikely to affect that universe of numerically small but potent institutions that Clark Kerr (1964) has described as the federal grant universities. In several cases, FIPSE did make grants to larger institutions, such as Bowling Green State University and the Grand Valley State Colleges, that, by means of the subcollege idea, were creating enclaves in which competence-based programs could be tried without seeking to swing an entire institution toward a novel pedagogic approach. It hoped, naturally, that what happened in the enclaves would infiltrate into other divisions of the institutions, but it made no effort to start a series of programs that might coalesce into something that would carry weight throughout an institution as a whole.

A notable and dramatic exception was the Curriculum of Attainments project at Florida State University in Tallahassee, where FIPSE took a chance that, by helping support a series of competence-based programs in disparate fields, a self-generating process might occur so that, once its support was withdrawn, the institution itself would not only carry on at least a substantial number of the enterprises but even expand them. What might happen at a major state university like Florida State could provide a model for other research-oriented universities and, what is more, by affecting the training of graduate students, begin a chain reaction that would influence the colleges, universities, and schools that subsequently employed these graduates.

One additional fact of educational innovation made an established university like Florida State of interest: Certain kinds

---

of the Curriculum of Attainments enterprise at Florida State University were candid and made exceptional and continuing efforts at objectivity. All the relevant data were made available to us. We met with complaining students and hostile faculty members, not only those we sought out but also at meetings arranged by our hosts. To everyone involved in the program, my deep appreciation.

Revisions of this chapter, based on the comments of many readers, have been facilitated by a grant from the Exxon Education Foundation, to which I am also indebted.

of pedagogic reform that are dubbed "innovation" may proceed with the best chance of success in relatively traditional pedagogic and cultural settings. A new institution, erected under the banners of nontraditional or dramatically innovative education, often attracts faculty members and students who, for a great variety of reasons, reject what they often characterize as traditional education. They bring to the new enterprise their private dreams (often based in fact on their unhappy personal experiences with traditional education), but these dreams then often collide. The "negative identity," in Erik Erikson's terms, of being against the traditional is not sufficient to overcome the difficulties of beginning any new enterprise, particularly if one of its commitments has been to one or another version of participatory democracy. (For several examples of this phenomenon, see Grant and Riesman, 1978.) But where faculty are for the most part already in place and where the student body is largely local and not attracted by promises of utter novelty and an overwhelming desire to be "with it," a departure from tradition may succeed if it proceeds cautiously and non-euphorically. Of course, it must promise enough to get itself started, but it must not make claims so extensive as to offend the powerful departments that dominate most major research-oriented universities. In such locales, quiet infiltration may win out while dramatic reforms seldom succeed, if indeed they ever start.

What made the competence-based Curriculum of Attainments enterprise at Florida State particularly intriguing was this: At even the most research-oriented universities, both public and private, faculty take seriously the teaching of graduate students and majors within their own orbit—more so than common legend would suggest. But unusually risky and demanding kinds of teaching, such as the Curriculum of Attainments would require, could prove a threat to one's visibility as a researcher and, hence, in the absence of great talent and furious energy, to the respect of one's disciplinary peers. And the very freedom of faculty that a major university provides (including the freedom to try out experimental courses) could at the same time be an obstacle to inaugurating a program that would not only ask more of faculty in the way of work but would carefully monitor their performance in ways to which they are accustomed when it comes to published scholarship but rarely when it comes to their effectiveness as teachers. If it was unlikely in such a university that one dramatically different competence-based enclave of students and faculty could influence the other segments of the institution, was it possible that more widely scattered bits and pieces of competence-based programs, which even at their height would be miniscule in comparison with the total educational enterprise on the sprawling Florida State campus, could develop a "critical mass" that would reform the entire university?

The fate of the Curriculum of Attainments would depend on a variety of factors—among them, the general budgetary situation and morale of public higher education in Florida, the prospects for faculty unionization within Florida's state university system, the kinds of communication that existed (to the extent that any did exist) among the diverse educational units of the campus, and the suspicions of those faculty who saw all educational experiments as endangering the standards that the university had continued and extended from its days as Florida State College for Women. For these faculty, all innovations were almost by definition ways of diminishing rigor and providing what the British would term "soft options" for students who should not be in a selective university in the first place. The enterprise could even be affected by the fate of Florida State's football team, important to the university's image with legislators and others. Despite these factors, however, FIPSE's gamble seemed worth the risk.

Prehistory

Significant to the gamble was the fact that Florida State University developed out of the Florida State College for Women, which had been founded at Tallahassee in 1851, two years before the land-grant University of Florida was established at Gainesville for men. Before the state became a center for tourism, phosphate mining, and citrus and other crops, let alone before it became a launching pad for such Americana as space flights and Disney World, Tallahassee and the northern part of the state were plantation country, not very different from rural south Georgia. Even today, northern Florida might be regarded as the only truly "southern" part of the state. The area in the Panhandle to the west of

Tallahassee—an area that, with legislative reapportionment, has rapidly lost influence to the more heavily populated regions such as Miami and Tampa–Saint Petersburg to the south—remains among its more conservative and traditional parts. In such an area, the pattern of a dual system of higher education between the sexes prevailed almost as long as the dual system between the races.

The Florida State College for Women early became a studious and scholarly institution, located as it was away from the resort areas and, though attended by some women of course for "social" reasons, lacking also the collegiate glamour mainly concentrated at the state's university. It possessed the first Phi Beta Kappa chapter in Florida and developed strength not only in such traditional female areas as teacher education, nursing, and social work but also and particularly in the liberal arts and sciences.

Its focus more than its intellectual character changed dramatically after the Second World War. In 1946–47, the state upgraded it to university status and made it coeducational, in part to accommodate the flow of new veterans. Under the driving leadership of Presidents Gordon Blackwell and Robert Strozier, it built on a strong foundation of scholarly development by amalgamating the former image of a women's college with that of a major research institution. It moved rapidly into the natural sciences, where large-scale federal funding was available to support new programs; it attracted such luminaries as Michael Kasha to its Institute of Molecular Biophysics; and it became a center of outstanding research in such areas as biochemistry, physics, and botany, as well as in the more experimental branches of psychology. It was the first university to adopt the entire PLATO program for highly sophisticated computer-assisted instruction that had been developed at the University of Illinois at Urbana–Champaign. And as part of a region-wide effort, it rose to a level where it could help stop the heavy "brain drain" of the most able southern students to major public and private northern institutions. (Also see Blackwell, 1962.)

At the same time, Florida State retained its legacy of the women's college era by emphasizing the arts. In the fine arts, it recruited some eminent painters. It built an architecturally outstanding theater building that offers facilities for a variety of performances on the Tallahassee campus. Its music school, third largest in the nation, attracted both performers and composers; their concerts made Tallahassee attractive for many faculty families and for other professional people in the area. Even at a time of general teacher surplus, the music school has been able to place students because of their outstanding training in a variety of skills and all-round capabilities.

During this period, a proposal natural for an upwardly mobile and ambitious institution, namely, to acquire a medical school, never received formal approval from the Board of Regents, and a trade-off appears to have allowed the newer and no less ambitious University of South Florida, with its large population center in the Tampa–Saint Petersburg area, to inaugurate the second state medical school. But Florida State did establish a law school, hoping for and in some measure attaining rapid distinction— not unmindful of the possibility of influencing the state legislature and the civil service by having, so to speak, friends at court who had been trained elsewhere than at the University of Florida.

Because of the rapid shift of population and resources to the South and West since the Second World War along with its own strong entrepreneurial leadership, Florida State has prospered. It has attracted faculty with "good" degrees from major universities in the Midwest, the East, and California, as well as in Europe and Asia, not primarily on grounds of warmth and scenery but because these faculty found colleagues who were stimulating and challenges that seemed worth tackling. (One well-known professor told me that he preferred teaching at Florida State because he was helping train a local elite in a part of the country that was desperately in need of one.) Among graduate students, its draw was less wide geographically but still considerably beyond the Southeast. And being over-applied at the freshman level by about two and one half to one, it was able to raise its qualitative standard for undergraduate admission well above the statewide floor, attracting "first-time-in-college" students from all over the state by an image of seriousness that to parents may have spelled sobriety as compared with Gainesville— the leading "party school" in the state. As an index of its cosmopolitan nature, 12 percent of its undergraduates were out-of-state students, many of them from sophisticated backgrounds, compared to 10 percent permitted on a state system-wide basis. With its off-campus residential programs for undergraduates in Florence and in London, as well as its research projects in Asia, the Middle East, Latin America, and elsewhere, it became part of the international network of "invisible colleges" that ties scholars together across institutional and even national boundaries.

During the 1960s, Florida State, like other institutions, was the locale for a variety of efforts at undergraduate curriculum reform, only a few of which took hold. Faculty members in Arts and Sciences proposed a subcollege similar to Justin Morrill College at Michigan State University, but the faculty senate did not approve. The Freshman Learning Experience (Flex), an interdisciplinary program in general education, brought five tutors together with forty-five undergraduates chosen as a cross section of volunteers, but it lasted only three years—it received inadequate publicity because it lacked strong faculty support and it generated little student interest because it was not radical enough for the late 1960s. Some faculty were dissatisfied with highly departmentalized and specialized teaching—for example, members of the Humanities Committee who felt that the university needed some kind of general education program—and the more inventive among them developed new courses in response to contemporary student concerns: for example, the very sophisticated courses on jazz and popular culture offered by W. H. Lhamon, Jr., of the English Department. At scattered points on the campus, individual faculty members began trying competence-based teaching even before the Curriculum of Attainments was conceived. But by and large these were isolated efforts, unrelated to each other and quite insufficient for a "critical mass" to support the morale, let alone to ensure the retention and promotion, of faculty members concerned with learning how to do a better job of teaching.

Beginnings

Stimulated in part by the Carnegie Commission report, *Less Time, More Options: Education Beyond the High School* (1971), the Florida state senate in 1972 passed a bill mandating time-shortened degrees in the state's colleges and universities. Owing to community college opposition, the bill was defeated in the house of representatives, but Florida's commissioner of education created a task force to investigate as one option for time shortening the three-year baccalaureate degree proposed by the Carnegie Commission. At this time, Daisy Parker Flory, who had come to Florida State when it was the women's college, was both dean and acting vice-president for academic affairs. A cheerful, energetic administrator who supported innovative faculty entrepreneurs, she knew that if the university came up with a good experimental design, the board of regents might give it funds to start new programs.

Also in 1972, the university recruited John Harris as director of its Division of Instructional Research and Services (since 1975, the Instructional Systems Development Center). Harris, an idealistic educator with an Ed.D. degree from the University of Tennessee, had earlier been involved in educational reform as associate director of the Office of Instructional Research and Development at the University of Georgia, and he had also worked with Georgia's state system of higher education. Before coming to Florida State, he had published an article entitled "Baccalaureate Requirements: Attainments or Exposures?" (1972) that contained the rationale for what would become the Curriculum of Attainments. Harris argued that the ordinary grading system had allowed institutions to become directionless: "Without explicit aims, institutions cannot very well delimit their societal responsibilities. Furthermore, without institutional criteria to credit and degree students, there is no way to evaluate the effectiveness of existing instructional programs and no functional guidelines for developing alternatives. . . . consequently, there are no points at which the process may be disciplined through feedback from its effects. . . . There is probably no way for an institution to break out of this dilemma short of actually commiting itself to awarding credit primarily on the basis of demonstrated and consensually evaluated attainment" (1972, p. 60). He believed that if institutions were committed to granting credit and degrees based on attainment, necessity would be the mother of invention as to how to achieve these aims through collective, rather than individualistic, faculty action.

Until Harris' arrival, the staff of the Division of Instructional Research and Service had seen themselves—and were correspondingly accepted on campus—as primarily a research and development group available to help those faculty members who wanted assistance for their own instructional purposes. Members of the division could provide design and technical assistance to faculty who made successful proposals for instructional improvement projects to the university-wide Council for Instruction. But President Marshall, eager to improve the quality of undergraduate education, encouraged Harris' own interests as a "change agent," and although many faculty members deeply resented Marshall's efforts to improve teaching, Harris saw himself as possessing a mandate to do more than wait for calls on his division's services. With Steven Keller, a doctoral student in the Department of Education, he wrote an essay, widely circulated to administrators and others, in which he contended that, in the coming era of accountability, employers and graduate schools would demand to know what students could do and would not be satisfied with a credential certifying the amount of time they had spent accumulating credit hours in the traditional way. (This essay has since been published, together with a bibliography of work that influenced Harris; see Harris and Keller, 1974.) Harris proposed what he termed a "Curriculum of Attainments," seeing it as a form for assessing not only what students could accomplish but also what faculty could "produce" in terms of outcomes, that is, of "value added." He would rule out the conventional assumption that, if students distinguished themselves after graduation, faculty and institution must have had a hand in their achievement.

Radical as it seemed, Harris' image of a Curriculum of Attainments was consonant with Florida State reality in one significant respect: Unlike other competence-based programs, it did not propose to help the unprepared and disadvantaged acquire academic credentials and the self-confidence that might attend certification of what they had learned. Harris' aim was to raise the ceiling, not to lower the floor. He saw the Curriculum of Attainments as asking students to achieve more than "mere" competence, hoping in this way to reverse tendencies toward slackness that in his judgment had developed in the late 1960s—an era when, with students increasingly insisting on doing their own thing, faculty had been free more than previously to do theirs, irrespective of the actual consequences for students. He was not satisfied with responses to this slackness in such self-paced instructional programs as the Keller plan or Benjamin Bloom's mastery learning, which added another freedom, namely, freedom to proceed at one's own pace, and which set a minimal goal, with faculty mentors serving as vaulting poles to help students get over barriers without reference to how long they took to prepare or how many runs they made. Harris wanted more than that. The Curriculum of Attainments would compel faculty to rethink what it was they were doing, a process that he hoped would encourage them to get rid of superfluities, especially of a preprofessional sort, and to concentrate on outcome-oriented conceptual clarity in their fields. They would turn themselves into coaches, with outside assessors judging their students' performance, and would thus avoid the traditional warfare between themselves and students over grades. Above all, students would assume greater responsibility for their own education, while faculty would assume greater responsibility for the coherence and integration of both professional and liberal arts programs.

Shortly after coming to Tallahassee, Harris recruited a Duke-trained counseling psychologist, Gary Peterson, whom he had met when Duke asked him to help plan a summer prefreshman program for its black students. Academically, Peterson is located in the Department of Human Services and Studies in Florida State's College of Education. There he obtained, and still retains, the status of associate professor; but three fourths of his time was devoted to Harris' Division of Instructional Research and Service, where Harris asked him to take over the task of finding faculty recruits for the prospective Curriculum of Attainments. Peterson, like other innovators, recognized that taking on such an assignment might jeopardize a career within his discipline as defined by his department, but he was willing to take a chance on the new effort, as at an earlier point in his life he had been willing to join the Peace Corps and go to Africa.

Under the umbrella for innovation provided by Dean Flory, a project committee was created to oversee the Curriculum of Attainments programs prior to their formal approval by the faculty senate—approval that could be delayed for eighteen months during which the programs would operate on a probationary basis. The committee did not seek to advertise the Curriculum of Attainments or broaden its appeal beyond the orbits that Peterson could reach on his own. But it secured permission from the faculty senate's Steering Committee for Peterson to submit a proposal, "The Curriculum of Attainments: An Alternative to Time-Based Degree Programs," to the board of regents of the state university system for funding, in response to the chancellor's mandate for the system's institutions to develop time-shortened degree mechanisms. Along with the College-Level Examination Program (CLEP), departmental tests, and advanced placement, the Curriculum of Attainments would be one of Florida State's efforts at shortening the time required for the baccalaureate.

But just when the expansive era of the "federal grant university" was coming to an end, neither the board of regents nor Florida's commissioner of education had the funds to support such proposals. When funds from the Carnegie Corporation of New York were not forthcoming, Harris was encouraged to secure a planning grant of $49,386 from FIPSE. This planning grant resulted in a prospectus to FIPSE that asked for financial assistance to establish pilot Curriculum of Attainments programs beginning with the 1974–75 academic year. These programs would come from diverse areas of the university; they would operate within existing educational units; they would be carefully monitored and assessed by an outside consultant (an educational psychologist); and their total number of students would be limited to 600.

Given the set of circumstances just delineated, FIPSE officials were rightly concerned whether Florida State University would itself become sufficiently committed to the Curriculum of Attainments so that the notion of competence-based education would not only continue beyond the individual funding for the initial programs but would spread to other educational units within the university. What would happen, FIPSE wanted to know, after the first programs were in operation? From this quite legitimate question, Harris and Peterson gained the impression that, in addition to the three pilot programs for the first year, they had to come up with perhaps another half-dozen programs for the second year, whether or not they could find suitable educational units. So they sought funds for about five more programs in the second year, with the possibility of additional ones in the third and final year of the requested grant. On this basis, their plan was funded.

FIPSE officials have denied any intention of pushing Florida State beyond what was reasonable in terms of available personnel and span of control; but whether the push towards enlargement in each of the three years came from within or without (or, as I am inclined to suspect, from both), the goal itself would seem in hindsight to have been misperceived. Neither the FIPSE officials nor the Florida State administrators could foresee the advantages of concentrating resources primarily on a few programs, particularly those where there might be enough student volunteers as well as already visible faculty mentors to help maintain momentum.

Meanwhile, Peterson had recruited two capable graduate students, Steven Smartt and Steve Wilkerson, who had visited department heads in the sixty instructional units at the university—in the professional schools as well as in Arts and Sciences—to explain the project and perhaps interest them in it. Twenty-three of the chairpersons had indicated a positive interest in trying out some sort of Curriculum of Attainments program, and the project committee chose nine departments from the twenty-three as the most viable prospects. In selecting these nine, the committee decided that professional fields with extant job analysis procedures for practitioners offered the best promise, since their departments would not have to fight over such inchoate competences as "what is a truly liberally educated person like?"

Peterson and his assistants then visited these nine departments a second time to make sure that the faculty members involved were genuinely interested and that their interest was realistic. This second screening led to a decision to proceed during the first year with programs in urban and regional planning, nursing, and marine biology—all three of them "applied studies." (Even marine biology, although housed within the Department of Biological Sciences, had potential vocational outlets with Florida's fishing industry and the state's Department of Natural Resources.)

Hindsight helps clarify the magnitude of the assignment undertaken by Peterson and his two graduate assistants in getting the three programs underway. First, hardly had the programs begun when John Harris resigned from his position at Florida State. He was more a philosopher of higher education, who saw in the Curriculum of Attainments a way of dealing with slackness in the great public universities, than a person given to working out the details in which all such programs become enmeshed, such as relations with the registrar, establishing new fee structures, figuring out how much time students are to be allowed to complete supposedly time-free programs, and overseeing the day-to-day work of evaluation. Trained in education, he could talk the lingo of behavioral objectives to FIPSE officials and to other project directors supported by FIPSE, but he had been deeply influenced by views of education in the United Kingdom. He thought of the Curriculum of Attainments on the one hand as a program of Oxbridge-like tutorials with the mentor preparing students for external examinations, and on the other hand as a program free of time and space, much like the British Open University—and with standards just as high. At any rate, his departure meant that competence-based education at Florida State had lost its chief theoretician.

Second, what Peterson and his assistants were offering to the leaders of the three educational units and, where appropriate, to cadres of their faculty members was not a program such as PLATO that, whatever its virtues and limitations, could be observed and rather readily explained. Instead, what they were presenting was an opportunity to pursue an ideal nowhere yet attained. Their program would focus on both long- and short-term outcomes in the practice of a profession or even of life itself, with no extant models of such a program actually in use in a setting even remotely relevant to that of Florida State. The history of curricular reform in America is strewn with plausibilities that, like versions of utopia, sound good on first hearing for those who find prevailing conditions inadequate or even intolerable; and thus John Harris' ideas sounded good—and still do, as do the writings of such other philosophers of the competence-based movement as Gary Woditsch. But in the diffusion of Harris' ideas to the various departments of Florida State, it was inevitable that the larger the span of control became, the less control could be exercised as to how individual faculty members or cadres would interpret and apply them.

Furthermore, in order to make an appropriate surmise as to

the quality of interpretations and applications one might expect from as many as nine different educational units in a multiversity, Peterson and those who worked with him would have to know more about a very diverse group of faculty than most of us know about colleagues inside our own department—in particular, they would have to know how these faculty look from the perspective of their associates and students. They would need more than hearsay knowledge of the legacies of past disputes and the internal politics of the various units—the factions, for example, within the School of Nursing. These matters had little enough to do with the Curriculum of Attainments as such but much to do with attitudes that would affect its fate. Yet they could not rely on the dean or chairman of a particular unit or department for this information. Such an administrator would most likely not only not be privy to all these latent themes but might, in fact, be kept in studied ignorance of them by his or her colleagues. Inevitably, then, the sponsors of the Curriculum of Attainments enterprise were sailing a boat not yet proved seaworthy, with a compass not adjusted to the particular territory and without navigational charts of tides and reefs beneath them, into what might look like safe harbors but what in effect were shoals and swift crosscurrents.

1974: The Three Initial Programs

Urban and Regional Planning. The planning committee for the Curriculum of Attainments project sought to begin with career-oriented programs where performance could be assessed with some measure of consensus; but it is difficult to imagine a field in which it would be harder to arrive at any consensus over a definition of competence than that of planning. Especially after losing its earlier mooring in the "hard" sciences and technology, the planning profession has come to lack consensus almost as much as sociology does, and it is incapable of distinguishing the question of who is its appropriate client from the question of who is competent. By the very nature of the field, it was nearly inconceivable that external assessors could be found whose verdicts about competence would be regarded as fair and reasonable either by faculty or students. If external juries were to help assess the competence of graduates, as the

Curriculum of Attainments proposed, would these juries consist of representatives of Florida land developers, of the many active environmental groups opposed to them, of local and regional planning authorities, or indeed of client or user groups that tangled with these authorities? Moreover, graduate planning departments had been attracting faculty from a variety of academic backgrounds, and these faculty often combined ideological combat with personal vendettas, sometimes exercised by the various factions on one another's relatively unprotected graduate students.

Although the Department of Urban and Regional Planning at Florida State consists of faculty trained in a variety of disciplines ranging from geography and environmental psychology to transportation, it has been able to resolve differences among them more amicably than some other schools. Lacking the influence of an engineering school on campus, it has put its emphasis on the social sciences and the human environment. Besides its four-course sequence for undergraduates of honors standing and its doctoral program, the department offers a two-year program leading to a master's degree (the usual terminal degree for professional planners)', and this program seemed to Edward McClure, chairman of the department, a natural possibility for a Curriculum of Attainments. Sixty to eighty students per year enter the program, and the faculty agreed that in 1974 sixteen of them could be admitted to a separate Curriculum of Attainments track without serious damage to the existing program. McClure avoided as much potential conflict as possible over the question of what planners should minimally know and what makes for a competent planner by focusing the Curriculum of Attainments on the first of the two years of the program, which contains its more academic aspects, and leaving untouched for the time being the second year, during which students are often engaged in internships in state or other planning agencies. He detailed two faculty members, Richard RuBino and Andrew Dzurik, as program coplanners to develop modular learning packages on such generic competences as "General Systems Theory" and "Information Systems in the Planning Process" that were not unrelated to the usual course work of the first year and for which they could serve as partial equivalents.

Perhaps inevitably, these generic competencies and the much

more concrete list of specific competencies were more closely related to the academic background common to planners with a social science orientation than to the performance of planning itself. For instance, what was designated as the "specific competency" for three credit hours under the heading of "Urban and Regional Systems" asked students to "demonstrate a comprehension of the concept of urban and regional systems and the factors and processes which influence and shape such systems." And this statement was followed by a learning guide that, for example, asked students to describe an innovation and diffusion process within cities in colonial urban systems and to "discuss, contrast, and evaluate factory-supply-based and demand-based theories of growth." For each such specific competency, a set of readings was set forth, some required and others recommended, but all by recognized leaders in the related fields of human ecology, economic growth, land use, theories of location, and history. Thus the historical readings ranged from Lewis Mumford on the development of the city in ancient times to Clarence Stein on the planned city of the twentieth century. This module was to provide one hour's worth of credit. (The translation of assignments into credit hours is a perennial problem of all the competence-based programs our project team examined as well as all those we read about.)

Unfortunately the planning program seems to have been accident prone even before it got under way. During the summer of 1974, McClure decided that he could no longer serve the department as its chairman, although he battled stoically against serious illnesses to meet his obligations to the Curriculum of Attainments program. RuBino and Dzurik were to have spent the summer working on learning packages in preparation for students' arrival that fall, but restrictions imposed by the congressional budgetary cycle made it impossible for FIPSE to give full assent to Florida State's proposal until midsummer. By that time, Dzurik had taken a year's leave of absence for 1974–75 and RuBino, who had already made extensive commitments to do consulting work, found himself assuming the department chairmanship from McClure and obligated to tutor some of the sixteen Curriculum of Attainments students on their arrival. Thus, when the students showed up, they found only four learning packages ready for them, and they therefore could not move ahead at their own speed, as they had been promised they would be able to do. Even after all the packages had been prepared and the students were ready for assessment on them, jury procedures still had not been worked out, and jurors were still unfamiliar with the kinds of questions that it was legitimate to ask under the novel dispensation of the program. The bookstore was unprepared as well, and there were the usual library inadequacies.

Nonetheless, one of the difficulties of the first year's students turned out to have serendipitous advantages. Because the modules were not ready ahead of time, the students were unable to accelerate individually and had to proceed at the same pace—this kept them together as a unit and fostered camaraderie. In addition, they had available to them what matters so very much in all programs, namely, what Trow (1975) has termed "private space"—a location not apportioned on some system-wide metrical or formula basis and available to be preempted for unspecified and unplanned purposes—in which they could meet informally and maintain a peer culture for discussion.

Student peer culture has very commonly become a forum for the nursing of grievances, and the culture that developed among the students in the program was no exception. They discovered that what might under more isolated circumstances have seemed to them their own stupidity could in fact be charged up to the logistical and intellectual bugs and hazards of the program itself. Some of the sixteen defended the program, and one of them, who took about half his work in it and half in more traditional courses, had no question about its superiority, even at the outset and before the program was straightened out. Yet the balance of rejection and acceptance was such that, while thirteen of the sixteen completed the first-year core requirements, only three of them elected to continue full-time in the Curriculum of Attainments format for the second year. For them, learning packages were developed along "non-specialist" planner lines, but the other students shifted over to various tracks within the regular program.

Despite the difficulties of the first year, RuBino, Dzurik, and McClure were prepared to carry on with a second cadre of new students in 1975. But some of the critical first-year students sought to talk the new students out of taking the Curriculum of Attainments option—a frank exchange that McClure did not seek to dampen—and at the same time the department's intake of new master's candidates that year dropped from around eighty to about sixty. Hence taking even fifteen of them—the number regarded by Gary Peterson as necessary for a "critical mass"—would be felt as a loss by some faculty, especially since these students were apt to be the more talented and adventurous. And this feeling of resentment against creaming off the supposedly better students into the Curriculum of Attainments was intensified by the state university system rule that no course could be offered with fewer than seven students in it. Thus the special program was seen as a threat that might lead to the reduction of several courses below the requisite minimum, quite apart from its depletion of the pool of good students other faculty sought. Thus it was decided that the second group of students would not pursue a Curriculum of Attainments for two full years. The combination of these faculty attitudes and the new students' encounters with the articulate students of the first year caused enrollment in the program to fall to nine volunteers in the second year, of whom one later dropped out. Two of the remaining eight were working part-time at Fort Myers. Their ability to participate in the Curriculum of Attainments, while illustrating its advantages of being cut loose from courses and specific locales, had the drawback for the program of leaving only six resident students to comprise the second cadre.

In contrast with the first group, which kept together as a social and intellectual unit during its second year despite the continuing involvement of only three of them in the Curriculum of Attainments, the second year's entrants did not proceed as a unit. With the program modules already on hand, some students proceeded rapidly, while others moved much more slowly, with the result that the cadre feeling of the first group never developed. The question then arose: If one assumes, as residential institutions have traditionally assumed, that one learns a great deal from one's fellow students and that in fact one learns best when one teaches fellow students, no matter how informally, are time-free and locale-free programs really optimal for residential students—or should they be planned especially for nonresidential students, such as housewives with small children or people working elsewhere full time, who cannot otherwise take university courses?

Added to this question of effectiveness was that of efficiency. Required to report to FIPSE on a semiannual basis, Peterson kept close track of the credit hour records of Curriculum of Attainments students for a "cost-parity" analysis of program efficiency. The state's payments to the university could not be made until the students' grades had actually been registered, and Florida State's registrar had to give incompletes to those students who, though they had obtained a learning package and perhaps spent much time with faculty mentors, had not yet gone through the jury assessment process and earned a grade. Many students were themselves inclined to delay this ultimate step in the process out of anxiety, not sure how other faculty members whose courses they had not taken might react, while their mentors themselves often cautioned delay because they, too, would be on trial during the assessments. And if a student did fail a particular assessment, a new one had to be devised—with great care taken to prevent the trauma of a second failure—and a new jury organized with all the scheduling problems this involved.

In Peterson's cost-parity analysis, the cost effectiveness of the competence-based urban and regional planning program—when compared with ratios of student credit hours and faculty involvement in the department's conventional program—was about 70 percent. That is, the Curriculum of Attainments program was nearly one third more costly per faculty member than the regular program. Peterson calculated that if a Curriculum of Attainments program had fewer than fifteen students in it, it would be almost impossible to achieve cost effectiveness, and the program would in addition lack the "critical mass" necessary for mutual peer support. At the same time, he concluded that if a program could maintain a steady flow of students, it could in time become cost effective, if not through actually saving money, at least through doing a better job for both students and faculty at no greater expense than regular programs. Even if the Curriculum of Attainments never met the hopes of the Florida legislature that it would save student and faculty time and hence money, it might someday reach a steady state in which it would cost no more than the regular program. But one must be extremely skeptical of "steady states" in academic life generally and even more so in such a field as planning, given its notorious lack of consensus. Ideas as to what planners ought to know will be constantly changing, and the half-life of carefully and painfully prepared modules will not be very great. Even in a field such as colonial history, which seems readily packagable, video-taped lectures do not last terribly long, as revisionist contemporary research adds to what is known about earlier periods, as well as offering new interpretations. In a field such as urban and regional planning, the hoped-for steady state will be long in coming if, indeed, it ever comes.

But it appears that Peterson's theory will not be tested further in the planning field, for with McClure's continuing illness and impending retirement, and the loss of outside funding, the department abandoned the Curriculum of Attainments as a separate program, even though it continues to use the modules from the project within its traditional program.

Nursing. In thinking about which Curriculum of Attainments programs would be the most viable to start with, it was not difficult for the project committee to conclude that nursing would be one, for Florida State's School of Nursing was a large and well-regarded school in a field with already developed procedures for on-the-job analysis. Moreover, some members of its faculty believed themselves to be the pioneers at the university in thinking in terms of competencies. They had spread the message in discussions at other schools of nursing, and they were consulted by other faculty at Florida State itself who were considering a Curriculum of Attainments program. Discrepancies exist between practitioners and faculty in nursing as they do in planning, but they are somewhat less polarized and publicly politicized. Nursing of course presents some of the same dilemmas that planning does concerning its clients—or, to put it another way, concerning the authorities entitled to judge what makes a good nurse and to assess the performance of nurses. Without the presence of a medical school in Tallahassee, however, the faculty of the School of Nursing felt that they were much freer to develop nursing as an advanced profession: a profession that has, in fact, entered the arenas of the social sciences, of group dynamics, and in this instance of competence-based education long before most medical schools have arrived at such a self-critical outlook.

Dean Shirley Martin of the school offered to begin a trial Curriculum of Attainments program for fifteen "generic nursing" students, as those students are called who, after a basic liberal education either at Florida State itself or perhaps at a community college, enter the school's upper division program that eventuates in a bachelor of science degree. Among the volunteers, a large proportion were from outside the state; a number were men, and several were black—despite the tendency for black students to stay away from "innovative" or "experimental" programs, given the greater likelihood of their being the first in their families to attend college and thus understandably preferring the presumably greater credibility of "regular" programs and, also quite understandably, wary of irregularities proposed by mainly white experimenters.

In Pauline Haynes, Martin found a faculty member willing, even eager, to act as mentor for the students, as later in Anne Belcher she was to find a worthy successor for the same role when Haynes' husband left Tallahassee for North Carolina and she accompanied him. During the summer of 1974, a number of faculty members produced rough drafts of learning packages for Haynes. These contained, on the one hand, a great deal of material concerning the role of the nurse and the profession of nursing—its history, its dilemmas, and its potential futures—and, on the other, abundant material on the basic sciences of physiology and anatomy and on the social sciences relevant to the various settings in which nurses find themselves. Despite an emphasis on performance in clinical settings, there was a large amount of basic "book learning" insisted upon, both in order to give the nursing students a sense of professionalism and, for the considerable number who wanted to go on to graduate school, the necessary scientific grounding for advanced study. (I was struck, as I had been in the urban and regional planning program, with how much these generic nursing students were supposed to learn in two years, and I concluded that they should not necessarily count on time-shortened degrees, although in fact several of them were able to finish one term ahead of time.)

As in the planning program, the materials were divided by generic and specific levels and then subdivided into modules. For example, under the general heading of "Health Hazards and the Surgical Experience," there were modules on blood therapy and postoperative complications, as well as more general discussions of what factors made for a safe patient environment in a hospital setting and the kinds of asepsis called for. Students were given a list of terms that they had to be able to define, such as *morbidity, antigen,* and *pathogenic,* along with standard textbook references on diagnostic procedures and nursing care. Each module included a "terminal competency," such as "knows the major health hazards to individuals and families throughout the life cycle and the epidemiological and preventive indications."

During 1974–75, the Curriculum of Attainments program in generic nursing developed relatively high morale, in contrast to that in planning, and achieved the best cost-effectiveness record of any of the special programs. But the program in generic nursing was discontinued after one year, and its advantages were put to use for quite a different category of nursing students instead, namely, registered nurses who had been out in practice on the basis of a hospital diploma or a two-year college degree and who now wanted to return for what they thought could be a time-shortened baccalaureate degree. A few of these nurses were returning to school out of a desire to advance to higher administrative responsibility or to be able to perform better the clinical work in which they were currently engaged, but most of them wanted a bachelor's degree as a basis for pursuing postbaccalaureate training.

For these nurses, the Curriculum of Attainments program had particular advantages. Its relatively time-free curriculum gave them more flexible field opportunities—for example, in hospital settings they could work at night or on weekends, when there were fewer nurses or physicians on duty and when, as a result, they were not only especially welcome but also freer to assume responsibility for patients. And its competence-based mode offered them the chance to show rapidly what they could do. Nonetheless, some problems arose. Many of the nurses were impatient with the learning packages because they felt humiliated by having to show, for example, that they could use a catheter or do a blood transfusion. But Peterson defended the insistence on such demonstrations on the ground that the university was certifying actual competence in the Curriculum of Attainments, not a person's say-so concerning competence, and that such demonstrations did not actually slow down people who really had acquired the skills. He had a point, for it was conceivable that, given the large range of ages and experiences of the returning registered nurses, some might have gotten rusty in one or another procedure, and it was even conceivable that having to demonstrate what in fact they did know would give them renewed confidence.

At the same time, a number of the registered nurses feared that because they were indeed already accomplished nurses in terms of actual experience, faculty members would demand from them a higher level of competence than they had asked from the generic nurses who were just entering the field. And they found themselves the object of envy by students not in the program. Since the registered nurses were not bound to attend courses, their peers outside the program felt that they were having an easier time.

If this freedom from time constraints was advantageous for some of the Curriculum of Attainments students, it also served to intensify the already heavy time demands on Anne Belcher, their chief mentor. She not only negotiated field opportunities for them in local hospitals, clinics, and agencies, but she also spent a great deal of uncompensated time in these settings with them so that she could assess their competence in bedside situations and give them continuous feedback about their performance in crucial areas. Helping them become more self-conscious as professionals and holding them to high but not pedantic standards of attainment, she performed a role of formative assessment for them, although she could have no vote in their eventual terminal examinations as competent practitioners.

The statistical cost-parity analysis of the nursing programs could not take account of the long-run costs in time of either Haynes or Belcher, who themselves hope to write something about their experiences with the Curriculum of Attainments but have not yet done so. Yet in terms of this analysis, the nursing programs came out much better than the other Curriculum of Attainments formats in comparison with the regular programs for which they provided alternatives. The costs of the nursing programs over two years were just slightly above parity (1.02), based on a comparison of student credit hours per faculty full time equivalent (FTE), as against the regular programs. The parity ratio was higher here than in any other program, partly because of the already high faculty-student ratios in the regular nursing programs, which use detailed clinical instruction in contrast to programs with conventional lectures for one or two hundred students at a time.

In the questionnaire survey administered to all Curriculum of Attainments students, the nursing students declared that the program was helpful to them, agreeing, for example, that it helped them "increase their ability to form more personal relationships with peers and instructors." They regarded as a valuable opportunity the very experience that some students might have found anxiety provoking: that of being required to prepare and then present material orally to a jury. This experience encouraged them to develop their communication skills and, when the process was successful, enhanced their self-confidence. And there is at least anecdotal evidence that the nurses emerging from the program have performed well in the variety of positions they have taken. Their mentors, at least, believe that they have done better than more conventionally prepared students. Even with the arrival of a new dean who wanted to put Belcher's very considerable energies to work in other phases of the School of Nursing than the Curriculum of Attainments and whose interests in the improvement of nursing education lay in a direction different from a competence-based approach, the program for registered nurses continues. However, the generic nursing program has admitted no new candidates to the original experimental group.

Marine Biology. The third of the first-stage programs was marine biology. It was at once the largest of the three, with forty-eight students enrolled during a two-year period, and, except for nursing, the most concentrated of any of the undergraduate Curriculum of Attainments programs in either the first or second stage. Its creator, Albert Collier, designed it as a holistic program that would bring together oceanography, geology, invertebrate zoology, and chemistry. He insisted that students learn on their own and that they relate their studies and initiation in research to practical situations in ecology or marine biology with which they might have to deal; and he gave the program a further practical focus by employing as his assistants graduate students who were themselves

working at the Florida Bureau of Water Resources Management
and the Bureau of Coastal Planning and Management.

The substantive content of the program described a series of
generic attainments—for example, a five-hour item in phytoplankton ecology declared that "the student will demonstrate through a
graded series of competency satisfactions that he has acquired a
mastery of the taxonomy, morphology, and ecology of the marine
phytoplankton consistent with his advanced undergraduate standing." These generic attainments were in turn broken down into
more specific attainments handled through a series of readings and
learning packages, by which students were expected to familiarize
themselves with everything from the tides to the intricacies of
cell biology.

Like the urban and regional planning students, those in
marine biology also had their own "private" space during their
first year. Thus the students had a room set aside for them and
were given keys not only to the laboratory reserved for them but
also to the Biology Learning Laboratory Resource Center that made
available cassette films, slide viewers, and the like for their use at
any time. For undergraduates at Florida State, this kind of treatment was anything but customary. At the same time, this private
space and the companionship that it fostered allowed the students
to do a good deal of peer teaching and to develop a sense of community that in turn set the level of effort they were willing to put
forth. As Hughes and his colleagues found in their work at the
University of Kansas (Becker, Geer, and Hughes, 1968), a group
of students can just as easily as any group of factory workers agree
from a sense of community to restrict their output; but at Florida
State in marine biology, their level of effort was high, and it was
kept so in part by the jury assessment process.

Some Curriculum of Attainments students understandably
felt that they were being discriminated against by faculty seeking
to trip them up to find weaknesses in their knowledge. But, by and
large, they came to accept the process, which worked like this:
Prior to appearing before a jury, students took a written examination; and if they passed, as virtually all of them did, in a few
days they appeared before a jury, which might keep them only a
half hour if it was obvious that they knew the material but consider-

ably longer if this was not so clear. One student recalled the strain of his first jury experience: "People boring in like that. . . . I'll never forget the question about what I would do if I had to dig a harbor in California: How would I keep it from filling up with sand, and so on and so forth. And every time I answered a question, another was asked." But he was not nervous about the next jury "trial," and he had already put his name up on the jury sheet that hung on the wall near the door of the laboratory. Collier himself saw the jury system as a mode of spreading sympathy toward the program among his fellow biologists, but recruiting jurors from the department was difficult. This difficulty perhaps reflected earlier conflicts concerning the directions in which the department was to move, but the conflicts also reflected a general disenchantment among Collier's colleagues with pedagogic experimentation. Collier had to look for jurors among oceanographers as well as among his colleagues and continued throughout the life of the program to find the task arduous.

One of the complaints that students had with the Curriculum of Attainments was that the self-discipline that self-teaching demanded was made more difficult by the competing pressure of the other courses required of them both in biological sciences and outside the field. Under the drumbeat of "regular" course work, Curriculum of Attainments packages were often the first to give way. But overall, students reported a high degree of satisfaction with the program. They declared that it helped them develop research interests, that they remembered better what they had learned in it than in their other courses, that it was "more relevant to the real world of professional activities" (Peterson, 1976, pp. 97–98), and that they would choose it again if they had the option.

The number of students in the marine biology program was more than sufficient for Peterson's estimate of cost-effective size, and yet the statistical data were discouraging. The fact that the students were taking work outside the program made all the more difficult a judgment as to cost effectiveness, since joint costs incurred by students could not easily be separated out, even on a theoretical basis. Still, in comparison with regular programs in biological sciences, the program was by far the most expensive of any Curriculum of Attainments effort, with a parity ratio of about 10 percent. This finding reflects the fact that for undergraduates the Department of Biological Sciences depends on large lectures, as against the more individualized and intensive work in the Curriculum of Attainments and in the professionally oriented programs in nursing and planning.

Not only the methods of teaching but the marine biology program and Collier himself were anomalies in a department that focused on graduate work and basic research and had the usual attitude of such a department toward "applied" undergraduate studies. Collier was the only marine biologist in the department at his appointment in 1965, and he remained the most practically oriented member of the department. But at the end of the 1976–77 academic year, he reached the point of retirement and was unable to interest the department in maintaining the program. In part, this lack of interest reflects the departure from Florida State of the department chairman, Peter Bennett, to the presidency of the Philadelphia Academy of Natural Sciences. Interested in innovation, and seeing the possibility of making use of Collier's unique talents, Bennett had not only encouraged the program but had found financial support for it from the Florida State administration beyond the money provided by FIPSE. His replacement, however, had no particular interest in carrying on the program.

In addition, senior faculty within the department feared that funds would be taken away from them for the program when it could no longer depend on support from FIPSE or the presence of Collier, who had carried it almost single-handedly as an uncompensated overload. Junior faculty were concerned that, if the program's competence-based mode of teaching should spread, it would interfere with their own professional advancement. Not only did department members see the program as less a new synthesis of disciplines than a series of dippings into complex but applied problems to prepare undergraduates for jobs—for example, as technical advisors to a fishing fleet—they noted that many more students volunteered for the program than could be taken into it and that these students were eager and highly motivated undergraduates. Thus, once the protective umbrella provided by Bennett was withdrawn, department members did not look around eagerly for a way of replacing Collier. Indeed, plans are now underway to transfer the whole marine biology program from Florida State to the University of South Florida in Tampa, for with Collier's departure, there is no one in biological science who cares to carry it forward.

1975: Stage II Programs

Four "second-stage" programs began operation in the academic year 1975–76, but plans for four others foundered. Two professional schools—library science and business—had promised to come into the project that year, but both withdrew. In the absence of new resources, the dean of the School of Library Science concluded that no faculty member could be released to undertake a Curriculum of Attainments project; and within the School of Business, no particular program seemed suitable to the dean for a Curriculum of Attainments effort. Two other departments, in vocational education and in leisure services, considered a Curriculum of Attainments program, but planning proceeded at a slow pace and neither advanced sufficiently to be in a position to recruit students. In vocational education, in fact, both the administrator of the prospective program and his assistant moved on to other institutions before it could be launched.

In the counseling psychology program of the Department of Psychology, Harold Korn put his undergraduate human relations course on a Curriculum of Attainments basis, with the aim of developing skills in observation and interpretation. Eight students volunteered for the course the first quarter, and eleven enrolled the second; but Korn's departmental colleagues treated his efforts with indifference, giving no response to his requests that they review his statements of attainment. In the Department of Religion, Charles William Swain attempted to establish a major in a Curriculum of Attainments format, but it drew only eight volunteers initially, four of whom dropped out during the first quarter; it was difficult to see how religion could sustain two parallel programs when only twenty-five students per year at most would be likely to declare a major in it. Although the School of Theatre began a program, it paradoxically did not put acting or the production of plays on a performance-oriented footing but instead the more traditional liberal arts field of theater history, which, together with the beginnings of a program in costuming, simply translated into Curriculum of Attainments terminology its usual syllabus of courses.

One other school with strong orientations toward performance, namely, the School of Music, also entered the Curriculum of Attainments project in its second year. Like theater, it did not select its most clearly performance-based segments—the training of soloists or of ensemble groups—where it might have been possible with reasonable consensus to judge at least minimal competence. Instead it chose its music education curriculum, where two thirds of the music students majored as a preparation for teaching in the schools and junior colleges. The music education program was closely geared to the expectations of the different school systems and community colleges that were looking for all-purpose music educators who could help students with specific instruments, could conduct marching bands, jazz bands, and "classical" ensembles of orchestras and choruses, and could perhaps even find time for a recital or two. The program was thus competence based in the way that many teacher education programs try to be.

The music education program was not offered entirely under Curriculum of Attainments auspices; instead, only the performance-oriented part of the program, in which students had to learn the basic techniques of every musical instrument, was included. The Curriculum of Attainments approach was launched under the enthusiastic auspices of Wesley Collins, assistant professor of music, who had come out of a career as a conductor, a high school band leader, and a performer in the Jackie Gleason band. He hoped that the Curriculum of Attainments could be a way of increasing the music education program's focus on jazz, both for its own sake and as an increasingly useful way of helping students get jobs as music educators, since they were more and more required to work with jazz groups in the schools. He also hoped that the program might endow some parts of the school with a greater conceptual sophistication. Thus the learning packages he developed sought to implant concepts that cut across the boundaries of different instruments. He did not want as heretofore to teach the rudiments of every instrument in isolation and expect students to master all of them at some modest level. What, for example, was common to all percussion instruments or to all strings? What problems of embouchure development or control of breathing did wind instruments share as a group? Collins designed a series of carefully graded and structured manuals as a guide to these learning activities. In the case of percussion, he worked out a careful table that listed the different kinds of percussion instruments, the various designs of each of them, and the forms by which they could be played and tuned. A typical specific competence would be, "demonstrates and explains the fundamentals of performance with a standard percussion instrument. Relevant factors to be included are holding and playing positions, developing performance techniques, and tuning procedures when applicable."

While certain attainments could be assessed by observing a student actually teaching a practice class, such as one made up of fellow students, the same goal could also be accomplished by videotape recordings. As at Alverno, each student had his or her videotape, allowing a cumulative record of progress as a performer, a teacher of music, and a conductor.[1] Or, to give another illustration, a student's awareness of the potentialities of various percussion instruments could be measured prior to jury assessment by a written examination where the topics would have to be mastered at a rate no lower than 80 percent. This was a higher minimum than that asked of the great majority of students, and because of the tremendous load of work put on the Curriculum of Attainments students —and on their mentors as well—only those most capable of self-pacing were in fact able to keep up with the planned sequences.

To put it somewhat ironically, Collins had to be responsible for requiring students to be responsible about their pacing. And, unfortunately, the progress of students in terms of learning packages completed was at least as ragged as the array presented by the poorest of marching bands. Despite his infectious enthusiasm and

[1] Videotapes played another important role. In the area of musical performance, students were shown by videotape what was minimally acceptable performance on an instrument, and then heard the same piece played at a level of high proficiency, either by an advanced student or a faculty member. This gave them a basis for judging whether or not they were ready for an audition—as well as reassuring many who would otherwise be frightened by the very high levels of performance attained by many students at the school, which is not only quantitatively large but, as mentioned earlier, qualitatively one of the more eminent in the country.

that of the graduate students who worked with him, and the fact that the Curriculum of Attainments students themselves worked in a cooperative way, this raggedness was evident in the results of the first year: Of eighteen students who entered the program, none of them completed all the sequences. According to Peterson's final report, "approximately six have completed twelve or more credit hours of [Curriculum of Attainments] learning packages, and another six have progressed less than twelve hours, while six have made virtually no progress" (1976, p. 17). All competence-based programs run the risk of laggard nonperformers; the programs tend to underestimate the capacity of human beings for procrastination. (As I have sometimes commented in talking with mentors and other faculty, I know that I must set deadlines for myself because I cannot depend on my own capacities as a self-starter; even if the spirit is willing, I have learned not to underestimate its capacity to be distracted!) But the temptation to fall behind was particularly great in music when, as in the case of a number of these students, they were also members of a wind ensemble or a marching band, doing some practice teaching, and seeking to develop greater competence on their own instrument. And, as in the theater history program, a student preparing for an upcoming performance outside the Curriculum of Attainments was inclined to put off work on the Curriculum of Attainments since this could always be postponed.

Collins is both a devoted teacher and a committed member of the faculty union. He was able to respond to both these dedications as long as the music department could afford, because of the grant from FIPSE, to give him released time in his role as mentor. But when these external funds ran out, the overload of work that he would have had to assume raised insurmountable problems for him. He abandoned the Curriculum of Attainments effort, and the School of Music dropped the project in the winter of 1977.

Accomplishments and Consequences

Given the way matters have turned out, it would be easy for critics at or of FIPSE to conclude that its gamble on Florida State University was a mistake. It early became clear that the congeries of intellectually disparate Curriculum of Attainments programs was not going to coalesce into a single program, let alone spread throughout the university as a whole. Indeed, the idea of expanding a few pilot programs into an entire curriculum would seem in retrospect to have been seriously misguided, assuming greater institutional loyalty and faculty localism than is consistent with either individual careers or departmental ambitions at major research universities. Even by the end of the first year, it was evident that any commitment of major segments of Florida State to a Curriculum of Attainments was tenuous, as illustrated by the several professional schools that decided not to participate or by a department such as religion, where it was impossible to sustain a program because of the few students per year who would be likely to declare a major in the field. In no field did the Curriculum of Attainments provide an entire major, making difficult any final judgment as to the contribution of competence-based education to students' understanding of a field as a whole. And few of the programs were true experiments. In both planning and nursing, the Curriculum of Attainments students were volunteers; in marine biology, the students chosen for the program could major in that subject in no other way. None of these voluntary programs was a true experiment in the sense that its participants could be compared to a control group, since by their very nature the volunteers were different from others, probably abler, usually more adventurous, and almost always more rebellious.

What appeared instead was a group of pilot programs, some with more and some with less professional focus, each related as spokes on a wheel to John Harris and then to Gary Peterson, but not related to each other in such a way as to create among either faculty or students in the university as a whole even a potential "critical mass" of people who were either devotees of the idea or had had some experience with its intricacies. And instead of some 600 students being involved in these programs by the end of the second year, as had been set as an upper limit in the proposal to FIPSE, the number participating never came close to that figure. By the end of that year, only 232 students had been involved—and these, as we have seen, only for limited parts of their academic programs.

In hindsight, it thus seems inconceivable that Florida State could have been incrementally converted to a Curriculum of Attainments model. Such a model asked too much of everyone involved.

It asked too much of faculty in terms of reorienting themselves and their graduate assistants for the complex tasks of mentorship, as noted by one informant in a letter afterwards: "So much of our undergraduate instruction is in the hands of graduate students, and they come and go so fast that it would have been all but impossible to break [their] mind set and teach them to be mentors, generation after generation." It asked too much of students in its novelty and in the hazards of what at the outset were intended to be primarily external assessments. Because it was seen by students as more difficult and demanding than regular course work, which they had learned how to manage and manipulate after many years of schooling, it drew insufficient numbers of volunteers; and especially for shy students, its jury assessment appeared as a formidable (though, in the opinion of our project team, valuable) ordeal. In addition, the model asked too much of leaders both in the programs themselves and in the university at large, for it would have required a commitment from them to stay at their jobs for a certain number of years in order to assure continuity—a commitment illegal to enforce under the Thirteenth Amendment and unlikely to occur, given what is in so many cases the short and unhappy half-life both of pedagogic innovators and of state university presidents and other key administrators.

Moreover, rather than concentrating only on those few programs, whether in nursing, marine biology, or music education, where performance could be assessed with some measure of consensus and where there might be enough student volunteers to make them cost effective, the project entered such notoriously conflict-ridden fields as planning and such underpopulated majors as religion. And no one seems to have adequately anticipated the possible disagreement or struggle over the question of who validates the judges—problematic, so far as I can see, in all competence-based programs aiming at more than routine skills. One dean at Florida State said that the Curriculum of Attainments would not work without a million dollars of outside funding—a most unlikely prospect—but it seems arguable that less than a million dollars would have sufficed to maintain the enterprise, if it had been concentrated on some of the more promising programs. These might have developed models of mentorship and assessment successful enough for transport to other large universities, even if departmental tariff boundaries and the systems of peer support and evaluations that they sustain would have prevented any large and long-term impact at Florida State itself.

Circumstances beyond the university's administrative control also took their toll. As federal support for research and for fellowships for graduate students declined during the 1970s, Florida's state university system was unable to compensate for this decline. On the contrary, having vastly expanded by beginning new upper-division and four-year universities, such as Florida International in Miami, West Florida in Pensacola, Florida Technological in Orlando, and North Florida in Jacksonville, as well as continuing to build up the University of South Florida in Tampa as the third major state university, the system was desperately pinched for funds during the entire time of the Curriculum of Attainments effort. Legislative support to supplement FIPSE funds was not forthcoming, although no one could have predicted that a fast-growing "sun belt" state like Florida would be harder hit in funds for public higher education than many others in the South or Southeast. Florida State, located as it is in the state capital, suffered particularly in this regard from the annual spring invasion of the legislators and their surrounding lobbyist flora. Strong pressure developed to bend the state's universities toward applied research, and a number of self-made populists within the legislature began to chide Florida State and the other universities as elitist and to urge that their expensive programs be sacrificed to the needs of the state's low-income in-migrants—the elderly who come to Florida to retire—and fixed-income residents, rarely rich enough to buy condominiums in the overbuilt coastal areas, rarely young enough to have children of college age, and more often a drain on the state's economy than a contribution to it. The liberal governor, Reubin Askew, did not prove himself the friend of higher education that liberals had hoped he would be; he was brave on race and integration, but few governors dare increase taxes today, and virtually all who have bravely done so have lost their jobs come the next election.

Nonetheless, the top leadership at Florida State wanted the Curriculum of Attainments to succeed. President Marshall and Vice-President for Educational Services Joe Hiett—the latter had

immediate charge of the programs—contributed some $20 thousand
toward part of the expense of Collier's participation in the marine
biology program; and Executive Vice-President Bernard Sliger was
prepared to support the project, at least as long as it did not drain
resources from other significant activities. But when President
Marshall announced his resignation in 1976, continuity of leadership was lost. His departure and that of other leading officials, even
if devoutly willed by many faculty, proved unsettling for the university as a whole. When Sliger was named president after a drawn
out and highly publicized search, he declared in an early statement
to the faculty that he wanted Florida State to become one of the top
twenty universities in the United States—an aim that would land it
well within the high-prestige circle of American universities, but one
that, while not necessarily inconsistent with experiments such as the
Curriculum of Attainments, did not make such enterprises a high
priority. In a fashion familiar at the level of the American presidency,
his administration sought to distinguish itself from its predecessor's
efforts at pedagogical improvement without necessarily putting an
end to those where interest and momentum already existed. It
sought to secure funds for faculty who were willing to work to improve undergraduate education. But in a situation that wavered
between retrenchment and stalemate, select graduate programs were
likely to receive the major share of whatever discretionary monies
could be salvaged. And in the years ahead, the hope that one can
simultaneously sustain a deep commitment to experimentally minded
undergraduate education and advanced graduate education and research is seldom likely to be realized. (I should add that I myself
share the frequently expressed anxieties of many about the fate of
graduate education and research in America in a time when there are
many temptations to intrastate leveling. These temptations are sometimes intensified by the renewed focus found everywhere, and rightly
so, on undergraduate teaching, but are also sometimes intensified by
populist politicans capitalizing on envy and resentment. See
Riesman, 1975.)

But even if it had been possible to anticipate all these
problems—and some observers did, in fact, anticipate many of
them—a judgment that FIPSE's gamble on Florida State was a
mistake would seem to me overly hasty. I must say that, beginning

as a skeptic, I was converted to a belief that what was happening at the university in the Curriculum of Attainments, despite variations among educational units, was potentially of major significance, even if what was produced, such as the elaborate learning materials in planning or nursing, might not be transferable to any other department. Even a rough impressionistic assessment of the impact of the project, beyond the cost-parity studies mentioned earlier, would indicate that Florida State is by and large a better place today because of the Curriculum of Attainments attempt. Peterson's questionnaire data from the students indicated relative satisfaction with all the programs. Even in urban and regional planning, the overall verdict of the students, despite their complaints about its original disorganization and their own inability to pace themselves, was that they had profited from it. They were, in fact, inclined to defend it from criticism—including, in many cases, their own. They recognized and appreciated that they had more than the usual amount of contact with faculty even in a department in which there was a good deal of contact already. And the alertness and aliveness of the students we talked to in the programs—their willingness to try to become more independent as learners—was impressive.

In addition, a relatively large number of Florida State faculty members (including graduate student planners and teaching assistants) were touched by the programs in one way or another. This group included thirteen mentors, thirty-two jury members, some forty-five tutors, and over a hundred faculty who served on various sorts of review committees. And even though it would take an archaeological dig to identify the shards of the programs that survive today, the nursing, religion, and urban and regional planning departments have all incorporated in their regular programs the instructional sequences developed in the Curriculum of Attainments in order to render their programs more coherent and internally consistent.

In Peterson's remarkably full and straightforward final report to FIPSE (1976)—a document of value to anyone attempting a similar venture elsewhere—he reviews the project's goals and seeks to assess the degree to which they were attained. The first of these goals was "to establish mastery standards for degree programs," and in the context of Florida State, such standards were indeed established. Attainments were geared to a level of mastery that in fact transcended what might be considered "mere" behavioral competence. In achieving Harris' hopes, the Curriculum of Attainments avoided the fears of its faculty critics, and it did not gain a reputation for being a "soft option." Instead, some students were attracted to it precisely because, given the allowance of a number of trials, they were permitted to earn no grade lower than B and could not choose to earn a lower grade by doing a lesser amount of work. The hurdle remained the same for all of them, although some might bound over it at a higher level than others.

Whatever Harris' and Peterson's original dreams for the endeavor, the Curriculum of Attainments did contribute to faculty development—a process that can hardly be called a fad, and one whose importance can only increase as faculty mobility diminishes. Faculty did not return to their departments completely unchanged from their experience as mentors. They had an opportunity to learn more about student learning, through the close tutorial supervision required by the program; and they were forced to think ahead of time as to outcomes, rather than proceeding on an ad hoc or catch-as-catch-can basis. Furthermore, in the best cases, as in nursing and urban and regional planning, not only did students have more chances to talk to one another and have more frequent contact with faculty than in most other settings but faculty members themselves had occasion to discuss with one another what they were doing. Some faculty were brought more closely together over substantive issues than they would have been in a regular departmental setting. Even faculty who were not mentors were influenced in their teaching by the existence of the program; for example, one of the original students in the urban and regional planning program, David Coburn, noted that the special sequences definitely influenced the teaching in conventional courses for the better. Thus, it is possible to argue that in a situation where the state university system can make no regular provision for sabbaticals, faculty renewal and improvement of teaching are more apt to come about through released time for working on a project such as the Curriculum of Attainments than through the more common—and, of course, from faculty members' point of view, more desirable—devices of assignment to a

European center for a term or a fellowship from the National Endowment for the Humanities.

In addition, the hope remains that the Curriculum of Attainments method can be applied in other fields at Florida State. Members of the Humanities Committee, chaired by Provost (now Dean) Robert Spivey, remain eager to improve the basic humanities sequence, possibly by putting it on a Curriculum of Attainments footing. And with the support of Roger Kaufman, director of the Center for Needs Assessment and Planning, Peterson has sought financial support for the development of a learning resource center to establish freshman courses on a competence basis, both for entering students who have learning deficiencies and for those who already possess and wish to demonstrate some of the desired competences. The Florida legislature has mandated that higher education institutions admit 10 percent of their students from those who do not meet traditional entrance requirements, and Peterson believes that a center modeled after the Curriculum of Attainments concept and applying its system of mentors, tutorials, and learning packages would help these students develop academic survival skills.

Besides working to aid entering students at both ends, so to speak, of the scale of aptitude, Peterson hopes to improve the articulation of community college transfers with the university. Given the restriction of freshman enrollments at all but one of Florida's four-year state universities, these transfer students comprise a large proportion of Florida State's student body. With the encouragement and interest of Vice-Chancellor Roy McTarnaghan, Peterson has been given the assignment by the Florida Articulation Coordinating Committee of exploring, along with William Wharton of the University of North Florida, the possibility that a competence-based education model such as the Curriculum of Attainments could be exported to an experimental pilot group of community colleges that would be connected in turn to an experimental group of either four-year or upper-division state universities. The situation is a politically delicate one. The graduates of community colleges naturally want two full years of credit for what they have done and do not want to pay for more than four years of post secondary education in order to secure a baccalaureate degree, while the universities, priding themselves on their selectivity and high standards, want to be sure that students' earlier work provides a sufficient base in the liberal arts and in basic skills for upper-division success. Finally, the state wants to avoid paying larger and longer subsidies and, if possible, even to shorten the process of undergraduate education, as it has already been shortened for many high school and some community college graduates by the CLEP examinations.

As a result, much of Peterson's recent effort has been devoted to the enormously intricate problem of taking a program not yet fully established—and, in fact, as we have seen, considerably attenuated if not altogether vanishing at Florida State itself—and persuading other institutions to adopt it as a mode of assessing both the aims of education and the credit to be given for various segments of it as students move from one institution to another. It is his hope that the Curriculum of Attainments can eventually prepare the way for an open university. (In principle, the idea behind this kind of curriculum should be exportable. Indeed, one of the problems it faced at Florida State was the fact that the individuals involved in it exported themselves before their programs were sufficiently developed to travel on the basis of their own substantive content and achievement.)

Beyond these outcomes at Florida State, and beyond potential effects at other institutions, the benefits of the Curriculum of Attainments also include what we have learned about competence-based education from this experience. First, we now know that professional or occupational programs are no more "natural" for a competence-based format than the liberal arts and sciences. One of the original goals of the Curriculum of Attainments was to establish a closer relationship between the curriculum and the world of work. But the short life of the programs established the fact—in a particularly disastrous way in the urban and regional planning program—that one cannot create an operational definition of competence—criterion-referenced and unequivocally assessed—simply because the tasks for which students are being educated are closely geared to specific occupational roles. In some occupations, little more consensus exists about these roles than in the academic disciplines. (The discussion on assessment in Chapter Four by Gerald Grant and Wendy Kohli suggests some of the as yet unsurmounted difficulties in this area.) It would thus seem that professional programs, geared toward practice by practitioners, are not necessarily more prepared to focus on competence and performance than are academic programs in arts and sciences. What did matter at Florida State was the initiative of individual faculty members and support for them by the chairpersons of their departments or deans of their schools. Peterson believes, however, that the real future of the Curriculum of Attainments lies less in the professional and vocational areas, where under other labels it already in some measure exists, than in the arts and sciences, where such a program might provide a kind of de facto honors college, drawing together intellectual and ambitious undergraduates and faculty members to match.

Second, if we did not know it before, we learned that developing a competence-based program means enforced decisions on what to leave out even more than on what to include. Faculty in many colleges teach their own subject as if it were the student's only requirement—so much so that in an earlier era I once commented that reading lists were the tailfins of faculty. The Curriculum of Attainments required, if not a closer fit with the world of work, though that was always hoped for, at least a closer fit with the way students actually work rather than the way in which they are assumed to work. Thus the learning packages or syllabi seemed to represent inevitable compromises among colleague groups fearful that "their" subject would be given short shrift in a potentially time-shortened and off-campus degree program. (Even this kind of senatorial comity did not always prevent an individual faculty member serving on a jury from seeking to prove that a particular student had not mastered the professor's subject, without which mastery, of course, one could not be thought of as truly competent.) The argument endemic to liberal arts colleges—how can you be an educated person without knowing Plato, Shakespeare, Afro-American history, and computer science?—must be answered quite explicitly in a competence-based program, even in such professional programs as urban and regional planning, where the question becomes, for example, how can you be an educated planner without familiarity with the writings, let us say, of Amos Hawley or, at another level, of Lewis Mumford? As a result of this tendency toward overloading in all academic programs, I do not see how students in a Curriculum of Attainments would be able to have time-shortened degrees rather than time-elongated ones, particularly if they also have to meet the course requirements of professors not participating in the program.

A third lesson concerns the difficulties of the mentor role. Although Peterson believes that with a steady flow of fifteen students a year, a Curriculum of Attainments program can become cost effective by doing a better job for students at no greater expense than a regular program, such a belief may take insufficient account of the psychological costs of mentorship. A mentor has something in common with a doctoral thesis adviser, as well as with a tutor— Harris recognized this—in a British university. But unlike either of these roles, it requires the expenditure of a great deal of time in creating learning packages and in negotiating and arranging for external assessment, with all the logistical difficulties this invariably involves in a busy university. (Surprisingly enough, an analysis of the time that mentors spent in various activities makes clear that they gave less time to either career or personal counseling of their students than to administrative tasks.) And, as we have seen, mentors are exposed to the judgments of their own colleagues concerning the adequacy of their teaching. Faculty are quite prepared to accept such judgments when it comes to their published research, but are usually unwilling to open up the privacy of their pedagogic work, despite the fact that they are supposed to be judged for retention and promotion in part on their adequacy as teachers.

Most professors even at major research universities derive a certain satisfaction from lecturing—and they often avoid its disappointments because they leave to their graders or teaching assistants the discovery of how little of what they believe they have taught has in fact been learned. They characteristically form a portrait of "*the* students" from those who act as a kind of front organization and conceal the hard core of the passive, the captive, and indeed the "no shows." But mentors have neither this buffer between themselves and actual student performance nor the customary psychological emoluments of lecturing. Their gratification is long postponed, as against the diurnal gratifications of the lecturer. They not only have to learn new roles that deny them such satisfactions but they require such special qualities as relative lack of narcissism, ability to endure frustration, persistence in the face of difficulty, and willingness to work cooperatively with other faculty in developing programs, as against the more characteristic academic norm of a scholar who (at least outside of the natural sciences) is accustomed to working in the privacy of the classroom and the solitude of the library.

Fourth, we have learned as much about the role of juror as that of mentor. For instance, jurors drawn from within the same school or department as the program in question have to learn new roles if they are not to sabotage the program by indifference or even by active hostility. They need to recognize that their role of juror is restricted to seeing whether the students in the program have met their assignments and can perform at the level of competence specified by the program. External jurors from the professions must avoid being overly critical on the basis of small points and should instead try to make overall judgments of a student's potential to become a competent professional who will continue learning long after graduation. In the nursing program at Florida State, for example, practitioners from the field tended to emphasize specific skills as opposed to interpersonal talent in nursing; here, as in other areas, practitioners from the "real world" were often less flexible and at times more "academic" than the faculty. As a result, members of the program faculty should serve on all juries to help see to it that students are not unduly prejudiced by the application on the part of other faculty or external jurors of standards irrelevant to the preparation they have been offered or to the direction taken by the program at large.

Another way to overcome some of these jury problems was illustrated in the urban and regional planning program during the 1975–76 year. The list of jurors for different learning packages was posted for the entire year, enabling students who felt anxious about their preparation to visit the jurors that they would come up against, perhaps to audit their classes, and otherwise to avoid the pitfalls of having jurors make demands for which they were totally unprepared. The students often had informal seminars with the prospective jurors, which led to their doing further reading or writing or both.

In this regard, Peterson advocates a policy that has struck this writer as desirable in other innovative settings as well, namely, establishing among colleague groups something akin to a common law of what is and is not permissible in a new and individualized program. For example, where students negotiate individual learning contracts with faculty members—whether at Johnston College of the University of Redlands in California, New College of the University of South Florida, or, indeed, at Hampshire College in Massachusetts—it seems important that both faculty members and students be present when particular cases are discussed, so that equitable, unit-wide standards are established and learning can be cumulative rather than episodic, just as in the judicial system judgments are refined by the accretion of case law. No such common law was established among the different Curriculum of Attainments programs. An honors grade in marine biology, for example, required a unanimous vote among jurors, whereas in music, nursing, and urban and regional planning, a simple majority sufficed. And, as Peterson observed, the sequence in which students were brought before a jury affected decisions. If an average student followed directly on the heels of a brilliant one, the jury's expectation was often too high—a problem analogous to that of inadequate seeding in a tennis or squash tournament.

Peterson's final report calls attention to one other unanticipated problem regarding jurors: the fact that many external jurors were "no shows" who took their duties so lightly that they did not even appear at the time specified for assessments, leaving in the lurch the faculty jurors, the nonvoting mentor, and, of course, the students, anticipating and prepared for an ordeal. External assessors were so unreliable that the money set aside for their compensation was generally not made use of, and except in nursing, where external assessment could occur in a hospital or clinic, the programs eventually abandoned the use of external jurors. In my experience, most practicing professionals enjoy the opportunity to be helpful to students (whether or not they are paid for it) and to serve temporarily in the role of professor. When I consider the seriousness with which, for example, Swarthmore's external examiners, who are always required for evaluations of its honors students, take their duties, preparing beforehand and giving students careful appraisal of their accomplishments and limitations afterwards, the casual behavior of the Curriculum of Attainments jurors seems especially perplexing. Although this problem at Florida State may have been unusual, its existence there is a warning as to possible hazards and the precautions that may be needed to ensure that busy professionals fully appreciate the seriousness of a commitment to serve as a juror.

Fifth and finally, we learned again the importance of leadership in the successful implementation of programs. Certainly without Edward McClure's power and interest as the initial department chairperson of the urban and regional planning program, the similar administrative backing of Shirley Martin in nursing, Peter Bennett in marine biology, and Wiley Housewright in music, the programs would not have won the amount of support they needed. With the departure of McClure, Martin, and Bennett, the retirement of Albert Collier in marine biology, and the withdrawal of Wesley Collins from the program in music, the programs inevitably lost the momentum they had developed.

In his final report, Peterson describes the requirements for implementing a Curriculum of Attainments program in a setting such as Florida State: not only consensus over criteria, procedures, and participants in the assessment process but also continual negotiation and compromise with traditional forms of education and authority. Peterson and other members of the Division of Instructional Research and Services were prepared to run interference for the mentors in the programs, helping them prepare modules and other pedagogic devices, untangling the complicated management of jury systems, and negotiating with the registrar, the librarians, and other supporting professional staff. This logistical aid proved imperative. As an illustration, the Curriculum of Attainments presented the registrar's office with problems in grading, timing, and even transcripts, since its students' records could not be computerized and thus had to be maintained by hand. The registrar's staff had seen so many experimental programs come and go that it was hesitant to make elaborate special arrangements for one more until assured that the program would expand and become a permanent feature of the university. While some staff members thought that the program mentors were seeking to bypass them, they saw Peterson as someone who understood their problems and sought to reduce them.

Plagued by the turnover of administrative and faculty leaders, the programs were lucky in two transitions: from Pauline Haynes to Anne Belcher in nursing, and from John Harris to Gary

Peterson in the program as a whole. Both in my own work in the field of more or less innovative higher education and in that of our project team, I have been impressed by the almost inevitable problem of what Max Weber termed "the routinization of charisma"— the succession from the pioneer evangelist, such as Harris, to the implementer, such as Peterson. Fortunately, it was Peterson, along with his graduate assistants, who had made contact with the department chairpersons who were the key figures throughout the development of the programs. Having worked with Harris in program planning and fund raising, as well as having followed the development of comparable programs elsewhere, he could take over from Harris without a moment's hiatus. Somewhat less visionary than Harris, and in some respects actually if not nominally in charge of the effort even before Harris left, he had a much more intimate sense of the details of its separate programs. He had his own quotient of idealism, but he kept it under wraps as a rather elegant but subdued persuasiveness. Among his advantages were his high intelligence, his shrewd judgment of men and measures, his diplomatic sensitivity to what was possible at Florida State, his gift for striking bargains with the department chairpersons and influential faculty that adapted the Curriculum of Attainments to their needs, or more correctly, their wants, and his ability to recruit from within a particular educational unit individuals to whom he could give support both directly and through the university structure.

With low morale prevalent throughout the university, anyone with high visibility who sought to do something out of the ordinary might have become a target for envy and suspicion. But Peterson's own academic and entrepreneurial goals were sufficiently fluid and responsive so that he did not come on the scene as an evangelist in the way that Harris seemed to some to have done. For one thing, he lacked the religious overtones, the philosophical and even theological penumbra that surrounded Harris. He was quiet and soft-spoken in manner and gentle in temperament; and at the same time, he was worldly enough to have assimilated a sufficient array of skepticisms so that no kind of opposition to competence-based education programs would come as a surprise to him. Thus he moved easily between the world of educational conceptualization and technology and that of the traditional liberal arts and sciences. Whereas in other institutions, directors of innovative programs have often managed on the one hand to attract disciples and on the other hand to polarize enmities, he won supporters rather than disciples and seems not to have awakened serious enmities.

But it was a considerable drawback to the Curriculum of Attainments that Peterson did not have tenure. His own Department of Counseling Psychology in the College of Education, where he teaches one-quarter time—although his full salary is paid by the Instructional Systems Development Center—did not see why it should have to acknowledge the services of someone whose efforts did not advertise the department so much as the university as a whole. For Peterson, in his vulnerable position as an assistant professor, his efforts on behalf of the Curriculum of Attainments were not always easy or, in terms of his academic career, promising assignments. (Peterson has since been promoted and given tenure, indicating recognition of his efforts on behalf of the Curriculum of Attainments and other work on a statewide basis.)

The significance of leadership was also demonstrated, finally, by the role of FIPSE. Its officials, who made arrangements for the grant to Florida State, monitored the progress of the grant, and served as colleagues or supervisors to the monitors, were men and women of high intelligence well aware of the risks they faced. They had enough experience with government to know that an auditor in the Government Accounting Office or some congressman or senator might seize on the grant and "expose" it as a waste of taxpayer money on a fanciful, even jargon-polluted operation that would save nobody any money and very few people any time. They knew academia enough to realize that the Curriculum of Attainments might be seen by some faculty as a misguided effort toward enforced accountability. Either way, its deficiencies would be negatively laid to the account of FIPSE itself (rather than being seen as in good part the result of overextension).

If FIPSE had been inhibited or intimidated by such anxious anticipations, it would clearly not have been doing the job for which it was created, namely, experimenting with the possibilities of improving postsecondary education. And if the lessons of the past are any guide, we need ever so many risky experiments that are provided both with money and, as in the case of Florida State, with really helpful advice and support from such an agency, for we are still very far from knowing how "improvement" actually occurs in postsecondary education or when, over the life cycle of students, faculties, and institutions, some movement toward it may have been attained. Nor do we know how to solve the whole congeries of problems that accompanies any large-scale innovation such as the Curriculum of Attainments, including how to sustain it after the founding cadre has either left or become exhausted, and new faculty members or mentors have arrived who did not themselves experience the excitement and frustration, the trial and error, of the original adventure into the pedagogic unknown.

Zelda Gamson

12

Assuring Survival
by Transforming
a Troubled Program:
Grand Valley
State Colleges

In trying to understand how a competence-based program gets off the ground with no outside funding in an existing institution, we should pay close attention to the struggles of the faculty members most involved in thinking through and designing the program. College IV at the Grand Valley State Colleges provides us with the opportunity to look at these struggles in the earliest stages of development. Barely past infancy, College IV has experienced since its birth in 1973 more than its share of disruptions, traumas, and advice about what is good for it—from career programs and liaison with community colleges and local businesses to better advertising and new seminars and classes. I certainly do not want to add my voice to this chorus of advice, except to say that competence-based education seems to have been a good way for College IV to give coherence and a rationale to its curriculum.

Located in the rolling hills of a rural area twelve miles west of Grand Rapids, Michigan, Grand Valley was established in 1960 and enrolled its first students in the fall of 1963, primarily from the western part of the state. From the beginning, it has had unusually close ties to the influential residents of this area, including former President Gerald Ford's adviser, William Seidman, who was a leader of the local group that pressed for a public four-year college in the Grand Rapids area and who served as its first board chairman.

Grand Rapids remains a rather conservative area with strong Dutch roots. A number of the administrators and faculty at Grand Valley share these origins and participate in the civic life of the Grand Rapids region. The institution seems to have minimized typical town and gown conflicts by sharing some of the traditional life-styles and values of its locale. Yet Grand Valley is an unconventional place in many ways. As one striking example, it has divided its approximately 6,000 students and 350 faculty among four very different undergraduate colleges and two graduate programs under the motto "Grand Valley Gives You a Choice." The original Grand Valley State College—the College of Arts and Sciences—remains the largest of the four, with an enrollment by 1976–77 of 4,200 students. Thomas Jefferson College opened in 1968 as an experimental arts-oriented college. William James College, which opened in 1971, combines an unconventional liberal arts program with career education. The youngest undergraduate unit, College IV, opened in 1973, the same year as the Seidman Graduate School of Business, and was followed in 1975 by the Graduate School of Education.

Each college has its own dean, faculty, student body, curriculum, grading system, and admissions procedures. Students in one college, however, may take courses in other colleges, and central services and facilities—the library, audiovisual services, computer, record keeping, admissions, financial aid, printing, and dormitories —are all shared. President Arend Lubbers, under whom the expansion of Grand Valley took place, has encouraged and supported the unique styles and missions of the colleges. His general philosophy of

administration is "each tub on its own bottom," which comes down
to keeping each of the colleges within its budget allocation and at
a student-faculty ratio of twenty-two to one. Should a college not
meet these conditions, Lubbers and his administrative associates
first ask its dean to straighten things out. Should the problems persist, they will then step in actively, though gingerly. Each of the
colleges in this system is protected from its sister colleges—and
for the three small undergraduate colleges, this usually means protection from the large College of Arts and Sciences—but of course
this system does not prevent backbiting or covert subversion, should
it be known that there is trouble in any one of the colleges. All these
forces have operated to some extent on College IV in its short life.
Equally important, state support for higher education in Michigan
has become less generous since the 1960s, a situation that caught
Grand Valley at the height of its development. Its expansion has
been curtailed sharply; and, as the newest college in the Grand
Valley galaxy, College IV has thus been placed in double jeopardy.

The Origins of College IV

College IV opened two years ahead of schedule—fortuitously
so, since it is unlikely that, given the severity of the more recent economic situation in Michigan and at Grand Valley, it could have
opened two years later. That it opened at all, and with the program
it had, speaks less to long-range planning on the part of Grand
Valley's administrators than to the strength of personal ties and
the ability of Grand Valley to capitalize on them. When a deanship
opened up at one of the existing colleges at Grand Valley in the
early 1970s, Robert Toft, director of the Science Curriculum Improvement Program at the National Science Foundation (NSF),
was recommended for the job by an assistant of President Lubbers.
At NSF, Toft had written a prospectus for a new program to
develop modular colleges attached to larger institutions. In his work
in the Science Curriculum Improvement Program, he had become
involved in encouraging the development of self-paced instructional
curriculums; he had, however, become disenchanted with the limitations placed on such curriculums when meshed with conventional

course structures. A better test of self-pacing, he thought, would be to modularize the whole curriculum; and thus he came to his Grand Valley interviews with an idea and a mission.

Toft's ideas did not endear him to the faculty members who interviewed him; both sides agreed that they were not meant for each other. However, during his interview with President Lubbers, Toft described his idea for a self-paced college, and Lubbers was sufficiently impressed to decide to open Grand Valley's fourth college ahead of schedule and to recommend Toft as its dean. College IV's hallmark was to be its unique "delivery system": it would rely almost completely on learning packages or "modules" rather than on conventional classes, and instead of grades, it would evaluate students in terms of mastery of these modules at a 90 percent level. Toft envisioned College IV as an open access unit of Grand Valley that would make a college education available to working people and housewives who could not attend a traditional institution. It would be open in two senses: not only could any high school graduate sign up for a module (typically worth a half credit), pay a modest fee ($5.75 per module in 1973), and be considered a College IV student but students could also enroll at any time and complete their academic work at any pace they wished.

The Grand Valley administrators saw Toft's modularized approach as a way of relating the institution even more closely than before to adult students. Time-free, self-paced instruction seemed ideally suited to a clientele that these administrators—several years ahead of the national trend toward "nontraditional" study—saw as a crucial new market. Toft's emphasis on the use of media and technology also fit well with Grand Valley's self-image as an institution for the twenty-first century, since it had already poured much money into the development of an audiovisual center with numerous electronic study aids.

Toft was hired in the spring of 1972 and given a full-time secretary, travel support, and a year to plan the new college. He immediately set to work writing proposals for outside funding and eventually got some $767,000 from NSF and FIPSE for a summer workshop prior to College IV's opening, implementation of the self-paced mastery-learning program, a visiting faculty program, and dissemination of the modular idea. Later, when the faculty of the college would turn to the idea of competence-based education as a solution to its problem with the modules, no such cushion of grants would be available to assure its survival.

Planning the Program

During the planning year, Toft also put a good deal of energy into publicizing the new college. Brochures, posters, and newspaper articles appeared both in state and out. Toft spoke on television and radio programs and traveled with Grand Valley admissions counselors on recruiting tours. Although Toft had his eyes on adult students, his publicity implied that there was something for everyone at College IV. An early advertisement in the Grand Valley State newspaper used the following phrases: "self-paced instruction," "modular curriculum," "mastery learning," "liberal arts," "profession oriented," "degree programs," "individualized instruction," "free design," "problem centered," "tutorials," "seminars" and "interaction." These phrases turned out to be more confusing than enlightening to potential students, who had a hard time understanding what College IV was about.

College IV was the first college in the Grand Valley cluster to have a dean before it had a faculty. This is a critical fact in understanding the college's early years. Toft had an almost completely free hand in recruiting his initial faculty, although the choice of disciplines was dictated by the NSF grant, which called for the development of science modules. Thus, advertisements listed jobs for a mathematician, a biologist, a chemist, a sociologist, and a psychologist, although these disciplines were later supplemented by positions in English and economics. Toft offered positions to seven people. All were given regular academic titles, although there was to be no tenure at College IV, and all expected to begin working on modules in the summer of 1973 during a two-month faculty workshop. Most of the seven had had some experience in the use of modules, and one of them, Milton Ford, had coordinated self-paced courses at Oklahoma State University and had prepared a module on how to write educational objectives. If anything can be called a "bible" at College IV, his "Writing Educational Objectives" comes closest, for it set the pattern for all other College IV learning materials.[1]

Much of the work of the faculty during the summer focused on reaching agreement on the format for all modules and on the hierarchies of subjects to be covered in each of the disciplines. By the end of the summer, they had forty-five modules on hand for entering students, covering introductory topics in the traditional academic subjects (chemistry, physics, English, psychology, sociology, biology, mathematics, geology, economics, and history), as well as two applied subjects (accounting and computer science). The modules took several forms: some were original self-contained packages; some were adapted from already existing self-contained instructional packages; some were study guides to textbooks and other library materials. The amount of new material generated by each of the seven depended as much on the existence and availability of self-paced modules from elsewhere as on their differing ambitions and energies. But because most of them objected to using other people's materials, many of which they viewed as unprofessional or ineffective, they had to prepare considerably more original modules than Toft had planned.

Producing and organizing the material was a prodigious task. Paper began piling up and secretaries were swamped. As the summer wore on, the pressure to produce modules meant that more of the modules ended up being study guides to standard texts rather than original organizations of the material. Toft's early plans to experiment with nonprinted media were dashed: faculty, pressed to produce modules, relied almost exclusively on the printed word. Meanwhile, there were bottlenecks in the central printing shop. The bookstore, which had just moved, was not processing the modules quickly enough for them to be available for students in the fall. "We found that our modules were being stacked in the back room, but not being priced and put on the shelf," Toft reported afterwards. "Since by this time the first day of instruction was upon us, an all-out effort was mounted to get the modules priced and on the shelves" (1976, p. 9). Even so, some of the

[1] For a recent review of the modular approach, see Keller and Koen (1976). Also important are Kulik, Kulik, and Smith (1976) and Mager (1962).

modules were priced mistakenly and some had parts missing. These were hardly exotic challenges, but it is in such shallow waters that captains of innovation run aground.

Problems of the First Year

The College opened officially on September 25, 1973. Although students could register throughout a two-day period, the bulk of them showed up early on the first day and waiting lines began to form. By the end of the first day, 100 students had registered and been assigned to faculty advisers who explained the College IV system to them. They were then free to go to the bookstore to purchase whatever modules they had signed up for. There was no formal orientation at this time. Meanwhile, the faculty had set up their schedules. They were to hold twenty office hours each week during the day and in the evening for tutoring and testing. The remainder of their time was set aside for writing modules.

A few students requested independent and small-group contract studies, but these students were rare. The more usual work was done through the modules, which typically carried a half credit or a full credit. (It was assumed that each half credit would entail approximately ten hours of student work.) After purchasing any of the module booklets from the bookstore and checking out tapes or films from the central audiovisual center, students could work on their modules at their own schedule wherever they wished. They were free to consult in person or by telephone with faculty during office hours and ask questions about any of the modules. There were no deadlines for completing the modules. Each module had a self-administered practice test. Credit for completion of the module was awarded when the student passed a mastery test at the 90 percent level; again, students decided when they were ready to take the test. If a student did not pass, faculty or tutors were available to diagnose weaknesses. The mastery test could be taken as many as three times; after three attempts, students had to pay additional tuition before they could receive more help on the material. College IV transcripts record only credits successfully completed.

Nondegree students were encouraged to enroll in College

IV, but the college also offered the B.A. or B.S. degree in the standard academic disciplines as well as in interdisciplinary and career-oriented areas. The majority of these majors, of course, had to be filled out with courses from the other colleges. For the bachelor's degree College IV initially required distribution credits spread across the following seven areas: communication skills, mathematical skills, study of the physical universe, study of life processes, man and his social systems, man and his thoughts, and man and his works. Like many new colleges, College IV also began with the idea of requiring comprehensive examinations in the senior year, but these were never given.

One hundred and fifty students enrolled during College IV's first registration and an additional 65 registered during the rest of the first quarter in 1973. During the term, these 215 students paid for 1,450 credits but, by the end of the term, they had mastered only 300 credits—1.4 credits per student. Taking 12 credits as a measure of full-time equivalency, 1,450 paid credits meant that College IV had 120 full-time equivalent students. But the large number of people who signed up for modules at the beginning was misleading since their completion rates were so low. Taking credits mastered as the measure, the college had only 25 full-time equivalents. In subsequent quarters, the college continued to carry many of these students without attracting enough new ones. The number of credits generated began to decline, a problem that can be traced directly to the self-pacing system and to a part-time student body. With no deadlines for completion, a student could sign up and pay for a module in one term but not complete the work by passing the mastery examination in that term. As with incompletes in a regular program, College IV could not count credits left over from earlier terms. This situation had several implications for College IV as a time-free, self-paced system. It made reporting awkward when students did not complete their work within the period normally expected. Without some kind of deadline, students would delay completion of their work and some would never complete it. More urgently, the low full-time equivalent ratio meant that the college had to attract a large volume of students, including a sufficient number of full-time students.

The central administration began to put pressure on Toft to

increase College IV's credit production. While Toft had some leeway because of the newness and unfamiliarity of the modularized approach, it was obvious that the budget was getting tighter and that College IV was nowhere close to the expected student-faculty ratio. Much energy went into finding new sources of students as well as into improving the progress of students already at the college. Advertising efforts were increased. Contacts were cultivated with the new continuing education office at Grand Valley. A local manufacturing firm in Grand Rapids agreed to provide space in its plant for College IV faculty to come one day a week to tutor and test employees. An anonymous gift of one thousand dollars helped to install College IV at the Kent County jail where inmates could work on modules for credit. Toft had also raised the possibility of bringing the college program to a variety of communities by means of a large van outfitted like a bookmobile.

But each of the solutions explored by College IV and the central administration brought new difficulties that were still unresolved as of 1977. Introducing deadlines undercut the time-free, self-paced character of the college. Increasing the number of students put an extra burden on faculty and tutors (part-time students do not necessarily see faculty part time). The mere presence of more full-time students did not necessarily mean that students would complete their modules more quickly. Further, if full-time students came to dominate the student body at College IV, they might alienate the part-time, adult students that College IV was initially designed to serve.

Student Characteristics

Careful surveys of College IV students were conducted periodically during the first two years by an evaluation team from Ann Arbor.[2] These surveys showed that the profile of College IV students was consistently different from the typical college popula-

[2] The grant from FIPSE enabled Toft to engage an evaluation team from Ann Arbor—Richard Heydinger, John Seeley, Margaret Talburtt, and Theodore Jolosky—that conducted surveys and interviews of faculty, students, and administrators between 1973 and 1975. Formative Evaluation Research Associates (FERA), as their organization is called, has been invaluable to me in the preparation of this case study.

tion. The first group of students, for example, was considerably older than a typical freshman class: almost two thirds were over twenty years old, and over 60 percent were working. Thus, College IV was a "second-chance" college for many people, who were attracted to the college precisely for the reasons Toft originally designed it. Most often they mentioned having come because of the opportunity to study on their own time and to get individual attention. Many said they were studying for intrinsic reasons, to expand themselves intellectually and to learn how to think critically and to communicate better, although an increasing percentage of those enrolled said that they were in College IV to improve their economic or occupational status. Construction workers came around on rainy days and set up study plans for the winter months; mothers on welfare brought their children to the campus daycare center; a secretary wanted to know how much education she could buy for the fifty dollars she had available; an elderly woman wanted to learn something about plants; the family of a mother of three gave her modules for Christmas.

There was, then, a close fit between College IV's flexibility and the kinds of students it attracted initially. Most of the students interviewed by the evaluation team expressed gratitude to and satisfaction with College IV. Typical comments were: "I wouldn't be in college if it weren't for College IV. The faculty will do anything to help you out." "College IV gives people a choice and suits people's personalities." "I'm satisfied because educational units are cut down in smaller sections where you can understand them and the class doesn't get ahead of you" (Jolosky and Talburtt, 1974).

Another theme also began to emerge from the interviews with students—procrastination. While they said they were pleased with the college, most were not pleased with themselves. Over half of the first group were not satisfied with their progress in completing modules and attributed their lack of progress to personal and situational reasons. There is a paradox here. While students valued College IV for the freedom and flexibility it gave them and while they recognized that success in such a system required high levels of self-discipline, a large proportion felt they did not know how to keep themselves going academically. And the college did very little to help them learn how to work independently. Students, of course, were free to consult with the faculty about these matters but the initiative had to come from them. Even so, not all the faculty saw the kind of counseling implied by the problem of procrastination as part of their jobs, and all of them were working furiously to produce more modular materials. Questions about modules were more easily dealt with than questions about how to study and how to arrange life to accomplish more.

The number of modules available to students had increased from 45 at the beginning of the school year to 125 in the winter term, and Toft (1976) later estimated that over 800,000 pages of modular materials had been printed by the end of the first year.

What College IV was doing in terms of total enrollment and credit production was very visible—with both intended and unintended consequences. The record-keeping system allowed more minute monitoring of student progress in College IV than is usually the case in a traditional college. Thus, it was possible for faculty and tutors to use the information for diagnostic and counseling purposes. At the same time, the relative ease of computing the total credits attempted and mastered meant that College IV's failure to produce enough credits was known not only within the college but more widely at Grand Valley.

By the beginning of the winter quarter, College IV could determine how many modules had been selected, how many tests had been given, and how many had been mastered. Biology, psychology and sociology were the most popular subjects, as measured by the average number of students signed up for the available modules. There was considerable variation in the average number of tests students took to reach mastery in each of the subjects, with biology, English and mathematics showing the most attempts, and accounting and speech requiring the least.

The college also began to attack the problem of procrastination in earnest. Toft and a student designed audiovisual orientation materials that described, in rather simple terms, what modules were, how they were organized in terms of behavioral objectives, and how necessary it was to keep up a rhythm of progress in the College IV system. But not until the second year, when one of the College IV students took the initiative, did the college invest in a personal orientation program, which included an interview with a student counselor as well as the audiovisual explanation of modularized instruction. Without such efforts to avoid the consequences of atomization, College IV might never develop the emotional glue to hold students, and everything seemed to work against it: the ease with which students could register and then disappear, the completely individualized modules, the lack of a clear focus in the curriculum, the pressure on the faculty to produce more materials, the personalities of the dean and some of the faculty, and even the architecture—faculty offices were tucked into a number of separate, narrow cul-de-sacs off a long corridor running along the first floor of a building used by other Grand Valley units. People were beginning to ask: Is this a college at all?

Growth of Faculty and Student Discontent

Because the faculty had no regular way to make decisions or share administrative tasks, the balance of power clearly lay on the side of the dean. This was not a problem at first, since there was broad agreement between the faculty and Toft about the goals and direction of the college. But by the end of the year, open criticism of Toft's management errors and brisk leadership style began to be voiced by the faculty. The dean's frequent absences from the college did not help matters, nor did the fact that the faculty were beginning to wear down from the heavy and multiple demands on their time. Moreover, some began to sense a certain lack of support from the central Grand Valley administration (Seeley, 1975).

A detailed analysis of faculty activities revealed that, on the average, faculty members were spending 52.6 hours per week on their work in the college, with the largest portion of time (60 percent) going into "teaching activities"—tutoring, counseling, contract study and seminars, and module construction. (Of these categories, module construction received the greatest amount of attention.) The second most demanding set of activities involved administrative tasks, which took an average of 14.5 hours per week of faculty time. There was a striking disparity between the amount of time faculty *did* spend on administrative matters and the time they *wished* to spend. Although College IV faculty said they wanted to spend only about 6 percent of their time on administrative activities, they estimated that they spent 15 percent of their time this way. In reality, or at least as measured by the weekly time logs, faculty were spending nearly twice as much time on administration as they thought they were and over four times more than they wanted to. And since each faculty member was the only person in his or her discipline, there was the additional pressure of having to be responsible for the total curriculum in a field. (For a comparison with other faculty workload data, see Parsons and Platt, 1968; Stecklein, 1961; and Yuker, 1974.)

Most of the students praised the faculty, but they blamed themselves for not benefitting more from what College IV offered. Nine months after the college opened, half of a sample of students said that they were considering dropping out or transferring from College IV either because there were not enough modules for them or because of poor progress in completing College IV work (Jolosky, 1974). In general, students with pacing problems had a hard time recovering. These students said they were having problems both in beginning and in completing the modules, a process Talburtt (1974) called the "downward spiral" of "non-pacing." The spiral began with an inability to get started on a module; the longer one was away from the module, the more guilt about procrastination; the more guilt, the less likely one was to turn to the module. Dropping out was the final step.

In the second year, three new faculty members were hired. More adjunct faculty were lined up to write modules and tutor College IV students, and more students began to request contract studies and group contracts. But the approximate full-time equivalent credits produced per faculty member in the college remained considerably lower than the Grand Valley average: Only 12.3:1 that winter. By spring the college was asked to reach three fourths of the overall average, or 15:1. Although credit-generating efforts continued through that year and a few new ideas bubbled up, additional problems also appeared. Relations with the Admissions Office, for example, became strained, to say the least. Toft claimed that the admissions counselors did not understand College IV well enough to explain it or were simply against it, while admissions people accused Toft of overestimating the potential market for a college as incomprehensible as College IV.

The Faculty Turn Toward Competence

During the winter of 1975, Toft announced that he was resigning to take a position as program development officer for Grand Valley State Colleges. Challenged over the past year by the faculty, Toft had already begun sharing power with them, and as the year passed, he increasingly refused to deal with problems that he felt the faculty should confront. The faculty, on their side, felt abandoned and exposed, but it was clear that they would have to take on more responsibility for the direction of the college. A Community Council was set up, including all full-time faculty, the dean, the assistant dean, and student representatives. Provision was made for a faculty chairperson, and five standing committees were given formal charges. A mechanism for the selection of the dean and a definition of the role of the dean were formally spelled out. These deliberations took a great deal of faculty time—if they had grumbled about the amount of committee and administrative work they were required to do the year before, that work was nothing compared to the herculean efforts required of them in 1974–75.

This was also the last year for the large grant from FIPSE. Afterwards, all regular College IV operations would be financed by institutional funds, and so the bulk of curriculum development had to be completed in this final year of the grant. The faculty was forced to confront what they were and what they should be. For the first time, they began working together on major policy decisions. They proceeded to tackle these questions in a straightforward, nonideological manner, a style undoubtedly reflecting their inclinations toward and experiences with behavioral objectives.

Their first step was to clarify and adopt a statement of the goals of the college. This document argues that the distinctiveness of College IV derives both from an emphasis on expanding educational opportunity for people who have hitherto been excluded from higher education and from a unique instructional system that allows temporal and spatial flexibility. College IV's two major objectives emerged as:

1. Training in the liberal arts. The dimensions of the liberal arts are defined as competencies exhibited by students.
2. An instructional system that is highly accessible and that accommodates diverse learning styles.

This statement of competencies was the first substantive identification of a unique College IV curriculum. It says that the college is to provide opportunities for students to develop cognitive skills, which include investigative skills, problem-solving skills, objectivity, analysis skills, critical thinking, the ability to synthesize, and effective decision making. It is also to provide: knowledge about and ability to use major social institutions, a historical perspective of events, a social-cultural perspective, an interdisciplinary perspective, and deep involvement in formal inquiry in at least one area. Students are to be given an opportunity to clarify their value systems; to develop self-motivation, goal direction, and self-confidence; and to deepen their esthetic sense. Social relationships are to help students develop social and political responsiveness and the ability to communicate effectively with others.

There had been discussion from the beginning about competence-based education at College IV. For example, six months after the opening of the college, Toft had written in an accreditation report: "A long-range consideration for the instructional program is that the degrees offered should be based not upon the accumulation of credits distributed according to a specific plan, but upon the demonstration of stated competencies . . . . we wish to work towards the articulation of specific competencies that would mark a broadly educated person. To the extent that we can describe these competencies, they will replace specific requirements within the curriculum leading toward a degree" (Grand Valley State Colleges, 1973a, p. 51). But the outcomes or competencies listed in the modules were not very different from those one would expect to find if English professors or biology professors decided to specify what they expected their students to know after studying some subject with them, and they were limited to these individual modules alone. The

1975 statement of goals was the first time that specific outcomes for the whole college had been spelled out. The process of writing it pointed the faculty in several—if not too many—directions. It made it possible for the faculty to explore the idea of a college-wide program, to agree that they should find out what progress other colleges had made with competence-based programs, and to commit a portion of a summer faculty workshop to a discussion of what a competence-based program might look like at College IV, before deciding whether to adopt it.

The goals document also left room for changing or expanding the curriculum and for establishing a degree structure that would fit the size and style of College IV. Essentially, the faculty chose a new degree structure that would be workable for a faculty of ten. They recognized that the college could not achieve any degree of stability while relying as much as it had on part-time, older students who were not coming to the college or completing modules at a rate to make the college cost effective. Nor did focusing on cross-registrants make much sense if College IV were to be something more than a service unit for Grand Valley. They decided instead to focus on full-time, degree-seeking students.

The final degree document drawn up late in the spring of 1975 was organized around a divisional structure—humanities, social sciences, and natural sciences. Students could major in any one of the divisions and fulfill most requirements within College IV or in a regular discipline from one of the other Grand Valley colleges. Beyond specific requirements for a concentration, all candidates for a B.A. or B.S. degree were required to do general distribution work in the concentration division, to take five credits across divisions, and to have up to ten credits in each of three basic competence areas—quantitative skills, investigative skills, and communication skills. Thus the way was clear in spring 1975 for a small competence-based program, although a new and possibly constraining divisional degree structure had been imposed on it.

The Beginnings of Competence-Based Education

During the faculty workshop that summer, the faculty balanced the need to move toward the competence-based program with the need to produce more modules for the small number of students who needed them to continue their work at the college. The faculty set aside one week for discussion of competence-based education. In typically straightforward fashion, the faculty quickly reached a consensus about the way they viewed competence-based education for College IV. Gary Woditsch, an expert on competence-based education from Bowling Green State University who attended the workshop along with other experts from Alverno College and Mars Hill College, encouraged the faculty by saying that they had already been engaged in competence-based education at the course level. They were accustomed to specifying outcomes and tailoring learning activities to the achievement of those outcomes. They were far ahead of most colleges that were beginning to move toward a competence mode. Their job, then, was to think through what competencies they, as a total college, wanted their students to achieve beyond the specific objectives in the modules. What "generic competencies" did they think their students should have when they left College IV? How did these fit together? How could they be connected to the modularized approach in general and to the specific outcomes already laid out in the modules?

The faculty divided into small working groups and, in two hours, each group had come up with overall structures for the competence program that were remarkably similar. All groups agreed that they should continue with the modules and the divisional degrees, but that these should be tied into a competence-based education program. Each group talked about generic competencies, such as communication skills, that would be "detachable" and independent so they could stand alone for students who might not necessarily want a College IV degree but, at the same time, these competencies would permit some merging with the existing curriculum and divisional degrees.

However, after the guests departed, it was clear that the apparent consensus was illusory. Several of the scientists objected to the college's putting much effort into a competence-based program when it had so much else to do. But after much discussion, the faculty decided that the competence-based program would be developed slowly over the next two years, that it would be integrated as much as possible with the existing modules or else be made detachable in a way that would not require basic restructuring of the modules, and that it would be subject to review by the Curriculum Committee and to a vote by the Community Council. The communications competence would be the first one tackled and would be viewed as a prototype for the development of others. In other words, the effort College IV would put into competence-based education would depend on what it took to get the communications competence program going.

By the third year, enrollments were looking up. In the fall quarter, full-time equivalents ran about sixteen or seventeen to one, and the average number of credits per student was up to 2.5. But the fall statistics also showed that the college had only nine full-time students enrolled for at least fifteen credits each (Heydinger, 1975b).

Then a bombshell hit College IV. An edict from the Veterans Administration that was intended to control abuses of veterans' educational benefits in colleges across the country classified the college as an independent study college, and veterans would now have to take twice as many credits in it to qualify for benefits. This ruling affected many innovative colleges around the country, and College IV—29 percent of its students were veterans—soon joined them in appealing it. Although it was not immediately apparent what the effects of the ruling would be, enrollments had drifted downward by the winter quarter.

The central administration began to take a more interventionist posture toward the college and complaints about College IV's favored position in credit production began to be heard more frequently from faculty in the other colleges. (For more on the controversy surrounding College IV, see "College Programs Rapped," 1975.) Over the Christmas holidays, the two vice-presidents of Grand Valley drafted a major planning document for the institution that opened a way out for College IV. They suggested that limits be placed on the number of new programs for the College of Arts and Sciences and that flexibility be encouraged in the other colleges, particularly in College IV. They recommended that College IV give more attention to the development of nonduplicating professional-technical programs and that it make efforts to appeal to recipients of associate degrees from local community colleges.

Within College IV, the heat was being felt. The faculty

drafted a long report that laid out what they believed the major emphases of the college should be, with the competence-based program an important component. Some faculty were still talking about developing more modules for students who had completed the existing ones, but this was becoming less acceptable among most of the faculty who were working either on the competence program or on the professional-technical program. Those faculty who had already reached the limit of their module-production energies were spending more time on other teaching activities, and there seemed to be a growing consensus that time would be better spent doing other things for the college than writing modules.

In January 1976, the college moved to its own building, which incorporated an open structure design that Toft had conceived. A large, central commons room with comfortable chairs, tables, and a testing area was ringed by small faculty offices, seminar rooms, and a laboratory. This arrangement produced a quantum increase in the sociability and visibility of people at College IV. Although it was clear that no major changes would occur at College IV until a new dean was selected, work on the competence-based program was going forward nonetheless. Two faculty members, both with experience in self-paced instruction at Oklahoma State University—Milton Ford in written communication and Paul White in oral communication—worked closely together on the communications competence program. They were able to provide support for each other at a time when the direction of the college remained unclear. The more they worked, the more they began to believe that they were developing a valuable model for the rest of the college to emulate. It would have been easy for them to start with the existing modules in English, but they chose a more difficult and ambitious path. First, they struggled with general statements of learning outcomes in the communications area. These statements became the basis for the rest of their work, which involved developing materials from imported learning packages, or from existing modules at College IV. They also planned to devise completely new learning materials. Finally came the problem of assessment, which proved more thorny than anticipated—a common occurrence in competence-based programs.

The communications competence program has since undergone several permutations, but from the beginning it included writing, public speaking, and social interaction competencies. The written communication competencies drew directly on modules Ford had written earlier, but the materials and assessments for the oral competencies were new. These began to move the college beyond its almost complete reliance on paper and pencil tests. White tackled the public speaking competence: using a videotape, he had students deliver short speeches and then rated them according to a scheme he had devised. Later, he was to build a whole course on spoken communication and turn to new materials to help him do it. He began to incorporate ratings by students into his assessments and to talk about using panels of outside assessors. Another faculty member, Christine Falvey, also turned to new sources for her work on interpersonal communication, eventually developing an assessment of interpersonal sensitivity based on videotaped vignettes produced at Michigan State University. Another technique introduced in the interpersonal communications competence was the use of face-to-face interviews.

What effects did the communications competence program have on students and on the college as a whole? According to White and Ford, students were beginning to see that communication skills went beyond the specific details of reading and writing. Students who went through the communications competence program began to get a sense of what was required for progress at the college and what the different modules added up to. They were beginning to find that the notion of "competence," as well as the assessments, helped them put together what before the advent of competence-based education seemed to be scattered, unconnected modules. As time passed, Ford and White began to see that their competencies were even more generic than they had originally thought, especially at the higher levels.

Another important recognition centered on assessment itself. While they were at the first stage in their work—stating the competencies and their components and running students through the lower-level assessments—Ford and White did not worry too much about their assessment tests. But as other problems were settled, they began to ask themselves whether they could really trust the assessments. Did they in fact measure "competence"? Would competence as measured on their tests transfer to other situations? How could they better simulate those other situations in their assessment instruments? Were the assessments missing some important elements? How could they assess oral communication as reliably as written work? Ford and White were beginning to get inquiries from around the country about "their" program at a time when they were still not sure they had it squared away. It was tempting to respond to those requests, and yet there was so much else to do.

Things were going less smoothly for David Bernstein who was the faculty member charged with developing cognitive skills competencies. It was not clear to him how to respond to the broad statement in the goals document that said College IV should "provide a setting and the training that will assist students in developing the following cognitive skills: problem solving, ability to analyze, critical thinking, objectivity, ability to synthesize, effective decision making." For a while, the task seemed to be an exercise in epistemology and, given his background in cognitive psychology, Bernstein was not averse to following that line. He reviewed the literature on cognition and kept in close touch with Gary Woditsch and his group at Bowling Green, since they had made some progress in defining and developing strategies for teaching problem solving and had gathered a vast amount of material. But unlike Ford and White, he was not able to turn to existing modules at College IV for help in his task.

Bernstein began to map the "cognitive area," as it had been broadly defined in the goals statement, by asking other College IV faculty members to describe what they saw as the generic skills required by their disciplines with respect to analysis, synthesis, decision making, objectivity, problem solving, and critical thinking. He also looked at techniques for teaching and assessing critical thinking skills. And when Paul Haas, an economist who had worked with Gary Woditsch at Bowling Green in designing a course in critical thinking, joined College IV in the spring 1976 term, the two men set about to define a model for conceptualizing critical thinking based on Haas' earlier work on problem solving. This attempt led them to see how closely tied their work was with what White and Ford were doing in communication. For example, one of the critical thinking competencies asked students to identify premises, assumptions, and conclusions in a persuasive essay. Doing this depended on mastery of the first-level communications competence: "reading comprehension ability to determine the main point of an essay and bases of support." At higher levels as well, students would be asked to demonstrate skills that rested on the ability to read, write, and speak effectively. As White and Ford framed the communication competence, its final stage would involve the ability to analyze.

From the beginning, Bernstein saw that he would have to involve College IV faculty in the critical thinking competence program. The existing curriculum would have to be examined in terms of the opportunities it afforded students to develop and apply critical thinking skills, and the assessment of student competence in these terms would have to come from the relevant faculty. Thus, it was obvious that developments in competence-based education could not be separated from what happened in College IV as a whole.

A New Dean and a New College IV

In March 1976, Douglas Kindschi, from Sangamon State University in Illinois, was offered and accepted College IV's deanship. He came with considerable academic and administrative experience. In addition to teaching mathematics at Sangamon, he had served as academic planning coordinator, director of academic planning, assistant vice-president for academic affairs, and dean of educational services. In these jobs he had established Sangamon's planning office and had worked on developing degree programs in interdisciplinary and professional studies. With his strong background within a new state institution with a reputation for innovativeness, he looked as if he had been sent providentially to College IV. And in a sense he had been—Toft knew him and had suggested him to other Grand Valley administrators.

Nearly everyone was pleased when Kindschi accepted the position, and he moved quickly to establish himself both with the College IV faculty and with the central administration. He spent time talking with the faculty about the directions in which he thought the college should move, thus laying the groundwork for major changes he would initiate the following year. While he asserted the primacy of liberal education, he thought it appropriate for College IV to help students, especially nontraditional ones, with career training. He accepted self-paced, modular instruction but thought that there were other ways of being accessible and flexible. The college needed strong *programs;* students did not understand nor did they get too excited about an instructional *method.*

Kindschi saw that the competence-based program could become the core of the College IV curriculum. It could be the intellectual force that would integrate its degree programs, since students would be required to complete the competence program before graduating. The competence-based program, in effect, was to become College IV's version of a distribution requirement. And it would reassure the faculty that their modular delivery system with its liberal arts contents would not be lost with the addition of professional programs.

By the beginning of the 1976 fall quarter, College IV had a new degree program, a new registration process, course-sized modules, a new grading system, deadlines for module completion, classes, and an unevenly developed competence-based program. Publications emphasized the competence requirements and the degree programs, which moved to the forefront of what was called "A College of Liberal and Professional Studies." The central administration gave Kindschi strong support by not pushing too hard on credit generation, by approving three faculty positions in the new professional-technical programs, and by encouraging him to move ahead with his plans.

All procedures were being regularized. By the end of a short revisionist period, so little remained of the original Toft program that people were beginning to talk about a "new College IV." Modules were "bundled" into course-sized chunks; the half-credit modules were absorbed into larger units, although most of these units did not consist of much more than the old modules stapled together (at first, symbolically, they were bundled with rubber bands). Registration procedures were tightened; the "banking" system, which left the choice of modules open, was eliminated, and students were required to sign up for specific modules or courses. They were encouraged to do this within the regular Grand Valley registration period, although it was still possible to register for self-paced modules any time during a term and get credit for them the following term. Time limits were placed on how long a module could be carried before a mastery attempt, and three levels of mastery (with three attempts possible) were introduced. The way was paved for College IV to amalgamate with the regular Grand Valley records system and, indeed, give students regular transcripts for the conventional part of their programs. (Competence achieved was logged separately from grades in courses and was to be indicated in an addendum to the regular transcript.)

Graduates of local community colleges were assured junior standing in College IV; for its new bachelor of applied science degree, they were required to complete the competence program and encouraged to enroll in a liberal arts major. Students in two new professional programs—occupational safety and advertising/public relations—were also required to complete the competence-based program and encouraged to work out a joint liberal arts concentration. The original bachelor's degree programs in social sciences, natural sciences, and humanities remained essentially as they had been, with the additional requirement of the competence-based core. Materials developed for the communications and problem-solving competencies the previous year formed the basis for courses in these areas. Other competence classes in value clarification and social interaction used some new materials that had been devised over the summer.

With the promotion of the competence-based program to the core of the College IV curriculum, it became imperative that the faculty hammer out its final list of competencies. Continued skepticism on the part of the scientists and ambivalence on the part of many others about whether a generic competence-based program could really replace a liberal arts distribution requirement led to a list of competence statements that combined both generic and disciplinary competencies. The generic competencies, patterned on other competence-based programs and on the previous year's work in communication and problem solving, included:

1. *Communication:* (a) Fundamentals of reading, writing, listening, and speaking; (b) composition of messages; (c) research and documentation; and (d) speech communication.

2. *Problem Solving:* (a) Critical thinking; (b) effective problem solving; and (c) formal inquiry.
3. *Social Interaction:* (a) Interpersonal interaction; and (b) organizations and management.
4. *Value Clarification:* (a) Identifying values; and (b) values and social conflict.
5. *Application of Basic Concepts:* (a) Concepts in the natural world; (b) concepts in the social world; (c) concepts in the world of ideas; and (d) quantitative applications.

As things stood in the spring of 1977, the faculty members responsible for each of the competence areas had produced a series of assessment guides addressed to students who might want to present themselves for assessment without taking a course, as well as students who wanted a preview of what was required in each of the competencies. These assessment guides were most clearly elaborated for communication and problem solving and at the lower levels throughout the competencies. Dates for assessment sessions were announced for the whole year, and students began to present themselves for assessment in 1976–77. Most students, however, signed up for the competence "readiness" classes or for self-paced modules. In almost all cases, competence was achieved in the framework of the courses, usually through paper and pencil tests or essay questions. The instructors of the courses assessed the students. When possible, many of the old modular materials were adapted to the competence courses. This was not possible in problem solving, social interaction and value clarification, where instruction took place in classes.

Purists in the competence movement might say that College IV's practices were questionable. First, the professional programs, a prime place for a competence-based approach, were not conceived in terms of competencies. Second, the conceptualization of the program did not appear to be based either on a view of students' future needs or on the liberal arts; rather, it appeared to be a pastiche of curricular compromises based on College IV's own particular needs. Third, most assessments were not performance-based nor were the competencies themselves, with a few exceptions, behavioral. Fourth, instruction was not separated from assessment, an ideal rarely achieved by competence programs at other colleges. But such judgments are unduly harsh. Like most "second-generation" adopters of innovations, the College IV faculty have chosen those aspects of competence-based education that fit their own needs and styles. The danger, of course, is that the essential features of a competence program—performance, verifiable assessment, and overarching outcomes—will become so misshapen as to be unrecognizable as competence-inspired. Most of the College IV faculty are aware of these problems and have kept in close touch with the leaders in the competence-based movement at Alverno and Bowling Green. College IV's competence-based program cannot be compared with the one at Alverno, which had a large cadre of faculty working for years on a redefinition of the liberal arts, but given its struggles for survival, the handful of faculty available to develop the competence program, the absence of extra development funds, and all its earlier disappointments, it is remarkable that College IV has come as far in a short time as it has.

The clear definition of its professional degree programs, the implementation of the competence program, and the introduction of classes have combined to produce more credits at College IV. In 1976–77, the college claimed 180 full-time equivalent students, compared to 160 in the highest quarter the previous year. The average number of credits taken increased from seven in 1976 to eleven in 1977. And with a good bit of help from the central administration, Kindschi was able to transfer fractions of some of the College IV appointments into other teaching departments; this, combined with the modest enrollment increases, brought College IV's student-faculty ratio almost exactly in line with Grand Valley's overall requirement.

In spite of difficulties, the College IV faculty were clearly relishing teaching classes—they had, after all, come to College IV because they were devoted to teaching. In the "old" College IV, the small number of students, along with the tight structure imposed by the modular format, prevented faculty from feeling as if they were really teaching. The "old Adam" had returned—to a degree that the administration became worried that the faculty would completely abandon the original core experiment, the modules! And classes brought a new atmosphere of camaraderie to College IV that even veteran College IV students—who complained bitterly about loss of flexibility and less faculty accessibility—applauded and enjoyed.

Conclusion: A New Lease on Life

Fearsome problems still remain at College IV. It is not clear that the professional-technical programs will attract a secure student base. What will happen to the divisional degrees is also unclear. The articulation between competence-based education and the career-oriented programs is still problematic, nor is it obvious that the still part-time and rather pragmatic student body will want to jump through competence hoops. How far a primarily liberal arts faculty can be stretched remains an open question; while many of them have shown great resilience, there is probably a limit. The same will be true of the new practitioner faculty who will staff the professional-technical programs. A more important question is whether most of the present and future faculty will be able to work within the competence-based part of the curriculum.

It is still too early to know whether, or how, these issues will work themselves out. Although elements from its past remained, College IV in 1977 was a new college. It reached this point because of a fundamental miscalculation about the appeal of a totally modularized, self-paced college to an unselected, part-time student body. To a large extent, an inexperienced and zealous leader who had selected an almost equally convinced faculty set in motion forces that prevented them from recognizing this mismatch. Problems with record keeping, materials, and recruitment, therefore, could be attributed to others outside the college rather than to the College IV system itself. Decisions in the early years were shaped by experiences with the atypical students who could benefit most from College IV's flexibilities and the accessibility of its faculty. These were the younger, usually full-time students, not the older, more burdened and insecure part-time people for whom College IV was primarily designed. At College IV, these people slipped away unnoticed—until their effects on enrollment statistics could no longer be ignored. There was little to hold them—no classes, no degree program that spoke to their possible interests and futures, and little that they could identify as a "college."

Heightened by pressure from the central administration, these realities led College IV to recognize that there are limits to flexibility. Breaking the "access barriers" and the "lockstep" of higher education does not automatically ensure a steady clientele. Free access also means free exit. Students are not generally attracted by a delivery system, even if it delivers education to them in a way that opens up possibilities that the traditional system cannot offer. Most students are not thrilled by the opportunity to study exclusively from modules—however flexibly in terms of time and place—nor does a modularized curriculum satisfy all their needs. Although it is claimed by some advocates of individualized curriculums that anyone can learn anything, given enough time, there is not enough time in most people's lives, particularly if they are adults, and the result is that "self-pacing" soon becomes "non-pacing." It is not enough to hand students modules; ways of socializing must be built into flexible, time-free colleges like College IV to an even greater extent than in more conventional programs.

It is also clear from College IV's experience that a modular curriculum is not "teacher-proof," nor does it appear to be a way of saving money. Most faculty will not depend exclusively on someone else's instructional materials, yet they also tire of spending large amounts of time writing their own when they want to leave a mark on students through their teaching (Toft, 1976). This means that materials devised by others will not be readily accepted or disseminated by college teachers. If this is so, then it limits the future diffusion not only of modular learning packages but of competence-based education as a whole, which has relied in its lengthy development on arguments for broad dissemination. (See Gamson, 1977.) Even the College IV faculty working on a "second-generation" competence-based program, who by necessity turned to experts in competence-based education around the country, discovered that approaches and materials developed elsewhere required extensive adaptation to their local situation. (For an overall assessment of other aspects of College IV, see Heydinger and Associates, 1977.)

The basic question for College IV is what it is to become. While it has succeeded in presenting itself in more coherent ways than at first, it has not yet settled on a conception of itself. The college includes a number of poorly integrated, possibly conflicting elements. It is a college of liberal and professional studies but so is the College of Arts and Sciences and, even more explicitly, William James College at Grand Valley State. The mixture of traditional elements (liberal arts and professional-technical courses) with non-traditional ones (a competence-based program and self-paced modules) is still unintelligible to most people. Without a clear conception of itself or a social philosophy, College IV will not be able to do much beyond responding expediently to what the future will bring. After all the trials of its short existence, it owes itself and its students something more.

Gerald Grant   Epilogue

New Methods
for the Study
of a Reform Movement

The Research Project on Competence-Based Education out of
which this book has grown was itself an experiment in social
research and an effort at reform of research methods. This final
chapter therefore treats the project itself as a "case" and gives a
concrete account of its conception and evolution in the hope of
indicating not only what we did but how and why we did it, so that
students of other movements can consider adopting our methods in
whole or in part. It explains how we arrived at our conclusions and
points to the limits of our generalizations, in order to ask whether
our approach justifies its cost in comparison with more common
ways of organizing a research enterprise. It illustrates the problems
that researchers are likely to encounter in evaluating reform programs, including those of confidentiality, reciprocity, and trust, and
it examines the politics of evaluation at the institutional and federal
levels. Finally, it analyzes the project and this book in light of larger
philosophical and epistemological questions that are inherent in all

social research but that are all too often ignored in reports of research.

Our research project was an experiment in the sense that it posed a test of the question: What is the best way to study an emergent large-scale social movement or educational reform in order to produce the greatest yield of useful knowledge to policy makers and potential participants in such a movement or reform—not merely descriptive information about particular programs but knowledge about what it would mean to foster more widespread adoption of the reform? The need for such an approach to the evaluation of broad-aim social programs and their potential consequences has been stated by Weiss and Rein, among others. In criticizing the mis-application of "controlled" experimental designs to evaluative research during the past decade, they have called for a more qualitative, process-oriented approach that would be "concerned with what form [an] action program actually [takes], and with the details of its interaction with its surroundings, from which may be formed an inductive assessment of its consequences" (1971, p. 296). Similarly, Parlett and Hamilton (1972) have urged adoption of "illuminative" methods of evaluation that are more concerned with description and interpretation than with measurement and predic-tion. Such evaluations would study how an innovative program operates, how it both influences and is influenced by its environ-ment, how those directly involved in the program perceive it, and what its most significant features, critical processes, and unintended consequences appear to be. This chapter attempts to show how our project constitutes a response to these proposals for new forms of evaluation and, at the same time, to illustrate how our inferences and generalizations about the competence-based education move-ment are grounded in field research rather than being the product of "armchair assessment" or typical social criticism.

Our project was also innovative both in the interdisciplinary character of our team and in the field research techniques we adopted. The more than a dozen original members of the team brought to it training in history, law, medicine, philosophy, psycho-analysis, English literature, education, and sociology. These multi-disciplinary foundations enriched our view of competence-based education, particularly since our inquiry was grounded in fieldwork by all members of the team, and our diverse beliefs and aims shaped our research method. This method may be unique in its combination of several elements: (1) repeated fieldwork at each site by one member of the team over a three-year period; (2) an agreement among team members to share all field notes from all site visits; (3) team visits to all sites so that every member of the team, while immersed in his or her own site, also did fieldwork relating to a cross-site theme at most of the others; and (4) a broad definition of the domain of research that included the agency funding the research as part of the legitimate field of inquiry.

Of necessity, this recounting of the history of the project must be made from my perspective as director of the project. But it is buttressed by considerable documentation: several thousand pages of field notes and correspondence; records of conversations with officials of the funding agency; three tape recordings of crucial discussions of method (the first, between members of the project team and officers of the agency when the project was under fire in its first year; the second, between the team and the subjects of our investigation midway in the project; and the third, among members of the team during a four-hour discussion at the end of the project); memoranda from all members of the team evaluating the strengths and weaknesses of the project from a methodological point of view; and, finally, a review of a draft of this account by the team members and several of the individuals mentioned in it.

No matter how much documentation is used, however, accounts of method are essentially first-person accounts, sometimes even confessional in tone. At its core, method is autobiography, and while research employs method in an attempt to rule out prejudice and idiosyncracy—to compensate, as it were, for autobiographical defects—an account of method reveals how one's scientific beliefs influence one's aims and what one lived through in attempting to realize them. It can also indicate what one believes about the nature of human action and why one has been persuaded to adopt a particular theoretical domain. If this chapter succeeds, the reader will sense both the drama and the confusion of our project, for our choices and decisions were not made under laboratory conditions.

Rather, we often acted with a sense of uncertainty, enmeshed in tension and conflict.

Genesis of the Project

In 1973, Thomas Corcoran, then a senior research fellow at the Educational Policy Research Center at Syracuse, obtained a one-year grant from FIPSE to investigate new curricular patterns in higher education. He and I conferred about nominees for a task force that he planned to assemble as well as about sites they might visit, but I declined Corcoran's invitation to join the task force because I was myself currently pursuing intense fieldwork for a study of reform movements in higher education. By the following spring, Corcoran's task force (including Audrey Cohen of the College for Human Services, Robert Birney of Hampshire College, Morris Keeton of Antioch College, and Zelda Gamson of the University of Michigan) had decided to focus efforts on competence-based education, and FIPSE had decided to earmark a large portion of its grants for competence-based reforms. After drafting a proposal for a follow-up grant, Corcoran was offered a position with FIPSE, which he accepted. Shortly thereafter, he approached me to see if I would be interested in assuming leadership of the project.

The project called for a study of innovation processes connected with the spread of competence-based education and giving practitionery program assistance. A task force at each college undertaking a competence-based program would jointly develop a process for monitoring the program and act as resources to one another, with technical assistance provided by Corcoran and two senior-level researchers at the Educational Policy Research Center. I thought that I should refuse Corcoran's offer to lead the project not only because of prior commitments but also because I did not feel qualified to assume Corcoran's technical assistance role. In addition, I lacked the personal relationships with experts in the field that Corcoran had developed in his exploratory grant—relationships important in coordinating a task force of competence-based practitioners.

A short time later, Corcoran reported that the deputy director of FIPSE, Russell Edgerton, wondered whether there were terms on which I might accept leadership of the effort. On further reflection, I decided that the opportunity to examine a major reform movement at an early stage should not be lightly dismissed. The research was congruent with my other interests, and, methodologically, an interesting possibility was beginning to form. I had recently contributed to a volume for the Carnegie Commission in which seventeen authors had been asked to write case studies of institutions that had experienced crises and transformations in the late 1960s and early 1970s (Riesman and Stadtman, 1973). Although some authors had exchanged drafts, the work was done largely in isolation and with no common framework. What if one had called the authors of that book together at the beginning, so that they could have discussed what kind of research ought to be done, developed conceptual frameworks, and remained in communication throughout their fieldwork? I reconceived Corcoran's proposal along those lines. If the project director's position was made half-time and the two senior research positions eliminated, funds would become available to engage a team selected for their research skills and analytic capabilities. Each member of the team would develop an analysis of some aspect of the competence-based movement in addition to writing a case study. These team members would be external to the institutions being surveyed, thus reducing the tensions possible between practitioners from an institution and the agency funding its programs. The work of the team members would be clearly labeled as research and analysis, with the technical assistance to the institutions largely eliminated.

As revised, the project would be an opportunity to address the problems of educating for competence in American society. This goal was stated as follows in the rewritten proposals: "The intent is not to evaluate programs as successes or failures, not to say in some absolute and definitive sense whether they "worked" or not. Rather, the intent is to investigate the way these programs have been conceptualized and operationalized, to discover how these settings have been created and evolved. The intent is to describe the programs, probe their assumptions, explore the pedagogic issues they raise, and in an open-ended way assess the range of impacts they may have" (Educational Policy Research Center, 1974, p. 2).

I told Corcoran that three years of funding would be needed to understand such a complex development, and some days later he called to say that Russell Edgerton was willing to continue discussions about the proposal under those conditions. When I met with Edgerton in Washington, I explained that, in order to study the competence-based movement, a project director would need authority to select a sample of institutions representing different levels of reform and programs preparing students for a wide range of occupations, whether or not such programs were operating under grants from FIPSE, as well as a free hand in choosing the members of the research team. Edgerton expressed some reluctance about these conditions, but did not oppose them outright. When we were joined by several other members of the FIPSE staff, however, and details of the revised proposal became clear to them, the tone of the discussion grew much more skeptical. One asked why a set of case studies and explorations of the issues could not be written on a one-year grant three years hence, thus eliminating two years of funding; he did not seem satisfied with my explanation that one cannot study the "evolution" of a movement on a post hoc basis and achieve the same results as those that accrue from immersion in the movement as it develops. Another scoffed that I proposed nothing other than writing a book: there would be no help to practitioners along the way, and FIPSE was not in the publishing business. While the revised proposal did retain some of the "assistance" function of Corcoran's plan by promising to provide feedback to practitioners and to share interim findings at two conferences, I was candid about the differences. I hoped the quality of research it planned would merit publication at least in part, if not in a book; and I pointed to several recent costly "action-oriented" projects of educational research that had resulted neither in worthy publications nor in much help to practitioners. This did not persuade my chief critic to change his view, and I left the meeting believing the odds were against my somewhat "bookish" project. But Edgerton asked me to spell out the intended outcomes of the project more clearly in light of the afternoon's conversation, and on returning to Syracuse I did so, listing five in an addendum to the proposal:

1. A set of case studies of the actual evolution over a three-year period of six to eight competence-based programs selected pri-

marily on the basis of their initial conceptual and programmatic diversity.

2. A synthesis of the ways that competence-based education has been conceptualized and operationalized, and of the critical issues associated with that process.
3. A study of the process of innovation at the institutional level and of the wider diffusion and growth of competence-based education.
4. A refined statement of the applicability, usefulness, and limits of the method of illuminative evaluation.
5. Providing useful feedback, when appropriate and desired, to the institutions participating in the study.

I was as surprised as anyone when two weeks later I received notice that the proposal had been approved and would be funded in its revised form. Although it was obvious that the staff at FIPSE was divided about the worth of the project, an enlightened view (from our perspective, at least) had prevailed. It would be funded for three years, and I was granted the conditions I regarded as essential: to include sites not funded by the agency, to choose the research team myself, and to draw a boundary between our research and FIPSE's monitoring of its own projects. To underscore this last requirement, it was agreed that no case-study materials, even in draft form, would be forwarded to FIPSE until the end of the second year of our project. This would ensure that our accounts would not be used to make decisions about whether projects should be refunded in the next funding cycle.

So-called contract research is in bad odor with many academics. Certainly the conditions under which any research is performed will significantly determine the outcomes. At one extreme the conditions can be such that researchers are virtually part-time employees of the agency and merely carry out quasi-administrative or management tasks. (Thus Horowitz, in his account of the cancelation of the highly controversial Project Camelot, traces much of the difficulty of that project to the failure of the social scientists involved to insist that they were more than hired hands for the Department of Defense: "The Army, however respectful and protective of free expression at the formal level, was 'hiring help' and not openly submitting military problems to the *higher* professional and scientific authority of social science" 1967, p. 36.) But it is also possible—and perhaps more often than traditionally oriented academics assume—to lay the groundwork for high quality work while under contract. Research contracts are open to renegotiation, however, and our agreements came unstuck from time to time as various officers of FIPSE attempted to interpret the proposal in light of what they regarded as more pressing or more useful ends. The boundary defining the researchers' independence had to be vigorously defended more than once.

The work of site selection began immediately. I read scores of proposals submitted to FIPSE in response to its call for experiments in competence-based education. Telephone interviews with a variety of researchers and practitioners led to other suggestions. Wendy Kohli, a member of the project staff, prepared an analysis of institutions developing programs they considered to be competence-based. We tried to identify the universe of institutions that consciously identified with the movement towards competence-based education (whether by the logic of internal developments, because it was required by the state, or in response to a call for proposals by FIPSE or some other agency). A more fundamental approach might have attempted to analyze all forms of higher education in America whether they called themselves competence-based or not. Yet, conceived as a study of a movement, this seemed appropriate though not ideal. And if the competence-based movement could be thought of as a Mississippi flowing through America, our aim was to sample its sources and headwaters, its branches and tributaries, as well as its relationship to other watersheds. However, all this was not thought through with precision. On the contrary, I proceeded in a rush—there was less than sixty days to recruit a staff, select a sample, assemble a team and make arrangements to get them into the field by the opening of most colleges in early September—partly using instinct and intuition and keeping several variables in mind. The sample of colleges selected ought to maximize diversity in the way that they initially conceptualized the problem of developing a competence-based program; a range of institutions by level, type, scope of program, and geographical location was desirable, and the programs ought to be representative of a wide range of career and occupational patterns. Although the proposal promised only eight case studies, twelve institutions were selected in anticipation of some attrition on our team and/or a refusal of some institutions to participate in the study. The twelve were: Alverno College in Milwaukee; Antioch School of Law in Washington, D.C.; College of Community and Public Service, University of Massachusetts at Boston; College for Human Services in New York City; Elgin State Mental Hospital in Illinois (which had pioneered a competence-based program for mental health paraprofessionals in conjunction with Northern Illinois University); Empire State College of the State University of New York; Florida State University in Tallahassee; College IV of the Grand Valley State Colleges in Allendale, Michigan; Justin Morrill College at Michigan State University in East Lansing; Mt. Hood Community College in Gresham, Oregon; Seattle Central Community College in Washington State; and the University of Toledo in Ohio. Nine case studies eventually were completed (Elgin State Mental Hospital, Empire State College, and Justin Morrill were dropped, and Syracuse University was substituted for Toledo), and our fieldwork extended, through short trips or interviews with faculty or administrators, to Bowling Green State University in Ohio; Florida International University in Miami; Mars Hill College in North Carolina; Our Lady of the Lake University in San Antonio, Texas; and Southern Illinois University in Carbondale. The five case studies in this volume illustrate the diversity in the competence-based education movement.

Creating the Research Team

After the sites had been selected, the critical task of assembling the team began. With only one exception, team members were asked to join the project with a specific site in mind. The exception was David Riesman. Out of long-standing collaboration, I consulted him as soon as I learned the project would be funded to ask if he would participate. Riesman agreed immediately, thus immeasurably enhancing the likelihood that other persons of quality would join, for his luster would obviously ease entrance to sites and help to certify the quality and seriousness of the project to external audiences. (Riesman's reputation paradoxically presented a method-ological problem at the site he eventually chose, Florida State University. Few people there had heard of the small competence-based program he came to study until he was introduced at a con-vocation of the whole faculty. As requests multiplied for Riesman to speak to various groups of faculty on the campus, he became a principal carrier—sometimes defender—of the innovation he sought to study. Typically, he turned this to advantage, seeing it as a unique opportunity to study the ecological relationships affecting the introduction of such an innovation.)

The ideal team to study the competence-based movement would have several characteristics: It would be composed of persons themselves representing a wide range of intellectual and practical competence who would bring an array of analytical perspectives to the investigation of competence. Members of such a team would be willing to do fieldwork (a requirement that was not modified even though several highly qualified persons whom I approached said they would join the project if they could be exempt). Members would also be congenial to both institutions and to one another, since the success of the team would depend on developing consid-erable trust, on being able to work together as a team in short bouts of intensive fieldwork, and in accepting critical peer evaluation of one another's work. And, finally, they ought to be sympathetic critics of the competence movement, neither avowed partisans nor implacable foes.

It sounds as though mere men and women could not people such a pantheon. Yet to a considerable degree, most of these high aims were realized. Initially the group included two persons outside academic life—one a practicing psychiatrist, the other a school superintendent. Most of the academics had had other careers—as lawyer, journalist, congressional assistant, military officer, school-teacher and Peace Corps volunteer, to name a few. In general, good matches were made with institutions. Thomas Ewens, for example, who taught philosophy at a small Jesuit liberal arts college and had lived in Milwaukee, took on the Alverno College assignment. Zelda Gamson, a sociologist at the University of Michigan, was quite knowledgeable about innovations in general and the experiments at the Grand Valley State Colleges in particular (in addition, she had been a member of the original Corcoran task force and so provided continuity with that work). Virginia Olesen, who agreed to do the case study of the nursing program at Mt. Hood Community College, had published a book-length study (Olesen and Whittaker, 1968) of the socialization and education of nurses. Not all achieved such a good fit, and compromises had to be made between qualities a particular researcher could contribute to the team and those that would be optimal at a particular site. But the matches were close enough so that only one of the researchers proposed was rejected by a site at the outset of the investigation, leading in that case to dropping the institution from the sample.

After both sample and team had tentatively been decided upon, it seemed best to call the president or dean or person chiefly responsible for the competence-based program in a given college directly, explaining the purpose of the study and the field work to be undertaken. If the response was favorable, I could then test reactions to the fieldworker proposed. The telephone call was often arranged as an "appointment"; the person called could then arrange a convenient time to talk and would have an opportunity to raise unanticipated questions. It also usually provided an immediate indication of whether the institution was inclined to participate. The conversation was followed the same day by a letter outlining the project in more detail, answering specific questions that were raised in the telephone conversation, introducing the fieldworker (through a copy of his or her vita), and enclosing other documents that may have been requested, such as copies of the project proposal and lists of other members of the team. In a few cases, host institutions wanted to impose special conditions (for example, one dean wanted to coauthor the case study with the fieldworker proposed; another wanted to choose the caseworker himself), but these requests were turned aside without apparent difficulty. In the end, eleven of the twelve institutions in the sample agreed to participate, and the stage was set for the beginning of fieldwork in September 1974.

If some of the institutions were hesitant, so were the researchers. Although a high proportion of the first choices for the team accepted, about half did so with reservations of various kinds. What these added up to was the message: "Well, it sounds interesting, even exciting, but I'll need a better sense of what I'm getting into before I can make a long-term commitment." Some were involved in competing projects, others were not sure their teaching schedules could be juggled, and still others had sabbaticals coming up. But all agreed to come to the first meeting. There was a price, however, for admission to that first meeting of the team, scheduled for late October: Each person was asked to make a visit to the field site before the team gathered, and to come prepared to report on it. A dull meeting would be a poor beginning. The best way to launch the project, as well as to insure a lively conversation, would be to begin with reports from the field, with opportunities for everyone to learn and teach on an equal footing. For the team's three-day meeting, held at a country inn in upstate New York, I had two principal outcomes in mind. The first was to secure commitments to the project on the part of those who came as "maybes." The second was to reach an agreement to share field notes. Near the end of the meeting, with some reluctance on the part of one or two members, we did reach that agreement, and our decision was to have important consequences for the team. It meant that members would be in virtually continuous communication between meetings, that peer pressures would operate to ensure fairly high levels of performance with respect to field work at each site, and that each would have an overview of developments.

The decision to share field notes led to one unexpected outcome, and that was to bar representatives of FIPSE from any of our meetings. Our team members felt that their presence would inhibit our discussions, since we could not share confidential field notes with them. Furthermore, even if FIPSE staff members were excluded from discussions of confidential material, our team felt that their presence at our meetings would destroy the researcher's credibility at each site (or at least at sites with grants from FIPSE), since the researcher would inevitably be suspect as a "spy" under those conditions, despite claims to the contrary. This outcome was troubling, since I had told FIPSE staff members that they could attend project meetings as observers, and I had also pointed out to the team that representatives of private foundations often attended meetings of projects they funded. But it quickly became clear that members of the team were unconvinced and felt strongly otherwise. Although I knew that this stand would cause distress at FIPSE, I concluded that to force my view was both untenable and undesirable if one wanted a team of colleagues who would share responsibility for the project rather than a set of "hired hands" who would passively do one's bidding. (See Roth, 1966, for a candid critique of the latter approach. Roth notes that "the product the hired hand turns out is not in any sense his. He does not design it, make any of the decisions about producing it or the conditions under which it will be produced, or what will be done with it after it is produced. The worker is interested in doing just enough to get by.")

Perhaps the best indicator of the outcome of the meeting was that within a few weeks all those who had not yet signed their contracts did so. Each promised to do ten to twelve days of fieldwork at his or her site each year, to participate in three of four team meetings annually, to write a case study, and to assist the project director in developing a conceptual framework for the study of the competence-based movement. Field notes at first trickled in but quickly became a torrent (more than two thousand pages in the first year), giving each researcher the sense, as Peter Elbow expressed it, "of having eaten a large dinner but not having had a chance to digest it." Such indigestion is endemic to fieldwork, but the discomfort was more acute in this instance because of the relatively large number of sites initially involved and the part-time commitments of the researchers, all of whom had other major responsibilities in addition to their work on the project. Individual assignments were budgeted on the average at about thirty-three consultant days a year, but team members often "donated" twice as many days to the project as they were paid for—a fact that had to be emphasized repeatedly to the FIPSE staff during budget negotiations, understandably sensitive as they were to Philistine attacks on presumably overpaid "jet-set" researchers.

A Search for Methods

Although a number of important decisions had been reached at the first meeting, some matters were left open quite intentionally. No interview guide had yet been developed, nor even a topical outline for case studies. To a large degree, each researcher was encouraged to interpret the broad aims of the proposal by his or her lights; no formulas or guidelines were presented as to what was meant by "the conceptualization of programs in competence-based education." (I expected to learn a great deal about what was relevant to such a movement by simply sifting the varied interpretations of researchers, who would differ among themselves about what was relevant.) One of the critical differences between qualitatively and quantitatively oriented researchers (if we may use those tired and inadequate terms for a moment) is that the latter generally assume that they know the nature of the system they are sampling. They seek to refine understanding of the system and to provide data to correct or improve its functioning—in other words, they seek prediction and control (Habermas, 1971, pp. 309–310). In contrast, qualitatively-oriented researchers do not assume they know the nature of the system. Their purpose is to discover and to describe it in such a way that the participants recognize it as a portrait of their world—a portrait that, if well done, will contain features the participants themselves may not have fully discerned. They seek not primarily to improve prediction and control of the system but to provide knowledge for more informed and conscious choices.

Members of the team were representative of the humanistic disciplines and the humanistically oriented social sciences, rather than such "hard" or quantitatively oriented disciplines as experimental psychology or economics. Thus the very terms *qualitative* or *quantitative* did not carry much weight with most members, although the more theoretically conscious sociologists among them were likely to refer to themselves as advocates of the qualitative school, more specifically as symbolic interactionists or practitioners of naturalistic sociology. These sociologists were by no means opposed to survey research or quantitative methods and in fact had used such techniques in the past, but they deemed them inappropriate as the primary form of investigation in this instance. All members of the team shared a view of the world that emphasized willful human agency—they saw the world as open and informed by human choice, as continually being remade. The team also agreed to explore topics by means of a free and relatively unstructured set of observational activities. A wide range of data would be sought from interviews, analysis of documents, and observation of meetings and classes, as well as through team visits. Each researcher would seek to describe the conceptualization and evolution of a particular competence-based program with the consciousness that his or her description would, as one piece of a mosaic, help us to understand and assess the nature of a much broader movement. There was a consensus that one ought to take a very liberal view, particularly in the initial stages of the inquiry, about what might be relevant to such an understanding. Though none of the team members was a professional anthropologist, most would have agreed with Malinowski that it is best to embark on fieldwork guided only by a "foreshadowed notion" of problem areas that may prove interesting.

As the notes began to flow back to Syracuse to be reproduced and distributed by mail to all, the variety of "foreshadowed notions" became evident. Each member of the team was analyzing the evolution of a competence-based program through a unique lens ground out of his or her training and interests. Thomas Ewens, a philosopher with psychoanalytic training, paid especial attention to the hermeneutics of the program at Alverno—when and with what kind of understandings did persons there begin to use the word *competence* and how did those understandings evolve over time? Zelda Gamson, long interested in the processes of innovation in higher education, was particularly sensitive to the ways that an innovation fulfilled institutional needs. John Watt, an historian, paid more careful attention than most other members to early documents and memoranda of competence movements. Virginia Olesen, a sociologist of the symbolic interactionist persuasion, inquired into how meanings were socially constructed by participants. David Riesman raised questions about the boundaries of the investigation by initially considering the widest possible context for understanding competence-based reforms. Peter Elbow, ever the humanist convinced of the need to honor concrete human experience and skeptical of abstract formulations of any kind, challenged all of us repeatedly, as he did by letter in responding to an earlier version of this chapter: "You talk as though it was interesting because we each had a different method—but some of us had no method at all—didn't know what a method looked like if it hit us in the face—we were scared and had a sense of not knowing which end was up."

Each researcher reading the notes was influenced to some degree by the foreshadowed notions of the others. In some cases, the awareness was expressly reflected in the notes by a comment that so-and-so would have approached an interview quite differently. (Over time, the parenthetical asides in the notes constituted a playful commentary on our various styles as fieldworkers, with all the private jokes and shorthand reference to signal events that one might find in a correspondence among good friends.) Or in team meetings, objections might be made to the use of specialized perspectives, such as psychoanalytic categories, that seemed inappropriate to analyze a particular phenomenon. Intersubjectivity or mutual infiltration of perspectives began to be operative on the consciousness of the group as a whole and to influence the way we established frameworks of analysis. Quite intentionally, there were no restrictions at the beginning as to the range of observations or to the way of generating the categories of observations. But at the end of the first year, some priorities had to be established and some limits set. Zelda Gamson devised a case study guide, and the group adopted it with few changes as a minimal outline of topics that every case study ought to treat. From the beginning, the necessity of some such guide was recognized, although members of the team varied in their eagerness or willingness to establish such categories at earlier stages. From another perspective, of course, this interdisciplinary, inductive approach could be seen as rather aimless mucking around, and such suspicions did play a role in a major crisis the team confronted, an event to be discussed in more detail later.

This guide helped structure the case studies without crushing flexibility of approach or overly restricting any researcher's decisions about salient themes at his or her site, and it undoubtedly reduced anxiety for some of the team members who had never written a case study. It was a straightforward outline of the basic content that the case studies should include: a description of the institution (size, character of faculty and students, significant academic structures, administrative and financial support patterns), an account of who introduced the competence-based program and of how it had developed, a specification of the competencies adopted and their rationale, a description of the ways faculty sought to assess competence in students, and an assessment of the scope and impact of the program. Some kinds of data might never have been collected in a uniform manner without development of the guide, although even at the end some gaps remained.

Fieldwork

The first and last (tenth) meetings of the team were the only two at which the team did not spend at least part of the time in fieldwork at one of the sites in the study. In a typical three- or four-day meeting, a day or a day and a half would be spent in fieldwork by all twelve members of the research team. Prior to the meeting, team members would have been receiving field notes from the worker at that site, along with catalogues and other relevant documents. The researcher responsible for that site, assisted by the project staff, arranged the fieldwork schedule, setting up appointments for interviews, arranging for classroom visits or access to files or records. At institutions such as the College for Human Services or Antioch Law School where students spent time in internships, arrangements were also made for up to half the team to accompany students to their field assignments. The researcher responsible for that site was told to look upon the entire team as research assistants for the portion of the meeting spent in fieldwork. Members of the team varied in the specificity of their directives, but in general schedules were arranged with care and always produced a bountiful harvest of field notes for the case writer. The team was mixed not only in its disciplinary affiliation but in background, age, and avocational competences, all of which were taken into account in fieldwork assignments. At Florida State, for example, two research assistants in their twenties talked with students, whereas David Riesman talked with the president and senior administrative officials on the campus. John Watt, an accomplished amateur musician, interviewed faculty in the music program, and Virginia Olesen, who had previously done participant observation in a nursing school, talked to the faculty in nursing. Thus the case writer could see and hear through others what might otherwise be denied him or her because of age or biology or the lack of common interests or expertise with those being interviewed. Teamwork of this kind is not unusual, of course, and consulting firms on contract to the government frequently put such teams in the field. But these are likely to be ad hoc teams thrown together for single visits, unable to develop the kinds of symbiotic relationships that the project team engendered over three years.

Some aspects of our method were invented on the spot and later formalized. For example, at the first team fieldwork visit to my own site, the College for Human Services, colleagues began spontaneously to question me about ambiguities or lacunae in my field notes. How did this event relate to that? Had I interviewed such a person about a particular event? Had I observed any of the sessions at which students were assessed on their performance of "constructive actions," as the performance tests were called at the college? Questions like these were later placed on the formal agenda of our meetings under the heading of "the witness box." They served the purpose of getting all members of the team sensitized to the fieldwork and as a means of constructive criticism of the fieldwork in an atmosphere that enabled the caseworker to think through the case freshly, often providing him or her with new insights into the latent significance of events. Use of the "witness box" was only a heightened form of the mutual adjustment that characterized the project as a whole. Each member's prejudices were open to correction by others, mitigating the dangers of bias that are present in all social research, as well as of the impressionism that, given our modes of work, was a particular problem for the team.

The team did not hold its meetings at the college being visited, and usually stayed at a hotel nearby. On the night preceding the fieldwork, the team invited everyone who would be interviewed the next day to a cocktail party at the hotel. This eased entrance of the team into the site, serving to introduce the researchers as persons, not just human tape recorders. At later stages of our research, when we had drafts of papers, representatives of the host institution were invited to join our discussions. In addition, we made an effort to provide feedback to those at the site. This sometimes took the form of presentations by members of the team, followed by questions from faculty and administrators, or of a private report by the case writer, either in person or by letter following the visit. The meetings usually ended with a postmortem analysis of the field experience, although some members of the team urged colleagues to save such analysis for field notes unfiltered by the group discussion. Some members managed to dictate their field notes during breaks between interviews or late in the evening the same day. In other cases retrieval had to be postponed until a day or two later, but long delays between experiences in the field and the recording of notes were not common, and the exceptions were usually quite noticeable in the quality of the notes.

I attempted to respond by letter to field notes as they came in during the first year, giving encouragement, making suggestions for next steps, and occasionally offering interpretations. As time went on, members of the team sometimes responded to each other's notes, and David Riesman in particular was extraordinarily conscientious in this respect. I tried to keep in touch with all members of the team by telephone and through memoranda, and there was a mailing of some kind virtually every week, whether a packet of field notes, a memo, or a journal article or two.

This was not traditional participant-observation in which a researcher might spend months or even years immersed in the local "culture." Most case studies were written on the basis of thirty days of fieldwork (including the team visit as the equivalent of ten to twelve "days"), and perhaps another fifteen to twenty days were spent in analysis of documents and materials from the site. Full-time participant-observation would have been prohibitively expensive, and it is questionable how much more would have been learned for our purposes. A more traditional anthropological style of fieldwork usually comes at a point early in a researcher's career—when the researcher is less rooted to a particular place or position and less expensive to employ. Fieldworkers at that point are also less experienced and knowledgeable. The project team was able to maximize experience and comparative scope through the part-time, in-and-out style we adopted. Such experience is invaluable in order to pierce what House (1974) has called the "ideology inherent in many proposals and regarded as absolutely indispensable in securing . . . funds because it says what the sponsors want to hear." In fact, because so much of the paper flowing between sites and Washington agencies is a semantic screen, an important function of the kind of research the project team engaged in is to get people talking more honestly and less grandiosely about the actual problems in the field, which are often obscured in the elaborate and mandatory "progress" reports. For example, David Riesman pointed out that experimenters at Florida State University felt they had to over-promise in order to meet FIPSE's expectations about expansion of their program, expectations that FIPSE later said it did not have. Experimenters at the site and officials in Washington were each, to some degree, acting with misperceptions of the other. As Virginia Olesen noted, the project team's style of research maximized both continuity, giving each researcher a three-year view of developments at his own and others' sites, and flexibility, enabling each field-worker to adjust strategies to the site and to periodically reassess the depth and frequency of data gathering. It demanded intensive and exhausting bursts of fieldwork, however, with the need for each researcher to pay attention to maintaining lines of communication with the site between trips. In such a fast-paced style in the field, as Olesen observed in a memorandum, every minute has a "data weight" attached to it: "One must move very quickly very early, which poses keen interactional skills, the possibility of inaccurate judgments, and the risks of failures or mistakes with little leeway to smooth over or patch up."

By the end of the first year, some members of the project were eager to discuss ways of integrating our findings and of achieving greater comparability of data. Based on a reading of the first six months of field notes, I drafted an outline of what seemed to be the emergent issues or critical features of competence-based education. To these I added other questions that I felt ought to be addressed in any intelligent analysis of the movement. Questions to be addressed were arranged under eight categories, or, as they came to be called later, critical issues. These dealt with such issues as images of competence, problems of acquiring and assessing com-petence, and the limits of the faculty's role in developing compe-tence. This was a rudimentary, first-level attempt to identify some of the major lines of inquiry. For example, the following questions came under the topic of the limits of the faculty's role:

- What is not teachable? Or what can be taught directly, what only indirectly?
- Can affective qualities be taught or stipulated as competencies? Can one speak of a competent lover, a competent mother?

- What are the logical levels of competence? What are differences of degree, what of kind, as one moves from the more specific to the more generic, from being a competent auto mechanic to a competent university president?
- Can one speak only of discrete competencies, or is it possible to specify the configuration, that is, how they are integrated?

I hoped that most members of the team would analyze some critical feature of competence-based education and write a paper about it in addition to his or her case study. While retaining responsibility for a particular case, each member would come to have a "specialty" in team fieldwork as we moved across all the sites. One member might pay particular attention to problems of assessment, and another to the processes of change generated by competence-based reforms. Although the outline was only a preliminary draft of what the final report might look like, most team members gave it a cool reception. The outline was interesting, but it was "too early" to begin to sort out the major issues. A few resisted the idea of doing such papers at all. They felt the report ought to have an introduction, a set of case studies, and a concluding summary chapter. Most agreed with the necessity for papers that analyzed the movement at a more general level, but a significant number felt that these should come after the case studies were completed. I agreed with the logic of such a view but argued that to wait until cases were written at the end of the second year of the study would crowd too much into the final year. Since the budget provided for only a fixed number of team meetings each year, I felt the team needed to use these to develop analyses and to criticize drafts. I believed in Rosalie Wax's (1971) realistic rule of thumb: Allow at least as much time for analysis and writing as one does for fieldwork. Hence, at the midpoint of the project (December 1975), writing ought to be underway, even though fieldwork would continue.

With the blessings of hindsight, one can see that such resistance to what were perceived as "laid on" topics (even though largely derived from the members' own field notes) was predictable. A project director should expect professionals to underscore their claims to autonomy and to exhibit the human tendency to be cautious in assuming specific responsibilities. Owing to my inexperience as an administrator, I did not realize this at the time, but my colleagues let me learn on the job. I decided, at any rate, to withdraw the outline because of the dissatisfaction it caused, but I also asked everyone to think more about it and respond by memo. What actually ensued was a negotiation process in which, by letter and phone, I began to sound out members about their preferences. I encouraged some to follow through on their first thoughts and discouraged others, according to my estimates of their strengths and capabilities. By the June 1975 meeting, most had staked out some general topic, and by the fall meeting some had submitted preliminary outlines of topics mutually agreed upon. At the same time fieldwork assignments increasingly reflected these preferences. Peter Elbow, for example, wanted to write about the way the advent of a competence-based program changes a faculty member's perception of his or her role, and so he spent much of his time in team fieldwork observing teachers at work and talking to them about such matters.

Renegotiation of the Project

The first year-end meeting developed into a confrontation with FIPSE over issues of who would "guide" the project towards what ends. It proved to be the first round in a crisis that would play itself out over the second year of the project. With the exception of the disgruntlement felt by FIPSE officials at being barred from team meetings, things had gone fairly smoothly for most of the year. Russell Edgerton, deputy director of FIPSE, responded favorably to the first draft of the critical issues (more favorably than the team itself). At a meeting with me midway in the year, he expressed satisfaction that the team had been organized and had begun work in the field with some dispatch, and hinted that although the work might not please everyone, he thought it was not a bad thing to have a group such as ours act as "conservative critics" of the movement. I would have preferred the phrase "unprejudiced critics" or "impartial analysts," but did not object to the word "conservative" if by that he meant the team had not been hired to promote competence-based education.

By late spring, however, somewhat different and mixed signals were emanating from FIPSE. In a discussion of budget proposals for the second-year renewal of the project, Edgerton and others at FIPSE expressed dissatisfaction with the project's approach to the critical issues, and one officer wondered whether the result would not be "just a bunch of essays" that had little connection with fieldwork. There was also criticism that it was unclear what the outcomes of the project would be and who would benefit from the research. Edgerton complained that at least some of the persons at the study sites were "confused." Since the members of the project were scheduled to meet in Washington in June in connection with team fieldwork at Antioch School of Law, a meeting with the FIPSE staff was scheduled. A week or two before the meeting, the FIPSE staff received draft copies of a report about the origins and current directions of FIPSE, prepared by two project team research assistants who, as part of the study, had interviewed FIPSE staff members about their role in the competence-based education movement. The report raised the temperature of the ensuing discussions close to the boiling point. Not surprisingly, it showed that experiments in competence-based education had claimed the largest proportion of FIPSE's budget in the preceding year but that the staff held varied opinions as to the nature and purpose of competence-based education—some perceiving it as a means to undermine a course-credit, time-served approach to earning a college degree, others as a means of institutional reform, and still others as a cost-cutting device. The report also indicated what was being fairly widely discussed among insiders in various Washington educational agencies at that time, namely that FIPSE might be absorbed in the new National Institute of Education and that its staff itself was divided about the pro and cons of such a reorganization. Although this was only a passing comment—three lines in a sixteen-page report—it angered at least one top FIPSE official, who told a member of the project team that the report could be used as a damaging document in a bureaucratic fight over FIPSE because it showed that its own staff was divided on one of its major special efforts. From the official's perspective, there were no such differences among staff members, and yet discussions with his staff during lunch prior to the meeting confirmed these differences of opinion. After lunch, the project team and the FIPSE staff were joined by Sister Austin Doherty of Alverno College, one of the sites in the study. She opened the discussion by asking members of the project team what, after nearly a year's study, they had learned. What could they tell her that would be helpful? Such a seemingly plausible question found no ready response. Instead, several of us explained that the team was still trying to sort out many issues and was consciously keeping an open mind about them, rather than trying to draw conclusions. Looking back, it is painfully obvious that this was the first direct encounter in a conflict that we did not comprehend in its full dimensions until much later. We should have anticipated that inductively oriented researchers would not be especially welcome in a movement dedicated to attaining more explicit statements of educational outcomes. In a sense, we were violating the central dogma of the movement we were studying. We were the enemy within the gate. (Although this conflict could not have been avoided, since it centered on our method, it might have been mitigated if I could have given more substantive responses. Researchers in the inductively oriented mode should anticipate that participants being studied will want some hints about the kinds of hypotheses that are beginning to form and ought to give them at least a general account as soon as they can.)

The discussion then turned to an expansion of themes that had been raised earlier by Edgerton in his talks with me, particularly the issue of what audience would benefit from our research. This reopened the question of the degree to which the project was primarily conceived as a form of technical assistance to the institutions under study or as an analysis of the underlying issues of competence-based education and their import for reform of higher education. Although a confrontation is not always the best way to approach an issue, I felt that pressure was building to reorient the project toward the former position, and I drew a hard line, saying the project could not serve those ends in the way some members of FIPSE's staff wished. In order to do so, the team would have to be selected on entirely different criteria (on their expertise in assessment or in particular curriculum areas, for example, rather than on their qualities as observers and analysts), and the project reconceived. The team, as presently constituted, could not succeed in either aim if it tried to do both. Underlying the discussion of this and a number of other issues was the plea that the team "open up" to include both practitioners and members of FIPSE's staff in future meetings.

The discussion revealed that FIPSE itself was divided about the worth and future directions of the project, and it seemed that positions for or against various definitions of the project were implicated in struggles for ascendancy within the agency. At the same time, differences of style and temperament were beginning to appear among members of the research team; under the pressure of fieldwork and the confrontation with FIPSE tempers had flared on several occasions. On the question of "opening up," for example, the team was divided; some members felt that to bring others to our meetings might violate confidentiality or too severely limit the scarce time the team had for its own work, while others felt that the practical and moral necessity to be responsive to FIPSE's concerns was overriding. The seams that had begun to show (in an earlier session one team member had heatedly attacked another for failing to properly plan the team's fieldwork at his site) now were beginning to pull apart. In such a situation, one should neither change one's suit too hastily nor pretend that nothing is amiss. One needs to look closely at the points of stress and decide what can be pulled together and what should give way to a new arrangement. Fortunately, the team had a final day to discuss matters privately. Out of that discussion came the agreement that we would hold to our definition of the project—even if this risked renewal of the project—and not attempt to accommodate demands to provide technical assistance, since we could not possibly fulfill them. A compromise was reached on the issue of opening our team meetings to others: it was decided that guests would be invited to every other meeting but that the number would be limited so as not to swamp the team or drain the energies of the central staff in conference planning.

In the weeks following the Washington meeting, FIPSE made two "suggestions." One would have required dismissing a member of the team on the grounds that her site was not really a competence-based experiment. The other, made somewhat later, was that I share an "edited version" of the field notes with the case study institutions as a way of providing feedback at the end of the first year. I declined to do either. In the first instance, I noted that the institution cited was selected largely on the grounds that it had given signs of moving toward a competence-based program. Hence, it provided a unique opportunity to observe an institution in transition. One would be able to learn just as much by discovering why the faculty turned away from competence-based modes as if they eventually embraced them. Arguing from analogy in the second instance, I asked how the FIPSE staff would feel if an edited version of notes taken by the project team during its interview of that staff were furnished to the head of Health, Education, and Welfare? The case study was intended to be the edited version of the field notes. But the agency's officer insisted that, although the proposal had specified a two-year deadline, an interim report was needed because some persons in the institutions were unclear about the purpose and "character" of the investigation. I was not then aware of such confusions, although I would later hear that complaint from the president of Alverno College. I noted that most members of the project had provided feedback during and after field visits but that they would not consider edited field notes an appropriate form of feedback. At the official's request, I did agree to ask members who had not yet made a report to do so in a manner each considered appropriate.

Thomas Ewens, the fieldworker at Alverno College, had also begun to hear complaints that the project had not lived up to its promises to provide feedback, but no one on the team was prepared for the crisis that ensued. Precisely in order to be responsive to requests for information, the meeting at Alverno in September 1975 included guests from four other sites as well as members of Alverno's faculty. An early draft of the chapter on competence in the liberal arts had been prepared by Ewens for the meeting, but president Read declared it was "nondiscussable." She queried us on what we meant by "competence-based education." Our response that this was the object of the study—precisely to discover what was signified by numerous initiatives being made under the label of "competence-based education"—was dismissed as unsatisfactory. Furthermore, project members could not respond to a request from a FIPSE official that we attempt on the spot a comparative analysis of the types of programs we were examining, since the logic of the work required that we complete the cases in the spring of 1976 and not begin comparative analysis until the third year.

This meeting was perhaps the low point of the project; members left it feeling frustrated and partially defeated. If anything, it confirmed the wisdom of those who had argued in June that we should resist demands to provide "feed" we didn't have. Alverno College called a moratorium on further field work by Thomas Ewens until it received a report on the team's fieldwork. We sent a forty-three-page report several weeks later but never received a reaction to it. In December, Alverno withdrew from the study. President Read politely explained that Alverno did not wish to be included in a study of competence-based education because it feared such inclusion would misrepresent the nature of its "Alverno Learning Process," as the faculty had come to prefer to describe its curriculum. But four other issues seem to have been involved. Although they took their most dramatic form at Alverno, they were not unique to that college, and in one form or another they are likely to arise in all research of this type. They are: (1) the actual or perceived role of the researcher as an agent of change, (2) the threat the researcher poses to the institution's image management, (3) the problem of exchange or reciprocity, and (4) the question of who defines the focus of the investigation. Each of them warrants at least brief attention.

The Researcher as Change Agent. Any researcher coming fresh into an environment has the potential for upsetting the local ecology. The power to ask questions can be used irresponsibly, and even when exercised with care can be perceived as a revolutionary act, as Socrates learned. With the aim of understanding the early conceptualization of the competence program at Alverno, Ewens began his work by conducting a set of extraordinarily perceptive interviews with a wide sampling of informants, including early opponents of the program. He had, of course, gone to the faculty dropouts (some of whom considered themselves "force-outs") who had resigned when the leadership at Alverno decided to put the entire college into the competence-based format. By the end of the first year's research, President Joel Read posed the issue as follows in a letter to Ewens:

> If . . . you take a statement from one of the persons you interviewed here at Alverno and attempt to cross-check it around the institution, it is altogether possible to raise what might have been only one person's

question into that of many persons, and thus, to make it an operative dynamic across the institution. Raising questions to levels of consciousness can be a fine art of manipulation or an unconscious politicization or both or neither. But, a person moving freely within an institution, responsible to no one but him or herself, and whose data is said to be held confidentially, can create an institution-wide dynamic which is outside the scope of management unless those responsible know that this is being done. Rumor [and] gossip . . . operate in most institutions and we all survive them like the bacteria we carry within our own organism. But, to deliberately introduce a free agent with the potential to make certain attitudes, approaches, perceptions more sharply focused and thus capable of altering the direction of an institution, can be downright dangerous—perhaps even irresponsible on the part of those answerable for the direction of the institution.

In an earlier letter, President Read had asked for a "clarification" of Ewens' role, saying, "There is a question then as to your position when you seem to be adopting the position of advocate of a particular point of view that exists within the college." In reply, Ewens denied that he was the advocate of any position and was astonished that his interviews would be so interpreted. With regard to her concern that he might be "complicating . . . the management of change," Ewens wrote:

With regard to your last paragraph, I can only say again that the role of a fieldworker is a difficult one. I am trying to observe a complicated process of change. But of course one cannot merely observe; one's presence, one's questions, one's reactions and interactions inevitably inflect upon and in some minimal way enter into the process itself. I would hope that this does not interfere with the task of those who are trying to manage the change. Indeed I think that the presence of a reasonably discreet outside observer may well facilitate that process in a number of different ways; it can give perspective; it can be therapeutic in allowing hostile or otherwise recalcitrant faculty to express their points of view; it can on occasion lead to new and fruitful questions being pursued. . . . As far as I am concerned, I hope some of these positive, auxiliary outcomes may be brought about, particularly now that I am beginning to know something of your situation at Alverno and of the situations at other institutions which are grappling with some of the same enormously difficult problems. Of course, I cannot guarantee these outcomes any more than I can warrant that unexpected and undesired outcomes will not advene; in neither case do they depend on me only.

Insofar as the research team could determine in its visit to Alverno College during 1975, Ewens had not in any way assumed an advocate's role nor had he been perceived as doing so by faculty. Yet I was told by one of the leaders of the competence-based experiment that she could not understand why Ewens "spent so much time looking into the dark corners" and (to her) so little time interviewing the "central persons." She went on, quite angrily, to say that she was "sick and tired" of hearing "over and over again" how the administration had supposedly "forced the program down everyone's throat." To some degree, an observer who interviews dropouts does stir up old scores and, no doubt, old guilts. But he or she may do this in an entirely unobtrusive way, serving as a neutral conduit of messages that otherwise would not reach the top because only the inflated "good" news that the leadership wants to hear gets passed up through official channels. Participant-observers often do give voice to those whose grievances have been officially silenced. For example, one of the nurses who was fired in the struggle recounted in Virginia Olesen's account of the competence-based program at Mt. Hood Community College wrote to her: "You and your case history were very important to us—made us feel that what we had accomplished was good and what we did was right."

The Threat to Image Management. Suspicions that researchers on the team were grinding special axes arose at other sites, and concern about the political impact of research was always present even when relations between institution and researchers were most cordial. Every institution is concerned about "image management" as well as "management of change." Just as researchers can arouse anxiety by altering or establishing new channels of communication internally, they present the even more potent threat of giving a less-than-flattering profile of the institution to the external world. Even if we set aside the problem of false or distorted representation, selective attention to one aspect of institutional life, no matter how sensitively portrayed, may be resented. In Alverno's case, it did seem odd for the president, after receiving numerous grants for the development of a curriculum publicly announced as competence-based, to cite as a principal reason for her withdrawal from our study that Alverno did not belong in our sample. Yet a president has a legitimate obligation—neglected at peril—to present the most favorable and attractive image of the institution to students, potential donors, and public agencies; and the competence-based label increasingly came to be perceived as a liability at Alverno. The public, however, also has a legitimate right to responsible accounts by qualified observers of educational experiments supported by their tax (and tuition) dollars, no matter what labels they appear under.

The question of the political impact of research goes deeper than issues of labels or cosmetics. The question of manipulation raised by President Read with reference to Ewens' interviewing can also be raised in relation to the institution's attempt to use the researcher for what it considers worthy ends. This dynamic also played itself out at several institutions in the study, most notably at the College for Human Services, where Dean Stephen Sunderland and, to a lesser degree, President Audrey Cohen were highly conscious of the potential impact of my research. A series of discussions with Sunderland came to a head when he made plain that he would not tolerate my presence if he did not think the College for Human Services would eventually benefit from my work. Expanding on this theme in a letter, Sunderland wrote that he viewed the relationship as a potential conversion experience: "I see you as part of a strategy that the college wishes to use to spread the word about the college's good works . . . and as a potential convert to the form of education and assessment that we see as necessary for a different kind of professional, social, and intellectual world." Sunderland was continually on guard whenever I was in the field, questioning "enterprises such as yours in terms of their usefulness in meeting the change goals of the college." At one point, he ushered me out of a tense meeting called by dissatisfied students on the pretext that my personal safety would be endangered, although I had previously established good relations with the students and was in fact invited to the meeting by them. It required several meetings with President Cohen for me to obtain permission to interview sources without "chaperonage" provided by Sunderland and to establish other ground rules I regarded as essential for responsible research, including access to records and random interviews with students and field supervisors.

The sharing of field notes by members of the project team was challenged by President Cohen, who wanted to know what images of the College for Human Services I conveyed to colleagues after my periodic visits to the college. She wanted an opportunity to counter any misleading information at an early stage. When I responded that to share notes with her would compromise confidentiality with sources, she argued that since they were being shared with others (that is, fellow researchers), why not with her? The analogy that I drew—that it was like doctors discussing notes about a patient in confidence—did not carry much weight with her since the College for Human Services sought egalitarian reforms in the professions that would deemphasize such claims of privilege on the part of professionals, whether they were doctors or researchers. In effect, the project team was not treating her as an equal! Realizing my analogy was a weak argument to advance in her court, I thus defended restricted circulation on other grounds, namely that field notes had a diarylike quality. They were dictated as "raw" material, often full of contradictions, free associations, conjectures, and highly tentative first interpretations to be checked against other evidence and subsequent observations. As president of the college, her memos to the faculty were public, but when she shared insights in meetings with a "kitchen cabinet" about various aspects of life in the college, such privileged conversations among a few intimates would be analogous to the sharing that went on among our team members through field notes. In such conversations, for example, a close colleague might tell her that one of her ideas was farfetched; team members similarly were able to open themselves to collegial criticism in this way.

Even social scientists do not always share raw field notes, however, and the perception that this practice gave a quasi-public character to interviews was troubling to others. President Joel Read, after a lengthy talk with Ewens about how the struggles within her religious community had affected reforms at Alverno, wrote: "I need some clarification on field notes. First of all, does everything become a part of field notes—that is, substance of conversations and so forth? Secondly, are all field notes of each project circulated to all other researchers on the other projects? What led to my questions was our lengthy discussion of the relation of my religious community to Alverno. I was willing to discuss that with you because of your background . . . but knowing the general lack of information, much less general lack of understanding of what religious congregations are all about, I did not consider our conversation a source for field notes. But I understand that some 200 pages of field notes already exist on us. I'd appreciate your comment."

Thomas Ewens, like most members of our project, had let it be known in conversations with sources that field notes were being shared in a confidential way among researchers. His reply could stand as a sensitive account of the discretion and self-censorship that members of the team exercised as they attempted to protect individuals even in such privileged communications as field notes:

> What goes into field notes varies widely depending on who is dictating them. Some are brief and laconic; others are quite detailed. Since conversations are a large part of the fieldwork, the substance of conversations is generally noted. Notes are circulated among the immediate members of our group with the understanding that they are strictly confidential. I have made this clear to everybody at Alverno who has asked me and almost everybody has. This is, of course, an extremely delicate matter and places the most stringent requirements of confidentiality and discretion on each one of us. It is, I think, because our group and the institutions which have agreed to cooperate with us share, in principle, the same commitment to the search for truth and understanding that our project, project members and, by im-

plication at least, our *modus operandi* were accepted to begin with.

With regard to our far-ranging conversation in July and other similar conversations: you and your colleagues have been extremely open with me and I have been told many things, often very intimate and personal, that I consider nobody else's business and would not put in any notes. There is a fine and delicate and supple discretion to be exercised here which would strain anybody's resources of practical wisdom. As a matter of fact I consider the background, history, habits, structures, goals and dynamics of the School Sisters of St. Francis an important factor in the changes that have and are being wrought at Alverno, as does almost everybody I have talked to. Nobody has spoken as insightfully and incisively as you have on certain aspects of that context; it has been very helpful to my own understanding and I would consider it important to share that understanding with others in an appropriate way.

The Problem of Reciprocity. In the end, the refusal of the team to supply field notes to Alverno was seen by its leaders as another indication of the project team's unwillingness to "interact" or provide what they considered adequate feedback. The issue of exchange or reciprocity—of what benefit the host institution receives in turn for its gifts of time, energy, and access to the researcher—has become increasingly salient in all forms of research. It is not unheard of today for researchers to be asked literally to buy their way in, even to pay for interviews or to promise that any royalties or proceeds from the research will be donated to a cause designated by the hosts. Researchers on projects of the type described here are sometimes referred to as "jet-setters," and are occasionally perceived in stereotypical terms as talking only to other researchers, mostly airborne like themselves, and serving no earthly practical purposes. No institution in the study demanded reciprocity in these terms, but the question of the quality and type of feedback provided was an issue in varying degree at most institutions, and most keenly at Alverno. After the Washington meeting in June 1975, Sister Austin Doherty asserted to Ewens that the project was not making good on its promises of feedback, and in September president Read told me that no one in our group seemed interested in giving feedback. "Are we just data?" she asked. "Why don't you want to interact?" In October, she told Ewens, "What I am telling you is that I don't want you to come out here until we have received some information. We have been very open and public; we have denied you nothing. But we do not know what your group is about." She insisted to Ewens that she wanted "more free sharing of information" as the research went on. Ewens indicated that this would be done in the case study the following spring but that he could not make daily reports, as it were, on his interviewing.

In response to concerns expressed at Alverno and from officials at FIPSE, I wrote to all institutions in the study, reemphasizing the provisions for sharing information in the study. I noted that institutions would be invited to criticize its conceptual framework, that special efforts at feedback would be made after each team visit, that each institution would have an opportunity to criticize early drafts of the case study, and that practitioners would be invited to join members of the project for discussion and development of the critical issues. President Read did not regard this letter as resolving differences over the feedback issue: "There is a difference of opinion regarding the methodology and approach of the task force, vis-à-vis the institutions participating in the project. . . . What is the evaluation intended to accomplish? What is its purpose? Who are the audiences? . . . To date, it is not possible to know where the project members are 'coming from.' While a general position on methodology is enunciated in the Case Study Guide, a working statement of your 'collective' philosophy of education and the current state of higher education is left to inference."

Questions about where the researcher is "coming from" often arise in participant observer studies and may reflect the simple human desire to know whether the observer is friend or foe, certainly an open issue in Sunderland's approach to me at the College for Human Services. But that did not seem to be the issue in the same sense at Alverno. In a five-page reply, I indicated that the inductive method used by the team, while loosely modeled on

Parlett's illuminative evaluation, allowed for differences of style and approach. I did not regard it as imperative for the group to share a " 'collective' philosophy of education." On the contrary, members were selected in part because they represented different views and perspectives, and each of them agreed to immerse himself or herself in the work of understanding a variety of attempts to conceptualize and practice competence-based curriculums. I noted that working papers on these issues would be prepared by the spring of 1976 and that "we hope they serve to create some useful dialogue among practitioners and ourselves about these issues." Then I turned to president Read's question about what audiences the project was addressing: "The audiences for this work are several. First, the institutions might benefit from sympathetic criticism and from the kinds of feedback described in my recent letter. Potential students might make more informed choices as a result of our work. Teachers and administrators in the broader higher education community may benefit by being able to vicariously 'visit' Alverno or the College for Human Services and other institutions where we are developing case studies. Policy makers may be influenced by our analyses. Those who have an interest in the processes of innovation would be another audience, and researchers with an interest in our methodology yet another."

The Problem of Who Defines the Issues. This question of whether practitioners themselves were the primary audience for the project's work was to receive sharp scrutiny within a few weeks. Institutions in the sample varied enormously, it turned out, in their expectations about the answer. I heard that officials at both Alverno and the College for Human Services were contacting other colleges in the study and raising questions about their continuance in it. At FIPSE, Edgerton warned me of the possibility that other institutions might follow their lead if they pulled out, in which case it would be difficult to justify continued funding of the project. In December, after Alverno did withdraw, Edgerton pressed hard for the point of view that the practitioners were the primary audience for the work and ought to have a major say in determining what issues we analyzed. In his eyes, "the proposal committed the project to a process for determining the issues (coordination of the conceptual framework with the evaluation personnel operating at the program level)' which seemed to guarantee that the issues which your team would concentrate on would be recognizable as important by the practitioners trying to put the programs into place."

Since our research was an inquiry into the actual difficulties practitioners encountered in attempting to conceptualize and devise competence-based instructional programs, members of the team felt that both the cases and the critical issues would be regarded as "important" by practitioners, although they would also reflect to some degree the particular interests and competencies of members of the team. Edgerton felt that some of the critical issues we had identified went too far in the latter direction and would result in essays "driven essentially by the interests of the author." But fair-minded persons could disagree about the degree to which a given critical issue was related to competence programs. For example, Edgerton cited the essay on the antecedents of competence-based education as an example of too tenuous a connection to the investigations at hand, yet members of the project were unanimous in feeling that it was important to trace the backgrounds of the movement, and practitioners, too, expressed considerable interest in the topic.

The argument seemed to turn on the question of what Edgerton meant by the phrase "determining the issues." Did the "guarantee" that practitioners would regard the issues as important mean in effect that he regarded them as holding a veto power over the researchers' definition of the critical issues? I asked him whether he would have refused to fund Abraham Flexner's investigation of medical schools because some practitioners did not regard Flexner's issues as important? Edgerton responded that it would depend partly on the boundaries of Flexner's research as originally agreed upon. I said that the commitments of the project were to consult and coordinate with practitioners but in no way did that imply any veto power. The boundaries of the project were set by the case study investigations, but the responsibility for identifying the emergent critical issues was primarily in our hands as researchers, and this was not a point that should be left ambiguous.

Yet Alverno's withdrawal, combined with the possibility that other institutions would pull out, generated considerable uncertainty about the continuance of the project. I did not want to take such a hard position without careful reflection and after that conversation sought counsel not only with members of the project but with colleagues at Syracuse, including Lawrence DeWitt, Sheila Huff, Bernard Kaplan, Maureen Webster, and Warren Zeigler. For the most part, these were persons who had had experience directing large-scale research projects in the social sciences. While offering helpful advice about strategy, they generally agreed the position we had taken was right in principle.

Edgerton's questions about the process for identifying the critical issues of the study were not naive ones, however. Edgerton had earned a doctor's degree in political science at Columbia and had taught for five years at the University of Wisconsin; he was not methodologically unsophisticated. Yet he was not particularly sympathetic to our method of avoiding prejudgments of realities, allowing issues to emerge, and reformulating the problems as our research proceeded. To us, the study was open-ended in that it permitted us to revise the explanatory scheme as we learned enough to know which variables deserved more attention and which less, as well as to discover hitherto obscure relationships among them. Edgerton wanted to define the boundaries of the research with more clarity and to get "closure" on the "product." We resisted his effort insofar as we perceived it as predetermining the focal issues of the research. Edgerton's warning had been written as a preface to his meeting with the project team scheduled for January 1976 at Florida State University. Considerable tension had built up prior to the meeting, since FIPSE had explicitly put the project on notice that renewal was not at all assured. The following excerpts of our discussion with Edgerton and Corcoran of the FIPSE staff convey some of the subtleties of a classic problem in a government-sponsored research project:

Grant: A good way to start is to ask you [Edgerton] what you see as the crucial, key issues.

Edgerton: I think that in a complex project in which divergent expectations exist within the Fund, your group, among project directors at the sites and between all those different parties . . . it seems to me that the most important thing . . . is to get as much closure as you can from this point forward on the product you are producing and communicate that to us and the project directors. . . . We need a sense of how the parts come together and what is the balance between the case analysis and the issue analysis.

Grant: You and I have talked about how they come together or connect. This morning's discussion (of the issues) was intended to show how we're grappling with these things. But I wonder whether it's a problem not of connective tissue but that you don't like the issues we've got. Your letter implies that the practitioners in these cases ought to have some veto power.

Edgerton: No, not veto power. . . . One of our expectations is that we expected the issues you would settle upon in your cross-site generalizations would be issues which the practitioners would recognize as important.

Riesman: I wanted to help the practitioners. But I ask myself who are the practitioners. The life of practitioners in this field is very short.

Ewens: Yes, what are we talking about. As Peter Elbow points out, what about all those people who think that CBE [competence-based education] is weird . . . if those practitioners are also part of the audience then that should be made very clear.

Edgerton: I think it is a very good point that the Fund may easily overreact to the constituency of the project and to the project directors (at the sites in the study) in particular. . . . But if you had to state a principle for inclusion or exclusion (of issues), what would you state?

Elbow: What is the point of exclusion? You raised some questions [in your letter] on historical background. But if all the project directors thought it was a waste of time to get background, it doesn't make me think so.

Edgerton: I can't imagine all of you not writing things that are valued. That's not the issue. In our view the [research project] had more boundaries, clear criteria of inclusion and exclusion. In the emergent method there are some points where you diverge outside of the study. . . . It's hard to know [from reading the project's statement of

	them] what the critical issues are. . . . I had a sense this morning that you yourselves don't know.
Gamson:	I think we don't know what the critical answers are, but we know what the critical issues are.
Olesen:	There are a lot of emerging themes here. Some of the emerging themes may seem enormously distant, but they are very closely tied to the everyday fieldwork in these sites, and they have emerged out of the definition of what is real for those people in that situation.
Edgerton:	I don't know how seriously you want us and the project directors to take your outline [of the critical issues] at this time.
Riesman:	Not as seriously as you did.
Edgerton:	How seriously should we take what you take seriously? We're talking about a kind of uneasy and turbulent environment and in some cases distrust.
Grant:	We had one institution withdraw. I don't see the distrust that you see. Most people understand what a case study is and what we are doing.
Olesen:	Russ [Edgerton], I want to take serious challenge on that issue. I don't think the rest of us [other than Alverno] have had problems of mistrust. But the fact that I could get in Mt. Hood after a serious rupture last summer indicates there is a modicum of trust. . . . I don't really think there are serious issues of trust in other sites.
Edgerton:	It seems to me that there are. There is a very common feeling across most of the sites that your agenda has not been revealed to them.
Olesen:	I think that is a fundamental problem of all fieldwork. There are always those questions [on the part of people at the site] "What are you people doing here?" Even if you told them two minutes before. I heard such questions nearly every day in three years of my participant observation study of the socialization of student nurses.
Corcoran:	There is another level. The fund [FIPSE] staff itself needs to know what you're up to.
Riesman:	You need ammunition; you need to defend us?
Corcoran:	Well, not necessarily. But we need to persuade col-

leagues back at the Fund that we know where you're going.

Edgerton: There's been a hell of a lot of trust [on the part of FIPSE towards the project] for a year and a half.

Watt: I'd be very surprised if College III (University of Massachusetts, Boston) wasn't one of the places you had to persuade. Last year it was a mine field. . . . I had no idea of the political complexities.

Corcoran: John [Watt], you have to understand our need to know because if you step on a mine, we get blown up.

Grant: I want to return to what are the boundaries. What we can write about is limited by the talents that we have, and the interests that we have. The critical issues are also bounded by doing case histories at specific institutions. There are boundaries or blinders in ourselves in the sense of our capacities to understand these institutions. Another boundary is indicated by the audience we visualize as composed of the wider kinds of practitioners and faculty at all institutions of higher education who might be interested in these issues—not just project directors at these ten sites.

Corcoran: We need some idea of the audiences you are trying to reach because we need to ask what is an effective way of reaching them.

Edgerton: Maybe I'm expecting too much, but it seems to me that you ought to be able to tell the Fund the extent to which you're looking for cost implications.

Olesen: I don't think we're going to have the time to dig into cost figures. I don't think they would give them to me.

Edgerton: There is no sort of hard line, rigid architecture. I'm just stating some general concerns and hoping they're accepted as genuine, valid concerns.

Gamson: There are going to be critical issues [that we'll identify] that however recognizable to the people at the sites will not be top on their list of critical issues and which might seem frivolous to them and not terribly relevant. I think we ought to recognize that.

The meeting was a major turning point for the project, and while no assurances were made about refunding, the tension eased perceptibly. Edgerton volunteered that "your own internal consensus and the research project is a lot further along and better than has been publicly communicated." As a result of participating in discussions of the issues, he was persuaded that "the analysis was really embedded in the cases and [that] that was the structure driving the report." He made a generous concession towards the end of the meeting: "I think we are as sensitive as you are in not wanting to impose process tactics that don't work. It was maybe an unwise attempt to try to get more active relationships between you folks and the project directors." Of course we felt that we had "active relationships" with sources at the sites—relationships that we in fact considered crucial when it came to the question of determining the critical issues. And the meeting had shown that this was the shared view of the project team, including such an experienced investigator as Virginia Olesen, who could tell Edgerton that what he saw as distrust of the team was to some degree to be expected in research of this kind.

Team members also left the meeting with greater appreciation for FIPSE's point of view and the political realities I faced in trying to satisfy multiple constituencies about the worth of the project. This made it easier for me to organize a spring meeting that would include about seventy-five practitioners from various competence-based sites. The project, up to this point, had to some degree been an unwitting victim of its own ethics. Our concern about confidentiality had led to barring the FIPSE staff from meetings, and since field notes were the principal "product" of the research during this first year, little was known about the quality or nature of the work underway. Edgerton was entirely correct in saying there had been a great deal of trust on the agency's side.

After the project team returned from the Florida meeting, a refined version of the critical issues outline was shared with all practitioners in the study and invitations went out for the spring meeting. At the same time—in late January 1976—a survey was made as a follow-up of Edgerton's concerns to see whether this statement of critical issues was "recognized as important" by practitioners. Since the spring conference would be organized around the critical issues as developed by the project team, practitioners were asked whether any topics of concern to them should be added to the conference agenda. Only one was suggested with any frequency—a request to pay more attention to the impact of competence-based education on the way that fees are charged and records are kept in institutions of higher education (subsequently incorporated in Zelda Gamson's analysis of processes of innovation). Within a few weeks it was evident that the distrust Edgerton referred to was apparent at two other sites. However, discussions with persons at those sites led in both cases to decisions to remain in the study. By late spring, nearly every member of the project had met the deadline for submission of first drafts of their case studies, and these received a generally favorable response both at the sites, where they were widely distributed, and at FIPSE. Better than 90 percent of those invited came to the project's June conference at Michigan State University, where in workshops with practitioners we invited criticism of early drafts or outlines of our papers on critical issues. During a panel discussion on the methodology of the project, participants in the case studies asked us about the timing of site visits, our role in offering practical advice to practitioners, the processes by which the research team had decided upon the critical issues, and the comparative validity of the case studies. Indeed, most of the issues discussed in this chapter were raised pointedly from the floor. We attempted to explain why we had proceeded as we had at each of our sites and how this had influenced our understanding of the critical issues.

The FIPSE staff, Edgerton in particular, felt the conference had been quite successful, but one problem remained: What was going to be done about the Alverno case study? Edgerton saw the issue partly in terms of due process. If the team had originally proposed to do three years of fieldwork, was it proper to go ahead and publish the Alverno case after only half that? I responded that the team was unable to carry out the commitment through no fault of its own; hence, the question really turned on whether there was a sufficient data base to complete some part of the intended work. I noted further that the due process provisions included a promise to circulate drafts of the case studies widely at the sites *prior to publication* to give any aggrieved party opportunity for redress as well as to provide for criticisms of other kinds and contrary interpretations of events. These provisions would be honored in the Alverno case, and it would be Alverno's responsibility to exercise such redress as it deemed appropriate. (As it later turned out, few responses were received from Alverno.) At the end of the Michigan meeting, Edgerton countered that since we differed, the matter should be arbitrated by appointing some panel or third parties to decide the issue. I declined the suggestion on the grounds that collegial peers had the responsibility to decide how and in what manner to make their research public. It would be a denial of academic freedom for some third group to decide what could or could not be published. Edgerton replied that researchers could decide at the end of the project to do or write whatever they wished, however the Fund had a responsibility to decide what it would pay for. This I readily acknowledged, but I did not think members of the project would agree to abort the Alverno case as a condition of third-year funding. Although FIPSE later asked two psychologists for their opinions of Ewens' Alverno draft, one of whom apparently disapproved of its "tone," it refunded the project for the third and final year without placing any conditions on the publication of the Alverno case.

Ethical Issues

Three other ethical issues became problems for us during the project and deserve mention here. The first involved prejudice or antipathy on our part toward individuals or programs being studied. Goodman (1976) is right when he says that we never see with "innocent eyes" but with the eyes of experience and prejudice, and most members of the team began their research with views of competence-based education already partially formed. Yet reality is more interesting and more complex than our stereotype of it, and (to follow Goodman) as we continue to learn, we bring new eyes to successive observations. Or, as David Reisman noted, not only is reality more complex than our stereotype of it but most observers are cultural relativists enough to have some empathy with things that in principle they may disapprove of. Others on the team felt the truth of the experience recalled by one member long after an early field visit:

> I still didn't know much about this competence-based thing and I frankly was, I now see, very snobbish about it. I really didn't think it was very important. . . .

> But when I met these people [two persons the researcher had interviewed and was moved by] I was sort of stunned by the reality of this. All of a sudden a lot of these things made sense. I saw itineraries coming into place, felt very humbled, recognized that I hadn't been looking at things . . . that sort of these habitual ways of seeing things filter reality, and you end up not seeing it. That made me, from then on, much, much more attentive and interested in what was going on . . . I strained much more; I recognized how little I knew about these things.

The matter of how deeply one disapproves or of how much empathy one is capable has ethical implications. It raises the question of whether a researcher should disqualify himself or herself on the grounds that his or her animus toward an institution, a person, or a movement destroys the ground needed for understanding. One strength of the team method is that team visits can be a way of both discovering and compensating for such animus. Animus between particular persons and the researcher is inevitable to some degree, and it became a noticeable factor in at least three cases, which were talked about openly on the research team. In one case, a researcher's antipathy for behavior modification techniques employed at one site was so strong as to be a topic of several discussions between him and the project director, and was eventually a significant factor in the researcher's decision to abandon the case study. This is not to argue that researchers must in principle approve of that which they write about—if that were true, then it would be extremely unlikely to find many researchers writing about authoritarianism or many other topics—but to recognize that, just as a psychiatrist might decline to take on a patient who rouses deep antipathies, a researcher should decline some cases, or, as in the case just mentioned, withdraw from others where prejudice or antipathy become apparent in the course of the work.

A second ethical issue that the team faced arose from its agreement to share field notes and write case studies. Several members of the team differed in their attitude toward use of actual names in the case studies. Some argued that it is generally unjustified to use names where informed consent has not been given. Yet even here it seems reasonable that actual identities may be revealed in some instances when they would serve to warn others in a convincing and authoritative way about an institution or agent that might do them serious harm or when the need of others to be informed about a person's intentions or policies overrides his or her desire for secrecy. It does not follow, however, that social scientists in the pursuit of truth may lightly decide such matters. In our study, we obtained the informed consent of most individuals by circulating drafts of our case studies to those named in them prior to publication. Thus, any objection to our use of a name or any feeling of invasion of privacy could be taken into account in revisions before publication.

Even if persons give informed consent, however, it is impossible for them to know in advance how they will be affected by what is published about them, and hence there is the possibility that they may be injured in some unforeseen way or suffer an unwanted invasion of privacy. Certainly there are some cases where a researcher is more "informed" about such possibilities of harm than is the supposedly "informed subject"; and in such cases, as David Riesman has pointed out, the researcher should warn the respondent of how the facts will look in print. But otherwise, the objection seems invalid that names should not be used even with informed consent. By not using names, researchers can actually diminish the autonomy of others. And if no names are used when consent has been given, then a researcher can be viewed as imposing anonymity on those who might prefer a share of the credit! Moreover, the use of real names holds a writer to higher standards of accuracy and makes contradiction of error more likely than do blanket disguises, which can sometimes lead to mistaken inferences that do more harm than if identities were given.

Another objection to the use of names sometimes raised among sociologists is more epistemological than ethical: some of them see sociological writing in terms of a structural analysis with generalizable meanings and interest that does not rely on the identification of particular groups and individuals. Such a view plants a flag at the far end of the spectrum running from "great man theories" to faceless "social structural" accounts, nonsensically declaring only the latter to be sociologically relevant. But both pre-existing social structures and the actions of individuals affect the course of social events. To write a case study of the reforms at the University of Chicago over the past forty years without ever mentioning Robert Maynard Hutchins would misrepresent reality.

The third ethical issue concerned our role as researchers and evaluators. At the final meeting of the team in May 1977, a discussion of the methodology of the project turned repeatedly to the discomfort researchers feel when asked to make judgments about persons or programs. Strong words were used, as in this excerpt from the transcript in which a team member describes a confidential conversation initiated by an administrator at one college:

> He wanted me to tell him who on the faculty he should be getting rid of, and I was really over a barrel because I knew I had to establish myself with him to do my field work. And he knew that. He really had me. I really hated him for it. I couldn't just be bland. I couldn't just say, Well, I'm sorry, professional ethics prevent that . . . it would be too much of a putdown. . . . I knew he was manipulating me, knowing that he could withdraw permission—the psychological permission —and really make it impossible to continue with the work. . . . I had to play a little bit his game . . . I would not rat on anybody, so what I ended up doing was not to ever say anything myself negative about anybody but when he said something negative I did not disagree, and I kept finding good things to say about some people. But at the end of the conversation he got an awful lot out of me and I felt dirty. I really felt—you know, I just felt guilty and inauthentic . . . disloyal, unprofessional.

If the researcher feels disloyal in such situations, so may the respondent, who feels he has told "too much." But feelings of inauthenticity and guilt often weigh heavier on the researcher, especially if he feels that he has wormed his way into an institution and into the confidence of the respondent. The researcher may experience such a relationship with respondents as a counterfeit friendship, one in which he or she withholds much while observing and gathering data. A member of the team who had never done field research of this kind expressed the internal struggle this way: "At first it was a question of trust. It felt [as though] they were doing me a favor to let me observe, to let me in, and my insecurity [was] doubled by the fact that not only was I not a professional fieldworker but I also didn't have a clue about [competence-based education]. So it seemed they were doing me a favor: it didn't seem as though I could say (almost think, even) anything bad about them. How could I be critical. How could I say they were screwing up when they are so nice, trying as hard as they can, and they have taken me into their confidence and let down their guard for me. It would be a personal betrayal."

The instrumental aspect of the relationship may be exposed when a researcher struggles with the human urge to put his or her arms around an interviewee who has begun to sob in the midst of recounting some trauma or when the respondent asks the researcher to take sides in an intrainstitutional battle, to cite two specific instances from our field notes. The researcher-respondent relationship is only a particular instance of the more general quality of modern life that requires us to treat other persons as members of categories. But the position of the researcher who makes repeated visits to an institution undergoing major change is especially vulnerable. Repeated encounters generate considerable trust. The researcher's sympathetic attempt to understand may be misinterpreted as support for a particular position. If help is then requested and denied, both sides can be hurt. The team member quoted earlier who felt she was being manipulated finally had to say, "Look, I feel very uncomfortable having this conversation and I really cannot give you what you want." This refusal created some strain temporarily but was accepted in the long term because one of the underlying conditions of the research was that appropriate feedback would be shared in an appropriate form—namely drafts of the case study— with all persons in the study. In the second example, the writer who raised the question of trust, increasingly came to feel, with the team's support, that his role as critic was both legitimate and needed. The project team was only "a passing intermittent shadow" when he began work at the site. But gradually the team became a crucial force "in giving me a bit more power to think critically . . . that is, I felt more and more connections, more and more support from the team."

The forgoing discussion should not obscure the fact that most relationships in the field are pleasant, and in a sense every good interview is an exchange. Moreover, there are many legitimate ways in which researchers can and do reciprocate. Faculty asked the assistance or advice of team members in innumerable ways, most often in connection with their work on competence-based curriculums, but not infrequently about personal matters or even help in finding a new job. Members of the team also responded to student requests for references or advice about graduate school.

Ethical dilemmas are unavoidable in research, and in some measure in all human encounters. In this study, it helped greatly to be able to talk about them and to draw on the counsel and support of other members of the team.

Lessons

Looking back, one wonders how we could have been so surprised by the conflicts we encountered during the project. Researchers who are bred to "expect" unanticipated consequences should not have been so dense—but we were. Our first surprise resulted from our failure to see how starkly the logic of our research methods contradicted the logic generating the reform we studied. As mentioned earlier, we proceeded by inductive and exploratory methods, discovering, testing, and modifying hypotheses as we enlarged our understanding, whereas most persons at the sites in the study proceeded deductively, deriving curriculums from highly specific sets of desired outcomes. Although such shorthand phrases do not capture the conflict so much as they suggest it, they represent the difference between a person on a hillside who wants to observe what happens when he lets go of a ball and another who wants to have the ball hit a particular target.

In addition to the tension generated by inductive versus deductive logics, we encountered some hostility growing out of differences in "local" versus "cosmopolitan" orientations. At sites where concerns were more local, we were likely to be perceived (to some degree correctly) as jet-setters who would get in the way without offering much practical help and whose research might result in negative publicity for the institution. In contrast, at larger, research-oriented institutions, where the outlook was more cosmopolitan, our respondents seemed to place a higher value on research for its own sake apart from any immediate utility it might have. They were more relaxed as to the nature and import of our research and felt less need for formalization of relationships or protection against institutional backlash. Their institutions were more financially secure and less dependent on tuition revenue; they were thus less worried than smaller schools about how the research would affect the institution's image.

The other major conflict—the confrontation with officials of FIPSE—was not so much totally unexpected as it was surprising in its intensity. Somewhat naively, we were not aware of the consequences of including FIPSE itself as a field site in the investigation of the competence-based movement, and we did not realize the degree to which our mode of operating turned the usual understanding of contract research on its head. The funding agency ordinarily sees the researcher as an instrument to accomplish some agency purpose or function, often to help the agency control or manage its field of operations more effectively, and in addition often seeks legitimation of its perceived role from the researchers. The need for great legitimacy was high at FIPSE, a young agency with no developed constituency that was attempting to make its way in Washington at a time when major reorganizations of federal education agencies were being proposed—under some of which FIPSE would be absorbed by other agencies. Research that would help ensure the success of its programs and reflect credit on the agency would be most desirable, while research that might reveal confusions about competence-based education outside and within the agency could be very threatening. Our project clearly fell in the latter category, and much of the concern about the need for feedback and clarification of what our research was "really about" should be read in that light. FIPSE had agreed to a set of conditions for our research that placed our project closer to the model of basic rather than contract research. It had agreed in principle to three years of funding (although subject to annual renewal) and to an inductive assessment of the movement. But in practice, as the politically sensitive import of these agreements was discovered, pressures were brought to modify the agreements. Yet, if there are any heroes in this story, they are the officers at FIPSE who, after all, continued to sponsor our research despite great misgivings. They were often forceful proponents of their own view, but they were not ideologues or blind empire builders. They tolerated dissent within the agency; they were willing to look at new evidence; and when we submitted the case studies of the project, they agreed that we had made good on our proposal and continued our funding.

What does one learn from such an experience? It might have been helpful if we had formed an advisory panel made up of a mix of "locals" and "cosmopolitans" who could have helped establish guidelines about feedback and could have reassured FIPSE about the progress of the research at a time when there was little "product" that could be made public. Perhaps even more importantly, we should have expected such conflicts and seen them as an opportunity to better understand the nature of the phenomena under study. In examining my own role, I now realize that I was at times much too defensive and had a tendency to be overprotective of the work of my colleagues. Although there were things to defend—and it is important to note, as Argyris (1971) has in another context, that a researcher who is easily manipulated is not respected—one needs to do so with as little armor and heat as possible. I did not always achieve this, and to the degree that I did, my colleagues deserve thanks for having had the courage to tell me to pull in my horns. But by the conclusion of the project, I feel that I had more of the competence that I needed at the beginning.

To turn finally to the question asked at the outset of this chapter: In what sense has this been a research project rather than a form of social criticism? It has not been research of a form that begins with a hypothesis that can be confirmed or denied. It has been a search into the foundations, understandings, meanings, and imports of the movement toward competence-based education. That search has been disciplined by the work of trying to understand and explicate to practitioners themselves a variety of actual experiments in competence-based education. Of course, as Becker and Geer remind us, "we often do not understand that we do not understand" what we have seen or what has been told to us (1972, p. 104). Our response as colleagues to each other's field notes—and later our direct observation at each site—helped make each of us aware of systematic distortions in our ways of perceiving. It is as though Robert Redfield and Oscar Lewis, the anthropologists who gave conflicting accounts of life in the village of Tepotzlan, were asked to reconcile their interpretations before publishing their work. In one or two cases conflict of this kind may have been a factor in a member's decision to leave the team. This element of self-selection means that some systematic bias or outlook may have characterized those of us who remained. But this bias was reduced by sharing drafts of the cases with participants at the sites, who forced awareness of omissions or alternative interpretations of events.

Research is a cooperative enterprise, and it is the disciplined process of cooperation, compelling systematic attention to evidence that does not "fit," that distinguishes it from social criticism, which is the reaction of a single sensibility to an object of perception or field of inquiry. This process of checking inference against "fact" and of compensating for observer bias was much stronger at the level of our case studies than at that of our cross-site analyses. At this thematic level, our research design is much weaker. We worked out the process of determining the critical issues informally, seeking a balance between what in our discussions we felt should be included in our report and what we felt we could do in terms of our talents, competence, and predilections. Thus when no one on the team seemed inclined to write about the issues of assessment, Wendy Kohli and I took on this assignment even though by background and training we did not feel at ease in doing so. Perhaps the team should have been augmented at this stage of cross-site analysis, but it would have been difficult to integrate new members at that point of time even if additional funds had been available. As a result, our critical issue chapters are mixed in form, some using the cases as the data for their analysis, while others merely draw on the cases for illustration. The latter, that is, are closer to the model of informed social criticism than of empirical research although even they are tempered by the process of mutual criticism.

Yet neither cases nor critical issues are replicable. Different persons working from our data might draw different inferences. In that sense, the work of our team is closer to the model of a jury than of a laboratory. It raises many hypotheses and settles few. In assessing such a process, one should ask how the jurors were selected, whether the process exposed hidden interests, whether they considered the relevant evidence, and, finally, whether they were competent to judge this evidence. Readers are now in a better position to assess these matters than I am. Nevertheless, I believe that the special merit in our approach is that our method is uniquely adapted to sorting out the larger implications and potential consequences of nascent educational reforms and thus can help both educators and policy makers better understand the complexities and costs of such movements at an early stage. It is, in other words, a method suited to the observation of a bandwagon while it is still moving slowly enough for careful appraisal.

Susan E. King

Assessment
of Competence:
Technical Problems
and Publications

The assessment of students is vitally important in any educational program. It can foster personal growth of students by helping them monitor their own performance and capabilities; it can credit and recognize their learning; it can provide information for program development, renewal, and quality control (Heydinger, 1975b). Careful assessment is particularly important in such nontraditional programs as competence-based education: Not only do they often need to "prove themselves" and build credibility for their unconventional methods and innovative objectives by demonstrating the quality of their students' learning but the very learning that can result from the use of suitable assessment techniques may be an intrinsic part of their methods and objectives. For educators who are planning or implementing a competence-based program,

the following review seeks to survey the basic technical problems
and literature relevant to assessment in such a program.

Terminology

Several different types of assessment are frequently discussed
in the literature, with different terms being used to denote assessment for different purposes. *Formative* assessment refers to assessments made throughout the course of the learning activity, often
for the purpose of providing feedback to the student and the
instructor. *Summative* assessment refers to assessments made at the
end of a learning activity, often for the purpose of determining the
sum of learning that has taken place. Popham (1973) provides a
very readable account of these two major types of assessment. *Ultimate* assessment stresses the ultimate purpose of assessment—for
example, the assessment of academic learning for the ultimate purpose of ensuring adequate on-the-job performance. Dean and
Waechter (1974) discuss this approach and list additional references for it.

Different terms are also used to distinguish between different
reference bases used in assessment. The term *norm-referenced* refers
to the use of the norm or average for some group as the standard
against which the performance of an individual is assessed, while
criterion-referenced refers to the use of a fixed standard or criterion
for assessment. (See Ebel, 1971; Block, 1971; or Burns, 1972b.)
Thus in a norm-referenced assessment of spelling, students might be
judged good spellers because they scored above the group average
on a spelling test. But in a criterion-referenced assessment process,
they would be judged good spellers only if they scored better than
a predetermined standard, such as 90 percent correct.

Distinctions are also made on the basis of the nature or
context of a particular assessment technique, such as between
group-administered and individually administered tests or between
projective tests and objective tests in which the true nature of the
item content is obvious. One important distinction of this type is
between *operant* and *inferential* forms of assessment (Dean and
Waechter, 1974) or *operant* and *respondent* forms (McClelland,
1973). In operant forms of assessment, the subject actually under-

takes or performs a task. This form is thus similar to what is frequently termed *performance-based* assessment. In inferential or respondent forms, all that may be required is a fairly passive response (hence McClelland's term "respondent"). An example here is the traditional paper and pencil test of an academic subject, from which an inference is drawn as to the extent of knowledge or ability possessed by the student.

A further distinction that is frequently found in the literature is that between *product* and *process* assessment or *product* and *performance* evaluation (see Burns, 1972b; Dean and Waechter, 1974; and Fitzpatrick and Morrison, 1971). This distinction is basically between assessing end products and assessing the means to these end products. In assessing the interviewing competence of counselors, for example, a product assessment might consider the information gained by a counselor from the interview as the product for assessment. However, equally important might be the process by which this information was gained; for example, did the interview heighten the sense of well-being of the client or did it make the person reluctant to return for further assistance?

Finally, the well-known terms *reliability* and *validity* are crucial in assessment literature. Reliability, as the term implies, refers to how reliable a particular test or technique is, in terms of whether scores on it are "consistent" (to use the term of Ebel, 1972) or likely to be reproduced if it is given at another time, or by another instructor/tester, or if a similar but alternative form of the test is used. One might well ask how assessment based on performance can be anything but reliable; yet performance must frequently be judged by observers in order for assessments to be made, and reliability can sometimes be attained only by fairly painstaking and sometimes costly training of those doing the observing.

The concept of validity is more complex. Whether or not a test is valid has sometimes been translated into the question, "Does it measure what it is supposed to measure?" (see, for example, Lindquist, quoted in Ebel, 1965, p. 377). An answer to this question may be attempted in a number of ways. The simplest, but least informative, way is to examine the contents of the test and see if it contains items that are related to what the test is supposed to measure—for example, athletic ability. If the items appear to be related, then the test is said to have *face validity*. A slight improvement on this approach is to see if the items also cover a sufficient range of those skills that are generally associated with athletic ability. If so, then the test is considered to have *content validity*. More sophisticated approaches to validity require the use of some other measure or rating as a criterion with which the athletic ability test scores may be correlated. One might, for example, get the physical education staff of a high school to rank all the students in terms of athletic ability. If those who score high on the test are also ranked high by the staff, the test can be considered valid; and because these two measures occur at about the same time, this form of validity is usually called *concurrent validity*. Another approach would be to use the test scores to predict future athletic success— for example, to predict athletic performance during college. If the test is found to be a good predictor it can be said to have *predictive validity*. Finally, one could decide upon some criterion with which to compare the test scores on the basis of the underlying construct that the test hopes to measure. Thus an attribute common to all athletic skills might be general body coordination, and a measure of body coordination could be correlated with the test scores. If those with good body coordination are found to score high, then the test is considered to have *construct validity*. (Standard texts such as Cronbach, 1960, and Ebel, 1965 and 1972, provide good discussions of approaches to both reliability and validity.)

Assessment in Competence-Based Programs

The literature concerned with assessment in competence-based education (see Burns, 1972a and 1972b; Redfern, 1973; Schmeider, 1973; Dean and Waechter, 1974; Quirk, 1974; and Palardy and Eisle, 1975) suggests some consensus about assessment in these programs. New forms of assessment are obviously needed in competence-based programs, and emphasis should be on operant (or performance-based) techniques, formative assessments that stress feedback to the student, and techniques directly involving the student, such as self-assessment or peer-assessment. In general, criterion-referenced techniques seem preferable to norm-referenced ones within competence-based programs.

Despite this seeming agreement, considerable disagreement remains. One issue concerns the desirability of specifying precise behavioral objectives. Many noted writers favor the specification of behavioral objectives in precise terms, both in order to clarify the aims of a course and in order to facilitate assessment (Bloom, 1956; Gagné, 1965b; Block, 1971); but McCelland (1973) and Skager (1973), for example, see such specific objectives as being too restrictive, and Ebel (1971) attacks their use as well as that of related criterion-referenced tests. He argues that "knowledge does not come in chunks that can be defined and identified separately" (p. 285) and that highly specific objectives are "unrealistic to expect and impractical to use except at the most elementary levels of education" (p. 281).

A related issue concerns the relative stress to be placed on assessment of products or processes. (See Fitzpatrick and Morrison, 1971; and Burns, 1972b.) Frequently products are more easily translatable into precise objectives, and thus may be stressed to the exclusion of less readily translatable process factors. But because "how things are done" and not just "that they are done" is frequently important, the need to consider process assessment is being more frequently recognized, as demonstrated by the many calls for new and better measuring instruments for such qualities as empathy and interpersonal communication skills (McClelland, 1973).

Some educators may think that few assessment problems exist in competence-based programs because they stress "doing" and performance. They may complacently assume that if a student can do a task then he has achieved competence. Such complacency grossly oversimplifies assessment by means of performance. Subjective judgments may vary among assessors, resulting in diminished reliability, just as the actual performance of the student may vary at different times, thus introducing the problem of which performance "counts" (Quirk, 1974).

Consider, for example, the assessment of competence in "tire changing." It is not sufficient to require that the student be able merely to change a tire. The performance must be carried out in such a way that the tire will remain inflated and safely in place even when driven at high speeds or on poor roads. If time is important, as in training pit crewmen for a racing-car team, a further condition might be that the tire change be performed safely within a prescribed time limit. In other situations it may be necessary to determine whether the student can perform the tire change in less than ideal conditions, with minimal equipment, or with unfamiliar tools. What constitutes a competent tire change is thus a complex matter but obviously much less complex than determining competence in such tasks as interviewing, counseling, or diagnosing.

A more serious problem is that of "atrophy" (to use Atkin's phrase quoted in Palardy and Eisle, 1975, p. 215), namely, the tendency of program objectives to become restricted to those that are most easily measured. An example would be for competence-based teacher training programs to stress proficiency in developing audiovisual aids rather than skill in communicating successfully with children—a skill more complex and difficult to assess. The poor state of the art of measurement, especially in affective areas, accentuates this danger, as Palardy and Eisle point out.

What then can be considered necessary for implementing adequate assessment procedures within competence-based programs? The first step is one that should be completed before the program commences, namely, a decision about the overall objectives of the program. If the program is designed to train nurses, the objectives must consist of those properties or skills necessary for competence in nursing. Obviously this specification of objectives is no small task. Without an accurate set of objectives as a guide to the competencies to be assessed, any assessment will obviously have little validity in terms of determining likely on-the-job competence.

Various methods can be used to determine suitable program objectives, including client responses to questionnaires, detailed job analyses, and recourse to expert opinions. Once these objectives have been determined, it is then necessary to decide how to ascertain whether students meet them. This may require refining the objectives into units or specifications amenable to assessment (bearing in mind the possible dangers of too rigid a specification) and then selecting reliable and valid measures for use in the assessment process.

A final decision concerns whether a required level of competency must be achieved in each and every area. Quirk (1974) discusses this problem in terms of two contrasting models—*regression* and *multiple-cutoff*. In the regression approach, poor performance in one or more areas can be compensated for by sound or superior performance in other areas. In the multiple-cutoff approach, minimal levels of performance are set for each area of competency and these levels must be reached in all areas. Under the multiple-cutoff approach, a medical student rated as deficient in bedside manner would not be certified as competent even though he has extraordinary medical knowledge or research skills, while under the regression approach, such knowledge or skills could compensate for the lack of bedside manner.

Next, the likely reaction of students and staff is worth considering in selecting assessment techniques. Reaction is likely to be positive if the technique seems relevant to the competence being assessed—that is, if it has "face validity." Trial runs with a particular technique may be useful in gauging reactions. Even quite gruelling assessment procedures are sometimes viewed favorably by those who experience them, as illustrated by the three-and-a-half-day assessment procedure of the U.S. Office of Strategic Services, whose candidates frequently commented that the experience had been one from which they had learned much about themselves (U.S. Office of Strategic Services, 1948). In a less demanding situation, the simulated experience offered by McGuire and Babbott (1967) was also favorably accepted by students because it offered them a situation in which to test their skills.

A final overriding consideration in selecting an assessment technique is the ratio of cost to benefit. Costs may involve time spent developing or refining a technique, recurrent time needed to use the technique (such as administrative activity or scoring), equipment or special staff needs (for example, computer time or a programmer if computer simulation is to be used or a panel of experts to observe task performance), and many other factors. Benefits may include added reliability or validity, the ability to assess several students at once, the opportunity to generate feedback to students, and the impact of the technique in improving student interest and motivation. Trade-offs will no doubt be necessary, for an ideal technique from the point of view of benefits may have exorbitant costs.

Taking into account their costs and benefits, the following assessment techniques might be considered for use in competence-based programs. (Publications useful in the preparation of this overview include Frederiksen (1962), Wilson (1962), Fitzpatrick and Morrison (1971), and CAEL's *A Compendium of Assessment Techniques* (1975).

The Critical Incident Technique (CIT). This technique is one of many outgrowths of wartime selection procedures that have relevance for modern-day assessment. Flanagan (1954) offers an excellent history of the technique from its use during World War II for aircrew selection to its postwar use in assessing the performance of dentists, industrial foremen, bookkeepers, the heads of life insurance agencies, salesclerks, and teachers.

The CIT requires preliminary determination of what constitutes desirable or undesirable behavior in a given job or position by observing people on the job, by asking workers in that field to report on their job and its characteristics, or by asking supervisors to report on crucial incidents that illustrate desirable or undesirable behavior. Critical incidents are thus formulated for a particular job or position. While amenable to use in many different situations, the CIT requires careful preparation of the initial list of incidents for any particular job or task. Its flexibility permits assessment (on the basis of the critical incidents) to be made by the student himself, his supervisors or instructors, or by other "experts." At Justin Morrill College, the CIT is apparently used as a technique for assessing experience gained from field trips oriented towards learning about a new social setting (such as a strange town) from a single visit (Duley, 1974).

The In-Basket Technique. According to Frederiksen (1962), the in-basket technique was developed by the Educational Testing Service under contract to the Human Resources Research Institute. The technique is generally referred to as a "situational test" (Frederiksen, 1962; Fitzpatrick and Morrison, 1971). The candidate is presented with the contents of an in-basket appropriate for a given job and is also provided with background information about the fictitious institution, staff, and clients that he must work with. The candidate is required to respond to the problems posed by the material in the in-basket, the responses being memos, letters, phone calls, and so forth. These responses are then evaluated—usually with the aid of scoring categories previously established.

Fitzpatrick and Morrison (1971) report use of the in-basket

approach in relation to the work of administrators (especially school administrators), school principals, and police lieutenants. Frederiksen (1962) gives a detailed account of its use in relation to the job of school principal. As Frederiksen points out, one advantage is that the situation is standardized for all candidates, whereas if real-life situations were used such standardization would not be possible. Disadvantages include the time and effort required to adequately prepare material for the exercise, possible difficulties in how responses should be scored (that is, what is a "correct" decision), and the possibility that certain candidates who work best by means of personal contact with their subordinates might be disadvantaged. The validity coefficients reported by Fitzpatrick and Morrison were not high but were sufficient to lead them to conclude that "the in-basket technique is at least a useful research tool, and probably has some validity for evaluation purposes" (1971, p. 245). Frederiksen, in his report on the technique's use with school principal jobs, comments that while some scoring categories were found to be unreliable, others had reliability coefficients ranging from .55 to .97.

Interaction Analysis. Systems of interaction analysis usually develop from a need to increase the reliability of observation. The Flanders system (Flanders, 1970) is one such verbal interaction analysis system that has been used extensively in research on teaching but that also has potential for use in assessment, as does the well-known Bales system for categorizing interaction in small groups. When properly used, these systems can lead to high interobserver reliability. But for such reliability to be achieved, observers must be carefully trained in the use of the system.

Interview. Although the interview has long been used as a means to obtain information from people and to make assessments concerning their personal qualities and skills, considerable debate exists in the literature as to the utility of the interview, as well as its reliability and validity. Some of this controversy stems from early debates concerning the accuracy of clinical versus statistical assessment techniques (Meehl, 1954). The debate continues, for one finds industrial psychologists, such as Blum and Taylor (1956), playing down the contribution of the interview as a predictive device, especially when other methods of information gathering may be more reliable and less costly. Certainly, if the sole function of the interview is to attain background information, more efficient techniques, such as the use of biographic data blanks, might be more suitable.

Grant and Bray (1969) conducted a study of the interview in terms of its contribution when used as one of an extensive battery of assessment procedures at an "assessment center." Their review of the literature reports some varied findings. The work reported from a study by Maysfield suggested that the interview was not reliable and valid as an estimator of mental ability. In contrast, however, the reported work of Ulrich and Trumbo suggested that the interview was most useful for assessing factors associated with interpersonal relationships and with motivation to work. This study, as reported by Grant and Bray, also concluded that structured interviews provided more valid information than did unstructured ones. In their own study, Grant and Bray concluded that the interview could contribute to the overall assessment process. Assessment of such personal characteristics as motivation and interpersonal skills seemed to be a particular contribution of the interview, and the validity of the information gained (using success in management and/or future salary increase as the predictive criterion) was considered by the authors to have been adequately established.

A further study by Newman, Howell, and Norman (1967), examined the ability of various techniques to predict success in a practical examination in dentistry. This study established that an interview of the candidate before a board of three officers, along with the assessment made from that interview, proved to be a better predictor of success in the practical dentistry examination than file records, scores on specific and general ability tests, and scores on four dental competency and knowledge tests. This suggests that the interview should not be totally discarded as an assessment technique, particularly if the interview can contribute to the assessment of interpersonal skills that are difficult to assess by other means. Possible drawbacks to the use of the interview are the danger of limited reliability and validity—especially if untrained staff are used as interviewers—and the cost of any extensive use of the interview for assessment, as the interview usually permits the assessment of only one student at a time.

Rating Scales. The term "rating scale" encompasses a wide range of roughly similar techniques of assessment. Remmers (1963) draws attention to scales of the following types: graphic, cumulative point, checklists, multiple-choice, forced-choice, sociometric, semantic differential, and Q-sort (also see readings in Whisler and Harper, 1962). The history of rating scales is again related to developments in selection and assessment procedures within the armed forces. While Paterson (1962) claims that the Scott Company used graphic scales prior to World War I, Remmers notes that the forced-choice method (in which the rater must choose between several described qualities of the individual or his job performance) was first used by the U.S. Adjutant General's Office during World War II. Cozan (1962) reports the results of a number of studies of the validity of rating scales using data from the armed forces and private industry. He reports validities as high as .60 for forced-choice ratings for store managers when an objective measure of units of production was used as the criterion, and of .75 for production foremen when supervisors' ratings were used as the criterion. Validity coefficients of up to .89 were reported for ratings for pharmaceutical salesmen.

Rating scales are usually used as a means of increasing the reliability of assessment by presenting a guide to the characteristics warranting consideration by the observer. The clarity with which these characteristics are presented will greatly influence this reliability. The appropriateness of the characteristics specified for consideration will no doubt determine the validity of the assessment made using the rating scale.

Simulation. Simulation offers a seemingly attractive method of assessing student competence. As Fitzpatrick and Morrison point out, the term "simulator" is usually used for "the most realistic and elaborate devices" while "trainer" is used for less sophisticated apparatus (1971, p. 239). Fitzpatrick and Morrison comment on two concepts crucial to discussion of simulation: comprehensiveness and fidelity. The former term refers to the range of aspects of the real-life situation that are simulated, the latter to how well an aspect is characterized in the simulation setting. These terms suggest that the question of validity of simulation might pose problems. Gagné comments on the validity of simulation: "To the extent that the simulator is 'real' the performance is 'real' " (Gagné, 1962b, p. 237).

Simulators are often used in cases in which the student or candidate cannot be permitted to perform in the real-life situation unless there is high assurance of success, as in the training and assessment of space-flight ground crews. Simulation has been used extensively here simply because practice in the real-life situation would be hazardous and extremely costly. The problem is that no real validation can be made of the assessments based on performance in the simulated situation. Any candidate who does not perform adequately at the simulation stage will obviously not get the chance to try his hand at the real thing. There is often a tendency to think of simulation as always requiring costly equipment. Simulation, however, could presumably be undertaken in less expensive ways, such as by using confederates to play certain roles. Such simulation might be useful in training counselors, doctors, and lawyers in interviewing skills. Simulation, in whatever form, has the probable advantage of appearing highly relevant to the student and of combining learning and assessment in one process.

Tab Technique. This is a highly ingenious method that seems particularly suited to both training and assessment in areas requiring some kind of diagnostic skill, whether medicine or electrical and mechanical repair work. A brief description of the problem is presented to the student (such as a television picture that will not remain stable), followed by a list of questions that the student may ask to gain further information. The answer to each question is covered by a tab. If the first question asked leads to an impasse, then a second question is selected. The aim is for the student to make a diagnosis by asking the minimal number of questions. The tab technique has been used as the basis for the approach developed by McGuire and Babbott (1967) to assess medical problem-solving skills. McGuire and Babbott see their approach as having greater flexibility, because it allows the student to follow through with his initial decision rather than having to backtrack to another question.

The technique has the obvious advantage of closely approximating the application of knowledge to real-life problems. This relevance may win student approval for the approach. But considerable time and effort may be required to construct suitable diagnostic problems and alternative questions, especially if the same group of students are to use the technique extensively. Scoring could be a further problem, for certain diagnostic problems might well be such that there is no obviously "best" approach to the solution.

Work Sample. Fitzpatrick and Morrison (1971), in their discussion of the work sample, describe it as a situational test in which the candidate performs some task that is obviously job related. Fitzpatrick and Morrison's review discusses simple work samples, as well as work samples of a more "troubleshooting" nature in which some deliberate fault in a system must be corrected. In Wilson (1962), assessment based on work samples was found to correlate from .13 to .50 with the criterion of pay scale for electrican's mates on submarines. These correlations are somewhat low, but the criterion used is obviously subject to question. Gordon (1967) reports on the use of language training work samples (designed to predict the likely success of the candidate in an intensive language course) as predictors of selection of Peace Corps members for overseas service. A correlation of .41 was reported, a value little different from any of the other predictors used. The work sample has the advantage of relevance but has the disadvantage of requiring large amounts of staff time if new work samples (especially of the troubleshooting type) are constantly required.

Traditional Techniques. As previously noted, it would be unfortunate to exclude from consideration the more traditional assessment techniques, such as the essay and the objective test. Each of these techniques has certain advantages and disadvantages, and in particular programs they may well serve an assessment need. Ebel (1972) presents an account of the various advantages and disadvantages of essay and objective tests. Major advantages of the essay are that a group of students can undertake the assessment exercise at the same time, and that the questions are such that individual interpretation and presentation is possible. Certainly the essay provides a suitable technique for assessment of writing skill and written expression. Major disadvantages include the problem of intermarker reliability, and lack of validity for the essay mark if that mark reflects some essentially irrelevant characteristic, as may well be the case if the marker makes the assessment on the basis of literary style or grammatical purity when, for example, the aim of the essay is to test historical knowledge.

Major advantages of the objective test are that it is easy to administer and score; it permits the assessment of groups of students at one time; and objective test items, if written by a skilled item constructor, are capable of testing levels of cognition quite high in

Bloom's taxonomy of objectives. Disadvantages are that the construction of sound items is time consuming and that it should ideally be accompanied by pretesting. Also, the most capable (or imaginative) students may be penalized for reading into the question more than even the item constructor had intended.

Despite these disadvantages, traditional assessment techniques may well serve a useful purpose in competence-based assessment. Certainly early in the training period they may serve as a relatively easily administered test to determine prior knowledge or familiarity with particular approaches to the task in question. Other traditional techniques, such as the oral examination, might also serve a useful purpose in assessment within competence-based programs, especially when the skill being assessed is related to competence in the area of verbal communication.

Techniques Incorporating a "Multi-Assessment" Approach. This somewhat ambiguous heading is meant to suggest that a number of techniques can be incorporated into one strategy, such as in the case of the assessment center, the expert panel, or the portfolio.

The assessment center approach is worth attention because it is being used to select personnel for large corporations, including IBM and the American Telephone and Telegraph Company (Huck, 1973). This approach, at least within the United States, apparently commenced with the selection program for wartime agents used by the Office of Strategic Services. Selection was made on the basis of performance in a program conducted at an assessment center. The actual tests ranged from standard paper and pencil tests of personality and ability, to interviews of both a standard and an "interrogation" type, and to imaginatively constructed performance tests (for example, how to successfully transport important equipment across a river, given certain conditions). Despite the presence of a full-time team of psychologists to observe the candidates and their performance, as well as to conduct the final overall evaluation of the candidate as a potential agent, follow-up studies that attempted to validate the assessment center ratings showed disappointing results. The researchers attributed these low validities to the lack of any clear specifications as to the type of work for which any one candidate was being considered. The authors of *Assessment of Men* (see under U.S. Office of Strategic Services,

1948), in which the details of the assessment center are outlined, consider this lack of clear specification as a major defect of the program and one that might account for the low validities, especially as one validity criterion used was the rating of the agent by his theater supervisor.

Huck (1973) provides an account of recent uses of assessment centers, and stresses the question of the validity of their assessments. He reports studies in which validity coefficients ranging from .44 to .71 were obtained for assessment center ratings when the criterion used was eventual position reached in the company for which the assessment was being conducted. He also reports the conclusion drawn by Byhams, based on a review of the literature, that validity coefficients as high as .64 might be achieved using assessment centers. Even if high validities might be expected from use of assessment centers for assessing potential (or even competence), they are costly ventures both in terms of initial establishment and upkeep. While large corporations or government agencies might well use such comprehensive assessment procedures, small colleges could probably not meet the costs of such an operation. Perhaps a local assessment center, funded and used by a number of institutions, might help solve this financial problem. The assessment center offers a prime example of the need to consider carefully the relative costs and benefits of any assessment technique or assessment program.

The expert panel might make use of a number of specific techniques for assessment. The approach might best be suited to the assessment of relatively complex competencies such as the competent presentation of a legal case in a mock trial. The approach essentially calls for an assessment by the experts on the panel. Observation, interviews, and presentation of written work by the candidate may all constitute input to the panel. The expert panel has the advantage of utilizing expert knowledge in a particular field for assessment purposes. The disadvantages include not only the cost of retaining the experts but the problems involved in ascertaining group opinion.

Finally, the portfolio is simply a collection of pieces of evidence to support the claim that learning has taken place. Empire State College utilizes the portfolio approach, especially to determine what credit should be given for prior learning. While the portfolio has the advantage of giving the student the opportunity to gather evidence on his own behalf and its preparation can thus itself be a learning experience, it also has the principal disadvantage of being a very time-consuming process for students and advisors. Again one faces the "trade-off," this time in the form of staff time versus the fostering of personal development for the student.

Publications

The following references about assessment are obviously far from comprehensive, but their purpose is to introduce the reader to major books and articles concerning assessment in industrial, military, and business settings—as well as in education—that may prove useful in designing assessment techniques in competence-based programs.* Some of these techniques are designed to assess skills that are common to a wide range of competencies—for example, problem solving or such interpersonal skills as empathy—by means of economical paper and pencil tests. The article by Mc-Clelland (1973) in particular provides an introduction to research on assessment techniques that may significantly influence the nature and effectiveness of competence-based education.

AIKEN, L. R., JR. *Psychological and Educational Testing.* Boston: Allyn and Bacon, 1971. An introductory book on psychological and educational testing that does provide some material on performance testing, discussing the in-basket technique and the tab technique.

ANTHONEY, W. A., GORMALLY, J., and MILLER, H. "Prediction of Human Relations Training Outcomes by Traditional and Nontraditional Indices." *Counselor, Education, and Supervision,* 1974, *14,* 105–112. This article reports on the use of work samples or training samples for the prediction of students likely to benefit from a course to heighten empathy in the counseling situation. It reports a previous finding by the principal author that gives a

---

* Since the annotations are intended to aid practitioners, the comments do not necessarily reflect the overall quality of the publications or their possible utility for other purposes.

correlation coefficient of .61 between ratings after a one-hour session in "empathy skills" and final training outcomes. The present study demonstrated that two "trainability indices" based on a paper and pencil test could be derived: One a trainability communication score from judges' ratings, and the second a trainability self-discrimination score that compared judges' ratings with self-ratings. The study claims to demonstrate that this new measure is a better predictor of success in empathy training than are traditional selection tests.

BEATTY, W. H. (Ed.). *Improving Educational Assessment and an Inventory of Measures of Affective Behavior.* Washington, D.C.: Association for Supervision and Curriculum Development, National Education Association, 1969. The inventory of affective measures in this small volume provides a listing of numerous tests in the area of affective assessment, along with brief test descriptions, but detailed comment on the tests is not provided. The introduction to the volume contains a number of articles by well-known writers in the assessment area.

BERG, I. *Education and Jobs: The Great Training Robbery.* Middlesex, England: Penguin Books, 1970. An interesting and provocative book that focuses on the general relationship between education and employment. While the book does not concern itself principally with specific testing and assessment issues, it does stimulate thought about the relevance of many of the educational requirements imposed on people wishing to enter certain jobs. It might prove useful to those who formulate entry requirements for occupations or determine necessary competencies for particular positions.

BLOCK, J. H. "Criterion-Referenced Measures: Potentials." *School Review*, 1971, 75, 289–298. This article is essentially a response to the article by Ebel in the same issue of *School Review*. While Ebel vigorously attacks criterion-referenced measures, Block defends their use and attacks norm-referenced tests as not telling enough about the student's capacities. Block argues that criterion-referenced tests ensure that every child completes a particular level of learning *before* proceeding to a higher level.

BLUM, M. L., and TAYLOR, J. C. *Industrial Psychology: Its Theoreti-cal and Social Foundations.* New York: Harper & Row, 1956. This text, written mainly for the industrial psychologist, gives information about a wide variety of testing and selection tech-niques. Since the authors make frequent use of existing data on test validity, the book also serves as a useful guide to other studies.

BOLTON, D. L. (Ed.). *The Use of Simulators in Educational Ad-ministration.* Columbus, Ohio: Merrill, 1971. A relatively specific book concerning the use of simulators in the area of educational administration.

BORICH, G. D. (Ed.). *Evaluating Educational Programs and Prod-ucts.* Englewood Cliffs, N.J.: Educational Technology Publica-tions, 1974. This recent book is more oriented to the problems of overall program evaluation than to assessment. But the reading by Sanders and Cunnningham offers a discussion of formative evaluation with special emphasis on techniques and procedures. This discussion lists such techniques as surveys, scaling, Q-sort, semantic differential, Delphi, sentence completion, observation, unobtrusive measures, and category and rating schemes.

BRAY, D. W., and GRANT, D. L. "The Assessment Center in the Measurement of Potential for Business Management." *Psycho-logical Monographs,* 1966, *80* (whole no. 625). This article dis-cusses the use of assessment centers, similar to those used by the Office of Strategic Services in World War II, as a means of determining business management potential. The more recent article by Grant and Bray (1969) gives wider coverage of the topic of assessment centers.

BURNS, R. W. "Achievement Testing in Competency-Based Educa-tion." *Educational Technology,* November 1972, pp. 39–42. In discussing what should be emphasized in assessment within com-petency-based programs, the author stresses the desirability of using criterion-referenced rather than norm-referenced tests. He also draws attention to the distinction between product and process evaluation.

BUROS, O. K. *The Sixth Mental Measurement Yearbook*. Highland Park, N.J.: Grython Press, 1965. This series of yearbooks offers one of the most comprehensive overviews of existing tests in almost all areas of psychological assessment. While paper and pencil tests are emphasized, projective tests are also discussed. Little attention is given to performance tests, perhaps because the yearbook is designed mainly for use by psychologists. Test descriptions, and sometimes detailed discussion of the merits of different tests, are provided.

CAMPBELL, D. T. "A Typology of Tests, Projective and Otherwise." In D. N. Jackson and S. Messick (Eds.), *Problems in Human Assessment*. New York: McGraw-Hill, 1967. The Campbell article offers a useful categorization system for examining the area of human assessment. Eight basic categories are suggested, all steming from three basic distinctions: whether the subject is aware of the true nature of the test, whether the response is direct or indirect, and whether there is a free or structured format.

CAMPBELL, J. P., DUNNETTE, M. D., and AVERY, R. D. "The Development and Evaluation of Behaviorally Based Rating Scales." *Journal of Applied Psychology*, 1973, *57*, 15–22. This article describes a variant of the critical incident technique for use in selecting department managers in retail stores. Little information is given in terms of predictive validity, as authors concentrate on validation by use of convergent and discriminatory validity.

CAMPBELL, R. J., KAGAN, N., and KRATHWOHL, D. R. "The Development and Validation of a Scale to Measure Affective Sensitivity (Empathy)." *Journal of Counseling Psychology*, 1971, *18*, 407–412. This article discusses an attempt to develop and validate an Affective Sensibility Scale (Empathy), which is essentially a paper and pencil test. Form B of the scale showed considerable concurrent validity with scores based on ratings by the therapist who had observed the prospective counselor and also showed significant predictive validity for "success as a counselor." The authors admit the need for additional work to refine the scale.

COZAN, L. W. "Forced-Choice: Better Than Other Rating Methods?" In T. L. Whisler and S. F. Harper (Eds.), *Performance Appraisal*. New York: Holt, Rinehart and Winston, 1962. This article reviews several studies of the validity of forced-choice rating scales and other rating methods. It looks at both military and nonmilitary findings and presents some surprisingly high predictive validity coefficients, but the material is now probably somewhat dated.

CRONBACH, L. J. *Essentials of Psychological Testing*. (2nd ed.) New York: Harper & Row, 1960. Frequently used as a basic text in psychology courses dealing with assessment and counseling, this book offers sound coverage of available tests, along with helpful advice for the novice test user. It discusses uses for tests and provides reliability and validity information.

DEAN, D. H., and WAECHTER, M. *Measurement in Competency-Based Education*. Gresham, Ore.: Mt. Hood Community College, 1974. Reports on assessment in Mt. Hood nurse training program. Some overview of assessment literature relevant to performance-based assessment is given. Discussion of distinctions among inferential-operant, norm-referenced, criterion-referenced, and formative-summative-ultimate tests.

DONOVAN, J. J. (Ed.). *Recruitment and Selection in the Public Service*. Chicago: Public Personnel Association, 1968. A text on public service selection that emphasizes paper and pencil tests. Little of real relevance.

DULEY, J. "Cross-Cultural Field Study." In J. Duley (Ed.), *New Directions for Higher Education: Implementing Field Experience Education*, no. 6. San Francisco: Jossey-Bass, 1974. A short chapter on assessment techniques used at Justin Morrill College (Michigan State University). Main reference is to critical incident technique as used in relation to field experience. Article also comments on student evaluation of the program by means of semantic differentials, value inventories, and so forth.

EBEL, R. L. "Criterion-Referenced Measures: Limitations." *School Review*, 1971, 75, 282–288. This article is of particular interest in view of the stress on criterion-referenced tests in competence-based programs. The author notes that criterion-referenced tests require "a degree of detail in the specification of objectives that is quite unrealistic to expect and impractical to use except at the most elementary levels of education" and that "knowledge does not come in discrete chunks that can be defined and identified separately." Author attacks criterion-referenced tests as not telling us all we need to know, difficult to obtain on a sound basis, and necessary only in a few important educational achievements.

EBEL, R. L. *Essentials of Educational Measurement.* Englewood Cliffs, N.J.: Prentice-Hall, 1972. This book is another basic text in the area of assessment, but emphasis is on educational testing rather than broader forms of psychological assessment. It offers a good coverage of statistical as well as practical techniques for improving assessment procedures and also compares the merits and drawbacks of certain types of tests, for example, essay versus objective.

FIELDER, F., and HARRIS, G. *The Quest for Foreign Affairs Officers —Their Recruitment and Selection.* New York: Carnegie Endowment for International Peace, 1966. This report summarizes the foreign service officer selection procedures. Preliminary selection is on the basis of a battery of paper and pencil tests (general ability, general knowledge, language potential), with the main selection being made on the basis of two-part oral examination: a "leaderless group" situation with other candidates, during which the candidates are observed, and an intensive individual oral exam before a panel. The report notes that the selection criteria used by panel members vary greatly.

FITZPATRICK, R., and MORRISON, E. J. "Performance and Product Evaluation." In R. L. Thorndike (Ed.), *Educational Measurement.* (2nd ed.) Washington, D.C.: American Council on Education, 1971. An excellent coverage of various product and performance assessment techniques—simulation, work sample, in-basket, and so forth. This article offers one of the broadest but also most detailed coverages found so far. The reference list is also very useful.

FLANAGAN, J. C. "The Critical Incident Technique." *Psychological Bulletin*, 1954, *51*, 327–358. This article reviews the history of the critical incident technique and also traces the many areas in which the technique has been used—from bookkeeping to dentistry and teaching.

FREDERIKSEN, N. "Proficiency Tests for Training Evaluation." In R. Glaser (Ed.), *Training Research and Education*. Pittsburgh: University of Pittsburgh Press, 1962. Frederiksen was one of the originators of the in-basket technique. His article lists a large number of techniques that can be used as proficiency tests and provides some useful references.

GAGNÉ, R. M. "Simulations." In R. Glaser (Ed.), *Training Research and Education*. Pittsburgh: University of Pittsburgh Press, 1962. This chapter discusses aircraft simulators, helicopters, large guns, complex electrical equipment (troubleshooting), complex weapon systems. Gagné offers a good history of the use of simulation but gives little concrete information concerning predictive validity of assessment made on the basis of simulated behavior.

GERBICH, J. R., GREENE, H. A., and JORGENSEN, A. N. *Measurement and Evaluation in the Modern School*. New York: McKay, 1962. A standard overview of educational assessment, although it does present a limited discussion of performance-type tests, a discussion not often found in such texts.

GLASER, R. (Ed.). *Training Research and Education*. Pittsburgh: University of Pittsburgh Press, 1962. The most notable chapters are those by Gagné on simulation, Frederiksen on proficiency tests, and Wilson on on-the-job tests and operational criteria.

GORDON, L. V. "Clinical, Psychometric, and Work Sample Approaches in the Prediction of Success in Peace Corps Training."

Journal of Applied Psychology, 1967, *51,* 111–119. This article provides data on the predictive validity of selection procedures used in the Peace Corps. The criterion variable is selection for actual overseas service. Procedures included: clinical assessment (.39 validity), work sample measures (.41)', psychometric measures (.37)', and brief assessment (.39). All were significant. Conclusion drawn: Use cheapest or quickest method since all are almost equally valid.

GRANT, D. L., and BRAY, D. W. "Contributions of the Interview to Assessment of Managerial Potential." *Journal of Applied Psychology,* 1969, *53,* 24–34. A good review of literature on the utility of the interview as a selection or prediction device. The article emphasizes the part played by the interview within an assessment center testing situation. Using data from the Bell Telephone Management Progress Study, the authors concluded that an unstructured interview in which questions were asked about family background, hobbies, work goals, position on social issues, and so forth made a useful contribution to the testing process, especially in terms of providing judgments about career motivation and interpersonal skills.

HOLMAN, M. G., and DOCTER, R. *Educational and Psychological Testing: A Study of the Industry and its Practices.* New York: Russell Sage Foundation, 1972. As a general overview of the testing "industry," this book gives some interesting information on who "controls" testing in the United States and on the legal considerations now related to testing.

HOOPES, R. *The Complete Peace Corps Guide.* New York: Dial Press, 1966. Essentially a handbook for the Peace Corps applicant and the Peace Corps worker.

HUCK, J. R. "Assessment Centers: A Review of External and Internal Validity." *Personnel Psychology,* 1973, *26,* 191–212. This review article provides good coverage of the literature on the validity of assessment center procedures for the selection of personnel for big business (IBM, Bell Telephone). Predictive validity coefficients from other studies are also reported.

JACKSON, D. N., and MESSICK, S. (Eds.). *Problems in Human Assessment.* New York: McGraw-Hill, 1967. This book emphasizes psychological assessment. The relevance of the readings varies greatly.

JOHNSON, D. W. "Affective Outcomes." In J. Walberg (Ed.), *Evaluating Educational Performance.* Berkeley, Calif.: McCutchan, 1974. Stresses affective outcomes of schooling and their measurement and reports on Minnesota School Affective Assessment test, which uses semantic differential items as well as agree-disagree items to test for cooperation and competition.

KELLY, E. L. "The Place of Situation Tests in Evaluating Clinical Psychologists." *Personnel Psychology,* 1954, *7,* 484–492.

KLINE, P. (Ed.). *New Approaches in Psychological Measurement.* New York: Wiley, 1973. Despite the promising title, this book contained little that was new or significant.

MC CLELLAND, D. C. "Testing for Competence Rather Than for 'Intelligence.' " *American Psychologist,* 1973, *28,* 1–14. One of the few articles to offer anything new on competence-assessment procedures. The author offers six characteristics he sees as suitable (or desirable) for tests assessing competencies and refers to certain empirical findings concerning the validity of both specific and general aptitude tests. This relatively nontechnical article also discusses the assessment of communication skills, patience, moderate goal setting, and ego development.

MC GUIRE, C. H. and BABBOTT, D. "Simulation Technique in the Measurement of Problem-Solving Skills." *Journal of Educational Measurement,* 1967, *4,* (1) 1–10. Discusses a variant of the tab technique. Account is of interest because of the generality or commonality of a concern with problem-solving ability.

MEEHL, P. E. *Clinical Versus Statistical Prediction: A Theoretical Analysis and a Review of the Evidence.* Minneapolis: University of Minnesota Press, 1954. A classic in the area of assessment, this

book is often cited for its attempt to evaluate the relative worth
of clinical and statistical techniques for predictive purposes.
Meehl's findings favored the statistical (or more "objective"
paper-and-pencil tests) approach (see Super and Crites, 1962;
and Stern, 1963). His work bears indirectly on the issue of overall judgmental versus specific and "objective" forms of assessment within competence-based programs.

MEYER, H. H. "The Validity of the In-Basket Test as a Measure of
Managerial Performance." *Personnel Psychology*, 1970, *23*,
297–307. In this study a maximum correlation of .37 was found
between the subjective estimate of "how well S handled Plant
Manager Position" during in-basket performance and on-job
rating for planning and administration. Although all other correlations reported were lower than this, author concludes favorably on the in-basket technique.

MILHOLLAND, J. E. "Theory and Techniques of Assessment." In
P. R. Farnsworth, O. McNemar, and Q. McNemar, *Annual
Review of Psychology*. Palo Alto, Calif.: Annual Reviews, 1964.
Article reports some interesting validity estimates for projective
tests, especially the Rorschach and Thematic Apperception Test.

MINER, J. B. *Personnel Psychology*. London: Macmillan, 1969.
A general text mainly for the use of industrial psychologists and
others concerned with selection of personnel. Of particular interest are the comments on specific tests of skill, and references to
the U.S. Department of Labor validity studies for components
of the General Aptitude Test Battery.

MOORE, R. F. (Ed.). *Compensating Executive Worth*. New York:
American Manufacturers Association, 1968. This book of readings focuses on the problem of how to identify and then compensate executive worth. Various articles trace the history of executive performance appraisal (trial ratings, overall performance
ratings, and, more recently, management by objectives). Management by objectives seems to have parallels with some aspects
of competence-based education (for example, specification of ob-

jectives, involvement of the candidate, and performance-based assessment).

MULLINS, C. J. "Development of Objective Personality Measures." Tri-Service Conference on Selection Research. Washington, D.C.: Office of Naval Research, 1960. Although essentially oriented towards the military and the selection of military personnel, this paper does discuss some interesting points.

National Society for the Study of Education. *Educational Evaluation: New Roles, New Means.* Chicago: University of Chicago Press, 1969. The chapter by Whitla reviews numerous findings on the validity of a wide range of tests (general ability, preference tests, personality tests) and is a very useful source of information.

NEWMAN, S. H., HOWELL, M., and CLIFF, N. "The Analysis and Prediction of a Practical Examination in Dentistry." In D. N. Jackson and S. Messick (Eds.), *Problems in Human Assessment.* New York: McGraw-Hill, 1967. A short article on the prediction of success in a practical exam in dentistry, using the interview, file evaluation (that is, records), verbal aptitude, spatial aptitude, quantitative ability, mathematical ability, and four specific tests of dental technique and knowledge as predictors. Interview provided best prediction, followed by the file evaluation.

NOWLIS, V. "Research with the Mood Adjective Checklist." In S. S. Tomkins and C. E. Izard (Eds.), *Affect, Cognition, and Personality.* New York: Springer, 1965. The study reported stresses validation of the checklist as a means of determining mood by use of the checklist to assess mood immediately after mood saliency has been increased (for example, by showing different films to different samples—comedy, tragedy, and so forth). Some support for the checklist is provided as a result of this study.

OSGOOD, C. E., SUCI, G. J., and TANNENBAUM, P. H. *The Measurement of Meaning.* Urbana: University of Illinois Press, 1957. This book reports the initial research on the semantic differential technique. The technique is widely used in research and could be considered for use in assessment when a relatively subtle or disguised assessment is needed. The technique requires the respondent to react to the concepts presented, using a continuum with polarized adjective pairs at the extremes (for example, client: good—bad, rich—poor). Duley notes the use of the technique as part of a program evaluation by students at Justin Morrill (see Duley, 1974).

PALARDY, J. M. *Teaching Today.* New York: Macmillan, 1975. A large number of readings that vary in quality and subject emphasis. Many of the readings are too general to be of great use, but Palardy and Eisle's "Competency-Based Education" contained some interesting points.

POPHAM, W. J. *Evaluating Instruction.* Englewood Cliffs, N.J.: Prentice-Hall, 1973. A teacher-oriented text that "practices what it preaches" in terms of having numerous exercises for summative evaluation purposes and specifying the objectives of each chapter. Perhaps a useful book for the reader who has little background in assessment.

QUIRK, T. J. "Some Measurement Issues in CBTE." *Phi Delta Kappan,* January 1974, pp. 316–318. Discussion of a number of issues related to measurement within competence-based teacher education. Some problems concerning simulation are noted, especially the instability of teacher behavior. The issue of whether to adopt a linear regression model (in which low performance in one area may be compensated for by high performance in other areas) or a multiple cut-off model (in which a minimum level must be achieved in *all* areas) is discussed.

REDFERN, G. B. "Competency-Based Evaluation: The State of the Art." *New Directions for Education,* 1973, *1,* 51–63. This article does not provide significant new information but traces some of the history of performance testing: trait rating, job descriptions, job standards, functions, performance objectives (product oriented), and stress on self-assessment.

REMMERS, H. H. "Rating Methods in Research on Teaching." In

N. L. Gage (Ed.)', *Handbook of Research on Teaching.* Chicago: Rand McNally, 1963. This article concentrates on various rating scale forms of assessment, with some emphasis on use in teacher evaluation. A useful list of various rating scales and of modifications of the rating scales approach: graphical, cumulative point, checklists, multiple choice, forced choice, sociometric, semantic differential, and Q-technique.

RUSSELL, J. D. "Assessment of Teacher Competencies." In J. E. Weigard (Ed.), *Developing Teacher Competency.* Englewood Cliffs, N.J.: Prentice-Hall, 1971. This article makes brief reference to a number of techniques that could be used to assess teacher competency—audiotape, videotape, interaction analysis, question-asking skills, instruction sequencing, creativity, and human interaction skills.

SCHMEIDER, A. A. *Competency-Based Education: The State of the Scene.* Washington, D.C.: American Council for Teacher Education, 1973. This publication actually does little to describe the state of competence-based education—at least in terms of assessment.

SHARON, A. T. *Planning the Development of Measurement and Evaluation Services for Use in Occupational Programs at Postsecondary Institutions.* Princeton, N.J.: Educational Testing Service (ETS), 1974. This report outlines attempts made by ETS to determine the need for new evaluation services, especially in occupational programs. The stress is very much on evaluating only those occupationally learned skills that overlap skills or knowledge taught in college courses—the emphasis is thus on transfer of credit. Although the report mentions the importance of affective variables, it claims that the state of the art does not permit their accurate assessment.

SKAGER, R. "Evaluating Educational Alternatives." In J. I. Goodlad (Ed.), *New Directions for Education: Alternatives in Education,* no. 4. San Francisco: Jossey-Bass, 1973. A general chapter that warns against the restrictiveness of the behavioral-objective approach in evaluation.

STERN, G. C. "Measuring Noncognitive Variables in Research on Teaching." In N. L. Gage (Ed.), *Handbook of Research on Teaching.* Chicago: Rand McNally, 1963. In reviewing a considerable amount of general assessment literature, this handbook stresses multivariate assessment and objective rather than clinical techniques. It discusses the problem of how to determine objectives, especially in regard to teacher education, and reports some of Gage's work on use of projective tests to predict teacher success.

SUPER, D. E., and CRITES, J. O. *Appraising Vocational Fitness.* New York: Harper & Row, 1962. This text provides an overview of fairly standard tests used for counseling and selection. Provides considerable test description, as well as reliability and validity data. Mainly directed toward the psychologist who wishes to select a test.

THORNDIKE, R. L. (Ed.). *Educational Measurement.* (2nd ed.) Washington, D.C.: American Council on Education, 1971. This book, which contains many readings by people well known in the field of psychological assessment, gives considerable attention to theoretical and statistical problems in measurement. The article by Fitzpatrick and Morrison (see separate entry) is very useful.

TOMKINS, S. S., and IZARD, C. E. (Eds.). *Affect, Cognition, and Personality.* New York: Springer, 1965. The main paper of interest in this volume of readings is that by Nowlis (see separate entry).

TRIVETT, D. A. *Academic Credit for Prior Off-Campus Learning.* Washington, D.C.: American Association for Higher Education, 1975. This report offers some up-to-date information about accrediting practices for off-campus experience. Most of the comment is general or directed at broad assessment issues.

TURNER, C. P. (Ed.). *A Guide to the Evaluation of Educational Experiences in the Armed Services,* Washington, D.C.: American Council on Education, 1968. This volume is simply a guide to transfer of credit for work done in military courses.

U.S. Government. *Peace Corps Handbook*. Washington, D.C.: U.S. Government Printing Office, 1961. A general guide for Peace Corps workers and Peace Corps applicants.

U.S. Office of Strategic Services. *Assessment of Men*. New York: Holt, Rinehart and Winston, 1948. A tremendously interesting account of selection techniques used by the Office of Strategic Services in selecting special agents. A three-day stay at a farmhouse with testers and testees in residence provided the test situation. Included were sentence-completion tests, health questions, vocabulary tests, personal history questions, projective questions, The Brook, The Wall, construction tests, interviews (stress), map memorization, and a test of critical sensitivity to things not seen before. Validity ratings ranged from .53 to .08 for the various components, and the program is generally seen as unsuccessful in achieving any real accuracy of selection.

WALBERG, H. J. *Evaluating Educational Performance*. Berkeley, Calif.: McCutchan, 1974. The paper by Johnson was found to be of most interest here (see separate entry).

WHISLER, T. L., and HARPER, S. F. (Eds.). *Performance Appraisal*. New York: Holt, Rinehart and Winston, 1962. This volume of readings presents some papers of historical interest that point to the early development of certain assessment techniques. The emphasis tends to be on appraisal of performance in military or industrial settings. The article by Cozan on forced-choice rating scales was of particular interest as it reported a number of validity findings (see separate entry).

WILSON, C. L. "On-The-Job and Operational Criteria." In R. Glaser (Ed.), *Training Research and Education*. Pittsburgh: University of Pittsburgh Press, 1962. Discusses rating scales and reports Jones' review (1950) of 2100 selection studies, of which only 426 report quantitative validity coefficients. Lists various assessment techniques, including operational performance measures, work samples, and ratings.

Wendy Kohli

Selected Annotated
Bibliography

ﾚﾚﾚﾚﾚﾚﾚﾚﾚﾚﾚﾚﾚﾚﾚﾚ

ARGYRIS, C. *Interpersonal Competence and Organizational Effectiveness.* Homewood, Ill.: Dorsey Press, 1962. The research presented in this volume is from a project that investigated the concept of competence in administrative settings in order to help an organization increase its administrative competence. The concept of administrative competence was analyzed and separated into two components: (1) intellective, rational, technical competence, and (2) interpersonal competence. The first deals with things and ideas: the second with people. The study focused on how to measure interpersonal competence within an organization and how to measure its impact upon the organization.

ARGYRIS, C., and SCHON, D. *Theory in Practice: Increasing Professional Effectiveness.* San Francisco: Jossey-Bass, 1974. This study addresses the issues around professional education based on effectiveness in professional action. Assuming a concept of human nature as "competence-oriented," it proceeds to develop action theories that will aid in practical professional intervention. The study is concerned with redesigning professional education to improve the *effectiveness of* professionals. Theories of

521

action are explored, and conditions for learning to enhance
effectiveness are addressed.

BERG, I. "Education and Performance," *Journal of Higher Education,* 1972, *43,* 192–202. Berg, also the author of *Education and
Jobs: The Great Training Robbery,* raises some provocative
questions about the value of and need for college credentials for
professional employment. He asks "whether college graduates are
increasingly likely to find themselves in vocations in which they
are required to perform in jobs falling below their expectations
with regard to challenge, mobility opportunity, and income
return" and "whether degrees and the qualities they presumably
represent enhance the performance of those who enter the
professions."

BETTELHEIM, B. *A Home for the Heart.* New York: Knopf, 1974.
The story of the creation of an atmosphere, or "home for the
heart," where a community of love, respect, and health thrives.
This community—at the Orthogenic School in Chicago—exemplifies "total milieu therapy" through which children previously
labeled as mentally ill or autistic have been returned to the world
to lead whole and healthy lives. Of particular interest to those
in the area of competence-based education may be the assessment of prospective staff members. The author here describes
assessment in its subtle and most human form.

BLOCK, J. H. "Mastery Learning in the Classroom: An Overview
of Recent Research." Mimeographed. Santa Barbara: University of California, 1973. A partial review of research since 1971
on mastery learning. It focuses on one topic—the use of mastery
learning concepts in the schools. In the first section, two major
approaches to mastery learning (Bloom's learning for mastery
and Keller's personalized system of instruction) are described and
contrasted. The second section discusses research on the cognitive
and affective learning outcomes of these approaches, and the
final section explores some of their effects on individual learning
differences.

BLOOM, B. S., (Ed.). *Taxonomy of Educational Objectives. Cognitive Domain.* Vol. I: New York: McKay, 1956. The culminative work of a committee of thirty-four educators and psychologists who met periodically from 1949 to 1953 with the task of organizing and writing the cognitive portion of a taxonomy of educational goals. This volume grapples with such issues as the problem of hierarchy in classification, what is knowable, and the problem of classifying educational objectives. The taxonomy is then presented, including sections on knowledge, comprehension, application, analysis, synthesis, and evaluation.

BLOOM, B. S. "Time and Learning." Thorndike Award Address, 81st annual convention of the American Psychological Association, Montreal, August 27, 1973. Bloom's central theme is time and its relationship to learning. Maintaining that all learning requires time and that time is limited, Bloom suggests that schools should reassess their use of time and investigate methods of learning that will be more effective and efficient for students, teachers, and institutions. He describes John Carroll's model of school learning and its basic thesis that time is a central variable in school learning and that students differ in the amount of time they need to learn a given unit based on a set of criteria.

BROUDY, H. S. "Can we Define Good Teaching?" *Teachers College Record,* 1969, *70,* 583–592. Broudy discusses the difficulties of defining good teaching and elaborates on the dichotomy between didactic and encounter teaching. The former, according to Broudy, is the kind of teaching for which outcomes, means, and criteria can be made explicit and will be the dominant mode in time to come. The latter form, after the model of the humanely cultivated person, may become possible as teachers are freed by technology, but here neither outcomes nor means nor criteria can be specified. Broudy maintains that the problem lies in getting people to do a kind of teaching that cannot be fully defined.

BROUDY, H. S. "A Critique of Performance-Based Education." Pamphlet No. 4 of Performance-Based Teacher Education Series.

Washington, D.C.: American Association of Colleges for Teacher
Education, May 1972. According to Broudy, performance-based
teacher education will produce persons capable only of didactic
teaching. The need for those who can design programs and build
contexts for learning calls for teacher education that is strong in
theory and evaluates learning on the basis of a student's understanding rather than performance.

BROWNLEE, C. G. "A Small College Looks at Competency." Council
for the Advancement of Small Colleges *Newsletter,* 1974, *17* (4),
9–12.

BROWNLEE, C. G. "Competency in Liberal Arts Education." Paper
presented to American Association of Higher Education National
Conference, Chicago, Illinois, March 11, 1974. (Can be obtained through ERIC Clearinghouse: No. ED 090-812.)

BRUNER, J. *The Process of Education.* Cambridge, Mass.: Harvard
University Press, 1960. This provocative volume on learning
and the curriculum has influenced educators at all levels of
teaching. Bruner addresses such issues as the "importance of
structure for learning," the need for "readiness for learning,"
and the place of intuitive and analytic thinking in learning.

BRUNER, J. *The Relevance of Education.* New York: Norton, 1971.
This volume of essays touches on many issues relevant to implementors of competence-based education programs. The author
puzzles over the "relationship between knowledge as detached
(competence?) and knowledge as a guide to purposeful action
(performance?)." He sees competence as self-rewarding and as
a form of motivation intrinsic to an activity. In the essay "The
Relevance of Skill or the Skill of Relevance," Bruner proposes
that the objective of schooling is to produce skill—"skill in
achieving goals of personal significance."

BURNS, R. W., and KLINGSTEDT, J. L. *Competency-Based Education: An Introduction.* Englewood Cliffs, N.J.: Educational
Technology Publications, 1973. This volume of eighteen papers

deals predominantly with teacher education, although much of what is presented is applicable to competence-based education as a general concept in education. The book moves from "basic theoretical assumptions and justifications to practical application." It also addresses some of the results of the implementation of competence-based education.

Carnegie Commission on Higher Education. *Less Time, More Options: Education Beyond High School.* New York: McGraw-Hill, 1971. This special report examines the "general flow" of students in and through the formal higher education structure and the role of degrees in this flow. It recommends change in degree structures to respond to new developments in higher education and supports time-shortened degrees and the acceptance of certain new degrees (doctor of arts and master of philosophy).

CARROLL, J. B. "A Model of School Learning." *Teachers College Record*, 1963, *64*, 723–733. This presents a conceptual model of learning to deal with factors affecting success in school learning and the way these factors interact. Carroll defines a "learning task" and suggests that *most* goals of the school can be expressed in this form. His model is intended to apply to all such tasks and is designed so that the basic concepts of the model are measured in terms of *time*. The goals that cannot be defined as learning tasks (attitudes, dispositions, and values) are not dealt with by this model, although they may be supported cognitively by related tasks. Perhaps the most implicit assumption in this model is that the degree of learning—other things being equal—is a simple function of the amount of time during which the pupil engages actively in learning.

CARROLL, J. B., and CHALL, J. (Eds.). *Toward a Literate Society: A Report From the National Academy of Education.* New York: McGraw-Hill, 1975. In addition to providing a concise diagnosis of the reading problem in America, this volume also reveals a strategy for remedying the problem with recommendations for specific legislative and administrative actions to implement that strategy. "The Political Implications of a National Reading

Effort" has some bearing on the political problem of accountability and competence-based education.

CHANAN, G. "Objectives in the Humanities." *Educational Research,*
1974, *16,* 198–205. The author argues that objectives are suitable to the teaching of the humanities and he seeks to discover a
mode of inquiry where this is so. He addresses the differences
between sciences and humanities and raises some pertinent questions that derive from "the nature of the humanities" rather than
from an "overgeneralized analogy with the sciences."

CHICKERING, A. *Education and Identity.* San Francisco: Jossey-Bass,
1969. In "Developing Competence," Chickering likens competence to a "three-tined pitchfork." Intellectual competence, phys-
ical-manual skills, and interpersonal competence are the tines,
and sense of competence is the handle. All aspects of competence
are analyzed separately, with Chickering maintaining that colleges
have the responsibility to systematically and rationally respond to
these components as separate elements of a larger whole. (The
entire book is recommended.)

CHICKERING, A. "Social Change, Human Development and Higher
Education." In E. McGrath (Ed.), *Prospect for Renewal: The
Future of the Liberal Arts College.* San Francisco: Jossey-Bass,
1972. The author maintains that three kinds of competence are
required for a successful and satisfying existence: intellectual
competence, professional or vocational ability, and interpersonal
competence. Furthermore, effective performance does not simply
depend upon *level* of competence; it is significantly influenced by
the self-confidence brought to the task. The implications of these
assertions for education are posited in this essay.

COLEMAN, J. (Ed.). *Youth: Transition to Adulthood.* Chicago:
University of Chicago Press, 1974. This report of the Panel on
Youth of the President's Science Advisory Committee challenges
the assumption that formal schooling is the best way to socialize
young people into adult roles. The main aim of the report is "to
stimulate the search for institutional inventions" that will ensure

that young people acquire the capabilities for fulfilling the demands and opportunities of adulthood. Implications for competence-based education at the high school and college level can be drawn from the findings in this report.

COLLEGE FOR HUMAN SERVICES. "Experiment in Competency-Based Education: A Total Program for Educating the Human Service Professional." Planning Paper No. 1. New York: College for Human Services, 1973. This document provides a general description of the program at the college—a program built around "performance objectives" in the areas of teaching and social work. The basic educational assumptions underlying this program are articulated, and the document concludes with an analysis of the educational design of the program built on a two-year time frame in which "practice, study and assessment" are carried out through curricular units or "clusters" built around various competencies.

COLSON, E. "Competence and Incompetence in the Context of Independence." *Current Anthropology*, 1967, *8,* 92–111. The focus within this anthropological study is on the way in which people perceive themselves as competent or otherwise. The author suggests that this perception refers to at least two factors: the "ability to compete with others" and the "ability to get things done in an effective way." Each implies both a standard by which the level of competency may be judged and someone to make the judgment. A distinction is made between technical competence (manipulation of materials processes) and political competence (manipulation of person and event) from a cross-cultural investigation. The author describes how the standards of competence change drastically as a society develops historically.

Competency-Based Undergraduate Education Project. Occasional Paper Series. Bowling Green, Ohio: Bowling Green State University. The first three papers in this series are Thomas Ewens' "Think Piece on CBE and Liberal Education," (No. 1, 1977), Mark Schlesinger's "Reconstructing General Education: An Examination of Assumption, Practices and Prospects" CUE Occasional Paper Series (No. 2, 1977), and Gary A. Woditsch's "Developing Generic Skills: A Model for Competence-Based General Education," (No. 3, 1977).

Competency-Forum. Elgin, Ill.: The Center for Human Potential. A regular newsletter dedicated to exploring developments in competence-based education.

CONNOLLY, K., and BRUNER, J. (Eds.). *The Growth of Competence*. New York: Academic Press, 1974. This book emerged from a conference on the growth of competence in infancy and childhood. Fifteen scientists met to discuss the concept of competence and ask questions that included: "What is competence and how do we use the notion?" "What are the principal dimensions of competence?" "Are certain skills more fundamental than others?" Among the more relevant essays in the text are: "Competence: Its Nature and Nurture;" "Competence and the Growth of Personality;" "Social Competence and the Educational Process," all three by Robert D. Hess, and "Competence, the Growth of the Person," by Bruner and Connolly. Although the authors are speaking particularly to the question of competence in childhood, general implications for adults and college education are apparent.

CROSS, K. P. *Beyond the Open Door: New Students to Higher Education*. San Francisco: Jossey-Bass, 1971. This analysis of the form and content of American higher education in relation to the "new students" of the 1970s illuminates the task of developing an education that will serve the needs of these students. Adults, ethnic minorities, and women are included under the rubric "new students." Their interests and attitudes about education and careers are analyzed, and suggestions are made for possible reforms that could accommodate this new clientele in higher education.

CROSS, K. P. *Accent on Learning: Improving Instruction and Reshaping the Curriculum*. San Francisco: Jossey-Bass, 1976. A synthesis from over a thousand studies of such important instructional techniques as mastery learning, self-paced modules, personalized systems of instruction, and interpersonal laboratory training. Cross advocates a curriculum requiring that all students achieve adequacy in working with (1) ideas, (2) people, and (3) things, as well as excellence in one of these three skill areas.

DORNBUSCH, S., and SCOTT, W. R. *Evaluation and the Exercise of Authority. A Theory of Controls Applied to Diverse Organizations.* San Francisco: Jossey-Bass, 1975. This volume, the result of a ten-year research program in formal organizations, develops a conceptual schema of evaluation and authority that is applicable to many kinds of organizations. Theoretical and empirical sections are interwoven nicely as the generality of theories is tested in an electronics plant, public school and university, hospital, student newspaper, football team, alternative schools and Roman Catholic archdiocese. Of particular interest to practitioners in competence-based programs is the analysis of evaluation (assessment) as a complex process with four distinct components: (1) assigning a goal to a participant, (2) determining criteria to be employed in evaluating task performance, (3) selecting the sample of *performances* or *outcomes* that will be inspected, and (4) assessing the sampled performance with the established criteria.

DOUVAN, E. "Commitment and Social Contract in Adolescence." *Psychiatry,* 1974, *37,* 23–26. The author analyzes the way in which an adolescent feels that to be competent is a commitment—a commitment to which she/he may be held; thus, it may be better to be incompetent. She discusses the way young people want to be loved "for ourselves alone," not because they are good or competent.

DRESSEL, P. L. *College and University Curriculum.* Berkeley, Calif.: McCutchan, 1968. This systemic focus on the college curriculum gives a thorough treatment of the developments and trends in education as they relate to liberal education (or disciplines), professional education, and graduate education. Questions of instruction and evaluation are spotlighted, and the competences to be attained by students are developed. The author presents six fundamental competences and how they may be attained, as well as suggests the evidence that may be needed to support their attainment.

DRESSEL, P. L. "Values Cognitive and Affective." *Journal of Higher Education* May 1971, *42*, 400–405. This editorial addresses the issue of the unification of the cognitive and affective domains of learning. For the author, "educated behavior always involves both affective and cognitive elements," and institutions of higher education must become more conscious of the role of values in the structure and content of the educational process.

DRESSEL, P. L., and MAYHEW, L. B. (Eds.). *General Education: Exploration in Evaluation.* Washington, D.C.: American Council on Education, 1954. A major portion of this volume is devoted to a report of the procedures and results of six intercollege committees. The committees, working on six objectives of general education accepted by all or most of the colleges, undertook to define the objectives more carefully, develop evaluation techniques, and collect evidence on student achievement.

ECKERT, R. E. *Outcomes of General Education.* University of Minnesota Studies of General Education, M. Maclean (Ed.). Minneapolis: University of Minnesota Press, 1943. This is a "first exploratory attempt" to discuss what the General College has accomplished and thus appraises the actual outcomes of a new curriculum. The volume argues that "the curriculum as it exists in *students* is the ultimate measure of any school's effectiveness." A chapter is devoted to the acquisition of socio-civic competence. This underscores the conviction that the college should "effectively prepare young people for the responsibilities and privileges of citizenship, both now and in their out-of-school years."

ELAM, S. *Performance-Based Teacher Education: What Is the State of the Art?* Washington, D.C.: American Association of Colleges for Teacher Education, 1972. This pamphlet constitutes an initial statement by the Committee on Performance-Based Teacher Education to clarify its concepts, to examine their potential and identify related problems, ambiguities, differences of opinion, and unanswered questions. Elam describes the five essential elements necessary for any performance-based teacher education program; states the characteristics implied in these essential elements; discusses the impact of the movement as it ranges through teacher education institutions, state departments of education, professional organizations and the communities they serve; and finally identifies a number of the advantages of the movement.

ELBOW, P. " 'A Competency-Based Management Program' at Seattle Central Community College." In G. Grant (Ed.), *On Competence: An Analysis of a Reform Movement in Higher Education.* Syracuse, N.Y.: Syracuse Research Corporation, 1977. This case study describes the attempt to use a federal grant to start a new program in a central city community college in a time of falling enrollment and budget cutbacks. The program is designed to provide a certificate in management to nontraditional students who are working as practitioners or are already working in management or supervisory roles in three human service areas: daycare centers; residential treatment centers or "halfway houses" of all sorts; and hospitals and other health care agencies. An interdisciplinary group worked out a core of management competencies needed in all three fields and organized them into eight courses where they would be taught and assessed.

GAGNÉ, R. M. *The Conditions of Learning.* New York: Holt, Rinehart and Winston, 1965. Learning is equated with "performance change" in this text. The author describes eight distinguishable classes of learning and the corresponding sets of conditions for learning that are associated with them. The eight classes are: signal learning, stimulus-response learning, chaining, verbal association, discrimination learning, concept learning, rule learning, and problem solving. According to the author, "Learning must be linked to the design of instruction through consideration of the different kinds of capabilities that are being learned."

GIARDINA, R. "The Baccalaureate: Defining the Undefinable?" *The Journal of Higher Education,* 1974, *45,* 112–122. Giardina maintains that a total reassessment of what the baccalaureate degree means is necessary if any attempt is to be made to change the character of degree requirements. Only by determining the types of competencies students should attain through an appropriate application of their affective orientations, values, and motivations, and by creating a degree program that will help to bring about these competencies can we reduce the time spent in undergraduate education without sacrificing educational quality.

GLADWIN, T. "Social Competence and Clinical Practice." *Psychiatry,* 1967, *30,* 30–43. The ideas presented in this article were drawn from a conference at the National Institute of Mental Health in 1965. The conference explored the ways "clinical interventions might be facilitated through placing a greater emphasis upon improving the social competence" of persons seeking or needing professional help. Social competence is referred to as "the ability of persons to participate effectively in the legitimate activities of their society" and is addressed in reference to social class and stratified social structure. The conference participants agreed that, for the development of social competence, there must be concern with the design of the "social pathways" through which one will travel and learn.

GLASER, R. "The Measurement of Learning Outcomes." *American Psychologist,* 1963, *18,* 519–521. This classic article calls for altered approaches to the measurement of learning outcomes. Achievement measurement is defined as the "assessment of terminals or criterion behavior." It involves the determination of the characteristics of student performance with respect to specified standards. Criterion-referenced measures of achievement or proficiency are used to assess the degree to which achievement resembles desired performance at any specified level.

GOODE, W. "Community Within a Community: The Professions." *American Sociological Review,* 1957, *22,* 194–200. The author maintains that a characteristic of each of the established professions, as well as a goal of each aspiring occupant, is "the community of profession." As the profession comes into being, it takes on the traits of a community. Socialization and social control in the professions are examined, and it is pointed out that "a client does not usually choose his professional by a *measurable criterion of competence* and after the work is done the client is not usually *competent* to judge if it was done properly. This puts the professional in a particularly exploitative position."

GOODE, W. "The Encroaching Charlatanism of the Emerging Profession." *American Sociological Review*, 1960, *25*, 902–914. The relationships among sociology, psychology, and medicine are explored to provide an illustration of the process by which an occupation moves toward professionalization. Goode notes that the process of professionalization and its concomitant changes are derived from "the knowledge base of an occupation and its service or collectivity orientation."

GOODLAD, J. I. *The Dynamics of Educational Change: Toward Responsive Schools.* New York: McGraw-Hill, 1975. This analysis of educational change rests on the assumption that schools are not mechanical organizations that can be broken down into distinct parts and studies but are ecosystems—whole organisms or natural systems of interdependent elements. Although this volume concentrates on innovations in the public schools, implications can be seen for higher education. The annotated bibliography is very helpful for those interested in educational institutions and change.

GRANT, G. (Ed.). *On Competence: An Analysis of a Reform Movement in Higher Education.* (2 vols.) Syracuse, N.Y.: Syracuse Research Corporation, 1977. This study, funded by the Fund for the Improvement of Postsecondary Education, includes nine case studies of colleges that chose to implement competence-based education programs. It also contains six essays on some common, critical issues that arose as these colleges instituted their new curriculums. The present volume (*On Competence*, Jossey-Bass, 1979) had its inception in the three-year study leading to this 1977 report.

GREEN, T. "The Undergraduate and the World of Work." In D. G. Trites (Ed.), *New Directions for Higher Education: Planning the*

Future of the Undergraduate College, no. 9. San Francisco: Jossey-Bass, 1975. This analysis of the relationship between education and "the world of work" suggests that a purely "nonvocational" view of liberal studies is necessary to understand this relationship.

HAMILTON, P. Memorandum Report, *Competence-Based Teacher Education.* Unpublished. Reproduced at Educational Policy Research Center, Stanford Research Institute, Menlo Park, Calif. 1973. This policy paper was commissioned by the U. S. Office of Education to study the movement toward accountability in teacher training (competence-based teacher education). The paper brings together the critical issues involved in competence-based teacher education, relates them to significant trends that could influence future policies, and suggests recommendations for future action.

HARRIS, J. "Baccalaureate Requirements: Attainments or Exposures?" *Educational Record,* 1972, *53,* 59–65. The question of degree granting in the undergraduate school is addressed. Should there be new criteria for the granting of degrees, and should degrees be based on *evaluated attainments* rather than *exposure* to subject areas? Harris makes the distinction between degree criteria and institutional goals, maintaining that an institution can seek to develop a total individual (affective domain); however, the degree criteria should be separate from this domain and be primarily cognitive.

HARRIS, J. "Assessment Measures Needed for CBE." *Peabody Journal of Education,* 1976, *53,* 241–247.

HARRIS, J. "The Competent College Student: An Essay on the Objectives and Quality of Higher Education." Nashville: Tennessee Higher Education Commission, 1977. This paper addresses the fact that too many people "enter the stream of adult life without having acquired . . . the skills and understandings essential for their own effectiveness."

HARRIS, J., and TROUTT, W. "Educational Credentials in American Society." Nashville: Tennessee Higher Education Commission, 1976. This paper describes the use of degrees, educational criteria, and other credentials in American society. A description of the present and anticipated roles of credentials is included, as well as a rationale of educational credentials.

HAYNES, P. M. "Competencies and Their Assessment." In *Instituting Competency-Based Degree Programs in a Large University.* Tallahassee: Center for Educational Design, Florida State University, 1975. This was a symposium held at the American Educational Research Association Annual Meeting, March 31, 1975.

HODGKINSON, H. "Issues in Competency-Based Learning." Mimeographed. Keynote address to National Conference on Competency-Based Learning, Cincinnati, Ohio, February 1974. Hodgkinson attempts to define competency-based learning and suggests that the impetus for its implementation stems from lack of faith in higher education. He deals with the development of mastery learning, as Bloom and Carroll have articulated it, and discusses six levels of general competence that provide a basis for many competency-based programs. Hodgkinson outlines problems that arise from competency-based education, such as the need to establish norm-referenced criteria with acceptable levels of difficulty, role problems of the faculty, poor measures of assessment, the need to develop an additive program rather than an array of self-contained courses with no direction, and the need to know more about the consequences of competency-based programs for institutions.

HOLDEN, C. "Employment Testing: Debate Simmers in and out of Court." *Science,* 1975, *190,* 35–39. A brief review of the employment testing controversy and legal attempts to correct employment testing abuses. The concepts of construct validity and "differential prediction" are analyzed in relation to "fairness" and minority recruitment. Implications for business and industry personnel selection procedures are presented.

HUFF, S. "Credentialing by Tests or by Degrees: Title VII of the Civil Rights Act and Griggs vs. Duke Power Company." *Harvard Educational Review,* 1974, *44,* 246–269. The author traces the evaluation of Title VII (Civil Rights Act of 1964 and the Equal Employment Opportunity Act of 1972) and the Griggs precedent (a test case of the principle that an employer has to prove employment tests are job related). She analyzes these implications for education in terms of the enrollment pattern, content, and function of public education.

INKELES, A. "Social Structure and the Socialization of Competence." *Harvard Educational Review,* 1965, *36,* 265–283. The author takes issue with socialization researchers over their failure to study socialization as a conscious process of training in anticipation of future social roles. Inkeles maintains that if we are to live in a modern, industrial setting, there are basic skills to be learned that will enable us to act as "competent" social beings. He suggests that it is up to the students of socialization to look at the differences among adults in this society to determine what is needed to prepare people competently for life in our constantly changing society and to question if in fact there may be qualities that give a person a general competence useful in all times and places.

JACKSON, D. N., and MESSICK, S. (Eds.). *Problems in Human Assessment.* New York: McGraw-Hill, 1967. A source book for professionals in education, sociology, and psychology who seek a cross section of thought on the problem of assessment. It includes classic articles by Robert Thorndike, Theodore Adorno, and Lee Crombach, as well as a presentation of research reports from contemporary literature.

JONES, N. "Antioch School of Law." In G. Grant (Ed.), *On Competence: An Analysis of a Reform Movement in Higher Education.* Syracuse, N.Y.: Syracuse Research Corporation, 1977. Antioch School of Law, which opened in Washington, D.C., in 1972, adapted the notion of competence to the area of professional education. This case study records the development of instruments for the assessment of lawyering competencies in a clinical setting, including the selection and specification of the competencies and the application of the evaluation instruments to the routine performance of students in the clinical component of the curriculum.

JOYCE, B., and WEIL, M. *Models of Teaching.* Englewood Cliffs, N.J.: Prentice-Hall, 1972. This volume, used by many competence-based curriculum specialists, identifies a range of models for teaching. These models are "approaches to creating environments for learning." They provide the teacher and curriculum-maker with the material to analyze, compare, and contrast so that their educational purposes may best be served. The models are subsumed under four main groups: (1) social interaction sources, (2) information-processing sources, (3) personal sources, and (4) behavior modification sources. The final section of the book draws out the implications of these models when they are used in actual educational settings.

KIMBALL, S. T., and WATSON, J. T. (Eds.). *Crossing Cultural Boundaries: The Anthropological Experience.* New York: Chandler, 1972. A collection of personal statements about fieldwork by approximately twenty contributors giving a comprehensive picture of *what* fieldwork is—not *how* to do it. It underscores the social and moral relationships involved in fieldwork.

KLEIN, R., and BABINEAU, R. "Evaluating the Competence of Trainees: 'It's Nothing Personal,'" *American Journal of Psychiatry,* 1974, *131* (7), 788–791. An exploration of factors that affect the participants in a process evaluating the professional competence of trainees in the mental health field. The authors draw on personal experiences with mental health trainees to delineate some of the rational and irrational components of the process and the dilemmas and conflicts for both the evaluator and the trainee; also, recommendations are made for clarifying roles and responsibilities for the individuals and the institutions involved.

KNOTT, R. "What is a Competence-Based Curriculum in the Liberal Arts?" *Journal of Higher Education,* 1975, *46,* 25–40. The

author begins the inquiry by formulating a model of the liberal
arts. He looks upon a liberal arts education "as a process that
develops specific human abilities rather than a set of studies with
inherent liberal qualities." He connects the liberal arts to competence-based curriculum by arguing that "the concern of liberal
education is the competent integration and utilization of required
competencies." From this initial connection, Knott proposes a
model of competence-based education that relies heavily on
Philip Phenix's patterns of meaning for its first component. A
second component is "a structure for promoting student mastery
of advanced skills in one special area." The third component
must include "a developmental scheme for effectively assisting
student maturation."

KOHLBERG, L., and MAYER, R. "Development as the Aim of Education." *Harvard Educational Review*, 1972, *42*, 449–496. The
authors offer an explanation of the psychological and philosophical positions underlying aspects of educational progressivism.
They contrast the progressivism identified with John Dewey
with two other educational ideologies, the romantic and the cultural transmission conceptions, that historically have competed
in the minds of educators as rationales for the choice of educational goals and practices. Kohlberg and Mayer maintain that
only progressivism, with its philosophically examined ethics,
provides an adequate basis for understanding the process of
education.

KOHLI, W. "Syracuse University." In G. Grant (Ed.), *On Competence: An Analysis of a Reform Movement in Higher Education.*
Syracuse, N.Y.: Syracuse Research Corporation, 1977. This case
study explores the interplay of three forces on the development
of the Redesign Program for Teacher Education at Syracuse
University. These three forces—federal educational policy, New
York State Education Department's mandates, and the university's preexisting involvement in competence-based teacher training—are analyzed. The study also details the changes in course
curriculum, as well as new modes of teaching and assessment,
that have resulted from the redesign efforts.

KRATHWOHL, D., BLOOM, B., and MASIA, B. *Taxonomy of Educational Objectives: The Classification of Educational Goals.* Vol. 2: *Affective Domain.* New York: McKay, 1964. The modeled partner of Vol. I, *Cognitive Domain,* this volume completes the Taxonomy of Education objectives. In addition to the classification scheme of receiving, responding, valuing, organization, and characterization by a value, this handbook focuses on such issues as the relation of the affective to the cognitive domain and the affects of this taxonomy on curriculum evaluation and research.

LIEBEIT, R. J., and BAYER, A. E. "Goals in Teaching Undergraduates: Professional Reproduction and Client-Centeredness." *American Sociologist,* 1975, *10,* 195–205. This article analyzes the efforts to refocus educational objectives in terms of client-centeredness and restructure the bureaucratic system of American higher education. The author indicates that "a client's reform of teaching" is possible if institutional policy makers continue to place "mounting emphasis on accountability to clients."

MC CLELLAND, D. C. "Testing for Competence Rather than for 'Intelligence.' " *American Psychologist,* 1973, *28,* 1–14. McClelland questions the validity of standard intelligence and aptitude tests as well as their "predictability" in relation to job performance and other worldly behavior. He proposes testing for competence rather than for intelligence through the use of criterion-sampling tests and that the assessment criteria be grouped in clusters of life outcomes (communication skills, patience, moderate goal setting, ego development). He suggests that this new testing movement should lead to a profile of an individual inclusive of ego and moral development and that tests should become a device for the mutual redesigning of the teaching/learning process.

MC CONNELL, T. R. "Problems Involved in Developing a Program of General Education." *Educational Review,* Supplement No. 16, 1947, *28,* 126–142. The author, involved with the General College at the University of Minnesota, maintains that "students should be expected to attain common *outcomes.*" These outcomes—defined in terms of *behavior*—must be evaluated for their attainment. This is a difficult task, for instruments have yet to be invented to adequately assess the student in relation to the outcomes; this, however, should not be used as a justification for returning to "credit-counting."

MC DONALD, F. "The Rationale for Competency-Based Programs." Mimeographed. Princeton, N.J.: Educational Testing Service, 1974. McDonald traces the roots of competency-based education to behavioral psychology and systems analysis and suggests that these origins account for three characteristics common to all competency programs. He maintains that competency-based programs should be developed in an analogous way to models that already exist and that the choice of the model should be based on very specific criteria. In conceptualizing such a program, McDonald finds it essential to distinguish between the *nature of teaching* and the nature of the *acquisition process* by which teaching competence is learned. According to McDonald, the rationale for competency-based programs is derived from a conception of the nature of what is to be learned and from a model of a system most likely to influence this acquisition. He points out that the model of these programs is basically a cybernetic one with a modular design as the technological device for implementing the model.

MC GRATH, D. (Ed.). "A Design of General Education." In *American Council on Education Series*. Vol. 8, Series 1 (18). Washington, D.C.: American Council on Education, June 1944. This report was meant to promote general education in the armed forces, but it was also directed toward civilian programs in the planning of postwar college experiences. Ten broad objectives of general education were articulated that warrant comparison with today's competence-based programs in the liberal arts. The committee said that performance at the level of the ten goals presupposed *knowledge* and understanding, *skills* and abilities, and *attitudes* and appreciation.

MC GRATH, E. J. "Careers, Values, and General Education." *Liberal Education*, 1974, *60* (3), 281–303. A plea for the renewal of the "historic function" of undergraduate education in a form suited to the present needs of our society. The author argues that liberal arts colleges must provide three services/functions (related to careers, values, and general education) simultaneously and in proper balance if the colleges are to survive.

MAC KINNON, D. W. "The Nature and Nurture of Creative Talent." *American Psychologist,* 1962, *17,* 484–495. Artistic and scientific creativity are explored in this essay. Such findings are presented as "persons who are highly creative are inclined to have a good opinion of themselves"; "there is a low correlation between intelligence and creativity"; and "the more creative a person is, the more he reveals an openness to his own feelings and emotions." With these provocative findings, the author addresses some implications of the nature of creative talent for the nurturing of it through the process of education.

MACLEAN, M. (Ed.). *University of Minnesota Studies of General Education.* Minneapolis: University of Minnesota Press, 1941–1943. This series represents an investigation of the General College at the University of Minnesota in an attempt to find out what has been achieved by one general education program designed especially for people of "just average scholastic ability." (If nothing else, this series will remind us that competence-based education has surfaced before in our history.)

MAGER, R. P. *Preparing Instructional Objectives.* Belmont, Calif.: Fearon, 1962. This little classic on behavioral objectives has become the foundation for many curriculums—especially competence-based ones. The author presents a now widely used approach to the task of goal specification that includes an examination of the "qualities of meaningful objectives," an attempt to define the "terminal behavior desired," and a manner of stating the criterion that will help recognize whether the behavior has been achieved.

MERROW, J. "Politics of Competence: A Review of Competency-Based Teacher Education." Washington, D.C.: National Institute of Education, 1975. The first part of this document reviews the history of teacher education in relation to the problem of public accountability. The author traces the origin of competence-based education in relation to this accountability issue and is critical of some aspects of this movement, including its costs, its "missing data base," and its "political and administrative problems." The second section of this report includes some responses to the first section that were made by educators and policy makers who are active in the movement toward competency-based teacher education.

Multi-State Consortium on Performance-Based Teacher Education. *Competency Assessment, Research, and Evaluation.* New York, Multi-State Consortium, 1974. A report of a national conference designed to "speculate and interact" on major issues related to the assessment of competence. The volume provides a conceptual framework for research and development, concentrates on the assessment of professional competencies, questions the effectiveness of performance-based teacher education programs, grapples with the effectiveness of given instructional strategies, and takes note of the social and political context of such programs.

NASH, R. J., and DUCHAINE, E. R. "A Future Perspective on Preparing Educators for the Human Service Society." *Teacher's College Record,* 1976, *77* (4), 441–471. This article attempts to "broaden traditional conceptions of teaching and learning so that educators can be more responsive to the range of human needs surfacing in the emerging human service society." The authors describe what an educator would be like in this human service society and suggest a "new professionalism" is in order that would foster the sense of political responsibility implicit in and required of all helping relationships.

NODDINGS, N. "Competence Theories and the Science of Education." *Educational Theory,* 1974, *24,* 356–364. A philosopher of education describes competence theories in the context of the free will and determinism debate. Some basic philosophical assumptions involved in the construction of competence theories are identified, and the significance of this type of theory for the development of educational science is addressed. The "competence theories" of Piaget and Chomsky are used to support claims about the nature of competence and its relation to performance.

O'CONNELL, W. R., JR., and MOOMAW, E. (Eds.). *A CBC Primer: Competency- Based Curriculums in General Undergraduate Programs.* Atlanta, Ga.: Southern Regional Education Board, 1975. This booklet, a report of a regional conference on competence-based learning, is designed to serve as an introductory discussion of the use of the "competency-concept" in general undergraduate programs. Contributors include Robert Knott, Ralph W. Tyler, Harold Hodgkinson, John Harris, and Richard Meeth.

O'TOOLE, J. *Work in America: Report of a Special Task Force to the Secretary of Health, Education, and Welfare.* Cambridge, Mass.: M.I.T. Press, 1973. This report examines the fundamental role of work in the lives of American adults. Chap. 5 is of particular importance to those in education because it deals with the relationships between work, education, and job mobility.

OUR LADY OF THE LAKE COLLEGE. *Competency Learning Project.* Unpublished compilation of reports by V. C. Duncan. San Antonio, Tex. Our Lady of the Lake College, 1975.

PACE, C. R. *They Went to College.* University of Minnesota Studies of General Education, M. Maclean (Ed.). Minneapolis: University of Minnesota Press, 1941. A desire to develop more effective education led to the inquiry into adult lives that is reported in this book. It was a study of the "extent to which young people leaving school have attained personal and social competence."

PETERSON, G. W. "A Strategy for Instituting Competency-Based Education in Large Colleges and Universities: A Pilot Program." *Educational Technology,* 1976, *16,* 30–34. The author describes the Curriculum of Attainments model for competence-based education that he and others have implemented at Florida State University. He argues that the "proliferation of pilot programs offers a means to incrementally and systematically introduce [competence-based education] degree programs" within large colleges and universities. The implementation and success of pilot programs must take into account the financial, personal, and institutional barriers existing in most systems of higher education.

PHENIX, P. *Realms of Meaning*. New York: McGraw-Hill, 1964. This volume by a professor of philosophy and education is "an attempt to elaborate a philosophical theory of the curriculum for general education based on the idea of logical patterns in disciplined understanding." After articulating the fundamental patterns of meaning (symbolics, empirics, esthetics, synnoetics, ethics, and synoptics), Phenix develops a curriculum for general education in reaction to these patterns of meaning. A central thesis of this book is that "knowledge in the disciplines has patterns or structures" and that an understanding of these typical forms is essential for the guidance of teaching and learning.

POLANYI, M., and PROSCH, H. *Meaning*. Chicago: University of Chicago Press, 1975. This volume of illuminating and provocative essays focuses on how the modern world has destroyed meaning. An implicit critique of positivism and behaviorism permeates the volume. The essay "Personal Knowledge" argues that a possible restoration of meaning may be provided through the development of the notion of personal knowledge. An integration of "personal" knowledge and "scientific" knowledge is necessary to come to any understanding. According to Polanyi, "The excellence of a distinguished medical surgeon is due not to his more diligent reading of textbooks (scientific knowledge) but to his skill as a diagnostician and leader—a personal skill acquired through practical experience."

POPHAM, W. J. (Ed.). *Criterion-Referenced Measurement in Education*. Englewood Cliffs, N.J.: Educational Technology Publications, 1971. This volume, a concise introduction to the general area of criterion-referenced testing, resulted from a symposium in 1970 at a meeting of the American Educational Research Association. Included are papers by Robert Glaser and W. James

Popham, leaders in this area of educational measurement. The implications and applicability of criterion-referenced testing are addressed.

President's Commission on Higher Education. "Establishing the Goals." In *Higher Education for American Democracy*. Vol. 1. Washington, D.C.: U.S. Government Printing Office, 1947. Poses objectives of general education that are very similar to those found in some current competence-based liberal arts programs and argues that the means for meeting these objectives are not limited to classroom book learning: "Formal courses are not the only sources of general education. There are a great variety of extra classroom resources in the university that should be used for educational purposes."

PRICE, K. "The Sense of 'Performance' and Its Point." *Educational Theory*, 1974, *24*, 313–327. This is the 1974 presidential address of the Philosophy of Education Society. The author speaks to the notion of teaching as a "performance." In doing so, he considers the concept of performance in terms of the many "senses" it carries. After a thorough conceptual analysis of performance and of teaching as a performance, Price concludes with the provocative assertion that "teaching is not a performance, not even the performance of a machine; and to treat it as if it were carries in its train confusion and false expectation."

RAE-GRANT, Q. A., GLADWIN, T., and BOWER, E. "Mental Health, Social Competence, and the War on Poverty." *American Journal of Orthopsychiatry*, 1966, *36*, 652–664. The skills and attributes of social competence are placed in the context of the urban poor "culturally deprived." The authors wonder if the quality and processes of today's educational institutions give disadvantaged students sufficient ego skills to cope with the stress and challenge of their lives. Furthermore, will technical competence in skilled or semiskilled trades be sufficient for "industrial competence"? They also question how the "culturally deprived" will acquire the more subtle attributes that are "vitally important for effective participation in the opportunities our society offers (middle-class attitudes)."

REBELL, M. *Teacher Credentialing Reform in New York State: A Critique and a Suggestion for New Direction*. New York: Study Commission on Undergraduate Education, 1974. This document analyzes and critiques the state of teacher credentialing and recent reform efforts in New York State. Of particular interest is the attempt to transfer teacher credentialing from a system based on credits earned to one based on demonstrated competence. The legal and educational implications of the transformation are presented and relevant legal cases are sighted to support the author's analysis.

RIESMAN, D. "The Problem of Competence: Obstacles to Autonomy in Play." In *The Lonely Crowd*. New Haven, Conn.: Yale University Press, 1961. In line with the theme of the entire book, this essay addresses the typologies of "inner-directedness" and "other-directedness" in relation to the "task of restoring competence to play." The author suggests that, with the advent of industrialization, specialization, and professionalization, men have forgotten how to play or have left it up to the professionals. He concludes by pointing out that childhood experience is most important in making true adult competence at play possible.

ROSNER, B., and OTHERS. *The Power of Competency-Based Teacher Education*. Boston: Allyn and Bacon, 1972. This report to the U.S. Office of Education made recommendations focusing on the necessary conditions for the development of competency-based teacher education and certification. It includes a description of a five-year program with specific activities and competencies that educational personnel would need to attain.

SCHEIN, E. H. *Professional Education*. New York: McGraw-Hill, 1972. This volume, sponsored by the Carnegie Commission, grapples with the changing work settings and clients of professionals and attempts to prescribe new directions for professional education. This prescription includes new learning modules that are designed either functionally by skill level or by type of career. The important thing is how the student *learns*. Furthermore, the faculty must "become more learning-centered" and be able to develop multidimensional performance evaluation systems that permit them to "discuss the students' accomplishments in concrete terms rather than in vague letter grades." Both students and future employers should be involved in determining the performance criteria.

SIMPSON, M. C., and SIMPSON, I. H. "The Psychiatric Attendant: Development of an Occupational Self-Image in a Low-Status Occupation." *American Sociological Review,* 1959, *24* (3), 389–392. The data in this brief article supports the hypothesis that people in "low-status occupations" can develop or maintain a favorable occupational self-image by focusing upon some highly valued aspect of the work situation. One could infer from this that competence for people in low-status occupations would be conceptualized quite differently from competence in more professional occupations. This contrasts with the "higher" professionals who develop a favorable occupational self-image through their formal training and the ideology that goes with it.

SKINNER, B. F. *The Technology of Teaching.* New York: Appleton-Century-Crofts, 1968. In "The Science of Learning and the Art of Teaching," the renowned behaviorist explicates the advantages of reinforcement techniques for learning and the implications of these techniques for classroom teaching. This and other essays in the book provide some fundamental learning theory and instructional methods for the more "behavioristic" competence-based programs.

SMITH, D. "Integrating Humanism and Behaviorism: Toward Performance." *Personnel and Guidance Journal,* 1974, *58,* 513–519. The current emphasis on performance criteria in training programs and in professional services poses a threat to the humanistically oriented helper. Humanists equate competence-based education with behaviorism and resist the demand for performance criteria. This article suggests a behavioral humanism as the desired solution to the dilemma, and it proposes some guidelines for formulating and implementing a synthetic system that would not jeopardize personal-professional integrity.

SMITH, M. B. "Exploration in Competence: A Study of Peace Corps Teachers in Ghana." *American Psychologist,* 1966, *21,* 555–566. This summarizes a study of a group of young people who were faced with a challenging assignment as the first group of Peace Corps volunteers. The particular form of "psychological effectiveness" (or competence) studied by the author seemed to have a coherent core of attributes: self-confidence, commitment, energy, responsibility, autonomy, flexibility, and hopeful realism. After addressing the general nature of competence, the author presented some interesting data on the various forms competent performance takes and the prediction of competent performance.

SMITH, M. B. "Competence and Socialization." In J. Clausen (Ed.)', *Socialization and Society.* Boston: Little, Brown, 1968. This article considers the bearing of socialization on the origins and development of competence. It is an attempt to "popularize" yet also clarify some of the issues that arise in conceptualizing the nature and development of competence. Smith presents alternative conceptions of competence and how they correlate with particular sociological role-status theories. He posits a provisional view of the "competent self" with particular attitudes and beliefs and suggests that this model may have transcultural relevance. Social structure and its bearing on competence are discussed in relation to power, respect, and opportunity.

SMITH, R. A. (Ed.). *Regaining Educational Leadership: Critical Essays on PBTE/CBTE, Behavioral Objectives, and Accountability.* New York: Wiley, 1975. This collection of essays, written for the most part by philosophers of education, provides a wide-ranging and often penetrating critique of competence-based education in the teaching profession. The various authors address conceptual, ideological, and moral problems.

SPADY, W. G. "Competency-Based Education: A Bandwagon in Search of a Definition." *Educational Researcher,* 1977, *6,* 9–14. The author analyzes the theoretical constructs implied in competence-based education and the characteristics that differentiate it from associated practice such as competence-based teacher education, mastery learning, and individualized instruction. The analysis treats competence-based education as "a data-based, adaptive, performance-oriented set of integrated processes that facilitate, measure, record, and certify within the context of flexible time parameters the demonstration of known, explicitly stated, and agreed upon learning outcomes that reflect successful functioning in life roles."

SPADY, W. G. "Critical Sociological Dimensions in Competency-Based Graduation Requirements." Paper presented at annual meeting of American Educational Research Association, 1975. This paper addresses the mandated graduation requirements in Oregon. Students must demonstrate "locally determined" competencies in three major areas, as well as complete twenty-one course credits. The author suggests that researchers have underestimated the range and consequences of the attempt to implement this mandate. Seven major areas for research are articulated, including resource allocation and utilization, basic functions of school systems, technical demands implied by minimum requirements, authority and decision-making structure, role responsibilities and structures, identifying educational and social values, and incentives and reward.

SPADY, W. S., and MITCHEL, D. E. "Competency-Based Education: Organizational Issues and Implications." *Educational Researcher,* 1977, *62,* 9–15. This article attempts to clarify, from a sociological perspective, the different bases on which schools could implement various competence-based education programs. It also analyzes the implication of such programs for the structure and functioning of the school's certification system.

SPAFFOR, I., and OTHERS. *Building a Curriculum for General Education.* University of Minnesota Studies of General Education, M. Maclean (Ed.), Minneapolis: University of Minnesota Press, 1943. This book responded to the need for a new curriculum that would address the characteristics and interests of the changing student body enrolling in colleges from 1930 to 1940. Concrete objectives for the college were established, including knowledge (as insight and understanding), skills and techniques, attitudes, interests, appreciation, and ideals. Evaluation was in relation to students' attainment of these objectives, not the attainment of mere facts.

STANTON, C. M. "Reflections on Vocationalized Liberal Education." *Educational Forum*, 1969, *40* (3), 297–302. The question is addressed, "What shall be the relationships of vocationally oriented programs to the more traditional disciplines?" The article suggests that faculties start redesigning the context and purpose of undergraduate curriculum along lines that have clearly met the needs of the "new clientele" in American higher education. The author suggests a "meshing of the traditional disciplines and the career programs to bring about a "complementary and integrated education."

STILES, U. "Liberal Education and the Professions." *Journal of General Education*, 1974, *26,* 53–64. The author plunges into his defense of the liberally educated professional by stating that "a liberal education is the taproot for all professional training and performance." Stiles criticizes the "accountability" demands being put on liberal studies and maintains that there are negative consequences resulting from the "stress on immediate, tangible results" that are supposed "to prove learning is taking place." He argues that this "behavioristic," performance-oriented learning leaves no room for "concomitants of learning experiences such as insight, inspiration, appreciation, and unexpected knowledge."

STRUENING, E., and GUTTENTAG, M. (Eds.). *Handbook of Evaluation Research.* Beverly Hills, Calif.: Sage, 1975. This two-volume handbook provides a comprehensive survey of the entire evaluation process. It was written to help social science researchers consider alternative approaches to program evaluation.

Study Commission on Undergraduate Education and the Education of Teachers. *Licensing and Accreditation in Education: The Law and the State Interest.* B. Levitov (Ed.). New York: Multi-State Consortium on Performance-Based Education, 1976.

This report addresses some key concerns of educators and policy makers with regard to licensing and certification. Michael Rebell, an attorney, analyzes the relationship of the law and the courts to teacher credentialing reform. Paul Pottinger attempts to codify some techniques and criteria for designing and selecting assessment instruments. Shelia Huff addresses the problem of institutional barriers that affect the implementation of competence-based programs, and Laurence Freeman examines the role of the state in teacher education.

STURNER, W. F. "An Analytic-Action Model for Liberal Education." *Educational Record*, 1973, *54*, 154–158. A truly liberal education should include not only a sampling of intellectual styles and contents but also *experienced encounters* with the applied aspects of these inquiries. This type of liberal education, according to the author, would cause the acquisition of certain transferable skills and abilities to be manifest in behavior and would develop the abilities for applying these skills to community needs.

TABA, H. *The Dynamics of Education*. New York: Harcourt Brace Jovanovich, 1932. This book presents the meaning and process of education in the context of the concept of becoming. By applying this concept to human experience in general and education in particular, the author provides "an alternative and corrective to the atomism pervasive in current scientific efforts at treating human phenomena." After articulating the concepts of becoming and analyzing the dynamics of learning, the author discusses the implications for curriculums of this integrative approach to education.

TAYLOR, F. W. *Scientific Management: Comprising Shop Management, The Principles of Scientific Management, and Testimony Before the Special House Committee*. New York: Harper & Row, 1947. (Originally published, 1911.) This text, containing "Shop Management" and Taylor's "Testimony Before a Special House Committee," also has his classic piece, *The Principles of Scientific Management*. Taylor argues that "the whole country is suffering through inefficiency" and that the remedy for this lies in "systematic management." He maintains that the best management is a true science and that the fundamental principles of scientific management are applicable "to all kinds of human activities."

THORNDIKE, R. L. (Ed.). *Educational Measurement.* Washington, D.C.: American Council on Education, 1971. Chap. 9 of this book is of particular import to those involved with competence-based or outcome-oriented education, as it examines the common performance tests and highlights such qualities as validity and reliability.

TIDBULL, M. E. "On Liberation and Competence." *Educational Record,* 1976, *57,* 101–110. The author makes an insightful analysis of the differing influences of gender on the drive for, and development of, competence. This analysis is attempted in order to provoke educators into thinking more about the environment they create for students, and for women students in particular. The intent of the article is to "encourage thinking on how best to promote the maximum unhomogenized development of both young women and men."

TRAVERS, R. M. W. (Ed.). *The Second Handbook of Research on Teaching.* Chicago: Rand McNally, 1973. This book chronicles the major achievements since 1960 in research on teaching. It provides guidance and coordination to researchers in this area and could lead to more sophisticated educational research.

TRIVETT, D. A. *Competency-Based Programs in Higher Education.* Washington, D.C.: American Association for Higher Education, 1975. This higher education research report surveys eight institutions that have implemented competence-based education programs. It explores various ideas about educational outcomes as a basis for defining what competence may or may not be. A helpful bibliography is included.

TYLER, R. *Adventures in American Education.* New York: Harper & Row, 1942. The two studies included in this book developed numerous instruments useful in assessing growth in regard to general education objectives.

TYLER, R. (Ed.). *Educational Evaluation: New Roles, New Means.* Chicago, University of Chicago Press, 1969. This yearbook of the National Society for the Study of Education describes and explains the developments taking place in educational evaluation and critically addresses their implications. Includes such informative essays as "Historical Review of Changing Concepts of Evaluation" by Jack Merwin and "Some Theoretical Issues Relating to Education Evaluation" by Benjamin S. Bloom.

U.S. Department of Health, Education, and Welfare. *Report on Higher Education.* Washington, D.C.: U.S. Government Printing Office, 1971. Known as the "Newman Report," after Frank Newman, chairperson of the task force formed to analyze the problems facing the higher education system in the 1970s, this document addresses the trends resulting from the growth and expansion of the higher education system. It expresses disenchantment with such trends as "growth of bureaucracy, overemphasis on academic credentials, isolation of students and faculty from the world, and a growing rigidity and uniformity of structure that makes higher education reflect less and less the interests of society." This document was influential in the movement toward competence-based education programs.

U.S. Office of Strategic Services, Assessment Staff. *Assessment of Men.* New York: Holt, Rinehart and Winston. 1948. This classic (out-of-print) volume is the account of how a group of psychologists and psychiatrists attempted to "assess the merits of men and women recruited for the OSS." This "novel experiment," concerned with the problem of predicting human behavior, followed the principles of Gestalt psychology in the design and implementation of selection procedures.

UNIVERSITY OF MINNESOTA, COMMITTEE ON EDUCATIONAL RESEARCH. *Effective General College Curriculum.* Minneapolis:

University of Minnesota Press, 1937. This volume focuses on the difficulty in evaluating the education of students in the General College at the University of Minnesota. The curriculum at the college relied heavily on behavioral objectives; thus evaluation had to be in relation to the attainment of these specific objectives.

VERMILYE, D. W. (Ed.). *Learner-Centered Reform*. San Francisco: Jossey-Bass, 1975. This volume of "Current Issues in Higher Education" includes essays by many who are involved in nontraditional learning in general and competence-based education in particular. K. Patricia Cross writes about the "learner-centered curriculums"; Harold Hodgkinson addresses the issues of evaluation in an attempt to "improve performance"; Jonathan Warren presents his ideas on "alternatives to degrees"; and Richard Meeth tackles the "restricted practice in funding that made it difficult to implement and develop nontraditional programs."

VERMILYE, D. W. (Ed.). *Lifelong Learners—A New Clientele for Higher Education*. San Francisco: Jossey-Bass, 1974. This volume of "Current Issues in Higher Education" focuses on lifelong learning and what it might mean to live in a "learning society." General themes related to "education, work, and the quality of life" are addressed by James O'Toole. Particular courses of action that institutions may take are treated by Robert Toft in "Designing a Performance-Based Module" and Ambrose Garner in "Performance-Based Campus." K. Patricia Cross, Morris Keaton, and Harold Hodgkinson contribute their views on the changing focus and foundations of American higher education.

WATT, J. "College of Public and Community Service (CPCS)." In G. Grant (Ed.), *On Competence: An Analysis of a Reform Movement in Higher Education*. Syracuse, N.Y.: Syracuse Research Corporation, 1977. The mission of this college, located in Boston, is to combine career education with a critical perspective on the liberal arts. This case study records the college's progress toward achieving these objectives through a competence-based curriculum that offers both skill and knowledge training along with work experience.

WENAR, C. "Competence at One." *Merrill-Palmer Quarterly,* 1964, *10,* 329–342. This article explores the concept of "executive competence" in relation to child development. A differentiated definition of this concept is developed including the following components: intensity (depth of involvement in an activity), persistence, and self-sufficiency. Competence for this author must be observed in relation to particular settings or activities to have a more realistic understanding of it. With this in mind, a final definition is arrived at: "Executive competence is the child's ability to initiate and sustain locomotor, manipulative, and visually regarded activities at a given level of complexity and intensity and with a given degree of self-sufficiency."

WHITE, R. W. "Motivation Reconsidered: The Concept of Competence." *Psychological Review,* 1959, *66,* 297–333. The author attempts a "conceptualization which gathers up some of the important things left out of drive theory," in the writings of C. L. Hull and Freud. White refers to competence as "an organism's capacity to interact effectively with its environment." The author's crucial argument is that "the motivation needed to attain competence cannot wholly be derived from sources of energy currently conceptualized as drive or instincts."

WIGHT, W. D. "Obtaining Competence with Competencies: A Case Study in Higher Education." *Educational Technology,* 1974, *14,* 46–48. This article, written by the director of instructional communications at Governor State University in Illinois, describes how that university applied the theory of competence-based instruction on a university-wide basis. The author examines the problems faced when this theory of education was applied and describes some of the solutions to these problems.

WILENSKY, H. V. "The Professionalization of Everyone?" *American Journal of Sociology,* 1964, *70,* 137–158. The author argues that the traditional model of "professionalism" is essential for understanding the increasing growth of professional organizations. Newer and "marginal" professions can be explained as deviations from this traditional norm. The author maintains that few occupations will achieve the authority of the established professions;

client-orientation undermines colleague control, and if everything is called a profession, then the structural form now emerging will be obscured.

WILLIAMS, C. T. *These We Teach*. University of Minnesota Studies
of General Education, M. Maclean (Ed.). Minneapolis: University of Minnesota Press, 1943. A report on the findings of an
international study of the abilities, interests, family backgrounds,
and problems of General College students. The assumption underlying the study was that a careful study of students is a prerequisite for adequate curriculum planning.

WILSON COLLEGE FACULTY. *The Concepts of Skill, Knowledge and
Insight*. Bombay, India: Wilson College, 1964. This penetrating
volume presents four parallel analyses of the concepts of skill,
knowledge, and insight and their relation to the structure and
function of higher education.

References

ALLEN, C. R. *The Instructor, The Man, and the Job.* Philadelphia: Lippincott, 1919.

ALVERNO COLLEGE. *Competence Assessment Program: Manual for Level 1.* Milwaukee: Alverno College, 1973a.

ALVERNO COLLEGE. "Historical Development of Competence-Based Learning at Alverno." Milwaukee: Alverno College, 1973b.

ALVERNO COLLEGE. *Catalogue, 1975–1976.* Milwaukee: Alverno College, 1975.

ALVERNO COLLEGE. "A Private College for the Woman Who Wants to Make a Difference." Milwaukee: Alverno College, n.d.

ANDERSON, D. S. "A Study of Professional Socialization." Canberra: Education Research Unit, Research School of the Social Sciences, Australian National University, 1973.

ANTIOCH COLLEGE. *School of Law Catalogue.* Yellow Springs, Ohio: Antioch College, 1975.

ARGYRIS, C. "Creating Effective Research Relationships in Organizations." In F. G. Caro (Ed.), *Readings in Evaluation Research.* New York: Russell Sage Foundation, 1971.

557

ARISTOTLE. *On the Parts of Animals*. (A. L. Peck, Trans.) Cambridge, Mass.: Harvard University Press, 1937.

BECKER, H. "The Nature of a Profession." In *Education for the Professions: Sixty-First Yearbook of the National Society for the Study of Education*. Chicago: University of Chicago Press, 1962.

BECKER, H., and GEER, B. "Participant Observation and Interviewing." In J. G. Manis and B. N. Meltzer, *Symbolic Interaction*. Boston: Allyn & Bacon, 1972.

BECKER, H., GEER, B., and HUGHES, E. C. *Making the Grade: The Academic Side of College Life*. New York: Wiley, 1968.

BELL, D. *The Reforming of General Education*. New York: Columbia University Press, 1966.

BENNETT, W. J., and DE LATTRE, E. J. "Moral Education in the Schools." *The Public Interest*, 1978, 50, 81–98.

BENNIS, W., and OTHERS. *The Planning of Change*. New York: Holt, Rinehart and Winston, 1976.

BERNARD, J. S. *Academic Women*. University Park: Pennsylvania State University Press, 1964.

BLACKWELL, G. W. "UF and FSU, 'Partners in Florida's Future.'" Phi Beta Kappa address, Tallahassee and Gainesville, Fl., May 1962.

BLOCK, J. H. "Criterion-Referenced Measures: Potentials." *School Review*, 1971, 75 (2), 289–298.

BLOOM, B. S. (Ed.). *Taxonomy of Educational Objectives: The Classification of Educational Goals*. (3 vols.) New York: McKay, 1956–1964.

BLOOM, B. S., and KRATHWOHL, D. R. *Taxonomy of Educational Objectives*. Handbook 1: *Cognitive Domain*. New York: McKay, 1956.

BLUM, M. L., and TAYLOR, J. C. *Industrial Psychology: Its Theoretical and Social Foundations*. New York: Harper & Row, 1956.

BOBBITT, J. F. *The Curriculum*. Boston: Houghton Mifflin, 1918.

BOBBITT, J. F. *Curriculum-Making in Los Angeles*. Chicago: University of Chicago Press, 1922.

BOBBITT, J. F. "Discovering and Formulating the Objectives of Teacher Training Institutions." *Journal of Educational Research*, 1924a, 10, 187–196.

BOBBITT, J. F. *How to Make a Curriculum*. Boston: Houghton Mifflin, 1924b.

BOBBITT, J. F. "The Orientation of the Curriculum-Maker." In G. W. Whipple (Ed.), *The Foundations and Technique of Curriculum-Construction*. Pt. 2. Bloomington, Ill.: Public School Publishing, 1926.

BODE, B. H. "Why Educational Objectives?" *Journal of Educational Research*, 1924, *10*, 175–186.

BODE, B. H. *Modern Educational Theories*. New York: Macmillan, 1927.

BODE, B. H. *Conflicting Psychologies of Learning*. Lexington, Mass.: Heath, 1929.

BOWEN, H. R. *Investment in Learning: The Individual and Social Value of American Higher Education*. San Francisco: Jossey-Bass, 1977.

BRADSHAW, T. K. "The Impact of Peers on Student Orientations to College: A Contextual Analysis." In M. Trow (Ed.), *Teachers and Students: Aspects of American Higher Education*. New York: McGraw-Hill, 1975.

BROWNLEE, C. G. "A Small College Looks at Competency." Council for the Advancement of Small Colleges *Newsletter*, 1974, *17*, 9–12.

BUCHANAN, S. *The Doctrine of Signatures*. New York: 1938.

BURNS, R. W. "Behavioral Objectives for Competency-Based Education." *Educational Technology*, Nov. 1972a, pp. 22–25.

BURNS, R. W. "Achievement Testing in Competency-Based Education." *Educational Technology*, Nov. 1972b, pp. 39–42.

BUTTS, R. F. *The College Charts Its Course*. New York: McGraw-Hill, 1939.

CALHOUN, D. H. *The American Civil Engineer: Origins and Conflict*. Cambridge, Mass.: M.I.T. Press, 1960.

CALHOUN, D. H. *Professional Lives in America, Structure and Aspiration, 1750–1850*. Cambridge, Mass.: Harvard University Press, 1965.

CALLAHAN, R. E. *Education and the Cult of Efficiency*. Chicago: University of Chicago Press, 1962.

Carnegie Commission On Higher Education. *Less Time, More*

Options: Education Beyond the High School. New York: Mc-
Graw-Hill, 1971.

CARO, F. G. (Ed.). *Readings in Evaluation Research.* New York:
Russell Sage Foundation, 1971.

CARO, P. W. "Report." In G. Peterson (Ed.), *Curriculum of Attainments: Final Report.* Tallahassee: Instructional Systems
Development Center, Florida State University, 1977.

CARTTER, A. M. "The Supply of and Demand for College Teaching." *Journal of Human Resources,* 1966, *1,* 22–38.

CENTER FOR EDUCATIONAL TECHNOLOGY. *Annual Progress Report,
1972–73.* Tallahassee: College of Education, Florida State University, 1973.

CENTER FOR EDUCATIONAL TECHNOLOGY. *Annual Progress Report,
1973–74.* Tallahassee: College of Education, Florida State University, 1974.

CHAPMAN, J. C. *Trade Tests: The Scientific Measurement of Trade
Proficiency.* New York: Holt, Rinehart and Winston, 1921.

CHARTERS, W. W. "Activity Analysis and Curriculum Construction."
Journal of Educational Research, 1922, *5,* 357–367.

CHARTERS, W. W. *Curriculum Construction.* New York: Macmillan,
1923.

CHARTERS, W. W. "Functional Analysis as the Basis for Curriculum
Construction." *Journal of Educational Research,* 1924a, *10,* 214–
221.

CHARTERS, W. W. "Principles Underlying the Making of the Curriculum of Teacher Training Institutions." *Educational Administration and Supervision,* 1924b, *10,* 337–342.

CHARTERS, W. W. *Basic Material for a Pharmacy Curriculum.* New
York: McGraw-Hill, 1925.

CHARTERS, W. W. "Review and Critique of Curriculum-Making for
the Vocations." In G. W. Whipple (Ed.), *The Foundations and
Technique of Curriculum Construction: The Twenty-Sixth Yearbook of the National Society for the Study of Education.* Pt. 1.
Bloomington, Ill.: Public School Publishing, 1926.

Chronicle of Higher Education, Aug. 7, 1978.

CLARK, B. R. *The Distinctive College: Antioch, Reed, and Swarthmore.* Chicago: Aldine, 1970.

CLARK, B. R., and OTHERS. *Students and Colleges: Interaction and*

Change. Berkeley: Center for Research and Development in Higher Education, University of California, 1972.

COLEMAN, J. S. *The Adolescent Society: The Social Life of the Teenager and Its Impact on Education.* New York: Free Press, 1961.

COLEMAN, J. S. *Equality of Educational Opportunity.* Washington, D.C.: U.S. Government Printing Office, 1966.

COLEMAN, J. S. "Differences between Experiential and Classroom Learning." In M. T. Keeton and Associates (Eds.), *Experiential Learning: Rationale, Characteristics, and Assessment.* San Francisco: Jossey-Bass, 1976.

COLLEGE FOR HUMAN SERVICES. *Final Report of the Women's Talent Corps New Careers Program: 1966–67.* New York: College for Human Services, 1968a.

COLLEGE FOR HUMAN SERVICES. *First Annual Report.* New York: College for Human Services, 1968b.

COLLEGE FOR HUMAN SERVICES. *Second Annual Report.* New York: College for Human Services, 1969.

COLLEGE FOR HUMAN SERVICES. *Third Annual Report.* New York: College for Human Services, 1970.

COLLEGE FOR HUMAN SERVICES. *Fourth Annual Report.* New York: College for Human Services, 1972.

COLLEGE FOR HUMAN SERVICES. *Two-Year Professional Program Leading to the Degree of Master of Human Services.* New York: College for Human Services, 1974.

"College Programs Rapped." *Ann Arbor News,* 1975.

A Compendium of Assessment Techniques. Princeton, N.J.: Cooperative Assessment of Experiential Learning, 1975.

COOPER, J. A. "Medical Education and the Quality of Care." *Journal of Medical Education,* 1976, *51,* 363–364.

COZAN, L. W. "Forced-Choice: Better Than Other Rating Methods?" In T. L. Whisler and S. F. Harper (Eds.), *Performance Appraisal.* New York: Holt, Rinehart and Winston, 1962.

CRONBACH, L. J. *Essentials of Psychological Testing.* (2nd ed.) New York: Harper & Row, 1960.

CROSS, K. P. "New Students in a New World." *Current Issues in Higher Education,* 1973, *28,* 87–95.

DAILEY, C., and OTHERS. *Professional Competences of Human Service Workers.* Boston: McBer, 1974.

DALE, E. "Historical Setting of Programmed Instruction." In P. Lange (Ed.), *Programmed Instruction: The Sixty-Sixth Yearbook of the National Society for the Study of Education.* Pt. 2. Chicago: University of Chicago Press, 1967.

DANIELS, A. K. "How Free Should Professionals Be?" In E. Friedson (Ed.), *The Professions and Their Prospects.* Beverly Hills, Calif.: Sage, 1971.

DAVIS, N. Z. "Proverbial Wisdom and Popular Errors." In N. Z. Davis, *Society and Culture in Early Modern France.* Stanford: Stanford University Press, 1975.

DEAN, D. H., and WAECHTER, M. *Measurement in Competency-Based Education.* Gresham, Ore.: Mt. Hood Community College, 1974.

DEWEY, J. *Democracy and Education.* New York: Free Press, 1966. (Originally published 1915.)

DODD, A. E., and RICE, J. C. *How to Train Workers for War Industries.* New York: Harper & Row, 1942.

DOENECKE, J. D. "Higher Education: The View of Insiders." *Libertarian Forum,* Sept. 1977, pp. 2–5.

DOOLEY, C. R. *Final Report of the National Army Training Detachments.* Washington, D.C.: War Department Committee on Education and Special Training, 1919.

DOOLEY, C. R. *How to Train Workers for War Industries: A Manual of Tested Training Procedures.* New York: Harper & Row, 1942.

DOYLE, B., and WARE, J. E., JR. "Physician Conduct and Other Factors That Affect Consumer Satisfaction." *Journal of Medical Education,* 1977, *52,* 793–801.

DREEBEN, R. *On What Is Learned in School.* Reading, Mass.: Addison-Wesley, 1968.

DRESCH, S. P. "Higher Education: External and Internal Dynamics of Growth and Decline." In J. D. Millett (Ed.), *New Directions for Higher Education: Managing Turbulence and Change,* no. 19. San Francisco: Jossey-Bass, 1977.

DRESSEL, P. L. *College and University Curriculum.* Berkeley, Calif.: McCutchan, 1968.

DUBERMAN, M. *Black Mountain: An Exploration in Community.* New York: Dutton, 1972.

DULEY, J. "Cross-Cultural Field Study." In J. Duley (Ed.), *New Directions for Higher Education: Implementing Field Experience Education,* no. 6. San Francisco: Jossey-Bass, 1974.

EBEL, R. L. *Measuring Educational Achievement.* Englewood Cliffs, N.J.: Prentice-Hall, 1965.

EBEL, R. L. "Criterion-Referenced Measures: Limitations." *School Review,* 1971, *75* (2), 282–288.

EBEL, R. L. *Essentials of Educational Measurement.* Englewood Cliffs, N.J.: Prentice-Hall, 1972.

EDUCATIONAL POLICY RESEARCH CENTER. "A Qualitative Study of the Evolution and Impact of Programs in Competency-Based Education." A proposal submitted to the Fund for the Improvement of Postsecondary Education, June 5, 1974.

EISNER, E. W. "Franklin Bobbitt and the Science of Curriculum-Making." *School Review,* 1967, *75,* 29–47.

ELAM, S. *Performance-Based Teacher Education: What Is the State of the Art?* Washington, D.C.: American Association of Colleges for Teacher Education, 1971.

ETZIONI, A. *A Comparative Analysis of Complex Organizations.* New York: Free Press, 1975.

FEATHERSTONE, J. "The Talent Corps: Career Ladders for Bottom Dogs." *New Republic,* 1969, *161,* 1–6.

FISHER, D. "Cost Parity Analysis." In G. W. Peterson (Ed.), *Curriculum of Attainments: Final Report.* Tallahassee: Instructional Systems Development Center, Florida State University, 1977.

FITZPATRICK, R. and MORRISON, E. L. "Performance and Product Evaluation." In R. L. Thorndike (Ed.), *Educational Measurement.* (2nd ed.) Washington, D.C.: American Council on Education, 1971.

FLANAGAN, J. C. "The Critical Incident Technique." *Psychological Bulletin,* 1954, *51,* 327–358.

FLANDERS, N. A. *Analyzing Teaching Behavior.* Reading, Mass.: Addison-Wesley, 1970.

FREDERIKSEN, N. "Proficiency Tests for Training Evaluation." In R. Glaser (Ed.), *Training Research and Education.* Pittsburgh: University of Pittsburgh Press, 1962.

FREEMAN, J. "Trashing: The Dark Side of Sisterhood." *Ms.,* 1976, *4* (10), 49–51, 92–98.

FREIDSON, E. *Professional Dominance.* Chicago: Aldine, 1970.

Fund for the Improvement of Postsecondary Education. "Program Information and Application Procedures—Special Focus Program: Education and Certification for Competence." Washington, D.C.: Fund for the Improvement of Postsecondary Education, Department of Health, Education, and Welfare, 1975.

GAGNÉ, R. M. "Military Training and Principles of Learning." *American Psychologist,* 1962a, *17,* 83–91.

GAGNÉ, R. M. "Simulators." In R. Glaser (Ed.), *Training Research and Education.* Pittsburgh: University of Pittsburgh Press, 1962b.

GAGNÉ, R. M. *The Conditions of Learning.* New York: Holt, Rinehart and Winston, 1965a.

GAGNÉ, R. M. "The Analysis of Instructional Objectives for the Design of Instruction." In R. Glaser (Ed.), *Teaching Machines and Programmed Learning II.* Washington, D.C.: National Education Association, 1965b.

GAMSON, Z. F. "Issues in the Diffusion and Implementation of Competence-Based Education." In G. Grant (Ed.), *On Competence: An Analysis of a Reform Movement in Higher Education.* Syracuse, N.Y.: Syracuse Research Corporation, 1977.

GAMSON, Z. F., and LEVEY, R. H. *Structure and Emergence: Proceedings of an Institute on Innovations in Undergraduate Education.* Publication No. 8. Ann Arbor: Center for the Study of Higher Education, University of Michigan, 1976.

GAVITT, J. P. "Lo, the Poor College." *Progressive Education,* 1931a, *8,* 264–266.

GAVITT, J. P. "Socrates on the Eight-Hour Shift." *Survey,* 1931b, *66,* 247–249.

GERTH, H. H., and MILLS, C. W. (Eds.). *From Max Weber.* New York: Oxford University Press, 1946.

GLASER, R. "Psychology and Instructional Technology." In R. Glaser (Ed.), *Training Research and Education.* Pittsburgh: University of Pittsburgh Press, 1962.

GLASER, R. "Implications of Training Research for Education." In E. R. Hilgard (Ed.), *Theories of Learning and Instruction.* Chicago: University of Chicago Press, 1964.

GLASER, R. (Ed.). *Teaching Machines and Programmed Learning II.* Washington, D.C.: National Education Association, 1965a.

GLASER, R. "Toward a Behavioral Science Base for Instructional Design." In R. Glaser (Ed.), *Teaching Machines and Programmed Learning II.* Washington, D.C.: National Education Association, 1965b.

GLASER, D. R., and GARDNER, F. M. "The Tab Item: A Technique for the Measurement of Proficiency in Diagnostic Problem Solving." In A. A. Lumsdaine and R. Glaser (Eds.), *Teaching Machines and Programmed Learning: A Source Book.* Washington: National Education Association, 1960.

GLAZER, N. "Conflicts in Schools for the Minor Professions." Harvard Graduate School of Education *Bulletin,* Spring 1974a.

GLAZER, N. "The Schools of the Minor Professions." *Minerva,* 1974b, *12* (3), 346–364.

GOODMAN, N. *Languages of Art.* Indianapolis: Hackett, 1976.

GORDON, L. V. "Clinical, Psychometric, and Work Sample Approaches in the Prediction of Success in Peace Corps Training." *Journal of Applied Psychology,* 1967, *51,* 111–119.

GRACE, A. G. *Educational Lessons from Wartime Training: The General Report of the Commission on Implications of Armed Services Educational Programs.* Washington, D.C.: American Council on Education, 1948.

GRAND VALLEY STATE COLLEGES. *College IV Self-Study for North Central Association Accreditation Team.* Allendale, Mich.: Grand Valley State Colleges, 1973a.

GRAND VALLEY STATE COLLEGES. "Report to the Fund for the Improvement of Postsecondary Education." Allendale, Mich.: Grand Valley State Colleges, 1973b.

GRANT, D. L. and BRAY, D. W. "Contributions of the Interview to Assessment of Managerial Potential." *Journal of Applied Psychology,* 1969, *53* (1), 24–34.

GRANT, G. "Universal B.A.?" *New Republic,* 1972, *166,* 13–16.

GRANT, G. (Ed.). *On Competence: An Analysis of a Reform Movement in Higher Education.* (2 vols.) Syracuse, N.Y.: Syracuse Research Corporation, 1977.

GRANT, G., and RIESMAN, D. *The Perpetual Dream: Reform and Experiment in the American College.* Chicago: University of Chicago Press, 1978.

GREENLEAF, R. K. *Servant Leadership: A Journey into the Nature of Legitimate Power and Greatness.* Paramus, N.J.: Paulist Press, 1977.

GUSFIELD, J. R. *Symbolic Crusade: Status Politics and the American Temperance Movement.* Urbana: University of Illinois Press, 1963.

HABERMAS, J. *Knowledge and Human Interests.* Boston: Beacon Press, 1971.

HACK, S. "A Statistical Report on the College for Human Services, 1967–1972." June 1973.

HARRIS, J. "Baccalaureate Requirements: Attainments or Exposures?" *Educational Record*, 1972, *53*, 59–65.

HARRIS, J., and KELLER, S. *Curriculum Innovation: Three Dimensions in Teaching-Learning Issues.* Knoxville: Learning Research Center, University of Tennessee, 1974.

HARTMANN, G. W. "The Field Theory of Learning and Its Educational Consequences." In N. B. Henry (Ed.), *The Psychology of Learning: The Forty-First Yearbook of the National Society for the Study of Education.* Bloomington, Ill.: Public School Publishing, 1942.

HAVELOCK, R. G. *Planning for Innovation through Dissemination and Utilization of Knowledge.* Ann Arbor: Institute for Social Research, University of Michigan, 1971.

HAWES, G. R. *Educational Testing for the Millions: What Tests Really Mean for Your Child.* New York: McGraw-Hill, 1964.

HAWKINS, L. S. "Training Tile-Setting Apprentices." *Journal of Educational Research*, 1926, *14*, 133–142.

HAWKINS, L. S., PROSSER, C. A., and WRIGHT, J. C. *Development of Vocational Education.* Chicago: American Technical Society, 1951.

HEFFERLIN, J. L. *Dynamics of Academic Reform.* San Francisco: Jossey-Bass, 1969.

HEYDINGER, R. B. "The Evolving College IV Student Body: January–June 1975." Dec. 9, 1975a.

HEYDINGER, R. B. "The Assessment of Student Performance: A Model and the Reforms." Paper presented at the National Conference on Higher Education, Chicago, 1975b.

HEYDINGER, R. B., and ASSOCIATES. "College IV: The Evolution of

an Experiment in Self-Paced Instruction." Ann Arbor, Mich.:
Formative Evaluation Research Associates, 1977.

HILGARD, E. R. "The Place of Gestalt Psychology and Field Theories
in Contemporary Learning Theory." In E. R. Hilgard (Ed.),
*Theories of Learning and Instruction: The Sixty-Third Yearbook
of the National Society for the Study of Education.* Chicago:
University of Chicago Press, 1964.

HILL, A. C. "Black Education in the Seventies: A Lesson from the
Past." *Journal of Negro Education,* 1970, *74,* 1339–1367.

HIRSCHMAN, A. O. *Development Projects Observed.* Washington,
D.C.: Brookings Institution, 1967.

HIRSCHMAN, A. O. *The Passions and the Interests: Political Arguments for Capitalism Before Its Time.* Princeton, N.J.: Princeton
University Press, 1977.

HOCHSCHILD, A. R. "Inside the Clockwork of Male Careers." In F.
Howe (Ed.), *Women and the Power to Change.* New York:
McGraw-Hill, 1975.

HOFFMANN, B. *The Tyranny of Testing.* New York: Crowell, 1962.

HOLMER, P. L. "Two Kinds of Learning." *Forum for Honors,* 1977,
8, (2), 12–20.

HOLT, H. "An Adventure in Old-Fangled Education." *Forum,* 1929,
82, 177–182.

HOLT, H. "The Rollins Idea." *Nation,* 1930a, *131,* 372.

HOLT, H. "We Venture on New Paths." *Journal of Higher Education,* 1930b, *1,* 503–506.

HOROWITZ, I. L. (Ed.). *The Rise and Fall of Project Camelot:
Studies in the Relationship Between Social Science and Practical
Politics.* Cambridge, Mass.: M.I.T. Press, 1967.

HOUSE, E. "The Politics of Evaluation in Higher Education." Paper
delivered at Workshop on Evaluation in Higher Education,
Indiana University, June 1974.

HOUSTON, L. P. "Black People and New Careers: Toward Humane
Human Service." *Social Casework,* 1970, *51,* (5), 291–299.

HUCK, J. R. "Assessment Centers: A Review of External and Internal Validity." *Personnel Psychology,* 1973, *26,* (2), 191–212.

HUFF, S. "Problems in Implementing Competency-Based Programs." Syracuse, N.Y.: Educational Policy Research Center,
Syracuse Research Corporation, 1975.

IDZERDA, S. "Evaluating the Rhetoric of Curricular Change." In *The Challenge of Curricular Change*. New York: College Entrance Examination Board, 1966.

JACKSON, D. N., and MESSICK, S. (Eds.). *Problems in Human Assessment*. New York: McGraw-Hill, 1967.

JENCKS, C., and OTHERS. *Inequality: A Reassessment of the Effect of Family and Schooling in America*. New York: Basic Books, 1972.

JOHNSON, B. L. "The Junior College." In G. W. Whipple (Ed.), *General Education in the American College: The Thirty-Eighth Yearbook of the National Society for the Study of Education*. Pt. 2. Bloomington, Ill.: Public School Publishing, 1939.

JOLOSKY, T. "Preliminary College IV Student Questionnaire Summary Nine Months after the Opening of the College." June 24, 1974.

JOLOSKY, T., and TALBURTT, M. A. *Descriptive Measures of the College IV Students*. Ann Arbor, Mich.: Formative Evaluation Research Associates, 1974.

JONES, N., and KOHLI, W. "A Brief History of the Fund for the Improvement of Postsecondary Education and Its Role in the Development of Competency-Based Programs." Syracuse, N.Y.: Educational Policy Research Center, Syracuse Research Corporation, 1975.

JONES, W. B. *Job Analysis and Curriculum Construction in the Metal Trade Industry*. New York: Teachers College Press, Columbia University, 1926.

JUNITZ, S. J. "Professionalism and Social Control in the Progressive Era: The Case of the Flexner Report." *Social Problems*, 1974, *22*, 16–27.

KARABEL, J., and HALSEY, A. H. (Eds.). *Power and Ideology in Education*. New York: Oxford University Press, 1977.

KEETON, M. T., and ASSOCIATES. *Experiential Learning: Rationale, Characteristics, and Assessment*. San Francisco: Jossey-Bass, 1976.

KELLER, F. R., and KOEN, B. V. *The Personalized System of Instruction: State of the Art*. Austin: Engineering Institutes, University of Texas, 1976.

KERR, C. *The Uses of the University.* Cambridge, Mass.: Harvard University Press, 1964.

KITSON, H. D. "Trade and Job Analysis as an Aid in Vocational Curriculum Building." In A. H. Edgerton (Ed.), *Vocational Guidance and Vocational Education for the Industries: The Twenty-Third Yearbook of the National Society for the Study of Education.* Pt. 2. Bloomington, Ill.: Public School Publishing, 1924.

KLIEBARD, H. M. "The Curriculum Field in Retrospect." In P. F. Witt (Ed.), *Technology and the Curriculum.* New York: Teachers College Press, Columbia University, 1968.

KNOTT, R. "What Is Competence-Based Curriculum in the Liberal Arts?" *Journal of Higher Education,* 1975, *46,* (1), 25–40.

KNOTT, R. *What Is a Competence-Based Curriculum?* Mars Hill, N.C.: Mars Hill College, n.d.

KOHLBERG, L. "Moral Development: A Review of the Theory." *Theory into Practice,* 1977, *16* (2), 53–60.

KOHLI, W. *Competency Goals, Method of Assessment, Scope of Program, Stage of Development, Student Clienteles, and Career Targets of CBE-Oriented Institutions.* Syracuse, N.Y.: Educational Policy Research Center, 1974.

KOHLI, W. "Syracuse University: Redesign Program for Teacher Education." In G. Grant (Ed.), *On Competence: An Analysis of a Reform Movement in Higher Education.* Syracuse, N.Y.: Syracuse Research Corporation, 1977.

KORNHAUSER, A. W. "A Plan of Apprentice Training." *Journal of Personnel Research,* 1922, *1,* 215–225.

KRAMER, M. *Reality Shock: Why Nurses Leave Nursing.* St. Louis: Mosby, 1974.

KULIK, J. A., KULIK, C. C., and SMITH, B. B. "Research on the Personalized System of Instruction." *Programmed Learning and Educational Technology,* 1976, *13,* 3–30.

LAZERSON, M., and GRUBB, N. W. (Eds.). *American Education and Vocationalism: A Documentary History, 1870–1970.* New York: Teachers College Press, Columbia University, 1974.

"Legal Service Assistants: Report on Legal Training Phase of a Joint Demonstration Program, 1969–70." New York: Columbia University Law School, 1970.

LEWIN, E. "Feminist Ideology and the Meaning of Work: The Case of Nursing." *Catalyst,* 1977, 10–11, 78–103.

LINCOLN UNIVERSITY. *Lincoln Masters Program in Human Services.* Lincoln University, Pa: Lincoln University, 1976.

LINDQUIST, J. *Strategies for Change: Collegiate Innovation as Adaptive Development.* Berkeley, Calif.: Pacific Soundings Press, 1977.

LINDSLEY, O. R. "From Skinner to Precision Teaching: The Child Knows Best." In J. B. Jordan and L. S. Robbins (Eds.), *Let's Try Doing Something Else Kind of Thing.* Arlington, Va.: Council for Exceptional Children, 1972.

LIPSET, S. M. *The First New Nation: The United States in Historical and Comparative Perspective.* New York: Doubleday, 1963.

MC CLELLAND, D. C. "Testing for Competence Rather than for 'Intelligence.'" *American Psychologist,* 1973, *28,* (1), 1–14.

MACCOBY, M. *The Gamesman: The New Corporate Leaders.* New York: Simon & Schuster, 1976.

MC GUIRE, C. H. and BABBOTT, D. "Simulation Technique in the Measurement of Problem-Solving Skills." *Journal of Educational Measurement,* 1967, *4,* (1), 1–10.

MC HALE, K. *Changes and Experiments in Liberal-Arts Education: The Thirty-First Yearbook of the National Society for the Study of Education.* Pt. 2. Bloomington, Ill.: Public School Publishing, 1932.

MAC KINNON, D. W. "The Nature and Nurture of Creative Talent." *American Psychologist,* 1962, *17,* 484–495.

MAGER, R. *Preparing Instructional Objectives.* Belmont, Calif.: Fearon, 1962.

MANIS, J. G., and MELTZER, B. N. (Eds.). *Symbolic Interaction.* Boston: Allyn & Bacon, 1972.

MANN, C. R. "The Technique of Army Training." *School and Society,* 1922, *15,* 228–232.

MANNHEIM, K. *Ideology and Utopia.* New York: Harcourt Brace Jovanovich, 1955.

MARIESKIND, H. "The Women's Health Movement." *International Journal of Health Services,* 1975, *5,* 217–223.

MEAD, M. *Culture and Commitment.* Garden City, N.Y.: Natural History Press, 1970.

MECHANIC, D. *Politics, Medicine, and Social Science.* New York: Wiley, 1974.

MEEHL, P. E. *Clinical Versus Statistical Prediction: A Theoretical Analysis and a Review of the Evidence.* Minneapolis: University of Minnesota Press, 1954.

MEETH, R. *Government Funding and Nontraditional Programs.* Washington, D.C.: Postsecondary Education Convening Authority, 1975.

MELTON, A. W. "Military Psychology in the U.S. of A." *American Psychologist,* 1957, *12,* 740–746.

MENDEL, W. M., and GREEN, G. A. "On Becoming a Physician." *Journal of Medical Education,* 1965, *40,* 266–272.

MERTON, R. K. "Insiders and Outsiders: A Chapter in the Sociology of Knowledge." *American Journal of Sociology,* 1972, *24,* 9.

MILLER, R. B. "Analysis and Specification of Behavior for Training." In R. Glaser (Ed.), *Training Research and Education.* Pittsburgh: University of Pittsburgh Press, 1962.

MILLMAN, M. *The Unkindest Cut.* New York: Morrow, 1977.

MT. HOOD COMMUNITY COLLEGE, ASSOCIATE DEGREE PROGRAM NURSING STAFF. *Articulation of Competency-Based Education in Nursing.* Proposal submitted to the Fund for the Improvement of Postsecondary Education, April 1974.

MT. HOOD COMMUNITY COLLEGE, ASSOCIATE DEGREE PROGRAM NURSING STAFF. *Articulation of Competency-Based Education in Nursing, Final Report.* Gresham, Ore.: Mt. Hood Community College, 1975.

NELSON, C. "Reconceptualizing Health Care." In V. L. Olesen (Ed.), *Women and Their Health: Research Implications for a New Era.* Washington, D.C.: National Center for Health Services Research, Health Resources Administration, Public Health Service, Department of Health, Education, and Welfare, 1976.

New York Times, Nov. 13, 1976.

New York Times, May 25, 1978.

NEWMAN, F. *Report on Higher Education.* Washington, D.C.: Office of Education, Department of Health, Education, and Welfare, 1971.

NEWMAN, J. H. *The Idea of a University.* New York: Doubleday, 1959. (Originally published 1852.)

NEWMAN, S. H., HOWELL, M., and CLIFF, N. "The Analysis and Prediction of a Practical Examination in Dentistry." In D. N. Jackson and S. Messick (Eds.), *Problems in Human Assessment.* New York: McGraw-Hill, 1967.

Northwest Association of Secondary and Higher Schools in Oregon, Report, 1972.

O'CONNELL, W. R., JR., and MOOMAW, W. E. *A CBC Primer: Competency-Based Curriculums in General Undergraduate Programs.* Atlanta, Ga.: Southern Regional Education Board, 1975.

OLESEN, V. L. "What Happens after Schooling: Notes on Post-Institutional Socialization in the Health Occupations." *Social Science and Medicine,* 1973, *7,* 61–75.

OLESEN, V. L., and WHITTAKER, E. W. "Role-Making in Participant Observation: Processes in the Research-Actor Relationship." *Human Organization,* 1967, *26,* 273–281.

OLESEN, V. L., and WHITTAKER, E. W. *The Silent Dialogue: A Study in the Social Psychology of Professional Socialization.* San Francisco: Jossey-Bass, 1968.

ONG, W. J. "Agonistic Structures in Academia: Past to Present." *Daedalus,* 1974, *103,* 229–238.

Oregon Journal, Aug. 27, 1975.

PALARDY, J. M., and EISLE, J. E. "Competency-Based Education." In J. M. Palardy (Ed.), *Teaching Today.* New York: Macmillan, 1975.

PARLETT, M., and DEARDEN, G., (Eds.) *Introduction to Illuminative Evaluation: Studies in Higher Education.* Berkeley, Calif.: Pacific Soundings Press, 1977.

PARLETT, M., and HAMILTON, D. "Evaluation as Illumination: A New Approach to the Study of Innovative Programs." Edinburgh: Center for Research in the Educational Sciences, University of Edinburgh, 1972.

PARSONS, T., and PLATT, G. *The American Academic Profession: A Pilot Study.* Cambridge, Mass.: Department of Social Relations, Harvard University, 1968.

PATERSON, D. G. "The Scott Company Graphic Rating Scale." In T. L. Whisler and S. J. Harper (Eds.), *Performance Appraisal.* New York: Holt, Rinehart and Winston, 1962.

PEARL, A. "The Human Service Society: An Ecological Perspective." In A. Gardner and others (Eds.), *Public Service Employment*. New York: Praeger, 1973.

PENNYPACKER, H. S., KOENIG, C. H., and LINDSLEY, O. R. *Handbook of the Standard Behavior Chart*. Kansas City, Kan.: Precision Media, 1972.

PERRY, W. C., JR. *Forms of Intellectual and Ethical Development in the College Years*. New York: Holt, Rinehart and Winston, 1970.

PETERSON, G. W. *Curriculum of Attainments: Final Report*. Tallahassee: Instructional Systems Development Center, Florida State University, 1976.

PETERSON, O. L., and OTHERS. "An Analytical Study of North Carolina General Practice." *Journal of Medical Education,* 1956, *31,* 10–15.

PETRIE, H. G. "Can Education Find Its Lost Objectives Under the Street Lamp of Behaviorism?" In R. A. Smith (Ed.), *Regaining Educational Leadership: Critical Essays on PBTE/CBTE, Behavioral Objectives, and Accountability*. New York: Wiley, 1975.

PHENIX, P. *The Realms of Meaning: A Philosophy of the Curriculum for General Education*. New York: McGraw-Hill, 1964.

POLANYI, M. *Personal Knowledge*. Chicago: University of Chicago Press, 1958.

POPHAM, W. J., and OTHERS. *Instructional Objectives*. Chicago: Rand McNally, 1969.

POPHAM, W. J. *Evaluating Instruction*. Englewood Cliffs, N.J.: Prentice-Hall, 1973.

POTTINGER, P. S. "Comments and Guidelines For Research in Competency Identification, Definition, and Measurement." Unpublished paper prepared for EPRC, June 1975.

POWELL, M. J. "Professional Self-Regulation: The Transfer of Control from a Professional Association to an Independent Commission." Paper presented at 71st annual meeting of American Sociological Association, New York City, 1976.

PRICE, D. DE S. *Science Since Babylon*. New Haven, Conn.: Yale University Press, 1961.

Quick-Training Procedures: Studies in Personnel Policy, no. 26. Supplement to Conference Board Management Record. New York: National Industrial Conference Board, 1940.

QUIRK, T. J. "Some Measurement Issues in CBTE." *Phi Delta Kappan,* Jan. 1974, pp. 316–318.

REDFERN, B. "Competency-Based Evaluation: The State of the Art." *New Directions for Education,* 1973, *1,* 51–63.

REMMERS, H. H. "Rating Methods in Research on Teaching." In N. L. Gage (Ed.), *Handbook of Research on Teaching.* Chicago: Rand McNally, 1963.

RICE, D. G. *Unit Instruction for Short-Period Training.* Boston: Civilian Conservation Corps, 1940.

RIEFF, R. "The Control of Knowledge: The Power of the Helping Professions." *Journal of Applied Behavioral Science,* 1974, *10,* 451–461.

RIESMAN, D., DENNEY, R., and GLAZER, N. *The Lonely Crowd: A Study of the Changing American Character.* New Haven, Conn.: Yale University Press, 1950. (Rev. ed., 1969.)

RIESMAN, D. "The Collision Course of Higher Education." *Journal of College Student Personnel,* 1969, *10,* 363–369.

RIESMAN, D. "Can We Maintain Quality Graduate Education in a Period of Retrenchment?" David Henry lecture, University of Illinois, April 1975.

RIESMAN, D. "Liberation and Stalemate." *The Massachusetts Review,* 1976, *17,* (4), 767–776.

RIESMAN, D. "Ethical and Practical Dilemmas of Fieldwork in Academic Settings: A Personal Memoir." In R. K. Merton, J. S. Coleman, and P. Rossi (Eds.), *Quantitative and Qualitative Social Research: Papers in Honor of Paul Lazarsfeld.* New York: Free Press, forthcoming.

RIESMAN, D., GUSFIELD, J., and GAMSON, Z. F. *Academic Values and Mass Education: The Early Years of Oakland and Monteith.* New York: McGraw-Hill, 1975.

RIESMAN, D., and STADTMAN, V. (Eds.). *Academic Transformation: Seventeen Institutions Under Pressure.* New York: McGraw-Hill, 1973.

RIPPA, A. S. (Ed.). *Educational Ideas in America: A Documentary History.* New York: McKay, 1969.

ROGERS, E., EVELAND, J. D., and KLEPPER, C. A. *The Innovation Process in Public Organizations: Some Elements of a Preliminary Model.* Ann Arbor: University of Michigan Press, 1977.

ROGERS, E., and SHOEMAKER, F. F. *The Communication of Inno-*

vations: A Cross-Cultural Approach. New York: Free Press, 1971.

ROSE, P. I. " 'Nobody Knows the Trouble I've Seen': Some Reflections on the Insider-Outsider Debate." Katherine Asher Engel lecture, Smith College, October 18, 1977.

ROTH, J. "Hired Hand Research." *American Sociologist,* 1966, *1,* 190–196. (Reprinted In N. K. Denzin (Ed.)', *Sociological Methods: A Sourcebook.* Chicago: Aldine, 1970.)

RUDOLPH, F. *Curriculum: A History of the American Undergraduate Course of Study Since 1636.* San Francisco: Jossey-Bass, 1977.

RUGG, H. "Curriculum-Making and the Scientific Study of Education Since 1910." In G. W. Whipple (Ed.)', *Curriculum-Making: Past and Present: The Twenty-Sixth Yearbook of the National Society for the Study of Education.* Pt. 1. Bloomington, Ill.: Public School Publishing, 1926.

RUZEK, S. *The Women's Health Movement: Finding Alternatives to Traditional Medical Professionalism.* New York: Praeger, 1978.

ST. JOHN'S COLLEGE. *Catalogue.* Annapolis, Md.: St. John's College.

SANTA, C. M., and BURSTYN, J. N. "Complexity as an Impediment to Learning: A Study of Changes in Selected College Textbooks." *Journal of Higher Education,* 1977, *58,* (5), 508–518.

SARASON, S. B. *The Creation of Settings and the Future Societies.* San Francisco: Jossey-Bass, 1972.

SCHMEIDER, A. A. *Competency-Based Education: The State of the Scene.* Washington, D.C.: American Council for Teacher Education, 1973.

SCHUSTER, G. "Introduction to Newman." In J. H. Newman, *The Idea of a University.* New York: Longmans, Green, 1960.

SEELEY, J. A. "College IV Strengths and Weaknesses: Faculty, Student Tutors, and Administrators View Their College in March 1974." May 12, 1975.

"Senators' Views Shock Postsecondary Education Fund." *Chronicle of Higher Education,* April 12, 1976, p. 3.

SIKES, W. W., SCHLESINGER, L. E., and SEASHORE, C. N. *Renewing Higher Education from Within: A Guide for Campus Change Teams.* San Francisco: Jossey-Bass, 1974.

SKAGER, R. "Evaluating Educational Alternatives." In J. I. Goodlad (Ed.), *New Directions for Education: Alternatives in Education,* no. 4. San Francisco: Jossey-Bass, 1973.

SMITH, R. A. (Ed.). *Regaining Educational Leadership: Critical Essays on PBTE/CBTE, Behavioral Objectives, and Accountability.* New York: Wiley, 1975.

SMITH, V. E. *The School Examined: Its Aim and Content.* Milwaukee: Bruce, 1960.

Southern Regional Education Board. "Research Study Points to Untapped Tax Capacity as a Potential Source of Added Postsecondary Funding." Atlanta, Ga.: Southern Regional Education Board, 1976.

SOWELL, T. "Black Excellence: The Case of Dunbar High School." *Public Interest,* 1974, *35,* 3–21.

SOWELL, T. "Patterns of Black Excellence." *Public Interest,* 1976, *43,* 26–58.

SPADY, W. G. "Competency-Based Education: A Bandwagon in Search of a Definition." *Educational Researcher,* 1977, *6,* (1), 9–14.

SPURR, S. *Academic Degree Structures: Innovative Approaches.* New York: McGraw-Hill, 1970.

STATSKY, W. P. "Field Report on Sixteen Legal Service Assistants Now Working in Nine Community Law Offices in New York City." New York: College for Human Services, 1969.

STATSKY, W. P. "Supervision Report on Sixteen Legal Service Assistants Now Working in Ten Community Law Offices in New York City." New York: College for Human Services, 1970.

STECKLEIN, J. *How to Measure Faculty Workload.* Washington, D.C.: American Council on Education, 1961.

STEVENS, R. *American Medicine and the Public Interest.* New Haven, Conn.: Yale University Press, 1971.

STRAUSS, L. *Liberalism, Ancient and Modern.* New York: Basic Books, 1968.

STRONG, E. K., and UHRBROOK, R. S. *Job Analysis and the Curriculum.* Boston: Houghton Mifflin, 1923.

TALBURTT, M. A. "Preliminary College IV Student Interview Summary Nine Months After the Opening of the College." June 24, 1974.

TAYLOR, F. W. *Scientific Management: Comprising Shop Management, The Principles of Scientific Management, and Testimony Before the Special House Committee.* New York: Harper & Row, 1947. (Originally published 1911.)

THORNE, B. "Professional Education in Law." In E. C. Hughes and others (Eds.), *Education for the Professions of Medicine, Theology, and Social Welfare.* New York: McGraw-Hill, 1973.

TOCQUEVILLE, A. DE. *Democracy in America.* London: Oxford University Press, 1946. (Originally published 1835.)

TODD, L. P. *Wartime Relations of the Federal Government and the Public Schools.* New York: Teachers College Press, Columbia University, 1945.

TOFT, R. J. "College IV: An Experiment in Alternative Higher Education." Report to the Fund for the Improvement of Postsecondary Education, Oct. 1976.

TOOPS, H. A. *Trade Tests in Education.* New York: Teachers College Press, Columbia University, 1921.

TROW, M. "Distractions." In B. Snyder (Ed.), *The Hidden Curriculum.* New York: Knopf, 1971.

TROW, M. "The Public and Private Lives of Higher Education." *American Higher Education: Toward an Uncertain Future.* Vol. II. *Daedalus.* 1975, *104*, 113–127.

TUMIN, M. "Valid and Invalid Rationales." In M. T. Keeton and Associates (Eds.), *Experiential Learning: Rationale, Characteristics, and Assessment.* San Francisco: Jossey-Bass, 1976.

TURLINGTON, R. B. *Student Acceleration in Florida Public Education.* Second Annual Report to the Florida Legislature and the State Board of Education, Feb. 28, 1975.

TURNER, E. V., HELPER, M. M., and KRISKA, S. D. "Predictors of Clinical Performance." *Journal of Medical Education,* 1974, *49*, 338–342.

TYACK, D. B. *The One Best System: A History of American Urban Education.* Cambridge, Mass.: Harvard University Press, 1974.

TYLER, R. "Historical Efforts to Develop Learning on a Competency Base." In W. R. O'Connell, Jr., and W. E. Moomaw (Eds.), *A CBC Primer: Competency-Based Curriculums in General Undergraduate Programs.* Atlanta: Undergraduate Educational Reform Project, Southern Regional Education Board, 1975.

UHRBROCK, S. "The History of Job Analysis." *Administration: The Journal of Business Analysis and Control,* 1922, *3,* 164–168.

U.S. Office of Strategic Services. *Assessment of Men.* New York: Holt, Rinehart and Winston, 1948.

VEYSEY, L. R. *The Emergence of the American University.* Chicago: University of Chicago Press, 1965.

WALLER, W. *The Sociology of Teaching.* New York: Wiley, 1932.

WATSON, G. "What Should College Students Learn?" *Progressive Education,* 1930, *7,* 319–325, 399–403.

WATSON, G. "Bearing of the Rollins Conference on the College of the Future." *Progressive Education,* 1931, *8,* 321–323.

WAX, R. *Doing Fieldwork.* Chicago: University of Chicago Press, 1971.

WEISS, R., and REIN, M. "The Evaluation of Broad-Aim Programs: A Cautionary Case and a Moral." In F. G. Caro (Ed.), *Readings in Evaluation Research.* New York: Russell Sage Foundation, 1971.

WHISLER, T. L., and HARPER, S. F. (Eds.), *Performance Appraisal.* New York: Holt, Rinehart and Winston, 1962.

WHITE, R. W. "Motivation Reconsidered: The Concept of Competence." *Psychological Review,* 1959, *6,* 297–333.

WHITEHEAD, A. N. *The Aims of Education and Other Essays.* New York: Macmillan, 1949.

WHYTE, W. H., JR. *The Organization Man.* New York: Simon & Schuster, 1956.

WILSON, C. L. "On-the-Job and Operational Criteria." In R. Glaser (Ed.), *Training Research and Education.* Pittsburgh: University of Pittsburgh Press, 1962.

WODITSCH, G. A. "Developing Generic Skills: A Model for Competency-Based General Education." CUE Project Occasional Paper Series, No. 3. Bowling Green, Ohio: Bowling Green State University, 1977.

YUKER, H. E. *Faculty Workload: Facts, Myths, and Commentary.* Research Report No. 6. Washington, D.C.: ERIC Clearinghouse for Higher Education, 1974.

ZALTMAN, G., DUNCAN, R., and HOLBEK, J. *Innovations and Organizations.* New York: Wiley, 1973.

Name Index

Subject Index

Academy for Educational Development, 303

Accountability, 14, 27–29, 100–102, 103, 153–155, 229

Achievement, distrust of, 47–50

Activity analysis, 80. *See also* Job analysis

Administration; and competence-based education, 63–65; and program initiation, 237, 252–254. *See also* individual institutions

Affective behavior, 507, 530; assessment of, 35–36; scale of, 509; tests of, 514, 518

Alverno College, 3, 5; Academic Task Force at, 270–278; administration of, 63–64, 267–271, 278–280, assessment at, 142–143, 145, 154, 156–159, 276–278, 284–288; curriculum at, 67, 96, 111–112; faculty at, 102, 246–247, 257–258, 266–278, 281–284, 289–298; institutionalization of, 255, 269–270; liberal education at, 167–170, 172, 177–179, 184, 186–188, 196; origins of CBE at, 230, 232,

235–236, 259–270; program initiation at, 238–240, 270–278, 280–290; students at, 12*n*, 33–34, 37–38, 40, 49, 296–298

Alverno Learning Process, 214, 216,

American Nurses Association, 205

Analytic competence, 273

Antioch School of Law, 3, 103–104; assessment at, 144, 145, 154; faculty at, 247; institutionalization of, 255; origins of CBE at, 33–35, 232–233, 235, 236; problems at, 278–280; professional education at, 142–143, 149, 209, 217–219; program initiation at, 240–241; students at, 40–42, 213, 250–251; study of, 536–537. *See also* Law

Army Trade Test Division, 73–77

Arts: competence levels in, 274–275, 283; performance training in, 391–393

ASEPTIC program, 355, 357

Assessment: analysis of, 529; attitudes toward, 139–147; impact on students of, 13, in liberal education, 173–176; of nonacademic

586